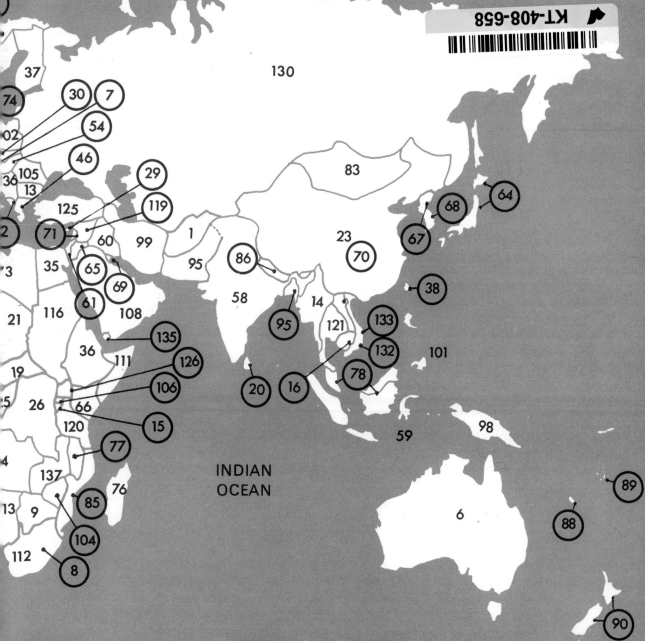

ARCTIC OCEAN

KT-408-658

130

37

74

30 7

54

46

02

29

119

36 105

13

125

2

71

60 99

1

23

86

70

68

64

67

38

35

65

69

58

14

95

133

61

108

121

132

101

21

116

135

20

16

78

36

111

126

19

106

59

98

26

66

15

120

77

6

137

76

85

88

89

13 9

104

112

8

INDIAN
OCEAN

90

Merry Christmas
1977. Love & Best Wishes
from Heather & David.

THE NEW WONDER BOOK
Encyclopedia

The New Wonder Book

Encyclopedia

Compiled and Edited by

GERALD E. SPECK
and
EUAN SUTHERLAND

With special contributions by
C. L. BOLTZ
MAURICE BURTON
DERYCK COOKE
P. J. FAULKES
HERBERT HOWARTH
LIONEL KOCHAN
DAVID S. KYLES
WALTER SHEPHERD
HEBE SPAULL
DUNCAN TAYLOR
G. H. VALLINS
K. R. WALLACE

WARD LOCK LIMITED

LONDON

© WARD LOCK 1967

Reprinted with corrections 1968

Reprinted 1969

Reprinted 1971

Reprinted 1972

Reprinted 1974

Reprinted 1976

ISBN 0 7063 1138 8

DESIGNED BY DAVID JOHNSON
FILMSET IN 10-PT. IMPRINT
BY
KEYSPOOLS LTD, GOLBORNE, LANCS.

PRINTED BY TOPPAN PRINTING COMPANY, SINGAPORE

How to use this Encyclopedia

No young reader should have any difficulty in using this book for the simple reason that it has been compiled in strict alphabetical order. CAPITAL letters are used to indicate that there is a separate entry devoted to that particular subject or person which the reader can refer to for further information.

An encyclopedia is rather like a living organizm in that it grows and changes from edition to edition. Now, you can be most helpful in maintaining the health and growth of this encyclopedia if you will write to the editor should you note something—no matter how small—you know to be incorrect or, more particularly, a subject which deserves more space or has been omitted altogether; in fact, anything you consider will improve the work's value and usefulness.

Acknowledgements

The Editor wishes to acknowledge fully the generous co-operation of the undermentioned in supplying photographs and data. Without their aid it would not have been possible to produce such a profusely illustrated book.

Alistair Duncan, Australian News and Information Service, Belgian Embassy, Bolivian Embassy, Brazilian Embassy, British Museum, British Rail, Canadian Embassy, Coventry Cathedral, Cypriot Embassy, Czechoslovakian Embassy, David Ashley, Embassy of Congolese Republic, Fox Photos, F. W. Lane, French Embassy, Japanese Embassy, Jodrell Bank, Jugoslavian Embassy, Kenya Information Service, Keystone Press Agency, Ministry of Information, Mount Wilson Observatory, National Gallery (London), National Portrait Gallery (London), P.A.—Reuter Photos, Paul Popper, Portuguese Embassy, Prue Dempster, Radio Times Hulton Library, Royal Astronomical Society, Royal Institution, Science Museum, Shell Photographic Unit, South African Embassy, Sport and General, Tate Gallery, Times Photos, United States Information Service, Victoria and Albert Museum.

Aa

AARD-VARK

This rather ungainly-looking mammal is a native of Africa. It has a tapering pig-like snout, donkey-like ears, a strong tail, a light covering of hair and powerful legs armed with sharp claws for digging into the mounds of termites on which it feeds with its long sticky tongue. It is solitary and nocturnal. The aard-vark is not an aggressive creature but runs for cover as soon as danger threatens. It is about 6 feet from tail to snout and weighs around 100 pounds. It is sometimes known as the 'African ant-bear'.

AARD-WOLF

Is native to S. and E. Africa and gets its name from its habit of living in a hole in the earth. It is related to the hyenas, and stands about 20 inches at the shoulders and some $2\frac{1}{2}$ feet long from tail to muzzle. It has a distinctive mane or crest which erects when it is attacked. In the main it feeds on insects, especially white ants. It is also known as a 'maanhaar-jackall'.

AARD-VARK is a termite-eating mammal, native to Africa. It is sometimes called an African ant-bear.

ABÉLARD, Pierre (1079–1142)

French philosopher and theologian. Born in Brittany, he dedicated himself to the pursuit of knowledge. His teaching was an appeal to reason against tradition, and made for him many enemies in the Church which ordered one of his books to be burnt. Although he was later appointed an abbot in Brittany he was repeatedly attacked for heresy and finally condemned in 1141. He died while on his way to Rome to defend himself in 1142. His love letters to the nun Héloise are famous.

ACADEMY

The name given to a gymnasium in a park and sports ground in ancient Athens. This gymnasium was called after a Greek named Academus. It was at the Academy that the philosopher PLATO taught nearly four hundred years before the birth of Christ. It continued to exist for many centuries and was only finally closed down in A.D. 529 by the Emperor JUSTINIAN. The most famous modern Academy is the Académie Française. In Britain the oldest Academy is the Royal Academy at Burlington House, London, founded in 1768 to encourage painters and sculptors by holding exhibitions of their work.

ACT OF PARLIAMENT

A law made by Parliament to which the Queen has given her assent. Another name for an Act is a Statute. When Parliament is discussing a proposed new law it is called a BILL and it only becomes an Act when the Queen has signed it.

ACTON, John Emerich Edward Dalberg, First Baron (1834–1902)

British historian. Born at Naples, he was brought up in England and finished his education at Munich University. He settled down in England as a Liberal Catholic journalist and Member of Parliament (1859–1865). After vainly opposing the dogma of Papal Infallibility (1871) he retired from public life and devoted himself to study and the writing of a *History of Liberty* of which only scattered parts appeared. He planned the Cambridge Modern History, but died before it appeared.

ADAM, Robert (1728–1792)

Scottish architect and designer. He became interested in Greek and Roman domestic architecture, and went to study the Emperor Diocletian's Palace at Spalato. This was the inspiration for his masterpiece, the Adelphi (demolished in 1936), though Adam produced a style peculiar to English architecture, elegant and restrained. Together with his brother James, Robert Adam also designed interiors for his houses, including furniture, giving them their peculiarly consistent and finished appearance. One of the examples that remains is Kenwood House in Highgate, London.

ADDISON, Joseph (1672–1719)

English essayist, poet, and man of letters. His greatest achievement was in the publication of *The Spectator*, a non-political paper centred on an imaginary club and its leading light, Mr Spectator. He and his club companions, like Sir Roger de Coverley, the old-fashioned country gentleman, fascinated the public for many years.

ADEN

An independent state and part of the Federation of South Arabia. It has a population of about 285,000 and an area of 75 square miles. Most of the fruit and vegetables produced in the Federation are sold through the market in Aden, and it is also an important port, where many oil-tankers call.

AEROPLANES

The main parts of an aeroplane are shown in the drawing on page 11. The wings support the weight of the aeroplane and keep it stable, and the fin and rudder control the direction of flight. The propeller or jet thrust moves the machine forward, and thus makes air flow past the wings. Because of the special shape of the wings and the angle at which they meet the airstream, a powerful upward force is produced. It is made up of two components: (i) the suction caused by the air flowing over the upper curved surface of the wing and (ii) the pressure of the air on the inclined lower surface.

The tailplane and elevators enable the pilot to fly in just what manner he desires. Thus a pilot can climb by opening the throttle and raising the elevators, and dive by depressing the elevators. The ailerons on the trailing edge of the wings allow turning and banking. Slots are devices to increase lift, and flaps both increase lift and act as air-brakes to slow the machine down; they are particularly useful in landing.

The aeroplane has played an important part in modern history, but it is too long to recount here; however, the following table gives some of the important landmarks in aviation history:

1783—First manned balloon ascent made by Pilatre de Rozier and the Marquis d'Arlandes.
1784—First balloon ascent in Britain made by James Tyler, at Edinburgh.

AEROPLANES Amy Johnson setting out on her record-breaking 9,900 mile flight to Australia.

1809—Sir George Cayley experimented with a glider in England.
1848—John Stringfellow built and flew the first powered model aeroplane. Power came from a small steam-engine.
1852—Giffard made a flight in an elongated balloon steered by a rudder and propelled by a steam-engine driving a propeller.
1896—Otto Lilienthal, known as 'the father of the aeroplane', killed in an accident after a series of gliding experiments in Germany.
1900—Zeppelin's first airship made its trial flight.
1903—Orville Wright made the world's first controlled, power-driven aeroplane flight at Kitty Hawk, North Carolina.
1905—First officially recorded flight was made by Wilbur Wright at Dayton, Ohio. He flew 11–12 miles in 18 minutes 9 seconds.
1906—Santos Dumont, in France, made the first officially recorded aeroplane in Europe.
1909—J. T. C. Moore-Brabazon (later Lord Brabazon of Tara) made first officially observed aeroplane flight in the British Isles.
M. Louis Blériot, a Frenchman, flew the Channel from Les Baraques.
1911—First airmail in the United States. Experimental airmail service operated between Hendon and Windsor in United Kingdom.
1919—John Alcock and Arthur Whitton Brown (both later knighted) made the first direct Atlantic crossing by air, flying from Newfoundland to Ireland, a distance of 1,890 miles, in 16 hours 12 minutes.

1926—Commander R. E. Byrd, with Floyd Bennett as pilot, flew from King's Bay, Svalbard (Spitzbergen), to the North Pole and returned in 15 hours.

1927—Colonel Charles A. Lindbergh, United States, made first solo crossing of the Atlantic, flying from New York to Paris.

1928—H. J. Hinkler flew from England to Australia, covering 12,250 miles in 15½ days.
'Southern Cross', a Fokker monoplane, with Captain C. Kingsford-Smith and C. Ulm, Australia, and H. W. Lyon and J. Warner, United States, flew from Oakland, California, to Sydney, Australia.
Juan de la Cierva of Spain flew by autogiro from London to Paris.

1929—Airship *Graf Zeppelin* made a world tour.
Flying-Officer H. R. D. Waghorn, Great Britain, won the Schneider Seaplane Trophy race at an average speed of 328·64 m.p.h.
Squadron-Leader H. Orlebar, Great Britain, set a world speed record of 357·7 m.p.h. at Calshot, England.

1930—Amy Johnson, Great Britain, completed 9,900 mile flight from London to Australia in 19½ days.

1931—Professor Auguste Piccard and Dr. Charles Kipfer ascended to record height of 51,775 feet at Augsburg, Germany, in a balloon.
Wiley Post, U.S. pilot, and Harold Gatty, Australian, as navigator, encircled the globe in 8 days 15 hours 51 minutes, a record-breaking 15,474-mile flight.

1931—Flight-Lieutenant G. H. Stainforth, Great Britain, made new seaplane speed record of 406·997 m.p.h. at Calshot, England.

1932—Miss Amelia Earhart flew from Newfoundland to Ireland in 13½ hours, the first solo flight across the Atlantic by a woman.
Auguste Piccard and Max Cosyns set altitude record of 53,153 feet in a balloon over Switzerland and Italy.

1934—Major W. E. Kepner, Captain A. W. Stevens and Captain O. A. Anderson, taking off from Rapid City, South Dakota, ascended to 60,613 feet in a balloon.
Lieutenant Francesco Agello made seaplane record of 440·68 m.p.h. at Desenzano, Italy.

1936—Amy Mollison flew from Lympne, England, to Cape Town, South Africa, in 3 days 6 hours 26 minutes, setting a new record.
Squadron-Leader F. R. D. Swain, Great Britain, set up new world's height record for landplanes of 49,967 feet.

1938—Two R.A.F. single-engined Vickers Wellesley long-range bombers established new world's distance record for landplanes of 7,162 miles by flying from Ismailia, Egypt, to Darwin, Australia.

1939—First commercial trans-Atlantic service begun by Pan American 'Yankee Clipper', flying by way of New York, Bermuda, Azores, Lisbon, Bordeaux, Marseilles and Southampton.
First British trans-Atlantic air mail service.
First jet plane, the German Heinkel He 178.

1941—First flight by British jet plane, the Gloster E.28/39.

1946—Group-Captain E. M. Donaldson, D.S.O., A.F.C., in a Gloster Meteor, raised the world's speed record to 616 m.p.h.

1947—Major Marion E. Carl, U.S. Marine Corps, flying a Douglas Skystreak jet plane, raised the world's speed record to 650·57 m.p.h.

1948—John Cunningham, Great Britain, set new altitude record for heavier-than-air craft in a de Haviland Vampire jet fighter of 59,445·5 feet at Hatfield, Hertfordshire.
Major Richard L. Johnson, United States Army Air Force, set a new world speed record by flying at 670·37 m.p.h.

1949—Squadron-Leader Trevor S. Wade, Great Britain, in a Hawker P.1052, flew from London to Paris in 20 minutes 37 seconds, an average speed of 618·26 m.p.h.
First flight of the 'Comet' jet airliner.

1950—John Cunningham and crew, Great Britain, flew from London to Rome in the 'Comet' jet airliner in 1 hour 59 minutes 37 seconds, an average speed of 447 m.p.h.

1952—B.O.A.C. 'Comet' inaugurated world's first jet-liner service, London to Johannesburg.

1953—Squadron-Leader Neville Duke set up new world speed record of 727·7 m.p.h. in a 'Hunter' at Tangmere.

1955—Colonel H. A. Hanes, U.S.A., set up unofficial speed record of 800 m.p.h. at Palmdale, California.

1956—Canberra flew from London to Cairo in 3 hours 59 minutes.
Peter Twiss flew Fairey Delta 2 at a speed of 1,121 m.p.h. near Chichester.

1957—U.S.A.F. Stratojets made non-stop flight round world in 45 hours 19 minutes.
Captain J. W. Kittinger made record balloon altitude flight of 96,000 feet.
English Electric P.1 exceeded world speed record of 1,132 m.p.h.

1969—Anglo-French 'Concorde', supersonic airliner, made first successful test flights.

AEROPLANES

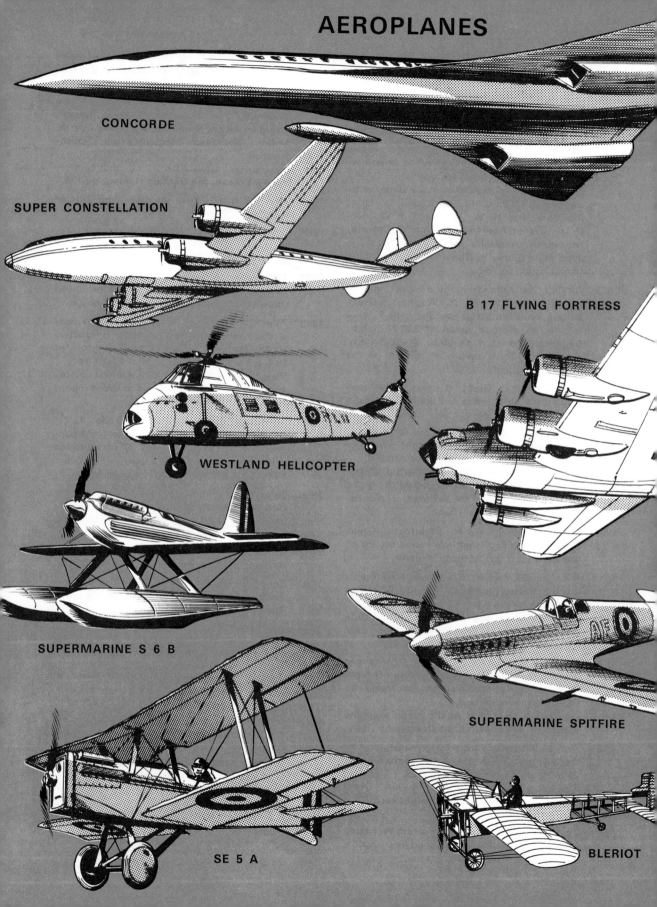

CONCORDE

SUPER CONSTELLATION

B 17 FLYING FORTRESS

WESTLAND HELICOPTER

SUPERMARINE S 6 B

SUPERMARINE SPITFIRE

SE 5 A

BLERIOT

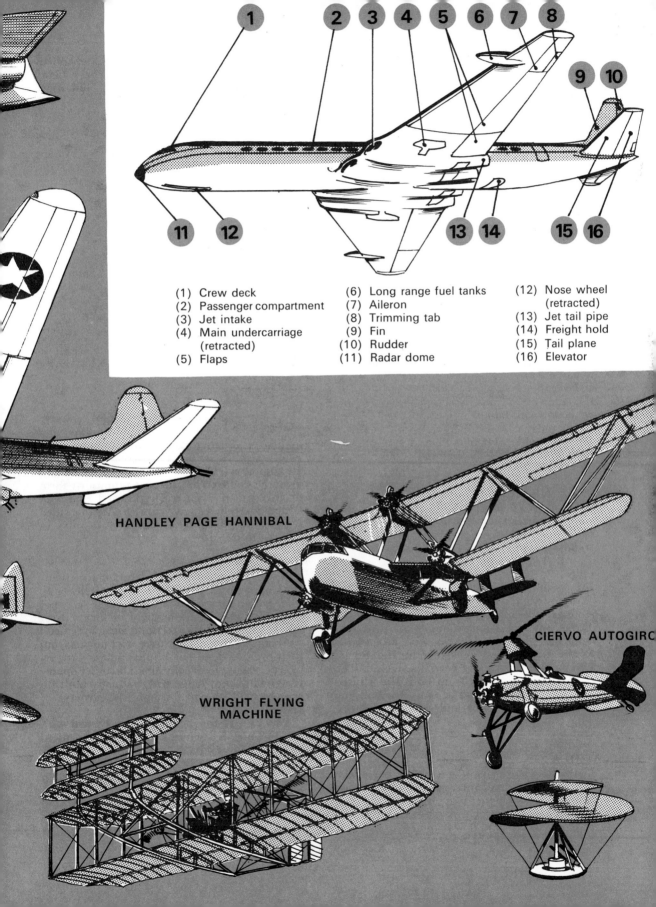

(1) Crew deck
(2) Passenger compartment
(3) Jet intake
(4) Main undercarriage
    (retracted)
(5) Flaps
(6) Long range fuel tanks
(7) Aileron
(8) Trimming tab
(9) Fin
(10) Rudder
(11) Radar dome
(12) Nose wheel
     (retracted)
(13) Jet tail pipe
(14) Freight hold
(15) Tail plane
(16) Elevator

HANDLEY PAGE HANNIBAL

CIERVO AUTOGIRO

WRIGHT FLYING
MACHINE

AESCHYLUS (525–456 B.C.)

Greek poet, and regarded as the founder of the Greek drama. He was greatly respected both by his contemporaries and by succeeding generations, and his plays continued to be produced long after his death. In the earliest of his remaining plays, the *Supplices,* the interest still centres around the chorus, though there is the beginning of some characterisation and plot. But in his last great work, the trilogy *Orestia,* there are traces of sympathetic character even in the humbler parts. His main themes are the sadness of human life; the power and the fearful anger of the gods; and their vengeance on sinners. He was especially adept at expressing slowly developing fear, and pointing contrasts. His other remaining plays are: *Persae, Seven against Thebes,* and *Prometheus.*

AESOP (c. 620–560 B.C.)

Author of fables about animals, which he wrote to show the follies and foibles of humans. For example: 'It is not only fine feathers that make fine birds.' He is supposed to have been a slave, though he was later freed and lived at the court of Croesus. Aesop probably did not write down his fables, and what we call *Aesop's Fables* today was based on a version by a 14th-century monk, Maximus Planudes, and probably contains much material unknown to Aesop himself.

AFGHANISTAN

A kingdom in Asia to the North and North-west of Pakistan [see map of INDIA]. It is a land of barren mountains and its capital, Kabul, stands on a river of that name. Although it is a little larger than France (250,960 square miles) it has only 13 million inhabitants, almost all of whom are Moslems. The people are of very mixed origins, the Pathans being amongst the most important. Next are the Tajiks, who are Persians and who speak that language; then the Uzbeks who are related to the people of Uzbekistan in the Soviet Union. Recently oil has been discovered. The country has had help from both the United States and the Soviet Union in building hydro-electric stations and irrigation works. The country exports dried fruits and lamb skins.

AFRICA

The second largest continent (about 11,500,000 square miles) and three times larger than Europe with about two hundred million people living in it. Until the making of the Suez Canal in 1860 it was joined to Asia by a narrow isthmus. At the end of the Second World War there were only three independent countries in the continent, the rest being governed by European countries. There are now nearly forty independent states.

AGOUTIS

Are rodents native to South and Central America and the West Indies. They are about the size of a rabbit but tail-less. Agoutis feed on leaves and fruits. They are much hunted as their flesh is considered a delicacy. A close relative is the 'paca'.

AGRICOLA-Georg BAUER (1495–1555)

German doctor, chemist and mining engineer. As a doctor he gave an account of miners' diseases and drew up rules for their safety and welfare. In the field of chemistry he explained how to prepare sulphur, nitric acid and sulphuric acid, and showed how artificial magnets could be made by hammering red-hot iron. His greatest work was in mining and contained in his magnificently illustrated book *De Re Metallica.* He has been called the 'Father of Metallurgy'.

ALBANIA

A small mountainous agricultural country of 11,100 square miles and over a million and a quarter inhabitants on the Adriatic coast whose neighbours are Yugoslavia and Greece. Its capital is Tirana. Since the Second World War the country has had a Communist form of government. When the Soviet Union and China quarrelled a few years ago Albania sided with China, the only Communist country in Europe to do so.

ALCHEMY

The ancient study from which modern chemistry has developed. The origins of alchemy, and even the source of the name, are not precisely known. The ancient civilizations of the Middle East had technologists and metal workers who learnt how to extract metals from their ores, to distil one liquid from a mixture, to get crystals out of solutions, and other operations. This knowledge was gradually built up and handed down through the groups of craftsmen.

Part of this knowledge was concerned with treating metals such as copper to make them look like gold or silver. At some stage, probably within the Greek colony in Alexandria, the craftsmen's knowledge became entangled in mumbo jumbo taken over in a crude form from the philosophers' mumbo jumbo about the 'principles' of matter. At this stage alchemists began to turn into magicians who used an obscure language with mysterious signs. They

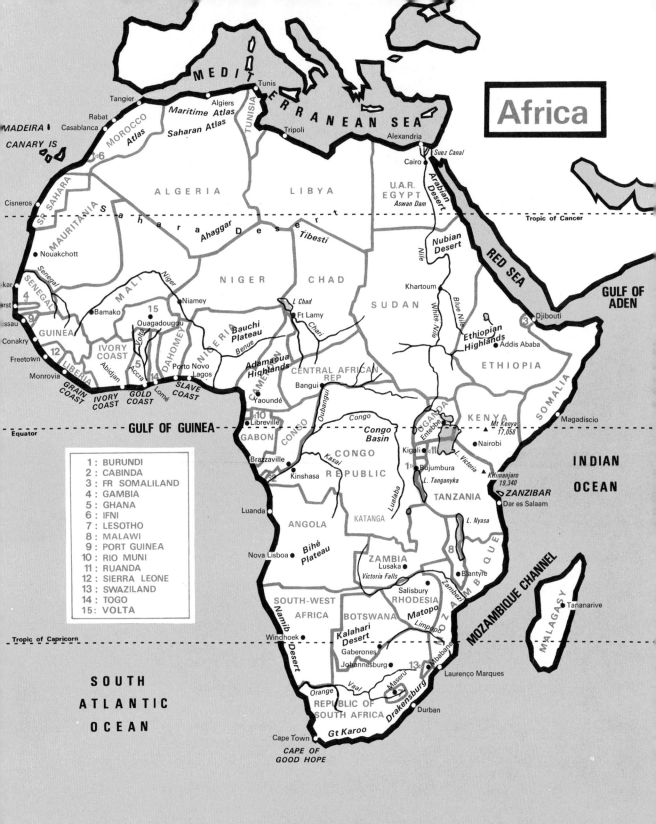

Africa

MEDITERRANEAN SEA

Tunis
Tangier
Algiers
Rabat
Casablanca
Tripoli
Alexandria
Suez Canal
Cairo

Maritime Atlas
Saharan Atlas
Atlas
MOROCCO
TUNISIA

MADEIRA
CANARY IS

SR SAHARA
Cisneros

ALGERIA
LIBYA
U.A.R.
EGYPT
Aswan Dam

Arabian Desert
RED SEA
GULF OF ADEN

Tropic of Cancer

MAURITANIA
Sahara Desert
Ahaggar
Tibesti
Nubian Desert
Nile

Nouakchott

Senegal
SENEGAL
GUINEA
Conakry
Freetown
Monrovia

NIGER
CHAD
SUDAN
White Nile
Blue Nile
Khartoum

Djibouti

Niger
Bamako
MALI
15
Niamey
L Chad
Ft Lamy
Chari
Benue
Bauchi Plateau

Ouagadougou
Volta
IVORY COAST
5
DAHOMEY
Porto Novo
Lagos
Accra
Lomé
14
Abidjan

Ethiopian Highlands
Addis Ababa
ETHIOPIA
SOMALIA

Adamaoua Highlands
CAMEROUN
Yaoundé
CENTRAL AFRICAN REP
Bangui
Oubangui
Congo

GRAIN COAST
IVORY COAST
GOLD COAST
SLAVE COAST
LIBERIA
12

Mt Kenya
17,058
KENYA
Nairobi
Magadiscio

Libreville
GABON
10
CONGO
Brazzaville
Kinshasa
Kasai
CONGO REPUBLIC
Congo Basin
Lualaba

UGANDA
Entebbe
Kigali
11
Bujumbura
L. Victoria
L. Tanganyka
Kilimanjaro
19,340
TANZANIA
ZANZIBAR
Dar es Salaam

Equator — GULF OF GUINEA

INDIAN OCEAN

Luanda
ANGOLA
Nova Lisboa
Bihé Plateau

KATANGA

L. Nyasa
8

MOZAMBIQUE

1: BURUNDI
2: CABINDA
3: FR SOMALILAND
4: GAMBIA
5: GHANA
6: IFNI
7: LESOTHO
8: MALAWI
9: PORT GUINEA
10: RIO MUNI
11: RUANDA
12: SIERRA LEONE
13: SWAZILAND
14: TOGO
15: VOLTA

ZAMBIA
Lusaka
Victoria Falls
Zambezi
Salisbury
RHODESIA
Matopo
Limpopo
Blantyre

MALAGASY
Tananarive
MOZAMBIQUE CHANNEL

SOUTH-WEST AFRICA
Namib Desert
Windhoek
Kalahari Desert
BOTSWANA
Gaberones
Johannesburg
13
Mbabane
Maseru
Laurenço Marques

Tropic of Capricorn

SOUTH
ATLANTIC
OCEAN

Orange
Vaal
REPUBLIC OF SOUTH AFRICA
Drakensburg
Durban
Gt Karoo
Cape Town
CAPE OF GOOD HOPE

ALCHEMY A print of an alchemist's laboratory showing the kind of apparatus he used.

claimed not merely to imitate gold but actually to make it from the baser metals. Attempts to generalize this mixture of technology, mysticism and charlatanry led to the dogmas of later alchemists. For instance, many ores were sulphides, and when these were treated by fire, sulphurous fumes were produced. So one of the 'principles' of *all* substances, they said, was sulphur. On the other hand, mercury seemed to remain unchanged through many operations. Consequently mercury became another of the 'principles'.

Thus alchemy reached its peak in the Middle Ages. Charlatanry flourished; many claimed to have the 'philosopher's stone' for transmuting any metal into gold. At the same time, in spite of all this—and there were of course grades of alchemist—knowledge of matter was advancing. ROGER BACON in England is credited with having discovered gunpowder as a result of his alchemical researches. Information on the production of acids and alkalies and salts was added to the body of knowledge.

In the 16th century a German alchemist who was also a physician, PARACELSUS, gave a new impetus to alchemy. He added a third 'principle', that of salt, to the other two. His contention that the human body was a sort of chemical laboratory led to the search for the elixir of life, the universal panacea and charm against death. Owing to his prestige in medicine many able men were attracted to the study of alchemy.

It was in the 17th century, though the magical side of alchemy persisted in decreasing importance for a century or so more, that the death-blow was really delivered to mumbo jumbo and magic and a fillip given to the truly scientific side of alchemical enquiry. This revolutionary change is associated with ROBERT BOYLE and his book *The Sceptical Chymist* published in 1661. The intellectual renaissance of the 17th century combined with immense technological and industrial expansion to cast into oblivion the old alchemy and found the new exact science of CHEMISTRY.

ALCUIN (735–804)

English scholar, born at York and educated at the school in that city. By 778 he was master of the school and its splendid library. Three years later he met the monarch CHARLEMAGNE at Parma; the emperor, interested in the development of education, invited Alcuin to join him. The offer was accepted, and Alcuin spent the remaining years of his life under the royal patronage, living and working in the courts and then the schools of the Continent.

ALDERMAN

The name dates back to Saxon times when older and consequently more experienced men were chosen to act as councillors. Today the term is given to those who may be considered senior members of COUNTY COUNCILS, COUNTY BOROUGH COUNCILS and BOROUGH COUNCILS. After a local government election the councillors elect some of their number to serve as aldermen. These are usually those who have already served for some years as councillors and it is one of the aldermen who is likely to be chosen MAYOR. Aldermen generally serve six years instead of only three as is the case with other councillors and half of them retire every three years. Apart from this their work on the council is the same as that of other councillors. About one quarter of the councillors are elected by their fellow councillors.

ALEXANDER the Great (356–323 B.C.)

King of Macedonia who spread Greek civilization wherever he conquered and who had the idea of forming a single community of the whole known world. Alexander was partially educated by the Greek philosopher ARISTOTLE. He was only twenty when he succeeded his father to the throne. He showed his military skill as a young man by conquering in turn Thebes, Persia, Syria and Phoenicia. In Egypt he founded the city of Alexandria and established Greek colonies in India. He finally returned to Babylon, intending to make it the capital of his Empire, but he died only eleven days after his arrival.

ALFRED the Great (c. 849–901)

King of Wessex, and defender of England against the Danes. When his fortunes were at their lowest ebb he retreated to the Athelney fens, but in 878 his armies defeated the Danes at Edington in Wiltshire. The Danish King Guthrum was baptised, and the country divided so that the Danes were confined in the north and east. This settlement enabled Alfred's successors to unite the whole country under their rule. In peace-time Alfred educated himself so that he could translate important works from Latin into Anglo-Saxon, and he probably began the *Anglo-Saxon Chronicle*. He started a new defensive system of fortified towns, and he designed some new ships to tackle the Danes at sea. He collected the laws of the earlier Kings of Wessex and Mercia and codified them into a single body, which provided the basis for a national law system in the next century.

ALGEBRA

The word algebra is of Arabic origin, getting its name from a mathematical book written A.D. 825, called *Hisab* **al-jabr** *wal muqabala*— the *Science of Equations*. The writer, Muhammad al Khwarizmi, also introduced the Hindu numerals into Europe. The usefulness of Algebra can be shown in the following problem —'A boy spends one fifth of his pocket money on sweets, a quarter on papers, saves a third and has sixpence ha'penny left. How much

does he get?' If we proceed to make an equation by letting x equal the unknown quantity, i.e., the pocket money in pence, then

$$x = \tfrac{1}{5}x + \tfrac{1}{4}x + \tfrac{1}{3}x + 6\tfrac{1}{2} \text{ pence}$$

Multiply $60\, x = 12\ x + 15\ x + 20\ x +$
by 60 $\qquad$ 390 pence
$\qquad 60\, x = 47\ x + 390 \text{ pence}$
$\qquad 13\, x = 390$
$\qquad\quad x = 30 \text{ pence}$
$\qquad \therefore$ pocket money was 2/6d.

An equation such as this is called a simple equation. When an equation contains an x^2 term, it is called a quadratic or an equation of the second degree; if it contains x^3 it is an equation of the third degree and so on to equations of the nth degree.

Early Egyptian manuscripts going back to 1600 B.C. show that they could solve certain problems by means of simple and even quadratic equations. But the number systems of the Egyptians, Greeks and Romans did not make concise mathematical statement possible and this is essential, for algebra is a kind of mathematical shorthand.

Take the equation $2x^2 - 5x + 6 = 0$. In the 15th century, this would have been written 2 *census et* 6 *demptis* 5 *rebus aequatur zero*. *Census* has to do with counting and in this case is meant to indicate squaring, *demptis* means subtract, *rebus* means together. There are no symbols for plus, minus, equals or for zero. There is no use of a letter for the unknown quantity. It was regarded as a great advance when Viete in 1595 could write instead: 2 *in* A *quad* — 5 *in* A *plano* + 6 *aequator* 0. There are still too many words; but we have signs for plus and minus and a letter for the unknown. It is said that François Viete solved an equation containing x^{45}. This would have been impossible without the improved notation. It remained for RENÉ DESCARTES, about the middle of the 17th century, to modernise and give us the version in completely symbolic form.

The Egyptians and Greeks could cope with equations of the first and second degree; for example EUCLID deals with the case of $(a + b)^2$ and $(a - b)^2$. He did this by calling the product an area. In the same way, cubic equations could be regarded as representing volumes. When it came to higher terms, mathematicians could not think of a corresponding meaning. Another difficulty since the time of Pythagoras was the irrational numbers i.e. numbers like $\sqrt{2}$ that never worked out exactly.

Arabic and Chinese mathematicians did not worry about the reality behind their equations to the same extent as the Greeks. Thus OMAR KHAYYAM could expand, i.e., multiply out $(a + b)^4$, $(a + b)^5$ and $(a + b)^6$. By 1300, Chinese writers could give the answer to

$(a + b)^n$ where n could be any whole number.

The influence of NEWTON on the mathematical discoveries of the 18th century was enormous. Following in his footsteps, progress was most rapid in applying the CALCULUS to mechanics. Then by the 19th century the division of mathematics into 'pure' and 'applied' developed. Algebra is the most fundamental part of pure mathematics. The student who wishes to understand the historical progress of algebra should read Lancelot Hogben's *Mathematics for the Million*.

ALGERIA

A republic in North Africa (847,550 square miles) nearly four times larger than France but with a population of 12 million, nearly all of them Arabs. A large area in the interior is part of the great Sahara desert and is uninhabitable except by a handful of desert nomads. The capital is Algiers on the Mediterranean coast. For more than a hundred years it was ruled by France and more than a million French people settled there and made it their home. After the Second World War the Arabs demanded that the country should become independent. As France was not then willing this led in 1954 to the beginning of war with France. In 1962 peace was restored and Algeria became independent.

ALPACA

A close relative of the LLAMA and a native of South America. It is smaller than the llama and has a fleece of at least 24 inches long from which the cloth known as 'alpaca' is woven. At the present time it is a domesticated animal.

ALPHABET

This word is made up from the names of the first two letters of the Greek alphabet—alpha (α) and beta (β). In the same way we speak in English of the ABC.

The English alphabet has twenty-six letters. Five of them, *a e i o u*, are called *vowels*—that is, the letters which have a 'voice' or sound of their own. The others are called *consonants*—that is, they have no voice or sound of their own, but can only be 'sounded with' (*con* = with, *sonant*, 'sounding') a vowel. Two letters, *y* and *w*, can be a vowel at one time and a consonant at another. Thus in *cycle, analysis, duty, suddenly*, *y* is a vowel; but in *youth* and *yellow* it is a consonant. In *swift, wife* and *which w* is a consonant, but in *crowd, knew* and *hawk* it is a vowel making one sound with another vowel.

Men first wrote, as we all do when we are very young, in pictures; and the letters of the alphabet have all come out of the far-off past

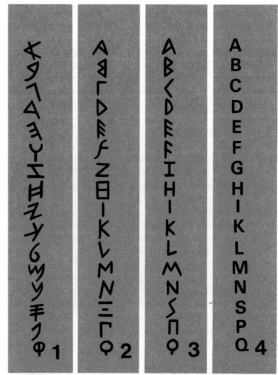

ALPHABET The four columns of characters above show the development of the main letters of our alphabet. Reading from left to right: Phoenician (1), early Greek (2), classical Greek (3) and Roman (4).

from certain pictures that had special meanings and uses. We are not altogether certain of them now, but it is generally believed that our letter *a* goes back to the picture of an eagle, *b* to the picture of a house, *n* to the picture of water (a wavy line $\sim$), and *o* to the picture of a man's eye. Our letters are those of the Roman alphabet, which was made up of letters simplified or altered from the Greek (thus α became *a* and β became *B*), and was first in use about six centuries before Christ.

Of course, our letters are not now pictures. They are symbols of certain sounds which can be arranged, like bricks and counters, in certain shapes or patterns. These patterns are called words, and the words are really the 'pictures', which can themselves be arranged in bigger 'pictures' called sentences.

Some languages, notably Chinese, still use pictures instead of letter symbols. This means that the Chinese has to know by heart several thousand signs before he can read a book. But we also have our difficulties. The chief one is to shape the words, to put the symbols or letters together, so that they represent the intended sounds. It is, in fact, the bugbear of spelling.

AMBASSADOR

A DIPLOMAT of the highest rank. British Ambassadors represent the Queen and the Ambassadors of other countries represent their Head of State, whether King or President. Because of this Ambassadors are always addressed as 'Your Excellency'. An Ambassador is sent to the capital city of a foreign State as his country's chief representative. The place where he lives and works is called an EMBASSY. Ambassadors and their chief assistants who are also diplomats have special rights and privileges and cannot be charged in a court of law in the country to which they are sent.

AMERICA

The name given to the two continents of the Western Hemisphere. They are joined together by an isthmus through which is cut the PANAMA canal. The isthmus, together with some adjoining islands, is referred to as Central America. North America, including Mexico, is a little less than twice the size of Europe. South America is a little smaller. Central and South America are often called Latin America because nearly all the people speak either Spanish or Portuguese, which are Latin languages. The name America is taken from the name of the Italian explorer, Amerigo VESPUCCI, who lived at the time of Christopher COLUMBUS.

AMPÈRE, André Marie (1775–1836)

French scientist who did important work in the field of electrodynamics and discovered the law which bears his name. The electrical unit of current strength is also named after him.

AMPHIBIA

Cold-blooded vertebrates with smooth, naked skins. They include newts and salamanders, frogs and toads. All are able to live both on land and in the water, breathing mainly by lungs when on land and through the skin when submerged in water. Most amphibia have four legs, but some have lost the hind pair and others are legless. They are classified into the 'Caecilians', with worm-like bodies and no legs, the tailed amphibia (newts and salamanders) and the tail-less amphibia (frogs and toads). Caecilians are found only in the tropics. The eggs of amphibia are, with few exceptions, laid in water and from them hatch the tadpoles, which breathe by gills.

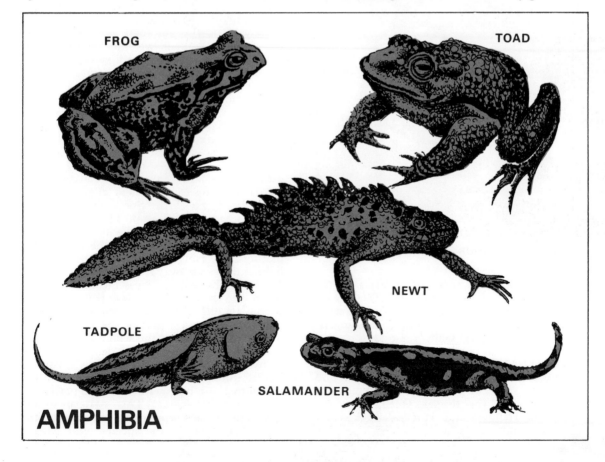

FROG

TOAD

NEWT

TADPOLE

SALAMANDER

AMPHIBIA

ANDERSEN, Hans Christian (1805–1875)
Danish writer of fairy-tales. Born in Odense, he was the son of a poor cobbler. A rather ugly child he used to listen enraptured to the tales of fairies and witches told by his grandmother. His own stories and plays won him such fame that the King of Denmark gave him a pension. This enabled him to travel to Germany, Spain and England where he stayed with Charles Dickens (1847). Of his many fairy tales the best known are *The Tin Soldier* and *The Little Match Girl*. The one called *The Ugly Duckling* is really an account of his own life. He died in Copenhagen.

ANGELICO, Fra (1387–1455)
Italian painter, born in Tuscany. He became a Dominican monk in 1407, and lived in the monastery of Saint Mark in Florence, where he produced many works, including the famous *Crucifixion with St. Dominic, Christ as a Pilgrim Welcomed by Two Dominicans,* and the great *Crucifixion.* In 1445 he was summoned to Rome by the Pope to decorate the Vatican, and in 1447 he painted *Christ as Judge* and *Prophets* in the cathedral at Orvieto. In 1448 he

ANIMAL BEHAVIOUR Grey wagtail feeding a young cuckoo

began his famous series of frescoes in the Vatican. His best works included *The Coronation of the Virgin* and *Christ in Glory,* the latter, containing 265 figures of saints and angels, now in the National Gallery, London.

ANGLO-SAXONS
People who came over from Germany and began to settle in England from about A.D. 450, i.e. after the Roman Occupation; the brothers Hengist and Horsa led the first invasion and settled in Kent. The legendary King Arthur was said to have united the Britons, the old inhabitants of the country, against the invaders.

Traces of the Anglo-Saxon language still exist in place names, e.g. Essex, the land of the East Saxons; Sussex, the land of the South Saxons; towns ending with 'ton' or 'ham'. Some local officials also date from these times, e.g. SHERIFF.

The Anglo-Saxon period in English history means from about A.D. 450 to A.D. 1066, the date of the Norman Conquest.

ANIMAL BEHAVIOUR
If we had to think about every action we have to perform life would be unbearable. Supposing when a speck of dust is coming towards your eye you had to stop and think now was the time to shut the eye, the eye would never be shut in time and you would always be suffering from specks in the eyes. Instead, we blink the eye automatically, and automatic behaviour of this kind is known as reflex action. Another thing is needed to keep our eyes in good condition: they must be kept moist. This is done by lowering the lids every now and then so that the moisture entering the eye through the tear-duct is spread evenly over the eyeball. This blinking, which goes on all the time we are awake, is also automatic or reflex. When we come to animals we find that very few animals show any real intelligence, or power to think, even in a simple way, and in most of them all behaviour is automatic.

The simplest form of behaviour is that known as the tropism or taxis. Unfortunately, scientists have given two names to the same thing and cannot agree among themselves on which to use. Tropisms may be of several kinds. Some animals move towards light, others move away from it. Some go downwards into the earth, others climb upwards away from the earth. Some move towards water, others away from it. The young queen ant, for example, shuns the light and stays buried in the earth, but when she is ready for mating these things are reversed, she seeks the light and flies up away from the earth. As soon as she has mated, she loses no time in going down into the earth, and away from the light. A tropism differs, therefore, from a reflex, for in the latter only a part of the body moves, whereas in a tropism the whole body moves.

It is not necessary here to deal with all the many kinds of behaviour; so we will confine our attention to one more only, the instinct. All animals are born with a definite pattern of instinctive behaviour. This pattern differs from one species to another, but is the same for all members of the species. Our garden

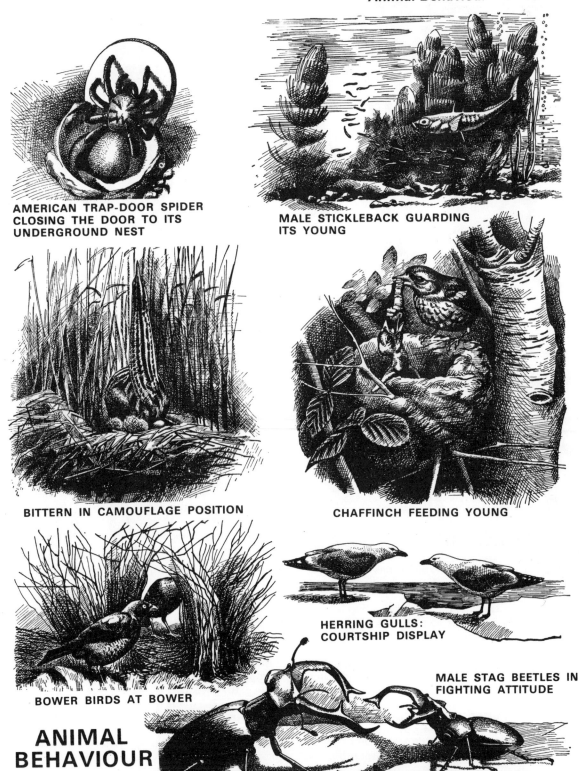

AMERICAN TRAP-DOOR SPIDER CLOSING THE DOOR TO ITS UNDERGROUND NEST

MALE STICKLEBACK GUARDING ITS YOUNG

BITTERN IN CAMOUFLAGE POSITION

CHAFFINCH FEEDING YOUNG

BOWER BIRDS AT BOWER

HERRING GULLS: COURTSHIP DISPLAY

MALE STAG BEETLES IN FIGHTING ATTITUDE

ANIMAL BEHAVIOUR

BLACKBUCK

IMPALA

WATERBUCK

ELAND

GERENUK
BUCK

DOE

KUDU

ANTELOPES

spider, the large diadem spider, has the instinct to build a web with radiating spokes covered with a spiral. All spiders of this species build webs of the same pattern, and the first web a spider makes is as good as the last. There is no improvement with practice. Moreover, the building of the web is not learned—it is innate or instinctive. Nest-building in birds is instinctive. If we find a bird's nest we can tell whether it was made by a thrush, a blackbird, a house-martin or a goldcrest by its shape and pattern.

Innate or instinctive behaviour is the result of something deep down inside the animal, but it usually requires something outside to set it going. We say that it needs something to trigger it off, and this something we call a releaser. The sight of food is a releaser, and the mouth watering is the result of an innate urge to feed triggered off by the sight of food.

Although behaviour is so largely automatic, there is even in the lower animals a certain amount which is not automatic. In the higher animals we call it intelligent behaviour, when the animal does something it has not done before, or solves a new problem by methods that are not instinctive. In the lower animals, such behaviour is rarely seen and is so far removed from what we normally call intelligence that we call it plastic behaviour. The difference between plastic behaviour and intelligence is, however, rather one of degree.

In recent years a great deal of time has been devoted to the study of the behaviour patterns of individual species. Especially outstanding in this field are Conrad Lorenz (he wrote *King Soloman's Ring*) and Dr. Tinbergen. The name of the branch of their particular science of behaviour is 'ethology'.

ANIMAL KINGDOM
A term used to include all animals both living and fossil. In so defining the term there are two difficulties attaching to the meaning of the word animal. To most people an animal is a MAMMAL. To the zoologist an animal is any living thing that is not a plant. This brings us to the second difficulty, that there are such things as plant-animals. These are mainly microscopic, one-celled organisms that behave in all respects like animals yet have chlorophyll and are able to manufacture their own food. Further than this, many animals are plant-like in appearance, such as sponges, sea-anemones, sea-mosses, and the like, and these were at first classified with the plants.

In classifying animals it is necessary to group into species those that look alike and behave in the same way. Related species are put into one genus, and several genera constitute a family. One or more families make up an order, orders are grouped into classes, and classes into phyla. An example will best explain this:

   KINGDOM: Animalia
    SUB-KINGDOM: Vertebrata
    PHYLUM: Chordata
    CLASS: Mammalia
    ORDER: Carnivora
    FAMILY: Felidae
    GENUS: *Felis*
     SPECIES: *leo*

The lion (*Felis leo*) belongs to the family FELIDAE (which includes tigers, leopards and cats). The family FELIDAE belongs to the Carnivora (flesh-eating animals). Carnivora are mammals, and so on.

ANTEATERS
A group of toothless mammals mainly native to the tropical regions of America. The best-known member of this family is the 'giant anteater'. It lives in S. and C. America. It is about 8 feet long from tail to snout, 2½ feet high and covered with long grizzled hairs. The giant anteater has a funnel-like head and a long sticky tongue which it uses to lick up the termites on which it feeds. It has, like the AARD-VARK, powerful forefeet for ripping open termites' nests and, when provoked, fighting with—and a dangerous animal it can be.

ANTELOPES
Even-toed hoofed mammals native mainly to Africa with a few in India. They include KUDU, NYALA, ELANDS, DUIKERS, WATERBUCKS, etc. They vary in size from the tiny Royal antelope to the large eland. They are all cud-chewers and live in various regions—open plains, forests, deserts, swamps and even on mountains.

ANTHROPOLOGY
Generally this term applies to the science of man in relation to his life, society, and environment, and is closely allied with archaeology, geography, folk-lore, and sociology. The two main branches of study are social anthropology and ethnology.

Social anthropology is concerned primarily with the study of the pattern of cultures and societies. It includes in its surveys such subjects as political organization, religion, marriage, law, kinship, technology, mythology, crime, language, etc. Ethnology deals with the classification of peoples so far as their racial and cultural features are concerned, and with the distribution and diffusion of races and cultures.

ANTIBIOTICS
Branch of medical science which has developed out of the discovery that PENICILLIN is capable of controlling diseases caused by bacteria. This was first observed by Alexander FLEMING in 1928 but it was not made on a commercial scale until 1941. Many are being discovered yearly as bacteria are quick to develop immunity to specific drugs.

ANTI-SLAVERY MOVEMENT
During the 18th century people in Britain began to feel ashamed that, while they lived in a country which had not known slavery for hundreds of years, slaves were still allowed in the West Indian Colonies. In 1790, it was estimated that British ships transported 38,000 Africans, and about half of these would have died during the journey, or in the early months of enslavement. The Quakers, especially Thomas Clarkson, helped to rouse public opinion. The younger PITT was sympathetic and encouraged by him, William WILBERFORCE, an M.P., pressed for action. The Danes had already forbidden the traffic in their colonies in 1802. In 1807 the British slave trade was forbidden, but it was not till 1833 that slavery in British colonies was abolished. Other colonial powers followed suit (e.g. France 1848, Holland 1863).

In the United States the victory of the North over the South in the Civil War (1865) brought freedom to the slaves of the southern states. *Uncle Tom's Cabin,* a moving story by Harriet Beecher Stowe, did much to stir the North into opposing slavery.

APES
More accurately 'great apes', are bigger and stronger than monkeys and have no tails. They include the GORILLA, ORANG-UTAN, CHIMPANZEE and GIBBON. All have long arms for swinging about in trees. When they walk erect they

APOSTLES as depicted by Giotto in his painting of the *Feast of Pentecost*.

support their weight on the knuckles of their bent fingers. In the main they are vegetable eaters although sometimes their food is supplemented with insects.

APOCRYPHA

Between the 3rd and 2nd centuries B.C., the Hebrew Scriptures, as they existed then, were translated into Greek for the benefit of the Greek-speaking Jews living in Alexandria, in Egypt. This translation is known as the 'Septuagint' (The Seventy) because seventy scholars are said to have worked on it. About A.D. 90, however, the Jewish religious leaders in Palestine decided to drop certain writings from their sacred scriptures, including some contained in the Septuagint. The Septuagint retained these writings, and thus included, along with other writings of Greek origin, books not found in the Jewish Bible. And these 'outside' writings form, in the main, the collection of 14 books and parts of books we call the Apocrypha, meaning 'hidden writings'.

The contents of the Apocrypha include historical works, such as First Maccabees, which gives a very valuable account of the Jewish war of independence against Syrian rule, between 168 and 164 B.C.; legendary writings, such as the Book of Tobit, which contains the famous story of Tobias and the Angel; and works of religious instruction and philosophy, such as the Wisdom of Solomon and Ecclesiasticus.

The ROMAN CATHOLIC CHURCH includes most of the Apocrypha in its version of the Bible, but it is seldom included in Protestant editions. When it is included, it is usually placed between the Old and New Testaments. The FREE CHURCHES make little or no use of the books of the Apocrypha, but Article IV of the CHURCH OF ENGLAND tells us the Church 'doth read them for example of life and instruction of manners.'

The Apocrypha is included in the Bible presented to the Sovereign during the Coronation Service.

APOSTLES

The word 'apostle' is almost exactly the Greek word *apostolos* which means 'one who is commissioned', a messenger with authority, an ambassador. In the New Testament it refers principally to the twelve disciples whom Jesus chose, at the beginning of His ministry, to be His companions and the special witnesses of His life and work, and His death and resurrection.

The original Twelve Apostles were Simon Peter, James and John, Andrew, Philip and Bartholomew, Matthew, Thomas, James the son of Alphaeus, Thaddeus, Simon the Canaanite and Judas Iscariot. Matthias was later elected to take the place of Judas who hanged himself after betraying Jesus.

The great St. Paul claimed to be an Apostle because, although he had not been a companion of Jesus, Jesus had appeared to him on the Damascus road. The title was also given to Barnabas, and certain others of the original followers of Jesus.

APULEIUS, Lucius (*c.* A.D. 125–?)

Roman writer. Born in North Africa, he was the son of a wealthy magistrate. After studying at Athens and Carthage, he used the wealth left him by his father to travel. He finally settled down in Carthage as a rhetorician where he died. (The date is unknown). His most famous work is *The Golden Ass* which describes the experiences of one Lucius whom an enchantress had turned into an ass.

AQUARIUM

A container, either a pond or some form of tank, in which fish, reptiles and plants are kept. There are two types of aquaria, the 'cold water' in which such fish as goldfish, minnows, sticklebacks, lizards, etc. can be kept and bred, and the 'tropical' or 'heated' aquarium for keeping angel fish, cichlids, paradise fish, etc. Any child wishing to start an aquarium should read a book on the subject as there is a lot to do and learn if the fish are to survive.

AQUINAS, St. Thomas (1226–1274)

Italian theologian. Born near Naples, of noble descent he studied at the monastery of Monte Cassino and at Naples University. He then became a Dominican friar (1243). After further study at Cologne and Paris he received his doctorate (1258). He spent the rest of his life teaching and writing and travelling in the service of his order. He died 1274 and was canonised 1323.

ARABIA

The Arabs inhabit what are today a number of different countries. These include IRAQ, JORDAN, SYRIA, LEBANON, SAUDI ARABIA, LIBYA, MOROCCO, ALGERIA, YEMEN and TUNISIA. Modern Egypt is also considered an Arab country.

Little of importance is known of the history of the Arabs before the birth of MOHAMMED in A.D. 571. The Arabs, inspired by his teaching, then set out to conquer their neighbours and to forcibly convert them to the new faith of ISLAM. Between A.D. 632 and A.D. 656 they conquered Syria, Egypt and Persia and later spread to North Africa and from there into Spain. The successors of Mohammed who ruled over the Arabs were known as Caliphs. In the 8th century the capital of the caliphs was moved from Damascus to Baghdad and the following century the famous Haroun al

over all the Arab countries, with the exception of Morocco. The Algerians freed themselves of the Turks in the 17th century. About 1830 Algeria and, later on, Tunisia came under French control. Morocco was a French protectorate from 1912–56, with the exception of a small part which came under Spain, Tangier becoming an international port and commercial centre.

It was not till after the First World War, when the Turkish empire came to an end, that the other Arab countries had an independent history of their own. It was decided that Arabia should be divided into several small countries and placed for a time under the LEAGUE OF NATIONS. These countries are now independent. Iraq, Syria and the Lebanon are republics. Saudi Arabia and Jordan are kingdoms.

ARBUTHNOT, John (1667–1735)

Scottish physician and wit. As a fashionable doctor he attended Queen Anne and many public figures, but he is best known for his wit and learning which made him the friend of SWIFT and POPE. He wrote *The History of*

GLASS COVER   **FLOATING PLANTS**

SUBMERGED PLANTS

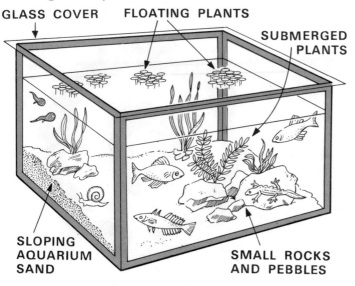

AQUARIUM A simple aquarium of the kind shown here is ideal for studying the behaviour of such animals as goldfish, minnows, sticklebacks, lizards and tadpoles.

SLOPING AQUARIUM SAND

SMALL ROCKS AND PEBBLES

Raschid, whose exploits are told in the *Arabian Nights*, was caliph. The Arabs at this time produced men of science and it was they who gave us the numerals we use today.

In North Africa the Arabs, or Moors, rose to great power and influence. They set up kingdoms under rulers known as Sultans and it was they who succeeded in conquering SPAIN in the 8th century.

The power of the Arabs declined with the rise to power of TURKEY in the 14th century. The Turks gradually extended their empire

John Bull in *Miscellanies in Prose and Verse*, and the *Memoirs of Martinus Scriblerus*, included in Pope's *Works*.

ARCHAEOLOGY

Branch of science (some prefer scholarship) concerned with revealing the nature of the societies and cultures of ancient man. During the past fifty years archaeology has considerably enlarged our understanding of man's prehistory; in fact, it has, from material evidence, created a clear picture of man's development

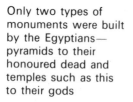

Only two types of monuments were built by the Egyptians— pyramids to their honoured dead and temples such as this to their gods

Excavation in progress at an Assyrian Temple with carved murals

Beauty was everpresent i civilization. Many of their masterpieces of sculpture architecture remain today including the Parthenon

during the past 40,000 years. Modern archaeology requires, in addition to the field archaeologist who excavates the find, the services of scholars to decipher hieroglyphic and similar writing, the historian, anthropologist and chemist. A recent development is submarine archaeology which has been made possible by the advances in aqualung apparatus. From the results already obtained it is safe to say that this will become an essential branch of archaeological research.

ARCHERY

Archery is a popular sport in many parts of the world, particularly in Great Britain where inter-county championships are contested every year.

Bows are between 5 feet and 6 feet in length, and arrows about 27 inches long and $\frac{1}{4}$ inch in diameter, with a nock in the untipped end and feather flights (best made from a goose's wing feather) at the other.

Archery targets are usually made of flat basketwork, 48 inches in diameter. On to this basketwork are painted circles, the middle one being in gold, the next red, the next blue, the next black, and the outermost one white. For purposes of scoring during a contest, gold counts 9, red 7, blue 5, black 3, and white 1. The range from archer to target varies according to the ages of the contestants and to whether they are men or women.

The strength of the bow is always measured in terms of pull, and a standard bow will have a pull of about 50 lb., that is, you would have

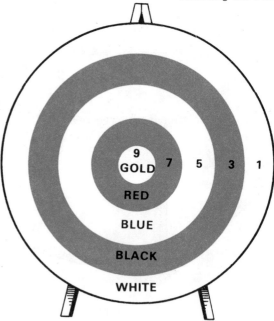

ARCHERY A marked target, see left.

to exert a pull of about 50 lb. to hold a bow-string back so that an arrow of about 27 inches has its tip just forward of the bow-grip ready for flight. The weight of the arrow itself is measured in terms of coins, just as it was in olden times. The most common one is known as a 'five-shilling arrow'; it weighs just what an old-time silver five-shilling piece used to weigh.

Pompeii and Mt Vesuvius which submerged the city with lava in AD 79

The pyramid is not solely an Egyptian structure— the Aztecs too built them between AD 1200–1600

In ancient times the sun ruled men's lives. Stonehenge was both a place of worship and a massive sun-dial

ARCHIMEDES of Syracuse (287–212 B.C.)

One of the world's greatest mathematicians and an outstanding engineer. His mathematical works included studies of spheres, cones, cylinders, spirals and irregular volumes. In mechanics he established the terms of levers and pulleys, and invented a method of raising water by turning a tube with a screw running through it [Archimedes Screw]. He also invented a military catapult for hurling rocks. Archimedes also discovered the law of flotation and the principle of specific gravity, which he used to test the purity of the gold in King Heiron's crown.

ARCTIC AND ANTARCTIC [See POLAR REGIONS]

ARGENTINA

A Spanish-speaking republic in SOUTH AMERICA and the second largest country on that continent. It is 1,084,360 square miles in area or five times bigger than France and has a population of about 22 million. It is a country of great plains, called pampas, where cattle and wheat are produced. There are some mountains of which the Andes are the most important. The capital is Buenos Aires.

Like many other countries of South America the country has seen a number of revolts which have led to changes in the government of the country. Between 1946 and 1955 the country was ruled by a dictator named Juan Peron. He was overthrown by the army and since then there have been other revolts.

ARISTARCHUS of Samos (310–230 B.C.)

One of the most distinguished astronomers of classical times. His plan of the solar system anticipated that of COPERNICUS 1,800 years later. He maintained that the universe was enormously larger than was then commonly believed. He taught that the moon shines by light reflected from the sun and revolves round the earth, and so correctly explained its phases.

ARISTOPHANES (c. 448–c. 388 B.C.)

Greek comic playwright and poet. In Athens, where he lived, great freedom of expression was allowed to the satirist, and there were no bounds to Aristophanes's criticism and mockery of personalities. At the same time he was a superb lyric writer, and his plays combined earnestness and uproarious comedy. Some of his best-known plays are *The Birds, The Frogs,* and *The Clouds.*

ARISTOTLE (384–322 B.C.)

Greek philosopher, biologist and political thinker. He worked under PLATO in his philosophic school, the ACADEMY at Athens, and was later invited to study at the court of Philip of Macedon, where he taught the young ALEXANDER. After the death of Philip, Aristotle founded his own school, called the Peripatetic school. In his writings he supplied many of the great topics which have fascinated scholars in succeeding generations, and the rules and terminology through which they could be discussed. These may be divided into the dialogues, in

MAYAN
Temple of Palenque

EGYPTIAN
Temple of Isis
Island of Philae

GREEK
Temple of Artemis
Ephesus

ARCHITECTURE

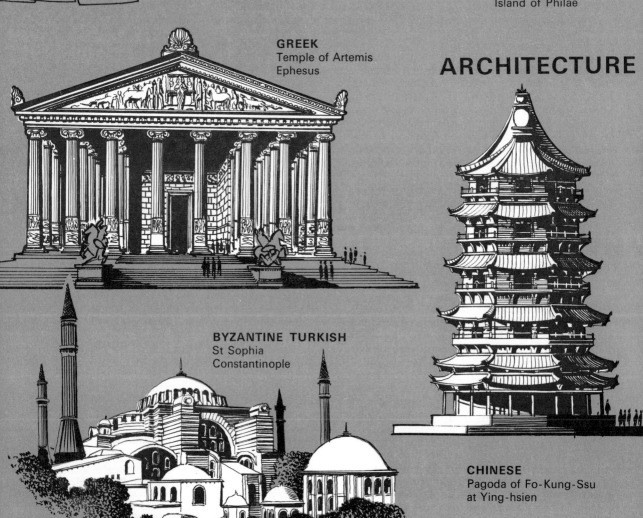

BYZANTINE TURKISH
St Sophia
Constantinople

CHINESE
Pagoda of Fo-Kung-Ssu
at Ying-hsien

ROMAN
Pont du Gard
Nimes

GOTHIC
Rheims Cathedral

INDIAN
Taj Mahal

**CONTEMPORARY
WESTERN HEMISPHERE**
U.N.O. Building
New York

ROMANESQUE
Worms Cathedral

which different views were discussed, though only fragments of these remain; the works like the *Constitution of Athens*; and the treatises on logic, physics, psychology, biology, metaphysics, ethics, and politics.

Aristotle was a vital influence on the medieval educational system, and in the movement in the universities known as 'scholasticism' his methods were used to try to reconcile worldy knowledge with the divine wisdom of the Bible. In the 13th century many of his works that were then unknown in Europe, like the *Politics* and the *Ethics*, were brought to the universities through the Arabs in Spain and Sicily, and through the Latin conquest of Constantinople.

ARITHMETIC

The oldest and the most practical branch of mathematics, and concerned only with numbers. As soon as early men learned how to write they developed a way of putting down numbers. The ancient Egyptians used a hieroglyphic (pictorial) method of representing numbers; ten was an open circle, hundred a curled palm leaf, thousand a lotus flower and so on.

The Greeks used an alphabetic system, α for one, β for two, and so on. The Romans used simple stroke marks for the first three numbers, but for five they used a 'V' sign which may originally have been represented by a hand; ten was two V's linked together.

The Roman, Greek and Egyptian number systems were very clumsy. The Egyptians for example could only multiply by two or by ten.

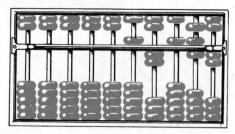

ABACUS The type shown here has been used in China since about the sixteenth century.

To help them work out their accounts the Greeks and Romans used an abacus.

Primitive tribes of the present day still count by fives because there are five fingers on each hand; Eskimos still count by twenties. Also, in the Middle Ages, twenty was a much used number, in fact we still keep the 'score' in such games as cricket, billiards, etc. The wants of a primitive people are naturally very simple. This is shown in their ideas of number. Thus a certain tribe of Australian aborigines

counts as follows: enea = 1, petchival = 2, petchival-enea = 3, petchival-petchival = 4.

The Babylonians perfected a system of measuring time and angles. Instead of basing the numbers on ten, as in the decimal system, they took the number sixty as the base. Now sixty has many factors, whereas ten is divisible by only two numbers—two and five. The Babylonian sexagesimal system, as it is called, survives in our measurements of time and angles. There are twelve months in the year, twenty-four (twice twelve) hours in the day, sixty minutes in the hour, and sixty seconds in the minute. In the Babylonian style,

$$\vee \quad \vee \quad \vee \qquad \overset{<}{<} \qquad \vee \quad \vee$$
$$60 + 60 + 60 \qquad 10 + 10 + 1 + 1$$

represents the number 202. They wrote these arrow heads in soft clay. It should be noted that the same arrow head can stand for sixty or for one according to its position at the beginning or at the end of the number. The idea that the value of the symbol depended on its position was a valuable contribution to arithmetic.

The decimal system as we know it today came to Europe through the Arabs, who in turn received it from the Hindus. The Arabic system only slowly ousted the Roman, and not until the 15th century was it in general use. The further development of using the decimal point to indicate fractions was the contribution of John NAPIER, who also gave us LOGARITHMS.

The fundamental processes of arithmetic are addition, subtraction, multiplication and division. The sign + (plus) is used to indicate the operation. Thus 5 + 7 means 7 added to 5. The answer 12 is called the sum. Using equal signs, we can write 5 + 7 = 12. Subtraction is the reverse of addition. The sign for subtraction is — (minus). Thus 12 − 7 = 5. The sign for multiplication is ×. Thus 7 × 5, means seven multiplied by five. The answer 35 is the product. Division is the reverse of multiplication and its sign is ÷. Thus

$$35 \div 7 = \frac{35}{7} = 5.$$

The student interested in the history of arithmetic should read T. Danzig's *Number*.

ARMADA

This is a Spanish word for a battle fleet, but it has become an English word too because the defeat of the Armada which Philip II of Spain sent against England in 1588, when Elizabeth was Queen, was one of the greatest battles in naval history. There is a story that

Francis DRAKE was playing bowls at Plymouth when the Armada was sighted and that he would not break off his game immediately but said: 'There's plenty of time to win the game and thrash the Spaniards too.' Anyway, the English seamen did 'thrash the Spaniards'. Afterwards a storm blew up and scattered the Spanish ships which were trying to escape. Some were wrecked as far away as Ireland and the west of Scotland. People are still searching for treasure which was thought to be on board a galleon that sank in Tobermory Bay on the Isle of Mull.

ARMADILLOS

Belong to a family of small mammals native to S. and C. America. They are distinctive because of the jointed bands of bony armour which extends from head to tail. This protection is a development of the skin and not a part of its skeleton. All armadillos are nervous creatures and roll themselves into a ball at the slightest sign of danger or attempt to bury themselves in earth. They are mainly nocturnal and feed on insects and sometimes eggs, small snakes and small rodents. The most common species is the 'nine-banded' armadillo.

ARMADILLO This is the nine-banded species.

ARMOUR—*See next page*

ARNOLD, Matthew (1822–1888)

Distinguished English poet and critic, and son of Thomas Arnold, the headmaster of Rugby School. Educated at Rugby and Oxford, he became an inspector of schools, and worked hard to improve secondary education in England, touring on the Continent to report progress there. Among his famous poems are *Sohrab and Rustum*, and *The Scholar Gypsy*, and his prose works include *Essays in Criticism* and *Culture and Anarchy*.

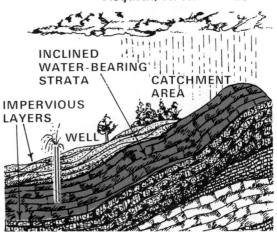

ARTESIAN WELL Section drawing showing strata.

ARTESIAN WELL

Type of well where water is forced to the surface by natural pressure. Such wells occur when an inclined aquifer (water-bearing stratum) is sandwiched between impervious strata and exposed at some point above the well to rain or other source of water-supply. The name derives from Artois, a town in France.

ARTIFICIAL RAIN

Natural rain is caused by water droplets which form a cloud becoming large enough to precipitate; cloud is formed of water droplets of approximately 1 to 10 microns radius and rain of water droplets of from about 100 microns to nearly 3 millimetres radius. This process can be caused or speeded up artificially by the following methods: (1) bombarding a cloud from above with dry-ice pellets, (2) saturating a cloud from below with silver-iodide smoke, and (3) injecting a cloud from below with water droplets. In certain arid regions of the U.S.A. and Australia the method (1) has had very positive results.

ASIA

The largest continent in the world, being about 16,000,000 square miles, with a population of over 1,000 million. It is separated from Europe by the Ural Mountains, from the American continent by the Bering Strait, by the Suez Canal from Africa, in the east by the China Sea, Sea of Japan and Sea of Okhotsk, and in the north the Arctic Ocean. [*See* map on page 88.]

ASQUITH, Herbert Henry, First Earl of Oxford and Asquith (1852–1928)

English Liberal statesman. Born in Yorkshire he was educated at Oxford. After a period at the Bar he entered Parliament as Liberal M.P.

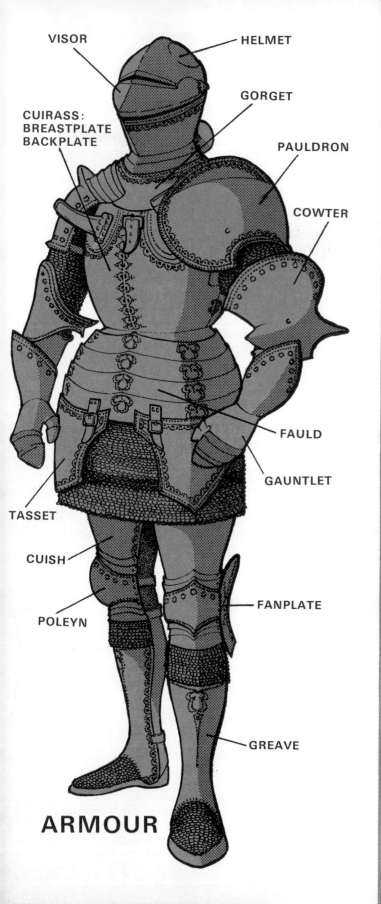

VISOR

HELMET

GORGET

CUIRASS:
BREASTPLATE
BACKPLATE

PAULDRON

COWTER

FAULD

GAUNTLET

TASSET

CUISH

FANPLATE

POLEYN

GREAVE

ARMOUR

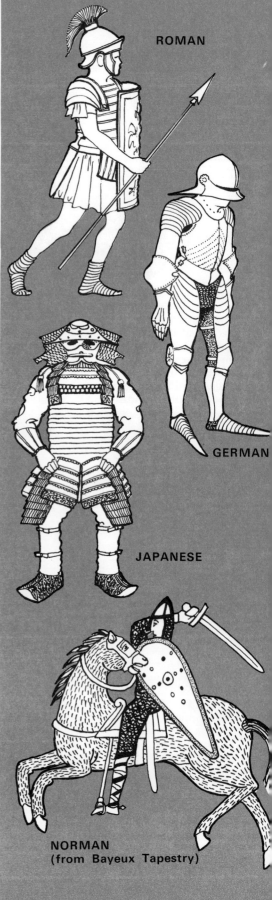

ROMAN

GERMAN

JAPANESE

NORMAN
(from Bayeux Tapestry)

for East Fife (1886). In 1892 he was Home Secretary under GLADSTONE and in 1905 Chancellor of the Exchequer when he laid the foundation of the scheme for old-age pensions. He was Prime Minister from 1908–1916. The first part of this period was marked by Asquith's Parliament Act (1911), which limited the power of the House of Lords, the question of Irish Independence, and the SUFFRAGETTES' demands for the vote. Later, Asquith led the nation during the Great War against Germany but was superseded in 1916 by LLOYD-GEORGE. He was created an earl in 1925 and resigned the Liberal leadership the following year.

ASSES
Related to the horse family and when domesticated are usually called 'donkeys'. They are smaller than the horse, have long ears, an upright short main and 'bray' rather than 'neigh'. The four main species are the Somali wild ass or African wild donkey, the 'Kiang' or Tibetan wild ass, the 'Onager' or Persian wild ass and the Mongolian wild ass.

ASSIZES
Courts which try the most serious crimes such as murder and burglary. They can also hear certain civil cases like libel and slander. Assize courts are branches of the High Court of Justice and are presided over by the Judges of the Queen's Bench Division. Assizes go back to the days of Henry II who divided the country into circuits and appointed justices to travel round the circuits to which they were appointed. Today the Judges are also appointed to districts called circuits and hold Assize Courts three times a year in the county towns and other large cities in their circuit.

ASSYRIA
The mountainous northern part of the land between the Tigris and Euphrates and seat of the ancient Assyrian civilization which reached great power in the 13th and 12th centuries B.C. Its outstanding kings were Assur-nasir-pal, Sargon and Sennacherib (Kings xviii 13). Throughout its history it was linked with BABYLONIA.

ASTRONOMY
The study of the heavenly bodies dating from the very earliest times; some of the first scientific astronomical observations were made by the Babylonians who recorded an eclipse in 2283 B.C. and the Chinese who about the same time mapped out the sky in constellations. In this encyclopedia the subject is dealt with under separate headings: NEBULA, PLANETS, RADIO-ASTRONOMY, STARS, SUN and TELESCOPE.

ATATURK, Kemal (*c.* 1880–1938)
Turkish general and statesman. Born in Salonica, the son of a customs official, he became an army officer and joined the nationalist 'Young Turk' movement. In the 1914–1918 war he defended the Dardanelles. At the end of the war he organized a national movement in Anatolia, summoned a National Assembly at Ankara and made war upon the Greeks in Asia Minor. He was elected President by the Assembly and in 1921 expelled the Greeks. He became the first President of the new Republic of Turkey and with the aid of the Turkish People's Party that he had founded, modernised the country.

ATLANTIC
The name given to a vast Ocean divided into the North and South Atlantic Oceans. It is approximately 31,830,000 square miles in area and its greatest depth is 30,250 feet. When a treaty, called the North Atlantic Treaty was signed in 1949 it was agreed that the North Atlantic meant north of the tropic of Cancer.

ASTRONOMY This dramatic photograph shows the 'Horse's Head' nebula in Orion. Taken at Mount Wilson with a 100-inch Hooker telescope.

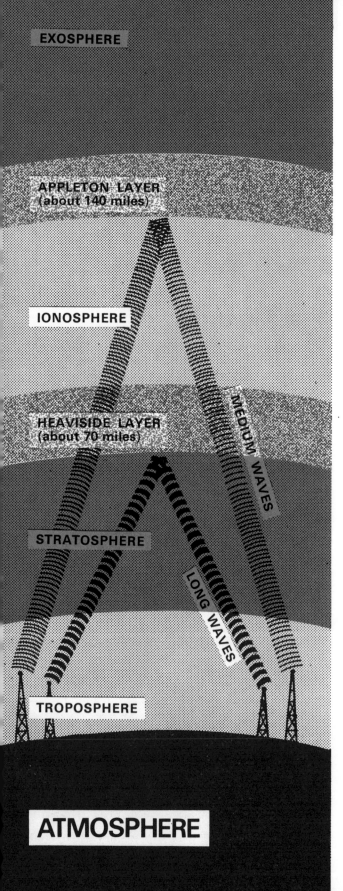

EXOSPHERE

APPLETON LAYER
(about 140 miles)

IONOSPHERE

MEDIUM WAVES

HEAVISIDE LAYER
(about 70 miles)

STRATOSPHERE

LONG WAVES

TROPOSPHERE

ATMOSPHERE

ATMOSPHERE

Blanket of air that surrounds our planet and is traceable at least 500 miles into space. Its principal constituents are nitrogen, oxygen, carbon dioxide, and water-vapour, but other and rare gases exist in very small proportions, for example, argon, neon, helium, krypton, and xenon. The average pressure of the atmosphere at sea-level is 14·5 lb. per sq. in.

The density of the atmosphere decreases until it reaches zero at its diffuse perimeter. Its temperature, however, decreases uniformly up to about seven miles from the Earth's surface, then abruptly remains constant. The region of decrease of temperature is called the 'troposphere' and the latter the 'stratosphere'; the imaginary surface separating the two being known as the 'tropopause'. [See WEATHER.]

The Appleton and Kennelly-Heaviside layers are electrically charged in the ionosphere and reflect RADIO waves.

ATOMIC ENERGY [See NUCLEAR ENERGY]

ATTACHÉ

A junior DIPLOMAT who is attached to an EMBASSY or LEGATION in order to learn the work of a diplomat and to help his AMBASSADOR. In addition to these junior diplomats important advisers may be appointed, or attached, to an Embassy to give advice to their Ambassador. There will, for instance, be high Army and Naval Officers and they will be called Army or Naval Attachés. Other experts may be chosen to give special advice so there may be a Commercial Attaché and a Press Attaché and so on.

ATTILA (A.D. 406–453)

King of the Huns, Attila proclaimed himself King of the Barbarians from the North Sea to the boundaries of China (445). He devastated the eastern portion of the Roman Empire and when he broke into the Balkan peninsula forced the Emperor at Byzantium to cede him territory and a huge tribute. In 451 he stormed westwards but was defeated at Châlons-sur-Marne in France where 200,000 men are said to have perished. He had made an unsuccessful attempt (452) to capture Rome itself. His empire fell to pieces at his death.

ATTLEE, Clement Richard, 1st Earl
(1883–1967)

English politician. He was educated at Haileybury and Oxford. Although called to the Bar (1905), he devoted himself to social work in the East End of London. He first entered Parliament in 1922 as Labour Member for Limehouse and had various posts in the Labour governments of 1924 and 1929. From

1935–1940 he was leading the Labour opposition in the House of Commons. During the war he served in CHURCHILL's coalition government (from 1943 as deputy Prime Minister). With the Labour electoral victory of 1945 he became Prime Minister. His period of office was characterized by widespread nationalization, by the introduction of the National Health Service, and by the granting of independence to India and Burma.

ATTORNEY-GENERAL
The chief law officer of the Government for England and Wales and is its legal adviser. In Scotland the officer who does this legal work is called the Lord Advocate. Under the Attorney-General are the Solicitor-General and the Director of Public Prosecutions. The Attorney-General is a Member of the Government and must always be a Member of the House of Commons. This means that when there is a change of government there is likely to be a change of Attorney-General.

AUDEN, Wystan Hugh (1907——)
One of the leading younger English poets whose influence during the 1930's was very considerable. He also wrote three plays with ISHERWOOD, and favoured the Republicans in the Spanish Civil War. He became an American citizen.

AUGUSTINE, St., of Hippo (353–430)
One of the greatest churchmen of all time. Born of a heathen father and a Christian mother, he studied philosophy at Carthage and was at last converted to Christianity thanks to his friendship with the Bishop of Milan, St. Ambrose. His greatest work, *De Civitate Dei* (*City of God*) is a powerful defence of the

AUROCHS The ancestor of domestic cattle.

AURORA Shimmering curtains of light seen at high altitudes in arctic regions.

Christian Church. His belief in predestination was taken up by the protestant reformers LUTHER and CALVIN.

AUROCHS
The ancestor of today's domesticated cattle. It was found mainly in Europe and N. Africa and became extinct in the early 16th century. The aurochs was a large animal standing at least 6 feet at the shoulder and had large curved horns. It is also known as the 'Urus'.

AURORA BOREALIS
The so-called northern lights *aurora polaris* or *aurora borealis* are seen in high latitudes in the arctic; in the antarctic *aurora australis* is seen. The aurora appears as bands of light in different colours, and is caused by the entry of solar particles into the earth's magnetic field. These consist chiefly of electrons which ionize the atmospheric gases at a height of about 100 miles, the excited atoms discharging light rays of various colours.

AUSTEN, Jane (1775–1817)
A Hampshire-born girl, who spent her life with her family, never marrying, never travelling abroad. She was the author of six novels, which are almost as quiet as her own life, but

BORNEO

Bandjarmasin

CELEBES

SUMATRA

rsan Range

Palembang

I N D O N E S

Macassar

FLORES

Djakarta Semarang

Surakarta

Surabaja

TIMOR

Krakatau ▲

Bandung

Jigjakarta

SUMBAWA

TIMOR SEA

JAVA

SUMBA

Darwin

AR

Daly

KIMBERLEY

Great Sandy Desert

N
TE

A U S T

Hamersley
Range

Gibson Desert

Mac

INDIAN

WESTERN AUSTRALIA

OCEAN

Great Victor
Desert

opic of Capricorn

S

Kalgoorlie ●

GREAT AU
BIG

○ Perth

○ Bunbury

Australia and New Zealand

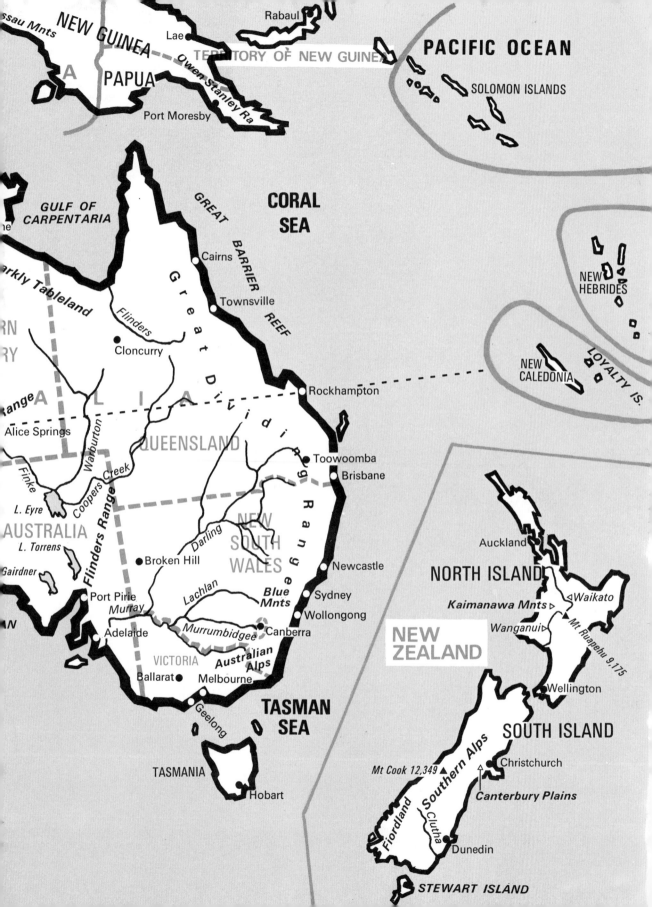

AUSTRALIA Surfing near the famous beach at Bondi, Sydney, New South Wales.

which have such sharp skill and humour that they now have admirers all over the world. The first of her published novels to be written was *Pride and Prejudice*, which she finished in 1797, but it was refused by the publisher at first and did not appear till 1813, while her second novel to be written, *Sense and Sensibility*, was the first to be published, appearing in 1811. Her other novels are *Mansfield Park, Emma, Persuasion* and *Northanger Abbey*.

AUSTRALIA

An island continent of 2,974,580 square miles which forms one of the British Dominions. If NEW ZEALAND and other islands which form part of the continent are included, the term Australasia is generally used.

The Commonwealth of Australia, including the island of Tasmania, is nearly as large as Europe but has only a little over 11 million inhabitants, most of them of British origin but there are about 50,000 native aborigines. Australia is made up of the following States: New South Wales (Cap. Sydney); Queensland (Cap. Brisbane); South Australia (Cap. Adelaide); Western Australia (Cap. Perth); Tasmania (Cap. Hobart). All these capital cities are ports, though Perth is served by the port of Fremantle which is a few miles away. An area, largely uninhabited but nearly as large as the States is the Northern Territory. Its capital is Darwin and another famous town is Alice Springs. The Territory does not yet govern itself in the way the States do. The federal capital is Canberra. Australia produces more wool than any other country in the world. The country also has rich supplies of gold, iron ore, lead and zinc and has a new and growing steel industry. One of the most important rivers is the Snowy in New South Wales and Victoria. A big new irrigation scheme is being carried out on this river and the Murray which involves taking the river waters through the mountains.

The first free immigrants arrived from Britain in 1793, the east coast of Australia having been discovered by Captain COOK about twenty years before. These settlers came to New South Wales which is thus the oldest State in Australia. In 1901 the six States were all united in a federation called the Commonwealth of Australia.

AUSTRIA

A small republic in central Europe (34,100 square miles), a little more than half the size of England and with a population of just over 7 million. Until 1918 Austria was the centre of the great Austro-Hungarian Empire. The capital is the beautiful city of Vienna on the River Danube. After the Second World War Austria was occupied by the four Allied Powers, the United States, the Soviet Union, Great Britain and France. In 1955 these four Great Powers signed a treaty with Austria which ended the occupation and the country became independent once more. She agreed to be neutral and not to join any military alliance. Austria is an agricultural country but she also produces iron and steel. She also has a flourishing tourist industry.

AUTOMATION

A modern method of manufacturing goods in which the processes are automatically controlled and regulated. There is, of course, nothing new in this, many branches of industry have for some time employed such means. The reason why it now claims so much attention is the rapid development during the past few years of electronics, which has been applied so successfully that some products can be manufactured entirely by automatic means—however, the day when cars will flow off a production line at the press of a button is still far off.

AVERRHOËS, Ibn-Ruoshd (*c.* 1126–1198)

Arab philosopher and physician. Born at Cordova, where his father was chief judge and priest. He succeeded his father as judge and was afterwards appointed chief judge of Mauretania (North Africa). Suspected of heresy, he was exiled, but later reinstated. He died in Morocco. He was a perceptive commentator on ARISTOTLE, and designed a medical system.

AVOGADRO, Amadeo (1776–1856)

Italian scientist who formulated what is now known as 'Avogadro's Law' which states that equal volumes of all gases at the same temperature and pressure contain the same number of molecules.

AZTEC

A powerful civilization which existed in Mexico between about A.D. 1200 and 1600. The people were originally a wandering Indian tribe, the Tenochcas, who settled in the lake district of Mexico. Four of their famous chiefs who built up this civilization were Itzcoatl (Eetz-co-atl), Montezuma, Axayactl (Ash-ay-ah-actl) and Ahuizotl (Ah-weet-zotl).

The Aztecs were outstanding craftsmen and artists. The city of Tenochtitlan (Te-notch-ti-tlan), was a magnificent sight with its gigantic stone temples and buildings, in fact, at the height of Aztec power it was as impressive as, say, Babylon or Thebes in Egypt; the great stepped temple was very like the ziggurat. They were equally skilled in working gold, mosaic and such materials as rock crystal.

Their religion was a form of nature-worship and exerted a powerful influence on them. It was observed with elaborate and, at times, bestial ritual. The two main gods were Huitzilopochtli (Weet-zeel-o-po-tchtly) and Tezcatlipoca (Tez-cat-li-po-ca). The priests conducted human sacrifices in honour of the gods.

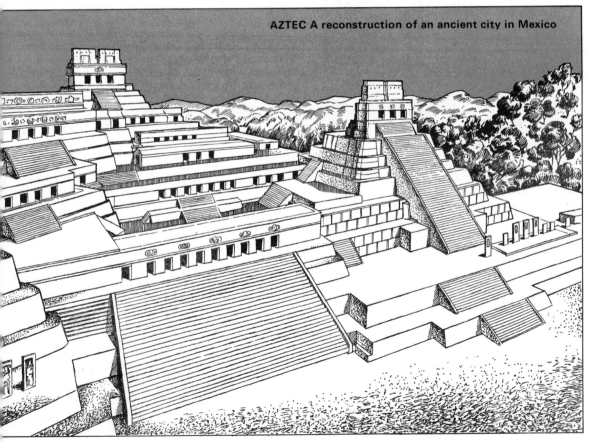
AZTEC A reconstruction of an ancient city in Mexico

Bb

BABOONS

These animals belong to the monkey family and are generally considered to be the most intelligent of the monkeys. Baboons live in groups or troops and prefer open country. They feed on many kinds of foods—roots, fruits, scorpions, beetles; in fact, a wide variety of insects. They have also been known to kill lambs. Baboons are very strong and extremely dangerous when roused—even lions respect the male baboon. They are found in Africa and Arabia; the Hamadryas baboon was held to be sacred by the ancient Egyptians. [*See* MONKEYS.]

BABOONS are the most intelligent of the monkeys.

BABYLONIA

The name once given to the alluvial plain (about 8,000 square miles) of the rivers Tigris and Euphrates, now known as southern IRAQ. In the Bible it is also called 'Shinar' and 'the land of the Chaldeans'. Later it was called 'Chaldaea'. Its main cities were Babylon, Lagash, Nippur and Ur. Two of its great leaders were Hammurabi (1792–1750 B.C.) and Nebuchadnezzar (605–562 B.C.).

BACH

Great family of German musicians, who lived in Thuringia, Germany, in the 17th and 18th centuries. The first-known musical member of the family was a miller, Veit Bach, who played the zither for his own amusement.

His sons and grandsons included some church-organists and excellent composers, but it was one of his great-grandsons who made the family name immortal—the great Johann Sebastian Bach, who was born at Eisenach in 1685. A brilliant organist, he held posts at various churches, finally settling at St. Thomas's, Leipzig. He produced a staggering amount of superb music, in particular the *St. Matthew Passion*, the *Mass in B minor*, two hundred cantatas, the six Brandenburg Concertos, a great deal of chamber music, and many suites for harpsichord and pieces for organ, such as the famous *Toccata and Fugue in D minor*. He died at Leipzig in 1750. His eldest son, Wilhelm Friedemann, is now regarded as a second-rate composer; the second son, Carl Philipp Emanuel was a brilliant harpsichordist and wrote some fine sonatas and symphonies. The youngest son, Johann Christian, is known as the 'London' Bach, because he settled in London for the later part of his life.

BACON, Francis, Lord Verulam and Viscount St. Albans (1561–1626)

English statesman and philosopher. Born in London, he was admitted to the bar in 1582. Under James I he was appointed attorney-general (1613), Lord Keeper of the Great Seal (1617) and Lord Chancellor (1618). He withdrew from public life after charges of corruption and bribery were made against him, and died in retirement. In his *Essays* (first published 1597), *Novum Organum* (1620) and *Advancement of Learning* (1605) he emphasised the importance of experiment and observation in science, which made him one of the founders of modern scientific method. He wrote: 'About Nature consult Nature herself.'

BACON, Roger (c. 1214–1294)

Franciscan friar, philosopher and scientist. Born in Somerset, he studied in Oxford and Paris, where he joined the Franciscan Order. He afterwards lectured at Oxford but was imprisoned in Paris on charges of heresy (1257). After his release he was again imprisoned (1277–1292). Apart from writing on natural science, he was especially interested in alchemy and optics. Like his namesake, Francis, he was also concerned with seeking scientific truth by observation and experiment.

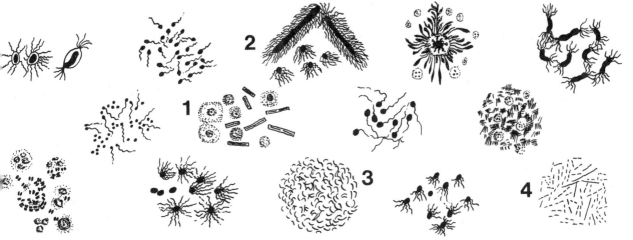

BACTERIA This drawing shows the many and varied forms of bacteria, some of which are harmful, others useful to man. 1, is the cause of anthrax, 2, typhoid, 3, cholera and 4, leprosy.

BACTERIA

Infinitesimally small, primitive organisms, consisting of one cell. Their average thickness amounts to one twenty-five-thousandth of an inch only. They do not contain any chlorophyll, but are, nevertheless, regarded as belonging to the plant world; in fact, they are in the same division as fungi. Their various activities include movement, the breaking down of complex substances, and the rebuilding of such materials. They also take in oxygen and give out carbon dioxide. Bacteria reproduce by simple division and at an incredible rate.

They are to be found in millions everywhere, including the human body. Some bacteria are infectious and spread harmful diseases; other kinds, however, are essential to the process of life itself. Some of the latter break down dead materials, others capture the nitrogen of the air and convert it into useful substances. Bacteria produce ferments and enzymes which are complex and necessary chemical changes in the human body.

Rod-shaped bacteria are called 'bacilli', bacteria with spherical shapes bear the name of 'cocci' and spiral forms 'spirilla'.

BADEN-POWELL, Lord (1857–1941)

British soldier and founder of the BOY SCOUT movement. Educated at Charterhouse and then joined the Army as a cavalry officer (1876). After serving in various parts of the world he won fame for his defence of Mafeking in the BOER WAR. Despite famine and sickness he held the town for 215 days against the Boers until he was relieved in May 1900. After the war he became inspector-general of cavalry (1903–1907). He founded the Boy Scout movement in 1908 with the aim of training boys in discipline, wood-craft and good citizenship. Two years later he founded, together with his sister, the Girl Guide movement.

BADGER

The common badger is a nocturnal animal, lying up by day in burrows called 'setts'. Its main foods are roots, bulbs and other vegetables, also eggs, mice, worms and—when it can—young rabbits. This wedge-shaped animal has long, coarse hair on its back which is grizzled with black and grey, the legs and belly are black, but the face is white with a broad black stripe on each side. The American badger is generally similar to the common badger but a little smaller and with a dark brown face with a central narrow white stripe.

BADGER just coming out of its sett at night.

BADMINTON

A game similar in play to tennis with the exception that a shuttle—a half-circle of cork in which feathers are fixed—is used. The court is also much the same, but small, and the net, although 5 feet above the ground, is only 30 inches deep.

Only the server scores and goes on doing so as long as the opponent loses rallies. The game consists of either 15 or 21 points and the winner of a set is the player who wins two games out of three.

Once the shuttle has been served (during service the racket must not be lifted higher than the waist) it is played until one of the players faults, that is, 1, the shuttle hits or passes under the net or fails to reach it; 2, the shuttle falls outside the court; 3, striking before the shuttle has passed over net; 4, hits the net with racket or any part of person; 5, fails to hit shuttle after passing over net; 6, hits the shuttle twice running or does not hit it properly. (Note—the player should hit the shuttle; he is not allowed to catch it on his racket and then propel it with a throwing motion.)

BAGEHOT, Walter (1826–1877)
English economist and journalist, and editor of the *Economist* newspaper. His special contribution was his scientific approach to matters that had not previously been handled in this way. His *English Constitution,* for example, analysed how the constitution actually worked, instead of merely repeating what the law said the constitution should be. In *Lombard Street* he approached the money-market in the same way.

BAHAMAS
An archipelago near the West Indies. They extend from the coast of Florida to Haiti and are a British colony. The capital is Nassau on New Providence Island. The islands are a favourite tourist centre.

BAIL
A term used when money is put down so that a prisoner can be set at liberty while awaiting trial. An arrested person will be brought before a MAGISTRATE and it will then be decided whether he is to be tried by a higher Court; that is, the Court of Quarter Sessions or the ASSIZES. The arrested person can ask for bail and if it is granted the Magistrate will say how much money is wanted as bail. If the person comes to Court when told, the money is returned but otherwise it is forfeited.

BAILIE
An officer in Scotland who serves a LOCAL AUTHORITY. His position is rather like that of an ALDERMAN in England and Wales. A bailie is also a MAGISTRATE.

BAILIFF
A term used to describe more than one type of law officer. The bailiff best known today is the sheriff's bailiff who is an under officer employed when the property of persons who have failed to pay their debts can be seized by order of the Court. Keepers of royal cities, like those of Westminster and Dover, are also called bailiffs, these being posts of honour.

BAIRD, John Logie (1888–1946)
Born at Helensburgh and showed marked inventiveness when quite young. His first (1925) experiments in television were very modest, consisting of transmitting shadow pictures. By 1928 he had successfully transmitted large-screen colour pictures. Baird was primarily concerned with mechanical scanning, using a Nipkow disc, not the cathode-ray tube method which is the basis of modern T.V. transmission and reception.

BALDWIN, Stanley, First Earl Baldwin of Bewdley (1867–1947)
English statesman. Son of a wealthy industrialist, he worked at first in the family business, entering Parliament as a Conservative in 1906. After a series of minor posts, he was Chancellor of the Exchequer in 1922–1923 and Prime Minister three times—1923, 1924–1929, and 1935–1937. The second of these periods was marked by the General Strike (1926) and the third by the abdication of Edward VIII (1936).

BALEARIC ISLANDS
An archipelago of small islands off the east coast of SPAIN which together form a Spanish province of some 1,930 square miles and population of about 440,000. The main islands are Majorca, Ibiza, Minorca and Formentera. The capital is Palma in Majorca.

BALI is famous for its traditional dancers.

BALFOUR, Arthur James, First Earl of (1848–1930)
British statesman. He entered Parliament in 1874 as Conservative member for Hertford, became First Lord of the Treasury and Leader of the House of Commons (1891), and held the office of Prime Minister (1902–1905). His Education Act entirely re-organized the administrative system of elementary and secondary education. During the Great War he was First Lord of the Admiralty and then Foreign Secretary (1916–1919). He led a very successful mission to the U.S.A. and also issued the so-called Balfour Declaration, establishing a Jewish National Home in Palestine (1917).

BALI
An island (2,530 square miles) east of Java and a part of the Republic of INDONESIA. It has a population of 1,500,000 and its produce is mainly agricultural. Because of the scenic beauty of the island and charming people it has been called the 'jewel of the East'. It has several active volcanoes. Bali's two important towns are Denpasar and Singaradja.

BALKANS
The name given to the most easterly of the three great peninsulars in the south of Europe. It is also the name of a range of mountains in that region. The name is sometimes used to describe the countries which occupy the peninsular, i.e. Yugoslavia, Albania, Bulgaria and Greece. Most of these lands were part of the Roman Empire in ancient times. Then in the 6th century there were invasions of Slav and Turkish, or Bulgar, tribes. The Slavs gradually developed separately as Serbs, Croats, Slovenes, Macedonians and Albanians. Later on there came Magyars, Slovaks, Ruthenians and Germans. These many different peoples were also of different faiths—Roman Catholic, Orthodox, Protestant and Moslem—and these differences led to much strife in the Balkans. Although for a short time there was, in the 14th century, a Serbian kingdom, this came to an end with the conquests of the Turks. It was not till after a war between Turkey and Russia in 1878 that Rumania, Serbia and Montenegro became free nations, but Bulgaria did not become independent until 1908.

When the First World War ended there was created in place of Serbia and Montenegro the much larger Yugoslavia, and Rumania also increased its territory. When the Second World War ended, Rumania, Bulgaria, Yugoslavia and Albania came under Russian influence and adopted Communism. In 1948, however, Yugoslavia, although remaining Communist, took up a more independent position and had more friendly links with western Europe. Albania became more closely linked with China and severed her connections with Russia.

BALLAD
The sort of song which a man at a fair or fireside might sing, but more especially it is the name given to certain memorable poems whose authors are not known and which seem to have sprung from the folklore of a region rather than from any one writer. The ballads of most of Europe have come down from the later Middle Ages. Often these ballads must have been sung, and a characteristic feature, the refrain, is probably a survival from the time when gatherings of men heard them sung and all joined in the refrain. The United States has many ballads, some being taken there by settlers from Europe, others coming into existence relatively recently and telling of modern events, such as the wave of unemployment of the late twenties.

BALLOT
A word which means a little ball but today it is used to describe secret voting. The origin of the word goes back to the days of ancient Greece when voters threw little coloured balls into a box, the colour of the ball showing how the voter intended to vote. Today the names of candidates at parliamentary and local government elections are printed on a paper and the voter puts an X against the name of the candidate for whom he wishes to vote. He then drops it into the ballot box.

BALZAC, Honoré de (1799–1850)
French novelist. He qualified as a lawyer, but when he refused to practise his parents tried to starve him into submission by allowing him very little money. Instead, he began to write, and became involved from time to time in business ventures which always left him in debt.

His main work was an enormously large output of novels—he wrote 85 in 20 years—most of which were designed to form part of the *Comédie Humaine*, intended to reflect a complete picture of contemporary life. The best of his work combines observation of minute detail with tremendously imaginative writing, and he was especially clever at portraying evil and misfortune. Two of his best novels are *Eugénie Grandet* and *Le Père Goriot*.

BANDICOOT
This small marsupial has limbs like the kangaroo's, but is very much smaller in size, in fact, the rat bandicoot measures about twelve

BANDICOOT A marsupial, native to Australasia.

inches from nose to tip of tail. It lives on the ground, nesting in hollows or burrows in the bush or plains, and feeds on small animals, insects, bulbs, roots and berries.

BANGLA DESH [*See* PAKISTAN]

BANK OF ENGLAND

The national bankers of Britain. It is also banker for other banks. It was first set up in 1694 by Act of Parliament and Royal Charter. It is the Bank of England which decides the Bank Rate and this in turn decides the rate of interest charged to borrowers by other banks. Only the Bank of England can issue bank notes in England and Wales. [*See* MONEY.]

BAPTISM

Although baptism has some connection with ancient Jewish ceremonial washing rites, the first person to use it as a sacrament seems to have been John the Baptist. 'Baptism' is a New Testament word, coming from a Greek word which means 'to dip in water'; and John the Baptist 'baptized' his followers by immersing them in the waters of the River Jordan. This was a public testimony on the part of the persons baptized that they had forsaken their former habits and ways, and intended to live lives dedicated to the service of God from then onwards. Before He commenced His public Ministry, Jesus came to John to be baptized, not because He had any sin to confess, but to signify His devotion to God's Will.

The Sacrament of Baptism is used, in one form or another, in almost every branch of the Christian Church today. Jesus Himself does not appear to have performed the ceremony, but His disciples certainly did; and it became the accepted rite of admission into the early Christian community. In Acts we find that a person had to acknowledge his sinfulness in the sight of God and profess belief in Jesus as his Saviour and Lord before being baptized and becoming a member of the Church. St. Paul likens Baptism to being buried with Christ and rising with Him into a new life of righteousness.

Since enough water for the total immersion of a new believer could not always have been conveniently available, it is almost certain that the early Church sometimes performed the ceremony of Baptism by sprinkling with water instead. By the end of the 2nd century, the practice had become established of baptizing infants and young children as a sign that they had been admitted as members of the Church.

BARBADOS

The most easterly of the West Indian Islands. It is twenty-one miles long and fourteen miles broad at its widest point and has a population of a little over a quarter of a million. It was a British colony from 1627 to 1966 when it was agreed that the island should become independent within the British Commonwealth. The capital town is Bridgetown.

BARBARY APE

This animal is a monkey and belongs to the macaque family. It is a powerful creature, its most important feature being the absence of a tail. The natural home of this monkey is North Africa, especially the mountainous regions of Morocco and Algeria. It was introduced into Gibraltar where it still lives under the protection of the Governor. Its main food is fruit and vegetables.

BARBARY SHEEP

This animal is closely related to the goat family and has a longish tail, large sweeping horns and a mane of long hairs on the throat and forelegs. It is found in Barbary and Kordofan in North Africa.

BAROMETER

An instrument for measuring atmospheric pressure. Its simplest form is shown in the drawing (1) and is known as a TORRICELLI tube after its inventor who discovered (1643) that air possessed weight and consequently exerted a pressure. In this instrument the atmospheric pressure acting on the surface of the liquid in the bowl (usually mercury) balances the fluid in the column; the space between the fluid level in the column and the end of the tube is exhausted of air. The tube is graduated to measure the pressure variations in inches or millimeters, or both. Another and more widely

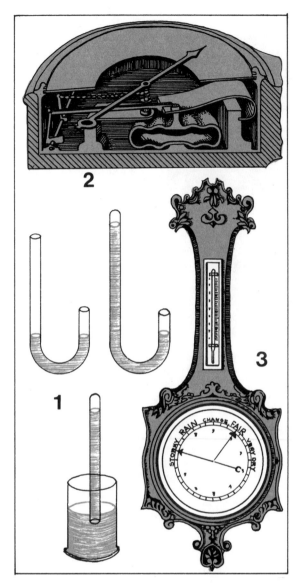

2

3

1

BAROMETER 1, examples of a barometer consisting of a simple tube. **2**, a section through an aneroid barometer showing the diaphragm and needle mechanism. **3**, a decorative wall barometer.

used type of instrument is the 'aneroid' barometer. [*See* drawing (2).] A 'barograph' is an elaborate form of aneroid barometer in which the movement of the diaphragm is permanently recorded on a continuous paper chart attached to a revolving drum.

BARRIE, Sir James M. (1860–1937)
Born at Angus, the son of poor parents. Although the author of many novels and plays, he is best remembered by young people for his play *Peter Pan*. He is buried at his native village of Kirriemuir, Angus.

BARTOK, Bela (1881–1945)
Hungarian composer. From an early age he was interested in and influenced by folk music; with Zoltan KODALY he made an extensive collection of east-European folk songs. His main works are *The Miraculous Mandarin, Bluebeard's Castle, Concerto for Orchestra*, several piano concertos and an outstanding violin concerto. Bartok also wrote some chamber music.

BASEBALL
American national game derived from 'rounders'. The main feature of the field is a square 90 feet long on each side; this is called the 'diamond'. The corners of the diamond are marked prominently and are the bases—home-base, from which the strikers (batsmen) do all their hitting, 1st, 2nd and 3rd bases.

Baseball teams consist of 9 players on each side, and, as in cricket, when one team is batting the other is fielding. The bat is about 42 inches long and only $2\frac{3}{4}$ inches in diameter at its thickest part. The ball is slightly less than 3 inches in diameter.

The play of the game is as follows. First the striker stands at home-base facing across the diamond. Right in front of him is the pitcher. Now the pitcher does not bowl in the cricket sense; he literally hurls the ball towards the catcher with every ounce of his strength. When the ball reaches home base the striker has to hit it so that it travels as far as possible. Then he starts running.

Once he is on the move, the striker is only safe when he is on a base. If when he is running from one base to another a fielder scoops up the ball and touches him with it, or when holding the ball touches any part of the base the striker is running to, then the striker is out. He is also out if the ball is caught direct from his bat. There is another way he can be out: if, the pitcher having pitched three 'strike' balls to him, he strikes at each ball and fails to run at least to first base, he is out at the third ball. If in striking he hits the ball out of the diamond behind the foul lines this counts as one of his three strikes. If the striker tips the ball and the catcher catches it, the striker is not out *unless he has made two unsuccessful strikes immediately beforehand*.

The striker scores if he hits the ball so well and truly into or beyond the diamond that he is able to run through all bases and back home in one go. This is known as a 'home run'. But should it happen that he does not have time to run further than 1st, 2nd or 3rd base without risk of being touched with the ball between bases, then he may stay on any of the bases he likes while another striker from his

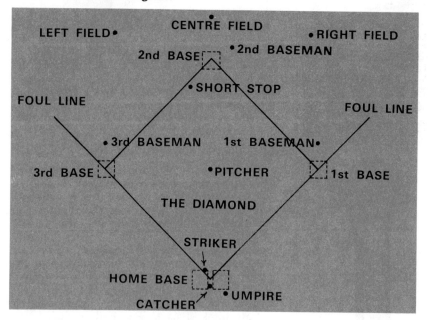

BASEBALL The layout and dimensions of a baseball field.

team takes a turn with the bat; he may then find an opportunity of completing his run to home base.

Thus it is possible for a batting team to have a man on each base, and if the striker strikes so that he himself can make a home run, then all the other men on intermediate bases can safely reach home base too, and 4 runs will be scored by their side.

An innings is completed when three strikers of a team are out, but as there are nine innings to a game each striker will have many chances with the bat during the course of it.

BASIC ENGLISH

A system by which the vocabulary of English is reduced, by the use of various word-relationships, to under a thousand words.

Thus if the words *dog* and *young* are included in the vocabulary there is no need for the word *puppy*; so it is left out. If you have *go* and *in*, there is no need for the word *enter*. The system was devised in the main by C. K. Ogden, and its purpose is to make English easily learnt by foreigners, so that it may become a world language. The word *Basic* itself is made up like this: **B**ritish, **A**merican, **S**cientific, **I**nternational, **C**ommercial.

BASKETBALL

In this game a team scores by putting the ball into its own goal instead of into its opponents'. The actual goals are called baskets, and each one is made of white net suspended from an iron ring 18 inches in diameter. The basket is fixed to a backboard so that the iron ring is

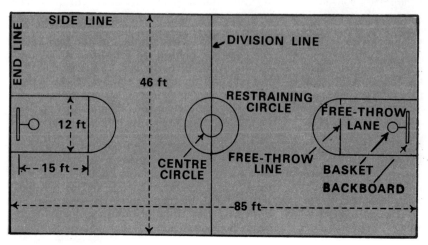

BASKETBALL The layout and dimensions of a basketball pitch.

BATS Flying mammals related to the rodents.

10 feet from the floor and 6 inches from the board at its nearest point. The backboards themselves are 6 feet wide by 4 feet high, and the lower edge is 9 feet from the floor.

The ball is similar to a soccer ball, and its circumference has to be between $29\frac{1}{2}$ and $31\frac{1}{2}$ inches. This gives it a diameter of about 10 inches. The ball must never be kicked; it must always be played with the hands.

A goal made in the course of ordinary play counts as 2 points, and a goal from a free throw counts as 1 point. A free throw is a penalty for infringement of the rules. The points are awarded to the team into whose basket the ball goes, no matter who puts it in. Whichever team has the most points at the end of the game is the winner.

BATS

These are MAMMALS and not birds whose fore-limbs have developed into wings which allow them to fly. Bats are divided into two groups, the insect-eating bats and fruit-bats or flying-foxes. Most bats are nocturnal. The erratic flight of bats has always interested man, and it is only recently that it has been properly understood. Science has discovered that a bat emits from its mouth a very high-pitched sound (usually called 'ultra-sonic') which is reflected back when it strikes an object ahead of it. This warns the bat to alter its direction of flight and so avoid the object. It is, in fact, a kind of sound radar system.

BAUDELAIRE, Charles P. (1821–1867)

French poet. Born in Paris, the son of a civil servant. He studied in Paris and Lyons but his early life was so irregular that he was sent to India (1841). On his return to Paris he became known amongst French writers and revolutionaries, and in 1857 he produced his masterpiece—a series of poems entitled *Les Fleurs du Mal* (Flowers of Evil). Baudelaire is also famous for his art-criticism and the French translation of Edgar Allan POE's works.

BAX, Sir Arnold (1883–1953)

Born in London. Of partly Irish descent, he was greatly attracted by the old Celtic legends, and many of his beautiful tone-poems, such as *The Garden of Fand* and *Tintagel*, are inspired by them. He also wrote seven symphonies, much chamber music, and many songs and piano pieces. He was Master of the King's Music from 1942 to 1953.

BEARDSLEY, Aubrey (1872–1898)

English artist, born in Brighton. He was a born illustrator in what is called the 'Art Nouveau' style. He illustrated Oscar Wilde's *Salome, Le Morte d'Arthur* and *Rape of the Lock*. Much of his work appeared in the *Yellow Book*, especially the cover designs. His early death robbed England of one of its most promising artists.

BEARDSLEY A cover design for the *Yellow Book*.

BEARS

These creatures are very often of large size and heavy build, with a very short tail, loose lips, and broad short feet provided with five toes, all close together, which have long, strong claws. Bears are found all over Europe and Asia, as far as Borneo, only in Morocco in Africa, all over North America and in the northern parts of South America. They are mainly vegetarian in diet, breed once a year and hibernate in the winter. Included in this family are the brown bear, grizzly bear, American black bear, polar bear, Himalayan black bear, honey bear, sloth bear and spectacled bear.

BEATITUDES

The word beatitude comes from the Latin word *beatitudo*, meaning 'blessedness', and a beatitude is a saying expressed in a manner often used in Hebrew Literature: it commences by describing something or someone as 'blessed'—or happy—and then goes on to explain why it does so. [See, for instance, Psalm 32, verses 1 and 2.]

Since the time of St. Ambrose, in the 4th century, however, the term 'beatitude' has been applied almost entirely to sayings of Jesus expressed in this way. Matthew and Luke both record some of Jesus's beatitudes, but whereas Luke only gives four, Matthew records eight, using them as an introduction to that great 'Christian Manifesto' known as the Sermon on the Mount (Matthew, Chapters 5–7). The first beatitude Matthew records is 'Blessed are the poor in spirit: for (or because) theirs is the kingdom of heaven'. This is followed by 'Blessed are they that mourn: for they shall be comforted'. And then comes perhaps the most well-known beatitude of all; 'Blessed are the meek: for they shall inherit the earth'.

BEAUFORT, Sir Francis (1774–1857)

British hydrographer who devised a scale of 13 wind strengths based on the number of sails a fully-rigged ship could carry. It was revised in 1905 and again in 1921. There are now 12 'Beaufort numbers', each embracing a small range of wind-speeds, '0' indicates less than 1 m.p.h. and '12' more than 75 m.p.h.

BEAUMARCHAIS, Pierre Augustin Caron de (1732–1799)

French dramatist, who first achieved fame as watchmaker to the king. He led a stormy life, had himself raised to the nobility, was condemned to civic degradation for attempting to corrupt justice, served in the secret service, and encouraged the American colonists in their war against England. His two famous comedies are *The Barber of Seville* and *The Marriage of Figaro*, better known to us through the operatic versions by ROSSINI and MOZART.

BEAUMONT, Francis (1584–1616) and FLETCHER, John (1579–1625)

These two poets and dramatists so successfully collaborated in a number of famous plays that we think of them as a pair. Beaumont was born in Leicestershire, Fletcher at Rye, Sussex; their work together lasted about nine years from 1607 onwards. Critics nowadays question whether in this relatively short time they could have done so much creative work as Jacobean publishers credited them with; but they certainly succeeded very happily in their collaboration on *Philaster* and *The Knight of the Burning Pestle* and other plays which still make entertaining reading and acting.

BEAVER

An aquatic animal with a wide, scaly, paddle-like tail and fully webbed feet which it uses for swimming. There are two species, the European and American. The European beaver lives, like a water-rat, in burrows in the banks of streams. The American beaver is the more interesting as it is this animal that makes dams of logs and branches, plastered with mud. These dams are to protect the beaver family from such animals as the coyote and cougar. Their food consists mainly of the bark of willow, poplars and other trees, but they also eat water lilies, grass and roots.

BEAVERS There are two species of this animal, one native to Europe and the other to America.

BEAVERBROOK, William Maxwell Aitken, First Baron (1879–1964)

British newspaper proprietor and politician. Born in Canada, the son of a Scottish presbyterian minister, gifted with great business acumen, he was a millionaire before he was thirty. Coming to England in 1910 he entered politics as M.P. for Ashton-under-Lyne and in 1918 was Britain's first Minister of Information. Between the wars he bought the *Daily Express* and the London *Evening Standard* and founded the *Sunday Express*, using them as exponents of his own attitudes in a popular and racy style. During the Second World War he was Minister of Aircraft Production and his dynamic energy was instrumental in producing the aeroplanes required to win the Battle of Britain.

BECKET, Thomas à (1118–1170)
Born in Cheapside, London, he studied at Merton Priory and Paris before becoming a Chancellor of England (1155) and Archbishop of Canterbury (1162). At this point his former friendship with King Henry II turned sour, as Becket turned from his devotion to the State and took an uncompromising stand on the rights of the Church. The centrepoint of the quarrel was Henry's demand that those who were in religious orders, which included almost all the educated people, should be punished by the royal as well as the Church courts for serious crimes, as, even in the case of murder, the Church did no more than to deprive a cleric of his status in the Church. Becket fled abroad from the King's wrath, but eventually the quarrel was patched up and he returned to England. But the Archbishop continued to excommunicate the King's servants, and an angry remark of Henry's, that he wished to be rid of 'this turbulent priest,' encouraged four knights to murder him in Canterbury Cathedral. He was canonised in 1172.

BECQUERELS
Family of French physicists. Antoine César Becquerel (1788–1878) was a pioneer in electro-chemistry and was the first to observe the photo-electric effect. Alexandre Edmond Becquerel (1820–1891), the son of Antoine, did important researches into light, photo-chemistry and the nature of phosphorescence. Antoine Henri Becquerel (1852–1898), the son of Alexandre, was one of the founders of modern physics. He discovered that uranium salts emit rays similar to X-rays; at first they were called 'Becquerel rays'. In 1900 he identified beta rays with cathode rays. He was awarded a Nobel Prize in 1903.

BEDE, the Venerable (*c.* 673–735)
Greatest name in Anglo-Saxon literature. He was born at Wearmouth and spent most of his life at the nearby monastery in Jarrow. In his *Historia Ecclesiastica*, written in Latin, he tells the story of Saxon times down till 731. On it we depend for almost all our knowledge of early English history. It was translated into Anglo-Saxon by King ALFRED.

BEERBOHM, Sir Max (1872–1956)
English writer and caricaturist. His drawings provide an excellent record of the social and literary life of his time, and some caustic comments on personalities. His best-known novel is *Zuleika Dobson*, a story of undergraduate life in Oxford.

BEETHOVEN, Ludwig van (1770–1827)
German composer, born at Bonn. At seventeen he went to Vienna, where he became a famous pianist and one of the greatest composers of all time. He had to struggle against poverty and at thirty began to go deaf, but he went on composing masterpiece after masterpiece until his death in Vienna. At the performance of his last and greatest symphony, which he himself conducted, he could not hear a note of the music, and had to be turned round to see the wild applause of the audience. His nine symphonies are generally reckoned to be the finest ever written, especially the 3rd, the *Eroica* (*Heroic*), and the 9th, in which a chorus sings of his faith in freedom and the brotherhood of mankind. Other outstanding works are the opera *Fidelio*, the *Mass in D*, fifteen string quartets and thirty-two piano sonatas.

BELGIUM
A small kingdom (11,800 square miles) in western Europe. It is the most densely populated country in Europe and although not much larger than Wales has more than nine million inhabitants. About half the people are Walloons and speak French and the rest, who live chiefly in the north, speak Flemish, a language very like Dutch. The capital is Brussels, the chief industrial town Liège and the chief port Antwerp. Belgium is an important industrial country with big engineering and shipbuilding works. She is also famous for her carpets, and grows sugar-beet, potatoes and other agricultural produce. Belgium is one of the three countries forming the customs union known as BENELUX.

BELL, Alexander Graham (1847–1922)
Scottish-American inventor. Improved and extended the work of his father on the education of the deaf. He initiated work on many inventions, the most outstanding being the transmission of speech by electric impulses—the telephone. The first message was transmitted in 1876. Bell also invented the phonograph or gramophone.

BELGIUM The old and the modern, two aspects of Brussels, the capital city of Belgium.

BELLINI, Giovanni (*c.* 1430–1516)
Venetian painter and member of a distinguished family of artists. He produced many fine religious works, and taught TITIAN. His *Agony in the Garden* is in the National Gallery, London.

BELLOC, Hilaire (1870–1953)
Anglo-French writer and poet. He was elected to Parliament as Liberal M.P. for Salford in 1906, but became disillusioned with politics, and did not seek re-election. He wrote travel books, historical studies and religious books, but is probably best-known for his nonsense verse for children—*The Bad Child's Book of Beasts* and the *Cautionary Tales*.

BELORUSSIA (or Byelorussia)
One of the fifteen republics which form the SOVIET UNION. The name means White Russia. Although part of the Soviet Union it is treated as a separate country and allowed to be a Member of the UNITED NATIONS as is also the UKRAINE. The capital is Minsk. The republic is about the size (80,000 square miles) of Great Britain but has only ten million inhabitants.

BENELUX
The name which the three countries BELGIUM, the NETHERLANDS and LUXEMBURG took when they formed a Customs Union in 1947. This means that they trade with one another as if they were a single country.

BENNETT, Enoch Arnold (1867–1931)
One of the most popular novelists of the first quarter of the twentieth century. Particularly celebrated for fiction set against the background of the 'Five Towns'—that is, the pottery towns of Staffordshire. He had been born in one of the 'Five Towns', Hanley, and brought up there, thus forming the impression that life was 'grey, sinister, and melancholy'.

BENTHAM, Jeremy (1748–1832)
British philosopher and social reformer. Born in London he graduated at Oxford and was later called to the bar. On the death of his father (1792) he became financially independent and devoted most of his time to study and research. He believed that the aim of the state should be to achieve the 'greatest happiness of the greatest number'. He helped to found University College, London, where his skeleton is preserved, dressed up in his own clothes.

BERKELEY, George (1685–1753)
Irish philosopher, born in Kilcrin, Ireland. Dean of Londonderry in 1724 and then went to America (1728–1731). He returned and was appointed Bishop of Cloyne in 1732. He founded a philosophy of idealism in which he stated that it is not possible to prove the

BIRDS The species above is the common European kingfisher.

BIRDS A Superb lyrebird of Australia on a mound which it has built to display its beautiful lyre-shaped tail. Lyrebirds have a wide vocal range and are superb mimics.

BIRDS A hummingbird hovering before feeding on the nectar of the tropical flowers. A hummingbird's wings beat at over 3,000 times per minute. Not only can they hover, but are the only birds who can fly backwards. There are over 200 species of hummingbird, the smallest being 2 inches long.

BIRDS The species shown here is the Emperor penguin of the Antarctic. After the female has laid her single egg the male takes over and hatches the egg. During this period the male starves in the most severe arctic weather. The females return to the sea.

BIRDS A pair of honey-guides of Africa. Although these birds feed on insects they are especially fond of honey which they have an instinct for finding. In parts of Africa certain species of honey-guide are protected by the natives who believe them to have magical powers.

BIRDS The whooping crane of
N. America. It is the tallest
bird in America, standing about
5 feet and has a wing spread
of nearly 8 feet.

BIRDS A pair of bowerbirds of
the species found in Northern
Australia. The bower is built
by the male for attracting
and mating with the female.
In many species the bowers
are surrounded with gardens
decorated with bright objects
gathered by the male.

existence of the material world about us as its reality is only in the mind of the beholder. His philosophical ideas are contained in *Treatise Concerning the Principles of Human Knowledge.*

BERLIOZ, Hector (1803–1869)

French composer. Born at Côte-St.-André. He showed an early liking for music, but his father, a doctor, made him study medicine. One sight of the dissecting-room was enough for him, however; he left the medical college and devoted his life to music. He became a great conductor, founded the modern style of writing for orchestra, and was one of the first composers to tell stories in music. His compositions are exciting and romantic, the best-known being the *Fantastic Symphony*, the overture *Le Carnaval Romain* (Roman Carnival) and the brilliant *Hungarian March.*

BERMUDA

The name given to the chief of about 100 islands known as the Bermudas or Somers Islands. They are in the west of the Atlantic Ocean and a British colony. Some land has been let to the United States and the Americans have reclaimed two square miles from the sea. The capital is Hamilton.

BESSEMER, Sir Henry (1813–1898)

Inventor of the process for making cheap steel and which still bears his name. The process consists of removing from the pig-iron such impurities as silicon, manganese and phosphorus. It is done by oxidizing the silicon and manganese by means of blasting air through the molten metal in the converter; the phosphorus is removed by its reaction with lime, which is added while the converter is blowing, and the magnesia or dolomite in the firebrick lining of the converter. The carbon in the pig-iron is removed during the process in the form of carbon monoxide, and dioxide, but as it is an essential ingredient of steel it is added later, as are such other ingredients as ferrosilicon and aluminium which act as deoxidizers, i.e., agents for removing any oxygen present after the process has been completed. The operation takes about twenty minutes. [*See* STEEL.]

BEVAN, Aneurin (1897–1960)

British Labour statesman, one of the thirteen children of a Welsh miner, who himself worked in the pits as a child. He became prominent in the South Wales Miners' Federation, and acted as miners' dispute agent during the 1926 General Strike. He was elected Independent Labour Party M.P. for Ebbw Vale

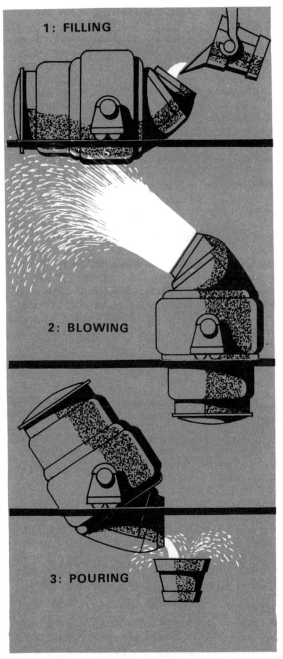

BESSEMER CONVERTER Three stages in the process of making steel in a converter. See STEEL.

in 1929, and joined the Labour Party itself in 1931. As Minister of Health in the Labour Government he introduced the National Health Service in 1948, but resigned over the proposed National Health charges in 1951. From then until he became 'shadow' Foreign Secretary in 1956 he was often in opposition to the established leadership of his party.

BEVERIDGE, William Henry, First Baron
(1879–1963)
British economist and statistical writer. Born
in India, where his parents were civil servants.
He helped to establish the first labour ex-
changes and to draft the first plan of unemployment insurance. During the Great
War he did important service at the Ministries
of Food and Munitions. Although a director
of the London School of Economics (1919–
1937) and Master of University College,
Oxford (1937–1945) and a Liberal M.P.
(1944–1945), he will best be remembered for
the *Beveridge Report* of 1942, which laid the
basis for all subsequent social security legis-
lation.

BEVIN, Rt. Hon. Ernest (1881–1951)
English politician and trade union leader.
Born in Somerset, he was orphaned at the
age of eight and began work at ten. He was in
turn errand boy, tram-conductor and van
driver, before entering on a trade union
career (1910). His first post was National
organizer of the Dockers' Union, where he
became known as the 'Dockers' K.C.', through
his skill in defending the dockers' interests.
He served on the General Council of the
Trades Union Congress (1925–1940) and was
instrumental in creating the Transport and
General Workers' Union. In 1940 he became
Minister of Labour. After the war he became
Foreign Minister in the Labour Government
of 1945. He held this post until 1951 when he
had to retire through ill-health.

BEWICK, Thomas (1753–1828)
English artist, born near Newcastle-on-Tyne.
He revived interest in black and white engrav-
ing and was a master wood-engraver. He illus-
trated many works with original wood-engrav-
ings, especially *History of Quadrupeds* (1790),
History of British Birds (1797) and John Gay's
Fables (1779).

BHUTAN
A small kingdom (18,000 square miles) to the
south-east of the Himalayas. It is rather more
than twice the size of Wales and has a population of about 700,000, most of them Buddhists.
It was formerly a protectorate of Great
Britain but is now a protectorate of India.
This means that although Bhutan rules itself
business with foreign countries is done on its
behalf by India. The capital is Punakha.

BIBLE
The word Bible comes from the Greek word
biblia, which means, simply, 'books'; and the
Bible itself is a collection, indeed a library, of

66 books translated into our own, and many
other languages. Our Bible is divided into two
sections: the Old Testament (39 books), and
the New Testament (27 books). The Old
Testament is mainly a record of God's
dealings with the HEBREW nation; the New
Testament tells of the life and teaching of JESUS
CHRIST, and the early days of the CHRISTIAN
CHURCH.

The original language of the Old Testament
was Hebrew (though certain small parts were
first written in Aramaic) and, as we have it
today, the Old Testament can be divided,
roughly, into three classes of literature: (1)
History and Law—Genesis to Esther; (2)
Poetry and Drama—Job to Song of Solomon;
(3) Religious Instruction (Preaching and Prophecy)—Isaiah to Malachi.

From the days of Abraham, the founder of
their race, and for perhaps a thousand years or
more, the Hebrews depended on their wise
men, and later on, their priests, to preserve in
their memory the largely unwritten religious
and historical traditions of their forefathers.
A start towards writing down these ancient
traditions seems to have been made in the
time of King David, about a thousand years
before Christ was born. The earliest written
records were cut or 'scratched' on to tablets
of clay, and, later, polished surfaces of wood
and metal.

Some time in the 9th century B.C., however,
about the time of the prophet Elijah, the first
important collection in writing was made of
the religious and historic traditions of the
Hebrew race. This collection was made in
Judah, the southern Hebrew Kingdom. About
a hundred years later, perhaps in the time of the
prophet Amos, another collection of very much
the same material was made in Israel, the
Northern kingdom. Later still, those two collections were combined into one.

As time went on, new materials for writing
were brought into use. In the time of the
prophet Isaiah, in the 7th century B.C., reference is made to rolls of 'books' which were
probably sheets of papyrus or parchment. By
the time of Jeremiah and Ezekiel, in the 7th
and 6th centuries B.C., these rolls of writings
were common, and probably all the Hebrew
sacred literature had been transferred by
scribes to such material by that period.

Shortly after the great Captivity of the Jews
in Babylon, or perhaps even while it still
lasted, a priestly writer, or writers, drew up a
further outline of the ancient Hebrew traditions and customs, in a rather heavy scholarly
style. This outline became known as the
Priestly Code or Code of Holiness; and some
hundred years later still, an unknown editor

BIBLE An early illustration of the 'Ascension'.

combined the Priestly Code with the earlier collection of sacred writings from Judah and Israel. And this final combination, made about 300 B.C., forms, in the main, the substance of what we now know as the first six books of our Bible. Modern Biblical scholars call this section of the Bible the *Hexateuch* from the Greek word *hex* = six.

Almost all the remaining 33 books of the Old Testament were also brought together gradually from the time of Ezra, about 450 B.C. onwards. The contents of some of these books, of course, date from much earlier than that period—the writings of great prophets such as Amos, Isaiah and Jeremiah, for instance. Before the end of the 2nd century B.C., the writing of the Hebrew Scriptures, the Jewish Bible, was practically complete. We call this wonderfully rich and inspired collection of sacred literature the Old Testament because it tells how God revealed Himself to man in ancient times, and how man grew in knowledge of God. It tells how, though man was frequently disobedient, and refused to listen to His voice, God was preparing the world for the new revelation of Himself which is recorded in the pages of the New Testament.

The original language of the New Testament was Greek, as it was spoken throughout most of the Roman Empire. Like the Old, the New Testament was brought together gradually, but over a period of about fifty, rather

than a thousand years. And, like the Old, the New Testament books were not written in quite the same order in which they appear in our Bibles today.

The earliest New Testament books are some of the Epistles (or letters) written by the great missionary, St. Paul between A.D. 50 and 61. At first, the early Christians were more concerned to win people's hearts to belief in Christ the Saviour of the World than to tell the story of the human Jesus and His everyday life. But, as time went on, a new generation was gradually replacing the one Jesus had lived with, and the need was felt for a permanent record of His life and work on earth. And that record is contained in the Four Gospels, which the 2nd century Church placed at the beginning of the New Testament, because they are by far the most important books of all.

The earliest Gospel (the word here means 'good news') was written by Mark, about A.D. 65. It is the shortest Gospel, and is mostly simple, matter-of-fact reporting. Next came Matthew's—perhaps A.D. 75—which is much more detailed than Mark's, and is obviously intended to commend the Christian faith to the Jews. Then, about A.D. 80, followed the Gospel by Luke, a medical man, probably of Greek descent, who had a cultivated mind and was a first-rate writer.

These three gospels are known as the *Synoptic* Gospels, because they can be considered as parts of a whole. Though differing in details, the three gospels all treat the story of Jesus's earthly life from much the same point of view. Scholars believe that before any of the Gospels were written, there existed a collection of 'The Sayings of Jesus' which was afterwards lost.

Lastly, perhaps shortly after A.D. 90, came the Gospel of John. This is very different from the Synoptic Gospels, and it has been discussed perhaps more than any other Biblical book. While it contains what appear to be vivid personal memories of Jesus's earthly life, it is mainly concerned with the deeper spiritual meanings behind the works and words of Jesus.

The Book of Acts of the Apostles which follows the Gospels, was also written by Luke, at about the same time as he wrote his Gospel. It is a very important record of the early days of the Christian Church, and, indeed, a valuable history of the Mediterranean area at that period.

The remaining books of the New Testament consist of more letters of St. Paul, and other writers. Finally, we have the strange and interesting Book of the Revelation written rather in the style of the Old Testament prophetic visions, such as we find in the Book of Daniel.

A translation into Latin of Old and New Testament Books, known as the Old Latin Version, dates, probably, to the 2nd century A.D. In A.D. 405, St. Jerome completed his great Latin version, the Vulgate.

Parts of the Bible were translated into English dialects from about the 8th century onwards, but the first English Bible was produced by John Wyclif (spelt 'Wycliffe' nowadays) in 1384. WYCLIFFE's Bible was based on the Vulgate, and many copies, all written out

Bible, in 1560. The Bishops' Bible appeared in 1568, during Elizabeth I's reign. Between 1582 and 1609, Roman Catholic scholars, now in exile in France, produced a new English Version from the Vulgate known as the Rheims and Douai Bible.

As a result of a conference at Hampton Court, London, called by James I in 1604, a committee of 47 religious scholars began work (about 1607) on an entirely new and improved English translation of the Bible. And in 1611 appeared the *King James Version*, known and

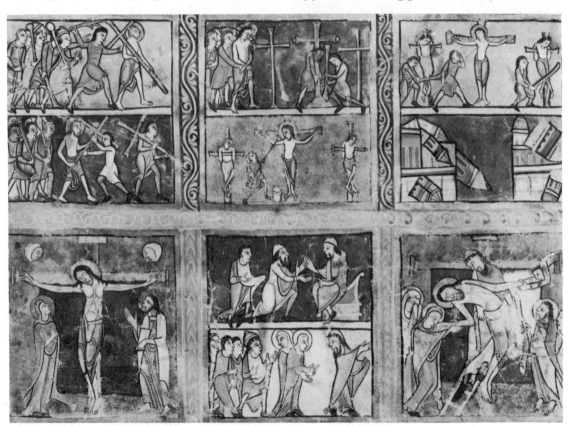

BIBLE A sequence of illustrations from a 12th-century *Book of the Gospels*.

by hand, were made. William TYNDALE produced in 1526, from the continent, where he was living in exile, the first printed English New Testament. He greatly desired to complete a new English Bible, translated from the original Hebrew and Greek, but he was martyred in 1536 before he could achieve his ambition. He may have known, however, that Miles Coverdale had produced the first printed English Bible in 1535. In 1538, Coverdale completed another version, known as the Great Bible.

From Geneva, where English Protestant scholars were living in exile, came the Geneva

used as the Authorized Version to this very day.

As time went on, however, new discoveries and fresh knowledge showed that some alteration and correction to the work of the King James translators was needed. In June 1870, a committee of 53 scholars commenced work on revising the 1611 Bible. They were joined by 31 American scholars in 1872. In 1885, the Revised Version (OT and NT) was published. 1901 saw a slightly different American Version appear.

In 1902, came Dr. Weymouth's New Testament in Modern Speech: and, in 1913, appeared Dr. James Moffatt's New Testament, followed in 1924 by the Moffatt Bible. In 1952 the Revised Standard Version was published in Britain and America, the product of 14 years of labour by 32 scholars at the Union Theological Seminary in New York. A version of the New Testament in contemporary English appeared in 1961, called the *New English Bible,* and this is now much used in churches all over the country. A further version in modern English (OT and NT), this time for Roman Catholics, was published in 1966, and is called the *Jerusalem Bible.*

The Bible is the most translated book in the world: the Bible, and parts of it, have now been rendered into a total of over a thousand languages.

BILL

A suggested new law in the form in which it is presented to Parliament. It remains a Bill until it receives the Royal Assent which means that the Queen has signed it. It then becomes an ACT OF PARLIAMENT.

There are ancient rules as to the way a Bill should be discussed by Parliament. A Bill can first be suggested, or introduced, either in the House of Commons or House of Lords though it is much more likely to be introduced in the House of Commons and if it is a Bill which states in what way some of the nation's money shall be spent it *must* be introduced in the Commons. The kind of Bill that is most likely to start in the Lords is one about which there is likely to be little disagreement.

There are different kinds of Bills. A Government Bill is one which the Government wants to be made law and usually a CABINET Minister introduces it. A Bill is said to be 'read' three times. The First Reading is a formal matter and there is no debate. The Bill is then printed so that when the Bill is discussed M.P.s can have copies of it. During the Second Reading there is a general debate and if the matter is an important one this continues for several days. A vote is then taken to see if the House wants to go on considering the Bill. If the House does, as is almost always the case, it then has to be considered in detail by a Committee of the House. If the vote should go against the Government it would be very serious and it might mean that the Government would have to resign or agree not to go on with the Bill. If the Government decided to resign it would almost certainly mean that there would be a GENERAL ELECTION. If the House wants to go on considering the Bill it can be considered in committee in one of two ways. It can be considered by a fairly small committee that meets in a committee room.

The committee will be made up of M.P.s of all parties. The advantage of this method is that several Bills can be considered in different committee rooms at the same time. But if the Bill is a Money Bill, saying how the nation's money is to be spent, or if all M.P.s want to be on the committee, then the method is rather different. All M.P.s remain in their seats and the SERGEANT-AT-ARMS removes the MACE from the SPEAKER'S table to show that the House of Commons is not in session: the Speaker leaves his chair and the Chairman of Committees takes charge. Then, each section, or clause, of the Bill is discussed in turn. The rules observed are such as might be followed by any committee and not the special rules of the House of Commons. When the Committee of the Whole House, as this is called, has finished its work for the day, the Sergeant-at-Arms puts the Mace back on the table, the Speaker takes his seat and the House of Commons is once more in session.

When the Committee has finished its work the Bill is reported to the House. This is especially important if the Bill has been discussed by a small committee as it gives others who were not on the committee the opportunity to speak. This may lead to some more amendments before the Bill is ready for the Third Reading. During the Third Reading it is possible for M.P.s to make quite small amendments such as a change in the wording of some clause to make it easier to understand.

The Bill then goes to the House of Lords where much the same procedure is gone through. When the Lords and Commons have agreed to any changes to be made the Bill is then ready for the Royal Assent. This is done by the Queen signing it and it thus becomes an Act of Parliament.

Not all Bills are Government Bills. An ordinary, or private, member can also introduce a Bill if the House agrees. LOCAL AUTHORITIES and other public bodies can have a private bill introduced on their behalf.

BILLIARDS

A game played with a cue, and three ivory balls on a baize-covered slate-table in which there are six pockets. A full-size table measures 12 feet by 6 feet $1\frac{1}{2}$ inches in Britain and 10 feet by 5 feet in the U.S.A. Cues range in weight between 16 and 18 oz.

Ordinary billiards is played with two white balls and one red ball. One white ball has two black spots on it and it is this spot-ball which is placed to start the game. The game is opened by placing the red ball on the billiard spot and the spot-ball anywhere within the 'D'. The second player starts by playing away from

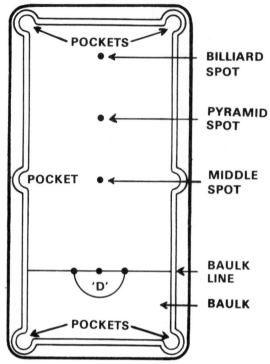

POCKETS

BILLIARD SPOT

PYRAMID SPOT

POCKET

MIDDLE SPOT

BAULK LINE

'D'

BAULK

POCKETS

BILLIARDS Layout of a full-size billiard table.

'baulk'. A player must hit another ball with his cue-ball or he forfeits 1 point; if the ball goes straight into the pocket he forfeits 3 points. The various ways of scoring are: potting the red into a pocket or by going into a pocket with the cue-ball after it has touched the red first (3 points); by doing the same with your opponent's white ball (2 points); by playing the cue-ball to strike both the other balls and termed a cannon (2 points). If the opponent's ball is potted it stays in the pocket throughout the break; when put back into play again it must be played away from baulk. A game is won by the player who first scores an agreed number of points—usually 100. In championship games this may be as high as 15,000. [*See* SNOOKER.]

BIOLOGY

A word derived from the Greek, *bios* meaning life and *logos* meaning study. Strictly speaking, therefore, a biologist should be one who studies everything connected with life and living things. This would, however, be a very wide subject indeed, so in practice the meaning of the word is restricted. It is usual, for example, to leave human beings out, even though they are recognized as belonging to the animal kingdom. Usually the word is given an even narrower meaning by excluding the study of animals and plants in the field, that is, in their

wild state. Even domesticated animals are left out since they are more properly the subject of study by the stockbreeder and others and by the veterinary surgeon. So we arrive at the seemingly absurd end, that the biologist, who should be studying living things, is usually found to be studying dead animals and plants in a laboratory. Perhaps this is not so absurd as it seems, and it helps us to arrive at, and understand, the real purpose of biology, namely, the study of the mechanism of life.

We do not yet know how life first began on the earth. Nor do we know what life itself is. Yet we are able to describe and to some extent explain how living processes work. Soon after men first began to study plants and animals seriously the microscope was invented. As a result it was possible to examine small specimens of living matter under the microscope. It was then seen that all parts of a living organism, whether plant or animal, were made up of very much smaller units, like bricks in a wall. The first tissues to be so examined were those of plants, and because these small parts looked, under the microscope, like the six-sided cells in a honeycomb, they were called cells. The study of plant and animal cells is called histology, *histo* being from a Greek word meaning a web or tissue.

Later it was found that a living cell was far from being a simple unit. As better and more powerful microscopes were invented, more and more of the fine structure of the cells could be seen. It was found that a cell was not just filled with a jelly-like fluid, as was first supposed, but is composed of a most complicated set of smaller parts. The fine structure of a cell is, in fact, far more complex than the most intricate piece of clockwork. The better the microscope, the more complicated the structure of the cell is seen to be. Cytology, as the study of the fine structure of cells is called, became a vast science on its own.

It is well known that the offspring of any plant or animal grows to be like its parents. It may not resemble its parents at first, as we shall see when dealing with INSECTS, but sooner or later it will. This gives an orderliness to life, and we say that a young plant or animal inherits the characters of its parents. The study of heredity, as we call this orderly resemblance of the offspring to the parents, is linked with the study of cytology. The fact that a child, or young animal or plant resembles or grows to be like its parents is due to minute particles in certain very small parts of the tiny cells that make up the body. The study of these minute particles, of the way they work and the effects they produce has grown into the tremendous science of GENETICS.

BIRDS Drawing of an archaeopteryx, the ancestor of the birds of today. It lived about 120 million years ago.

Biology includes, therefore, not only the study of the organs of living things, or the anatomy, and the chemistry of these organs, known as physiology, but also the sciences of histology, cytology, and genetics. It also includes the study of how things reproduce and grow; it includes the study of their life histories, from the egg or seed to the full-grown animal or plant. Finally, it takes in the study of how one plant has given rise to other plants, and one animal to another animal throughout the millions of years that living things have existed on the earth.

BIRDS

Warm-blooded vertebrates whose bodies are covered with feathers. The ancestor of the present birds was the 'archaeopteryx' who lived during the late Jurassic Period, that is, about 120,000,000 years ago.

Most birds can fly but some, like the ostriches, have probably never been able to fly, and others, like the penguins, have lost the ability to fly, although it is certain that their ancestors could do so.

Birds' skeletons are very light, the bones being hollow and strengthened inside by fine struts of bone. Added to this, there is a system of air-sacs connected with the lungs that help to lighten the body still further. Although the legs and feet are like those of reptiles, from which birds are believed to have been evolved, the forelimbs or wings have become markedly altered. There are the usual bones of the arm, but the wrist bones are few in number, and there are merely traces of three fingers out of the usual five.

The muscles which raise and lower the wings are very large and may make up nearly one-fifth of the total weight of the body. They are fastened at one end to the keel-like breast-bone. In birds that do not fly the breast-bone is more nearly normal.

A bird's feathers are of two kinds, the smaller contour feathers that cover most of the body, and the large flight feathers in the wings and tail, the latter acting mainly as a rudder. Every year the feathers are moulted and replaced by new feathers, and in some species there may be more than one moult in a year.

All birds lay eggs, a nest usually being built in which they are incubated. Some birds lay one egg only each year, others like the pheasant may lay up to twenty.

BISMARCK, Otto, Prince Von (1815–1898) Most famous of German statesmen and founder of the German Empire. Born in Brandenburg of an old Prussian family. He entered the Prussian diplomatic service (1851) and filled various high posts in Frankfurt, Vienna, St. Petersburg and Paris. His great opportunity came when he was appointed Prussian Prime Minister and Foreign Minister. The policy that he now began to pursue culminated in the foundation of the German Empire and the unification of Germany. In 1866 Prussia crushed Austria, after ensuring the latter's isolation and thus made herself the dominant power in Germany; and in 1870–1871 Prussia defeated France. Bismarck was the first Chancellor of the Empire and now concerned himself mainly with internal policy. In 1890 he was displaced by Kaiser Wilhelm II. [*See* GERMANY.]

BISON

Belongs to the family of wild cattle. It is distinguished by its mane and thick woolly hair over the front of its body and forelegs. There are two species, the European bison or wisent, and the American bison or buffalo.

BIZET, Georges (1838–1875) French composer, born in Paris. He is chiefly remembered for his exciting Spanish gipsy opera, *Carmen,* and the music he wrote for the play by Daudet, *L'Arlésienne.* He also wrote a lively symphony.

AVOCET

CROWNED CRANE

WEAVER BIRD

DODO

CASOWARY

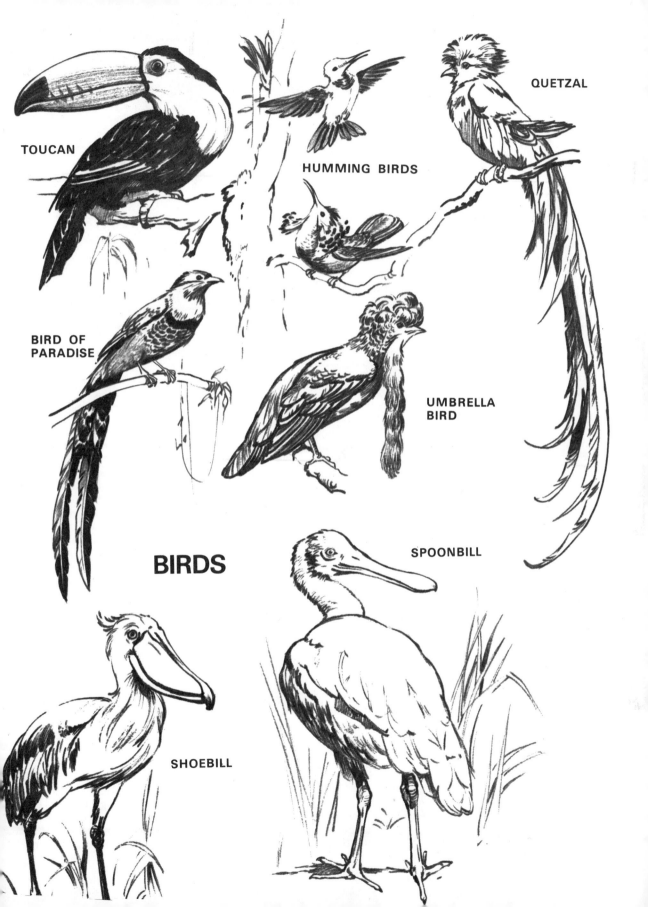

TOUCAN

HUMMING BIRDS

QUETZAL

BIRD OF
PARADISE

UMBRELLA
BIRD

BIRDS

SPOONBILL

SHOEBILL

BLACK, Joseph (1728–1799)

Scottish chemist whose work did much to lay the foundations of quantitative analysis. He suggested (1767) that a bag filled with hydrogen would rise in the air. As a result of his researches into the nature of heat he concluded that it must be some subtle kind of fluid and put forward the 'caloric' theory (1760) of heat. He first recognized 'latent' and 'specific' heat.

BLACK DEATH

In the year 1349 a deadly disease spread through Britain. Those who caught it vomited blood and broke out in boils. On their skin dark blotches appeared. The disease was called the 'Black Death'—'Black' because of the blotches and 'Death' because those who caught it nearly always died. Between one-third and one half of the population of England perished. Many villages and small towns were left without a single inhabitant.

BLACK ROD

The Royal Messenger who carries messages from the Queen and the House of Lords to the House of Commons. His office goes back to the 14th century and he gets his name from the Black Rod, surmounted by a golden lion, which he carries as a symbol of his office. When the Queen has given the Royal Assent to a BILL it is Black Rod who is sent to tell the Commons to come to the House of Lords to hear the Royal Assent announced.

BLAKE, William (1757–1827)

An outstanding genius alike as a poet and as an artist. A Londoner. At the age of 12 he was already writing poetry, and within a few years had composed poems great in their very simplicity. When he was 16 he was engraving pictures of sincerity and strength. He needed little teaching, and throughout his long life of seventy years he went on constantly writing and drawing, often in poverty, from the resources of his imagination—or his 'visions', which seemed to him quite real.

You will find two different sorts of poem in his books; short rhyming poems, especially in *Songs of Innocence* and *Songs of Experience*; and complex, visionary, non-rhyming poems, called *The Prophetic Books*. He published his poems himself with his own illustrations. The original editions of them are now very precious because of the magnificent pages in which his drawings and verses are combined.

BLANK VERSE

Form of poetry which has served our writers very usefully, especially when they have been working for the stage. 'Blank' indicates that

BLAKE A typical example of his visionary drawing.

the lines do not rhyme. The lines are of equal length—of ten syllables divided into five metrical groups each made up of an unstressed syllable followed by a stressed syllable. Open a volume of Shakespeare's plays and look at the verse speeches; most of them provide examples of blank verse. When Prince Hal rejects his old friend Falstaff he says:

I háve lŏng dréam'd of sŭch ă kínd of mán,
So surfeit-swell'd, so old, and so profane;
But being awak'd, I do despise my dream.

(The first line in the quotation has been specially marked for you here, to show how the ten syllables are divided and how in each pair or foot the unstressed syllable, ˘ , comes before the stressed syllable, ´ .)

BLIGH, William (c. 1753–1817)

Nicknamed 'Breadfruit Bligh' because he discovered breadfruit while accompanying Captain COOK on his second voyage, 1772–1774. In 1787 he was sent in H.M.S. *Bounty* to bring breadfruit to the West Indies and on his return the following year mutiny broke out on the ship and Captain Bligh, with some others, was set adrift. After a voyage of over 4,000 miles in an open boat he landed in the East Indies. The mutiny on the *Bounty* was the inspiration for Byron's poem *The Island*.

BLOW, Dr. John (c. 1648–1708)

English composer. Born at Newark. A choirboy at the Chapel Royal of King Charles II, he became organist of Westminster Abbey. This post he generously gave up in favour of his great pupil, Henry PURCELL, taking it over again on Purcell's death; he died at Westminster. His music consists mainly of church anthems and songs, an outstanding exception being the fine masque, *Venus and Adonis*.

BLUNDEN, Edward Charles (1896———)

English nature poet and critic. His poetry includes *Pastorals* and *The Waggoner and Other Poems*, and *Undertones of War* is perhaps his best prose work. In 1966 he became Oxford Professor of Poetry.

BOBCAT

This aggressive animal belongs to the lynxes and is found in North America from Canada to Mexico. It is quite small, and has been described as an 'over-grown house cat', which it is like in its mewing, yowling and caterwauling. It is also known as 'bay lynx' or 'wild cat'.

BOCCACCIO, Giovanni (1313–1375)

Italian writer. Born probably in Paris, the son of a Florentine merchant. He is best known for his work *Decameron* (completed 1358). This is a collection of a hundred prose tales supposedly told by a group of Florentine nobles in withdrawal from the plague of 1348. Because of their form and style Boccaccio has been termed 'the father of the modern novel'. In his own day the *Decameron* influenced Chaucer's *Canterbury Tales*.

BOER WAR

'Boer' is a Dutch word meaning 'farmer' and it used to be the name by which the Dutch colonists in South Africa were known. The Boers founded a colony at the Cape of Good Hope in 1652. In 1814 the British paid six million pounds for it and Dutch Guiana together. It then became a British possession. The Boers later moved north and founded the Orange Free State and the Transvaal, but distrust between the two peoples remained. In the Boer War (1899–1902) the Boers were defeated and lost their independence, but in 1910 the Union of South Africa was established with British and Boers in equal partnership. [*See* SOUTH AFRICA.]

BOHR, Niels (1885–1962)

One of the world's foremost atom scientists. Born at Copenhagen. Studied at Cambridge and Manchester. Collaborated with Lord Rutherford to produce the planetary theory of atoms according to quantum theory. In 1943, when Denmark was over-run by Nazis, Bohr was smuggled out of his country on a fishing boat and escaped to Sweden. From there he was flown to England and then to America where he joined the scientists working on the atom bomb.

BOLIVIA

A republic in the north-west of South America. It is 415,000 square miles, nearly twice as large as France, with a population of over 4 million. It is a mountainous country in the Andes. About two-thirds of the people are Indians, descendants of the INCAS, and they speak their own languages. The people of European origin speak Spanish. The country takes its name from Simon BOLIVAR, a great South American patriot. Bolivia has many minerals the chief of which is tin. The capital is La Paz.

BOLIVIA La Paz, capital of Bolivia and the highest capital city in the world.

BOLIVAR, Simon (1783–1830)
Born in Venezuela and grew up to be a soldier and revolutionary leader who was eventually responsible for the liberation from Spanish rule of Venezuela (1824), Colombia, Equador, Panama, Peru (1824) and Bolivia. The last-named was called after him. His achievements were due to his personal qualities and to the energy and fire with which he tackled his problems. He was an adventurous and romantic figure who undoubtedly did more than any other one man to influence the history of South America.

BONAPARTE, Napoleon (1769–1821)
French Emperor and military leader. Born at Ajaccio, Corsica, he received his military education in France and was a captain by the age of twenty. In 1794 he served in Italy with the French Revolutionary forces with such distinction that he was made a general and the next year appointed commander-in-chief. A series of brilliant successes followed. He defeated the Austrians at Campo Formio (1797), led an expedition to Syria and Egypt (1798) and when he returned to France declared himself First Consul (1799). He reformed the French administration and published the *Code Napoleon*, the basis of modern French Law. In 1804 he was crowned Emperor. Although defeated at sea by the English at Trafalgar (1805), he won land victories against Austria, Russia and Prussia. He had now reached the climax of his career as virtual master of Europe. The tide turned when the invasion of Russia was a failure (1812) and

when the Peninsular War in Spain went against him. In 1814 the Allies entered Paris and forced Napoleon to abdicate. He was sent to Elba but escaped and gathered his old army about him. He was finally defeated at Waterloo (1815) and exiled to the island of St. Helena in the south Atlantic where he died.

BONGO
A distinguished-looking antelope having massive horns twisted into about one complete spiral. It is about four feet high, is chestnut in colour and has white stripes running over its body. The bongo lives in the forested districts of Central Africa.

BONNARD, Pierre (1867–1947)
French painter, born at Fontenay-aux-Roses. He was a leading member of a group of artists known as the 'Nabis', but later developed a more impressionistic style. He was an outstanding colourist and excelled in his nudes and interiors. Bonnard also illustrated books and produced lithographs.

BOOTH, William (1829–1912)
English religious leader, born in Nottingham. Originally he was a Methodist minister, but in 1865 set up the Christian Mission. This he organised on military lines and in 1878 founded the SALVATION ARMY.

BOROUGH
A town which has a MAYOR and has been given a Royal Charter. The citizens elect a Borough Council, or Corporation, and the Councillors when elected choose certain of their number to serve as ALDERMEN. One of the aldermen is usually chosen to be Mayor. Borough Councils come under COUNTY COUNCILS, except the new London Boroughs. BOROUGH COUNCILS collect the RATES in their area to help pay for the many services which they have to provide. Some of the money so collected has to be paid over to the County Council. Amongst the services which Borough Councils must provide is the collection of refuse and the provision of welfare clinics. They also build houses and provide public libraries. Not all Borough Councils carry out exactly the same work because in some cases the duty may be carried out by the County Council and in others by the Borough Council.

BORROW, George (1803–1881)
English traveller, linguist and author. While he was articled to a firm of Norwich solicitors he acquired a knowledge of many European tongues, ancient and modern, including Romany, the language of the gypsies. Later he took

BONGO Lives in the forests of Central Africa.

to the roads as a wanderer himself. He became famous when *The Bible in Spain* was published in 1843, and *Lavengro* and *Romany Rye* are the products of his English travels.

BOSCH, Hieronymous (*c.* 1450–1516)

A Dutch painter, he spent most of his life in s'Hertogenbosch. Bosch's paintings display a fantastic and haunting vision not far removed from some modern surrealist artists. His imagery was no doubt drawn from medieval symbolism, the meaning of which is lost to us. Among his most outstanding works are *Earthly Paradise* (Prado, Madrid), *Seven Deadly Sins* (Prado, Madrid) and *Ship of Fools* (Louvre, Paris).

BOTANY

The branch of science devoted to the study of plants. Plants have been used for feeding, clothing, and healing mankind from time immemorial, but it was not until the Middle Ages in Europe that plants were studied by herbalists with a view to recording and describing them. The need for clear description led to an interest in external, and then in internal structure. Nehemiah Grew (1628–1711) described the structure of stems, and used the word 'cell' for the basic component of plant tissues. This in turn led to a consideration of how a plant lives, and it was Stephen Hales (1677–1761) who showed that plants must be built of materials absorbed from the air. Joseph PRIESTLEY (1779) showed that in sunlight plants gave out oxygen, and thus prepared the way for work on photosynthesis and related subjects.

Meanwhile, LINNAEUS (1707–1778) in Sweden produced a classification of plants of the world and laid the foundations for modern classification. As the microscopes of the 17th century were improved, so more detail of the structure of plants was observed, and this led naturally to examination of the processes of sexual reproduction and these were mainly worked out by the end of the 19th century.

In 1859 Charles DARWIN produced his now famous book, *On the Origin of Species by means of Natural Selection*, and this drew great attention to variation, heredity and evolution. Gregor MENDEL in 1865 put forward his theories of inheritance, but the importance of these was not realized until 1900. Sutton in 1902 showed how Mendelian inheritance could be explained by the behaviour of chromosomes in cell division, and since that time there has been a tremendous expansion of work on this subject.

Modern botany thus includes many different, but related, branches. A large part is systema-

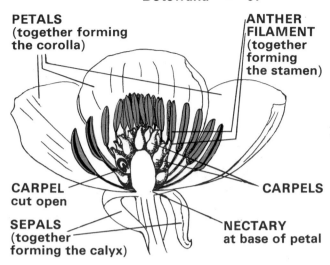

BOTANY Structure of a flowering plant

PETALS (together forming the corolla)

ANTHER FILAMENT (together forming the stamen)

CARPEL cut open

CARPELS

SEPALS (together forming the calyx)

NECTARY at base of petal

tics, and this covers the description and classification of all plants of all groups, which range from flowering plants, pines and other conifers, ferns, mosses and algae, to fungi and bacteria. Morphology deals with the forms of plants, and Developmental Morphology (Ontogeny) deals with the way in which plants grow. Anatomy is concerned with internal structure. Cytology is the study of cell structure and is an important aid, through the examination of the chromosomes, to the understanding of Genetics, the study of heredity [*see* BIOLOGY]. Physiology is concerned with the life processes of plants. Ecology deals with the relation of plants and their environment, and Plant Geography with the occurrence and dispersal of plants throughout the world.

Botanical science plays an important part in modern life. Branches of applied botany include Economic Botany (the study of useful plants), further sub-divisions of which are Agricultural Botany and Forest Botany. Genetics is applied in plant breeding, and the study of fungi and bacteria make important contributions to plant pathology, that is, the study of plant diseases. Physiology has helped greatly in agriculture in its work on plant nutrition. Lastly, Microbiology (study of micro-organisms such as yeasts and bacteria) has shown these to be important agents for the manufacture of chemicals, including vitamins, for example riboflavin, and antibiotics such as penicillin and streptomycin.

BOTSWANA, formerly **Bechuanaland**

An African State within the BRITISH COMMONWEALTH. It lies between South Africa and RHODESIA. Although it is slightly larger (220,000 square miles) than France it has less than half

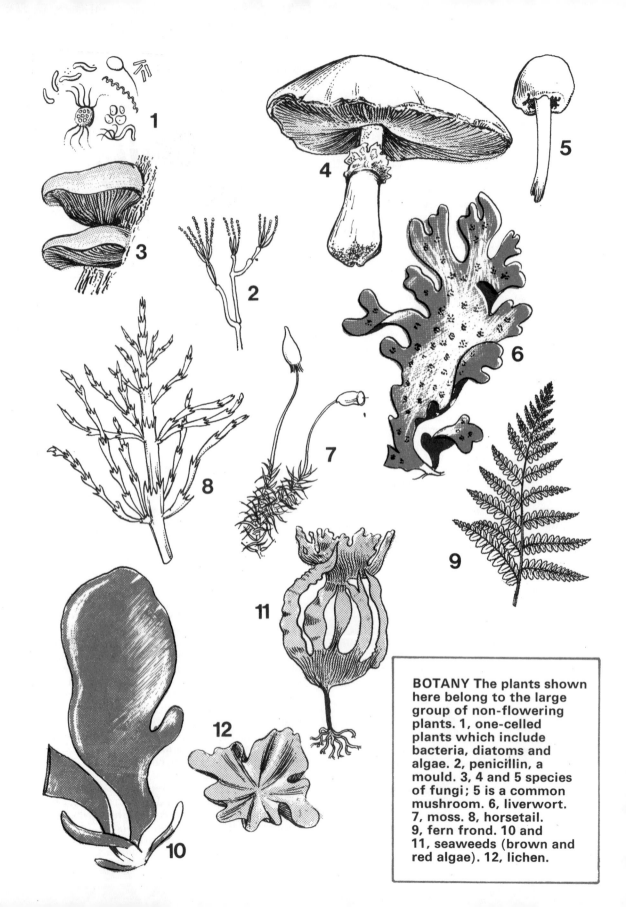

BOTANY The plants shown here belong to the large group of non-flowering plants. 1, one-celled plants which include bacteria, diatoms and algae. 2, penicillin, a mould. 3, 4 and 5 species of fungi; 5 is a common mushroom. 6, liverwort. 7, moss. 8, horsetail. 9, fern frond. 10 and 11, seaweeds (brown and red algae). 12, lichen.

a million inhabitants. The country was formerly a British PROTECTORATE but in 1966 it became independent and took the new name of Botswana. Its Prime Minister is Seretse Khama. The capital is Gaberones.

BOTTICELLI, Sandro (*c.* 1444–1510)

Italian Renaissance painter of the Florentine school. Started as a goldsmith's apprentice, and produced classical as well as religious subjects. His greatest works were: *Primavera*, painted for Lorenzo de Medici, *Fortitude*, in the Uffizi Gallery, *The Birth of Venus*, *The Annunciation*, and *The Magnificat*. His *Mars and Venus* is in the National Gallery, London, together with the *Nativity*.

BOUCHER, François (1703–1770)

French painter. He won the Grand Prix at the age of 20, and after studying in Italy he became the most fashionable painter in France. He produced many pictures, etchings and tapestry designs, and was appointed director of the famous Gobelins tapestry factory. There are many fine examples of his work in the Wallace Collection, London.

BOXING

A game of skill where two opponents, equally matched and following well-defined rules, take part in a friendly attempt to outwit each other's punching prowess.

Physical fitness is an essential and for this there must be training and adequate rest and sleep. The first and easiest exercise is deep breathing. This can be done at all times but best when walking or running in the open air. Skipping is also of value. P.E. instruction gives muscle strength to arms, legs, back and stomach, while vaulting and other exercises give the necessary light freedom of movement. Home-made equipment such as a punch pad, improves speed and timing, while exercises on the punch bag ensure that blows are delivered with power.

The basis of boxing is good balance and easy footwork. The stance, or sparring position, should be as follows:

Arms Left elbow bent, close to the body and behind left glove which is held with the thumb uppermost. The right glove is just below the chin with the knuckle part toward the opponent and the right elbow tucked in.

Legs Comfortably apart, with weight of body balanced evenly on both feet—left leg slightly bent.

Body Left shoulder directed toward opponent; chin tucked in.

Feet Left foot pointed in the direction of opponent, right heel raised. The left heel may

BOTTICELLI Section of his *Nativity*.

be raised or ready to be raised; weight of body equally on the ball of both feet.

Footwork The above position should be adopted whenever possible in readiness for moving. On going forward the left foot leads and is followed by the right; on retiring the right foot is moved first and is followed by the left. When moving to the right—the right foot comes first, followed by the left; and when moving to the left—the left foot comes first followed by the right.

The first basic punch is the straight left. Starting from the sparring position, the leading foot of the attacker should be in a line between the toe of his opponent's leading foot and heel of his rear foot. In this way, if the punch is straight, it will contact the target. The punching arm from shoulder to fist should be in a straight line with the left foot and to get the most effect from the delivery of a straight left, it must follow the direction in which the foot is pointing. The development of a good left hand helps correct balance, style, footwork and judgement of distance to be acquired and will stand the boxer in good stead when learning the more advanced blows, such as the hooks or uppercuts.

(The boxer who stands naturally with his right arm and leg forward is known as the 'southpaw'. He is the looking-glass reflection of the conventional type.)

Appearance is important also. The hair

should always be well cut. A plain vest completely covering the chest and back must be worn by amateur boxers; shorts should be fairly loose; light gym shoes or boxing boots must be worn with ankle socks which, if possible, should be white.

In competitive boxing, marks are awarded for scoring blows—any fair blow delivered with the knuckle part of the closed glove, either hand hitting, with force, the target area (the front or sides of the head or body above the belt—an imaginary line drawn from the top of the hips through the navel). Blows on the arm do not score. Aim to be first with the punch; anticipate an opponent's moves and beat him in speed to the punch; learn of the science of the game—slipping, swaying, counter punching, leading an opponent on, boxing on the retreat.

The most important thing is to box with people of as many styles as possible, learning from each, and trying out new punches or ways of evasion. After boxing, or following exercises, there should always be a sponge down or a shower, finishing with a stimulating rub down with a towel.

The information given above is for international amateur boxing.

BOYLE, Robert (1627–1691)

Born in Ireland and son of the Earl of Cork. He is best remembered for his work on the physics of the atmosphere; the relations between the volume and pressure of gases— the well-known Boyle's Law of gases. His experiments on air under low pressure led to work on the nature of combustion and he nearly anticipated the chemists of the 18th century and their discovery of the chemical nature of air. His best known work is *The Sceptical Chymist*. He is often called the 'father of modern chemistry'. Died in London.

BOY SCOUTS AND GIRL GUIDES

World-wide movements which were founded by Lord BADEN-POWELL in 1908 and 1910. The purpose of both bodies is to develop character and good citizenship on non-political, non-denominational lines. In the United Kingdom there are about 509,000 scouts and 557,000 guides.

Both scouts and guides wear uniforms. In 1966 it was decided to change the uniform and also to change the names of the different sections into which the age groups are divided. Instead of shorts, scouts wear long tapering trousers. Cub Scouts are replacing Wolf Cubs and Senior and Rover Scouts are now known as Venture Scouts. Most scouts are under sixteen years of age.

BRAGG, William Henry (1862–1942)

British physicist who together with his son, William Lawrence Bragg (1890———) founded the science of X-ray crystallography—the study of crystal structure by X-ray analysis. They were awarded a Nobel Prize in 1915.

BRAHE, Tycho (1546–1601)

Danish astronomer. Although he did important work in the field of observation he rejected the Copernican system in favour of his own in which he attempted to put the earth back in the centre of the solar system. He suggested that the other planets revolved about the sun, which carried them round the earth. His assistant was KEPLER.

BRAHMS, Johannes (1833–1897)

German composer. Born at Hamburg. He became a great friend of Schumann, who gave him much help and advice; and when Schumann died, he took care of his wife and children. He eventually settled in Vienna, where he produced his masterpieces, and it was there that he died. An outstanding pianist, he wrote two powerful concertos for the instrument, as well as four mighty symphonies, one of the world's few great violin concertos, much chamber music, and many beautiful songs and piano pieces.

BOYLE Often called the 'father of modern chemistry'.

BRAILLE, Louis (1809–1852)

Born near Paris, and became blind when he was three years old. He became an instructor at an institute for the blind in Paris and developed what is now known as the 'Braille System' of reading and writing for the blind, which was published in 1829. This system is adopted all over the world and is used for figures and music as well as reading and writing. The principle is that of dots embossed on the paper and felt with the tips of the fingers.

CHAMELEON This slow-moving animal belongs to the lizard family. They are found in S. Asia and Africa, especially Madagascar where the horned chameleon lives. The main physical features of a chameleon are its swivel eyes, split toes and lightning-quick tongue.

REPTILE A flying lizard of the kind found in the jungles of S.E. Asia. The wings are really scaly membranes.

SNAKES The species shown here are rattlesnakes of the New World. They belong to the pit viper family of snakes. The rattle is a series of hollow segments at the end of its tail which when violently shaken makes a whirring sound.

AMPHIBIANS *Above*, a pair of tree frogs. This group of frogs is
well adapted because of its toes for living a life in trees.
Many species are found in tropical regions of America. *Below*,
a blind salamander or 'siren'. This species inhabits sub-
terranean caves and because of the blackness has virtually no eyes.

CROCODILE The specimen shown above
is a baby Nile crocodile. The adults
of this species grow to about 12–16
feet in length.

TURTLE This illustration shows a turtle lumbering its way up
a beach to lay its eggs. It scoops out a deep hole in the sand,
deposits its eggs and then covers the hole in again. When
the young turtles hatch out they crawl up through the sand and
make their way to the sea; frequently they are caught by seabirds.

BRAZIL A view of Brasilia the new capital and the most modern capital in the world.

BRAQUE, Georges (1882–1963)

French painter, born at Argenteuil. Initially a decorator's apprentice, he was very much a self-taught artist. He was one of the leading members of the 'Fauve' school of modern painters. About 1909 he became friendly with PICASSO and together they developed the 'Cubist' style of painting. After the First World War he developed a style which was based on reality but integrated with cubist vision. Braque was a meticulous painter and at their best his canvases are a perfect balance of design and colour.

BRAZIL

The largest country (3,289,000 square miles) of South America and about the same size as the United States. It has rather more than 66 million inhabitants who are of many different races. The chief river is the Amazon which is navigable through nearly two thousand miles of Brazilian territory. The country has vast forests and is rich in minerals. Its chief export is coffee, half the world's supply coming from Brazil. The capital is the new city of Brasilia, which is 600 miles north-west of the former capital of Rio de Janeiro. Brazil's largest city is Sao Paulo which has nearly four million inhabitants.

Brazil was discovered by a Portuguese, Pedro Alvares Cabral, in 1550. Brazil was ruled by the Portuguese for several centuries and became independent only in 1820. For a time the country was ruled by an Emperor but became a republic in 1889. As in some other countries of South America there are revolts from time to time, usually led by the Army, one of these revolts being as recent as 1964.

BRECHT, Bertholt Eugen Friedrich (1898–1956)

German playwright and poet. He was born in Augsburg, but fled from Nazi Germany in 1933, settling at last in Hollywood. A Marxist, he was brought before a Senate sub-committee for un-American activities in 1946. In 1948 he settled in East Berlin where he founded the *Berliner Ensemble*. He intended his plays to be social experiments rather than entertainments, so he made sure that his audiences remembered that his actors were actors and not the characters they represented by, for example, having them stumble over their lines. His writing could be powerful or lyrical, and there is a great range of expression in his poetry. One of Brecht's early and very successful works was *The Threepenny Opera* adapted from John Gay's *Beggars Opera* and with music by Kurt Weill. *Mother Courage* and *The Good Man from Setzuan* are two of his plays.

BREUIL, Abbé H. E. P. (1860–1961)

French archaeologist and the world's most outstanding authority on the art of prehistoric man in Europe and Africa. Among his best-known work is that concerned with the cave paintings discovered by four schoolboys at LASCAUX, France, in 1940.

BRIDGES, Robert (1844–1930)

English poet. First a doctor but later devoted his whole time to poetry. Poet Laureate (1913) and O.M. Best-known work is *The Testament of Beauty* which was not published until his eighty-fifth year and which expresses his long experience of life. He was also a sympathetic critic of Milton and Keats.

BRITISH BROADCASTING CORPORATION (BBC)

The only body in Great Britain which is allowed to transmit sound broadcasts. It shares with the INDEPENDENT TELEVISION AUTHORITY the right to transmit television services.

Sound broadcasting began in Britain in 1922. Parliament then decided that the right to broadcast should be given to a new company called the British Broadcasting Company but in 1927 the present Corporation was formed to take over the work from the company. In 1937 the BBC inaugurated a television service but this was suspended during the war and not resumed until 1946. The cost of the BBC service is met by a charge for a licence which every owner of a radio or television set must pay to the Post Office. Parliament decides how much of this money shall be handed over to the BBC. Parliament also gives a grant to the BBC to pay for broadcasts to other countries.

BRITISH COMMONWEALTH

A free association of independent States, all of whom recognize the Queen as Head of the Commonwealth. Some members of the Commonwealth, such as Australia and Canada, accept the Queen as Queen of their country as do the people of Britain. Others are republics and one—MALAYSIA—is a kingdom. The British Commonwealth today is made up of twenty-three Member States. Because they are independent States they are all allowed to become Members of the UNITED NATIONS.

The British Commonwealth of free nations has developed from the older Empire when Britain ruled many overseas territories as colonies or protectorates. It was during the reign of Elizabeth I that the foundations of the British Empire were laid. In 1583 a colonizing expedition, under Sir Humphrey Gilbert, sailed for Newfoundland and the island was annexed by Britain. In 1607 the East India Co. established the first trading stations in INDIA and this eventually led to the establishment of British rule in that country. Not long after this the first British settlements were made on the Canadian mainland. It was not till the end of the 18th century that the first British immigrants settled in AUSTRALIA and not till the 19th century that Britain established colonies in Africa.

When some of the older colonies were granted the right to govern themselves it was recognized that they were no longer possessions of Britain and therefore a new relationship between Britain and her former colonies had come about. So in 1932 the Statute of Westminster was passed which gave the self-governing colonies the name of Dominion and new rights as nations. Since the Second World War nearly all the former colonies and protectorates have been given the right to govern themselves and to become members of the British Commonwealth.

BRITISH EMPLOYERS' CONFEDERATION

An organization which unites nearly all those who employ labour in industry and commerce, except for the nationalized industries such as the railways and mines. The big engineering firms, for instance, will belong to the Engineering Employers' Federation and so on. These federations, or associations, will affiliate to the British Employers' Confederation so that all employers can unite, when they wish to do so, to protect their interests. When the Government wishes to know what are the views of both sides of industry it asks the Confederation to speak for the employers and the TRADES UNION CONGRESS to speak for the workers. Each year, when the INTERNATIONAL LABOUR ORGANIZATION holds its conference the Government asks the Confederation to appoint the employers' delegate and the TUC to appoint the workers' delegate.

BRITISH HONDURAS

A British Crown Colony in Central America. It is rather larger (8,868 square miles) than

BRITISH HONDURAS is covered with dense forests which contain valuable mahogany trees.

Wales and has just over 90,000 inhabitants. Most of the country is covered with forests which contain valuable trees such as mahogany and cedar. Another tree is the chicle from which chewing gum is made. The capital is Belize.

BRITTEN, Benjamin (1913——)
English composer. Born on St. Cecilia's day at Lowestoft. He finds inspiration in the music of PURCELL, many of whose works he has arranged, and in the life and countryside of his native Suffolk. His operas *Peter Grimes* and *Albert Herring* are both set in that county, and he has founded a Musical Festival at the little Suffolk town of Aldeburgh. For the Coronation of Elizabeth II he composed the opera, *Gloriana*. Several of his compositions, especially the cantata *St. Nicholas* and the *Spring Symphony*, contain parts for children's voices, and his stage-entertainment, *Let's Make an Opera*, was written specially for children. He has written a *Young Person's Guide to the Orchestra*, and is also a fine song writer. His *War Requiem* sets to music the poetry of the war-time poet Wilfred OWEN.

BRONTË, Charlotte (1816–1855),
Emily (1818–1848), and **Anne** (1820–1849)
These were three of six children born to an Irish parson in a West Yorkshire moorland village. Two other sisters died; these three girls wrote novels and poems now famous all over the world. Charlotte offered her early novels to a publisher under the masculine pseudonym of Currer Bell; her first effort, *The Professor*, was rejected, but her second, *Jane Eyre*, obtained deserving success. Emily's *Wuthering Heights* appeared under the pseudonym of Ellis Bell. Anne, who used the name Acton Bell, is not so famous as her sisters, but her novels, too, have quality.

BROOKE, Rupert (1887–1915)
Born at Rugby. This poet, who died early in the First World War at Skyros while on the way to the Dardanelles, caught the public imagination in England and is still remembered most for his patriotic sonnets of 1914. Some of his sayings are memorable, above all his declaration that there are three fine things in the world: 'one is to read poetry, another is to write poetry, and the best of all is to live poetry'.

BROWN, Ford Madox (1821–1893)
English historical painter. Born at Calais. He became closely associated with the PRE-RAPHAELITES in London, and his paintings became celebrated for their bright colours and

BRONTË Charlotte, the author of *Jane Eyre*.

naturalness. Among his best-known works are *Christ Washing Peter's Feet* (National Gallery, London), *Work* (Manchester Art Gallery), *The Last of England* (Birmingham Gallery), and his 12 frescoes depicting the history of Manchester are in Manchester Town Hall.

BROWNING, Robert (1812–1889) and
BARRETT, Elizabeth Moulton (1806–1861)
Robert Browning was born into a rich family which was sympathetic enough to let him follow no profession but that of poet. To gain worldly and literary experience he travelled over Europe and read widely. When he was 32, and beginning to win a reputation, he met Elizabeth Barrett, who, herself a poetess, had been described as 'the second most accomplished woman of the day'. The two married by elopement (against an opposition from Mr. Barrett that has become legendary), and, living thereafter chiefly in Italy, enjoyed until her death one of the happiest marriages of which there is record. Following her death Robert continued, though lonely, his chosen work of writing, and in this period attempted the long successful novel-in-verse, *The Ring and the Book*. Apart from this the poems of his which we most read today are his dramatic sketches of characters, particularly of characters from the past, like the painter Fra Lippo Lippi. Of his wife's work we most read the so-called *Sonnets from the Portuguese*. Her poem in defence of Italian freedom, *Casa Guidi Windows*, should also be read.

BRUCE, Robert (1274–1329)
Scottish national hero. He supported at first Edward I, King of England, in his struggle against the Scots, but then transferred his loyalty to Wallace, the popular leader in the Scottish War of Independence. Finally, in

BUDDHA Founder of the Buddhist faith.

1306, Robert crowned himself King of Scotland. But the struggle against the English continued. They were not decisively defeated until 1314 at the Battle of Bannockburn when Robert overthrew an English army three times the strength of his own forces. His success liberated Scotland from all fear of a re-establishment of English supremacy. In 1328 by the Treaty of Northampton his title as King of Scotland was officially recognized.

BRUCKNER, Anton (1824–1896)
Austrian composer, born in Ansfelden. Was first a church organist and later a concert organist. He settled in Vienna and devoted himself almost entirely to composition. He wrote nine symphonies, a Te Deum, a Requiem and other works. He was influenced by both BRAHMS and WAGNER. Until quite recently Bruckner was not very highly regarded outside Austria, but now his work is coming more and more into the concert repertory.

BRUEGEL, Pieter, the elder (c. 1525–1569)
Known as Peasant Bruegel. A Flemish landscape painter, he visited Italy, and developed a highly individual style of painting landscapes and peasants. In a number of his pictures he showed the horrors of the Inquisition. His *Massacre of the Innocents* illustrated the massacre of Flemish villagers in wintertime. In the main Bruegel's landscapes are full of vitality and gaiety. Bruegel's son, also Pieter, worked in a style very similar to his father's; in fact, he often copied his paintings.

BRUNO, Giordano (c. 1548–1600)
Italian philosopher. Started life in the Dominican Order but was forced to leave this because of his advanced views. He was the first Western thinker to conceive the heavens as limitless, empty space. He supported the work of COPERNICUS and opposed the older ideas, especially those of ARISTOTLE. He was burned at the stake by the INQUISITION.

BUCHAN, John, 1st Baron Tweedsmuir (1875–1940)
Scottish author and statesman. He was a member of the publishing firm of Thomas Nelson, and was director of information under Lloyd George during the First World War. He served as M.P. for the Scottish universities from 1927 to 1935, when he became Governor-General of Canada.

His books include some of the most gripping adventure stories ever written. *Prester John* is set in South Africa, where he had served under the high commissioner, and *Huntingtower* in the Scottish border country. Even better known are the spy thrillers like *The Thirty-nine Steps* and *Greenmantle*.

BUDDHA, Prince Siddartha Gautama (c. 567 B.C.–c. 487 B.C.)
Founder of the Buddhist faith, born in northern India, the son of a rajah. The suffering he saw around him made such an impression on him that he left his wife and his kingdom and turned to a simple life of contemplation. He believed that life on earth must always be unhappy, but that by following the Buddhistic rules man could eventually attain 'Nirvana' or 'Bliss' by losing his separate identity and merging with the universal. The unholy man, after his death, must pass through other existences before he can reach 'Nirvana'.

In India, Buddhism has been superseded by the Hindu religion and the religion of Islam. But it is still strong in Tibet (Lamaism), Ceylon, Burma, Thailand, China (Ch'an Buddhism) and Japan (Zen Buddhism). It has greatly influenced many modern Western writers, especially Aldous Huxley.

BUDGET
A term used to describe a sum of money which it is expected will be needed for a certain purpose. It is chiefly used to describe the money which the nation is expected to need to carry on the work of government for a year. The nation's Budget is presented to Parliament by the Chancellor of the Exchequer every Spring. Because the reckoning is not made from January 1st but usually from April to April this is spoken of as the financial year.

BULGARIA

A republic in Eastern Europe that borders the Black Sea. It is rather smaller (43,000 square miles) than England and has a population of just over 8 million. Its people speak a language known as Slavonic, the group to which Russia belongs. It is chiefly an agricultural country and grows tobacco, grapes and attar of roses. Recently important industries have developed, particularly steel and coal. The capital is Sofia. During the Second World War Bulgaria sided with Germany and at the end of the war the country was occupied by the Russian Army. Since 1947 the country has had a Communist form of government.

BUNSEN, Robert Wilhelm (1811–1899)

German scientist, born in Gottingen. Bunsen's work ranged very widely, but he is best remembered for the gas burner which still bears his name. With KIRCHOFF he founded the study of spectrum analysis. He discovered the elements caesium and rubidium, and methods for separating yttrium and erbium. Bunsen also worked in the electrical field and devised a wet battery, known as a 'Bunsen' cell.

BUNYAN, John (1628–1688)

English writer. Born near Bedford. He was a travelling tinker and in 1644–1645 fought in the Civil War with Cromwell's forces. He joined a nonconformist sect in Bedford (1653), but was imprisoned in 1660 for twelve years as an unauthorised preacher. He was again imprisoned in 1673, during which time he began to write *The Pilgrim's Progress* (published 1678), the work by which he is still remembered. It is an allegory describing Christian's progress from the City of Destruction to the Celestial City. Its homely language and lively dialogue and description have made it a classic.

BUOYS

Anchored floats used in marine navigation. They are of various shapes and colours, each being designed for a particular duty. *Channel buoys* mark the approach to the entrance of a channel and are usually pillar or landfall buoys. These are followed by a number of can-shaped buoys to port, and conical-shaped buoys to starboard. *Spherical buoys* usually denote the presence of an obstruction. *Special buoys* are used for marking wrecks, quarantine stations, telegraph cables, and as mooring buoys.

BURBANK, Luther (1849–1926)

American plant-breeder, whose experiments led to the introduction of numerous new species of flowers and fruits, particularly plums. He recorded his methods and discoveries in a number of books.

BUOYS

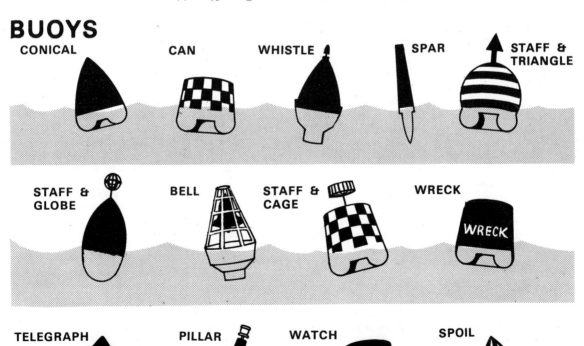

CONICAL   CAN   WHISTLE   SPAR   STAFF & TRIANGLE

STAFF & GLOBE   BELL   STAFF & CAGE   WRECK

TELEGRAPH   PILLAR   WATCH   SPOIL

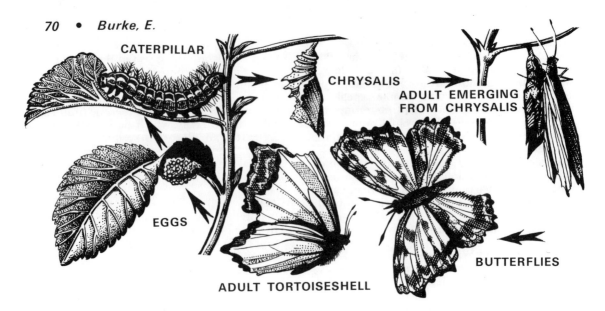

CATERPILLAR

CHRYSALIS

ADULT EMERGING FROM CHRYSALIS

EGGS

BUTTERFLIES

ADULT TORTOISESHELL

BUTTERFLIES The series of changes (metamorphoses) in the life of a butterfly.

BURKE, Edmund (1729–1797)

Anglo-Irish statesman, essayist and political theorist. He became a Whig M.P. in 1766, and was one of the leading lights of the Whig party until 1790. He strongly opposed George III's attempt to control the Government through subservient ministers like Lord Bute and Lord North, and in 1780 made proposals designed to limit the corrupt influence of the Crown. In *Thoughts on the Cause of Present Discontents* (1770) he described such a ministry as 'a faction ruling by the private instructions of a court against the general sense of the people', but he believed that the country should be ruled by the landed aristocracy in the interest of the nation and commerce. He opposed the coercion of the American colonists, as he believed it would go against British interests (*Speech on Conciliation*, 1775), but he was quite out of sympathy with the French Revolution (*Reflections on the Revolution in France*, 1790), for he believed no good could ever come of violently overthrowing a government, even a government as tyrannical and divisive as that of the Bourbons. This led him to break with Charles James FOX and the young Whigs. Burke also played a leading part in the impeachment of Warren HASTINGS.

BURMA

A republic in south-east Asia that is rather larger (262,000 square miles) than France. It has over 20 million inhabitants who are nearly all Buddhists. Most Burmese are farmers, rice being both grown and exported. Her forests produce valuable timber, particularly teak. The country is rich in minerals, the most important of which is oil. Another valuable mineral is ruby. The capital is Rangoon, and Mandalay is an important city.

For many years Burma was governed by Britain as part of India. During the Second World War the Japanese invaded Burma and occupied it. When the war was over Burma decided that she did not wish to remain in the British Commonwealth and so she and Britain signed a treaty to bring this about. This was followed by a period of civil war in the country. After the war was over a new government introduced a number of social and economic reforms.

BURNE-JONES, Sir Edward (1833–1898)

English painter. Born in Birmingham. After studying at Oxford, where he met William MORRIS, he worked with ROSSETTI in London, and the two became the leading exponents of a new phase of Pre-Raphaelitism. Burne-Jones based many of his pictures on the stories about King Arthur and the Greek Myths. His original style of drawing was a powerful influence on later artists both in England and on the Continent. His *King Cophetua and the Beggar Maid* is in the Tate Gallery, London, and his *Star of Bethlehem* in the Birmingham Art Gallery. He executed many designs for stained glass windows, and these are to be found in a great many English churches.

BURNS, Robert (1759–1796)

Scottish poet, the son of a farmer at Alloway in Ayrshire, who was influenced as a child by the popular songs and ballads he heard from an old woman called Betty Davidson. Failure in both farming and love turned him to poetry, and his reputation was soon established in the literary circles of Edinburgh. Later he was appointed an exciseman by the Government, which gave him a regular income. His radical sympathies are expressed in songs like *A Man's a Man for a' That*, and he favoured the French Revolution for a time. No other poet can equal the fun-loving, passionate, bawdy beauty of his poetry and songs, written in his local dialect, from the noisy, superstitious pieces about witches and warlocks (*Tam o' Shanter*) to the patriotic and the sentimental (*Auld Lang Syne*).

BURUNDI

A small republic in Africa near the Congo. It is a little larger (10,700 square miles) than Wales and has a population of a little more than 3 million. It was formerly part of the territory known as Ruanda-Urundi which was governed by Belgium as an INTERNATIONAL TRUST TERRITORY of the UNITED NATIONS. It is an agricultural country, producing chiefly coffee and cattle. The capital is Bujumbura.

BUTLER, Samuel (1835–1902)

British satirist, grandson of Dr. Samuel Butler, headmaster of Shrewsbury. In 1859, he abandoned the idea of going into the Church, went to New Zealand to breed sheep, and wrote a book about his experiences. Returning to England in 1864, he settled down to writing, and during the next thirty-eight years wrote criticisms of DARWIN's theories, travel books, a biography of his grandfather, translations of the Iliad and the Odyssey, and literary criticism. But his greatest work is *Erewhon*, in which he satirised the hypocrisy and stupidity of the society around him—for example, in the imaginary land of Erewhon people are punished for being ill, while those who commit crimes are given sympathy and treatment. *The Way of All Flesh*, an autobiographical novel, is Butler's most widely read work.

BUTTERFLIES AND MOTHS

INSECTS which belong to the order *Lepidoptera*, hence the name lepidopterist for a collector of these insects. It is not always easy to tell the difference between a butterfly and a moth as they are both typical insects. However, two characteristics which are reliable guides are: 1, a butterfly always has a narrow waist while most moths are solid round the middle, and 2, in a butterfly the antennae or feelers are thickest at their tips, like clubs, while in moths they are very varied in shape but always taper to a point. A male moth always has thicker feelers, often beautifully branched like fronds or feathers.

One of the most fascinating things about these insects is their life-cycle or metamorphosis. From the first or egg-stage it changes to a caterpillar, then into a pupa or chrysalis and finally into a beautiful adult insect.

BYE-LAW

A rule which a Borough or County Council, or some other public body, is allowed by Parliament to make. People who break a bye-law can be punished by a fine.

BYE-ELECTION

An election that has to be held unexpectedly because of the death or retirement of an M.P. or Councillor.

BYRD, Richard Evelyn (1888–1957)

American scientist and explorer. He started his career in the American navy, but took up flying, and in 1926 flew over the North Pole. In 1927 he flew the Atlantic from New York to Paris and in the following year led an expedition to the Antarctic in the course of which he flew over the South Pole. He made further expeditions to the Antarctic, in 1933, 1939, and 1946, mainly to collect meteorological and other scientific information necessary for our understanding of the world's weather.

BYRD, William (1543–1623)

English composer of the time of Queen Elizabeth, born probably at Lincoln. A pupil of Thomas Tallis, he became organist of Lincoln Cathedral, and was generally acknowledged to be the greatest composer of his time. His musical compositions include many magnificent anthems for both the Roman Catholic and Church of England services, some fine madrigals and fantasias for viols, and a lot of delightful dances and variations on popular songs for virginals.

BYRON, George Gordon, Lord (1788–1824)

English poet. A lame, handsome Englishman, who, from the time of a first long tour in the Eastern Mediterranean at the age of 21, fell in love with the Mediterranean climate and manners, spent much of his life on its coasts, and was one of the most romantic figures of the early 19th century. While he had a bad reputation with his own countrymen, he won the admiration of readers of poetry on the Continent, especially when he became a champion of liberty; and when he died with the Greek forces who were struggling to liberate their land from Turkey, he became a legend. See Byron's collected poems, particularly *Childe Harold, Manfred* and *Don Juan*.

RED ADMIRAL

LIGHT BLUE

CAMBERWELL BEAUTY

MARBLED WHITE

TRODES CROESUS

STRIPED
HAWKMOTH

CINNABAR

BROAD-BEARDED
BEE HAWK

LARGE FOOTMAN

BUTTERFLIES
AND MOTHS

OLEANDER

GARDEN TIG

Cc

CABINET

A body made up of the chief Government Ministers who are chosen by the PRIME MINISTER. The exact number of Cabinet Ministers varies according to the decision of the Prime Minister, but it is usually about twenty. Some Ministers, such as the CHANCELLOR OF THE EXCHEQUER and the LORD CHANCELLOR are always Cabinet Ministers but in some cases there is no firm rule. The meetings of the Cabinet are held in strict secrecy and no Member is allowed to express disagreement with any policy decision reached by the Cabinet and announced to Parliament. If he wishes to do so he must resign. All Cabinet Ministers are members of the PRIVY COUNCIL and for this reason they are given the title 'Right Honourable'.

The origin of the Cabinet goes back to the days of Charles II. When a Privy Council met, the King would ask a few members to come with him to a little room called a 'cabinet' to discuss some matter and then report back to the Privy Council. When George I, who could speak no English, came to the throne, he asked his Prime Minister, SIR ROBERT WALPOLE, to preside over the Cabinet in his place. Since then it has been the rule for Cabinet meetings to be presided over by the Prime Minister.

CABOT, John (1450–1498)

Italian navigator, born in Genoa. In 1484 he came to England with plans to find a westerly route to the Orient, and in 1496 Henry VII granted him and his three sons letters patent to set sail and discover 'whatsoever isles, countries, regions or provinces . . . which before this time have been unknown to all Christians'. Cabot discovered Newfoundland and Nova Scotia, though he thought that they were part of Asia. His second son, **Sebastian Cabot** (c. 1476–1557) sailed from Seville in 1525 down the coast of Brazil and explored the River Plate. In 1553 he set out from England to find the north-west passage to the East, some of the expedition reached the White Sea, and a visit to Moscow established trade links with England.

CAEDMON

We know very little about Caedmon, except that he was living in Northumbria around A.D. 670, yet we think of him as one of the fathers of English poetry, on account of one of the most beautiful traditions that have come down to us from the ANGLO-SAXON age. It seems that it was a custom in the evenings, when work was done, for men to sit and chant poems. Caedmon used to keep away from these gatherings, since he could not sing. One night an angel came to him in a dream, and told him to sing. 'What shall I sing? I know nothing.' 'Sing the beginning of created things,' was the reply. So he sang the story that is told in Genesis; and the gift of putting into poetry the text of the Old Testament remained with him after that. He was received into the Monastery at Whitby by the Abbess Hild, and there devoted his life to religious duties and his gift of song.

CABOT The navigator who discovered Newfoundland and Nova Scotia thinking them part of Asia.

CAESAR, Gaius Julius (c. 102–44 B.C.)

Greatest of Roman soldiers and statesmen. Born in Rome of an aristocratic family, he devoted his early life to politics and the army. After forming a triumvirate with Pompey and Crassus in 60 B.C., Caesar's campaigns of the next ten years extended the Roman Empire to Germany, France and Britain, which he invaded in 55 B.C. and 54 B.C. Caesar's demand that he be made the consul of Rome now brought him into conflict with Pompey. In the ensuing civil war Pompey's forces were crushed and from 45 B.C. Caesar ruled as sole ruler in Rome (Imperator). Although he planned many administrative and domestic reforms, Republican plotters killed him in 44 B.C. on the grounds that he was aiming at a tyranny. Apart from his military genius, Caesar stands high as orator, writer, jurist and architect.

CALCULUS

A branch of higher mathematics discovered by NEWTON and LEIBNIZ, and includes the differential and integral calculus. The differential calculus is concerned with the rate of change of variable quantities; that is, velocity is the rate of change of position in relation to time. In general terms it is expressed as

$\dfrac{\text{distance}}{\text{time}} = \dfrac{s}{t}$, but in terms of the differential

calculus only infinitesimal increments of the quantities (known as variables in pure mathematics) are considered, and are defined by placing in front the symbol d, thus ds means an increment of distance, dt an increment of

time, and $\dfrac{ds}{dt}$ an increment of velocity. From

the diagram it will be seen that this is equivalent to the slope of the curve.

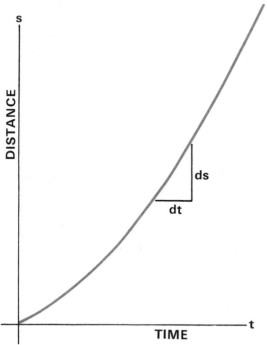

CALCULUS Slope of curve equals velocity

The integral calculus is concerned with determining the laws relating variables when the rate of change, that is, the differential, is known. The operation of integration is expressed by the symbol ∫. A practical introduction to this branch of mathematics is contained in L. Hogben's *Mathematics for the Million* and in several other popular books, among them S. P. Thompson's *Calculus Made Easy*.

CALDERON de la Barca, Pedro
(1600–1681)

Spanish dramatist, born in Madrid. He studied at the University of Salamanca, served with the Spanish Army, was ordained a priest and in 1663 was appointed chaplain to Philip IV of Spain. He wrote more than two hundred plays of many types of which those written after his entry into the Church were all on sacred subjects.

CALENDAR

We take it for granted that if we want to know the date or the day of the week we can tell it by looking at the calendar. Or if we want to know the time, a clock will tell us the hour, minutes and perhaps the seconds. How did these divisions of time come about?

The word 'calendar' comes from the Roman Calends or Kalends which was the first day of the month. Upon the Kalends was based the Roman method for dividing time into hours, days, months, etc.

Primitive man divided the twenty-four hours into darkness and light, and the year was divided into the time for planting or for gathering in the harvest. The times of the new or the full moon were other divisions of time. As people became more civilized they needed more accurate means of measuring divisions of time.

The ancient Egyptians were probably the first to work out a calendar. They had a lunar month; that is, they noticed that there were thirteen new moons in a year so they used thirteen months. Later, however, they divided the year into twelve months of thirty days each. But it was found as years went by that there was something wrong with their calendar for, as astronomers now know, the year really consists of 365 days plus about four hours. So in time the Egyptians improved things by adding an extra day every fourth year—Leap Year. It is thought from ancient Egyptian inscriptions that the calendar was probably introduced about 4241 B.C.

It was the Romans who gave the names of the months which we still use. It was they, too, who decided that the day should begin at midnight. Although the Roman Kalends had been in use for some time before Julius CAESAR began his rule they had become very muddled. So Julius Caesar, with the help of an astronomer, began to reform the calendar. One change was that the year should begin on January 1st instead of in March. To commemorate his work the seventh month was named after him, July. One mistake was made in the Julian calendar and that was that Leap Year occurred every third instead of every fourth year. This

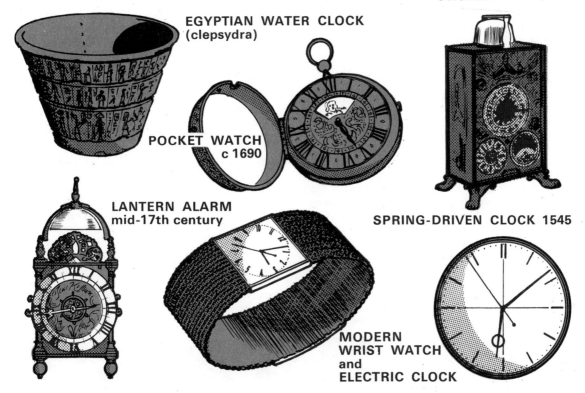

EGYPTIAN WATER CLOCK
(clepsydra)

POCKET WATCH
c 1690

LANTERN ALARM
mid-17th century

SPRING-DRIVEN CLOCK 1545

MODERN
WRIST WATCH
and
ELECTRIC CLOCK

was corrected by Augustus Caesar in the year 8 B.C. and he named the eighth month after himself.

Although the calendar was by now very similar to the one we still use it was about eleven minutes too long. In the course of centuries these minutes became days; so in 1577 Pope Gregory XIII appointed two astronomers to help him reform the calendar. The result of this reform was that ten days had to be dropped in the year it was introduced. One country after another adopted the Gregorian calendar, Britain not adopting it till 1752 when ten days were dropped in September of that year. Russia did not adopt the Gregorian calendar until the Bolshevik Revolution in 1917. The Orthodox Church still keeps Christmas and Easter according to the old Julian calendar. The custom of dividing the years into those before Christ and after Christ was first adopted in the year 540.

The names of the days of the week which we still use were given by the Anglo-Saxons, though some are similar to Roman ones. Except for the two first they were named after pagan gods. The Saxon names were Sun's Day, Moon's Day, Tiw's Day, Woden's Day, Thor's Day, Frigg's Day and Saterne's Day.

Unlike the other divisions of time the grouping of days into weeks has nothing to do with astronomy. It was the Jews and their neighbours who first grouped days together to form a week.

The dividing of time into hours, minutes and seconds is told today by clocks. The first method of telling the time was done by means of sun-dials. The earliest forms of shadow clocks of which we know were those used in ancient Egypt. There is a reference to a sundial in Isaiah xxxviii, 8. The ancient Egyptians also used a kind of water clock. This measured time by the quantity of water discharged through a small opening in a vessel and known as a 'clepsydra'.

It is not known for certain who invented the first mechanical clock but it is thought that it was a Benedictine monk named Gerbert who afterwards became Pope Silvester II. He made a clock for Magdeburg in 996 which had a weight for motive power. The oldest existing clock in England is one in Salisbury Cathedral which was made in 1386 but it is known that the Cathedrals of Westminster, Canterbury and St. Paul's all had clocks by the 13th century. The first pocket timepiece or watch was probably made at Nuremburg at the beginning of the 16th century. The invention of the watch was made possible by the substitution of a mainspring for suspended weights. The first watches had only an hour hand, the minute hand being added towards the end of the 17th century.

CALVIN, John (1509–1564)
Swiss religious reformer. The early part of his life was spent in France, during which time he led the life of a scholar rather than an evangelist or preacher. He was greatly influenced by Martin LUTHER, and one of the most controversial points in his teaching was the simplicity and austerity which he urged people to follow in both everyday life and church ritual.

CAMEROON
A federal republic on the West coast of Africa. It comprises nearly 184,000 square miles, more than twice the size of France, and has a population of about five million. Its capital is Yaounda and its biggest town is Douala. Before the First World War most of the territory was ruled by France on behalf of the LEAGUE OF NATIONS. After the Second World War it came under the UNITED NATIONS as an International Trust Territory. In 1960 the territory became an independent country. A small part of the Cameroons was ruled by Great Britain on behalf of the United Nations

Indo-China (now CAMBODIA, LAOS and VIET-NAM) had fought a bitter war against the French. Nearly all the people are farmers.

CAMELS
There are two species, the 'Bactrian' camel (*Camelus bactrianus*) of Central Asia and the 'Arabian' camel (*Camelus dromedarius*) of the Arabian deserts. The Bactrian camel is a sturdy animal and has longer hair to withstand the cold of the Asian deserts. It has two humps. The Arabian camel has only one hump and is a slimmer and swifter animal. Camels feed on coarse desert vegetation. Living in regions where food is scarce they have developed humps of a fatty substance to draw on for sustenance. Camels are close relatives of the LLAMAS.

CAMPBELL, Sir Malcolm (1885–1949)
British racing motorist. Set up a series of world records which established a leading place for Britain in the world of automobile engineering. In 1924 he reached a speed of 146·157 m.p.h.,

CAMPBELL, Sir Malcolm in *Bluebird*. In 1935 he raised the world speed record to 301.129 m.p.h.

and when French Cameroons became independent this small territory decided to join with the larger one. The country produces cocoa, cotton, timber and aluminium for exporting abroad.

CAMBODIA
A kingdom in south-east Asia and is part of what used to be French Indo-China. It is nearly 66,000 square miles, rather more than twice the size of Scotland, with a population of about six million. The people are mixed, some being like those of MALAYSIA and others who came originally from India. They are nearly all Buddhists. The country became independent in 1954 after the countries of

and, in 1935, 301·129 m.p.h. in *Bluebird*, making a new land speed record nine times during this period. In 1939 he also set up a speed-boat record of 141·74 m.p.h. In 1931 he was knighted for his achievements. His son, **Donald Campbell** (1921–1967) broke the world water speed record on Ullswater in 1955, and, in 1964, he put the official water speed record up to 276·33 m.p.h. in *Bluebird* on Lake Dumbleyung, Western Australia.

CAMUS, Albert (1913–1959)
French writer. His father was a farm-labourer in Algeria, and repeated illness interfered with Camus's education and early career. He joined

the French resistance movement during the Second World War, and later edited the left-wing newspaper *Combat* with SARTRE. His novel *L'Etranger* is nihilistic, that is, set in a world in which nothing seems to have any sense or meaning. This was followed by further novels, including *La Peste* and *La Chute*, and some plays.

CANADA

The largest (3,560,238 square miles) and oldest British DOMINION. It lies north of the United States from which it is separated for a considerable distance by five great lakes, one of them, Lake Superior, being the largest fresh-water lake in the world. The country is a little larger than the United States. There are about 19 million inhabitants most of whom speak English except those in the province of Quebec who speak French. The country has a federal system of government and is divided into ten provinces, each of which has its own parliament or legislative assembly. The federal parliament which makes laws for the country as a whole is at Ottawa. The Parliament consists of a Senate and a House of Commons. The ten provinces are: Ontario; Quebec; Nova Scotia; New Brunswick; British Columbia; Prince Edward Island; Manitoba; Alberta; Saskatchewan and Newfoundland. Newfoundland with Labrador, only joined Canada in 1949. In the north of Canada are two vast almost uninhabited territories, the Yukon and the North-West Territories. Canada's largest cities are Montreal in Quebec and Toronto in Ontario. Other important cities are Edmonton (Alberta), Winnipeg (Manitoba), Hamilton (Ontario) and the port of Halifax (Nova Scotia).

Canada is the world's leading supplier of timber and she is one of the chief wheat growing countries in the world. She has many minerals and has more nickel, aluminium, asbestos and platinum than any other country.

Canada's two most famous rivers are the Mackenzie and the St. Lawrence. After the Second World War, in co-operation with the United States, Canada decided to make of the St. Lawrence River a Seaway which has turned the city of Montreal into a seaport.

Canada was discovered by the Italian explorer John CABOT, in 1497 and during the following century the French established settlements in Quebec. In 1613 the British attacked the French at Port Royal and this was the beginning of constant fighting between British and French for control of Canada. The first British colony in Canada was Nova Scotia, but it was not until the last battle with the French in 1759 that the British, under General WOLFE, obtained final control of all Canada.

CANADA Logs in the form of a circular boom floating down a river. Over 12½ million logs are transported in this way every year.

Between 1812 and 1814 there was fighting between the United States and the British in Canada, but this ended in agreement between the two countries to keep the frontier unarmed —the only unarmed frontier in the world. In 1867 an Act was passed by the British Parliament which set up a federal government for all the Canadian colonies as the Dominion of Canada.

CANALETTO, Antonio (1697–1768)

Italian painter, born in Venice. Followed his father as a scene-painter. His earliest works are dated from 1720 and are views of Venice— the subject with which he will always be connected. Canaletto worked for some time in England, and the finest collection of his work is the Royal Collection. He was the first to use the camera obscura—a mechanical/optical device used for making accurate drawings, especially topographical subjects.

CANARY ISLANDS

Better known as the Canaries, they are a group of islands in the North Atlantic Ocean that belong to Spain. The largest is Teneriffe, capital Santa Cruz, and the next largest Gran Canaria, capital Las Palmas. The islands export tropical fruits and tomatoes. Their combined land area is 2,807 square miles and population about 900,000.

CAPYBARA

The largest rodent on earth and native of South America—fully-grown it can measure over 48 inches long and 20 inches at the shoulder. Capybaras are social animals, moving and feeding in troops. Their main foods are grass and water plants. They live on river banks and are expert swimmers. For all their size they are timid creatures, scurrying for cover at the slightest disturbance.

CARACAL

A lynx-like animal of the cat family. It is found in wide areas of Asia and Africa. It has short, tawny brown fur and tufted blackish ears. The caracal preys on small creatures, like hares, peacocks, cranes and the like. In India the caracal is trained to hunt in the same way as the cheetah.

CARACTACUS (*c.* A.D. 50)

British chieftain who fought defensive battles against the Roman invasion at Wallingford, Colchester and Shropshire. He was finally captured and, with his family, taken to Rome, where their lives were spared by the Emperor Claudius. It is thought that Caractacus died in Rome about A.D. 54.

CAPYBARA Largest member of the rodent family.

CARAVAGGIO, Michel Angelo Merisi (1569–1609)

Italian painter. After studying in Milan and Venice, he founded the naturalistic school in Rome, and his models were distinguished by their individual character. His most famous paintings were *The Card Players* and *Gypsy Fortune Teller*. His *Christ and the Disciples at Emmaus* is in the National Gallery, London.

CARIBOU [*See* REINDEER]

CARLYLE, Thomas (1795–1851)

British historian and author. Born at Ecclefechan, Dumfries-shire where his father was a mason. After studying at Edinburgh University (1809–1813) and working as a schoolmaster (1816–1818), he became a journalist, author and historian. From 1834 he lived in London, where he died. Although it was some time before he became known he was eventually recognized as one of the greatest writers of the 19th century. His best known works are *History of the French Revolution* (1837), *Cromwell's Letters and Speeches* (1845), and *History of Frederick the Great of Prussia* (1858–1865).

CARNEGIE, Andrew (1835–1919)

American industrialist and philanthropist. Born of humble parents in Dunfermline, he emigrated to America with his family in 1848. After various poorly paid jobs he joined the Pennsylvania Railroad as a telegraph operator. He rose rapidly, laying the foundation of his later fortune by introducing sleeping cars on the railway and by his investments in oil-fields. He established various iron and steel industries in Pittsburgh and elsewhere, amassing an immense fortune. On retiring in 1901 he founded many philanthropic funds for such purposes as the Scottish Universities, public libraries and the like as well as the Carnegie Endowment for International Peace.

CARNOT, N. Sadi (1796–1832)

French physicist, born in Paris. Published his *Reflections* (1824), in which he dealt with the relationship of heat and energy, especially so far as heat engines are concerned. He formulated a law for the operation of an ideal engine; the law is known as 'Carnot's Cycle'.

CARP

Originally native to the Caspian and Black Seas, this fish is now widely distributed. It has large scales, a long dorsal fin and barbels on the upper jaw. Normally it is about 12–14 inches long, but some forms have been developed which weigh some 55 pounds and over 3 feet in length; an example of this is the 'golden' carp of Japan.

CARROLL, Lewis (1832–1898)

Pen-name of Charles L. Dodgson and now justly famous wherever children's books and humorous poetry are loved. It is said that from the room where he studied (his subject was mathematics) in the college library at Christ Church, Oxford, he used to see the Dean's small daughter playing on the lawn below, and that this first gave him the idea of *Alice's Adventures in Wonderland*. This was followed six years later by *Alice through the Looking Glass*. His stories twist and turn like the incidents of a dream, and interspersing them are gay and delightful verses. *The Hunting of the Snark* is a longer nonsense poem, equally delightful. He was also an excellent photographer.

CARTWRIGHT, Edmund (1743–1823)

English cleric and inventor, born at Marnham. Arising from a visit (1784) to a cotton-spinning mill at Cromford, Cartwright turned his mind to the possibility of a mechanical weaving machine. This he completed in 1787 and set up his own factory at Doncaster, but it was properly tried out by a Manchester mill in 1791. Cartwright also invented a wool-carding machine and improvements in methods of rope making.

CATHEDRAL [*See* next page]

CATHODE-RAY TUBE

This electronic apparatus consists essentially of an electron gun which causes a thin beam of electrons to strike a fluorescent screen at the flattened end of the tube and so cause a spot of light. The intensity of the spot is controlled by a control grid. In the electrostatic type of C.R.T. two pairs of deflector plates are placed in the line of the beam and by applying suitable voltages to these the electron beam can be deflected as required. The magnetic type of C.R.T. has an external system of coils which develop magnetic fields and by applying electric currents to the deflection coils the electron beam's position and hence the spot of light on the screen can be changed. In TELEVISION the changing light signals are applied to the control grid so that the spot of light varies in intensity, while deflection circuits are provided at the receiver to cause the spot of light to trace a pattern of light on the screen and so build up the required pictures.

CATS

These felines are distributed all over the great continents of the world from north to south, but do not extend beyond Borneo and are absent from Madagascar and Australia. Their habits are very similar wherever they are found. For preference they kill their own prey,

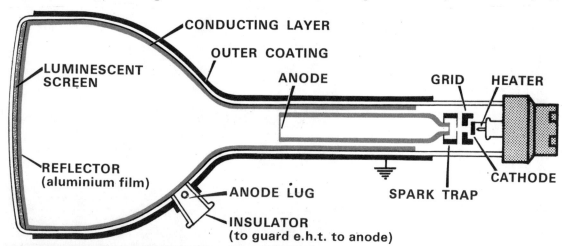

CATHODE-RAY TUBE Simplified diagram showing the construction of this electronic apparatus.

CATHEDRALS

**WEST FRONT OF
SALISBURY CATHEDRAL**
▼

▲ **FLYING BUTTRESSES AT
SALISBURY CATHEDRAL**

▶
**CAPITAL
DECORATED
WITH LEAVES
IN WELLS
CATHEDRAL**

**TOWER OF
GLOUCESTER CATHEDRAL**
▼

▼**NOTRE DAME
ON THE SEINE, PARIS**

which consists mainly of any mammals or birds they can catch, but many eat frogs, fish, insects and even carrion at times. Usually they catch their prey by stalking or by lying in wait for the animal until it moves within springing distance. Owing to their short jaws, they can never secure their prey with a quick snap, but strike it down or grab it with the paws before seizing it with the mouth—watch your cat catch a mouse. There are a great many species, but apart from the house cat, the best known are the LION, TIGER, PANTHER, LEOPARD, JAGUAR, PUMA and cheetah.

CATULLUS, Gaius Valerius (*c*. 84–54 B.C.)
Great Roman lyric poet, born at Verona. He is known for his bitter attacks on many of his contemporaries, including Julius CAESAR; and for the beautiful lyric poetry inspired by his mistress Lesbia. His writing was heavily influenced by Greek and, especially, Alexandrian poetry.

CAVELL, Edith Louisa (1865–1915)
Born in Norfolk, took up nursing, and at the outbreak of the 1914–1918 war was matron of a hospital at Brussels. She sheltered and helped a number of British, French and Belgian prisoners to escape, for which she was eventually imprisoned and finally shot. She is most widely known for her remark '*Patriotism is not enough.*'

CAVENDISH, Henry (1731–1810)
British chemist and physicist, born at Nice. In 1766 Cavendish published three important papers on the properties of gases. In one he included an account of the production of hydrogen by the action of mineral acids on metals. He was the first to identify hydrogen

as a distinct gas and described its properties. Around 1771 he carried out work on electrical forces. He devised ways of measuring the capacity of conductors and condensers, and compared the electrical conductivity of different metals. Henry Cavendish discovered the composition of water by exploding a mixture of oxygen and hydrogen. He did not publish these results until 1784.

CAVY
The name given to the wild kind of guinea-pig found in the forested regions of South America. The best known is the 'Patagonian' cavy. It is very much like a hare and the larger species grow to some 36 inches in length. Cavies live in burrows and are extremely timid.

CAXTON, William (1422–1491)
First English printer, born in Kent. He was apprenticed to a rich silk mercer in 1438 and finished his term of service in Bruges. He then engaged in commercial negotiations for Edward IV with the Dukes of Burgundy and from 1471–1476 acted as a commercial adviser. It was probably at Cologne about this time that he learnt the art of printing and where he printed his first book, a translation of a French romance. In 1476 he set up his own printing works at Westminster where he printed some eighty books. The *Dictes or Sayengis of the Philosophres* was printed in England in 1477. He also printed Chaucer's *Canterbury Tales* and Malory's *Morte d'Arthur*.

CELTS
Celtic tribes, that came originally from central Europe, invaded Britain in two waves—the Goidels in the late Bronze Age, and the Brythons and Belgae in the Iron Age. The Celts

CELTS An artist's impression of a Celtic settlement of the Iron Age period.

CÉZANNE A view of Mont St. Victoire, near Aix, Provence. This mountain was a favourite subject of Cézanne.

must have come in considerable numbers, for by the time of the Roman invasion almost all the inhabitants of Britain and Ireland had the Celtic language and culture. The DRUIDS were their religious leaders, and the Celts produced fine bronze-work. After the Romans had left, the Britons in the south called on Saxons from the Continent to help protect them against the ravages of the Picts and Scots, but the Saxons later turned against the Britons and drove them into the highlands in the west.

Some of the Celtic culture was preserved in these parts of the country, notably in their languages—Irish, Gaelic, Welsh, Cornish and Manx. The first three are still spoken quite extensively today.

CERVANTES An engraving of an incident from Cervantes' novel *Don Quixote de la Mancha*.

CENSUS
The counting of the people of a country. The first census in Great Britain was taken in 1800. Since then a census has usually been taken every ten years, but the census of 1951 was the first in twenty years.

CENTRAL AFRICAN REPUBLIC
An independent state in Africa just north of the Equator. It was formerly a French colony and was then known as 'Ubanghi Shari'. It is a little larger (234,000 square miles) than France but has only one and a quarter million inhabitants. The capital is Bangui, near the border with the CONGOLESE REPUBLIC. The country is a member of the FRENCH COMMUNITY.

CERVANTES Saavedra, Miguel de
(1547–1616)
Spanish writer. Born at Acalá de Henares. He led a very adventurous life as a soldier and lost the use of his left hand at the battle of Lepanto. Although Cervantes wrote a number of works, his fame rests on his novel *Don Quixote de la Mancha*.

CEYLON
A Dominion within the BRITISH COMMONWEALTH. It is an island, at the southern tip of India and is about half the size (25,330 square miles) of England with over 10 million inhabitants. Its capital is the important town of Colombo. The people of Ceylon are of different origins, the most numerous being the Singhalese, who are Buddhists, and the Tamils, who came originally from India and are mostly Hindus. In recent years there has been trouble between the two groups. Ceylon was the first

country in the world to have a woman as Prime Minister—Mrs. Bandaranaika. The country is famous for its production of tea. It also has precious stones.

CÉZANNE, Paul (1839–1906)
French painter. Born at Aix-en-Provence. After studying with PISSARO, he exhibited at the Impressionist show in 1874, but developed his own original style, blending impressionism and classicism. He produced many pictures of landscapes and flowers, along with some fine portraits. His oils and water colours alike were distinguished by vivid colouring. He exerted a great influence on modern artists. His *Le Jardinier* is in the Tate Gallery, London.

CHAGALL, Marc (1887———)
Russian painter, born in Vitebsk, Russia. Trained in Leningrad (then St. Petersburg) and went to Paris in 1910. Returned to Russia in 1917 where he headed an academy but returned to Paris in 1923 where he has since remained except for a short period in the U.S.A. His subjects are the fantasy world of Russian/Jewish folklore and his colours rich and luminous. One of his most outstanding works are the paintings for the ceiling of the Paris Opera House.

CHAMBER MUSIC
Music written for performance in a chamber, or large room, by a small combination of instruments, as opposed to that written for performance in a big concert hall by a full orchestra. The most common forms of chamber music are: the sonata for piano with one other instrument; the piano trio (piano, violin, cello); the string quartet (two violins, viola, cello); and the quintet (string quartet with an extra instrument). Combinations of six, seven, eight or nine instruments are called sextets, septets, octets and nonets respectively; larger combinations are described as 'ensembles'.

CHAMBERLAIN, Sir (Joseph) Austen (1863–1937)
British politician. Born in Birmingham, the son of Joseph Chamberlain. He held the posts of Chancellor of the Exchequer (1903) and Secretary for India (1915). But he is best known for his initiation, when Foreign Secretary, of the Locarno pact (1925) which attempted to reconcile France and Germany.

CHAMBERLAIN, Joseph (1836–1914)
English politician. Born in London in 1836, he worked as a screw manufacturer in Birmingham where he soon made a large fortune, retiring from business in 1874. Already well

CHAMBERLAIN, Neville. Returning to Britain after his meeting with Hitler in 1938 and waving the non-aggression pact which he had signed.

known in Birmingham public life as mayor, he entered Parliament in 1876 for the Liberals and held various offices under GLADSTONE. He won his reputation as Secretary of State for the Colonies (1895–1903).

CHAMBERLAIN, Neville (1869–1940)
British politician. The son of Joseph Chamberlain. He was active in Birmingham business circles and municipal politics, becoming Lord Mayor in 1915. Returned to Parliament for the Conservatives in 1918 he was successively Chancellor of the Exchequer (1923), and Minister of Health (1924). He became Prime Minister in 1937. In 1938 his appeasement policy towards Germany and Italy was much criticized. After the unsuccessful British campaign against the German invasion of Norway in 1940, Chamberlain resigned. He died the same year.

CHAMPOLLION, Jean Francis (1790–1832)
French scholar who, by studying the ROSETTA STONE, first deciphered ancient Egyptian hieroglyphic writing. His findings were published in 1824.

CHAD
A republic in North Central Africa that is more than twice the size (487,920 square miles) of France and has a population of a little more than two and a half million. It was formerly

CHAMELEON A ponderously slow reptile with a swift and deadly accurate tongue.

a French colony and is now a Member of the FRENCH COMMUNITY. The capital is Fort Lamy, south of Lake Chad.

CHAMELEON

This creature is a REPTILE and belongs to the lizard family. There are over 80 known species most of which are in Africa and Madagascar. The main characteristics of this ponderously slow reptile are its split toes specially adapted for grasping, its swivel eyes and its extremely long and deadly accurate tongue for catching insects. Much is said about its ability to change colour; in fact, it is not all that significant, the range being from green to yellow to greyish. The average species is under 6 inches long, but there are a few of up to 24 inches, including the tail.

CHAMOIS

This small fleet-footed mammal has features which are common to both goats and antelopes. It is native to alpine regions, especially Austria and Switzerland. Its most recognisable features are its short hooked horns. An adult measures about 30–36 inches at the shoulder. The 'shammy', a soft leather for cleaning, was originally made from chamois skin.

CHANCELLOR OF THE EXCHEQUER

The CABINET Minister who looks after the nation's money. It is the oldest office in the Government and goes back to the days of Henry I. In those days the Chancellor sat at a table covered by a chequered cloth to receive the taxes which were at that time collected by the sheriffs. The Chancellor is regarded as the most important Minister after the PRIME MINISTER and is the Second Lord of the Treasury, the Prime Minister being the First. It is the Chancellor of the Exchequer who presents the BUDGET to PARLIAMENT.

CHANCERY

One of the three Divisions of the High Court of Justice. The LORD CHANCELLOR is its head though he does not himself act as one of the judges. One of the chief duties of the Chancery Division is to act as guardian to children and young people who have inherited property. Such young people are called 'Wards in Chancery'.

CHANNEL ISLANDS

A group off the north-west coast of France that have belonged to Britain since the Norman Conquest. There are nine islands, of which the most important are Jersey, Guernsey, Alderney and Sark. Jersey and Guernsey are famous for their breeds of cattle. The islands also grow tomatoes, potatoes and flowers for export. There are about 100,000 inhabitants and the islands govern themselves. The Channel Islands total 75 square miles.

CHARDIN, Jean Baptiste Siméon
(1699–1779)
French painter. Regarded as one of the greatest French colourists, Chardin produced honest and well-observed still lifes and domestic interiors—usually small in size. He was for a time the teacher of FRAGONARD.

CHARLES I Condemned and executed in Jan. 1649.

CHARLEMAGNE (Charles the Great) (742–814)

Eldest son of Pepin III of France, and himself later King and Emperor. He extended his empire into Italy, and fought many wars there, in Dalmatia, Germany and Spain. His campaigns against the Moors in North Spain are chronicled in the *Chanson de Roland* and many legends grew up round the adventures of Charlemagne, who in addition to his warlike pursuits, was also a scholar. In spite of the almost perpetual wars and battles in which France was involved, the reign of Charlemagne is noted for an advance in the arts, craftsmanship, and scholarship.

CHARLES I, King of Great Britain and Ireland (1600–1649)

Son of James I, married the French Catholic Princess Henrietta Maria. He was made King in 1625, became the tool of Buckingham until the latter was murdered (1629), and then fell under the influence of his wife. For eleven

CHARTISM A print of a Chartist demonstration.

years he ruled without Parliament, with Laud and the Earl of Strafford as his advisers, and using the Courts of Star Chamber and High Commission. Forced loans and ship money alienated the English, while the Scots were angered by Laud's attempt to impose episcopacy on the Church of Scotland. Charles summoned a Parliament—'the Short Parliament'—but it refused to grant him money to fight the Scots, and John Pym demanded that he redress Parliament's grievances. The 'Long Parliament' impeached Laud and Strafford and demanded that the King appoint better advisers. In reply, Charles took the fatal step of trying to imprison five members of the House of Commons. In 1642 he declared war on the Parliamentarians from Nottingham. After four years of Civil War his army was destroyed at Naseby (1645). Taken to London in 1648 he was tried as a 'tyrant, traitor and murderer', and, though he refused to plead, condemned to death and executed in Whitehall, January 30th, 1649.

CHARTISM

A movement of working-class people in the middle of the 19th century. They signed a Charter demanding equal electoral areas, universal suffrage, payment of M.P.s, no property qualifications for M.P.s, secret ballot and annual parliament. Chartism was the product in the 1830s and 1840s of the depression among the artisans, like the handloom weavers, whose jobs could now be more cheaply done by machines, and the Chartists believed that the reforms they demanded would enable them to influence a government which they rightly thought was prejudiced in favour of the employers. But the depressed trades gradually died out, many people channelled their enthusiasm towards the Anti-Corn Law League instead, and Chartism passed away. Nevertheless, the modern Labour Movement grew out of the Chartist agitation.

CHATEAUBRIAND, François René, Vicomte de (1768–1848)

Politician and pioneer of the French Romantic Movement. In *Le Génie du Christianism* he described the appeal of the Christian religion, and said that of all religions it was 'the most poetical, the most favourable to freedom, art, and letters.' His *Mémoirs d'Outre-tombe* is an autobiographical work. In politics he favoured the Bourbons, and was made ambassador to Great Britain (1822) and Minister of Foreign Affairs (1823–1824).

CHATTERTON, Thomas (1752–1770)

English poet. He began to write documents, which he claimed were medieval, and which quite took people in, beginning with a description of the mayor of Bristol opening Bristol bridge in 1248. Later he made up *The Rise of Painting in England, written by T. Rowley in 1469, for Master Canynge,* and some poems by the same imaginary author, which temporarily deceived Horace Walpole, and began a controversy that lasted 80 years. These creations show Chatterton to have been a poet of real genius. In 1770 he moved to London and wrote satires, essays and stories, and had his play *The Revenge* put on stage. But in August, when he was penniless and starving, he poisoned himself with arsenic.

CHAUCER, Geoffrey (*c.* 1345–1400)

The greatest English poet of the 14th century, and today regarded as one of the greatest of all time. Coming from East Anglia, he found noble patrons and became attached to the Court, which he served as a courier to France and Italy. Up to the age of forty he frequently travelled on royal business. After that, posts were found for him in London, where he was able to write his poetry, which was welcomed by the king and court. His masterpiece is *The Canterbury Tales*—a series of stories told by pilgrims who are journeying together from London to the shrine at Canterbury. The series was never completed.

CHEETAH

Member of the CAT family and ranges over most of Africa, Iran and Central India. It is the swiftest animal on earth over short distances and often mistaken for a LEOPARD.

CHEKHOV, Anton Pavlovich (1860–1904)

Russian writer. Born at Taganrog in South Russia, he was the son of a liberated serf. He entered Moscow University as a medical student. He practised only a short time and soon turned to writing. One of his most charming stories is *The Lady with the Dog*, and his plays include *The Seagull, Uncle Vanya, The Three Sisters,* and *The Cherry Orchard.*

CHEMISTRY

That branch of science concerned with discovering the elements of which substances are composed and how these elements are combined to form chemical compounds. All pure substances—solid, liquid, or gas—in the universe are either elements or chemical compounds made by the combination of two or more elements. For example, chalk is a compound of the element calcium, the element carbon, and the element oxygen. Impure substances may consist of mixtures of elements, of elements and compounds, or of compounds. The process of finding out the elements of which a compound is composed is called chemical analysis. The process of combining elements together to make compounds is called synthesis.

Ninety-six elements have so far been discovered, ranging from hydrogen, the lightest, to curium, the heaviest. The smallest unit of an element is an atom. The weight of an atom of one element in relation to that of an atom of oxygen, taken as 16, is called the atomic weight. On this basis the atomic weight of hydrogen is 1·008 and that of curium 242. Furthermore, the elements may be arranged in a list of increasing weight, starting from hydro-

CHEMISTRY A laboratory-scale cell for producing fluorine, a valuable chemical element.

gen, the position in the list being the atomic number. Thus hydrogen has atomic number 1, helium 2, lithium 3, and so on up to curium, atomic number 96. This list can be arranged into groups in what is called the periodic table. Members of one group have similar properties. Thus Group VII has fluorine, chlorine, bromine, and iodine, all of which have a number of chemical properties in common. In this way a classification of elements is possible and systematization is brought into what was once merely a collection of facts about the preparation of chemicals and their properties.

As a simplification of chemical language each element is given a symbol, e.g. chlorine is Cl, hydrogen H, oxygen O, etc. With these symbols a compound can be represented by a formula. Calcium carbonate is thus $CaCO_3$, meaning that one atom of calcium, one of carbon, and three of oxygen combine to make one molecule of calcium carbonate. Any division of a molecule leads to different substances. If chalk is heated, for instance, it loses carbon dioxide (CO_2) and is left as lime (CaO). This reaction can be put in the form of an equation:

$$CaCO_3 = CaO + CO_2$$

Such an equation is a statement of a known reaction; it is not a mathematical device for prophesying what reaction will take place.

In general substances can be divided into salts, acids, and bases. An acid contains hydrogen and is such that the hydrogen can be replaced by a metal. When this happens, the result is a salt. Zinc and sulphuric acid produce hydrogen and a salt, zinc sulphate:

$$Zn + H_2SO_4 = H_2 + ZnSO_4.$$

A base, or alkali, is most simply defined as a substance that combines with an acid to form a salt or salts without the release of hydrogen. Sometimes a group of atoms act together as if they were a single element. The group SO_4, for instance, does this in sulphuric acid. Such a group is called a radical.

The whole of chemistry consists of the description of substances and how they are made, the search for laws governing chemical reactions, and the understanding of chemical combination.

CHESS

Reputed to have been invented in India some 1,500 years ago, and to have been introduced into Europe by Arab invaders of Spain in the 8th century. It was popular at the time of the Crusades. Canute and William the Conqueror are said to have played it. The game is played on a board of 64 squares. It is a very intricate game and has been likened to fighting a battle,

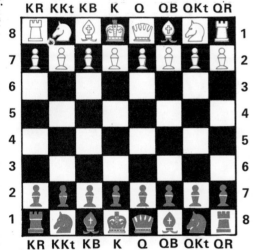

CHESS Layout of the chessmen at the start.

with a king at the head of an army consisting of his queen, various officers and a number of men, in fact the main aim of play is to force the opposing player's king into such a position that it cannot avoid being captured. This position is termed 'checkmate'. As can be seen from the diagram the chessmen are arranged like two opposing armies. Note that the board is so placed that each player has a black square to his left in the row nearest him. The various pieces are: in the two squares of the middle of the back row are the King and Queen; the Queen is the piece standing on its own colour (white Queen on white square). Next to these

are two Bishops, one on each side. Next to the Bishops are the Knights, and in the corners are two Castles, more commonly called Rooks. The front row is simply filled with ordinary soldiers called Pawns. Because of the complexity of the game the young reader should seek further guidance from an experienced player. A useful introduction is Joan Moloney's *Make and Play Chess*.

CHESTERTON, Gilbert Keith (1874–1936)

English journalist and writer. He attacked the materialism and pettiness of the Victorians, though in his literary studies, which included *Browning*, *Dickens* and *The Victorian Age in Literature*, he appreciated the talents of the great Victorians. He wrote both serious and comic verse. Everyone has read *The Donkey*, for example. His most popular stories were the detective novels about 'Father Brown'.

CHEVROTAINS

Dainty little creatures without horns and about the size of hares. They inhabit the forests of tropical Asia and Africa. Being timid and defenceless, they lie up by day in sheltered places, only venturing out at dusk to feed on vegetable plants. They are sometimes called 'mouse deers'.

CHIANG KAI-SHEK (1886——)

Chinese political and military leader. Served with SUN YAT-SEN during the 1911 revolution and later became leader of the nationalist government. He opposed the communists and had to flee to Formosa (Taiwan) in 1950 where he organized opposition to MAO TSE TUNG.

CHILE

A republic in South America which lies between the Andes Mountains (which separate it from Argentina) and the shores of the south Pacific. It is the narrowest country in the world, stretching from north to south for 2,800 miles but at no point is it wider than the county of Sussex. Its estimated area is 290,000 square miles. It has a population of about seven and a half million. The capital is Santiago and the chief port Valparaiso. Chile is an important copper producing country and she also has much coal. She owns Easter Island on which are ancient mysterious stone figures.

CHILTERN HUNDREDS

The districts of Stoke, Burnham and Desborough in Buckinghamshire. In olden times the King appointed a Steward to prevent bands of robbers over-running the forests of the Chiltern Hills. The office of Steward still

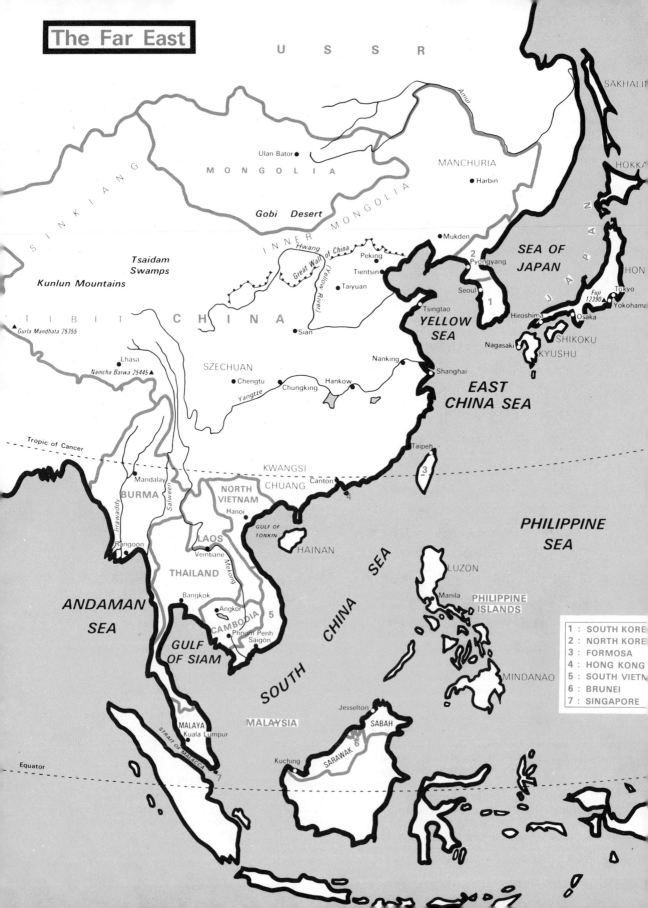

The Far East

U S S R

SAKHALIN

MONGOLIA

Ulan Bator •

MANCHURIA

• Harbin

Gobi Desert

HOKKA

INNER MONGOLIA

S I N K I A N G

Tsaidam
Swamps

Kunlun Mountains

Hwang

Great Wall of China

• Mukden

2

Peking

Pyongyang

Tientsin

Seoul

SEA OF
JAPAN

HON

T I B E T

C H I N A

Tsingtao

1

Fuji
12390 ▲ Tokyo

Taiyuan

Yokohama

Hiroshima

Osaka

▲ Gurla Mandhata 25355

• Sian

YELLOW
SEA

Nagasaki

SHIKOKU

KYUSHU

Lhasa

Namcha Barwa 25445 ▲

SZECHUAN

Nanking

Hwang (Yellow River)

• Chengtu

Hankow

Shanghai

• Chungking

Yangtze

EAST
CHINA SEA

Tropic of Cancer

KWANGSI

Taipeh

3

Mandalay

CHUANG

Canton

4

BURMA

NORTH
VIETNAM

PHILIPPINE
SEA

Irrawaddy

Salween

Hanoi

LAOS

GULF OF
TONKIN

HAINAN

Rangoon

Veintiane

Mekong

THAILAND

LUZON

ANDAMAN
SEA

Bangkok

Angkor

CAMBODIA

5

Phnom Penh

Saigon

SOUTH

Manila

PHILIPPINE
ISLANDS

GULF
OF SIAM

CHINA

SEA

1 : SOUTH KORE

2 : NORTH KORE

3 : FORMOSA

4 : HONG KONG

5 : SOUTH VIETN

6 : BRUNEI

7 : SINGAPORE

MINDANAO

MALAYA

Kuala Lumpur

MALAYSIA

Jesselton

SABAH

STRAIT OF MALACCA

SARAWAK

6

Kuching

Equator

7

nominally exists although there is no work for him to do. So when a M.P. wants to cease to be a Member he asks to be made a Steward of the Chiltern Hundreds. This is because a M.P. cannot resign from Parliament but if the Queen appoints him Steward he cannot also be a M.P. As soon as the M.P. is made Steward he at once resigns and so the office is vacant for any other M.P. who may wish to apply for it.

CHIMPANZEE

One of the most man-like of the apes. It lives in the forests of West and Central Africa. Chimpanzees are more arboreal than the gorillas, better climbers, and much more active both in trees and on the ground. When climbing they never leap from branch to branch, but either move along using hands and feet, or swing arm over arm, never letting go with one hand until the other has made a firm grip. When they descend quickly, they drop from bough to bough, checking their fall with their hands as they come down. A fully-grown male measures about 60 inches erect and weighs around 400–500 pounds—its armspread being about 90 inches. There are three forms, the smallest being the 'pygmy' chimpanzee.

CHINA

One of the largest countries in the world (4,300,000 square miles) having a bigger population than any other country. It is believed to be about 700 million. The country is considerably bigger than the United States and is divided into 26 Provinces. These include

CHIMPANZEE A native of West and Central Africa.

CHINA The Great Wall of China which was built about 200 B.C. and is some 1,200 miles long.

Inner Mongolia, Manchuria and Tibet. The capital is Peking which has a population of more than 4 million. Shanghai, the chief port, is even bigger with over 6 million. The most important rivers are the Yangtse, the Yellow and the Canton at the mouth of which is the city of that name. China is rich in minerals, though most of them are not yet fully used. They include coal, copper, lead and zinc but most of the people are farmers.

China has the oldest civilization in the world and her people have invented many things, including paper and gunpowder. China has for centuries made beautiful porcelain which for this reason is known as 'china'. China's recorded history goes back to the year 2200 B.C. when they were already an advanced nation inhabiting the Yellow River Valley. One of the most famous of the early Chinese Emperors was Tsin Shi-hwang who about 200 B.C. built the Great Wall of China, part of which remains to this day. Between the 14th and 17th centuries a line of Emperors, known as the Ming dynasty, ruled China and during this time Chinese art, particularly porcelain, flourished. The Ming dynasty was succeeded by the Manchu dynasty, the last line of Emperors to rule over China.

In 1900 a Chinese terrorist society, known as the Boxers, tried to throw out all foreigners in China. This led to fighting between the European and Americans against China. China had to agree to give Europeans special rights.

In 1911 the country became a republic under Dr. SUN YAT-SEN. From that time onwards there was constant civil war. In 1931 the Japanese made war on China and Manchuria. After the Second World War civil war again broke out and the Communists, under their leader, MAO TSE-TUNG, were able to conquer the country. The nationalist forces under General CHIANG KAI-SHEK, took refuge in FORMOSA, or Taiwan, and claimed that they were still the rightful government of China.

CHINCHILLA

This rodent is best known for its lovely soft silver-grey fur which is much valued for making coats and furs. It is about the size of a squirrel, the head and body being about ten inches long and the tail about five. The chinchilla lives in burrows in the Andes of Chile and Bolivia.

CHIPMUNK

Another name for the American ground squirrel or striped gopher found in Asia and North America. Chipmunks differ from the ordinary squirrels in that they live in burrows in woods and open spaces.

CHIPPENDALE, Thomas (1718–1779)

Born in Yorkshire but came to London where he became one of the most famous English cabinet-makers and carvers. His chairs are perhaps most well-known, but he also designed settees, and mirrors, and lesser numbers of tables, cupboards and bookcases, and, thanks to his book of designs, the *Gentleman and Cabinetmaker's Director*, his work was widely copied.

CHINCHILLA Lives in burrows in the ground.

CHOPIN, Frédéric François (1810–1849)

Polish composer, born near Warsaw. He spent much of his life in Paris, where he became the most famous pianist of his time and the founder of the modern style of piano-playing. Although very poor and of delicate health, he gave many concerts to raise funds for refugees from Poland, which was at that time overrun by the Russians. Some of these he gave in London in the last year of his life; he died in Paris, aged only thirty-nine. His studies, Preludes, Waltzes, Mazurkas and other pieces are some of the most frequently performed of all piano music.

CHRISTIAN DEMOCRATIC PARTY

The name given to a political party to be found in a number of European countries. In these countries it is quite usual for people belonging to a particular religious denomination to form their own political party, something which is not done in Britain where people join the political party of their choice regardless of their religion. The Christian Democratic Party is the Roman Catholic party and is especially strong in France, Belgium, Italy and the German Federal Republic.

CHRISTINA, Queen of Sweden (1626–1689)

Succeeded to the throne of Sweden when she was only six years old, and assumed power in 1644. She showed great interest in the arts and philosophy and, eager for more personal freedom, abdicated her throne in 1654 in favour of her cousin, Charles Gustavus. She became a Roman Catholic and lived in Rome. Later, she tried to regain her throne and also to take the crown of Poland. She died in Rome.

CHURCH MUSIC

From the time of the spread of Christianity until the 16th century, the religion of all European countries was Roman Catholic, and all church music was written for the Roman Catholic Church. Two types of composition were common during this period: the motet (a setting of words from the Bible, in a Latin version) and the mass (a setting of the Catholic Church Service, which was also in Latin). Composers who wrote great works of this kind were PALESTRINA, Victoris, Thomas TALLIS and William BYRD. (The masses of later Protestant composers, such as BACH and BEETHOVEN, were written as religious music in the general sense, and were not intended for use in the Catholic Church Service). After the Reformation, the churches of all countries which accepted it replaced Latin by the country's own language: in England, motets in English were henceforward called anthems, and the mass was replaced by the service, a setting of the English words of the church service. Tallis and Byrd, whose lives stretched over the period of change, wrote some fine anthems and services, as did Orlando GIBBONS, Dr. John BLOW, and Henry PURCELL after them. The cantata is another church composition which came into existence at this time; it is a kind of anthem in several sections. The ORATORIO is not a church composition, being written for the concert hall.

CHURCHILL, Sir Winston Leonard Spencer (1874–1965)

British statesman. Born at Blenheim Palace, grandson of the seventh Duke of Marlborough, he was educated at Harrow and Sandhurst. Entering the Army in 1895 he served in Cuba, India, the Sudan, and was a war correspondent in the Boer War (1899–1900). Entering politics in 1900, as Conservative M.P. for Oldham, he changed to the Liberals in 1905. After a series of ministerial posts he became First Lord of the Admiralty (1911) where he remained for the earlier part of the Great War. In the post-war period his principal position was Chancellor of the Exchequer (1924–1929). He was excluded from the National Governments of 1931–1939

CHURCHILL giving his famous victory sign.

on account of his opposition to the policy of appeasing Germany and Italy. But when the Second World War came, he was appointed First Lord of the Admiralty. After the resignation of Neville CHAMBERLAIN in May 1940, Churchill became Prime Minister of an all-party coalition. As the supreme director of the war effort, and the main architect of the alliance with Russia and America, he led the nation to victory over Germany and Japan. But he was defeated at the Polls in 1945, and did not become Prime Minister again until 1951. He resigned the office of Prime Minister in 1955. Apart from his political activities Churchill has also found time for numerous writings including the monumental *A History of the English-Speaking Peoples,* and also for painting.

CHURCH OF ENGLAND

Ethelbert, Saxon King of Kent, welcomed St. Augustine when he landed in Kent in A.D. 597, permitting him to use the ancient British Church of St. Martin's, Canterbury, and Augustine became the first Archbishop of Canterbury. Under the Archbishop and his successors, the Roman Church spread rapidly.

In 664, at the Synod of Whitby, the King of Northumbria decided in favour of the ROMAN CHURCH rather than the Celtic Church, with its monastic ideal. This decided the form of religion that was to last in England until the REFORMATION.

The great cleavage came in Henry VIII's

CHURCH OF ENGLAND Thomas Cranmer one of the founders of the Church of England.

reign, when he repudiated the spiritual authority of the Pope.

Thomas CRANMER, Archbishop of Canterbury, became one of the chief architects of the Church of England [*see* PRAYER BOOK]. On the death of Edward VI, his half-sister, Mary Tudor, ascended the throne in 1553, and commenced a Roman Revival, which ended in the burning at the stake of many 'heretics', including Cranmer.

Her reign was short-lived. Elizabeth, her half-sister, rose to power. Queen Mary I died, and under Queen Elizabeth I the attempt was made to establish a national church which steered a middle course through the ever-growing conflict between Puritan (extreme Protestant) and Roman Catholic elements.

During the reign of Charles II (1660), the Anglican Church became the 'Church of England by law established', and is still the 'established' Church in England today. It is the Mother Church of a world-wide communion of Episcopal Churches, the principal Assembly of this Anglican Communion being the Lambeth Conference (since 1867) which meets approximately every ten years under the presidency of the Archbishop of Canterbury.

There are over 12,500 parishes in England, each of which has a parochial Church Council elected by parishioners on the Electoral Roll (baptized Church members). Apart from salaries of Chaplains to the Forces, the Church of England today receives no direct State Funds, its revenue coming from voluntary offerings, investments and legacies.

CHURCH OF SCOTLAND

The greatest name in early Christian history in Scotland is that of St. Columba who landed on the Island of Hy (Iona) with his followers in A.D. 563. Two hundred years previously, St. Ninian, a Cumbrian, ordained bishop in Rome, had founded the church and monastery of Whithorn in Galloway. As against Celtic Christianity, the Roman Church gained ground steadily in Scotland especially during the reign of Malcolm Canmore and his English Queen, Margaret.

The foremost figure in the Scottish Reformation when it came was John KNOX, who became in 1559 the champion of Presbyterian Protestantism. A year later the Scottish Parliament accepted Knox's Confession of Faith and thenceforward Scotland was a Protestant country.

Presbyterianism is based on the government of a church by Elders (Greek, *presbyteros*) of whom the minister of the church is one—a 'chief among equals'. He and the Elders form the Kirk Session, to which is entrusted the spiritual welfare of the parish.

Each year in May, the Supreme Council of the Church meets in Edinburgh; this is known as the General Assembly and the President is called the Moderator of the General Assembly of the Church of Scotland. In 1843 Thomas Chalmers founded the Free Church of Scotland, and four years later came the United Presbyterians. The latter united with the Free Church in 1900 to form the United Free Church. The year 1929 saw the reunion of the United Free and the Established Church, although some United Free Congregations refused to join.

The Church of Scotland is the Mother Church of Presbyterian churches in many parts of the British Commonwealth, and it strongly supports Missionary work in many lands.

CICERO, Marcus Tullius (106–43 B.C.)

Roman orator, politician and writer. He was trained in law, and when consul in 63 B.C. foiled Catiline's plot. But he violated the rule that only the people in assembly had the power to condemn to death, and had to flee the country. Later he was forgiven, and sent as governor to Cilicia. He sided with Pompey against Julius CAESAR, but Caesar afterwards allowed him to return to Rome. He took no part in Caesar's murder in 44 B.C., though he deplored the continuation of his despotism through the person of Mark Antony. Antony, Octavian and Lepidus had him proscribed and he was murdered by their soldiers near his villa at Formiae. His real greatness was in his oratory and writing: in the pathos and wit of his speeches as a lawyer; in his treatises, such as *On the Republic*, *On the laws* and *On old age*; and in his letters, which, by their detail and frankness, provide a living image of Rome in the 1st century B.C.

CIMABUE (?1240–1302)
Italian painter, and reputed teacher of GIOTTO. The only certain work of Cimabue is in Pisa Cathedral, most other works being at best attributed to him.

CITY
The description given to an important town. British towns can only describe themselves as cities if they have had permission to do so from the Queen, or reigning sovereign. Most British cities have a cathedral.

CIVIL SERVANTS
People who are employed by the State and who are paid by money which Parliament has agreed shall be used for that purpose. Civil servants do not all work in Government offices. They also include postmen and some policemen. Civil servants are not allowed to be Members of Parliament.

CLAUDE LORRAINE (1600–1682)
French landscape painter, born at Lorraine. As a young man he went to Rome, where he became servant and colour-grinder to the landscape painter Augustino Tassi. In 1627 he secured the patronage of Pope Urban VIII, and quickly became famous. Claude's landscapes influenced the art of most of his successors. The book in which he kept tinted drawings of his paintings and the names of the purchasers is in the Duke of Devonshire College, Chatsworth. His real name was Claude Gelée.

CLAUDIUS I (10 B.C.–A.D. 54)
Nephew of Emperor Tiberius and born at Lyons. Proclaimed emperor following the assassination of Caligula. Although studious, he was a weak man who allowed power to pass into the hands of his military leaders. It was during his reign that Rome finally settled Britain. He was poisoned by his wife Agrippina to secure the accession of her son NERO.

CLEMENCEAU, Georges (1841–1929)
French republican patriot and statesman, born in Mouilleron-en-Pareds, La Vendée. Elected to the Chamber of Deputies in 1876 as leader of the Radical Party. In 1906 he became Prime Minister and Minister of the Interior. He created a Ministry of Labour, inaugurated a scheme of social reform and accomplished the separation of Church and State. Played an indispensable part in inspiring the French to victory in the Great War. Clemenceau was nick-named 'The Tiger' on account of his ferocity in debate and his vigour in overthrowing ministries.

CLEOPATRA, Queen of Egypt (69–30 B.C.)
Ousted by her co-sovereign and brother, Ptolemy, Cleopatra gained the help of Julius CAESAR, who replaced her on the throne. She bore Caesar a son, and travelled to Rome, but returned home after his murder (44 B.C.). Mark Antony became infatuated with her—she is supposed to have been one of the most beautiful women that ever lived—deserted his wife, Octavian's sister, and went to live in

CITY A view of the Palace of Westminster which houses both chambers of Parliament.

Alexandria. But Octavian defeated their forces at the sea-battle of Actium, and they both took their own lives, Antony falling on his sword and Cleopatra allowing an asp to bite her. Her story is told by Shakespeare in *Antony and Cleopatra* and by G. B. Shaw in *Caesar and Cleopatra*.

CLERGY

Although the word 'Clergy', which signifies 'men in holy orders', should, strictly, be applied only to priests of an Established Church, it now usually refers to all ordained Christian ministers—as opposed to the 'laity' or ordinary church members. A number of ecclesiastical positions, however—most of them honorary—are held by laymen.

An Archbishop is the senior Bishop of a Province, i.e., a fixed number of Dioceses. Nowadays a Roman Catholic Archbishop is usually known as a 'Metropolitan', i.e., Bishop of the chief church of the 'metropolis' or 'capital' of the province. There are two Provinces in the Church of England; Canterbury (29 Dioceses) and York (14 Dioceses). The Archbishop of Canterbury, Primate of all England, has the privilege of crowning the Sovereign at Coronations. The Archbishop of York, Primate of England, has the privilege of crowning the Sovereign's Consort.

A Bishop. In New Testament times, the word 'Bishop' usually referred to an 'Elder' of the Church, but in time the Bishop became the highest order in the Catholic Church, East and West. A Bishop is the spiritual head of a Diocese, a fixed territory, sometimes also called a 'bishopric', or 'see'. He supervises the general conduct of all the religious activities within his Diocese, ordaining priests and deacons, confirming children, preaching sermons, and regularly visiting all the Churches and clergy under his charge. In England, a Bishop is elected by the Crown, and is usually consecrated to his office by the Archbishop of the Province in which his particular Diocese is included. Bishops form the 'Lords Spiritual' in the House of Lords.

Archdeacons and Deacons. Originally a 'chief deacon', the rank of Archdeacon has risen to become next to a Bishop. His main duties are the general administration of that part of a Diocese allotted to him, and the supervision of maintenance work on church buildings and furniture. The office of Deacon, on the other hand, has gradually diminished in responsibility, until today, in the Anglican and Roman Churches, a Deacon is usually regarded as a 'student priest', most Deacons being ordained to the priesthood after a year. Certain Free Church lay officials are known as Deacons.

A Canon. Originally applied to one living a semi-monastic life, the word now usually refers to a member of a Cathedral Chapter, in both the Anglican and Roman Catholic Churches.

A Cardinal is the highest ranking official in the Roman Catholic Church, next to the POPE —who elects all Cardinals to their office.

A Curate is one who has the care of souls, a priest—usually applied nowadays to the assistant of a Rector or Vicar. In France the word *curé* is still applied to the parish priest.

Deans (*a*) Originally a monastic term, the word 'Dean' is now applied to the Head of a Cathedral Chapter, i.e., the assembly of clergy known as Canons, who govern the management of a Cathedral. The Chapter is the Bishop's executive council. The Dean usually has complete charge of the arrangement of services in his Cathedral, and the supervision of the building and property. (*b*) A Rural Dean, usually a specially chosen parish priest, supervises on behalf of his Bishop, certain affairs of the 'deanery'—that part of the diocese in which he exercises special charge.

A Minister is 'one who serves', and the word is applied fairly generally to all clergymen— 'minister of religion' being a recognized occupation for official purposes.

A Parson is, strictly speaking, a Rector, but now applied to clergymen in general.

A Pastor is 'one who has care of a "flock"'— frequently applied to clergymen.

A Prebendary is a resident clergyman of a Cathedral, receiving a *prebend*, or endowment, from his Cathedral.

A Priest is a clergyman; a minister of public worship. In earliest times and in every land, the priest was the 'one who offers sacrifices'.

A Rector is the parish priest living in a Rectory and entitled to *all* the ecclesiastical income of his parish.

A Vicar is a parish priest who occupies his post 'in place of' a Rector; living in a Vicarage and entitled to a *proportion* of the parish's ecclesiastical income.

CLERK OF THE PEACE

A county lawyer who gives advice to the Justices of the Peace when persons accused of wrongdoing are brought before them. The Clerk also keeps the records of his county.

CLIVE, Robert (1725–1774)

Principal founder of the British Empire in India. Born at Market Drayton in Shropshire he was dull at books as a boy but famous for his daring. He is also said to have formed a small army of boys and imposed a tax on the shopkeepers of Market Drayton if they did not

CLIVE Founder of the British Empire in India.

want their windows to be broken. When 18 he entered the service of the East India Company in Madras, first as a clerk and later as an ensign. After various minor campaigns, his victory at Plassey (1757) in revenge for the imprisonment of the British in the Black Hole of Calcutta by the Nawab of Bengal, won this province for the British Empire. He returned to India from 1765–1767, reformed the Civil Service and improved the army. But when he returned to England, powerful enemies attacked his conduct in India. He died by his own hand.

CLOUD

Condensed water vapour floating in the air above the earth. According to the International Cloud Atlas the following principal cloud formations are recognized:

Upper Clouds (average altitude: 9,000 metres).

Cirrus: Detached, featherlike clouds.

Cirro-stratus: A thin, white cloud sheet.

Intermediate Clouds (between 3,000 and 7,000 metres).

Cirro-cumulus: Small rounded masses of white clouds (mackerel sky).

Alto-cumulus: Larger rounded masses, arranged in groups.

Alto-stratus: Dense sheet of grey or bluish clouds.

Lower Clouds (2,000 metres).

Strato-cumulus: Large masses of grey cloud.

Cumulo-nimbus: Dense layer of dark shapeless clouds (rain clouds).

Clouds of Diurnal ascending currents.

Cumulus: Apex, 1,800 metres; base, 1,400 metres. Thick cloud with flat base and dome-shaped upper part.

Cumulo-nimbus: Apex, 3,000 to 8,000 metres; base, 1,400 metres. Great masses of cloud in the form of mountains.

High fogs, under 1,000 metres.

Stratus: A uniform, foglike cloud in the air.

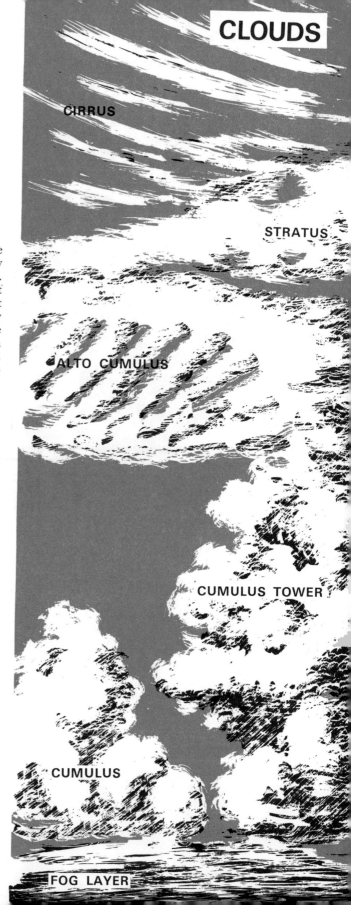

CLOUDS

CIRRUS

STRATUS

ALTO CUMULUS

CUMULUS TOWER

CUMULUS

FOG LAYER

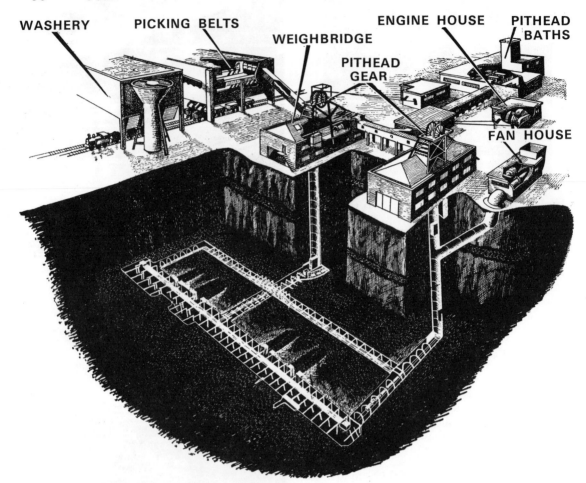

WASHERY   PICKING BELTS   WEIGHBRIDGE   ENGINE HOUSE   PITHEAD BATHS   PITHEAD GEAR   FAN HOUSE

COAL. A cut-away drawing of a modern coal-mine showing how the shafts are sunk and worked. At one time coal was used almost entirely for heating. Today coal is a source for thousands of by-products.

COAL

A black mineral consisting chiefly of carbon derived from the wood and foliage of primitive trees. The coal forests flourished about two hundred million years ago on vast swamps at the mouths of rivers. The trees were related to our present-day club-mosses, ferns and horse-tails, but they were equal in size to modern forest trees. Great thicknesses of fallen trunks, dead branches and leaves accumulated on the ground and became buried in the mud brought down by the floods. Under the weight of the deposits above them, they slowly changed to coal.

COASTGUARD SERVICE

Chiefly a life-saving organization. It comes under the Ministry of Transport and keeps watch at danger points around the coast. If a vessel is in distress it will, when necessary, give assistance by rocket life-saving apparatus. It works closely with the Royal National Life-boat Institution.

The coastguard service grew out of a coast force established in 1798 which patrolled the coast to prevent smuggling. Until 1831 the service came under H.M. Customs and in the 19th century it was taken over by the Admiralty. It has since been re-organized several times and after coming for a time under the Board of Trade it was recently brought under the Ministry of Transport.

COBBETT, William (1763–1835)

British author and journalist. Born in Surrey of peasant stock, he worked on his father's farm before joining the Army (1783). Discharged as sergeant-major (1791) he began his career as political journalist in Philadelphia and was thrice prosecuted for libel. On his return to England he started Cobbett's *Weekly Political Register* (1802). In 1832 he was elected

M.P. for Oldham. He was a vigorous reformer and champion of the farm-labourer. In his *Rural Rides* (1830) he gave a picture of the poverty and plenty of English village life, written in a vivid, popular style.

COBRA [*See* SNAKES]

COCTEAU, Jean (1891–1963)
A man of remarkably diverse talents, who had success as an actor, film director, poet, playwright, novelist and critic. Notable among his novels is *Les Enfants Terribles* and, among his films, *Orphée* and *La Belle et la Bête*.

COLERIDGE, Samuel Taylor (1772–1834)
One of those poets who has written little, but whose two or three best works are outstanding. His father, a country clergyman at Ottery St. Mary, died when he was nine, and from then onwards he seemed throughout his life to be lonely and unattached. He had brilliant ideas, expressed them brilliantly in conversation, but found it hard to persevere in a set task or to fulfil his plans in action. But he did complete *The Ancient Mariner*, a poem different from anything that had been written in English before it, telling a story powerfully and hauntingly. His short fragment *Kubla Khan* and the unfinished *Christabel* are equally fine. With WORDSWORTH he published (1798) *Lyrical Ballads*.

COLLINS, William Wilkie (1824–1889)
English novelist, and son of the Victorian landscape painter William Collins. He was called to the Bar in 1851, but preferred literature to the law, and became a pioneer in the field of detective fiction. Two of his best-drawn characters are the villainous Count Fosco in *The Woman in White*, and Sergeant Cuff in *The Moonstone*.

COLOMBIA
A large republic in the north-west of South America whose shores are washed by both the Atlantic and Pacific Oceans. It is more than twice the size (440,000 square miles) of France and has a population of a little over 15 million. The capital is Bogota. Colombia takes its name from Christopher COLUMBUS who discovered it in 1502. It remained under Spanish rule until 1824, when, as the result of a revolution led by Simon BOLIVAR it became independent.

COLOUR
Strictly speaking, colour is a private sensation. If two people look at a pillar-box, each says it is red, but there is no way of proving that each one is having the same sensation because each has been trained from infancy to call that particular sensation red. This fact brings difficulties that have troubled colour scientists for centuries. However, following Sir Isaac Newton [*see* SPECTRUM] it is possible to deal with light of different wavelengths in a scientific way and use the terms applicable to colours. Thus we can speak of red light, green light, etc. without any fear of being misunderstood.

The wavelengths of visible light, i.e. the distance from crest to crest of the wave by means of which the light travels, range from about 0·00004 centimetre to about 0·00007 centi-

COLERIDGE The author of *The Ancient Mariner*.

metre. It is more convenient to deal in Angström units, one such unit being a hundred-millionth of a centimetre. We can then say the wavelengths of visible light range from about 4,000 Angström units to about 7,000 Angström units. The light of the shortest wavelength looks violet and that of the longest looks red.

The colour of an object is caused by the fact that material of the object absorbs some wavelengths from the light falling on it. For instance, a piece of grass, when white light falls on it, absorbs the longer wavelengths and reflects the rest, with a little absorption at the violet end as well. So the light reflected looks green, but it is not monochromatic [*see* SPECTRUM]. We judge the colour by the mixture and give it the name of the chief, or dominant, wavelength present. Thus the dominant wavelength of the light from green grass could be 5,200 Angström units. But it might be 5,400 Angström units, or in fact one of quite a number of wavelengths all of which produce a green sensation. The only way to find out the actual dominant wavelength is to use scientific apparatus such as a colorimeter or a spectrophotometer.

Dominant wavelength is not the only fact by

means of which we judge colour. For example, an orange reflects light with a dominant wavelength of about 5,900 Angström units. But if we take a paint of exactly the same hue and then mix black with it, the dominant wavelength is still the same but the appearance has been changed. It looks darker and if dark enough may even be brown. So the lightness of a surface is an important factor in determining colour sensation. This is measured in terms of the proportion of light reflected. In other words, the luminance factor of the surface has to be known. Furthermore, the colour depends on how much of the dominant wavelength is present. This quantity is called the purity. In addition to these factors, there is the quality of the light being used. For instance colours look different in electric light from what they do in daylight.

There are thus four measurable factors in determining a colour in physics—dominant wavelength, purity, luminance factor, colour of the illuminant. The first three of these correspond to our sensations of hue, saturation, and lightness. In other words the dominant wavelength of the reflected or transmitted light determines the hue, the purity, or amount of dominant wavelength, and this determines what we call the saturation, and the luminance factor determines how light or how dark the object appears. By relating the physical facts to the facts of our sensations in this way, the scientific study of colour is made possible.

COLUMBUS, Christopher (1451–1506)

Italian navigator, born at Genoa. Inspired by the adventures of MARCO POLO Columbus sought a westerly route to the East. After seeking the aid of Portugal, Spain, England and France, his scheme was eventually supported by the King of Spain. On his first voyage (1492) Columbus discovered Watling Island and Cuba, and on his second, (1493) the WEST INDIES. The third voyage ended in Columbus being taken prisoner, after he had discovered the South American mainland, and returned to Spain. During a fourth voyage he sailed along the south side of the Gulf of Mexico. He died in poverty at Valadolid, and unaware that he had discovered the New World.

COMENIUS, Johann Amos (1592–1671)

Czech educational reformer. Born in Moravia, he later became a schoolmaster. He was invited both to Sweden and to Hungary to advise on educational systems. He also came to England at the invitation of Parliament, but the outbreak of the Civil War drove him to Sweden (1642). He died at Naarden near Amsterdam. As an educationalist he stressed that languages should be taught by conversation, grammar being ignored until simple words and phrases had been learnt. He also thought that the use of pictures would make it easier to learn foreign words.

COMET

A comparatively light heavenly body with a luminous tail of gaseous matter which is thought to be ejected from the comet's body by the pressure of the sun's radiation as it approaches the solar system. The length of the tail varies, but can reach lengths exceeding

COMET Position of its tail round the sun.

the distance of the earth to the sun. Comets follow either elliptic paths round the sun or parabolic paths towards or away from the sun. At one time it was thought that they came from outside our galactic system, but now it is known that many belong to it. Perhaps the best known is Halley's Comet which was first studied and predicted by Edmund HALLEY (1656–1742).

COMMANDMENTS, The

Probably the oldest part of Hebrew tradition. They are the foundation upon which the Religion of Israel was built and developed; and they have profoundly influenced the ideals of many nations to this day. The story of how Moses received them from God on Mount Sinai, of how Moses found that, in his absence, the Israelites had made a Golden Calf as an object of worship; and how God gave Moses the Commandments a second time, is told in Exodus and Deuteronomy. The Commandments themselves are set out in Exodus, Chapter XX, and Deuteronomy, Chapter V. Scholars know them by the Greek term 'Decalogue'—The Ten Words.

COMMUNIST PARTY

In Great Britain a small political party and for some years has not succeeded in getting its candidates returned to Parliament. Communists believe that all industry and all land should be owned by the State and that the ultimate aim should be 'From each according to his ability and to each according to his needs.' In Russia, China and other Communist countries it is the party which rules the country and no other party is allowed. Communists all over the world look to Karl MARX who lived and wrote in the middle of last century, as the founder of their philosophy.

COMPUTER

An automatic, electronic machine designed especially for the rapid solution of very complex and time-consuming mathematical problems. Also referred to as an 'electronic brain'. There are various types of which the two most important are the *digital* computer and the *analog* computer. The digital is the larger, more expensive type used in science, business and industry. It handles figures (digits) similar to the way an adding machine does. It produces a special numerical result by breaking down a problem into a succession of the four arithmetical operations of addition, subtraction, multiplication and division, by any of the procedures known in numerical analysis.

The analog computer uses physical quantities as 'analogs' to the variables being solved.

COMMANDMENTS An early print of Moses receiving the Commandments from God on Mount Sinai.

It handles continuous data such as charts and curves. Each point on a curve is the analog of the information plotted, just as distances along a slide rule are analogs of numbers. The analog computer produces other charts or curves which are usually less precise than the digital results. This type of computer is used mostly in technological studies.

CONCERTO

Musical composition for a solo instrument (for example, violin or piano) with orchestra. It is usually built on the same plan as the symphony, and may be written for any instrument. Sometimes there are two (or even three) soloists, in which case it is described as a double (or triple) concerto.

CONDOR

A species of vulture native to South America —especially the Andes—having a wing-spread of about 9 feet. Although like the vultures it is mainly carrion-eating, it will attack small animals like lambs. Its main physical feature is its bold red head—the male has a ruff round the base of the neck and a growth on top of its head.

CONDUCTOR (music)

Musician who directs the performance of a piece of music, standing in front of the players and indicating his wishes with a short stick, known as a baton. Until a hundred years ago, conducting was nearly always done by composers. In early times they used a scroll of paper; later they kept time by thumping the floor with a heavy staff, sometimes drowning the music in their excitement. (The French composer, LULLY, who worked at the court of King Louis XIV, once hit his foot instead of the floor, giving himself a bruise from which he died!) BACH, HANDEL and MOZART directed from the harpsichord; after that, the principal violinist directed from his seat in the orchestra. The baton came into use in BEETHOVEN's time, and the modern type of conductor arose who is not himself a composer, but only directs performances of other men's music.

CONFIRMATION

In the Anglican, Eastern, Lutheran, Roman, and other churches, Confirmation is the ceremony in which those baptized shortly after birth, 'confirm' the Baptismal Vows made for them by godparents, and so are admitted into full church membership. A Sacrament in the Roman Church, Confirmation is administered not later than seven years after Baptism. The Eastern Church administers it immediately after Baptism. It is not a Sacrament in the

Anglican Church, and candidates are usually aged between 14 and 18. A Bishop performs the ceremony by laying his hands on the candidate and invoking the Holy Spirit as comforter and strengthener.

CONFUCIUS (Kung Fu-tse) (551–479 B.C.)
Chinese philosopher and meditator, whose doctrine of tolerance and simplicity influenced Chinese, and also Western, civilization. He taught his disciples what he considered to be the principles of good conduct, both in individual lives and government, and was the first exponent of the 'do as you would be done by' attitude.

CONGER EEL [*See* EELS]

CONGO
The name of one of two countries that take their name from the great river of that name which flows through both countries. To avoid confusion the name of the capital city is usually also given, in this case Brazzaville. The republic (129,960 square miles) is bigger than Great Britain but has less than a million people. Before it became independent in 1960 the country was ruled by France and was then known as the Middle Congo.

CONGOLESE REPUBLIC
One of two republics (*see above*) that take their name from the Congo River. It is a vast country (905,580 square miles), nearly a third the size of the United States. From 1885 to 1960 the country was under Belgian rule. Because Africans had been given no opportunity to study at Universities when the country became independent there were no doctors, lawyers or other professional people. This led to grave trouble and for several years, at the request of the Congolese, the UNITED NATIONS gave special help with the administration of the country and in training Africans in skills of all kinds. The Congo is rich in copper, found in the province of Katanga, which adjoins ZAMBIA. The country is the world's chief supplier of cobalt and has important supplies of uranium. The capital is Kinshasa (formerly Leopoldville).

CONGRESS
The name given to the central government of the UNITED STATES. It has two houses, the Senate and the House of Representatives. Because the United States is what is known as a federal state, the American Congress only makes laws which must apply to the whole country. Other laws, such as those relating to education, health and marriage are made by

Above, CONGOLESE REPUBLIC A rich copper mine in the province of Katanga. *Below*, CONGRESS The House of Representatives in full session.

the separate legislatures, or parliaments, of each of the fifty-one States which make up the Union. The House of Representatives is elected in much the same way as the House of Commons in the British Parliament. It consists of 435 members who are elected every two years. The Senate is made up of two Senators from each of the fifty States. They serve for six years. One important difference between Congress and the British Parliament is that neither the President of the United States nor any members of his Cabinet are allowed to be members of either House.

CONGREVE, William (1670–1729)
Born near Leeds but educated in Ireland, Congreve came to London to attempt, in his early twenties, to make his fortune as a playwright. Congreve's first play to be performed—at Drury Lane in 1693—was *The Old Bachelor*. John DRYDEN wrote verses to welcome it, saying that he found in Congreve's style the beginning of an age of perfection in the use of the English language. Other plays followed including his masterpiece, *Love for Love*, in 1695, and *The Way of the World* (1700). His particular talent was for the comedy of manners, set among the rich and fashionable people of the day.

CONRAD, Joseph (1857–1924)
British novelist. Born of Polish parents in the Ukraine, he joined the crew of a French ship when he was 17. After twenty years at sea, he turned to writing and settled in Kent. He was able to use his experiences of the sea as material for his books, and *Lord Jim* and *An Outcast of the Islands,* for example, are set in the seas and jungles of Singapore, Borneo and Sumatra. The charm and individuality of his style is partly due to the fact that he could speak three languages fluently.

CONSERVATIVE PARTY
The name of one of the largest and oldest of the political parties in Great Britain. The party developed from the Tory Party of the 17th century. This was made up of those who supported the King and his Court at a time when the country was divided in its allegiance. The name Tory is still sometimes used to describe Conservatives. The British Conservative Party depends for its chief supporters very largely on leaders of industry, although it has a more progressive outlook in regard to social reform than do the conservative parties on the continent. It agrees, for instance, with the need for what is now called the 'Welfare State'. It is opposed to the nationalization of industry and believes in encouraging private enterprise in all sectors.

CONSTABLE, John (1776–1837)
English landscape painter. Born in Suffolk and the son of a rich miller. His painting *The Hay Wain* was exhibited at the Louvre in 1824, where it created a sensation. In his own day he was appreciated more in France than in England; he was not admitted to the Royal Academy until 1829. However, he is now recognized as one of the very greatest English landscape painters. *The Cornfield, The Hay Wain* and *The Valley Farm* are in the National Gallery, London.

CONSTABLE *The Cornfield,* a magnificent landscape.

CONSTITUENCY
The name of a district which has the right to elect a Member to Parliament. The number of constituencies changes slightly from time to time as the result of boundary changes. The present number is 630.

CONSUL
Someone sent to a foreign country by his Government and whose chief duty is to look after anyone from his country who may be in need of help. In some cases people may need a permit, called a visa, to allow them to travel from one country to another. In this case it is the consul who gives a visa to those wishing to enter his country. Because a Consul, unlike an AMBASSADOR, is concerned with helping ordinary citizens, it is often necessary to have several consuls in a single country. As Britain is a great seafaring country, British sailors may sometimes need help and so there are British consuls in all the chief ports of the world.

COOK, Capt. James (1728–1779)

Famous English navigator. The son of a farm-bailiff, he entered the Navy in 1755 after sailing before the mast in the Norway and Baltic trades. After surveying and charting New-foundland and Labrador, he was invited to command an expedition to the Pacific to observe the transit of the planet Venus over the face of the sun. On this voyage New Zealand was circumnavigated and Australia visited, the east coast being annexed under the name of New South Wales. On his next voyage Cook discovered the Society Islands, the New Hebrides and New Caledonia in the Pacific. On his third voyage he made many discoveries as far north as the Behring Strait, but was killed at Hawaii in the Sandwich Islands.

COOK A print of Cook's expedition to the Pacific.

COOPER, James Fenimore (1789–1851)

American novelist. His series, the Leather-stocking Tales, which include *The Last of the Mohicans*, records the life of the Red Indians in the 19th century.

CO-OPERATIVE MOVEMENT

The name given to different kinds of co-operative societies. The best known and most usual in Great Britain are those called consumer societies. This means that the co-operative store is owned by the people who consume, or use the goods sold by the society, that is to say by the customers. This is done by giving each member a share of the profits in the form of a dividend on the amount of his purchases during the year. There are about 900 co-opera-

tive societies in Britain and between them they have nearly 13 million members. The largest society is the London which has more than a million members and is the largest co-operative in the world. The shops of these societies are to be seen in every town.

Amongst other kinds of co-operative societies, some of which are to be found in Britain, are the producer societies. They are owned by the people who produce, or make, goods which the society sells.

The most important producer societies are agricultural ones. Farmers join such a society in order to use modern methods which they might not be able to afford to do individually. The society may, for instance, operate a modern dairy, or a slaughter house or tractor station which all the farmers in the neighbourhood, who are members, can use.

In many of the poorer, or developing, countries this type of agricultural co-operative society is becoming increasingly important. Poor farmers may be able to buy seed, fertilisers and other necessities through a co-operative society much more cheaply than if each bought the goods separately. They may be able to erect good storage buildings for their grain where the members can bring it to be properly packed for the market. In some countries co-operative housing societies are formed to help the members to obtain houses more cheaply. Fishermen's co-operatives may make it possible for the fishermen to use modern fishing boats and craftsmen of many kinds may form co-operatives in order to share workshops with proper equipment.

COPERNICUS, Nicolaus (1473–1543)

Polish astronomer, born at Thorn, Prussia, and considered to be the father of modern astronomy. He was dissatisfied with the complexity of Ptolemy's system and adopted that of ARISTARCHUS in placing the sun in the centre of the solar system and the planets—including earth—revolving round it. This work *De Revolutionibus Orbitum Coelestium* was published in 1543, but a century passed before it was generally accepted.

COPTIC CHURCH

The Copts are the Christian descendants of the ancient Egyptians. Christianity was introduced to Egypt through the Greek-speaking settlements founded there by the Greek Empire. The Coptic Christians claim to have received their faith from no less a person than St. Mark, whom tradition names as the first Bishop of Alexandria.

By persisting in a view of Jesus's nature (the 'Monophysite Heresy') condemned by the

Council of Chalcedon in 451, the Coptic Church became detached from the ROMAN CATHOLIC CHURCH; and after North Africa was overrun by Moslem armies in the 7th century, the Copts found themselves cut off from the Christian world. The Coptic Church, however, still survives in fair numbers in Cairo and other parts of Egypt, having preserved in its long isolation its ancient forms of worship.

CORELLI, Arcangelo (1653–1713)
Italian composer, born near Milan. Is important in the history of music as the composer who introduced the violin in favour of the viol. BACH composed a fugue based on Corelli subjects in his honour.

CORMORANT
Sea bird which nests on coasts, but is sometimes found on estuaries and rivers. It lives almost exclusively on fish which it dives for. It is a large bird, growing up to 36 inches long.

CORN LAWS
> The Corn Laws are the greatest scourge
> That has been since the flood,
> Enacted since the time of George,
> Whose reign was that of blood!

These lines, written early in the reign of Queen Victoria show how people in the towns felt about the Corn Laws which were intended to help British farmers by restricting the import of corn from abroad. A number of Corn Laws had been passed in the reign of George III but they were not the first. There had been Corn Laws since 1361. But in the 19th century the inhabitants of the quickly growing towns demanded cheaper bread and the Corn Laws were repealed in 1846.

CORNEILLE, Pierre (1606–1684)
French dramatist. He was one of the 'Five Poets' whom the Cardinal de RICHELIEU used to write down his ideas, though the Cardinal became jealous of the success of Corneille's first great play, *Le Cid*. Today his plays may seem rather formal and artificial, but his writing has a beauty and a dignity unmatched by any other playwright. *Le Cid* is based on the youth of the Spanish hero who fought the Moors in the 11th century. *Polyeucte* and *Cinna* are two of his greatest plays.

CORONER
A person, usually a doctor or lawyer, who is appointed to enquire into the death of someone who has died, or who is thought to have died from some unnatural cause. When a coroner holds a court there may be a jury and if in the opinion of the jury someone is believed to be guilty of the murder or manslaughter of the dead person then the coroner must send that

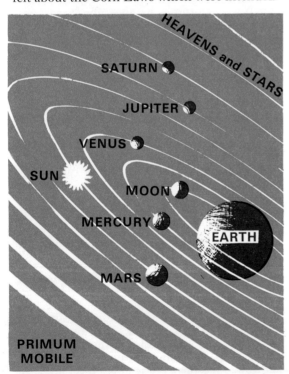
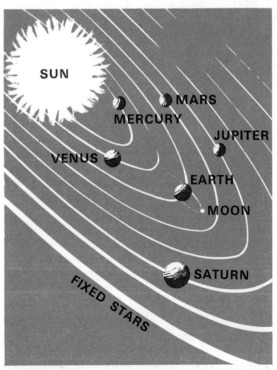

COPERNICUS *Left*, diagram of the solar system as conceived by Ptolemy and *right*, by Copernicus.

COROT A typical landscape by an artist who was direct and used a simple range of colours.

person to prison so that he can be brought before the ASSIZES for trial. In addition to enquiring into unusual deaths a coroner also has to enquire into treasure trove and to decide to whom the treasure belongs. In the City of London the coroner may also enquire into the cause of a fire.

COROT, Jean Baptiste Camille
(1796–1875)
French landscape painter. Born in Paris. Apart from three visits to Rome, he spent most of his life in Fontainebleau or Ville d'Avray. Although he only made his fortune late in life, he was well-known for his charitable works, and gave money to the poor of Paris. Corot is regarded as the greatest of the Barbizon school (named after a village which was a favoured spot for nature painters) of landscape painters, and his paintings are famous for their directness and simple colour range.

CORREGGIO, Antonio da (1494–1534)
Italian painter, named after the small town of Correggio where he was born. His early style was greatly influenced by LEONARDO DA VINCI. One of his famous works is the fresco he painted on the inside of the cupola of the Cathedral at Parma—the *Assumption of the Virgin*—which TITIAN praised. His *Ecce Homo* in the National Gallery is a very delicate and beautifully coloured painting.

CORTÉS, Hernando (1485–1547)
Spanish soldier. In 1518, he began the conquest of the Mexican Empire with a tiny force of men and a handful of horses and brass guns.

He approached the water-bound capital in 1519 and carried off the King, Montezuma. But the people rose up against him, and the Spanish and their allies were routed as they tried to flee from the city along the causeways that led to the shore. Later he returned with a much larger force, besieged the city, and destroyed it (1521). MEXICO was renamed New Spain with Cortés as its governor (1522), and he sent expeditions into Guatemala and Honduras. Cortés died in obscurity in Spain.

COSMIC RAYS
These consist of particles and radiations that reach the earth from outer space. Such radiations were unknown before 1910 and were not investigated satisfactorily until the American scientist R. A. Millikan started work in aeroplanes, on mountain-tops, and in balloons in 1923. The modern study of cosmic rays did not start until an instrument called the GEIGER-MULLER COUNTER, which is a detector and measurer of any radiation that electrifies a gas when passing through it, was readily available. The first important fact in this modern study was that there was much less cosmic radiation near the earth's equator than in higher latitudes. This fact showed that the radiation could be charged particles such as electrons.

Later work has shown that there are two forms of cosmic radiation, known as showers and penetrating radiation. The former has been shown to consist of electrons. The latter consists of particles much heavier than electrons and called mesons. These at sea level are very penetrating, more penetrating than any known radiation from earthly sources.

Both the electron showers and the mesons are believed to be created by still other particles that come into the earth's atmosphere from outside. The emission is continuous and every minute at sea level approximately one ray passes through every square centimetre.

COSMOGONY

That branch of ASTRONOMY concerned with the origin of the universe. There are many cosmogonies, some largely mythical and restricted to accounts of the origin of heaven and earth, others more scientific, such as the nebular hypothesis, originated by LAPLACE, which attempts to account for the origin of the solar system.

More recently Lemaitre proposed the 'big bang' theory of the origin of the universe which took place some 10 to 40 billion years ago. As the result of a primordial explosion of a highly compressed cloud or blob containing all the mass we see today, spreading out as galaxies through universal space, the universe is still expanding.

The latest addition to cosmogony theories is that of the 'continuous creation hypothesis' which states that the universe is being created continuously by the formation of new hydrogen ions at an extremely slow pace. Thus the universe is in a 'steady state' of creation.

COSMOGONY The spiral nebula 'M 74' in Pisces

COSTA RICA

A small republic in Central America on the peninsular which—except for the Panama Canal—joins Central to South America. It is less than half the size (19,650 square miles) of England and has a population of about one and a half million. The capital is San José. The country has the highest standard of living in Central America and more people can read and write there than in any other country of Latin America. In 1948 the country abolished its army. Its main products are coffee, bananas and sugar cane; recently cattle raising has been introduced.

COULOMB, Charles A. De (1736–1806)

French physicist. He studied the distribution of electric charges over variously shaped conductors, and showed that a charge spreads itself by self-repulsion. He also devised a method of measuring 'electric density' and used it to describe the electrical potential on the surface of a spherical conductor. The unit of electrical charge, the coulomb, is named after him.

COUNCIL OF EUROPE

The name of an organization set up in 1949 to enable the countries of Western Europe to work together more closely. Its headquarters are in Strasbourg, France. It has a Consultative Assembly which brings together M.P.s from the Parliaments of all the countries that belong to it. Great Britain is allowed to send 18 M.P.s and these always include some from all three parties represented in Parliament—Labour, Liberal and Conservative. The M.P.s from other Parliaments are chosen in a similar manner. A smaller body, called the Council of Ministers, brings together Cabinet Ministers, usually the Foreign Ministers, from the Member countries and it is they who make final decisions as to what shall be done.

COUNSELLORS OF STATE

Certain members of the Royal Family who, by Act of Parliament, may be appointed by the Queen to carry out certain duties when she is abroad or if she should be ill. An Act of Parliament in 1953 named the Duke of Edinburgh as Regent if the Queen should be permanently ill or if the Prince of Wales should succeed to the throne before he became of age to rule in his own right.

COUNTY BOROUGH COUNCIL

The LOCAL AUTHORITY in a city or large town. The Council does all the work done by a BOROUGH COUNCIL and all the work by a COUNTY COUNCIL in the case of other towns.

COUNTY COUNCIL

The chief LOCAL AUTHORITY in a county. A few counties that are bigger than others have been divided; for example, there are three in Yorkshire and two in Sussex. This means that there are rather more administrative counties than there are geographical ones in England and Wales. In all areas, except Greater London, the County Council is responsible for providing a POLICE force. They are responsible, too, for education and certain other services which benefit the whole county. In addition they have to supervise the smaller local authorities in their area except COUNTY BOROUGHS and in London the London Boroughs do not come under the GREATER LONDON COUNCIL. County Council elections are held every three years.

COUPERIN, François (1668–1733)

French composer, born in Paris. He came of a well-known family of musicians and known as 'Couperin le Grand'. Perhaps his most important work was for the harpsichord, an instrument on which he wrote a standard work. At 25 he was organist in Louis XIV's chapel at Versailles and later organist at St. Gervais, Paris.

COURBET, Gustave (1819–1877)

French painter, born at Ornans. His work ranged from landscapes to nudes to scenes of everyday life to still lifes, all done in a vigorous naturalistic style. He was involved in the revolution of 1848 and the Commune of 1871. After the latter he was imprisoned and fined for aiding the destruction of the column in the Place Vendôme.

COWARD, Noel (1899——)

English actor, playwright and composer. Plays like *Hay Fever* and *Private Lives* are witty

COWARD Actor, playwright and composer.

satires on English life in the 1920s and 1930s. He has produced several films, and wrote the song *Mad Dogs and Englishmen*.

COWPER, William (1731–1800)

Following a two-year period of insanity at the age of 32, Cowper retired to the fen country and lived a withdrawn life, writing much poetry of simplicity, of charm, and sometimes of wisdom and power. Cowper's most famous poem—so famous that it is often familiar to people who do not know its author's name—is *John Gilpin*.

COYOTE

A member of the WOLF family and native to North America. It lives mainly on small mammals, birds and reptiles—sometimes a lamb. Its howls, whines and yaps are familiar in the American West, although it is widely hunted as a sheep killer—an accusation which has been shown to be unfounded. The coyote is also known as the 'prairie wolf' and 'brush wolf'.

COYPU

Also known as the beaver rat; is rather like a small beaver, with webbed feet, but has a long rat-like tail. It is common in the Argentine where it lives in burrows in the banks of streams and lakes. Coypu fur is known as 'nutria' and is used as a substitute for beaver fur.

CRABS [*See* CRUSTACEANS]

COYPU whose fur is known as 'nutria'.

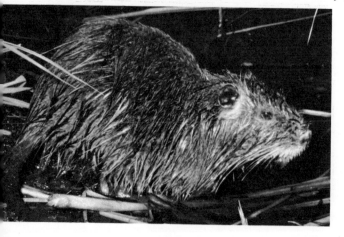

CRANACH, Lucas (1472–1553)

German painter, born at Kronach. Went to Vienna and then to Wittenburg as court painter to Frederick the Wise, Elector of Saxony. He was a close friend of Martin LUTHER whose portrait he painted a number of times. Cranach painted many religious subjects in addition to some outstanding nudes. He was also a wood-engraver after the style of DÜRER.

CRANMER, Thomas (1489–1556)

Found favour with King Henry VIII by his views and statements on divorce. He also did much to encourage the translation of the Bible and to see that a copy of it in English was placed in every church; and he carried out various changes in the prayer book. Archbishop of Canterbury in 1533. One of the leading figures of the English REFORMATION, he was burnt at the stake for treason and heresy during the reign of the Roman Catholic Queen Mary.

CREED

(Latin *credo*, 'I believe'). A fixed statement of belief. The only 'creeds' the early Church used were the simple confessions of faith required from candidates for Baptism. The Anglican Prayer Book contains three Creeds:

1. The Apostles' Creed, recited during Anglican Morning, Evening and Baptismal Services. Opening 'I believe in God the Father Almighty, Maker of heaven and earth' and proceeding to state the principal points of Christian Doctrine, such as 'And in Jesus Christ His only Son our Lord . . . (He) Was crucified, dead, and buried . . . The third day He rose again . . . I believe in the Holy Ghost, the Holy Catholic Church . . . .'

2. The Nicene Creed, recited during Anglican Communion. The Nicene is a more detailed statement than the Apostles' Creed, commencing 'I believe in one God, the Father Almighty . . .' and continuing 'And in one Lord Jesus Christ . . . in the Holy Ghost . . . who proceedeth from the Father and the Son . . . And I believe in one Holy Catholic and Apostolic Church. . . .'

3. The Athanasian Creed is really a Latin Hymn (a canticle) entitled *quicumque vult*, which though not written by Athanasius himself, is reasonably styled 'The Faith of Saint Athanasius', since it states Christian doctrine as he expressed it.

CRETE

Island of 3,200 square miles in the Mediterranean, mostly mountainous, and a part of GREECE. This island's fame rests upon the excavations of the palace of Minos at Cnossos

CRETE Reconstruction of the Palace of Minos at Cnossos. Excavated by Sir Arthur Evans.

which revealed an advanced civilization at least 4,000 years old; this site was excavated by Sir Arthur Evans. The present population is about 500,000 and the main cities Candia and Canea.

CRICKET

Ball-game which can be considered the national sport of Britain, but also played extensively by many countries within the British Commonwealth.

There is no standard size or shape for a cricket ground, but its boundaries must be clearly marked before a match begins. In the middle of the ground lies the actual pitch, which is 22 yards long and 10 feet wide. At each end of the pitch is a white line, called the bowling crease, and in the middle of each is placed the wicket. Each wicket consists of 3 stumps with 2 bails on the top; it is 9 inches wide and 28 inches high. The wickets are placed opposite and parallel to each other. Parallel with each bowling crease, and 4 feet down the pitch, is the popping crease.

The game is played with a bat which must not be more than $4\frac{1}{2}$ inches wide or 38 inches long, and with a ball weighing between $5\frac{1}{2}$ and $5\frac{3}{4}$ ounces and measuring between $8\frac{13}{16}$ and 9 inches in circumference.

According to the rules each team has two innings, although in one-day matches probably only one innings will be played by each side. Each team has a captain, and before the game

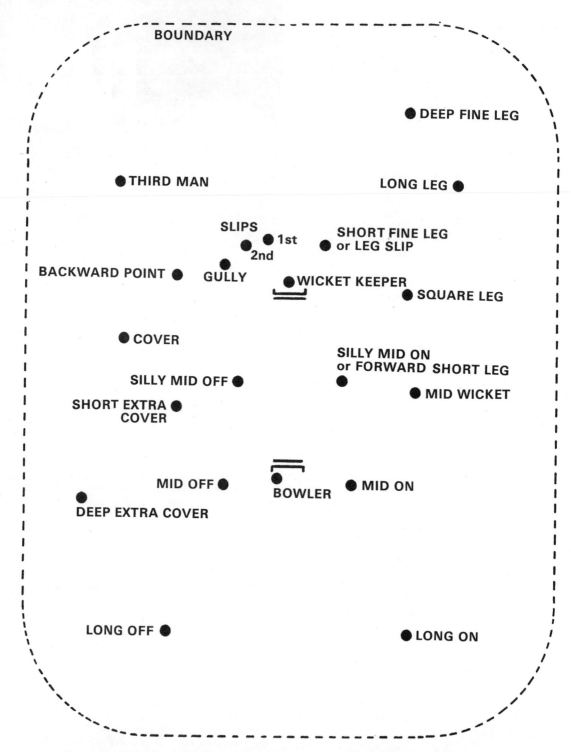

CRICKET. Above are shown 21 fielding positions, including bowler and wicket-keeper, considered by many experts of the game as standard. Although there is no standard size for a cricket ground, the boundaries must be clearly marked. The actual pitch must measure 22 yards long by 10 feet wide, bowling creases marking the ends.

begins one captain tosses a coin and the other calls heads or tails. The winner of the toss decides whether to bat or field first.

The whole of the fielding side take the field and remain there throughout the opposing side's innings. The batting side open their innings with 2 players. When one of these is out, he is followed by another, and this continues until 10 men have been given out, unless the captain 'declares' the innings closed before this happens. The game is won by the side scoring the greater number of runs in the innings added together. If the scores are equal, the result is a tie; if any innings is unfinished, the result is a draw.

The game is begun when one of the fielding side starts to bowl from one end of the pitch to the opposite wicket, which is defended by one of the batsmen. The other batsman stands at the bowler's end, and takes no part in the play except to run when necessary.

The bowler bowls an 'over' of 6 balls, at the end of which another member of the fielding side bowls from the other end. A bowler is not allowed to bowl 2 overs in succession.

Apart from the bowler, the members of the fielding side are placed in various positions by their captain. One of these, called the wicket-keeper, stands behind the wicket towards which the bowler is bowling, and crosses to the other end of the pitch at the end of each over. Both the batsmen and the wicket-keeper are allowed to wear pads and gloves for protection.

A run is scored each time the batsmen, after a hit or at any time while the ball is in play, cross and make good their ground from end to end.

Any number of runs may be scored at a time. After crossing, each batsman must put his bat, or some part of his body, on the ground, over the popping crease towards which he is running before turning and starting on another run. When he fails to do this, 'one short' is signalled and the run is not scored, although the second run will be. If a batsman is 'run-out'—this will be explained later—the run which was being attempted is not scored. If a batsman is out as a result of being 'caught', no runs made after that hit are scored.

If the ball crosses the boundary of the ground after bouncing, 4 runs are scored. In this event, runs already scored by the batsmen when the ball crosses the boundary are not counted. If the boundary results from an over-throw or the wilful act of a fieldsman, however, the 4 runs shall be added to those already made at the time of the throw or act. If the batsman hits the ball so that it clears the boundary line without a bounce, 6 runs are scored.

If a fieldsman wilfully stops the ball with

CRICKET The MCC's Jubilee Match of 1837.

his cap or other article of clothing or object, 5 runs are awarded to the batting side and added to any runs already scored. In this case the batsman do not change ends.

Runs scored after the ball has been hit by one of the batsmen are credited to that batsman. All other runs are called 'extras', and count equally in the innings total.

There are four kinds of extras: no-balls, wides, byes, and leg-byes.

A no-ball is an improper delivery by the bowler. A no-ball counts as one run unless runs are otherwise scored off it in the normal way. A no-ball does not count in the over.

A wide occurs when the bowler bowls a ball so high over or wide of the wicket that it is out of the batsman's reach. Again, a wide counts as one run unless runs are otherwise scored off it, and does not count as a ball in the over.

When a normal delivery passes the batsman without touching his bat or his person, any runs scored are counted as byes. If a normal delivery touches any part of the batsman's dress or body other than his hand, any runs scored are counted as leg-byes. If, however, the batsman deliberately deflects the ball with any part of his person, no runs are scored. Byes and leg-byes count in the over just like any other balls.

The ways in which a batsman can be out are the following:

(*a*) Bowled. If the wicket is bowled down by a legitimate ball. This applies equally if the ball first touches his bat or person.

(*b*) Hit Wicket. If, in playing the ball, the batsman hits down his wicket with his bat or any part of his person, or his cap falls on and breaks the wicket.

CRICKET Three great batsmen in action. *Top*, Wally Hammond, *centre*, Don Bradman and *bottom*, Garry Sobers.

(*c*) Run Out. Either batsman is 'run-out' if, in running or at any time while the ball is in play, the wicket is put down while he is out of his ground; that is, if no part of his bat in hand or of his person is grounded behind the line of the popping crease. If the batsmen have crossed, the one running towards the broken wicket is out; if they have not crossed, the batsman who has left the broken wicket is out.

(*d*) Stumped. If, in receiving the ball, the batsman is out of his ground, but not attempting a run, and the wicket is put down by the wicket-keeper, or if the wicket is broken by the ball rebounding from the wicket-keeper's person, the batsman is out 'stumped'.

(*e*) Caught. The batsman is out 'caught' when the ball, after contact with the bat or the hand holding the bat (excluding the wrist), is caught by a fieldsman before it touches the ground and is held under control.

(*f*) Leg Before Wicket (L.B.W.). The batsman is out L.B.W. if he intercepts the ball with any part of his person except his hand, provided that:

(i) the ball would otherwise have hit the wicket;

(ii) the ball did not first touch his bat or hand;

(iii) the ball pitched either on a straight line between the two wickets or on the offside of the batsman's wicket;

(iv) at the moment of impact the part of the batsman's person that intercepts the ball lies on a straight line between the two wickets.

It does not matter if the height of the ball at the moment of impact is above that of the bails, provided it would have hit the wicket, nor does it matter what part of the body is struck other than the hand.

(*g*) Handled the ball. If the batsman touches the ball in play with his hands, except when they are holding the bat, and except when he does this at the request of one of the fieldsmen, he is out 'handled the ball'.

(*h*) Hit the Ball Twice. If, except for the purpose of guarding his wicket, the batsman wilfully strikes the ball after it has already once struck his bat or any part of his person, he is out 'hit-the-ball-twice'.

(*i*) Obstruction. If either batsman wilfully obstructs the opposite side he is out 'obstructing-the-field'. If the obstruction prevents a ball from being caught, it is the striker who is out even if the obstruction was done by the other batsman.

A batsman cannot be out bowled, hit-wicket, stumped, caught, or L.B.W. from a no-ball, but can be run out.

The ball is said to be 'dead' when it finally settles in the hands of the bowler or wicket-keeper; when it reaches the boundary; when it lodges in the dress of a batsman or umpire; on the call of 'over' or 'time'; when a batsman is out; or when a fieldsman is penalised for stopping the ball illegally. After the ball is dead, no runs may be scored and neither batsman can be out. The ball ceases to be dead when the bowler starts his run or bowling action.

A substitute may run for a batsman who is unfit, or take the place of a sick or injured fieldsman, provided that he is correctly dressed for his position, but he may not bat or bowl.

Two umpires are appointed for each game, and all decisions are made by them. They stand

CROCODILES

These fearsome animals are reptiles and closely related to the alligators. Crocodiles differ from alligators in that the fourth tooth of the lower jaw fits into a notch in the upper jaw giving the creature a permanent grin. In alligators the fourth tooth fits into a pit. Both these creatures feed on almost anything they can overpower. The largest living crocodile is the 'salt-water' crocodile of Australasia which can reach a length of 30 feet. The 'caimans' of South America are relatives of the alligator and 'gharials' or 'garials' of India are crocodiles; these have long slender snouts.

CROCODILE Has a permanent grin because the fourth tooth in its lower jaw fits into a notch in the upper jaw.

one at each end of the pitch, the umpire at the bowler's end normally standing directly behind the wicket, and the umpire at the other end away from the wicket in a straight line with the popping crease.

The umpire decides whether a batsman is out, but only after an appeal has been made. He calls 'over' and 'time', and signals boundaries, extras and short runs to the scorer. In addition to a signal he must shout 'no-ball' immediately one is delivered.

The captain is responsible for choosing the batting order, changing the bowlers, and arranging the field, although this last is usually done in conjunction with each bowler. He must also instruct his team on tactics, telling the batsmen when to play defensively and when to hit out or take chances. If he wins the toss he decides whether his team shall bat or field, also he has to judge—an important decision—when to declare an innings closed.

CRIVELLI, Carlo (?1430–1495)
Venetian painter, best known for his religious paintings in a late Gothic style. Worked most of his life in the central region of Italy known as the 'Marches'. One of the best collections of his work is in the National Gallery, London.

CROME, John (1768–1821)
English landscape painter. Born at Norwich and founder of the Norwich school of water colour artists. The son of a weaver, he became apprenticed to a sign painter, and subsequently earned a living by giving drawing lessons and making a few sales. Most of his life was spent in Norfolk. Crome's landscapes are noted for their simplicity and beauty.

CROMWELL, Oliver (1599–1658)
Lord Protector of England. Born at Huntingdon and educated there and at Cambridge. He became an enthusiastic Puritan, and spoke for the Puritans in the Parliament of 1628, and in the Short and Long Parliaments (1640). When the Civil War broke out (1642) he built up a body of highly disciplined troops, the 'Ironsides', and his cavalry charges brought victory to the Parliamentary Party at the battle of Marston Moor (1644). At Naseby (1645), he led the victorious 'New Model Army', and his military power began to overshadow the authority of Parliament. Cromwell might have come to terms with Charles I, but the King's plotting made this impossible, so he brought him to trial and signed his death-warrant. Cromwell's victory at Worcester (1651) ended

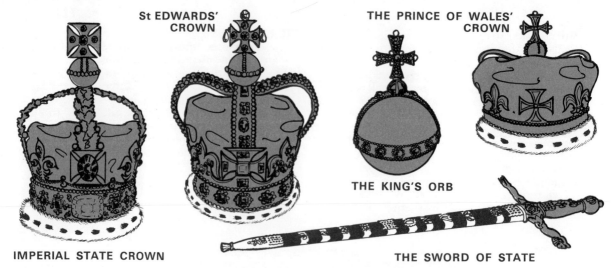

St EDWARDS' CROWN

THE PRINCE OF WALES' CROWN

THE KING'S ORB

IMPERIAL STATE CROWN

THE SWORD OF STATE

the Civil War. He was declared Protector (1653), and troublesome Parliaments were dismissed. Cromwell reorganized the Church, encouraged the universities, reformed the law, and pursued a successful foreign policy in the interests of British trade and of a Protestant Europe. But his system of government collapsed at his death.

CROMWELL, Thomas (*c.* 1485–1540)
English statesman, the son of a blacksmith. He became agent and secretary to Cardinal WOLSEY, and entered Parliament. He advised Henry VIII to break with Rome and declare himself head of the Church. Further to this, he aimed to make the King's power absolute, and promised him untold riches, and as a means to this he counselled Henry to dissolve the monasteries and brutally destroyed those—like MORE and Fisher—who would not go along with him. His unpopularity and his fall from Henry's favour led to his imprisonment in the Tower, and he was beheaded on Tower Hill.

CROOKES, William (1832–1919)
British scientist, born in London. In 1861 he discovered thallium, and in 1878 demonstrated the particle nature of cathode rays in a tube of his own invention. Later he did research into the nature of radioactive substances.

CROQUET
A ball-game played on a court the layout of which is given in the diagram. The playing equipment is 4 balls (coloured red, blue, yellow and black), 4 clips similarly coloured to fix on

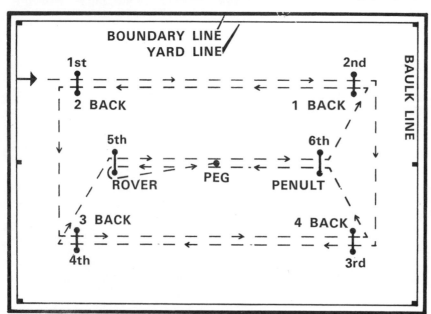

CROQUET The boundaries of the court-line should be either 35 x 28 yards or 30 x 24 yards.

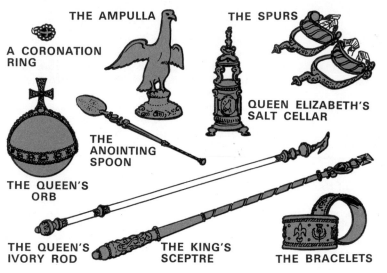

A CORONATION RING

THE AMPULLA

THE SPURS

THE ANOINTING SPOON

QUEEN ELIZABETH'S SALT CELLAR

THE QUEEN'S ORB

THE QUEEN'S IVORY ROD

THE KING'S SCEPTRE

THE BRACELETS

CROWN JEWELS This priceless collection of royal jewels can be seen in the Tower of London. The Imperial State Crown contains over 3,000 precious stones.

to hoops, and either 2 or 4 mallets according to the number of players. The ball must be struck with one of the end-faces of the mallet and never with the side of it.

An opponent's ball can be deprived of a clear run through the hoops by a 'roquet', hitting it with the player's own ball so that it is driven out of its advantageous position. This is followed by a 'croquet', when the player's own ball is placed so that it just touches the ball roqueted, and is struck so that the opponent's ball moves, no matter by how little. The player then makes another stroke, provided he has not failed to move the other ball. If a ball passes through a hoop in the wrong direction it does not count; the player must go on playing that ball until it eventually goes through in the right direction. Should a ball go over the boundary-line, it is picked up and placed on the yard-line at a point nearest to where it went out of the court. If it comes to rest between a boundary-line and a yard-line, then it is played from where it lies, if it is the striker's ball, or placed at the nearest point on the yard-line if it is his opponent's ball.

The striker goes on playing after a successful roquet or croquet or after his ball has passed through the proper hoop in the right direction. If he fails to do any of these things he loses his turn and his opponent then plays. When the opponent fails to make a roquet, take a croquet, or pass his ball through the proper hoop, then the first player plays again, and so on.

Four balls are used in Croquet. When only two players are playing, each player has 2 of the balls, one playing the Red and Yellow, the other playing the Blue and Black. Each player is equipped with 2 clips which correspond to the colours of the balls he is playing, and he places these clips on the tops of the next hoops he has to play for the first time round (hoops marked first to sixth on our diagram) and on the sides of the hoops and on the Peg the second time round (hoops marked one-Back to four-Back, Penult and Rover). When the game starts all 4 clips will be on the top of the first hoop. When starting to play, all balls must be played on to the court; after that, each player may play either of his balls just as he chooses.

When four players are playing, they are divided into 2 teams of two each, and each player has only one ball which he is allowed to play. The two players of a team do not have to play alternately; either player can play when it is the turn of his team to do so, but he must only play his own ball and not his partner's. Which partner of a team plays at the beginning of a turn is a matter to be decided by the partners themselves.

In ordinary games, that is, in games which are not part of an organized competition or for which no referee has been appointed, each player is responsible for the correct placing of his clip or clips on the right hoops, or for placing it on the next hoop the ball has to be played through.

If a player can so play one ball that it hits his other one and sends it through its proper hoop, he scores that hoop. But if he knocks one of his opponent's through, the latter scores the hoop—or even the Peg if that is his next target.

CROWN JEWELS

This priceless collection is kept in the Tower of London. The principal items are: the Ampulla, Coronation Spoon, Queen Elizabeth's Salt-cellar, St. Edward's Crown, Royal Sceptre with the Cross, Large Orb, Queen's Sceptre with Cross, Sceptre with Dove, Small Orb, Queen's Sceptre with Dove, Queen's Ivory Rod, Bracelets, St. Edward's Staff, Circlet of Queen Mary of Modena, Coronet of the Prince of Wales, Sword of State, St. George's Spurs,

Sword 'Curtana', Mace of Charles II, State Crown and the Coronation Ring.

The State Crown contains 2,783 diamonds, 277 pearls, 18 sapphires, 11 emeralds and 5 rubies. The most magnificent of these jewels is the Black Prince ruby in the front of the crown. Next comes Edward the Confessor's sapphire, which now shines from the cross on top of the crown. Third comes the Stuart sapphire, and fourth the second largest piece of the Cullinan diamond, known as the Second Star of Africa, which occupies the front of the band. The largest portion of the Cullinan diamond, and the largest cut diamond in the world, is mounted in the head of the Sceptre with the Cross, a symbol of the Sovereign's dignity, power and justice. The original Cullinan diamond was the largest which has ever been found and measured four inches in length and weighed more than one and a half pounds.

CRUIKSHANK, George (1792–1878)

English artist, born in London. An outstanding caricaturist and book illustrator. Illustrated the novels of Sir Walter SCOTT and later those of Charles DICKENS; perhaps his most outstanding work was the illustrations to Dickens's *Oliver Twist*.

CRUSADES

In 1096 a number of expeditions set out from Europe for the Holy Land, inspired by the call of Pope Urban II. Their aim was to recapture the Holy City of Jerusalem from the Mohammedans. The soldiers wore a red cross on their shoulders and so, from the Latin word *crux*— a cross—they were called 'crusaders'. The first crusade succeeded in capturing the Holy City (1099) and in founding the Latin Kingdom of Jerusalem, covering much of Palestine and Syria and protected by a series of defensive castles. But in 1187 Jerusalem fell to the Mohammedans again. The third crusade (1188) in which Richard I of England, 'the Lion Heart', took part, came very near to success. The fourth crusade was the most damaging, for it was turned against Byzantium, the old capital of the Eastern Empire, instead of against the Saracens, and the imperial city was plundered. Jerusalem was again held by the Christians for fifteen years thanks to the treaty made by the Emperor Frederick II with the Sultan of Egypt in 1229.

CRUSTACEANS

These are a class of invertebrates with jointed legs and includes the crabs, lobsters, crayfish, shrimps, barnacles and similar animals.

Lobsters are closely connected with the crayfish and both differ from the crabs by their long bodies, extremely long feelers and fan-shaped tails. The largest lobster, the American lobster, weighs 30 pounds and measures up to 36 inches in length. The common European lobster is much smaller, weighing on an average 5–6 pounds.

Crabs are much rounder, their eyes are set on movable stalks and they have five pairs of legs, the front pair forming grasping claws. There are many different species of crab and not all are aquatic, some live on land like the 'ghost' crab found in Florida. The strangest crab is the 'hermit' crab. This species has no hard covering and to protect itself from its enemies it uses the cast-off shells of other creatures. Hermit crabs range in length from 1 to 18 inches.

CRYSTALS

Many substances are built of precisely similar units added to one another in succession, just as a wall is built of precisely similar bricks. Such substances are called crystals. The unit may be one in which the atoms are at the corners of a cube, in which case the crystal is said to be a cubic crystal. In actual fact, this does not mean that the resultant large crystal will necessarily be a large cube, for the formation may be extended more in one direction than in the other two, or more in two directions than the other one. In addition, in the natural formation of crystals, atoms of other elements may join with those of the parent crystal unit, thus causing a distortion in the form. Furthermore, the unit cubes may form larger cubes and these cubes be assembled symmetrically into other geometric shapes.

The basic crystal forms are divided into seven types: triclinic, monoclinic, orthorhombic, rhombohedral, hexagonal, tetragonal, cubic. Common salt forms cubic crystals whereas sugar forms monoclinic crystals. Quartz forms hexagonal crystals, and these may be seen on the inside of flints.

The study of crystal forms was much advanced by means of X-RAYS and more recently by the use of electrons. When X-rays are passed through a crystal the picture formed gives an indication of the arrangement of atoms and molecules as well as the distances and directions between them. This sort of X-ray crystallography is the occupation of many of our leading physicists.

Crystals are formed not only by inorganic substances but by organic substances as well, even though the final form gives no hint to the naked eye or the microscope that the structure is actually crystalline.

Crystals of many substances can be made by dissolving some of the substance in hot water

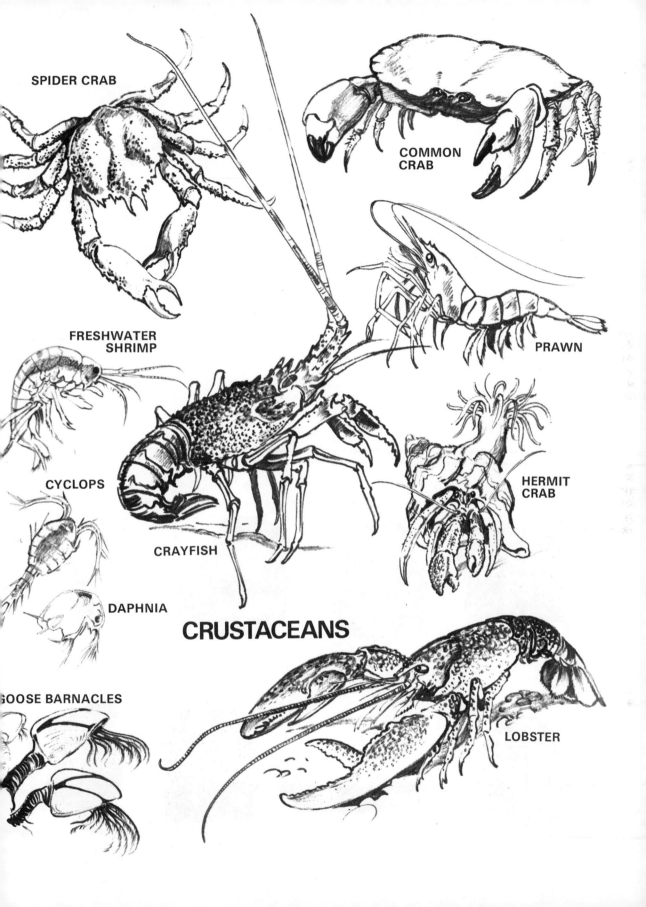

SPIDER CRAB

COMMON CRAB

FRESHWATER SHRIMP

PRAWN

CYCLOPS

HERMIT CRAB

CRAYFISH

DAPHNIA

CRUSTACEANS

GOOSE BARNACLES

LOBSTER

and then evaporating the solution until a very concentrated solution is formed and then cooling it. Crystals then separate out. One of the easiest to treat in this way in order to witness crystals being formed is copper sulphate.

CUBA

An island (44,178 square miles) in the Caribbean which is rather smaller than England and has a population of about six and a half million. The capital is Havana. Its chief products are sugar and tobacco.

The island was discovered by Christopher COLUMBUS in 1492. It was a Spanish colony until 1898 when the United States, as the result of a war with Spain, gained control of the island and it was not till 1909 that it finally became independent. In 1933 a Cuban Army officer, General Batista, seized power and ruled despotically till 1959. By that time the country had become very poor and in 1959 he was forced to abdicate by Dr. Fidel Castro who brought about changes that were similar to those in Communist countries. This angered the United States who refused to trade with Cuba and so Cuba turned to the Soviet Union for help.

CUCKOOS

There are over a hundred species of this bird and not all have the habit of the common cuckoo of Europe of leaving its parental responsibilities to other birds. The common

CUCKOO The common cuckoo of Europe.

cuckoo is rather hawk-line in appearance which may be the reason why it finds it easy to lay its eggs in other birds' nests. However, most other species build their own nests and rear their chicks. They vary in size from the small, brilliantly colourful cuckoos of Africa and the Pacific islands to the large—almost pheasant-sized—'channel-bill' cuckoo of Australasia.

CUMMINGS, Edward Estlin (1894–1962) American writer and painter. *The Enormous Room* describes his wartime experiences in France. In his poetry he omitted the normal

CRYSTALS A selection of useful and valuable minerals in their natural crystal form.

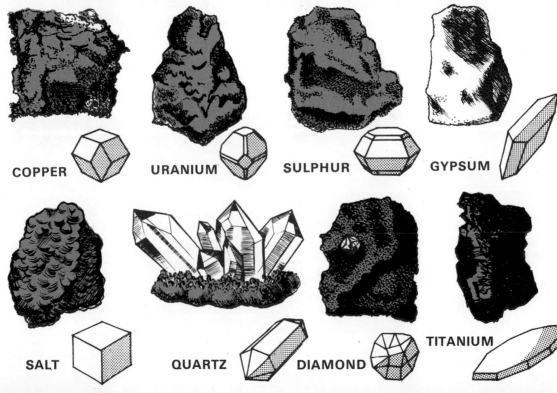

COPPER   URANIUM   SULPHUR   GYPSUM

SALT   QUARTZ   DIAMOND   TITANIUM

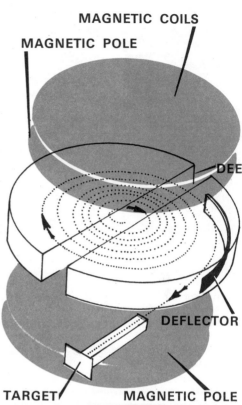

MAGNETIC COILS

MAGNETIC POLE

DEE

DEFLECTOR

TARGET   **MAGNETIC POLE**

CYCLOTRON Simplified diagram of a cyclotron, a device for accelerating nuclear particles.

use of capital letters, and arranged the words on the page with an eye to their appearance as much as to their meaning.

CURIE, Marie S. (1867–1934)
French scientist, born in Warsaw. In 1895 she married the French scientist, Pierre Curie (1859–1906), with whom she worked until his untimely death. In 1898 they discovered polonium in pitchblende—and suspected the existence of radium which they discovered and separated in 1902; in 1910 M. Curie isolated metallic radium for the first time. Pierre Curie and his brother Jacques discovered the piezo-electric effect in 1881. Marie and Pierre Curie were jointly awarded a Nobel Prize in 1903 and Marie Curie a further Nobel Prize in 1911.

CURZON, George Nathaniel, Marquis Curzon of Kedleston (1859–1925)
English statesman. First entered Parliament as Conservative M.P. for Southport (1886). His rise was rapid. He was Under-Secretary for India (1891–1892), Under-Secretary for Foreign Affairs (1895–1898) and Viceroy of India (1898–1905). In 1911 he was created

Earl. During the Great War he became a member of the small war cabinet of Lloyd George and Government leader in the House of Lords. He was Foreign Secretary 1919–1924.

CUTTLEFISH [*See* OCTOPUSES]

CYBERNETICS
Study of control and communication mechanisms in machines and animals. It covers all automatic control devices, selectors, relays, robots, and computers, and also the corresponding physiological mechanisms such as those of automatic balance, reflex action, and cerebral association. The application of cybernetics to electronic computers may possibly throw light on the function of the brain.

CYCLOTRON
Apparatus invented by Professor E. O. Lawrence for accelerating heavy particles like protons and deuterons in order to give them high energies and thus provide very energetic projectiles for atomic bombardment. The idea of the device is that a stream of particles (protons or deuterons) is made to circulate in a spiral and is given an acceleration by means of an

CYPRUS Nicosia, the capital of Cyprus.

alternating supply feeding two electrodes, called dees, the frequency of the alternation being such that the polarity of the dees is reversed just when the particles have reached half the way round their circle. Cyclotrons and other similar accelerators are an essential part of every establishment where atomic research is carried out.

CYPRUS

A large island in the Mediterranean that is a little less than half the size (3,572 square miles) of Wales and with a population of a little over half a million. Rather more than three-quarters of these are Greek-speaking and Christians, the others being Turkish-speaking and Mos-lems. The capital is Nicosia.

Cyprus was a British colony from 1918 to 1959 when the country became an independent Member of the British Commonwealth. For some years before this there had been very serious trouble between the Greeks and the Turks. When the country became independent it was agreed that the two groups should each manage their own local affairs. The President of the country is the leader of the Greeks on the island, Archbishop Makarios. In 1964, however, more trouble between the two groups occurred and the UNITED NATIONS was asked to help keep the peace between the two sides.

CZECHOSLOVAKIA

A republic (53,700 square miles) in central Europe that is slightly smaller than England and has nearly fourteen million inhabitants. The people speak a Slavonic language related to Russian. About half of them are farmers and the rest are employed in industry. The country is famous for its glass and china. The capital is Prague in the province of Bohemia and another important city is Brno, a big industrial centre.

In the Middle Ages much of what is now Czechoslovakia formed the Kingdom of Bohemia but during the Thirty Years War (1618–1648) it became part of the Austro-Hungarian Empire. After the First World War, under the leadership of Thomas MASARYK and Edward Benes, the country became independent again and took the name of Czechoslovakia. After the Second World War the country adopted a Communist form of Government.

CZECHOSLOVAKIA A panoramic view of Prague, the capital, in the province of Bohemia.

Dd

DAGUERRE, Louis Jaques Mandé (1789–1851)

French scientist who discovered the first photographic process and who is considered the 'father of modern photography'; the prints are known as 'daguerrotypes'. He was also connected with the invention of the 'diorama' a popular Victorian entertainment.

DAHOMEY

A small republic on the Gulf of Guinea in West Africa. It is a little smaller (47,000 square miles) than England and has a population of about two million. The capital is Porto Novo but a more important town is Cotonou. Dahomey was a French Colony from 1892 until the country became independent in 1960 when it decided to join the FRENCH COMMUNITY.

is contained in his classic work, *New System of Chemical Philosophy* (1808). [*See* CHEMISTRY.]

DANCE

Of all the arts of man the dance is the most ancient and most widely practised. Its great antiquity is proved by cave paintings some 20,000 years old which depict primitive man performing a magical dance. For its distribution it is enough to say that it would be impossible to find a primitive anywhere in the world which does not perform some type of dance.

Originally, the dance served a magical purpose, that is, it was a part of a ritual that was performed to assure the safety and well-being of the group or tribe. Even today such primitive peoples as the Australian aborigines and pigmies of the Belgian Congo perform dances

DANCE Californian Indians performing a sacred dance. Many of their rituals date back to before the arrival of the white man in America

DALI, Salvador (1904——)

Spanish painter. After a period of painting abstract subjects he became a surrealist. An accomplished draughtsman, he produces paintings of a dream world, with special emphasis on plastic watches. Recently he has turned to religious subjects; his *Christ of St. John of the Cross* is in the Glasgow Art Gallery.

DALTON, John (1766–1844)

English chemist, born at Cockermouth. Although he was interested in many sciences, particularly meteorology and colour blindness, his most famous work was in laying the foundations of the modern theory of the atom which

to make them successful in hunting. Further, some of the dances we know as folk-dances served a similar purpose. In ancient Greece, Rome and Egypt the dance was purely religious, and still is in India and Japan.

Dancing as we understand it is only a few hundred years old and is what could be called a social activity for pleasure and entertainment. Among the best known of these are the minuet, gavotte, waltz, mazurka, bolero, fox-trot, tango and the multitude of modern forms.

The highest form of dancing in the Western world is the ballet. Originally this formed part of an opera (and still does in many operas) and did not appear as an art in its own right until

DANCE a traditional Portuguese folk-dance, Such dances are performed throughout the world, especially among peasant communities. The most performed folk-dance is connected with the gathering in of the harvest. Most folk-dances are concerned with some aspect of day-to-day life.

the 18th century, and then through the work of Jean Georges Noverre. Although the ballet was popular in Europe, it was in Russia that it reached its peak; in fact, the renaissance in ballet was started by the Russian, Sergi DIAGHILEV, when he brought his famous company to Europe in 1909. Since that time many countries have developed their own national ballets, particularly France, America and Britain.

DANEGELD

'Geld' means 'gold' and 'Danegeld' was originally the money which was paid to the invading Danes, particularly by Ethelred II, 'the Redeless' (978–1016), to avoid fighting them. Later it became a tax paid to the King of England to pay war expenses.

DANELAW

That part of north-east England which the Danes occupied, beginning about A.D. 850. Town names ending in -by (Whitby), -wick (Runswick), and -toft (Lowestoft) are of Danish origin and are found in the former Danelaw. The division of Yorkshire into 'Ridings' is also a Danelaw survival.

DANTE, Alighieri (1265–1321)

Greatest Italian poet. Born at Florence, where his father was a lawyer. Through becoming involved in the internal politics of his native city he was falsely sentenced to death in 1302. He escaped and for some years was a wanderer in North and Central Italy. Returning to

Florence in 1310, he was soon forced to go into exile again. He spent his last years at Ravenna, where he died. His fame rests on *La Divina Commedia* (The Divine Comedy). It is divided into three parts—Inferno, Purgatory and Paradise—and is in the form of a vision in which Dante is led by the Latin poet Virgil through the Inferno and Purgatory to Paradise.

DANTON, Georges Jacques (1759–1794)

One of the leaders of the French Revolution, and co-founder of the Cordeliers Club, an important meeting-place for the Revolutionaries. Danton's encouragement helped the people of Paris to defend themselves against the Prussians and the Royalists in 1792. He voted for the death of the King, was an original member of the Committee of Public Safety, and helped to set up the Revolutionary Tribunal that inaugurated the Terror. He also helped to destroy the moderate Girondin party in 1794, but the next year he himself was tried, and, in spite of his eloquent defence, condemned to death.

DARIUS

The name of three Persian kings, of whom the most famous, known as Darius the Great, reigned from 521 till 486 B.C. He was one of the greatest rulers of the East and built many inscribed monuments from which we know his history. He did much to bring about the civilization of his country and empire, and was eventually defeated by the Greeks at Marathon.

DARLING, Grace (1815–1842)
English heroine. Born at Bamborough in Northumberland, the daughter of the lighthouse keeper on Longstone, one of the Farne Islands. On September 7th, 1838, together with her father, she rowed out to a rock where nine survivors from the wreck of the *Forfarshire* had found a foothold, and rescued them from their peril. For this heroism she was awarded a gold medal by the Humane Society.

DARWIN, Charles (1809–1882)
Born at Shrewsbury. His father was a doctor and his grandfather was Josiah Wedgwood of pottery fame. From his earliest youth he was an enthusiastic naturalist, and went as unpaid naturalist on the ship *H.M.S. Beagle*. Darwin was away five years during which time he collected such an enormous quantity of materials on animals and plants that it took some twenty years to examine and collate it. The result was his famous book, *The Origin of Species*. Many branches of thought were influenced by this work: religion, science, philosophy and economics. It should be noted that Darwin's ideas met with bitter opposition when they were first published. However, he achieved great fame in his lifetime and was buried in Westminster Abbey. [*See* EVOLUTION.]

DAUDET, Alphonse (1840–1897)
French novelist, born at Nîmes. His works show his great admiration for DICKENS and THACKERAY. *Tartarin de Tarascon*, about the people of Provence, is probably the best-known of his works in England.

DAUMIER, Honoré (1808–1879)
French painter and cartoonist, born in Marseilles. In 1832 he was sent to prison for six months for a political cartoon. He produced nearly 4,000 lithographs. He also painted about 200 small canvases, but did not receive recognition as a painter until he was an old man and blind, living in a cottage given to him by COROT.

DAVID, Jacques Louis (1748–1825)
French historical painter, born in Paris. He won fame with *Blind Belisarius Asking Alms*, and became court painter to Louis XVI. During the French Revolution he was a member of the Republican Convention and voted for the king's death. At this time he painted the *Assassination of Marat*. Sentenced to the guillotine, he escaped execution because of his fame as an artist. Appointed first painter to Napoleon. Among his most famous paintings are *The Rape of the Sabines*, *The Oath of the Horatii* and *The Death of Socrates*.

DAVY, Sir Humphry (1778–1829)
Born at Penzance. He intended entering the medical profession but turned to chemistry after reading LAVOISIER'S work. He joined the Pneumatic Institute at Bristol and here discovered the anaesthetic property of laughing gas. At twenty-three he went to the Royal Institution where he remained for the rest of his life. Of his many scientific discoveries, perhaps the most famous, was the miner's safety lamp, based on his discovery that a flame will not pass through metal gauze.

DEBUSSY, Claude (1862–1918)
French composer, born near Paris. His music has a strange, mysterious character, generally described as 'impressionistic'. His best-known compositions are the tone-poem *L'après-midi d'un faune* (The Daydream of a Faun), an opera *Pelléas and Mélisande*, several orchestral suites, such as *La Mer* (The Sea) and *Nocturnes*, and many piano pieces, including the popular *Clair de Lune* and a *Children's Corner Suite*, written for his little daughter.

DEER
The name given to those animals who grow antlers and/or long, tusk-like upper teeth (canines). Belonging to this family are the red deer, wapiti, Indian sambar, chital, fallow deer, elk or moose and roebuck, to mention only a few.

DEER A sambar deer, a native of India.

DE GAULLE President of the Third Republic and leader of the French Forces in World War II.

DEFOE, Daniel (1660–1731)
English author, born in London. He is sometimes described as the first English journalist. Defoe wrote on almost every sort of subject. Pamphlets on politics, pamphlets on religion, records of travels (notably *Tour Through Great Britain*), translations, histories, seemed to fly from his pen. His most famous work, which has been read by generation after generation, is *Robinson Crusoe* (the first part of it was published in 1719), while his novel *Moll Flanders* is one of the landmarks in the growth of English fiction.

DEGAS, Edgar (1834–1917)
French painter, born in Paris. After exhibiting in the Salon of 1865, he became friendly with MANET and other Impressionists and thereafter exhibited with them. He served in the French army during the Franco-Prussian War and then stayed for a time in New Orleans. After producing historical paintings, he abandoned oils for pastel, and his paintings of ballet-dancers, theatres, cafés and race-track scenes are world-famous. He also produced excellent bronzes of dancers and horses.

DE GAULLE, General Charles (1890–1969)
French soldier and statesman. He became famous during the 1939–1945 war as leader and organizer of the Free French Forces outside France and in the course of the war led many successful military campaigns. In 1944, he headed the liberation forces that entered Paris, and was head of the provisional government, though he soon retired from politics. The political confusion of the Fourth Republic in the 1950s encouraged him to return to power, and in 1958 he became President of the Fifth Republic and resigned in 1969. His policies included withdrawal from former colonial possessions, opening up trade and improving relations with the Eastern Bloc countries and South America, and vast economic expansion at home.

DELACROIX, Ferdinand Victor Eugène (1798–1863)
French historical painter, born at Charenton, Department of the Seine. Following his first work *Dante and Virgil,* which he exhibited in 1822, he became leader of the French Romantic movement. In 1824 he painted *Massacre of Scio,* and in 1834 after visiting Morocco he painted *Women of Algiers.* Delacroix was one of the greatest French colourists. His first success *Dante Crossing Acheron in Charon's Boat,* ranks as a milestone in the history of art.

DELIBES, Léo (1836–1891)
French composer, born at St. Germain-du-Val. Composer of light, gracefully melodic music. His best-known works are the ballets *Sylvia* and *Coppélia,* and his opera *Lakmé.*

DELIUS, Frederick (1862–1934)
English composer, born at Bradford. Of German descent, he lived at various times in England, Norway, Germany and America (on an orange-plantation in Florida), finally settling in France, where he died. At about fifty he became blind and paralysed, but bravely continued composing with the aid of Eric Fenby, who took down his music from dictation. His compositions have a dream-like quality, and each breathes the atmosphere of the country in which it was written; his tone-poems *Brigg Fair* and *On Hearing the First Cuckoo in Spring* belong to the English country-side, *Eventyr* to Norway, *Appalachia* and *Sea-Drift* to America, and *Paris* and the Violin Concerto to France.

DEMOCRACY
A word used to describe government for the people by the people. It comes from two Greek words *demos* = people and *krateo* = rule. It was the Greeks who first gave to the world the idea of democracy in their city-states in which all the citizens took part in government. It is only during the past two hundred years, however, that gradually the power to choose their own kind of government has passed from a small and favoured group to the

people of the country as a whole. Even today not all people agree as to the meaning of the word 'democracy'. In the Soviet Union and Eastern Europe the term 'People's Democracies' is used to describe a form of government which is not regarded as democratic in Britain and other western countries.

DEMOCRATIC PARTY

One of the two great political parties in the UNITED STATES. Its origins go back to the days when the United States became independent. The Democratic Party was formed to see that the federal Government did not have too much power over the separate States that make the Union. After the American Civil War the southern States almost always voted for the Democratic Party because the northern States, against whom they had fought, had been led by a Republican President, Abraham LINCOLN. After the American Civil War the people of the southern States were much poorer than those in the north which is why the Democratic Party in modern times has been more interested in providing national undertakings, like roads and electricity, out of national funds. The Democratic President who did much to help the less fortunate was Franklin D. ROOSEVELT who introduced reforms just before the Second World War that came to be spoken of as the 'New Deal'. [*See* REPUBLICAN PARTY.]

DEMOCRITUS of Abdera (460–361 B.C.)

Developed and elaborated the atomic theory of Leucippus. He pictured atoms as minute hard balls of different sizes in a constant state of agitation.

DENMARK

A small kingdom in North Europe and is one of the Scandinavian countries. It is 16,608 square miles in area, about twice the size of Wales, and has a little over $4\frac{1}{2}$ million inhabitants. The capital is Copenhagen. The people are among the most prosperous in the world. The country is famous for its dairy produce, much of it being exported to Britain. [*See* SCANDINAVIA.]

DE QUINCEY, Thomas (1785–1859)

English writer. He ran away from school to wander in Wales, and then began his writing career in London. He became the friend of COLERIDGE, SOUTHEY and WORDSWORTH, and most of his work was in the form of articles for *Blackwood's* and other magazines. His greatest work, *Confessions of an Opium Eater,* tells how ill-health and poor nerves led him to take opium, and describes the terrible effects this produced, and the suffering he endured when the danger of death made it necessary for him to cut down his dose.

DESCARTES, René (1596–1650)

French mathematician and philosopher, born near Tours. He came of a wealthy family and took up soldiering as a career. It was while lying in bed one morning that his attention was

DEMOCRATIC PARTY President Roosevelt (President 1933–45) addressing a joint session of Congress.

DICKENS A reproduction of one of the original illustrations by Phiz to Dickens' *Pickwick Papers.*

drawn to a fly hovering in a corner of the room. As he watched it, Descartes realized that the position of the fly could be fixed by its distances from the walls and ceiling. Or if two dimensions were used the position of a moving point could be defined by the distances from two axes at right angles. This discovery can be regarded as one of the greatest single steps ever made in mathematics. A new geometry was born, Cartesian or analytical geometry. He achieved great fame during his lifetime and as a result was invited to the court of Queen CHRISTINA of Sweden. The post of tutor there involved teaching at five o'clock in the morning. For one of Descartes' disposition this proved too great a strain. He died in Stockholm at the early age of 54.

DETERGENT

A substance with cleansing properties. However, today the word generally refers to the substances made from petroleum and coal-tar by-products. Ordinary SOAP is made from edible fats, while detergents are obtained from petroleum and represent a direct saving of food. Furthermore, for many purposes they are better than traditional detergents owing to certain characteristics, such as penetrating and dispersing powers and their freedom from scum. They are instantly soluble and equally effective in hard, soft or salt water. These detergents are also highly efficient wetting agents; they make water wetter and speed up processes involving scouring, mixing or rinsing with water.

DE VALERA, Eamon (1882———)

Irish national leader. Although born in New York, he was brought up in Ireland. During the Dublin Rising of Easter 1916 he commanded an insurgent battalion. He was sentenced to death but eventually pardoned. De Valera's party (*Fianna Fail*—Soldiers of Ireland) won a majority in the Irish Parliament (1932) which it retained until 1948. But by 1937 he had cut all ties linking the Irish State to the Crown and had established the independent Republic of EIRE.

DEW

Waterdrops deposited on exposed cool surfaces. This moisture is partly derived by condensation of water vapour in the air and partly by evaporation from warm ground (radiation). Plants also give out waterdrops through their leaf pores. The level beyond which the temperature of a surface must be reduced in order to obtain water deposits is known as the 'dew point'.

DIAMOND

Precious mineral in crystalline form of extreme hardness. An allotropic form of carbon. Diamonds are always found as single crystals. Their brilliancy and fire originate in the stone's high refractive power, but are only displayed after faceting. Diamonds are mined in Africa, India, and South America. They are mostly found in alluvial deposits a long way from the place where they originated. Their weight is measured in carats and many big stones are valuable. On account of its extreme hardness, diamond is the only material used for cutting diamonds. Faceting of precious stones, cutting and drilling of various materials are all done by diamond or powdered diamond. Artificially-made diamonds are made but used for industrial purposes.

DIAGHILEV, Sergi Pavlovich (1872–1929)

Russian impressario. Took his company, the Ballet Russe, to Paris (1909) and created a new interest in ballet in Western Europe. Perhaps his most valuable contribution to ballet was the creation of modern ballets set to the music he commissioned from modern composers and in settings by modern artists. His three most famous ballets are *The Firebird, Petrouchka* and *The Rite of Spring*, all by STRAVINSKY. Among the famous dancers in his company were Pavlova, Karsavina, Nijinsky, Lopokova and Massine.

DIAZ, Porfirio (1830–1915)

Mexican general and politician. He distinguished himself as a soldier in the Mexican Civil War (1855–1860) and was promoted general. He also played a leading part in the resistance to the French invasion of Mexico under the Emperor Maximilian and in 1867 took Mexico City. Then he retired from public life but returned in 1876 when he was elected President, which post he held for many years. Although Diaz degenerated into a dictator, he brought order to the country. But in 1911 a revolt drove him into exile. He died in Paris.

DICKENS, Charles (1812–1870)

As a boy in London Dickens experienced the humiliation and physical suffering of growing up in poverty. His father had been in prison for debt, and at the age of twelve Dickens worked in a factory for boot-blacking. He never forgot the miseries of this period of his life. By the use of his pen, and by his lectures and readings (in which he had great dramatic skill) he became famous, influential and rich, and indeed a public idol, being known as 'the Inimitable'. Dickens was a master of humour, both in dialogue and in the picturing of somewhat strange people; was a master of words, and loved to write descriptions of an exaggerated but highly atmospheric kind; and filled the mind of his readers with pity at the injustices and sad things of life. In recent years readers have been stirred to turn to his pages again after seeing film versions of, for example, *Oliver Twist*, or seeing television versions of such masterpieces as *Great Expectations* and *David Copperfield*.

DIDEROT, Denis (1713–1784)

French philosopher, novelist, playwright, and critic. His *Pensées Philosophiques* was burnt by the Parliament of Paris in 1746 and he was imprisoned in 1749 for his *Lettres sur les Aveugles*. This led on to his great work, the *Encyclopédie,* which took 20 years to complete, and in which he tried to collect all the new ideas and the new scientific techniques that were circulating, and to employ all the important writers of the day including VOLTAIRE, Montesquieu, J.-J. ROUSSEAU, and Turgot. The authoritarian government and the Church were outraged, and the *Encyclopédie* was suppressed in 1759. Nevertheless, Diderot managed to produce 35 volumes, though he had to complete much of the work single-handed.

DIESEL ENGINE [*See* INTERNAL COMBUSTION ENGINE]

DINGO

A wolf-like wild dog native to Australia. It is thought that this animal was introduced by natives from south-east Asia. It stands about 24 inches at the shoulder and is some 48 inches long, including its bushy tail. It is a savage killer of sheep and for this reason, killed on sight.

DINOSAURS

Group of giant reptiles which lived in the Mesozoic era between 50 and 175 million years ago. They formed the principal group of land-living animals and attained incredible lengths of up to 100 feet. From fossils found in Mesozoic rock formations many different kinds of dinosaurs have been reconstructed. Some were carnivorous and attacked the vegetarian dinosaurs which were protected by thick

DINGO Wild dog native to Australia.

CAMPTOSAURUS

TRACHODON

TYRANNOSAURUS

BRONTOSAURUS

PODOKESAURUS

DINOSAURS

IGUANODON

ANKYLOSAURUS

SCELIDOSAURUS

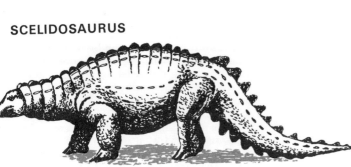

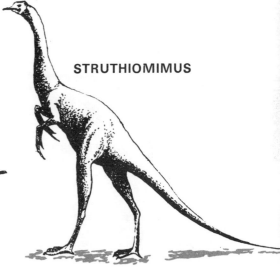

STRUTHIOMIMUS

STEGOSAURUS

TRICERATOPS

plated hides and spines. Some used their long tails as a support and counterbalance to their long necks; others progressed partly submerged in water. The reasons why these giant reptiles vanished from the earth cannot be certain. It may well be that they were too specialized to adapt themselves to a changing earth.

DIOCLETIAN (243–313)

Roman Emperor (284–305), born in Dalmatia of a humble family. He was proclaimed Emperor by the troops at Chalcedon in 284. As the barbarian threat increased, he found it necessary to divide the Empire first into two and later into four divisions: Italy and Africa, under Maximilian; Britain, Gaul and Spain, under Constantius; Illyricum and the Danube valley, under Galerius; retaining the East for himself. He attempted to revive the old religion, and fiercely persecuted the Christians as their Church was outside the control of the State. In order to strengthen the Empire, Diocletian sacrificed public participation in politics and organized a system of highly centralized bureaucracy in its place. In 305 he retired from public life, and settled at Spalato (Split) where his magnificent palace inspired Robert ADAM many centuries later.

DIOGENES (412–323 B.C.)

Greek Cynic philosopher. The dissolute youth was struck by the ascetic teachings of Antisthenes, and we are told that he changed his ways and began living in a tub, believing that virtue was only to be found by avoiding all physical pleasure. Captured by pirates, he was sold as a slave in Crete, where, asked what his trade was, he replied that he was a governor of men and would like to be sold to a man who needed a master. This is effectively what happened, and Diogenes soon gained his freedom and became tutor to his master's children. ALEXANDER THE GREAT is said to have been so impressed with him that he once remarked: 'If I were not Alexander, I should wish to be Diogenes'.

DIPLOMAT

Someone sent to a foreign country as one of the representatives of his country. Diplomats are of different ranks. The most important is an AMBASSADOR. Next is the ENVOY or Minister. A country will decide whether the chief representative shall be an Ambassador or an Envoy. Today it is nearly always an Ambassador. Next to the Ambassador is the Counsellor. There will also be Secretaries of Embassies of which there are three ranks—First, Second and Third. Last of all there are ATTACHÉS.

DISNEY, Walt (1901–1967)

American artist and film producer, born in Chicago. His first successful film cartoon was *Mickey Mouse* (1928) which was followed by a series known as the *Silly Symphonies*. Moved on to full-length feature films, the most successful being *Snow White and the Seven Dwarfs* and *Fantasia*. In more recent years he produced several wild-life films, the best-known being *The Living Desert*.

DISRAELI, Benjamin, Earl of Beaconsfield (1804–1881)

English statesman and novelist, born in London. He entered Parliament in 1837 and became Prime Minister in 1868 and again from 1874 to 1880. He secured for Queen Victoria the title Empress of India and also obtained control of the Suez Canal Company. Abroad, his policy was determined by the interests of the British Empire, and at home by the need to give the working classes a stake in the country through social reform. His novels, of which *Coningsby* and *Sybil* are the most important, are lightly written and express his political beliefs.

DIVISION

A term used to describe a vote taken in the House of Commons. A vote can be taken without a division if the wish of Members is quite clear and they do not wish for a division. When a division about some matter has to be taken the SPEAKER asks Members to say either 'Aye' or 'No'. If it is quite clear that nearly everybody is shouting 'Aye', the Speaker says 'The Ayes have it,' but if some call out 'The Noes have it,' he orders a Division. Then all the Members must go into one of two lobbies, one on the Speaker's right and the other to his left. Bells ring all over the great building and this sends Members hurrying to the lobbies. As the Members pass through the turnstiles into one or other of the lobbies they are counted.

DODECANESE

A group of islands which form part of GREECE. They include Rhodes, Astipalaia, Karpathos, Kassos, Nisyros, Kalymnos, Leros, Parmos, Kos, Symi, Khalki and Tilos. The group are sometimes called the 'Southern Sporades'.

DOGS

These animals belong to the family *Canidae*. They are adapted for swift running in pursuit of prey, have long jaws for snapping and are flesh-eating. Contained in this family are the wolves, jackals and foxes. The domesticated dog is certainly one of man's earliest pets and is thought to have descended from the WOLF.

AFGHAN HOUND

POODLE

SALUKI

BOXER

CORGI

ALSATIAN

DOGS

LABRADOR RETRIEVER

BASSET HOUND

SPANIEL

COLLIE

SEALYHAM

IRISH SETTER

DACHSHUND

DOLPHIN

A mammal, like the whale, and *not* a fish. It averages about 7 feet long and is found in most seas of the world. In recent years dolphin pools have been set up in marine parks and, because of the apparent intelligence of these mammals, have become very popular.

CEYLON, SIERRA LEONE, JAMAICA, TRINIDAD AND TOBAGO, KENYA and MALAWI. The other Members of the Commonwealth are most of them republics who have a President as their Head of State but recognize the Queen as Head of the Commonwealth. The special rights of Dominions were described in the Statute of

DOLPHIN This beaked-nosed species is the Ganges river dolphin, the best known of the river dolphins.

DOMESDAY

Domesday Book or Domesday, though written in the days of William the Conqueror, can still be seen in the museum of the Public Record Office, Chancery Lane, London. It is a record of the great survey which William's officials made twenty years after the Conquest to find out what property his subjects held, so that he could be sure that he was getting all the services and revenue that were due to him. Its name, pronounced 'Doom's Day', was acquired later when people found that it spared no one and there was no appeal from it—like Jehovah at the Day of Judgment.

DOMINICAN REPUBLIC

An independent country on the island of Hispaniola in the West Indies. It shares the island with the republic of HAITI. It is 19,322 square miles in area, nearly three times the size of Wales, and has a population of 3 million. The capital is Santo Domingo, for a time called Ciudad Trujillo. The country was a Spanish colony until 1821. From 1916 to 1924 the country was occupied by America. From 1930 to 1961 the country was under a dictator named Trujillo. There has in recent years been trouble between the Republic and Haiti.

DOMINION

The name given to those countries belonging to the BRITISH COMMONWEALTH which govern themselves and which accept the Queen as their sovereign and Head of State. These are the UNITED KINGDOM, AUSTRALIA, NEW ZEALAND,

Westminster passed in 1931. The Dominions have their own Parliaments and are allowed to be Members of the United Nations. Instead of exchanging Ambassadors with one another Members of the Commonwealth exchange High Commissioners who have just the same rights and privileges as AMBASSADORS.

DONATELLO (1386–1466)

Italian sculptor, born in Florence. He was the most distinguished sculptor in Italy in the 15th century and was greatly revered by MICHELANGELO. He was an apprentice of GHIBERTI, the designer of the famous doors of Florence Cathedral, and worked on the sculptural side of that building for some thirty years. Among his most outstanding works are *St. John Evangelist, St. George Killing the Dragon,* the mausoleum of Pope John XXIII and *David*. Donatello was the first to show the true range of sculpture in low relief.

DONIZETTI, Gaetano (1797–1848)

Italian opera composer, born at Bergamo. His work displays beautiful melody and humorous touches in the plot, though the tremendous speed at which he wrote produced inevitable faults. His outstanding works are *Don Pasquale, L'Elisir d'amore, La Fille du regiment,* and *Lucia di Lammermoor*, the last based on SCOTT's border country novel, *The Bride of Lammermoor*.

DONNE, John (1573–1631)

English poet, born in London. When Shakespeare's plays were winning popularity, Donne was a young man, studying in Lincoln's Inn, taking part in naval expeditions, and writing poems of fire and fantasy. These early poems, known as the *Songs and Sonnets,* are now regarded as the most passionate of Elizabethan lyrics. Donne later took up theology, and turned his natural cleverness to account by winning success in religious controversy and then, later, great popularity as a preacher. The last years of his life (he was Dean of St. Paul's after 1621) were devoted to dramatic public sermons and the writing of intense religious poetry.

DORÉ, Paul Gustave (1833–1883)
French artist, born in Strasbourg. He was a distinguished draughtsman and one of the most prolific illustrators of the 19th century. He illustrated many classics including Shakespeare and Cervantes. His drawings of the poor districts of London are moving and authentic records of that time.

DORMOUSE
This animal is about the size of a house-mouse, but is fawn in colour and has much hair on the tail. It is found in thickets and hedges, and fattens itself on nuts, beachmast and acorns before retiring for its winter sleep, which is spent in a compact nest of leaves, sometimes in earth. In the spring the female builds a nest for her young, usually in a bush.

DOSTOIEVSKI, Fyodor (1821–1881)
Russian novelist, born in Moscow he studied military engineering and then became an officer in the Russian army. Arrested in 1849 for belonging to a socialist society and exiled to Siberia for four years. On his return to Russia he was harassed by gambling debts and had to write furiously in order to pay them off. He also travelled widely, especially in Germany.

DRAKE Commander of the British Fleet who defeated the Spanish at Gravelines in 1588.

His novels, of which the most notable are *Crime and Punishment* (1866), *The Idiot* (1869) and *The Brothers Karamazov* (1880), are all written in a fast, vigorous style. They are inspired by a mystical sympathy with the poor and express deep religious belief.

DOUGLAS-HOME, Sir Alexander Frederick (1903———)
British Conservative statesman, educated at Eton and Oxford. He entered Parliament in 1931, became Commonwealth Relations Secretary in 1955, and Foreign Secretary in 1960. There was some surprise in the country when he succeeded MACMILLAN as Prime Minister in 1963. He made history when he renounced his peerage and fought in a by-election for a seat in the House of Commons while he was still Prime Minister. He resigned the leadership of the Conservatives after their defeat in the 1964 General Election, and his successor, Edward Heath, was chosen by a new system of election within the party.

DOWLAND, John (1563–1626)
English lutanist and song-writer. He toured and worked abroad, associating with English Catholic friends whom he later denounced in order to restore his damaged reputation in England. Returning to England he produced the first volume of *Songes or Ayres of Foure Partes with Tableture for the Lute* (1597). The other two volumes appeared while he was in Denmark, but he returned to produce his *Lachrymae* in 1605, and became lutanist to Charles I in 1625.

DOYLE, Sir Arthur Conan (1859–1930)
British author. He was trained in medicine, but his poor income led him to writing, and he began on a series of stories about Sherlock Holmes, the master-detective, and his less observant companion, Dr. Watson, including *The Adventures of Sherlock Holmes*, and *The Memoirs of Sherlock Holmes*. He also wrote historical romances, scientific novels, *Rodney Stone*, a novel about boxing, and some works on spiritualism.

DRAKE, Sir Francis (1540–1596)
Elizabethan seaman, born in Devon. As a youth apprenticed to the sea. Between 1570 and 1573 he made three voyages to the West Indies during which he sacked Portobello and Vera Cruz, accumulating a considerable fortune. In 1577 he was the first Englishman to sail round the world. Queen Elizabeth knighted him in 1581 and four years later gave him command of a fleet with which he led many assaults on Spanish ships and Spanish coastal

towns. He defeated the Armada off Gravelines on its way to England (1588). He died at Portobello when on a voyage to the West Indies.

DREISER, Theodore (1871–1945)
American novelist, who carried on the tradition of austere realism associated with 19th-century authors like ZOLA. His novels include *Sister Carrie* and *Jennie Gerhart*, both of which were strongly criticized, and *An American Tragedy*.

DREYFUS, Captain Alfred (1859–1935)
French officer, falsely accused of espionage. He entered the army and rose to the rank of artillery captain attached to the General Staff. On the basis of a forged document he was arrested for selling military secrets to the German government and sent to Devil's Island (1894). Years of public agitation followed in which 'L'Affaire Dreyfus', as it came to be known, divided almost all France into those who fought to establish his innocence, and those who exploited French anti-jewish sentiment against Dreyfus. Emile ZOLA and Clemenceau were amongst Dreyfus's foremost supporters. He was pardoned in 1899, and declared innocent in 1906.

DRUIDS
Religious leaders of the Celtic people who were very powerful in Britain and Gaul before the

DUCCIO'S altarpiece *The Virgin and Child*.

Roman occupation. Julius Caesar wrote an account of the druids in his book *The Gallic Wars*. [*See* CELTS.]

DRYDEN, John (1631–1700)
Born at Aldwinkle. Ranked with Milton as Britain's greatest poet in the second half of the 17th century. From the time he settled in London on completion of his university course, he devoted himself to professional writing. The only play of his to be acted at all frequently today is *All for Love*, on the subject of Antony and Cleopatra. Of his poems, his satires are much read. They are: *Annus Mirabilis*; *Absalom and Achitophel*; *MacFlecknoe*; *Religio Laici* and *The Hind and the Panther*.

DUCCIO Di Buoninsegna (c. 1255–1319)
Italian painter, founder of the Sienese school. His religious paintings broke from the old tradition, and brought a new human appeal. His finest work is the double altar in Siena cathedral, completed in 1311. The citizens of Siena were so pleased and proud of the altar that they carried it to the cathedral in procession.

DUCHAMP, Marcel (1887–1968)
French artist. He has exerted a considerable influence on modern artists, especially in America where he has lived for many years. His most important painting is *Nude Descending a Staircase*, a work which caused an uproar when it was first shown in the Armoury Exhibition (U.S.A.) in 1913. For the past thirty years he has done little or no creative work.

DUCKBILLED PLATYPUS [*See* PLATYPUS]

DUCKS
Aquatic birds which belong to the same family (Anatidae) as the swans and geese. They usually have small heads, long necks, rather heavy bodies, short tails and short stout legs; each foot has three webbed toes and a hind toe. In the southern hemisphere both sexes have similar plumage, while in the northern hemisphere the males (drakes) are more brightly coloured. They feed mainly on aquatic plants which they obtain from the bottom of shallow water; diving ducks, however, feed on mussels, etc., for which they dive considerable depths.

DUCTLESS GLANDS
Ductless or endocrine glands of the HUMAN BODY are the glands of internal secretion. They secrete chemicals, pouring active substances (hormones) directly into the blood-stream instead of into ducts. These juices maintain

SCAUP

COMMON
SHELL DUCK

SHOVELLER

TUFTED DUCK

PINTAIL

GARGANEY

DUCKS

POCHARD

MALLARD

WIDGEON

EIDER DUCK

RED-BREASTED
MERGANSER

health, control growth and help the nervous system in its work. They also play a most important part in the make-up of every individual.

The main ductless glands, which are scattered about the body, are the thyroid and parathyroids; the pituitary; the adrenals; the ovaries and the testes.

The pancreas, the stomach and intestine are strictly speaking not ductless glands although they also secrete very important chemicals.

The pancreas, for instance, produces a digestive juice which it pours into the duodenum with which it is connected by a duct. Apart from this, however, it also produces the important hormone insulin, which prevents diabe'es.

The function of the ductless glands has been studied by experimental methods and it was found that removal or suppression of their secretion leads to definite physical and mental changes.

The thyroid, which lies in the neck, produces the hormone 'thyroxin' which is necessary to normal development and health. An inactive thyroid gravely affects growth and development in a child. An over-active thyroid, on the other hand, results in nervousness and over excitement.

The task of the parathyroid glands, which are attached to the thyroid, is to maintain the calcium in the blood at a steady level.

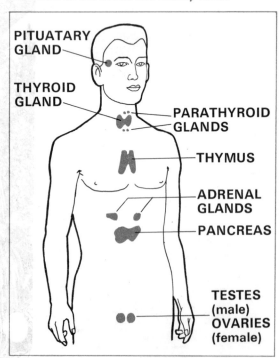

DUCTLESS GLANDS Their location in the body.

PITUATARY GLAND

THYROID GLAND

PARATHYROID GLANDS

THYMUS

ADRENAL GLANDS

PANCREAS

TESTES (male) OVARIES (female)

DYCK a portrait of Agostino Pallavicino

The tiny pituitary gland, situated at the base of the brain, is divided into two lobes. It produces more hormones than any other endocrine gland and, furthermore, controls the activity of all the other glands. The anterior lobe of the pituitary secretes a growth hormone and several other hormones, which act on the thyroid and the suprarenal glands. It also affects the sex glands, the female milk-secreting glands and one of its hormones raises the sugar content of the blood. A hormone produced in the posterior lobe acts on smooth muscles causing them to contract. Over-activity of the pituitary produces enormous growth (giants), under-activity produces dwarfism.

The hormones of the male and female sex glands are necessary for normal development of the sex organs, for reproduction and for the formation of normal personality.

The hormone adrenaline is produced by the two adrenal glands which sit on top of the kidneys.

DUFY, Raoul (1877–1953)
French painter. His paintings are freely realistic, brightly coloured and rather light-hearted. He favoured subjects like racecourses, regattas, seaside fronts––in fact, any subject with colour and movement. He was a notable book illustrator and designed fabrics and ceramics.

DUGONG
A large ungainly mammal which inhabits the Indian Ocean and Australian Seas. It is never found very far off shore and lives on seaweed. The dugong is very skilled in the use of its flippers, employing them not only to direct

food into its mouth and balance in the water, but, and this is interesting, to hold its baby to the breast to feed. It is thought that the dugong may account for the legends and tales about mermaids and sirens.

DUIKERS
Members of the ANTELOPE family and widely found in Central and Southern Africa. The name duiker, which comes from the Dutch and means 'diver', describes the behaviour of these antelopes who, when approached, dive or plunge into the undergrowth.

DUKAS, Paul (1865–1935)
French composer, born in Paris. Studied at the Paris Conservatory and was later a professor there. His most popular work is *The Sorcerer's Apprentice*--used by Walt Disney in his *Fantasia*. His considered masterpiece is *Ariadne and Bluebeard*, an opera on a work by Maurice MAETERLINCK.

DUMAS, Alexandre (1802–1870)
French novelist and dramatist. He wrote fast-moving adventure stories, set in historical backgrounds, of which the most famous are *The Three Musketeers, The Count of Monte Cristo* and *The Black Tulip*. His play *Henry III and his Court* marked the beginning of the era of romantic drama.

DUNS SCOTUS, John (*c.* 1265–1308)
Scottish medieval philosopher born in Roxburghshire. He wrote commentaries on the Bible and Aristotle, as well as works of logic, metaphysics and theology. He appears to have become a Franciscan monk and to have studied and lectured at Oxford and Paris. His skill in debate won him the title of Doctor Subtilis (the subtle doctor). His theological opponents were especially the followers of St. Thomas AQUINAS, who labelled Duns's supporters 'Duns's men' from which the modern word 'dunce' is derived.

DURER, Albrecht (1471–1528)
German painter and engraver. Born in Nuremburg and son of a goldsmith. Between 1494 and 1505 he produced a number of copper engravings, including *Adam and Eve, The Prodigal Son*, and *Nativity*, and the famous woodcuts for the *Apocalypse, Great Passion* and *Life of the Virgin*. In 1506 Durer visited Venice, where he painted the *Feast of the Rose Garlands* and *Christ Crucified*. From there he went to Bologna. On returning to Germany, he was appointed court-painter to the Emperor Maximilian. His copper engravings *The Knight, Melancolia,* and *St. Jerome in His Study* are regarded by many as the greatest of all copper engravings. Durer was the inventor of etching, and worked in wood, ivory, stone and metal. During his last years (1521–1528) he produced his famous painting *Unknown Man*, also *Madonna and Child with St. Anne* and *Virgin and Child*.

DVORAK, Antonin (1841–1904)
Czech composer. He began life helping his father in their butcher's business. Later, after a musical training at Prague, he was encouraged by BRAHMS. During his period as Director of the New York Conservatoire he composed his ever popular Ninth Symphony, *From the New World*. Other works include opera and chamber music.

DYCK, Sir Antony Van (1599–1641)
Dutch artist, born in Antwerp. He was an assistant to RUBENS and travelled widely, especially Italy and England. He settled in England in 1632 and was patronised by Charles I who gave him a knighthood. He was a prolific painter of portraits, some of his best works being those of Charles I mounted on a horse.

DURER Woodcut from the 'Life of the Virgin'.

Ee

EAGLES

Birds of prey which belong to the same family (Accipitridae) as the buzzards, kites, harriers, vultures and ospreys. The Golden Eagle chiefly inhabits mountainous regions, but is also found in forest areas. In the British Isles it is mainly confined to the Highlands of Scotland. The nest is large and built of sticks in a tree or ledge of a cliff. Two or three eggs are laid.

EARTH

One of the nine planets of the SOLAR SYSTEM. It revolves on its own axis, and moves round the sun in an orbit located between Mars and Venus. Its physical characteristics are: diameter at equator 7,926·5 miles; diameter at poles 7,900 miles; mean distance from sun 93,000,000 miles; weight or mass $5·87 \times 10^{21}$ tons; revolves on axis every 23 hrs. 56 mins.; revolves round sun every 365 days 6 hrs.; length of orbit round sun 584,000,000 miles; water surface 141,050,000 square miles; land surface 55,786,000 square miles; mean density 5·5 that of water.

EARTHQUAKE

A local shaking of the earth's crust, which may be violent enough to throw down tall buildings. Sometimes large cracks appear in the ground, and straight roads or railway tracks may be broken or forced into fantastic curves. Most earthquakes are caused by the slipping of the rocks deep underground, a very small movement being sufficient to cause great havoc.

ECHIDNA

An egg-laying mammal native to Australasia. Its body is covered with spines mingled with brownish grey hair. It averages about 18 inches. The echidna has a beak-like muzzle which it

EAGLES

IMPERIAL EAGLE

GOLDEN EAGLE

HARPY EAGLE

SHORT-TOED EAGLE

WHITE-TAILED or SEA EAGLE

uses to feed on ants and termites—it has no teeth. It is a nervous little creature which burrows rapidly into the earth at the slightest sign of danger with its powerful spade-like claws. It is also known as the 'spiny anteater'.

ECLIPSE

Phenomenon that takes place when the sun, moon, and earth are in direct line (*see* diagram). The eclipse of the sun viewed from the umbra is said to be total, and partial when viewed from the penumbra. The moon is eclipsed when the earth is in direct line between the sun and moon.

INCAS. The capital is Quito and the chief river the Upper Amazon. Ecuador owns the GALAPAGOS ISLANDS in the Pacific.

EDDINGTON, Sir Arthur Stanley (1882–1944)

Astronomer and mathematician. Born at Kendal of a Quaker family. He early showed brilliance in mathematics. In 1913 he became Plumian Professor of Astronomy, Cambridge. He did much to spread Einstein's ideas. His greatest work was concerned with the internal constitution of stars.

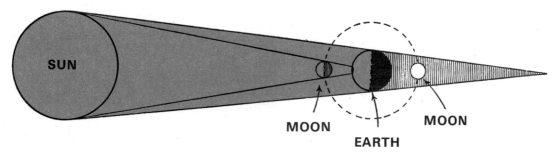

ECLIPSE The in-line positions of the earth, moon and sun during a 'total' eclipse.

ECOLOGY

The conditions under which plants and animals live (their environment) vary from place to place. Different kinds of plants and animals can more readily live and reproduce under certain conditions. The result is that animals and plants are found only in certain places.

For example, there are different groups of plants which live on seashores, in salt water, in fresh water, on sandy soil, and on chalky soil. Further, seashore plants of the tropics are different from those of temperate regions. Lastly, the modes of life of plants of one general environment are complementary. In an oak woodland, bluebells flower before the oaks put out their leaves and shade the ground. The same thing is observed in the animal kingdom; for example, the animals of the forest differ from those of the desert; animals of the highlands differ from those of the lowlands; shallow water fish differ from deep water fish; and so forth.

The study of plants and animals and their modes of life in relation to their environment and to one another is called ecology. 'Ecology' comes from the Greek word for 'house', so ecology is the study of plants in their homes.

ECUADOR

A republic on the Pacific coast of South America (225,000 square miles) about the size of France. It has a population of some 5 million, about a third of whom are descendants of the

EDDY, Mary Baker (1821–1910)

Founder of the Christian Science Movement. Originally a teacher she was dogged by ill-health and as normal medicine proved of little value she turned to faith healing and made a remarkable recovery. After this she and her husband devoted themselves to this method of healing. She wrote *Science and Health With Key to the Scriptures* (1875) and established the publishing house which still publishes *The Christian Science Monitor*.

EDEN, Sir Robert Anthony, Earl of Avon (1897——)

British politician. He was educated at Eton and Oxford. During the Great War he won the Military Cross. Entering Parliament in 1923 his first position was Parliamentary Under-Secretary to the Foreign Office (1931). Later he became Foreign Secretary (1935), but resigned when he disagreed with Neville CHAMBERLAIN'S appeasement policy (1938). He again became Foreign Secretary during the war and was Sir Winston CHURCHILL'S right-hand man in the War Cabinet. He lost office when the Conservatives were defeated in 1945 but with their victory in 1951 again became Foreign Secretary. On the retirement of Sir Winston Churchill he assumed the role of Prime Minister (1955). In 1956 he ordered British forces to occupy the Suez Canal Zone in order to protect British interests, but this action was condemned by the United Nations.

Eden resigned early in 1957 and was succeeded by Harold MACMILLAN.

EDINBURGH, Prince Philip, Duke of (1921——)

Consort of Queen Elizabeth II. The son of Prince Andrew of Greece, his early life was spent in exile and he was educated at various schools in Paris, Germany, England and Scotland. He joined the Royal Naval College at Dartmouth as cadet (1939) and served in the Navy throughout the war, rising to command two destroyers. He was also mentioned in despatches. In 1947 he became a British subject, changing his name from Prince Philip of Greece to that of Philip Mountbatten. In November that year he married the then Princess Elizabeth in Westminser Abbey and was created Duke of Edinburgh. He has shown interest in the promotion of British technology, in the advance of science, and in finding interesting and healthy pursuits for young people to follow.

EDISON, Thomas Alva (1847–1931)

American scientist and inventor, born at Milan, Ohio. Although Edison's interests were very wide his greatest contributions to applied science are: the carbon filament electric lamp, the phonograph, and the development of the dynamo for the generation of power. Edison received no university training; in fact, other than the education he gained from his mother he was mainly self-taught. It is interesting to note that he was greatly influenced by Michael FARADAY whose background was not unlike his own.

EELS

These snake-like creatures are fresh- and salt-water fish and found almost all over the world. They have very tiny scales or none at all and vary in size from the common eel to the huge conger and moray eels which may grow up to 10 feet long. The common eel spawns in the Atlantic in a region near the Sargasso Sea. When the eggs hatch the young eels or 'elvers' make their way back across the ocean to rivers or streams or ponds, a distance of 3,000 miles.

The notorious 'electric eel' is in fact a relative of the catfish and not a true eel. It is toothless and swallows its food whole. Not very much is known about its habits. The average-sized electric eel has an electrical discharge of between 300–400 volts, enough to stun an adult man, and people have been known to be killed by the shock. They inhabit the rivers of South America.

EGYPT [*See* UNITED ARAB REPUBLIC]

EHRLICH, Paul (1854–1915)

German bacteriologist. Born in Silesia. Discovered 'Salvarsan', the cure for venereal disease. It is sometimes called compound '606', for it was the 606th compound tested. In 1908 he shared the Nobel Prize for Medicine.

EINSTEIN, Albert (1879–1955)

Born at Ulm, Germany, of German-Jewish parents. As a boy he showed no signs of outstanding intelligence. However, when he attended the Gymnasium at Munich he soon revealed an unusual grasp of mathematics. When his parents moved to Italy, Einstein attended a technical school at Zürich. Not

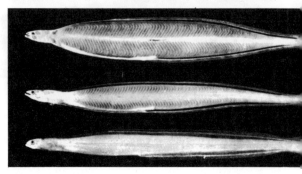

EEL This photograph shows three stages in the growth of a young eel or 'elver'.

being a Swiss citizen he could not continue his studies and became a private tutor. Later he entered the Swiss Patent Office, and it was while here that he published his two epoch-making papers, *The Special Theory of Relativity* (1905) and *The General Theory of Relativity* (1910). By 1919 his fame was established. He was appointed Director of the famous Kaiser Wilhelm Institute, Berlin. After Hitler seized power Einstein was forced to leave Germany and he accepted a post at the Institute of Advanced Studies at Princeton University (U.S.A.). His theories not only revolutionized our ideas of the universe, but made possible the development of atomic energy. Einstein was a kindly man who desired that science be used for man's betterment. He was also a fine violinist.

EIRE [*See* IRELAND]

EISENHOWER, Dwight David (1890–1969)

American President and military leader. Born in Texas of a humble family and brought up in Abilene, Kansas. After a variety of jobs he entered the military academy at West Point, leaving there in 1915. After serving in the Great War he became a staff officer in Washington and from 1933–1939 served with GENERAL

MACARTHUR as military adviser to the Philippines. In 1942 he was appointed United States Commander for the attack on French North Africa and in 1944 Supreme Commander of the Allied Expeditionary Forces. As such he led the Allied Armies to victory over Germany (1944–1945). After the war he was in turn Army Chief of Staff, President of Columbia University and Supreme Commander of the North Atlantic Treaty forces (1950). In 1952 he was elected Republican President of the U.S. and in 1956 was elected for a second term.

ELAND

Belongs to the family of ANTELOPES and has spirally twisted horns, like a gimlet. There are two species, the common eland and Lord Derby's eland, both are found in Africa.

ELECTRIC CURRENT

Electricity in motion. In the atoms of metallic substances there are a number of 'free' electrons (negatively charged particles) which wander in the spaces between the atoms of the metal. The electron movement is normally without any definite direction and cannot be detected. The connection of an electric battery produces an electric field in the metal and causes the free electrons to move or drift in one direction, and it is this electron drift which constitutes an electric current.

It must be noted that the electrons, being of negative polarity, are attracted to the positive terminal of the battery and so the actual direction of flow of electricity is from negative to positive, that is, opposite to the conventional direction usually adopted.

ELECTRIC MOTOR

A machine for converting electrical energy into mechanical energy.

In the electric generator, which is similar in construction to an electric motor, the coil generates power when moved through a magnetic field. Now, if an electric current is passed through the coil it creates its own magnetic field which reacts with the main magnetic field of the permanent magnets. The effect of this is an increase of the field on one side and a decrease on the opposite, the result being that the magnetic field pushes the coil round on its axis for half a revolution. If the current in the coil is reversed it moves a further half revolution thus completing one turn. In a motor the armature is so designed that the current is reversed in the coils every half revolution.

Electric motors have a wide variety of uses: compact motors drive small tools as well as fans, sewing machines, and so on; larger units drive machine tools, refrigerators, etc.; and the giants, developing 15,000 h.p. or more, are used for very heavy work.

ELECTROLYSIS

Process of splitting up a compound in a state of solution by the passage of an electric current through it. Pure water is a good electrical insulator, but when certain chemicals, common salt, sulphuric acid, sodium hydroxide, etc., are dissolved in it, the solution will conduct an electric current. The elements of the compound are normally held together by chemical affinity which is really an electric force, but when disolved in water it is split up into charged particles or ions. This splitting up into ions is known as dissociation, and the theory assumes that normally as many molecules of the compound are being reformed as are being split up.

When an electromotive force is supplied to two electrodes immersed in the solution (the electrolyte) the positive ions move to the negative electrode (the cathode) and the negative ions move to the positive electrode (the anode). The charges are neutralized at the electrodes and the particles are released to be deposited on the electrode or react chemically with whatever is present.

The process of electrolysis has many industrial applications. Aluminium is obtained cheaply from its ores (previous to the electrolysis method of extraction aluminium was a precious metal); copper is refined; electroplating is carried out; chlorine is obtained from sea water; and heavy water is prepared in bulk.

ELECTRO-MAGNET

Consists of a large number of turns of wire wound on a soft-iron core of high permeability. When an electric current is passed through the coil a strong magnetic field is formed. The disconnection of the current reduces the magnetic effect. Examples of the use of the electro-magnet are the lifting magnets fitted to cranes in steel foundries, magnetic clutches, and telephone and telegraph relays.

ELECTRO-MAGNETIC WAVES

Circuits carrying high-frequency oscillating currents radiate energy in the form of two inter-dependent fields, an electric one and a magnetic one, each field tending to maintain the other. The changing magnetic field giving rise to the electric field, and the changing electric field creating the magnetic field. The radiation is said to consist of electro-magnetic waves which travel through space at the speed of light, i.e., 186,284 miles per sec. or in metric units 299,796 million metres per sec.

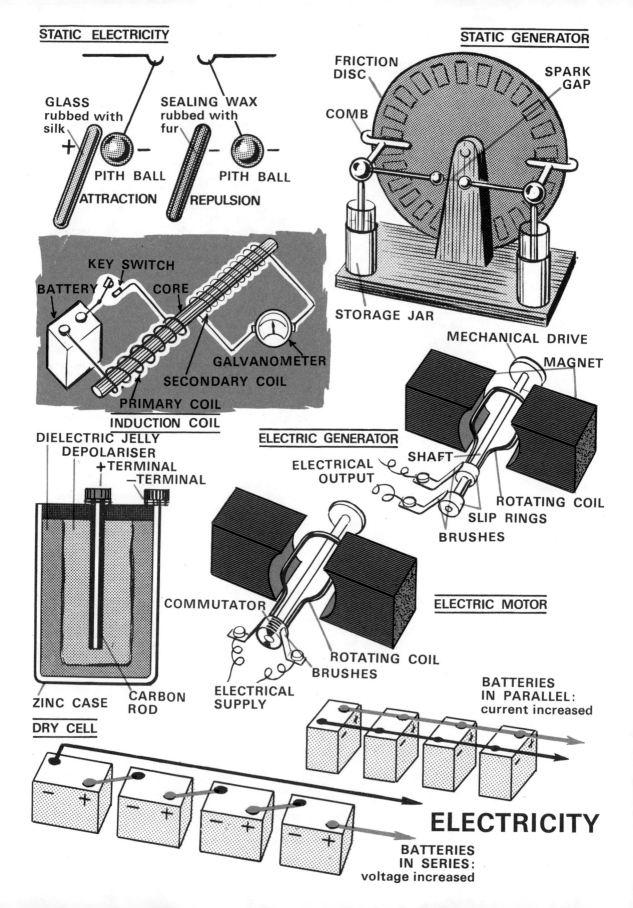

STATIC ELECTRICITY

GLASS rubbed with silk

SEALING WAX rubbed with fur

+   −   PITH BALL   ATTRACTION

−   +   PITH BALL   REPULSION

STATIC GENERATOR

FRICTION DISC

SPARK GAP

COMB

STORAGE JAR

KEY SWITCH

BATTERY   CORE

GALVANOMETER

SECONDARY COIL

PRIMARY COIL

INDUCTION COIL

MECHANICAL DRIVE

MAGNET

SHAFT

ELECTRIC GENERATOR

ELECTRICAL OUTPUT

ROTATING COIL

SLIP RINGS

BRUSHES

DIELECTRIC JELLY
DEPOLARISER
+TERMINAL
−TERMINAL

COMMUTATOR

ELECTRIC MOTOR

ROTATING COIL

BRUSHES

ELECTRICAL SUPPLY

ZINC CASE   CARBON ROD

DRY CELL

BATTERIES IN PARALLEL: current increased

ELECTRICITY

BATTERIES IN SERIES: voltage increased

MAXWELL, by means of applied mathematical methods, and on the basis of the experimental work carried out by FARADAY (who earlier had proved experimentally the relation between magnetic and electric phenomena), postulated the existence of electro-magnetic waves and that they were of the same nature as light, conversely that light waves were a form of electro-magnetic wave. Maxwell's purely mathematical theory was proved experimentally by Heinrich Hertz some eight years after Maxwell's death; these experiments formed the foundation of RADIO and TELEVISION technology.

ELECTRON
Fundamental particle of electricity and matter. It was discovered by Sir J. J. THOMSON in 1897. The electron carries a negative charge. Electrons exist in all atoms as planetary particles revolving around the nucleus. These planetary electrons can be ejected by heat, as in thermionic emission, by radiation, as in photo-electrical emission, by chemical action, and under the stress of high voltage, as in the cold-cathode discharge tube. Electrons can also be emitted from the nuclei of atoms, in which case they travel at high speed, and are known as beta particles. It has a mass of approximately $1/1840$ of that of a hydrogen atom, i.e., 1.673×10^{-24} gm. The charge on it is approximately 4.8×10^{-10} electrostatic units. [*See* NUCLEAR ENERGY.]

ELECTRONICS
Branch of electrical engineering which deals with the theory and practical application of the movement of electrons in space (in a vacuum or a gas) and such solids as selenium, galium and arsenide; the latter is a very recent development in electronics. It includes the study of RADIO, TELEVISION, RADAR, etc.

The first phase of this important branch of science extended from about 1870 to the early years of the present century. During this period scientists carried out the work which proved the existence of the electron and its electrical properties, outstanding were Sir William CROOKES and Sir J. J. THOMSON. The electron itself was named (1881) by G. Johnstone Stoney, an Irish scientist. The most far-reaching discovery of this period was made by T. A. EDISON and since called the 'Edison effect'. While experimenting with an incandescent electric lamp, Edison noted that an electric current passed from the filament to a metallic conductor he had put in the glass bulb, and flowed in *one* direction only. This was put to practical use by Sir J. A. FLEMING in his valve to detect wireless waves (1905)

The second phase, from about 1905 to 1935,

saw the rapid development of radio and wireless telegraphy. The most important discovery being Lee de Forest's triode valve (1907).

The third and present phase saw the growth of electronics in almost every field of human activity; home, office, field, factory, hospital, education and entertainment.

ELECTRON MICROSCOPE
A type of MICROSCOPE in which the specimen is illuminated by electrons focused by means of specially shaped magnetic fields. The electrons serve the same purpose as light in the ordinary optical microscope, but are employed because, when considered as waves, they have a very much smaller wavelength than light and can, consequently, be used to observe specimens very much smaller than could be observed with light, for example, viruses and large molecules. The electron image cannot be directly seen by the eye, but is made visible by means of a fluorescent screen similar to that used in television receivers. Photographs are obtained by allowing the electrons to fall on to a photographic plate.

ELECTROPHORUS
Simple piece of apparatus used in the laboratory to obtain a number of charges of static electricity from a single initial charge. It consists of a thick ebonite disc held in a brass sole, and a brass

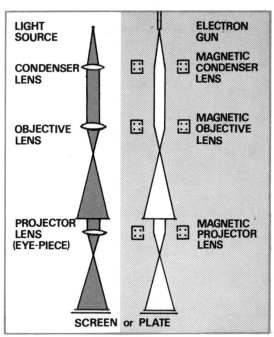

ELECTRON MICROSCOPE This diagram compares the lens system of an ordinary optical microscope with an electron microscope.

disc with insulated handle. The ebonite disc is charged by rubbing with fur and the metal disc is brought near and allowed to pick up an induced charge which can be lifted and conveyed where required.

ELECTRO-PLATING

Process of depositing by electrical means one metal upon another. An electric current is arranged to flow from immersed plates (the anodes) to the object to be plated through a metallic solution (the electrolyte). The anodes are of the same metal as that in the electrolyte and are slowly dissolved into it. The metal ions are attracted to the objects being plated and there give up their electric charges and deposit themselves on the surface. Silver, nickel, copper and zinc are the metals most commonly used in this process.

ELECTROSCOPE

Instrument used to detect the presence of electric charges. It is based on the fact that like charges repel each other, that is, in the case of a charged body being brought in contact with the instrument the gold leaves will part owing to the repulsion of like charges on them.

ELEPHANT

This animal differs from all other land animals in size, and in the lengthening of the nose and upper lip to form a trunk. There are two species, the Indian or Asiatic elephant and the African elephant. The Indian species has a bulging forehead, rather small ears, and the tip of its trunk has a finger-like lobe which closes down on the lower lip. The African species has a rounded, sloping forehead, large flapping ears, and the end of the trunk is formed like two lips. The most important difference, however, lies in the teeth, which are much more complicated in the Indian elephant. A bull elephant measures up to about $10\frac{1}{2}$ feet and weighs between 6,000 and 8,000 pounds. Both kinds of elephants live in herds, and feed on the foliage of trees, grass, canes, fruit, bark, tubers and the like. An elephant in captivity will drink up to fifty gallons of water per day.

ELGAR, Sir Edward (1857–1934)

English composer, born at Broadheath. He restored to English music the greatness it had lost since the death of Purcell, notably with his *Enigma Variations* (a set of musical portraits of his friends) and his oratorio *The Dream of Gerontius*. He also wrote two powerful symphonies, and two fine concertos for violin and cello. His motto for composers is worth remembering: 'There is plenty of music in the air all around us; all one has to do is to take some'. Elgar also wrote some popular music, the best-known piece being *Pomp and Circumstance*.

ELIOT, George, pen name of Mary Anne Evans (1819–1880)

English novelist. The daughter of a Warwickshire land-agent, she had a severe religious upbringing. As housekeeper after her mother's death she had found time for studying German, Italian and music, and for wide reading. She showed a talent for writing herself, became an editor on the *Westminster Review*, and in the literary circle which this opened to her she met G. H. Lewis, with whom she was to spend the greater part of her life.

She began her first story, the *Scenes of Clerical Life*, after a trip abroad with Lewis, and this was followed by *Adam Bede, The Mill on the Floss, Silas Marner, Middlemarch* and others, which leave us detailed images of the way of life in the Warwickshire countryside during the 19th century, and studies of characters that are humorous, profound and meticulously precise.

ELIOT, Thomas Stearns (1888–1965)

Born at St. Louis in the United States, and educated at Harvard. He fell in love with the culture of Europe, and, after further studies at Oxford and in Paris, settled in London. In 1927 he became a naturalized British subject. His best-known poem, *The Waste Land*, was published in 1922; his first full-length poetic play, *Murder in the Cathedral*, in 1935; and his very fashionable poetic play, *The Cocktail Party*, in 1950. In 1948 he was awarded both the Order of Merit (O.M.) and the Nobel Prize for Literature.

ELIZABETH I, Queen of England (1533–1603)

Last of the Tudor monarchs, and daughter of Henry VIII and Anne Boleyn. At the age of 25 she became Queen, after a period of imprisonment under her sister Mary. During Elizabeth's reign, the Church of England was established as an independent Protestant church, its doctrine based on the 39 Articles and its service on the Book of Common Prayer. Elizabeth aimed to make peace on all sides and to prevent foreign interference in English affairs, though she supported Protestants in France and Scotland. She kept Mary, Queen of Scots imprisoned for 19 years, but the numerous Catholic plots which centred on her eventually led to her execution (1587). The persecution of Catholics in England was one of the factors that annoyed Philip of Spain,

ELEPHANT The species shown above is an African elephant; note the very large ears.

whose great Armada was nevertheless defeated by a hastily summoned English fleet under Sir Francis DRAKE and others. Towards the end of her reign she began to have difficulty with Parliament, which had more inflated ideas about its powers than she had and quarrelled about royal expenditure. The vociferousness of the Puritans was also increasing. Though she had her favourites, notably Robert Dudley, Earl of Leicester, and Robert Devereux, Earl of ESSEX, she never married.

ELK
Also called a moose, is the largest of the deer family, and is found in the forested districts of North America, Asia and Europe, but is now very rare in Europe. It feeds on foliage, twigs, mosses and water plants. It is fond of the water and during hot weather stays in rivers and lakes for long periods.

EMBASSY
The home and office of an AMBASSADOR. An Embassy is regarded as part of the territory of the country represented by the Ambassador. This means, for instance, that a British policeman could not enter the French or American Embassy in London if he were chasing a burglar or other suspected criminal, any more than he could go to France or America to arrest him. What has to be done when a suspected criminal escapes to the embassy of a foreign country is to ask for what is called an order for EXTRADITION.

EMPEDOCLES (c. 495–435 B.C.)
Greek philosopher, born in Sicily. A great advocate of the experimental method in science. Argued that every idea should be tested. By this method was the first to show that air is a substance. Empedocles adopted the traditional theory that matter was composed of four elements, earth, air, fire and water. He accounted for the varieties of substances in the world by the forces of 'love' and 'hate'—attraction and repulsion—harmony and discord.

EMU
The national bird of Australia and the second largest bird on earth. It is flightless and an adult reaches a height of about 60 inches, the female being the larger. Emus are rather dull-coloured and live mainly in open grasslands in small flocks feeding on vegetable matter. The emu lays from seven to twelve eggs, but it is the male who sits them and cares for the young birds.

ENCLOSURES
The medieval system of agriculture was based on the open-field (divided into strips which were shared among the tenants for cultivation) and the common pasture where everyone grazed their animals. But from the middle ages to the 19th century, landlords sometimes withdrew the common land from their tenants and fenced it off for their own purposes, especially during the last years of the 18th century, when people discovered that enclosed land was more productive, for a proper rotation of crops could be used, and the land fertilized by grazing animals between crops. Enclosure caused the poor country people great suffering, for they were deprived of their means of livelihood. Bitterly they said:
> 'The law locks up the man or woman
> Who steals a goose from off the common;
> But leaves the greater villain loose
> Who steals the common from the goose.'

ENERGY
Capacity of a body to overcome resistance and do work. There are a number of forms of energy, e.g., kinetic energy of a body in motion; potential energy possessed by a body by virtue of its position, e.g., a coiled spring or body placed above the earth's surface; atomic energy or fission. [*See* WORK.]

ENGELS, Friedrich (1820–1895)
Co-founder with Karl MARX of scientific socialism. Born in Barmen (Prussia), son of rich textile manufacturer. Together with Karl Marx published *The Communist Manifesto* in 1848. Although a successful textile manufacturer he was all his life an active socialist, and supported Marx financially. He wrote a number of books, two of the best-known being *Scientific Socialism* and *The Origins of the Family*.

ENGLAND

The southern and larger part of the island of GREAT BRITAIN. Its nearest point to the Continent is Dover where the distance across the English Channel is 21 miles. Its greatest length is from Berwick, Northumberland, to the Lizard, Cornwall, which is 425 miles. In England more people are crowded into a small space than is the case almost anywhere else in Europe. There are rather more than 44 million people in England. Out of every hundred about eighty live and work in towns.

London, the chief city, is the third largest city in the world and with New York and Rotterdam is one of the three largest ports in the world. It has a population of more than 8 million. The River Thames, on which London stands, is the longest river in England and the most important. Birmingham, the second largest city, is the centre of the hardware industry and Manchester is the chief commercial city in the north. Liverpool and Southampton are two of the chief ports. [*See* GREAT BRITAIN.]

History :

Though a good deal is known about the CELTS who lived in England for several centuries before the birth of Christ, England's written history begins in 55 B.C. when Julius CAESAR tried to conquer the land. It was finally conquered by the Emperor Claudius in A.D. 85. The Roman occupation lasted till about A.D. 446. Soon afterwards Angles, Saxons and Jutes arrived from the continent and eventually conquered practically the whole of England; the Angles gave their name to England. In the 9th century Danish warriors invaded much of England, but King ALFRED managed to contain them in the north and west, and they were eventually assimilated into the English nation. While England had been divided into many kingdoms in the early 9th century—Northumbria, Mercia, East Anglia, Kent and Wessex—during the 10th century it became a unified Kingdom. In 1017, Canute the Dane conquered the country and became King.

In 1066 the Normans, under William the Conqueror, invaded England and set up a new dynasty, or line of kings. The Normans replaced the decentralized and variable Anglo-Saxon feudalism with their own highly centralized system, and degraded many Anglo-Saxon freemen to the dependent rank of 'villein'. Henry II and Richard I not only ruled England but also the greater part of France. John's loss of the French possessions, and his arbitrary behaviour caused by financial difficulties led to the signing of MAGNA CARTA.

About fifty years later PARLIAMENT began to develop. During the 14th century there began the Hundred Years War with France and soon afterwards there was civil war in England—the Wars of the Roses. During the reign of HENRY VIII the English Church for the first time became independent of Rome. During the reign of ELIZABETH I the beginnings of the British Empire were laid as the result of the discoveries made by British navigators. After the death of Elizabeth in 1603 the crowns of England and Scotland were united when the Scottish king became James I of England. During the reign of CHARLES I a serious quarrel arose between the King and Parliament and this led to a revolution under Oliver CROMWELL and the execution of the King. From 1649 to 1660 England was a republic called the Commonwealth. In 1707, during the reign of Queen Anne, England and SCOTLAND joined together with a single parliament. England led the world during the 19th century in the changes known as the INDUSTRIAL REVOLUTION. The stories of the First and Second World Wars are told under the heading WORLD WARS.

ENTOMOLOGY

The science of INSECTS in all their aspects, such as their evolution, distribution and classification. The class of insects belongs to the phylum of arthropods and falls into twenty orders, comprising among others the beetles, bugs, lice, dragonflies, moths, butterflies, and bees. The number of species of insects is enormous and nearly half a million are known, but it is estimated that there are about three million species of insect in existence.

ENVOY

Also known as a Minister Plenipotentiary, is a DIPLOMAT who ranks second after an AMBASSADOR. Countries which do not have much business with one another may decide to exchange Envoys instead of Ambassadors. The home and place of business of an Envoy is called a Legation.

EPIC

A long poem with an heroic subject or a subject of high importance to mankind. The two oldest works which have come down from the Greeks are epics: the *Iliad* and the *Odyssey* of Homer. The first tells of the war between Greeks and Trojans and the participation of the gods on behalf of their favourite heroes on either side. The second tells of the ten years of wandering which Odysseus the Greek suffered in returning home from Troy.

Every great language has its one or two epics. From Old English the epic which has come down to us is *Beowulf*. In our English of later

AMERICA/CANADA
The Niagara Falls are
divided by Goat Island
into two falls; the
American Falls seen
above (about 1,000 feet
wide and 165 feet high)
and the Canadian Falls
(about 2,500 feet wide)
and 160 feet high).

AMERICA
The Bryce Canyon in
the United States.
It is a magnificent
example of erosion by
sun, wind and rain
of sandstone.

ISRAEL
A view of
Jerusalem showing
in the foreground
'The Dome of
the Rock' in the
Kidron Valley.

SOUTH AFRICA
A village of
round thatched
huts near Durban.
The people who
live in these
villages work on
the nearby farms.

AUSTRALIA A view of Sydney showing the up-to-date docks. Sydney is the oldest and largest city in Australia.

AUSTRALIA A typical sheep farm in New South Wales. About 160 million sheep are reared every year on such farms and the wool is Australia's main export.

NEW ZEALAND Much of New Zealand's landscape is mountainous and in such regions sheep are reared and their wools and meat exported. The high peak is Mount Cook which rises to a height of 12,000 feet.

INDIA A village in the northern region of India. The crop growing near the village is barley. Such villages depend wholly on the success of their crops. Periods of drought can often mean starvation to such people.

England And Wales

times the two great epics are Spenser's incomplete *Faerie Queene,* which illustrated through knightly tales the virtues of the true gentleman, and Milton's *Paradise Lost,* which in order to 'justifie the wayes of God to men' tells the story of the Garden of Eden.

The word epic can also be used to describe novels, plays, or films which have a distinctively high historical theme. So Tolstoy's *War and Peace,* with Napoleon's invasion of Russia for its background, is sometimes called epic; and so are films like *Cleopatra,* which deal with the important events of history in great detail.

EPICURUS (341–270 B.C.)

Greek philosopher, born on the island of Samos. He opposed the teachings of the Platonists as mystical. Instead he insisted that knowledge of the world can be obtained only by studying the behaviour of matter. He taught that all natural phenomena can be explained by the motions of atoms, and that it was not necessary to refer to the 'gods', who were concerned only with the life of the soul. He also thought that pleasure was good, hence the word 'epicurean'.

EPSTEIN This modelled bust is typical of Epstein's strong, fluid sculpture.

EPIDIASCOPE

An optical instrument for projecting images on to a screen and similar to the ordinary lantern. Its particular use is for projecting on a screen such things as pages of a book, natural history specimens (beetles, moths, etc.); in fact, any suitably sized solid object. It can also project lantern slides.

EPIGRAM AND EPITAPH

An epigram is a short, witty and pithy piece of prose or verse, like 'It is a wise father that knows his own child', and

'Hope springs eternal in the human breast; Man never is, but always to be, blest.'

An epitaph is an inscription on a tombstone. Here is a famous one, which is to be seen in Elgin Cathedral:

'Here lie I, Martin Elginbrodde:
Have mercy on my soul, Lord God,
As I would do, were I Lord God
And Ye were Martin Elginbrodde.'

EPSTEIN, Sir Jacob (1880–1959)

American-born sculptor who lived in England from 1905 until his death. Born in New York, he moved to Paris (1902) and then to England. His early work was strongly influenced by the art of primitive peoples and was attacked and abused when exhibited—especially his sculpture *Rima* (1925). He will no doubt be remembered for his outstanding talent as a portrait modeller of such people as Einstein, Smuts, Churchill, and many other leading personalities.

ERASMUS, Desiderius (1466–1536)

Dutch scholar, born at Rotterdam. His writings on the Greek and Latin classics did much to stimulate interest in these fields. Although belonging to the order of Augustinian monks, he strongly criticized the out-of-date traditions of the Church and urged people to get closer to the BIBLE and early Christian teachings.

ERITREA [*See* ETHIOPIA]

EROSION

The surface of the earth is carved into hills, valleys, mountains, plains and other forms of scenery, and the general process by which this is done is called erosion. Erosion starts with the weathering of the rocks, and is carried on by ice, water, and even wind. Glaciers carve out U-shaped valleys in the rock. Rivers carve their valleys by washing away the loose soil and stones, and then using these as tools with which to grind out deeper valleys. They widen their valleys by wandering from side to side, and also remove a good deal of mineral matter dissolved in their water. Erosion by the sea takes place chiefly between low and high tide-levels, where the constant raking in and out of the beach pebbles wears a level platform on the rock beneath. In times of storm the sea beats against the cliffs, hurling stones at the rocks and forcing its way into narrow fissures and caves. In this way it may accomplish a great deal of destruction in a very short time,

EROSION The San Juan river (USA) has cut itself a channel 1200 feet below the level of the plain.

but even in calm weather it is always at work. When the waves approach the shore at an angle they remove the beach by rolling the pebbles along the shore, unless this is protected by 'groynes'.

Rain and frost help to break down the rocks, and the land surface is worn away by the action of rain, melting snow, ice and frost. In desert areas, the wind wears down the rocks by driving sand against them, and causes the sand-dunes to drift.

ESPERANTO

A language made up of about 2,600 common words drawn from important European languages and spelt phonetically. It was invented by Dr. Z. Zamenhof, and was intended to further communication between peoples of the world, but has not attained great popularity.

ESSEX, Robert Devereux, Second Earl of
(*c.* 1566–1601)
Elizabethan soldier and courtier, born in Herefordshire. He was educated at Cambridge and later took part in several expeditions against the Spaniards and Portuguese. He soon became a favourite of Queen ELIZABETH I, was appointed Master of Ordnance, Earl Marshal and Chancellor of Cambridge. He was sent to Ireland as Governor-General (1599), but when he failed to suppress the Irish rebels the Queen dismissed him from office and imprisoned him. He then entered into a plot to secure the dismissal of the Queen's advisers and raise London in revolt. For this he was accused of treason and executed.

ETHIOPIA

Formerly called Abyssinia, is in north-east Africa, and covers an area of about 400,000 square miles; that is, nearly twice as large as France. It has a population of nearly 22 million, most of whom are Christians belonging to the Coptic Church. There are also many Moslems and some pagans. The country is wild and mountainous. Ethiopia is principally an agricultural country, growing such crops as maize, cotton, coffee, fruits and tobacco, and breeding cattle. The chief river is the Blue Nile and the capital is Addis Ababa. The country is ruled by an Emperor. In 1936 Italy, under Mussolini, conquered Ethiopia and the Emperor, Haile Selassie, took refuge in England. In 1940 he returned to his country to fight on the side of the Allies and became Emperor again the following year. In 1952 Eritrea, which used to be an Italian colony, became federated to Ethiopia. This added to the country a new area of land nearly as big as England.

EUCLID (*c.* 365–275 B.C.)

Greek and may have been a pupil of ARISTOTLE. His work, the *Elements of Geometry*, laid down how geometry was to be taught for over two thousand years. How much of the books were original is difficult to say; they may have been the collected and edited work of his predecessors. Euclid also wrote books on astronomy, music and optics.

EUGENICS

Branch of science developed by Sir Francis Galton (1822–1911) and concerned with the physical and mental characteristics of men and women resulting from selective and non-selective breeding.

EUPHEMISM

This word comes from a Greek root meaning 'pleasant'. It means a pleasant word for an unpleasant or embarrassing thing. We use a euphemism when we wish to be polite. Thus we sometimes say of a fat man that he is 'stout', or 'putting on weight', or is 'getting a corporation'. So we often avoid the words *die* and *dead*; we say 'pass away' and 'at rest'. Euphemism is not to be confused with *euphuism*, which is the kind of artificial and flowery language used particularly by John Lyly (who lived in Shakespeare's time) in his book *Euphues*.

EURIPIDES (*c*. 480–406 B.C.)

Greek dramatist. Born at Phyla on the island of Salamis, he was at first probably intended to be a professional athlete and secondly a painter. But he soon took to writing for the stage. In 455 B.C. he exhibited his first tragedy and in 441 B.C. he won the drama prize. He achieved this feat another four times. He wrote about 90 plays in all but only 18 have survived. These include *Hecuba, Orestes,* and *Electra*.

EUROPE

The continent which forms the north-west part of the Old World. It is a little larger (1,903,000 square miles) than the United States, its greatest length from north to south being 2,400 miles, and its greatest breadth from east to west being 3,000 miles. It is separated from Asia by the Ural Mountains in Russia and by the Bosphorus at Istanbul, Turkey. There are about 500 million people living in Europe.

EUROPEAN ATOMIC ENERGY COMMUNITY (EURATOM)

An organization set up in 1957 as part of the EUROPEAN ECONOMIC COMMUNITY. Its purpose is to create a powerful industry for the peaceful use of atomic energy.

EUROPEAN ECONOMIC COMMUNITY

Better known as the Common Market, this organization was set up by a treaty signed in Rome in 1957 by France, Germany, Italy, the Netherlands, Belgium and Luxemburg. Discussions before this had taken place not only between these six countries but with seven others who eventually decided not to join but to form the EUROPEAN FREE TRADE ASSOCIATION. The Common Market countries are sometimes called 'The Six'. They are getting rid of trade barriers between their countries and each agrees not to make any special trade arrangements with other countries in whatever part of the world, except by agreement with their fellow members of the Community.

Before the Treaty of Rome was signed there had been set up the European Coal and Steel Community and it was later agreed that this and the EUROPEAN ATOMIC ENERGY COMMUNITY, as well as the Economic Community itself, should be ruled by the same Authority. This Authority is called the European Parliament. The Parliament leaves to a Council of Ministers the task of organizing the work of the Community. If the Members disagree over some legal matter they can refer it to the Court of Justice which the Community has set up. During 1965 and 1966 there was serious disagreement between France and the other Members of the Community which made it difficult for the Community to do its work satisfactorily.

EUROPEAN FREE TRADE ASSOCIATION (EFTA)

An association of seven European nations set up in 1959 to promote free trade amongst themselves. They are sometimes referred to as 'The Seven'. These States agreed gradually to get rid of tariffs on the industrial goods which they imported from one another so that by 1970 there would be no such tariffs. Each one is quite free to put tariffs on goods from countries which do not belong to the Association. The seven countries are the United Kingdom, Sweden, Austria, Denmark, Norway, Portugal and Switzerland. Finland became an associate member. All these countries had originally planned to join the EUROPEAN ECONOMIC COMMUNITY but could not agree with all the plans that were made, but many are re-applying for membership.

EVEREST, MOUNT

Highest mountain in the world, 29,028 feet in the Himalayas. After many attempts to climb it (dating back to 1921), it was successfully climbed by an expedition led by Colonel John Hunt. The flags of Britain, India, United Nations and Nepal (the country in which Everest is situated) were planted there by the New Zealand climber Mr. (now Sir) Edmund Hillary and the Sherpa guide Tiger Tensing,

EVEREST Tiger Tensing on the summit of Everest which he climbed with Sir E. Hillary.

just four days before the coronation of Queen Elizabeth II on June 2nd 1953.

EVOLUTION

A term used to describe the theory, held by the majority of scientists, to explain how the earth became peopled with such a great variety of plants and animals. The idea is not a new one and scientists centuries ago were already coming to this view, but it was Charles DARWIN who first put it on a scientific foundation. We may go further and say that it is only through this theory that we can explain the many puzzles and riddles presented by living organisms.

Modern science leads us to believe that life began on the earth about 1,500 million years ago, and that from the living matter then formed all the plants and animals now living, and all those that have ever lived and which we know only from their FOSSIL remains, have descended or evolved. It is not possible to prove this to everybody's satisfaction but all that we see or know points to its being correct.

The first great difficulty in proving the theory lies in the fact that all rocks more than 500 million years old contain no fossils or only the merest traces. So the record of what living things were like during a period of 1,000 million years has been lost for ever, largely because the changes that have taken place in those older rocks have destroyed any fossils there may have been. In the Cambrian rocks, as those 500 million years old have been called, as well as in those formed later, there are usually plenty of fossils, representing the remains of plants and animals now extinct. The only reasonable explanation of these fossils is in the beginning of time all plants and animals were of very simple form, and that as time went on they became more and more complicated. This the story of the rocks.

There are living today about two million different plants and animals known to science, and probably nearly half that number still to be discovered and named. Some are of microscopic size, others are large. The blue whale weighs up to 174 tons and the giant redwood trees stand up to 385 feet high. Some plants and animals live less than a day while the giant tortoise may live for 200 years, and the oldest living tree known is 4,900 years old. Some things live on land, others in the earth. Many live in the sea, from the shore down to a depth of six miles, others are found in fresh water, in streams, ponds, rivers and lakes. Some are simple, others are complicated. As we study this bewildering variety of things, living in different ways and in different places, often so dissimilar to look at and behaving in such different ways, one thing begins to strike us. This is, that there is similarity of pattern running through the whole of the plant and animal kingdoms. It is like a pattern on a carpet, now disappearing, now clear, but always there and making a whole if we have the patience to trace it.

Another striking thing is that the stuff of which all living things are made, the protoplasm as we call it, is essentially the same, whatever the plant or animal we are dealing with. So, in spite of the gaps in our knowledge, we have strong reason for believing that all plants and animals, whatever their size and shape, are related and form one large family.

The general view is that at some time in the dim and distant past, microscopic plant-animals, consisting of a single cell only, came into being. These were not only able to feed themselves but to reproduce themselves, probably by simply splitting in two. In the course of time changes began to appear in some of them which made them better fitted to overcome the difficulties of living. Those creatures in which such beneficial changes occurred would be the more likely to survive and to reproduce their kind. On the other hand, those less well fitted to life tended to die out.

This weeding out by natural circumstances is called natural selection. It can be best understood by what takes place when we breed rabbits. In every litter there will be some that are darker and some that are lighter than others. If we want all dark rabbits, we keep the dark ones and get rid of the rest. By this artificial

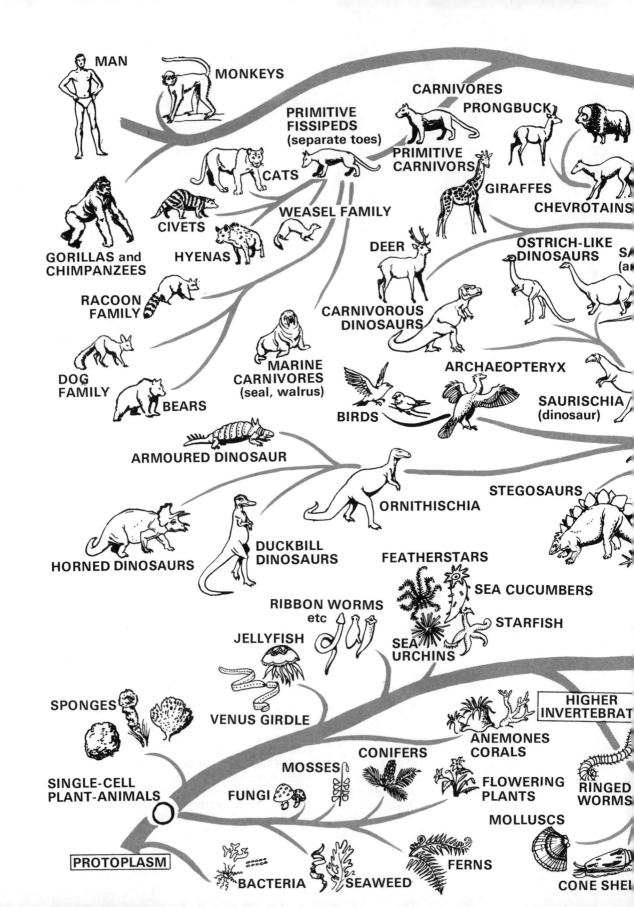

MAN

MONKEYS

CARNIVORES

PRONGBUCK

PRIMITIVE
FISSIPEDS
(separate toes)

PRIMITIVE
CARNIVORS

CATS

GIRAFFES

CHEVROTAINS

WEASEL FAMILY

CIVETS

HYENAS

DEER

OSTRICH-LIKE
DINOSAURS

GORILLAS and
CHIMPANZEES

RACOON
FAMILY

CARNIVOROUS
DINOSAURS

MARINE
CARNIVORES
(seal, walrus)

ARCHAEOPTERYX

DOG
FAMILY

BEARS

BIRDS

SAURISCHIA
(dinosaur)

ARMOURED DINOSAUR

STEGOSAURS

ORNITHISCHIA

DUCKBILL
DINOSAURS

FEATHERSTARS

HORNED DINOSAURS

SEA CUCUMBERS

RIBBON WORMS
etc

JELLYFISH

STARFISH

SEA
URCHINS

SPONGES

HIGHER
INVERTEBRAT

VENUS GIRDLE

ANEMONES
CORALS

CONIFERS

MOSSES

SINGLE-CELL
PLANT-ANIMALS

FUNGI

FLOWERING
PLANTS

RINGED
WORMS

MOLLUSCS

PROTOPLASM

FERNS

BACTERIA

SEAWEED

CONE SHEL

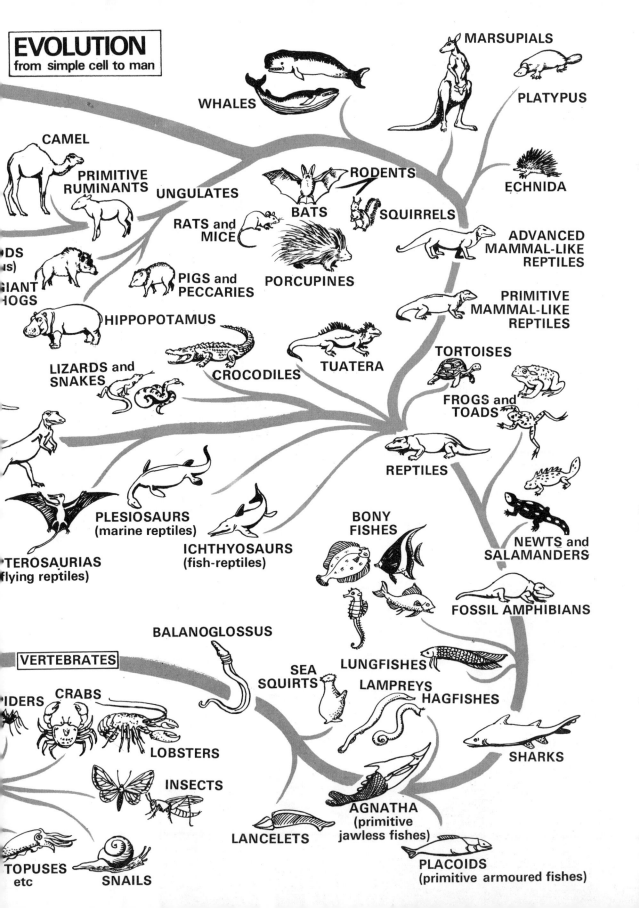

EVOLUTION
from simple cell to man

MARSUPIALS

PLATYPUS

WHALES

ECHNIDA

CAMEL

PRIMITIVE
RUMINANTS

UNGULATES

RODENTS

BATS

SQUIRRELS

ADVANCED
MAMMAL-LIKE
REPTILES

...DS
...s)

RATS and
MICE

...IANT
...OGS

PIGS and
PECCARIES

PORCUPINES

PRIMITIVE
MAMMAL-LIKE
REPTILES

HIPPOPOTAMUS

LIZARDS and
SNAKES

CROCODILES

TUATERA

TORTOISES

FROGS and
TOADS

REPTILES

PLESIOSAURS
(marine reptiles)

ICHTHYOSAURS
(fish-reptiles)

BONY
FISHES

NEWTS and
SALAMANDERS

...TEROSAURIAS
(flying reptiles)

FOSSIL AMPHIBIANS

BALANOGLOSSUS

VERTEBRATES

SEA
SQUIRTS

LUNGFISHES

LAMPREYS
HAGFISHES

...IDERS

CRABS

LOBSTERS

SHARKS

INSECTS

AGNATHA
(primitive
jawless fishes)

LANCELETS

...TOPUSES
etc

SNAILS

PLACOIDS
(primitive armoured fishes)

selection, it is possible to breed darker and darker rabbits or to breed for long ears, long fur, or any other character. All our domestic varieties of animals have been bred, or selected in this way, and it is assumed that something of this sort happens under natural conditions. For example, in a litter of wild rabbits there may be an occasional light-coloured or even white baby, or a dark or nearly black one. A white or a black rabbit shows up very clearly in a field, more clearly than the sandy-coloured rabbits, and they are much more likely to be seen and killed by buzzards or other enemies. So there is a natural selection in favour of sandy-coloured rabbits.

This is but a simple instance. Others are not so easy to explain in a few words, but the same rules apply. In every family the young ones differ slightly from each other. They are said to vary. Some of these variations will hold an advantage in the struggle to live, others a disadvantage and those having them are less likely to survive and have families of their own.

The first obvious objection to this idea, that evolution has taken place by a natural selection acting upon small variations, is that it would take a long time. But 1,500 million years is a long time, so long that it is very difficult to imagine: the lifetime of a man as compared with 1,500 million years is as a camera exposure $\frac{1}{15}$ thousandth of a second compared with twenty-four hours.

In judging the speed at which evolution has taken place, however, we must reckon with something else, that is the sudden changes which take place and which are called mutations. This was first discovered by a Dutch botanist named de Vries. He noticed that certain seeds of the evening primrose grew into plants that were sufficiently like the parent plant to show where they came from and yet were markedly different. A sudden change had taken place overnight, so to speak.

There are many gaps in the story of evolution, but sufficient is known to justify our accepting it as a theory. It is the only theory by which we can explain satisfactorily all the curious things we see in the world.

EXTRADITION

The handing over of a person accused of a crime, who has fled to another country, to the Government of the country where the crime was committed. This procedure is necessary because policemen cannot follow criminals to foreign countries. It is the duty of the police in the country to which the criminal has gone to arrest him and, if there is an extradition order, to hand him over to the police of the other country. If a person has broken a law because to obey would be against his conscience then most countries, like our own, would refuse to extradite him because he would be regarded as a refugee from oppression and not as a law-breaking criminal.

EYCK, Hubert Van (*c.* 1370–1426) and **Jan Van** (*c.* 1390–1441)

Brothers, and founders of the Flemish school of painting. The 24-panel altarpiece, known as *The Adoration of the Lamb* in Ghent Cathedral, is their masterpiece, though it is not known which parts each painted. Jan van Eyck is believed to have painted the portrait of *Arnolfini and his Wife*, and the picture called *Man in a Red Turban*, both of which are in the National Gallery, London.

EYCK A section of Jan Van Eyck's famous painting of *Arnolfini and his wife*.

Ff

FAHRENHEIT, G. D. (1686–1736)
German scientist, born in Danzig, and served his apprenticeship at Amsterdam where his important work was done. He devised his thermometer scale with the temperature of a freezing-mixture of ice and salt as 0° and human blood-heat as 100°. This made the boiling point of water 212°, and after this had been accepted careful measurement showed that blood-heat is really 98·4°. He also devised the modern type of hydrometer, a device for determining specific gravity of fluids.

FAIR ISLE
A small rocky island, midway between Shetland and Orkney, Scotland. It is famous for its brightly patterned knitted goods, such as jumpers and pullovers, that are made by the islanders.

FALCONS
These birds of prey are close relatives of the EAGLES and HAWKS. The best known of the true falcons is the 'peregrine' falcon used in the sport of falconry. There are a number of species of this bird and all have a compact body and long pointed wings of up to 3 feet wing spread. Falcons are vicious killers, swooping on their prey with amazing speed. They do not build a nest but lay their eggs in a scooped out shallow.

FALKLAND ISLANDS
A British Crown Colony in the South Atlantic made up of some hundred islands, the largest of which are East Falkland (2,610 square miles) and West Falkland (2,090 square miles). There are a little over 2,000 inhabitants who are of British origin. The chief town is Stanley. South Georgia, an island 800 miles to the south-east, is a dependency of the Falklands.

FALLA, Manuel de (1876–1946)
Spanish composer, born in Cadiz. Was a devoted student of Spanish folk music, his own compositions being greatly influenced by it. Among his most important compositions are *La Vida Breve* (a national opera), *The Three-cornered Hat* (first produced by DIAGHILEV), *Love the Magician* (a ballet) and *Nights in the Gardens of Spain* (for piano and orchestra).

FANTIN-LATOUR, Henri (1836–1904)
French painter, born at Grenoble. An accomplished portrait painter but painted a number of still lifes and flower pieces rather in the Dutch manner. Was greatly influenced by such romantics as WAGNER and painted some strange figure compositions.

FARADAY, Michael (1791–1867)
Born near London of very humble parents. At the age of 13, he was given the job of errand boy to a bookbinder. He made the most of this opportunity to read, and among books that particularly interested him were some on chemistry and electricity. One of the bookbinder's clients happened to give Michael,

FARADAY lecturing before the Royal Institution.

then 21, a ticket for some of DAVY's lectures at the Royal Institution. He was so fascinated by his glimpse into the world of science that he was emboldened to write and ask Davy for a job. Davy responded to the evident sincerity of Faraday's appeal, and young Faraday was taken on, at first in a very humble capacity, then, when Davy retired, Faraday became Director of the Royal Institution and held this post till ill health compelled him to retire. He was a born experimentalist. Considering his lack of mathematical training, his insight was astonishing. His first interest was chemical and he made many discoveries which in themselves would have made him famous. But it is his discovery of electro-magnetic induction that is so very important as it led directly to the electric generator and motor. The greatest honour in the scientific world, the Presidency of the Royal Society, was refused by Faraday.

FARÖE ISLANDS
Group of islands in the Atlantic and part of DENMARK. The total area of the islands is 540 square miles and the population 35,600. The capital is Thorshaven. The islanders have their own government (Lagting) and two representatives in the Danish Government (Folketing).

FAR EAST
A term used to describe the countries of CHINA, KOREA, JAPAN, BURMA and THAILAND.

FARNE ISLES
A group of small islands off the coast of Northumberland that are now a bird sanctuary. [See Grace DARLING.]

FAULKNER, William Harrison
(1897–1962)
Leading American author, whose complex novels show a very individual and concentrated style. The Sound and the Fury and Requiem for a Nun are both well-known. He was awarded a Nobel Prize for literature in 1949.

FAURÉ, Gabriel Urbain (1845–1924)
French composer, born in Parniers. Was a teacher of composition at the Paris Conservatory, among his pupils being RAVEL. He was a prolific composer in most fields of music. One of his most performed works is his Requiem, composed in 1887.

FAWKES, Guy (1570–1606)
English conspirator, and central figure in the Gunpowder Plot. He served with the Spanish forces in the Netherlands (1593–1604). Fawkes was a zealous Roman Catholic and in 1604 became involved in a plot to blow up the Protestant King (James I), his ministers and Parliament, so that in the resulting chaos the Roman Catholics, headed by the plotters, could seize power. A vault under the House of Lords was stored with barrels of gunpowder, but an anonymous letter was received by Lord Monteagle which warned: 'Though there be no appearance of any stir, yet I say they shall receive a terrible blow this parliament, and yet they shall not see who hurts them.' On 4th November, 1605, Fawkes was discovered in the vault preparing for the explosion. He was executed in 1606.

FEDERAL and FEDERATION
Words used to describe a particular form of government. Some very large countries, like the United States, Canada, Australia and Brazil, prefer to let different parts of the country have their own parliaments or legis-latures and their own governments. There is, however, a central government which makes the laws and does the work which must apply to the whole of the country. The opposite to a federal state is a unitary one. This describes the form of government of the United Kingdom.

FEISAL I, King of Iraq (1885–1933)
Arab ruler. Born in Rahab, he became deputy in the Turkish Parliament (1913). During the Great War he took part in the Arab national movement against the Turks. Although appointed King of Syria (1920) he was deposed after only a few months' rule. However, he became a candidate for the vacant throne of Iraq and was elected King (1921). Later he negotiated Iraq's membership of the League of Nations and a Treaty of Alliance with Great Britain (1930). He died in Switzerland (1933) and was succeeded by his son, Ghazi.

FENCING
The origins of fencing are very ancient, for they go back to the time of the medieval tournaments when mounted knights fought each other with lances. Today, fencing is a very modern and athletic sport, though the language of fencing is French, as it has been for very many years. One of three weapons may be used—the foil, the épée or the sabre. The foil has a quadrangular, flexible blade, and valid hits are made with the point on the trunk only. Both men and women can use this weapon, but foilplay is subject to rather complex rules and conventions. The épée is the duelling sword, and has a large bell guard and a stiffer, triangular blade. A hit with the point is valid on any part of the opponent and, if both fencers are hit, priority is determined on time alone. Foil and épée competitions are judged with an electrical apparatus. The sabre has a flattened blade and hits may be made with the edge ('cuts') or the point anywhere above the waist. The use of the sabre is governed by similar rules as at foil. It is not as dangerous as it may sound, for the swordsman is well protected by his canvas jacket and breeches, and his mask and glove.

FERMAT, Pierre de (1601–1665)
French mathematician, born at Toulouse. One of the greatest mathematicians, he did much to prepare the way for co-ordinate geometry and the CALCULUS. His most important work was on the theory of numbers.

FERMI, Enrico (1901–1954)
Italian physicist, born in Rome. Most of Fermi's work was done in the field of NUCLEAR

ENERGY. As early as 1939 he was exploiting the possibilities of using controlled atomic energy. His greatest contribution was the designing of the first nuclear pile which came into operation at Chicago in 1942. He was awarded a Nobel Prize in 1938.

FEUDALISM

The general name given to the social systems that predominated in Western Europe in the middle ages, the main feature of which was that men held land from other men for their own use in return for certain services.

In Anglo-Saxon England, men often depended on a lord for protection and help, but they generally owned their own land and the

In return for their fiefs, vassals gave certain agreed services to their lords. For the free tenants, these would include: the duty to look after their lord's interests in all things; military service (the number of day's service required and the details of how the vassal was to be armed were specified in the contract); the obligation to attend his lord's court--important because courts were a source of profit in the middle ages; the duty to ransom his lord if he was taken captive; and the duty to advise his lord, which in the case of the barons meant attending the King's Council. The vassal recognized his dependence and obligation to his lord by the ceremony of paying him homage on his knees and taking an oath of fealty

FEUDALISM The killing of Wat Tyler who led a revolt against the excesses of the feudal lords. He was killed by the Lord Mayor of London after meeting Richard II to abolish serfdom.

services they gave in return were not very burdensome. But, with the coming of the Normans in 1066, a harsher kind of feudalism was introduced.

In theory, feudal society resembled a pyramid. At the top was the King, the head of state and the sole owner of land. Immediately below him were the tenants-in-chief or barons, who held large areas of land from him in which they held their own courts and from which they extracted their income. Below the tenants-in-chief came further strata of tenants, and at the bottom were the serfs who probably held their houses, beasts and farming implements of their lords as well as their land. In the feudal relationship, the superior is called the lord and his dependant a vassal, and the land the vassal holds of the lord is a fief.

(faithfulness). The burdens of the serfs were very heavy, and as well as having to grow their own food, they also had to help their lord regularly in his fields and give him extra help at seed-time and harvest-time.

Though we call it a system, feudalism allowed of great variety. The number of services to be rendered varied, and the burden on the serfs was less heavy in one manor than in another. When the Church held lands of a lord, it avoided many of the feudal services. It had its own courts, for example, and also, as it never died it never had to pay 'relief'--a sum of money which a vassal had to give to his lord in order to inherit his father's lands.

Feudalism disappeared gradually from the 12th century onwards. Men began to pay a sum of money to their lord with which he could hire a mercenary, instead of serving in battle themselves. A strong and centralized government began to send its judges and sheriffs into the shires and to collect taxes directly from the people within the domains of the great lords. The knights of the shire elected to Parliament showed that people other than the barons could help in government. Only the feudal tenure of land survived the middle ages, and was not formally abolished until 1660, though it had long been obsolescent.

FIELD, John (1782–1837)
Irish composer, born in Dublin. Was something of an infant prodigy, giving his first public piano recital at 9 years. He was highly regarded in his lifetime as a composer, especially for his piano concertos. He was the first to introduce the 'nocturne', a style taken over by CHOPIN.

FIELDING, Henry (1707–54)
English writer, born near Glastonbury. He has rightly been described as the 'father of the English novel'. His greatest work is *Tom Jones* which also has been set as an opera by Vaughan Williams, and made into a film. His other novels are *Joseph Andrews, Jonathan Wild* and *Amelia*.

FIJI
A British Crown Colony that consists of a group of more than 300 islands in the South Pacific, of which 106 are inhabited. The population is nearly half a million, the people being of very mixed origins. The majority are Indian, the Fijians coming next. The capital is Suva on Viti Levu. Under a new constitution the Fijians have a good deal of self-government.

FINLAND
A republic in Northern Europe, rather more than half the size (130,165 square miles) of France and with a population of about $4\frac{1}{2}$ million. The Finnish language, which is called Suomi, is related to Hungarian and Estonian. The capital is Helsinki. Nearly three-quarters of the country is covered with forest and this fact makes Finland, apart from Russia, the chief timber producing country in Europe. The Aaland Islands in the Baltic Sea belong to Finland. [*See* SCANDINAVIA.]

FIRST-AID
The emergency treatment given in cases of accident or sudden illness and may be carried out by people with an adequate training before a doctor can be found. Training in first-aid includes a knowledge of the structure and working of the body. When a large blood vessel is severed a considerable loss of blood will take place unless immediate treatment is carried out. This loss of blood is known as a haemorrhage. Naturally this is not uncommon in serious accidents. The breaking of bones, known as fractures, also occurs in these circumstances. The efficient treatment of a fracture by someone trained in first-aid may make the setting of the bone much easier for the doctor to carry out. The accidental swallowing of poisons and drowning are examples of other emergencies in which the first-aid worker can be of great help in the saving of life.

FISHES
Marine animals which belong to the class *Pisces,* and are widely distributed in fresh and salt water. It is estimated that there are about 25,000 species.

The body of a fish consists of a head, trunk and tail. The boundary between head and trunk is marked by the position of the gills. The head bears the usual sense organs; mouth, nostrils (the sense of smell being highly developed in fishes), eyes and ears (there is no external ear, only an inner ear).

A fish swims by wagging its tail, that is, the muscular part of the body lying between the trunk and tail fin. The dorsal and anal fins act as keels to keep the fish on an even course. The pelvic fins assist in maintaining balance and act as bilge keels. The pectoral fins are sometimes used for swimming but generally serve for balancing and steering—they can also be used for stopping or slowing down.

A most important feature of this animal is its method of breathing. This it does by taking water into the mouth and passing it across the gills which absorb oxygen and pass it to the blood stream. At the same time carbon dioxide is given out. Incidentally, the water expelled from the gill-slits assists the forward motion of the fish.

The scales of fish are arranged like tiles on a roof. In some, such as eels, these are so small that they look more like a skin. In some fishes it is possible to tell age by the rings on the scales, rather as the age of a tree is estimated.

Many fishes, for example, the herring, spawn some 50,000 eggs each year. These sink to the bottom to lie on the sand and the parents take no further notice of them. Some fishes are more careful and build nests; the stickleback does. Others, like the skate, keep their eggs in a leather-like case. Again, some fishes retain their eggs inside the body for their early development so that the young are already formed when they enter the world. See illustration on pages 158–9.

FISHING FLEETS

Many hundreds of vessels ranging from small sailing smacks to large powerfully engined trawlers make up the fishing fleets which are engaged in the daily task of winning from the seas the vast quantity of fish which form so important a part of every nation's food supply.

The trawler uses a large trawl net which she lays down over the sea-bed and tows for a period. It is then hauled on board and the catch is emptied. The fish are sorted, cleaned, placed in ice and packed in boxes in the hold. The operation is repeated until a full load has been obtained. These voyages usually last from three to four weeks.

Another method is drift-net fishing. This is carried on by drifters who stream their nets to catch herring and mackerel. They drift for a period to allow the fish to swim into the meshes, then the catch is hauled on board and placed in the hold. They repeat the operation until loaded, when they make for their home port. As they are only at sea for a short while there is no sorting or cleaning necessary, so when the fish arrive they are unloaded, and cleaned at the docks.

Inshore fishing for prawns, shrimps, crabs, lobsters, oysters and other small fish is also carried on from the many ports around our coasts in small motor and sailing boats.

FITZGERALD, Francis Scott Key
(1896–1940)

Leading American novelist of the inter-war period. He reflects the spirit of the thirties in America, to which he gave the name of the 'jazz age', capturing the restless search for excitement, and the break-up in human relationships that this caused. The unfinished novel *The Last Tycoon* is a brilliant portrayal of the brashness and competitiveness of the Hollywood film industry. *The Great Gatsby, Tender is the Night* and *This Side of Paradise* are all widely read.

FIVES

This game dates from the 14th century at least, and is derived from the French *Jeu de Paume*. It was known in England at one time as 'hand-tennis'. There are two styles of fives recognized in Britain; that for the Eton game and that for the Rugby game. It is the latter which is described here.

The court is not unlike a SQUASH court. The main differences are that no precise dimensions are given for a fives court, and that no lines are drawn on the floor of the court. Otherwise, as in squash, the court consists of a 'front wall' (the wall the players normally face), a 'right-side wall', a 'left-side wall' and a 'back wall'. On the front wall a board is fastened horizontally at a height varying from 3 to $4\frac{1}{2}$ feet above the ground according to the heights and ages of the players.

Although the following description applies to the two-handed or single partners game, it should be understood that fives can be played by four people making two sets of two partners.

Fives is also like squash in the way it is played—the ball has to be hit up against the front wall above the board so that it bounces back, either direct or after bouncing against a side or the back wall, for one's opponent to play next. Instead of using a racket for striking the ball, only the hand and forearm may be used. It is best *not* to play the game without gloves. Although these have some disadvantages, the regulation gloves will be found quite

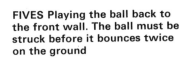
FIVES Playing the ball back to the front wall. The ball must be struck before it bounces twice on the ground

FISHES

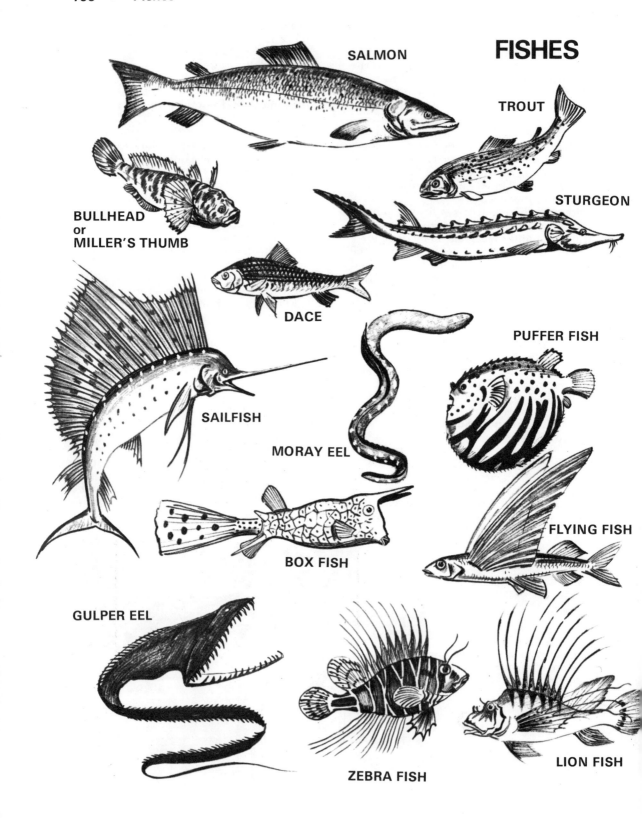

SALMON

TROUT

STURGEON

BULLHEAD
or
MILLER'S THUMB

DACE

PUFFER FISH

SAILFISH

MORAY EEL

BOX FISH

FLYING FISH

GULPER EEL

ZEBRA FISH

LION FISH

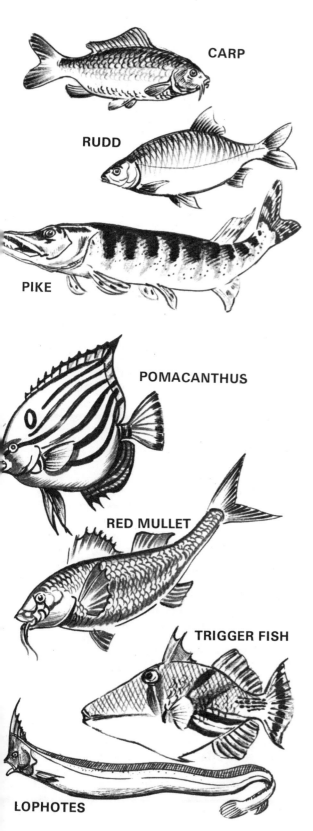

CARP

RUDD

PIKE

POMACANTHUS

RED MULLET

TRIGGER FISH

LOPHOTES

comfortable. Each player strikes the ball alternately, and the one who fails to strike it back to the front wall above the board loses a point. The ball must be struck before it bounces twice on the ground, of course.

The player who is serving has to strike the ball so that it hits the front wall above the board and then the side wall furthest from him before it bounces on the ground. The player who has to return the service must hit the ball so that it first hits the side wall from which the ball came, then the front wall above the board. After the service and its return, each player in turn strikes the ball on to the front wall, either directly or after it has hit a side or the back wall, and the rally goes on until one player fails to return the ball properly.

The player who returns service *must* strike the ball so that it first hits the side wall from which it came to him. If, instead of doing this, he returns the ball to the front wall or to the opposite side wall first, the return is known as a 'blackguard'. The server, who is next player after a blackguard, may refuse to play the ball, in which case he gains a point; or he may call out 'taken', and play the ball as though it had been returned properly, in which case he does not gain a point unless he wins the rally. If the server has only one point to make to win the game, he is not allowed to take a blackguard.

The game is begun by the two players playing a preliminary rally--the winner of this rally serves first. The thing to remember about scoring is that *only the server can score points,* and he goes on scoring them so long as he wins rallies. The moment he loses one, his opponent becomes server; and he in his turn scores only as long as he wins rallies. When he loses one, he also loses the service, which goes back to the first player.

A game is won by the player who first scores 15 points. But should it happen that the players make 14-all, then the game cannot be won unless one of the players wins two points in succession.

FIZEAU, A. H. L. (1819–1896)
French physicist, born in Paris. Made important advances in the field of optics and in 1849 successfully measured the speed of light by reflecting a beam of light through the teeth of a rotating cog.

FLAMINGOES
These elegant and colourful birds live in very large flocks in shallow reaches of water. The oddly-shaped bill is to·enable it to feed by sifting the food from mud on water bottoms. During this operation the bird's head is almost upside down. The flamingo lays a single egg

which both female and male take part in hatching. The nest is a simple nest mound of up to 18 inches high.

FLAMSTEED, John (1646–1719)

English astronomer, born near Derby. He was appointed 'Astronomical Observator'—now known as the 'Astronomer Royal'—in 1676. It was at this time that he began his great catalogue of the stars, which was his most important work and which occupied him until his death.

FLAUBERT, Gustave (1821–1880)

French novelist, who trained as a lawyer but preferred writing. He insisted that every word he wrote should be the most apt word available, and every phrase perfectly exact, which often meant that it took him a week to finish a page. He was a realist, that is, he aimed at a perfect representation of life in his works, and this aim was certainly achieved in his novel *Madame Bovary*.

FLECKER, James Elroy (1884–1915)

English poet, born in London. He not only loved the Near East but really knew it from working there, and understood the character of its peoples as few Englishmen have done. Suffering from tuberculosis, he eventually had to retire from his Consular post in the Levant to Switzerland, where he died. He left a number of poems and two plays, one of which, *Hassan*, is a wonderful re-arrangement of certain great Arabic legends as a modern drama.

FLEMING, Sir Alexander (1881–1955)

Born at Loudoun in Ayrshire. When he was 8 years old he had to walk 4 miles to school. At the age of 11, he went to Kilmarnock Academy,

FLEMING He isolated penicillin in 1938 and shared a Nobel Prize for Medicine in 1945.

then at 13 he joined his brother, a doctor, in London. Fleming continued his education at the Regent Street Polytechnic. He showed no particular aptitude for science and left the 'Poly' to become a clerk in a shipping office. Then when he was 20, he was left a small legacy and he decided to take up medicine. He became a student at St. Mary's Hospital where he remained. His great discovery is the isolation and cultivation of the mould *Penicillium notatum*. This was in 1938. A few years later, the search for the active factor was taken up at Oxford. Two other scientists shared with Fleming in the isolation of PENICILLIN—Dr. Florey, and Dr. Chain. All three shared the Nobel Prize for medicine in 1945.

FLEMING, Sir Ambrose (1849–1945)

Born at Lancaster. Fleming took his degree at University College, London, and later returned there to become Professor of Electrical Engineering. This was in the eighteen-eighties when EDISON and others were working on filament lamps. In 1904 he invented the thermionic valve—so called because electricity could only pass one way between the filament and a cylinder placed round it. He was made a F.R.S. in 1892 and knighted in 1929. [See ELECTRONICS.]

FLINT

A very hard black mineral with a white crust. It is deposited by water in chalk hills, and consists of a substance called silica derived from the skeletons of fossil sponges. Flints washed out of the chalk by rivers or the sea soon become rounded pebbles and usually turn brown.

FLOWERING PLANTS

These fall into two distinct classes, the Gymnosperms (plants with seeds not enclosed in an ovary), and Angiosperms (in which the seeds are enclosed in an ovary).

The Gymnosperms include pine, spruce, yew and juniper, all of which are conifers or cone-bearing plants. The cones are of two kinds, those which produce pollen and those which produce ovules. After pollination, the ovule-bearing cones grow larger and then dry up so as to shed the winged seeds. Conifers are important to us because they provide wood, resin and turpentine.

The Angiosperms are divided into 'monocotyledons' and 'dicotyledons', in which the embryos have one seed leaf and two seed leaves respectively. Another big difference between the two groups is the ability of the stems and roots of dicotyledons to increase in thickness by what is known as secondary growth, so as

INDIA *Above,* a village potter throwing water pots on a simple wheel. Making things in this craftsmanship way is a traditional feature of Indian village life. *Below*, a camel working a simple water wheel for the irrigation of crops. The Indian Government is making great efforts to replace these primitive methods with modern systems of irrigation.

JAPAN The terraces in the foreground are used
for growing oranges. On the plains such crops
as wheat and barley are grown.

MALAYA
A typical
village. A
third of the
world's rubber
is grown in
Malaya.

YUGOSLAVIA
The medieval walled town of Sveti Stefan. It is connected to the mainland by a narrow causeway.

ITALY
The Bridge of Sighs in Venice. The main canal in this city of canals is the Grand Canal, and branching from it are about 150 smaller canals.

SPAIN
A windmill on the island of Majorca, one of the Balearic Islands off the east coast of Spain.

BRITAIN
A view of London looking over Trafalgar Square to the River Thames. Centre left is St. Martins in the Fields and just below the National Gallery.

FORD Pioneer of the motor car in America

to form woody annuals, shrubs and trees.

The characteristic reproductive part of the Angiosperms is the flower, which is a special branch bearing floral leaves (perianth) sometimes composed of distinct petals and sepals, stamens, and one or more ovaries with stigmas for the reception of the pollen. Pollen is commonly transferred by wind or insects, and many flowers have special shapes, colour, nectaries, and scents which make them suitable for particular insects.

Useful plants belonging to the Monocotyledons are grasses (including fodder grasses such as rye grass; cereals such as wheat; bamboo; and sugar cane), palms, especially coconut and oil palms, plants of the ginger family, various bulbs grown for flowers, and bananas.

A great number of Dicotyledonous plants are useful. They yield timber, such as oak and mahogany, rubber, resins, gums, tannins, spices such as cinnamon, medicines such as senna, drugs such as morphine, fruits such as apples and oranges, vegetables such as potatoes, and beverages such as tea and coffee. [*See* BOTANY.]

FOCH, Ferdinand, Marshal of France (1851–1929)

French soldier. Born in Tarbes, the son of a lawyer and revenue official, he entered the army in 1870. By 1912 he had risen to become divisional General and Director of the Ecole de Guerre (School of War). During the Great War he took part in the battles of Ypres (1914 and 1915) and Vimy Ridge (1915). In March 1918 he became generalissimo of the Allied armies, and succeeded in driving the Germans back and winning the war.

FOLK MUSIC

The songs and dances of the common people of any country, composed in the distant past and never written down, only passed from father to son by ear, the names of the composers being forgotten. A typical example is the popular *Greensleeves*. With the spread of popular commercial music, these songs and dances began to die out and in the last 50 years a great effort has been made to preserve them by musicians who visit isolated country districts and take them down from people who can still remember and sing them. Many thousands have been collected by various people, especially in England by Cecil Sharp and in the Hebrides by Marjory Kennedy-Fraser.

FOOD

Supplies energy for the normal working of the HUMAN BODY. There are three types of food, namely fats, carbohydrates and proteins, and an adequate amount of each one is necessary for health. Fats are found specially in milk and butter, proteins in lean meat and cheese and carbohydrates in sugar, fruit and starchy foods. Most foods cannot be used by the body until they have been digested. After digestion the food materials pass in the blood stream to different parts of the body, where they are used by the body cells and blood.

FORD, Henry (1863–1947)

American automobile manufacturer of Irish extraction. Starting as a penniless mechanic's apprentice, he developed his interest in mechanics, produced a petrol-driven car in 1893, and founded the Ford Motor Company in 1903. Later he produced aircraft and tractors, became famous as a pacifist in the First World War—he tried to negotiate peace in Europe—and was known for the high wages he paid his employees.

FORD, John (1586–1639)

One of the numerous dramatists who wrote striking, if sometimes exaggeratedly violent, plays for the London stage in the generation after Shakespeare and Ben Jonson. He had a reputation for melancholy, celebrated in the couplet

'Deep in a dump John Ford was alone got,
   With folded arms and melancholy hat',

and the titles of his plays, such as *The Lover's Melancholy* and *The Broken Heart,* are in accord with that.

FORMOSA

Also known as Taiwan, is a mountainous island off the southern coast of China of 13,800 square

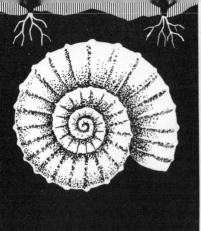  

FOSSILS Top: Water and chemicals act on the shell, replacing its particles with solid mineral. In time, the shell becomes a perfect replica in stone. Bottom: As the fish decays, it leaves a hole in the soil. After the ground has hardened, the hole fills with mud forming a 'cast'.

miles area, less than half the size of Scotland. The population is about 11½ millions, most of them Chinese. The capital is Taipeh. Formosa's main export is camphor. In the main the country is agricultural but has important fisheries. From 1895 to 1945 it was under Japanese rule. In 1945 Chinese forces, under CHIANG KAI-SHEK, occupied it. In 1949 Chiang Kai-Shek's army in China was defeated by the Communist forces and his army took refuge in Formosa where they have remained ever since.

FORSTER, Edward Morgan (1879–1970)
English novelist, educated at Tonbridge School and at Cambridge. He attacked the attitudes and way of life of the English middle-classes, as preserved in the Civil Service, the Church, and the Public Schools, and his books point the contrast between the conventional products of these institutions and the spontaneous and intelligent people whom he admired. *Howards End* and *A Passage to India* are two of his most successful books.

FOSSILS
The material signs of ancient life preserved in the rocks, and they may consist of the actual hard parts of the creatures themselves, or simply be impressions left by creatures which have since disappeared. The most common fossils are sea-shells and their impressions, but when the shells themselves are present they

are not in their original state. They have become 'fossilized' or altered in some way that has caused them to be preserved. Usually this is the replacement of their perishable materials by crystalline minerals, and this is done grain by grain (by percolating water) so that even the minutest details are preserved. Bones become fossilized in the same way, but with wood and other plant remains it often happens that all the substances of the fossil disappears except the carbon in it, and this needs no further preservation. Fossils may be found in limestones, clays, shales, and many other rocks, and can often be picked out of seaside cliffs. [*See* EVOLUTION and GEOLOGY.]

FOUCAULT, Jean B. L. (1819–1868)
French scientist, born in Paris. Made important contributions in several branches of physics. With H. FIZEAU made the first photograph (daguerrotype) in 1845. His best-known work was on demonstrating the rotation of the earth by means of a 200-feet long pendulum, suspended from the roof of the Panthéon, Paris. A similar pendulum can be seen in the Science Museum, London. He also made important advances in the GYROSCOPE.

FOUQUET, Jean (*c.* 1420–1482)
French painter, born at Tours. The leading French painter of the 15th century and court painter to Charles VIII from 1475. He was

especially famous for his portraits and miniatures, and designed some sculpture. One of his best-known works is *The Man with a Glass of Wine* in the Louvre.

FOX, Charles James (1749–1806)

Famous English statesman and orator, born in London. He first entered Parliament in 1769 and from 1775 was known as one of the leaders of the Whigs. He was Foreign Secretary in 1782 and again in 1806. Although he was not in favour of forcing the American Colonies to stay under English rule, and championed many liberal causes, including the French Revolution, Fox's sincerity became suspect due to his coalition with his former enemy Lord North in 1783, and his prospects for office were mined by his continual demand for the reduction of the political influence of the King. From 1784 he was the determined opponent of PITT in all but a few causes, and their verbal battles in Parliament became legendary. In 1806 he tried to negotiate peace with Napoleon. Only a few days before his death that same year he brought in a bill to abolish the slave trade.

FRAGONARD, Jean Honoré (1732–1806)

French painter. After studying in Italy from 1755 to 1761, he was admitted to the Royal Academy of Painting and Sculpture for his *Corésus and Callirhoé*. Afterwards he produced paintings of love and gaiety intended for the court of Louis XVI, including *The Swing,* now in the Wallace Collection, London.

FRANCE

A republic and the largest country (212,890 square miles) in Europe, except for the Soviet Union. It is one of the important countries of the world that are called the Great Powers. The country is three and a half times bigger than England and Wales. At its greatest length it is 600 miles and at its greatest width 540 miles. There are over 46 million people living in France. The capital is Paris on the River Seine. The French language is one of those described as a 'Romance' language. France is the second greatest wine-producing country in the world, and Burgundy and the area around Bordeaux contain the most sought-after wines. But France also has big cities and important industries, and during the years since the war there has been a rapid transition from an agricultural to an industrial economy. The chief industrial city is Lyons and the chief port, Marseilles, on the Mediterranean.

France formerly had a large Empire in Africa but these colonies and protectorates are now independent states. [*See* FRENCH COMMUNITY.] She also ruled a large area in south-east Asia known then as French Indo-China [*see* CAMBODIA, LAOS and VIETNAM]. Today France's overseas territories consist of islands in the West Indies and in the Atlantic and of French Guiana in South America.

History:

In Roman times the country we now know as France was called Gaul.

In the 5th century A.D. the country was conquered by barbarian tribes, and one of these tribes, the Franks, gave it its later name. CHARLEMAGNE ruled over France, Germany and Italy, and was crowned Holy Roman Emperor at Rome in 800. But, after his death, the Empire began to break up, and the power of the monarchy declined, until the country was ruled by great feudal lords who refused all obedience to the King. One of these lords was Henry Plantagenet, Henry II of England (1154–1189), who ruled more of France than the French King himself.

During the centuries which followed, France and England were often at war with one another. After one war the French king Philip IV, agreed that his daughter, Isabel, should marry the English prince who later became Edward II. Years later this marriage led to the Hundred Years War between England and France. This was because Edward III claimed in vain that he was the heir to the French throne through his mother, Isabel. It was during this war that there arose one of the greatest figures in French history, the Maid of Orleans, JOAN OF ARC. The English had won the battles of Crécy, Poitiers and Agincourt when she led the French forces to victory. The English were expelled from France in 1453.

During the next hundred years France was constantly at war. The troubles abroad were followed by religious quarrels at home. The extreme Catholic party, led by the Guises and Catherine de Medici, widow of the French king, Henry II, planned a massacre of the Protestants, or HUGUENOTS, on St. Bartholomew's Day, 1572. This was followed by civil war and in 1589 Henry of Navarre, who favoured the Huguenots, became King Henry IV. By the Edict of Nantes he allowed freedom of worship. His grandson, Louis XIV, during whose long reign there were constant wars with Holland and Spain, revoked the Edict and caused great numbers of Huguenots to flee to England and other countries, taking with them their industries and skills.

The harsh rule of the Bourbons and the aristocracy, which held back the growth of industry and trade, and the poverty of the peasants, caused the middle-classes and the peasants to rebel in 1789, and the period that we call the French Revolution began. The middle classes took over the government and abolished the monarchy in 1792, and King Louis XVI was guillotined in 1793. That year, England joined the war against the French Republic, though by 1797 France had become a dictatorship under NAPOLEON BONAPARTE, who eventually assumed the title of Emperor. Napoleon embarked on a campaign of conquest of Europe and although for a time successful, he was finally defeated at the Battle of Waterloo in 1815 and banished by the British to St. Helena.

It was not till 1870 that the Third Republic, the form of government under which France is still governed, was set up. This was at the time of the Franco-German War, in which Germany was victorious.

At the beginning of the 20th century Britain and France became better friends than at any previous period in their history, and an agreement between them, called the Entente Cordiale, was signed in 1904. When the First World War began in 1914, therefore, Britain and France were allies. They were allies, too, when the Second World War broke out in 1939. In 1940, in the face of German successes, the French army surrendered and a government which collaborated with the Germans was set up in Vichy under Marshal PÉTAIN. However, a French underground resistance movement was formed in France to help the allies and in Britain a French army force, under General DE GAULLE, was organized which fought with allied troops.

After the war France fought a bitter war in Indo-China which resulted in the end of her rule there. Later on she was involved in war in ALGERIA. It was during this war that General de Gaulle came to power in France in 1958. A new constitution, setting up what is called the Fifth Republic, was then agreed to which brought about important changes in the way France governs herself.

FRANCE, Anatole (1844–1924)
French author, born in Paris he was of very liberal mind and lent support to ZOLA's defence of DREYFUS. One of his most famous books is *Penguin Island*, a political satire. He was awarded a Nobel Prize for Literature in 1921.

FRANCHISE
The freedom to vote. In Great Britain everybody above the age of 21, with a few special exceptions, is allowed to vote. Each CONSTITUENCY keeps a list, called an electoral roll, of people who are allowed to vote in that constituency.

FRANCK, César Auguste (1822–1890)
French composer, born in Liége. Studied at the Paris Conservatory and later taught the organ. Composed much music, especially for the organ and orchestra, but is remembered mainly for his only symphony.

FRANCO, General Francisco (1892——)
Dictator of SPAIN. He rose to power during the Spanish Civil War (1936–1939) on the side of the Insurgents. Was closely associated with MUSSOLINI and HITLER at that time but did not openly align himself with the Axis Powers in the Second World War.

FRANKLIN, Benjamin (1706–1790)
American statesman, scientist and man of letters. He was born in Boston and started work in a printer's shop. Later he did a considerable amount of writing, and carried out scientific experiments. He became involved in politics, helped draft the Declaration of Independence (1776) and gained French support for the war against England. Later he negotiated the 1783 peace treaty, and helped frame the new constitution of the United States.

FRAUNHOFER, Joseph von (1787–1826)
German physicist, born at Straubing (Bavaria). Studied and explained the dark lines in the solar SPECTRUM and suggested as a result of his observations of the spectra of stars that they could be classified according to these lines. Also made important advances in optical instruments, especially the manufacture of lenses.

FRAZER, Sir James George (1854–1941)
Famous British scholar and anthropologist. He is especially known for his studies in the religion and magic of primitive peoples incorporated in his most famous book *The Golden Bough*.

FREDERICK II, The Great (1712–1786)
Born in Berlin and son of Frederick I, Frederick II of Prussia was a most enlightened ruler. He was an educated and scholarly man, preferring the French to the German way of life, and was a more civilized personality than his predecessors. Under his rule Prussia developed economically and industrially and much was done to improve the conditions of the peasants. The arts and sciences also flourished and the French influence which Frederick imposed did much to civilize the Prussian way of life. In addition he was a brilliant military leader and took a leading part in making Prussia one of the leading military powers in Europe.

FREUD The founder of 'psychoanalysis'.

FREE CHURCHES

Those Protestant Churches in England and Wales which are not established as is the Church of England. Members of such churches were formerly called 'dissenters' and are still frequently called 'non-conformists'—a term originally applied to those clergy who left the Church of England after the restoration of Charles II, rather than conform to the new Act of Uniformity.

The principal Free Churches are:

The Baptist Church which arose in England probably about 1612. Baptists hold generally to standard Protestant doctrine, but their principle of belief is *Believer's Baptism*; i.e., though Baptists 'dedicate' infants, they maintain that baptism should only be administered to someone old enough to realize what baptism stands for. Almost invariably, Baptists are baptized by complete immersion, minister and candidate standing about waist-high in water, in the Baptistry; the minister then dipping the candidate below water level for an instant.

The Congregational Church traces its origin to the Elizabethan reformer, Robert Browne, who founded a Protestant sect known as the Brownists. The name Congregationalist came into use during the Civil War period, when they were also known as 'Independents'. The outstanding Congregationalist principle is the complete independence of each separate congregation in all respects—including such matters as doctrine, discipline and membership. As an organization, the Congregational Church is purely a voluntary association of like-minded Christians; each local church being answerable, finally, to Christ alone. Women are eligible for the Congregational ministry.

The Methodist Church. 'The people called Methodists' owe their origin to a little group of Oxford undergraduates who collected around John WESLEY, and whose spiritual zeal and earnestness contrasted sharply with the religious apathy and indifference of their times. The name Methodist was first applied to them in 1729, because of the methodical way in which they carried out their programme of Scripture study, prayer, visiting the gaols, and educating slum children.

Mention should be made, too, of the Presbyterian Church of England, the Moravian Church, and the Countess of Huntingdon's Connexion. All the above-mentioned Churches associated in England in 1940 to form the Free Church Federal Council, which thus represents about seven million Free Church members in Britain. The principal Free Churches have important associated churches in Scotland and throughout the world.

FRENCH COMMUNITY

The name given to the association of States chiefly in Africa, that were formerly part of the French Empire and which on becoming independent, decided that they would like to work closely with France. It was set up in 1958 when General DE GAULLE first became President of FRANCE. Some of the countries have since ceased to be Members but they still have close trading links with France.

FREUD, Sigmund (1856–1939)

Austrian doctor who founded the science of PSYCHOANALYSIS. His work has not only been very important in the scientific study of the unconscious mind, but has had great influence in such fields as art, literature and education.

FRIENDLY SOCIETIES

Voluntary associations for the purpose of giving help to their members in times of distress, such as sickness or unemployment. Their work is much the same as that of an insurance company. Members pay regularly into a fund which is used to provide help.

There were friendly societies, called *collegia*, in the days of ancient Rome. In the Middle Ages the Craft Guilds organized funds for their fellow craftsmen if they were ill or they were too old to work. They also paid for the funerals of those who died. By the middle of the 17th century the guilds were no longer so active but it was at this time that a new type of friendly society was formed. This was called the General Sea Box and it was formed in 1643. A few years later another friendly society called the Landsman's Box was formed. The 'Box' was a big chest in which the funds were kept. The first writer to call these funds friendly societies was Daniel DEFOE, the author of *Robinson Crusoe*. He tried to encourage the formation of more such societies. These early societies were quite small and took the form of village clubs. It was Huguenot refugees who were largely responsible for their introduction to England, although they had been known in Scotland since 1555. The large nation-wide societies were not, however, formed in either country till the 19th century. Some of these big societies were called 'Orders', such as the Oddfellows, Forresters, and so on.

In order to make sure that Friendly Societies are conducted in a business-like way Acts of Parliament have been passed from time to time which lay down rules for their conduct and supervision, the earliest going back to 1829. The National Insurance Act when it came into force in 1948 made a great deal of difference to the Friendly Societies. For the Act provides benefits similar to those of the Friendly Societies. But although not so many people belong today as formerly many are glad of the extra help which the societies give them.

A special kind of friendly society is the Building Society which lends money to those who wish to buy or build a house. This is usually done by means of a mortgage and means that the society keeps the deeds of the house until the money that has been lent has been repaid with interest. The building societies get their money chiefly from the general public who buy shares, or deposit money, in them. All Friendly Societies must be registered with the Chief Registrar of Friendly Societies.

There are friendly societies and building societies in many other countries besides Britain.

FROBISHER, Sir Martin (1535–1594)
English seaman and explorer. He went in search of the North-West Passage, which was thought to lead to Cathay and India, commanding two expeditions with this purpose. In 1585 he was vice-admiral to Sir Francis Drake in his voyage to the West Indies. He was knighted for his action against the Spanish Armada.

FROEBEL, Friedrich Wilhelm August (1782–1852)
German educationalist who originated the 'kindergarten' system for teaching young children. A Froebel training is now one of the recognized qualifications for a teacher of young children and Froebel-trained teachers are found throughout the world.

FROISSART, Jean (c. 1333–c. 1405)
French chronicler. Born at Valenciennes, he became secretary and companion to various rulers, including Queen Philippa (the wife of Edward III of England), Edward the Black Prince, and various rulers in North Italy. He was present at the battles of Crécy and Poitiers and died at Chimay. His Chronicles are in four books and trace the main events in England, Scotland, Ireland, France, Flanders,

Rome and Spain from 1325 to 1400. They are the greatest of medieval histories and are most interesting for the deeds of chivalry that they vividly describe.

FROST, Robert (1875–1963)
American poet, born in San Francisco. The body of his work consists of realistic scenes of country life in New England. *Birches* and *Mending Wall* are two of his poems. He lived for some years in England and it was while there that he won recognition as an outstanding nature poet.

FRY, Christopher (1907——)
English dramatist. He began as a schoolmaster, but eventually worked full-time in the theatre. The remarkable thing about his plays is the use of free-verse. See his *The Lady's not for Burning,* and *Thor, with Angels.*

FUGUE
Musical composition for any instrument or combination of instruments. It is based entirely on one tune, which is played alone at the beginning and appears in various disguises during the progress of the music. Usually it is preceded by a piece of simpler character called a prelude or toccata. The greatest fugue composer of all time was J. S. BACH.

FULMAR
One of the most common sea birds of the northern hemisphere. The bird is nearly 20 inches long and is predominantly grey and white in colouring. They nest in colonies on sea cliffs and lay only one egg. Its main food is fish, but will eat any fatty substance which might come its way.

FULTON, Robert (1765–1815)
American inventor, born at Little Britain. Originally intended to be an artist, but abandoned this for engineering. He experimented with a number of designs—including a submarine—with the support of the English and French Governments. He returned in 1806 to America from Europe and built the paddle-steamer *Clermont* which plied between New York and Albany.

FUSELI, Henry (1741–1825)
Swiss artist, born in Zurich. Originally a clergyman but turned to art, studying in Berlin, London and later in Rome. Fuseli's work has great movement and extravagance, and was devoted to Shakespearean subjects. He was friend and mentor to William BLAKE. He was elected to the Royal Academy in 1790 and was its keeper from 1804 until his death.

Gg

GABOON

A republic on the Atlantic coast of West Africa that was formerly ruled by France. Although larger (101,400 square miles) than Great Britain it has a population of less than half a million. It is a Member of the FRENCH COMMUNITY.

GAINSBOROUGH, Thomas (1727–1788)

English painter, born at Sudbury. At the age of 14 he was apprenticed to a silversmith in London. In 1745 he returned to Sudbury and married, and from then on in Ipswich, Bath and London he achieved growing fame, until he became the rival of Sir Joshua REYNOLDS. He produced, in addition to his portraits, some of the finest landscapes, but these were little appreciated in his day. Gainsborough's works are famous for their elegance, delicacy and lightness. Among his best pictures are: *Perdita* (in the Wallace Collection, London), *The Blue Boy, Lady Innes, The Mall, The Morning Walk, The Market Cart.*

prolific writer; his medical works alone comprised 131 books. These dominated medicine for over twelve hundred years. They survived so long because, as in the case of ARISTOTLE, his views harmonized with the teaching of the church. Galen saw evidence of Divine providence in every detail of the body's working. His views, particularly in physiology, though far from correct, prevailed down to the time of HARVEY.

GALILEO (1564–1642)

Italian physicist, born at Pisa. Galileo was a born experimentalist and soon gave up his medical career to devote himself to mathematics and physics. But he was still a medical student of 18 when he made his first great discovery— a triumph of observation. During a service in the cathedral, he watched the swinging of a lamp suspended from the roof by a long chain, and discovered the value of the pendulum for the exact measurement of time. He had to time the swings with his pulse as watches had

GABOON A typical open market at Lebamba. Such markets are not only places where goods are bought and sold, but social centres for the women.

GALAPAGOS ISLANDS

A group of islands in the Pacific that is about 650 miles west of ECUADOR to which they belong. They are noted for the giant tortoises which live there and their name is taken from the Spanish word for tortoise. Charles DARWIN visited the islands to study the unusual animal life.

GALEN (A.D. 130–200)

Born in Asia Minor of Greek parents. After much wandering, he settled in Rome, where he became physician to the Emperor. He was a

not yet been invented. Galileo had not been a professor of mathematics long before he made his famous experiment of dropping weights from the top of the leaning tower of Pisa, to show that all bodies fall at an equal speed. This was a direct challenge to Aristotelian doctrine which asserted that the heavier the object, the faster it fell. Galileo went on to prove his point by further experiments. He made his university colleagues look ridiculous and unfortunately from this time on his very success made him many enemies. He almost anticipated NEWTON in his work on motion.

Thus he showed the path of a projectile such as a cannon ball was a parabola. He was interested in every branch of physics, and invented the first thermometer. It was what we would call an air thermometer. It is in astronomy, however, that his greatest discoveries were made. It was by chance that he heard of a new toy—a spy-glass from Holland. In Galileo's hands, this was perfected into the first TELE-SCOPE with a magnification of 30. With this new instrument he found that the surface of the moon was covered with craters and mountains, while the sun instead of being without a blemish, as taught hitherto, contained dark spots. He observed the moons of Jupiter revolving round their parent planet.

The enemies of Galileo charged him with heresy and he was brought before the Inquisition in 1615. His defence was brilliant but availed him little and to save his life he was forced to 'abandon and cease to teach his false, impious, and heretical opinions'. This was not the end of his studies, though deafness and blindness impeded his work.

GALLUP POLL

A system designed to gauge the state of public opinion, first used by Dr. George Gallup of the American Institute of Public Opinion in 1935. The idea is to question a fair sample of the population of a country or area about their opinions so as to discover what the people as a whole think. In Britain, gallup polls are used to predict the results of GENERAL ELECTIONS and BY-ELECTIONS.

GALSWORTHY, John (1867–1933)

English novelist, born at Combe, Surrey. Galsworthy's greatest work is *The Forsyte Saga*, one of the most outstanding novels of all time, and a useful record of the way of life of the class that ruled Britain before the Great War. He wrote a number of plays all of which were concerned with some social problem, for example, the conditions of convicts in *Escape* and anti-semitism in *Loyalties*.

GALVANI, Luigi (1737–1798)

Italian doctor, born at Bologna. Noted the movement of frogs' legs which led to the discovery of animal electricity and opened up important fields of research into electricity. His findings were published in his *De viribus electricitatis in motu musculari* in 1791.

GALVANOMETER

Instrument used for the detection and measurement of an electric current. It is essentially a laboratory instrument consisting of a magnetic needle and a coil of wire so arranged that the

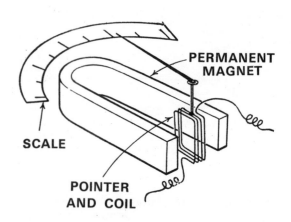

GALVANOMETER Diagram showing the principle and main parts of this measuring instrument.

needle is deflected when a current flows in the coil. A galvanometer can be used as a sensitive current detecting device only or as a measuring instrument, the angle of deflection of the needle being used to measure the current flowing.

GANDHI, 'Mahatma' (Great Soul) (1869–1948)

Indian national leader, born in Kathiawar, India. He was the son of a merchant, and became a lawyer, practising in India and South Africa. In 1919 he took over leadership of the Indian national movement for independence. He developed the methods of non-co-operation and non-violent civil disobedience. He also used the tactic of fasting in order to further his aims. He underwent several terms of imprisonment, but was eventually able to play a large part in the negotiations for Indian independence (1946–1947). He was assassinated in 1948 by an extreme nationalist Hindu who thought Gandhi had made too many concessions to the Moslems. [*See* INDIA.]

GANNET

Sea bird which looks somewhat like a large seagull—its length being about 3 feet. It has a milk-white plumage with a tinge of buff on head and neck and blackish wing tips. It breeds on the Atlantic coasts of Europe and North America. Gannets catch fish by 'dive-bombing' from about 200 feet. They nest in huge colonies and both parents take part in the incubation of the single white egg.

GARIBALDI, Giuseppe (1807–1882)

Italian patriot and liberator. Born in Nice, the son of a sailor, he had to flee from ITALY when involved in a revolt at Genoa (1834). He escaped to South America, where he engaged in various wars of liberation. He returned to Italy in 1848 but again had to flee when the national insurrection he led was a failure. He took refuge in New York. When war against the Austrians broke out, he was again in Italy. His most famous victory was the conquest of Sicily and Naples, which he then handed over to Victor Emmanuel as King of a united Italy. In 1862 and 1867 he was unsuccessful in capturing Rome from the Pope.

GARRICK, David (1717–1779)

English actor, born at Hereford, and studied classical languages under Samuel JOHNSON. He first appeared on the stage in 1741, and in the same year the theatre-going public deserted Covent Garden and Drury Lane to see him at Goodmans Fields playing *Richard III*. Later he became both actor and manager at Drury Lane. Garrick was probably the most versatile actor England has ever produced. He was buried in Westminster Abbey.

GASKELL, Elizabeth Cleghorn (1810–1865)

English novelist. She was the daughter of a Unitarian minister, and was brought up at Knutsford in Cheshire, which she idealized in *Cranford*. She married a Unitarian minister in Manchester, but when her child died in 1844 she looked to writing to distract her, and began *Mary Barton*. In this book she bravely criticized the lack of sympathy of the Manchester employers for the situation of their working people during the 'hungry forties', and the work became very popular, bringing her into contact with Dickens. Later novels included *Ruth* and *North and South*.

GANNET Famous for its 'dive bombing' tactics.

GAUGUIN, Paul (1848–1903)

French painter, born in Paris. Up to the age of 35 he was a successful business man, but gave this up to be a full-time painter. He was closely associated with Van GOGH with whom he lived at Arles. Gauguin's later life was spent in the South Seas where he did some of his greatest paintings. He died in the Marquesas Islands.

GAUSS, Karl Friedrich (1777–1855)

One of the three greatest mathematicians of all time, was born in Brunswick, Germany, and became known as the 'Prince of Mathematicians'. At the age of 19 he demonstrated for the first time that a circle can be divided into seventeen equal arcs by elementary geometry. In 1801 he published *Disquisitiones Arithmeticae* on the theory of numbers, and six years later became director and professor of astronomy at the Observatory at Göttingen. He formulated the method of least squares, devised a solution for binomial equations, proved the law of quadratic reciprocity, and founded the mathematical theory of electricity. The *gauss*, the electromagnetic unit of magnetic induction, is named after him. He carried out researches in astronomy, optics, magnetism, and electricity.

GAUTIER, Théophile (1811–1872)

French poet and novelist. Born at Tarbes in the Pyrénées, he was educated at Paris and at first intended to become a painter. But inspired by the French Romantic Movement he turned to poetry and the novel. He defied convention and used to wear a cherry-coloured waistcoat, green trousers, and a grey overcoat lined with green satin. He became one of the leaders of the school of 'art for art's sake', giving much more attention to style than to content.

GAY, John (1685–1732)

English dramatist, born at Barnstaple. One of the circle of friends around POPE and SWIFT in the early 18th century. A humorous and well-beloved figure, he won a special place for himself in English literature when he wrote *The Beggar's Opera*. It is said that Swift put into his head the idea of a comedy set in Newgate, a London prison. Gay worked with relish and the result was a play, or light opera, of a kind unknown before. In 1729 Gay wrote a sequel, *Polly*, which was, however, prohibited.

GAY-LUSSAC, Joseph Louis (1778–1850)

French scientist, born at St. Leonard. His important work was in the field of gases and one fundamental law of gases still bears his name. It states that when gases combine to form other gases they do so in the simplest proportions by volume, and the volume of the product is a simple fraction or multiple of the constituents.

GAZELLES

A group of small delicate ANTELOPES of Africa and South Asia. Their natural home is treeless plains and hot deserts, and their sandy brown hides make them inconspicuous in such surroundings. They are notable for their incredible speed and leaps. Gazelles have ringed horns which sweep back into a lyre shape.

GECKO

One of a large family of LIZARDS. Geckos live in trees, houses, in the ground and on the ground, and are insecting-eating reptiles active at night. Some—not all—have adhesive pads on their toes which enable them to run up and down walls and over ceilings. Geckos are tropical animals being very abundant in the Far East.

GEESE

These birds are waterfowl and related to DUCKS and swans. They were early domesticated by man as evidenced by the paintings and carvings of the ancient Egyptians and Romans. It is thought that geese pair for life and breed in nests on small islands or mounds. The female lays from four to six eggs which take about a month to hatch. (People should be warned that geese with a young brood can be very vicious if disturbed.) The best-known species of geese are the Greylag goose, Lesser Snow goose, Greater Snow goose, Canadian goose and Barnacle goose. The domestic goose has been bred from the Greylag goose.

GEIGER-MULLER COUNTER

Device for detecting and counting such fundamental particles as beta and alpha particles. In its simplest form it consists of a cylinder containing a wire electrode along its axis. A high voltage is applied across the gap from cylinder wall to wire. Some gas at low pressure is let into the cylinder before it is sealed. If a beta particle enters the cylinder it collides with gas molecules and releases many electrons, all of which move towards the wire because of the electric field created by the applied voltage. This movement constitutes an electric current. The resultant effect of one beta particle, therefore, is a surge of current. This can be made to operate a mechanical counter or light a lamp. The Geiger-Muller or, simply, the Geiger counter is probably the most widely used piece of apparatus in the physics of radiation and nuclear particles.

GEMSBOK

A member of the ANTELOPE family and belongs to the group called 'oryxes'. Its natural home is the African veld. The gemsbok is a greyish-brown creature with blackish stripes and long rapier-like horns which sweep back some 48 inches; the female has the larger horns. It is one of the swiftest animals.

GENERAL ELECTION

The term used to describe the election of a new House of Commons. Since 1911 it has been the rule to have a General Election at least every five years. It can be held more often. If a majority of M.P.s vote against the Government on an important matter the PRIME MINISTER may go to the Queen and offer his resignation and that of his government. Or if for some other reason the Government thinks the nation should have the chance to vote in an election without waiting for the end of five years the Prime Minister can ask the Queen to dissolve Parliament, but in that case neither the Prime Minister nor the Government resign before the result of the General Election is known. This would also be the case if the General Election was held because it had become due. If the Prime Minister has resigned because his Government has been defeated in the House of Commons the usual thing is for the Queen to send for the Leader of the Opposition and ask him to form a government. He will probably agree to do so but at the same time he will ask her to dissolve Parliament so that the nation has a chance to approve the new Government.

Today almost every adult above the age of 21 has the right to vote during a General Election. When the result of the election is

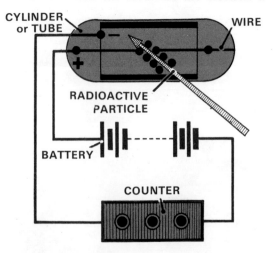

GEIGER-MULLER COUNTER An instrument for detecting and counting fundamental particles.

GENETICS

DIAGRAM OF ANIMAL CELL STRUCTURE labels:

- CYTOPLASM
- CHROMATIN NETWORK
- NUCLEUS
- NUCLEAR MEMBRANE
- NUCLEOLUS
- NUCLEO PLASM
- CENTROSOME
- VACUOLE

**DIAGRAM OF
ANIMAL CELL STRUCTURE**

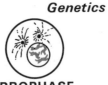

PROPHASE
Chromosomes thicken and split lengthwise: nuclear membrane disappears: spindle forms

METAPHASE
Chromosomes line up at equator

ANAPHASE
and migrate to spindle poles

TELOPHASE
Spindle disappears: cell body divides: nuclear membranes reform

INTERPHASE
Two fully formed daughter cells

STAGES IN MITOTIC CELL DIVISION

---

known the Queen sends for the leader of the party that has most seats in the new Parliament and asks him to become Prime Minister and to form a new Government. [*See* BALLOT.]

GENETICS

Science concerned with the study of the inborn properties and the inborn differences which determine heredity. Such studies are closely linked with relevant subjects, such as cytology, reproduction, breeding, etc. It is evident that the implications of genetics for evolution in general are of the greatest importance.

The physiological fundamentals of genetics are described under the heading BIOLOGY and are therefore only referred to here.

The united male and female germ cells which form the beginning of each individual, contain all the genetic material which controls the future individual animal or plant. The basis of every part of the future organism is found in the two germ cells which play equal roles in their hereditary influence.

The chromosomes (*q.v.*) in the nucleus of each germ cell consist of a number of rod-shaped bodies which differ from each other and are formed from genetic material, known as genes.

The genes, themselves the heritable factors, consist of nucleoproteins and are ultra-microscopic, but each chromosome is composed of many thousands of separable genetic elements, which are visible under the microscope.

When the male and female germ cells fuse, the chromosomes pair together, each pair carrying the same genes, arranged in identical order. The fertilized egg then undergoes a cell division, known as mitosis during which all chromosomes and therefore all genes are doubled. In consequence, new chromosomes are formed, bearing new strings of genes, visible as split chromosomes. In the continued cell division, two daughter cells with identical number of genes to the parent cell are formed. As the nucleus of each cell of the individual contains a double set of identical chromosomes and as the egg and sperm cell contain only half that amount of chromosomes, it is evident that a reduction of chromosomes must have taken place. This reduction or meiosis occurs during the formation of the ripe egg and its objective is evident; if a chromosome reduction would not take place, the progressive accumulation of chromosomes in following generations would completely fill the cells.

Present-day genetical theory assumes that differences which develop in individuals in a uniform environment are caused by different genes. Such differences arising by a sudden change of one or more genes are called 'mutations'. A mutated gene continues to be propagated in its changed state until a new mutation

GEOLOGICAL PERIODS

Period	Geographical Conditions	Plant Life	Animal Life
ARCHEOZOIC	Extensive mountain building —volcanic action.	Possibility of simple algae.	—
PRE-CAMBRIAN 1,125,000,000	Sedimentation—mountain building.	Sea-weeds.	Small jelly-fishes, sponges, polyps.
CAMBRIAN 450,000,000	Sinking sea floor. Sands and mud deposited in troughs. Warm water conditions Land of desert type.	Sea-weeds develop a calcareous (containing limestone) framework.	By end of Cambrian all main divisions of invertebrates existed in the seas, graptolites, trilobites, brachiopods, molluscs.
ORDOVICIAN 375,000,000	Land submergence. Volcanoes erupt on sea floor.	Calcareous sea-weeds.	Sponges, corals, sea-urchins, star-fishes, lingula, sea-snails, trilobites, branched graptolites.
SILURIAN 335,000,000	Troughs and depressions deepen — deposition keeps pace with subsidence. Warm climate.	The earliest known land plants appear in Australia — already well adapted.	Reef-building corals, crinoids, abundant brachiopods, shrimp-like crustaceans, sea-scorpions. First vertebrates (the fish-like Jaymoytius).
DEVONIAN 300,000,000	Earth movements cause rise of mountain ranges which are worn down to form the 'Old Red Sandstone'.	Late Devonian included ferns, horse-tails, and seed-ferns.	Rapid evolution of backboned animals— some fishes had lungs. Amphibia come into existence. Wingless insects.
CARBONIFEROUS 250,000,000	Widespread, clear, shallow seas. Warm seas and warm land climate.	Scale trees and seed ferns flourish in swamps. Formation of coal beds.	Abundant fauna of foraminifera, crinoids, brachiopods, molluscs. Fishes, especially sharks, abundant. Large insects, e.g., giant dragonflies.
PERMIAN 205,000,000	Lofty mountains, shrinking of inland seas. An 'Ice Age'.	Many groups become extinct. Conifers increase.	Sharks survive—great variety of reptiles, some mammal-like.
TRIASSIC 170,000,000	Largely desert with hot dry climate. More moist towards end of period.	Conifers, cycads and ferns develop.	Crustaceans, scorpions, long fish, large amphibians, land reptiles (some carnivorous), early mammals.
JURASSIC 135,000,000	Mountains now reduced to low hills. Seas spread over large areas.	Maidenhair trees, 'the age of cycads'.	Dragonflies, grasshoppers, termites, flies. Freshwater snails. First frogs and toads. Giant reptiles, e.g., dinosaur, flying pterodactyls, turtles. First true mammals.
CRETACEOUS 95,000,000	Seas transgressed widely over the land.	First flowering plants on land (similar to fig and magnolia).	Fish life modern in aspect. Dinosaurs dominated life on land. Mammals still inconspicuous. First marsupials.
PALEOCENE 80,000,000	Sea floors raised and chalk formations become land. Vast out-pourings of lava.	Herbaceous flowering plants and grasses.	Invertebrates now almost modern. Early whales and sea cows. Mammals attain dominance on land.
EOCENE 50,000,000	Basins of deposition, e.g., London and Paris basins.	Deciduous trees dominant.	All main groups of placental mammals are now found.
OLIGOCENE 42,000,000	Uplift more pronounced. Alps begin to develop.	Grasslands increase.	Insects of every type. Bats. Small elephants. A horselike animal.
MIOCENE 25,000,000	Himalayas, Andes, Rockies and Alps are formed.	Prairie grasses well established.	Wading birds. Rhinoceros, larger elephants. Primitive anthropoid apes.
PLIOCENE 8,000,000	Continents take present form.	Number of plants in Europe.	Man-like apes on up-grade, including the upright Australopithecus.
PLEISTOCENE 500,000	The Ice Age.	Many plants driven south.	Tool-making man, i.e., Pithecanthropus. Ancestors of domestic animals.
RECENT 50,000	Retreat of ice.	Cultivated plants.	Man (*Homo sapiens*).

may change it yet again. Organisms with such mutant genes (mutants) are used for breeding purposes. Direct genetical adaptation to environment (Lamarckism), previously believed in, has not been justified and it would now appear that inherited variations on the one side and external conditions on the other, select individuals which contain satisfactory combinations of genes.

A more frequent origin of variations than those caused by mutations, is the exchange of corresponding bits of chromosomes originating from the two parents in such a way that not all the genes of that chromosome need be transmitted. This process called 'crossing-over' during the egg and sperm formation ends in a recombination of genes in the same chromosome, thus giving rise to new variations.

It has been shown that each individual has two genes for each character, derived from the male and female germ cell respectively. The individual is called 'homozygous' if the two genes are alike; 'heterozygous', if one of the genes is a mutant gene, both then termed alleles.

In such cases the influence of one gene can be 'dominant' to the other or 'recessive', the latter seemingly being totally excluded. The characteristics of one parent can thus be recessive but will reappear in later generations, according to definite rules and in a definite ratio. A number of such rules of heredity were first laid down by MENDEL and are recognized as Mendel's laws.

GENETS
Animals related to the CIVETS, but are much smaller, with longer tails and shorter legs—they live most of the time in trees. The common genet is still to be found in Spain and the south of France. Other members of this family are only to be found in Africa.

GENGHIS KHAN (*c.* 1162–1227)
Mongolian chieftain and warrior. Conquered most of China, Turkistan and Afghanistan. Was the grandfather of Kublai Khan, the founder of the Chinese Yuan Dynasty and immortalised in Coleridge's poem, *Kubla Khan*.

GEOGRAPHY
Branch of science which deals with surface of the earth and the physical phenomena which occurs thereon, together with animal life, plant life, industry, commerce and peoples. It will be clear that geography depends to a large degree on other sciences; for example, chemistry, physics, biology, geology, meteorology, anthropology, social sciences and economics.

GEOLOGY
That branch of science concerned with the study of the earth's crust. The earth has been in existence for thousands of millions of years and in that time has undergone many changes, some gradual, some sudden. Animals and plants have lived and died and disappeared altogether as species. Metals and metallic compounds have been heated and compressed and changed into crystals. Animal skeletons have been preserved. Vegetation has been heated and compressed. The result of these changes can be seen in the configuration of the earth's surface into hills, mountains, valleys, oceans and rivers, in the fossilized remains of extinct animals, in the existence of minerals now of great value to modern man, especially COAL, which is the compressed remnant of primeval forests. The study of all these things comes into geology.

As a science geology has existed for about a century and a half since James Hutton wrote his famous book *The Theory of the Earth* in 1785. It has developed so rapidly, especially because of the arguments about evolution and the need for exact knowledge of rock formations, that today no practising geologist would claim to know the whole of geology. So it has become divided into sections. The section called physical geology deals with the conditions that are needed to form rocks and rock-changes. Stratigraphical geology deals with the laying down of rocks in sequence; in other words, historical geology. PETROLOGY is concerned with the minute analysis of rocks and their constituents, usually by means of chemistry and microscopy. Palaeontology deals with the plants and animals that have existed in the past and are now known only by their FOSSILS. Geochronology is concerned with dating and uses the most advanced techniques made available by the advances in nuclear physics.

GEOMETRY
Mathematical study of space and those elements that compose it, i.e., points, lines, planes, and volumes [*see* EUCLID]. Plane geometry deals with points, lines, and planes (two dimensional), solid geometry with bodies possessing volume (three dimensional), and conic sections: the curves formed when a plane cuts a right cone, i.e., circle, ellipse, parabola, and hyperbola. Analytical geometry, which was developed by René DESCARTES, consists essentially of defining and describing a point, line, plane or volume in terms of co-ordinates and expressing the relationship in terms of algebraic equations, e.g., $a^2 = x^2 + y^2$ is the equation of a circle where x and y are co-ordinates on the circle and a the radius. [*See* NON-EUCLIDEAN GEOMETRY.]

GEOPHYSICS

The application of physics, chemistry, geology, etc. to the study of the materials composing the earth and its atmosphere. So important has this subject become that the period from July 1957 to December 1958 was devoted to the special study of the physical nature of the earth and the atmosphere, and called the International Geophysical Year (I.G.Y.).

GERENUK

This is an unusual member of the ANTELOPE family because of its extraordinary long neck. Its coat is reddish-brown with a broad dark-brown band down its spine. The horns of the male are ringed and curve forward towards the tip. It lives in East Africa. It is also called Wallers' gazelle.

GÉRICAULT, Théodore (1791–1824)

French painter, born in Rouen. Not only did he introduce romanticism into French painting but many technical innovations such as painting directly on canvas. He was an outstanding painter of horses. Géricault's most outstanding work is *Raft of the Medusa* now in the Louvre.

GERMAN, Sir Edward (1862–1936)

English composer, born at Whitchurch in Shropshire. Although he composed symphonies, rhapsodies, etc., he is best known for his light operas, especially *Merrie England* and *Tom Jones*.

GERMANY

A large country in central Europe. It is rather smaller than it was before the Second World War, some part now being included in Poland and some in the Soviet Union. Because the war-time Allies have not been able to agree about the future of Germany the country has been divided into separate republics. The eastern part is Communist and the ally of the Soviet Union and the western part is the ally of the countries belonging to NATO.

German Federal Republic, or Western Germany, is rather larger (95,770 square miles) than Great Britain and has a population of about 58 million. The capital is Bonn, on the River Rhine, other important cities being Hamburg, Dusseldorf, Hanover, Frankfurt-on-Maine and Munich. Part of Berlin is under the control of the Federal Republic although it is surrounded by the territory of East Germany. Germany is one of the most highly industrialized countries in the world. She has coal and iron, chiefly near the River Ruhr, and has a big steel industry. Amongst the many things she manufactures and exports are motor vehicles, machine tools and chemicals.

East Germany, or Democratic Republic of Germany, is smaller (41,380 square miles) than England and has a population of a little more than 17 million. The capital is East Berlin, other important cities being Dresden and Leipzig. Many of the people are farmers but there are big new steelworks at Fursten-burg-on-Oder and at Calbe.

History :

German recorded history begins at the time of the Roman Empire when the country we now call Germany was inhabited by a number of different tribes of whom the chief were the Goths, the Franks, the Vandals, the Lombards, and the Saxons. It was the Goths who invaded Rome in A.D. 410, and the Vandals sacked Rome in 455.

In the 9th century CHARLEMAGNE succeeded in uniting the tribes of Central Europe. After his death, when Germany and France became separate countries, there was much unrest in Central Europe. Germany was not a single country although the election of a sovereign as Holy Roman Emperor did give some unity to the country. For four and a half centuries the Emperors were elected by the King of Bohemia, the Count Palatine of the Rhine, the Duke of Saxony, the Margrave of Brandenburg, and the archbishops of Mainz, Cologne and Trier.

An important event in German history was the Protestant Reformation, led by Martin LUTHER, in the 16th century. This led to great controversy as to whether the Emperor should be a Protestant or a Roman Catholic and this brought about the Thirty Years War in the 17th century. At the beginning of the 18th century another important change came about when Prussia was made a kingdom with Frederick the Great on the throne. The troubles during the Napoleonic wars made the Germans think about becoming a single nation.

About 1860 Prussia had a famous statesman named BISMARCK and it was he who planned to bring about the setting up of the German Empire under the leadership of Prussia. His plans were helped by the Franco-German war of 1870 and it was the following year that William I of Prussia was crowned Emperor, or Kaiser, of Germany.

After the defeat of Germany at the end of the First World War in 1918 the country became a republic. There followed a period of hardship for the Germans, and in 1933 Adolf HITLER became Chancellor. He and his followers called themselves National Socialists, or Nazis. Under Hitler's dictatorship many Germans, particularly Jews, suffered persecution either for their opinions or their race. Hitler planned to make Germany the most powerful country

GEYSER 'Old Faithful' in Yellowstone Park, U.S.A.

poser of popular songs. Later studied music in Paris. He composed hundreds of popular songs and several large-scale works, especially *Rhapsody in Blue* (piano and orchestra), a piano concerto, *American in Paris* (orchestral piece) and *Porgy and Bess* (the first American folk opera).

GETTYSBURG ADDRESS

Speech made by Abraham LINCOLN at Gettysburg, site of one of the great battles of the American Civil War (1863). It is Lincoln's classic and concise summary of what he saw to be at stake in the war, and of what he thought to be the aspirations of the American people. It contains the famous phrase 'government of the people, by the people, for the people'.

GEYSER

Spring of natural hot water which periodically plays like a fountain. Rain-water runs down through cracks in the crust of the earth until it reaches heated rocks like those found beneath volcanoes. Here it boils into steam, and all the water above it is suddenly blown high into the air—sometimes as much as 200 feet. The best-known geysers are 'Old Faithful' in Yellowstone Park, U.S.A. and the 'Great Geyser' in Iceland.

GHANA

Formerly the Gold Coast, this is a republic within the BRITISH COMMONWEALTH. It is slightly larger (92,100 square miles) than Great Britain and has a population of nearly 7 million. The capital is Accra and another important city is Kumasi in Ashanti. A new harbour was opened at Tema in 1962 and it is now one of the largest in the South Atlantic. When the country became independent in 1957 the former INTERNATIONAL TRUST TERRITORY of British Togoland was allowed to become part of Ghana. The country is one of the chief cocoa producing countries and is rich in minerals, including gold and bauxite. The Volta River is being dammed to produce hydro-electric power and this will enable aluminium to be produced from the bauxite.

The country's first Prime Minister and President was Dr. Nkrumah, but in 1966 he was deposed by the Army whilst he was on a visit to China and a new government was set up.

GHIBERTI, Lorenzo (1378–1455)

Florentine sculptor and designer of the magnificent bronze doors of Florence Cathedral depicting scenes from the Old and New Testaments. He also designed some stained-

in Europe and his aggressive plans led to the outbreak of the Second World War. When the war was over and Hitler and his followers dead or captive, much of Germany lay in ruins.

After the Second World War the four chief Allied countries—the United States, the Soviet Union, the United Kingdom and France—sent their armies to occupy the country. They divided Germany into four parts. Berlin, the capital, was occupied by all four countries. When it was thought the time had come to let Germany once more rule herself Russia and the other countries could not agree. So in 1954 America, Britain and France agreed that their part of Germany should be entirely independent and the German Federal Republic became a separate country. The Russians arranged for the setting up of the German Democratic Republic in their part.

The Soviet Government and the western countries have constantly disagreed about the administration of Berlin. This led in 1948 to the Russians blockading the roads and railways leading to Berlin and in 1961 to the erection by them and the East Germans of a wall between East Berlin and West Berlin.

GERSHWIN, George (1898–1937)

American composer, born in New York. Started his career as a jazz pianist and com-

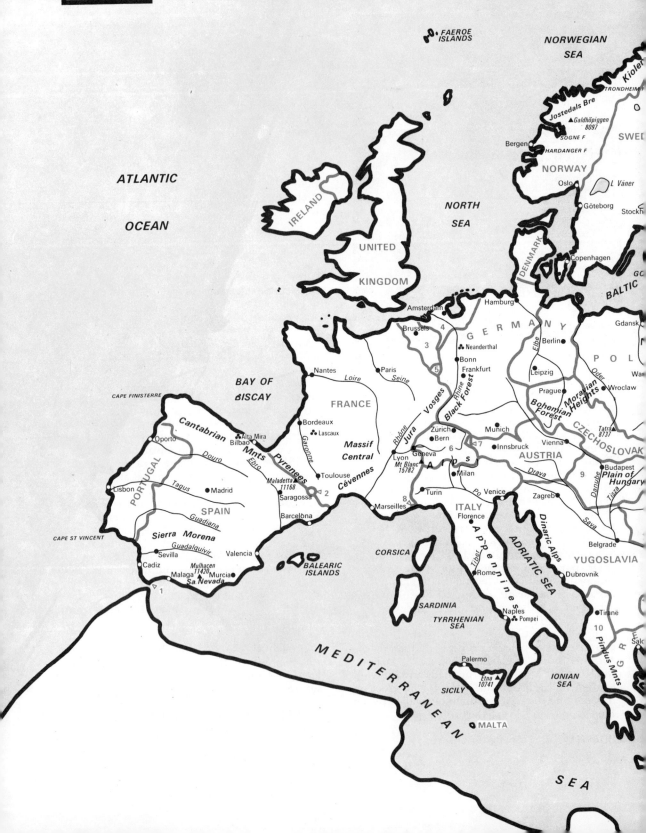

Europe

FAEROE ISLANDS

NORWEGIAN SEA

LOF ISLAN

TRONDHEIM

Jostedals Bre

▲ *Galdhöpiggen* 8097

SOGNE F

SWED

Bergen

HARDANGER F

NORWAY

Oslo

L. Väner

Göteborg

Stockh

ATLANTIC

OCEAN

IRELAND

NORTH SEA

DENMARK

Copenhagen

BALTIC

GO

UNITED KINGDOM

Amsterdam

Hamburg

Gdansk

Brussels

4

G E R M A N Y

Berlin

POL

3

Elbe

Leipzig

Wa

Neanderthal

Bonn

Oder

Wroclaw

Nantes

Paris

Loire

Seine

5

Frankfurt

Prague

Moravian Heights

BAY OF BISCAY

FRANCE

Rhine

Vosges

Black Forest

Bohemian Forest

CZECHOSLOVAK

CAPE FINISTERRE

Bordeaux

Lascaux

Massif Central

Rhône

Jura

Zürich

Bern

Munich

Innsbruck

Vienna

Tatra 8737

Cantabrian

Alta Mira

Bilbao

Mnts

Pyrenees

Toulouse

Garonne

Lyon

Mt Blanc 15782

A l p s

6

7

AUSTRIA

Oporto

PORTUGAL

Douro

Ebro

Cévennes

2

Geneva

Milan

Drava

9

Budapest

Plain of Hungary

Lisbon

Tagus

Madrid

Maladetta 11168

Saragossa

Turin

Po

Venice

Tisza

Danube

Zagreb

Sava

SPAIN

Guadiana

Barcelona

8

Marseilles

ITALY

Florence

Adriatic Sea

Dinaric Alps

Belgrade

CAPE ST VINCENT

Sierra Morena

Guadalquivir

Valencia

CORSICA

Tiber

Rome

YUGOSLAVIA

Sevilla

Cadiz

Malaga

Mulhacen 11420

Murcia

Sa. Nevada

1

BALEARIC ISLANDS

A p p e n n i n e s

Dubrovnik

Tirane

SARDINIA

TYRRHENIAN SEA

Naples

Pompei

IONIAN SEA

Pindus Mnts

10

G R E

Salc

M E D I T E R R A N E A N

Palermo

Etna 10741 ▲

SICILY

MALTA

S E A

NORTH CAPE

BARENTS
SEA

Lapland

nekaise
965

KANIN
PENINSULA

KOLA
PENINSULA

U
r
a
l

WHITE SEA

OF BOTHNIA

FINLAND

R
E
P
U
B
L
I
C
S

M
o
u
n
t
a
i
n
s

L Onega

Helsinki

L Ladoga

European

Plain

Leningrad

GULF OF FINLAND

Tallinn

ESTONIA

Volga

Riga

ATVIA

Central

Moscow

S
O
C
I
A
L
I
S
T

UANIA

Vilnius

Russian

Minsk

BYELORUSSIA

Volga Heights

Pripet
Marshes

Pripet

Desna

Uplands

Kiev

UKRAINE

U
N
I
O
N

O
F

S
O
V
I
E
T

Volga

MOLDAVIA

Kishinev

Dnieper

CASPIAN

SEA OF
AZOV

Crimea

Caucasus

Elbrus 18480

BLACK   SEA

GEORGIA

ARIA

Mountains

SEA

Istanbul

BOSPHORUS

Tbilisi

AZERBAIJAN

Yerevan

Ankara

Mt Ararat
12945

ARMENIA

Sakaria

Kizil Irmak

U

R

L Tuz

Erciyas
12850

K

E

Euphrates

Y

L Van

Toros Mnts

CYPRUS

Nicosia

1	:	GIBRALTAR
2	:	ANDORRA
3	:	BELGIUM
4	:	NETHERLANDS
5	:	LUXEMBOURG
6	:	SWITZERLAND
7	:	LIECHTENSTEIN
8	:	MONACO
9	:	HUNGARY
10	:	ALBANIA

glass windows in the cathedral and produced a number of outstanding sculptures, most of which are in his native Florence.

GHIRLANDAIO, Domenico (1449–1494)
Florentine sculptor, famous for his frescos, and the fact that MICHELANGELO was one of his pupils. Ghirlandaio worked on frescos in Florence and Rome. He also produced many portraits.

GIBBON
The smallest of the APES, and lightly built with long legs and arms. It spends most of its time in the tree tops. When on the ground it walks upright on its legs and does not support itself by the knuckles, as does the CHIMPANZEE. Also it can, especially when young, run very fast, holding its arms aloft to balance itself. The gibbon eats fruit, leaves, insects, spiders, eggs and small birds. It is extremely noisy and lives in the East Indies, ranging from Assam to Cochin, China and Borneo.

GIBBON, Edward (1737–1794)
English writer, born at Putney. Widely travelled, and while in Rome conceived the idea of writing what was to be one of the widest read books of history, *The Decline and Fall of the Roman Empire*. The three volumes of this work covered the period from the Emperor Trojan (died A.D. 117) to the fall of Constantinople to the Turks (1453). It is recognized as a great work of literature as well as history.

GIBBONS, Grinling (1648–1720)
English woodcarver, born in Rotterdam. He was woodcarver to Charles II and employed by Christopher WREN for decorations in St. Paul's Cathedral. His woodcarvings are outstanding for their truly sculptural quality.

GIBBONS, Orlando (1583–1625)
The last of the great English composers of the time of Queen Elizabeth. Born at Oxford. A choirboy at King's College, Cambridge, he became organist at Westminster Abbey. He wrote many fine church anthems and several madrigals, including the beautiful *Silver Swan*.

GIBRALTAR
A rocky promontory at the southern tip of Spain, $3\frac{3}{4}$ miles long and $\frac{3}{4}$ mile wide. The Straits of Gibraltar connect the Mediterranean Sea with the Atlantic Ocean. Gibraltar has a population of nearly 25,000. It is an important British Naval base and has belonged to Britain since 1713. In recent years there has been some trouble with Spain over the future of the Rock as they would like Britain to hand it back.

GIDE, André Paul Guillaume (1869–1951)
French writer, one of the leading lights of his generation. He was awarded the Nobel Prize for Literature in 1947. See the novels *L'Immoraliste, La Symphonie Pastorale, Les Faux Monnayeurs*, etc.

GILA MONSTER
One of the few venomous LIZARDS, found in the desert regions of Arizona and Mexico. A fully grown gila monster can measure up to 24 inches long. It has a yellowish or pinkish skin marked with black bars.

GILBERT AND ELLICE ISLANDS
A group of islands in the West Pacific Ocean which form a British colony. They include Christmas Island. There are about 50,000 inhabitants.

GILBERT AND SULLIVAN OPERAS
The popular stage-works which go under this name are the combined effort of the playwright, William Schwenk Gilbert (1842–1900), and the composer, Arthur SULLIVAN. Sullivan was already an established composer of serious music when he met Gilbert in 1871; most of his symphonies and church compositions have been forgotten, however, and his fame rests on the works he produced in collaboration with Gilbert. The Savoy Operas, as they are called, brought both men wealth, fame, and a knighthood. The most famous of them are: *The Mikado, The Gondoliers, Iolanthe, H.M.S. Pinafore, The Pirates of Penzance, Patience* and *The Yeomen of the Guard*.

GILBERT, William (1544–1603)
English physician and physicist, born at Colchester. He did important pioneer studies into the nature of magnetism as described in his work *De Magnete* published in 1600. He also coined the term 'electricity' to describe the property of amber for attracting light objects—the Greek word for amber being 'electron'.

GILLRAY, James (1757–1815)
English artist and caricaturist. Studied at the Royal Academy. Perhaps one of the most devasting caricaturists of all time. No person or institution was safe from his cutting wit, especially George III and those surrounding him. He produced thousands of drawings.

GIORGIONE, or Giorgio Barbarelli (c. 1478–1510)
Venetian painter, born at Castelfranco Veneto. Studied art in Venice under Giovanni BELLINI,

and had TITIAN as a fellow-student. Little is known about his life, but he developed a new style of painting, intimate and romantic. He produced mostly scriptural and pastoral works, including the famous altarpiece at Castelfranco, and *The Three Philosophers*.

GIOTTO DE BONDONE (c. 1267–1337)

Italian painter, and architect, born at Vespignano near Florence. A shepherd's boy, he was discovered while sketching his flock one day by Giovanni Cimabue, the founder of the Florentine school of painting, who was so impressed by Giotto's pictures that he made him his pupil. Giotto's works include the frescos depicting the life of St. Francis in the Church of St. Francis at Assisi, the frescos in the Arena chapel at Padua depicting subjects from the Life of Christ and the Virgin, the *Navicella* mosaic and the altarpiece at St. Peter's, Rome, and the frescos in the Church of Santa Croce, Florence. Giotto was one of the first artists to turn from the stiff Byzantine style of painting and to copy from nature. He depicted the Apostles as real people, and all his figures were graceful, natural and lifelike. He was appointed master of the cathedral at Florence and city architect in 1334, and he designed the campanile.

GIRAFFE

A ruminant closely related to the OKAPI. The most striking feature is its very long neck. Other things which should be noted, however, are the short horns which are tipped with hair, small ears, and long lips and tongue, both used for plucking foliage on which giraffes live; mostly they feed upon the acacias. Giraffes are found in many localities in Africa, south of the Sahara Desert.

GIRAUDOUX, Jean (1882–1944)

French poet, novelist and playwright. He is best remembered today for his plays, which were based on the Greek myths and biblical stories, and in which he satirized modern life—*Electra, Ondine, Tiger at the Gates, Duel of the Angels*.

GIRTIN, Thomas (1775–1802)

English watercolour artist. In his short life he revolutionized watercolour painting, and had a great influence on TURNER. His work was mainly landscape subjects executed with a deeply poetic feeling for his subject in bold colourful washes.

GLACIER

River of ice occurring in mountainous regions above the snow-line. Where great thicknesses of snow accumulate, the weight of the top snow compresses the lower layers into ice, and if this is resting on a slope it begins to slide slowly downwards. As it moves the glacier scours out for itself a deep, U-shaped valley, grinding the rocks beneath it to a fine powder which forms 'boulder-clay' or 'till'. Boulders and stones fall from the sides of the valley on to the ice and get carried along with it. When the snow-line is reached the ice melts and the rocks resting on it are deposited in a heap called a moraine.

GLADSTONE, William Ewart (1808–1898)

One of the greatest Parliamentarians and Liberals of the 19th century. Born in Liverpool, and the son of a merchant, he was at first anxious to enter the Church but followed his father's will and entered politics. He first became an M.P. in 1832 and (except for a break in 1846–1847) remained a member until 1895. He occupied the highest offices of state, being President of the Board of Trade (1843), Chancellor of the Exchequer (1852–1855), and Prime Minister (1868–1874, 1880–1885, 1892–1894). Amongst his more important measures were the Disestablishment of the Irish Church (1869), the Irish Land Act (1870), the Ballot Act (1872), and the Reform Act of 1884, which gave the vote to the agricultural labourers. His two Home Rule Bills for Ireland were unsuccessful. Gladstone was a man of great energy and found time from his political activities to write numerous works on theology and the classics.

GIRAFFE The long neck of this ruminant enables it to feed off the leaves of acacia trees.

GLASS

Hard, transparent material obtained by the fusion (melting) of certain silicates and an alkali, and cooled at a rate which avoids crystallization. The chief raw materials for glass are fine sand and limestone, alkali is furnished by carbonates of potash and soda ash. The qualities and physical characteristics of glass are varied by the addition of certain substances, usually oxides, e.g., cut glass contains lead oxide, glass of high refractive index barium oxide, and glass used in electrical and thermal apparatus boric oxide.

GLAZUNOV, Alexander (1865–1936)

Russian composer, born in St. Petersburg (Leningrad). At first was greatly influenced by national Russian music but later became more sympathetic to European styles. Composed a great deal of music, including eight symphonies.

GLINKA, Mikhail (1803–1857)

Russian composer, born in Smolensk. He has been described as 'the father of the Russian National School of composition', his music drawing largely on the folk music of his country. His most famous compositions are the two operas, *A Life for the Czar* and *Russlan and Ludmilla*.

GLOW-WORM

A luminescent INSECT which is in fact the wingless female (hence the reason why it is always found grubbing about in grass) of the species *Lampyris noctiluca*. The pale greenish light comes from the abdominal region.

GLUCK, Christoph Willibald Von (1714–1787)

Composer of operas, born in Bavaria. Although widely travelled he spent the greater part of his life in Paris and Vienna where he died. His great contribution to opera was to marry the musical with the dramatic. His best known works, which are still performed, are *Alcestis, Iphigenia in Aulia, Iphigenia in Tauris,* and *Orpheus and Eurydice.*

GOA [*See* INDIA]

GOATS

This group of animals belong to the cud-chewing family of animals, and the wild kinds are usually called IBEXES. Mostly their horns curve upwards and backwards but there is one, the markhor, with horns twisted like a corkscrew. All males have a beard or 'goatee'. They are found in Europe, North Africa and Central Asia.

GOBI DESERT

Arid desert area of some half a million square miles in Central Asia. During the past few years the MONGOLIAN PEOPLES REPUBLIC has done much to reclaim and develop the region for agricultural purposes.

GODWIN, Mary Wollstonecraft (1749–1797)

English writer, born in London, she had at first to earn her living by teaching. She then worked for a London publisher as reader and translator. Turning to authorship, she published *Vindication of the Rights of Man* in defence of the French Revolution, but is most famous as a pioneer of women's rights, especially in education. She expressed her views in *Thoughts on the Education of Daughters* and *Vindication of the Rights of Woman.* Her daughter Mary married the poet SHELLEY, and wrote *Frankenstein* and *Valperga.*

GOETHE, Johann Wolfgang Von (1749–1832)

Born at Frankfurt, and educated at Leipzig and Strasbourg. The greater part of his life was spent in the service of Charles Augustus, Duke of Saxe-Weimar; for ten years he was the Duke's chief adviser. Goethe wrote poetry, drama, novels and made important contributions to botany and the theory of evolution. His greatest work was *Faust*, an adaptation of MARLOW'S *Dr. Faustus*, which was finished only a few weeks before his death. It tells the story of Faust, who offers his soul to the devil if the devil can give him happiness in return.

GOG AND MAGOG

Two large sculptured figures in the Guildhall, London. They were destroyed during the Blitz and restored in 1954. One legend has it that they were two giants who were brought to London to act as royal porters at the gates of the palace. Another story is that they represent a Saxon and an Ancient Briton.

GOGH, Vincent Van (1853–1890)

Dutch painter, born in Brabant. He trained unsuccessfully as a Methodist preacher in England, and, as an evangelist among the Belgian coal-miners, he was distrusted by the employers and derided by the miners. Unfortunate love-affairs further unsettled him, but he turned to painting, was helped to study in Paris by his brother Théo, and met GAUGUIN and TOULOUSE-LAUTREC. Many of his best paintings, like *Sunflowers* (now in the Tate Gallery), owe much to the startlingly bright colours of the landscapes around Arles, in Provence. 1889–1890 he spent in an asylum after he had cut off his own ear, and in July

1890 he shot himself and died two days later, ending an unhappy life. But Van Gogh was one of the founders of the modern Expressionist style in painting, and his strong use of colour and vigorous strokes make his paintings unmistakable.

GOGOL, Nikolai Vasilievich (1809–1852)

Russian novelist and dramatist. His famous comedy *The Inspector General* was a biting attack on the official class of the day, and the novel *Dead Souls* is the most precise picture we have of Russian provincial life in the early 19th century.

GOLD

Valuable metal and 79 in the table of elements. Its chemical symbol is Au and atomic weight 197·2. From most ancient times it has been highly valued, particularly for ornaments and decorations.

Gold is to be found in minute quantities throughout the earth's crust, even in the sea, but in this state is of little use to man. Gold as we understand it is mined from lodes (a metal-bearing vein of rock) or from gravel deposits in river beds which have been washed out of gold-bearing rocks. The richest gold deposits are in the Transvaal (South Africa), Rocky Mountains (America and very widely distributed along this mountain chain) and, this is of recent development, the Ural Mountains in the U.S.S.R.

GOLDONI, Carlo (1707–1793)

Italian dramatist. Born in Venice, he was the son of a physician. Although intended originally for the law, he soon took to play-writing. His first attempts were tragedies, but he made his mark as a comic writer; the best known is *The Landlady*. He created a new school of comedy based on lively dialogue, humorous characters and domestic life. He died in Paris.

GOLDSMITH, Oliver (1728–1774)

Born in Ireland, he studied at Trinity College, Dublin, wandered over Western Europe, and eventually made a living by journalism in London, where he became one of Dr. Johnson's circle. His poems *The Traveller* and *The Deserted Village*, his novel *The Vicar of Wakefield*, and above all his play *She Stoops to Conquer* are among the masterpieces of English literature.

GOLF

The basis of golf is very simple. It is to hit a ball with a club from one place (called a 'tee') into a small hole in another place (called a 'green') in the fewest number of strokes.

The ball is very small. According to the rules, it must not weigh more than 1·62 ounces avoirdupois and must not be less than 1·62 inches in diameter. It is generally made of rubber and is painted white so that it can be more easily seen.

With regard to clubs, no exact measurements are given, but there are one or two things about them which are forbidden. No club may have any springs or other mechanical devices which will give added force to a ball when struck, and the head of the club must not be in the shape of a mallet. Also, the length of the club-head from toe to heel shall be greater than the breadth from the striking face to the back.

Golf is played on a golf course, which is a large area of ground laid out in a certain way. It has 18 tees, 18 greens and 18 holes; each tee, green and hole combined, is generally referred to as a 'hole'. Holes (in the latter sense) are irregular in length (about 100 to 500 yards), and each one has certain definite characteristics. First there is the tee, which is a flat piece of lawn on which the ball is placed in readiness for being struck towards the green. Between the tee and the green is a 'fairway', a strip of cropped grass down which the player should play. If he plays off this fairway, his ball goes into the 'rough', that is, uncropped grass from which further strokes are very difficult.

Between tee and green are what are known as 'hazards', natural and prepared. Natural hazards are such things as ponds, trees and clumps of bushes. Prepared hazards, usually placed uncomfortably close to the green, are known as 'bunkers'. They are awkwardly-shaped pieces of ground (small depressions and hills) lined at the bottom with fine sand.

The green is a small piece of fairly level lawn, and somewhere in the middle of it is the hole itself, $4\frac{1}{2}$ inches in diameter, at least 4 inches deep, and marked with a flag on a pole so that a player driving off from the distant tee can see it easily.

On the tee, the ball is raised a little from the surface of the ground by supporting it on a tee-peg. The ball is hit with a club so that it goes in the direction of the distant green.

Rules which every player ought to learn are:
(1) No player shall play his ball while it is still moving from a previous stroke, or pick it up or touch it while it is in play, that is, from the time it is driven off from the tee until it is played into the hole on the green, except for purposes of identification and for cleaning the ball on the green. Penalties: for playing a moving ball, loss of the hole; for touching the ball, one stroke added to the score.
(2) If two balls lie within a club-length of

each other, one may be lifted until the other has been played; the lifted ball is then replaced on the spot from where it was picked up.

(3) A player must not move or bend fixed or growing objects on the course in order to play a ball which lies awkwardly. Penalty: loss of the hole.

(4) If a player accidentally plays his opponent's ball and it is not discovered until after his opponent has played a substitute ball, he loses the hole.

(5) If the ball becomes lost or is found to be unplayable where it lies, the player shall drop another ball within two club lengths of where the ball lay, but not nearer the hole, and then add 2 strokes to his score; or play his next stroke as near as possible to the spot from which the original ball was played, adding a penalty stroke to his score.

(6) If a ball becomes so damaged that it is unplayable, it may be replaced after the player has told his opponent of his intention to play a new ball. The new ball is played from the spot where the old ball came to rest.

(7) If a ball lies in a hazard, nothing shall be done to improve its position for playing the next stroke. Penalty: loss of the hole.

(8) If a ball comes to rest in water (a pond, for example) he may drop another ball near by so that the water is still between the ball and the green; he then adds one stroke to his score.

(9) If a ball comes to rest in casual water (rain water which has collected on the course) he may remove it to a spot as near as possible to where it lay on ground which avoids these conditions, but not nearer to the hole on the green than were it first lay. It should be noted that this does not apply if the casual water lies in a hazard. There is no penalty.

(10) When playing on the green towards the hole, a player may have the flagpole removed from the hole as he approaches.

Apart from the lone player who goes round the course for exercise, two or three players may play each other. Alternatively, four players (two to each team), may play, each team having one ball or two. The order of play when driving off is alternate, each player playing his strokes in an agreed order and playing his own or his team's ball. The player whose ball is farthest from the hole plays the next stroke. If any player plays out of turn, he or his team loses the hole. There is no penalty for playing out of turn, except that the shot may be recalled.

Concerning scoring, as the object of the game is to strike a ball from tee to hole in as few strokes as possible, the player or team with the *fewest* number of strokes per hole is the winner of the hole. Over the entire course of 18 holes (or twice round, making 36 holes),

the winner of most holes is the winner of the match.

Sometimes players score in another way—the lowest number of strokes over 18 or 36 holes, irrespective of individual holes won, wins the match. Occasionally players who do not have much time to spare will play only half a course, 9 holes.

There are numerous types of golf clubs and the selection is largely a matter of the player's individual choice, but he cannot carry more than 14 clubs during any match.

GONIOMETER
Instrument for measuring the angles of a crystal. There are two types, the contact goniometer used for large crystals and the reflecting goniometer for small crystals; the latter is a high-precision optical instrument.

GOPHER [*See* CHIPMUNK]

GORDON, General Charles George
(1833–1885)
Military leader, born at Woolwich. He became known and admired for his bravery and Christian principles. His qualities of leadership made him universally popular with the men who served under him. He served in the Crimea, China, and Egypt, and was governor of the Sudan. He was captured and killed during the siege of Khartoum after holding out for a remarkable length of time, and shortly before relief arrived.

GORILLA
The largest of the man-like APES, a large male having a standing height of up to $5\frac{1}{2}$ feet and weighing about 600 pounds; the female is much smaller. It inhabits the equatorial forests

GOYA A detail showing the brilliant quality and character of Goya's portrait painting.

of Africa, particularly the Belgian Congo, where it is protected. It is untrue that gorillas are fierce and carry off natives. They are, in fact, inoffensive, making off into the forest when man approaches. If they and/or their family are attacked, however, they can be terrible antagonists.

GORKY, Maxim (1868–1936)
Russian writer. During his early life he was a wanderer, or perhaps more correctly, a tramp. However, it was his knowledge of tramps and vagabonds that enabled him to write some of the finest short stories ever written. He was accorded the highest honours by the Soviet government and was a close friend of Stalin. His best-known books are *Mother, My Childhood, Reminiscences* and the play, *The Lower Depths*.

GOUNOD, Charles François (1818–1893)
French composer, born in Paris. Was greatly interested in early sacred music and wrote many religious compositions. His fame perhaps rests on his opera *Faust* which is still popular. He lived in London for five years during the Franco-German War.

GOVERNOR
Within the British Commonwealth, one who acts as the Queen's representative in a colony. In a colony where the people are able to manage most of the affairs of the colony themselves the Governor's duties will be fewer than in those where he has to make many of the decisions. In the DOMINIONS the Queen is represented by a Governor-General who carries out, in the Queen's absence, the same kind of functions as does the Queen herself. Because a Governor, or Governor-General, represents the Queen, he is addressed as 'Excellency'.

GOYA Y LUCIENTES, Francisco José de (1746–1828)
Spanish painter and etcher. Born near Saragossa. After studying in Madrid and Rome, he settled in Madrid and was commissioned to paint a series of tapestry designs for the royal manufactory at Santa Barbara. The charm, gaiety and quality of these oil paintings brought Goya to the King's attention, and in 1786 the artist was appointed court painter and began a series of portraits in which he brilliantly, and often cruelly, revealed his subjects' characters as well as their appearance. His series of etchings, in particular the *Disasters of War* series, were as candid as his portraits. Goya is regarded as the greatest painter of his age and the forerunner of the great French painters of the 19th century. Among his distinguished

sitters was the Duke of Wellington. His *Tauromaquia* prints of bull-fight scenes are universally renowned.

GRAHAME, Kenneth (1859–1922)
Scottish author, he retired from his post at the Bank of England because of ill-health in 1908. His *Wind in the Willows*, a story about river-side animals—Rat, Mole, Badger and 'the intelligent Mr. Toad'—has long been a favourite with children. *The Reluctant Dragon* was filmed by Walt Disney.

GRAMPUS
Also known as the 'killer whale'. It feeds on sea-birds, seals, porpoises and fish, and has been known to kill and eat Greenland whales. Its eating capacity can be gauged by the example of one grampus of 21 feet in length which when caught had in its stomach 14 seals and 13 porpoises. [*See* WHALE.]

GRANITE
Rock formed by the cooling and crystallizing of minerals which have been melted by the interior heat of the earth. The three chief minerals in granite are called quartz, mica and felspar. Granite may be grey or pink, according to the colour of the felspar it contains.

GRASSHOPPERS [*See* INSECTS]

GRASSES
These plants are distributed throughout the world and belong to the family Gramineae. They are easily recognized, but as they lack the well-known parts such as petals and sepals, they are often thought not to be flowering plants. The unfamiliar parts are usually only modifications of more well-known ones in flowering plants. Grasses include sugar cane, wheat, millet, rice, bamboo, rye and barley. Esparto grass is used in the manufacture of high-quality paper. (See drawing on page 184.)

GRAVES, Robert Ranke (1895——)
English poet and novelist, and son of an Irish folk-verse writer. *I, Claudius* and *Claudius The God* are novels set against the background of ancient Rome. Another pair of novels—*Sergeant Lamb of the Ninth* and *Proceed, Sergeant Lamb* relate the adventures of a British Soldier involved in the American Revolution.

GRAVITATION
Sir Isaac NEWTON, in pondering over the question of why things always fell towards the earth and why planets followed elliptical paths round the sun, eventually stated the

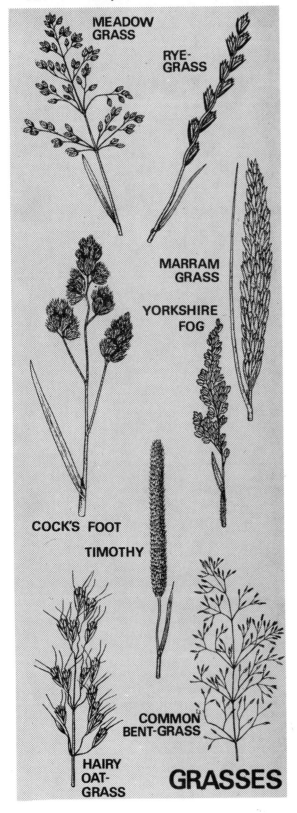

MEADOW GRASS

RYE-GRASS

MARRAM GRASS

YORKSHIRE FOG

COCK'S FOOT

TIMOTHY

COMMON BENT-GRASS

HAIRY OAT-GRASS

GRASSES

most general law of all physics, one without exception. This law is known as the law of gravitation.

The law states that every body attracts every other body with a force that is directly proportional to the masses of the two bodies and inversely proportional to the square of the distance between them. This means that if a billiard ball weighing 100 grammes is resting on the table and 20 centimetres from a second billiard ball weighing 50 grammes then there is an attractive force between them proportional to 50×100 divided by 20^2. The answer to this is 12·5. This answer does not give the actual force of attraction. To get this the answer must be multiplied by a figure called the constant of gravitation, which on the system of units above is 6·6576 divided by a hundred million. This constant is a universal constant. Similarly, the earth is attracting the first billiard ball and it is likewise attracting the earth. At the same time the earth is attracting the second billiard ball and this is also attracting the earth. In fact *every* body attracts *every* other body according to the law of gravitation. [*See* RELATIVITY.]

GRAY, Thomas (1716–1771)
English writer, born in London. Professor of History at Cambridge and close friend of Horace WALPOLE. His output of poetry was not very great, and he is best remembered for *On a Favourite Cat Drowned in a Tub of Gold Fishes* and *An Elegy Written in a Country Churchyard*; the churchyard in question was Stoke Poges where he was buried.

GREAT BARRIER REEF
Longest coral reef in the world, stretching over 1,200 miles and located in the Coral Sea off the coast of Queensland, Australia. The magnificent coral gardens and tropical marine life have been closely studied during the past few years by aqualung divers and underwater cameras; several colour films have been made and should be seen by all interested in natural history.

GREAT BRITAIN
The seventh largest island in the world and is in the North Atlantic Ocean. It consists of the three united kingdoms of ENGLAND, SCOTLAND and WALES. Its greatest length is 605 miles, its greatest breadth 360 miles and its area is 87,818 square miles, excluding the islands. The term British Isles is used to describe the archipelago off the north-west coast of Europe which includes many groups of islands as well as Great Britain itself. The chief groups are the SCILLY ISLES off the south-

west of England and the Orkneys, Shetlands and Hebrides off Scotland. The chief single islands are the Isle of MAN, Anglesey and the Isle of Wight. The CHANNEL ISLANDS are a possession of Great Britain but are not part of the British Isles.

Great Britain is the chief steel-producing country in Europe and one of the main ship-building countries in the world. The chief ship-building district is the Clyde estuary in Scotland. Britain is rich in coal, the chief coal mines are located in Northumberland and Durham, Lanarkshire in Scotland, and South Wales. Britain is one of the chief textile countries. Lancashire produces cotton and Yorkshire woollen goods. London, on the River Thames, is the third largest city in the world and is the capital. In 1966 important deposits of natural gas were discovered in the North Sea and this is expected to make an important difference to Britain's supply of fuel.

GREATER LONDON COUNCIL

A new local government body that came into being in April 1965. It replaced the former London County Council and Middlesex County Council as well as taking in part of Essex, Kent, Herts and Surrey. The area of the new Council is five times bigger than that of the former London County Council. The work of the Council is rather different from that which the L.C.C. formerly did as some work has been taken over by the BOROUGH COUNCILS within the area. These Boroughs are all much bigger than the former ones and some of them have taken new names. There are 32 Boroughs within the Greater London area. Twelve of these are called the Inner London Boroughs. They cover the area of the former L.C.C. and, acting together, are responsible for education in that area. Each of the other twenty Outer London Boroughs is responsible for education in its own area.

GREAT LAKES

Five lakes (fresh water) which lie between the border of the U.S.A. and Canada. They are Lake Superior (largest lake in the world), Lake Michigan, Lake Huron, Lake Erie and Lake Ontario; Lake Michigan is in American territory. Among the important ports and in-dustrial towns on the banks of these lakes are Detroit, Chicago, Cleveland, Toronto and Fort William. Since the opening in 1959 of the St. Lawrence Seaway [*see* CANADA] ocean-going vessels have been able to reach ports on the lakes.

GREBE

A family of diving birds with a straight and rather long bill, and legs set rather back-wards. Their nests are made of aquatic plants on inland waters. They lay from 3 to 6 eggs, depending on the species. The most distin-guished bird of this family is the 'Great Crested' grebe and the smallest the 'Little' grebe or 'dabchick'.

GRECO, El, properly Domenico Theotocopouli (1541–1614)

Spanish painter, born in Crete. In Italy, he was a pupil of TITIAN and studied with MICHELANGELO. He moved to Toledo in the 1570s and his series of pictures in the church of Santo Domingo el Antiguo, which included *The Stripping of Christ before the Crucifixion*, brought him to the attention of Philip II. Gradually he developed a strangely individual and mystical style—striking colour contrasts, and figures elongated and distorted to increase their emotional impact. El Greco had consider-able influence on VELASQUEZ and later on MANET and the Expressionists. The body of his works have remained in Toledo, though the National Gallery has the *Purification of the Temple* and *Christ's agony in Gethsemane*.

GREECE

A kingdom in south-east Europe about 51,180 square miles and has rather more than 8 million inhabitants. The capital is the ancient city of Athens whose people gave to the world the idea of democracy. The second largest city is Salonika. Among the more famous of the

GRECO'S painting of *The Agony in the Garden*.

GREECE Amphitheatre at Delphi, one of the many vast theatres where Greek drama was born.

Greeks Islands are RHODES, CRETE and Patmos. The Greek people, whose language is descended from that used by the ancient Greeks, are Christians belonging to the GREEK ORTHODOX CHURCH. Most Greeks are peasant farmers who grow and export tobacco and fruit. Currants take their name from the Greek city of Corinth where they were first grown. Greece is also an important seafaring nation.

History :

The Greeks of ancient times were divided into three great families—Ionians, Aeolians and Dorians. It was the Ionians of Asia Minor who first developed Greek science, literature and art. By 700 B.C. Greek trade was flourishing and the following century the city of Athens became the centre of Greek culture which was to influence European civilization for all time. The Persians, under Cyrus and DARIUS, tried unsuccessfully to conquer Greece. As a result of repeated attacks by the Persians the city states of Greece formed a confederation and this led to the building of an Athenian Empire under the Greek leader, PERICLES. But war developed between Athens and her rival, Sparta. This war, called the Peloponnesian War, lasted from 431 to 401 B.C. The war was followed by the rise to power of Philip of Macedon and his son, ALEXANDER THE GREAT, who ruled not only Greece but a great empire that stretched into India. The Empire did not last long after Alexander's death and in 146 B.C. Greece came under Rome.

After the fall of Rome Greece was invaded by the Goths and Vandals, and in the 6th century by the Slavs. Greece formed part of the Byzantine Empire until the 13th century and in 1460 the country was conquered by the Turks. It remained under them until 1821. In that year the Greeks rose in rebellion against the Turks, but it was not till 1830 that Greece became completely independent. British people sympathised greatly with the Greek people and some, including Lord BYRON, the poet, went to Greece to help them in their fight for freedom.

Greece became a monarchy after her liberation though some Greeks wanted a republic and this later on led to some trouble and discontent. For eleven years after the First World War the country was, in fact, a republic. In 1941 Italy invaded Greece and so Greece became one of the Allies. For a short period after the war was over there was civil war in the country which added greatly to the sufferings of the people. Gradually Greece was able to recover and to rebuild the country.

GREEK ORTHODOX CHURCH

The word orthodox means, 'sound in doctrine, upholding established teachings'; and the Greek (more correctly, the Eastern) church considers itself alone to be orthodox, in that it regards the doctrinal decisions of the seven Ecumenical Councils [*see* ROMAN CATHOLIC CHURCH) as unalterable and binding on all Christians. The official cause of separation between the Eastern and Western churches was, and still is, an addition made to the Nicene Creed probably in Spain about 589.

The Orthodox Church includes the Ecumenical Patriarchate of Constantinople, the Patriarchates of Alexandria, Antioch and Jerusalem, the Churches of Greece and Russia, the

Holy Monastery of Sinai, and seven other independent communities. The Patriarch (the word comes from the Latin *pater*, father, and the Greek *arche*, rule) of Constantinople still has an honorary precedence throughout the Church.

The Eastern Church rejects the authority of the Pope and the idea of Purgatory. Its principal feast is Easter, its main fast, Lent. Its central service is the Eucharist; its vestments correspond to those of the Roman Church. Monastic life is prominent in the Eastern Church, based, mainly, on the famous 4th-century Rule of Basil the Great. Today the Orthodox Church has some 144 million members.

GREENAWAY, Kate (1846–1901)

English artist and book-illustrator, well-known both in England and on the Continent. Her greatest success was with children's books, like *Mother Goose* and *Mother Goose Rhymes*, which she illustrated with charming coloured drawings of children in early 19th-century costume, and for which she also wrote the text. She also designed Christmas cards, birthday cards and calendars.

GREENE, Graham (1904———)

British author. His portrayal of underworld figures, like the hired killer in *A Gun for Sale*, and of men trapped in unhappy situations by the regularity of their own lives (*The End of the Affair*) is not surpassed by any other author. A Catholic himself, Greene shows many of his characters struggling with the implications of their religion. His crime and suspense stories are among the most exciting ever written— *Brighton Rock*, for example, and *The Third Man*, which ends with a chase through the dark sewers of Vienna, after the crook Harry Lyme.

GREENE, Robert (1558–1592)

English dramatist and poet. He is regarded as one of the founders of English drama, though his plays are rather tedious. *Pandosto* gave Shakespeare the basis of the plot for *The Winter's Tale*, and when Greene talked of 'an upstart crow, beautified with our feathers' in *The Groat's Worth of Wit Bought with a Million of Repentance* he may have been accusing Shakespeare of claiming credit for his own lines.

GREENLAND

The largest island in the world except for Australia. It is in the Arctic Ocean and is about 132,000 square miles. Only a small part, rather larger than Britain, is ice free and so can be inhabited. There are a little over 34,000 Greenlanders, most of whom are Eskimos. Greenland belongs to DENMARK, but the United States has the right to build air bases. Cryolite comes from Greenland and in 1948 important discoveries of lead were made.

GRENVILLE, Sir Richard (c. 1541–1591)

Famous Elizabethan seaman. Born of an old Cornish family, he commanded Raleigh's expedition to Virginia. In 1591, as Vice-Admiral of a squadron sent to the Azores to intercept the homeward-bound Spanish fleet, Grenville's ship, *The Revenge*, was cut off from the rest of the squadron. For many hours his men fought hordes of Spaniards. Grenville himself was mortally wounded in the battle. TENNYSON'S ballad *The Revenge* celebrates the battle.

GREY OF FALLODON, Edward Grey, First Viscount (1862–1933)

British statesman. He became Foreign Secretary in 1905, his policy being friendship with the United States, a defensive alliance with Japan and co-operation with France. By these means his aim was to maintain European peace, which he thought most threatened by Germany. On the eve of the First World War he tried to organize a conference to settle the dispute between Austria and Serbia. When this attempt failed he had no alternative but to declare war on Germany in support of France and Belgium. He remained Foreign Secretary until 1916 when his eyesight began to give way and he had to retire.

GRIEG, Edvard Hagerup (1843–1907)

Norwegian composer, born at Bergen. Norway's best-known composer, his music is still very popular, especially his piano concerto and the incidental music to the play *Peer Gynt*. He wrote many songs.

GRIMM, Jakob Ludwig Karl (1785–1863) and Wilhelm Karl (1786–1859)

German philologists and students of folk-lore. Both were born at Hanau in Hesse-Cassel. Their lives were largely spent together. After being librarians at the town of Cassel they went to Göttingen University as lecturer and librarian respectively. They were dismissed on political charges and then became Professors at Berlin University. The first volume of their collection of fairy tales was published in 1812 and the second and third volumes in 1814 and 1822. The tales have been translated into many languages and have made the Brothers Grimm a household word. They also compiled a German dictionary and wrote works on German mythology.

GRÜNEWALD, Mathias (*c.* 1480–*c.* 1530)
German religious painter. He worked under the patronage of the Archbishop of Mainz and specialized in paintings of the 'Passion of Christ'. His *Crucifixions* are in a number of museums. A great colourist, his tragic paintings portray with outstanding realism the agony of Christ. His great masterpiece is *The Isenheim Altarpiece* now in the museum in Colmar, Alsace.

GUANACO
Wild species of LLAMA.

GUARDI, Francesco (1712–1793)
Italian painter, born in Venice. Most of his paintings are of Venice but done in a free style suffused with light and colour—quite different from the architectural works of CANALETTO.

GUATEMALA
A republic in Central America which adjoins MEXICO and BRITISH HONDURAS. It has an area

GUILLOTINE
Machine used in France for beheading, that is, carrying out capital punishment. It is named after its designer, Joseph Ignace Guillotin, who introduced it during the Revolution, but similar machines had been used in Britain and the Continent since the middle ages. The name is also used for machines used for cutting various materials, for example, paper and sheet metal.

GUINEA
A republic in West Africa which has an area of 96,865 square miles. It was formerly part of French West Africa. It has a population of 3 million and its capital is Conakry. The country produces bauxite and iron ore.

GULF STREAM
Warm oceanic current which starts in the Gulf of Mexico, flows through the Straits of Florida and merges with the North Atlantic Drift. The south-westerly airstream that comes from warm regions and passes over the

GUNPOWDER PLOT
This was led by Robert Catesby and its purpose was to replace James I by one of his younger sons. The plot was foiled on Nov. 5th, 1605.

of about 42,040 square miles and has about 4½ million inhabitants of whom the majority are Indians. The capital is Guatemala City. The country produces coffee, bananas and chewing gum. For many years Guatemala has quarrelled with Britain over the neighbouring territory of British Honduras which she wants Britain to give to her.

GUERICKE, Otto von (1602–1686)
German physicist, born at Magdeburg. He invented the first air pump and demonstrated air pressure by means of spheres. Guericke also made the first frictional electric machine, using a large sulphur ball, and made studies of comets.

surface waters of the Atlantic Drift, brings the warmth inland to influence the climate of Britain and western Europe.

GUNPOWDER
Invented in China about the 9th century A.D., and introduced to Europe in the 14th century. Roger BACON probably experimented with it. Its first use in warfare was at the Battle of Crecy. It is a mixture of salt-petre (75%), sulphur (10%) and carbon (15%).

GUNPOWDER PLOT
A secret plot organized during the reign of James I by a group of people led by Robert Catesby. Its purpose was to place one of the

King's younger sons on the throne. It had the support of some Roman Catholics who were suffering persecution under the harsh religious laws of the time. To hasten their plans the plotters persuaded one of their number, named Guy FAWKES, to arrange for thirty-six barrels of gunpowder to be hidden in a cellar under the Houses of Parliament and to set light to them when Parliament met on November 5th, 1605. The plot was discovered and the ringleaders put to death. Ever since then, on November 5th, bonfires have been lit and fireworks let off in celebration of the fact that the plot failed.

GUTENBURG, Johann (*c.* 1397–1468)

German printer, born at Mainz. He is considered to be the first printer in Europe to print with movable type. In 1454 Gutenburg published a Bible using metal types.

GUYANA

A British Dominion, formerly known as British Guiana. It took the name Guyana when it became independent in 1966. It is in the north of South America and covers an area of 83,000 square miles but has only a little over half a million inhabitants. Its capital is Georgetown at the mouth of the Demerara River. The river gives its name to the sugar that is grown on its banks. The population is nearly evenly divided between people of Negro descent and of Indians from the Indian subcontinent. There has been serious trouble between the two groups from time to time.

GWYNN, Nell (1650–1687)

Of obscure beginnings she started by selling oranges outside the Drury Lane Theatre in London and then became an actress and dancer. Although uneducated, she had great wit and charm, and was a close friend of King Charles II. It is said that it was she who persuaded him to found the Chelsea Hospital.

GYMNASIUM

Generally used to describe a place where atheletic exercises can be taught and practised. In Germany and some other continental countries a gymnasium is a school which prepares young people to enter a university.

The reason the word gymnasium is used so differently in Europe today can be understood when it is realized what the earliest gymnasiums were like. The gymnasium was started in ancient Greece for the training of youths. They were sports grounds which had baths attached and rooms for discussion and conversation. Teachers, particularly philosophers, used to visit their pupils at the gym-

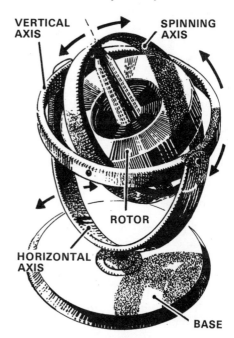

GYROSCOPE in its simplest form. The non-magnetic compass used by mariners is basically the same.

nasium and hold discussions with them. The most famous gymnasiums were the ACADEMY, the Lyceum and the Cynosarges.

GYROSCOPE

Well-balanced wheel spinning at a comparatively high speed of revolution and supported so as to have freedom in three planes. The wheel is so mounted that only one point—its centre of gravity—is in a fixed position, the wheel itself being free to turn in any direction about this point. Its two main physical characteristics are: (1) gyroscopic inertia, i.e., property which causes it to maintain its position in space regardless of how the supporting base is turned, and to resist any force tending to turn its spinning axis in a new direction, and (2) precession, i.e., property of a gyroscope which, when a couple is applied, causes it to move in a direction at right angles to the applied couple and also at right angles to the axle of the spinning wheel. These unique properties of the gyroscope can be controlled in such a manner that it will seek and maintain an indication of the true geographic north. Such an application is termed a gyro-compass and is now used in the navigation of aircraft and ships as it is in no way affected by the earth's magnetism as is a magnetic compass. Other aircraft instruments, such as the direction indicator, automatic pilot, horizon indicator, and turn-and-bank indicator, are based on the gyroscope.

Hh

HABEAS CORPUS
This term means 'you must have the body', and is a written order commanding a man to be brought into court to see that he has not been wrongly imprisoned. The Act of Habeas Corpus was passed in 1679, and ever since then, except when suspended during times of national emergency, it has been regarded as a vital British liberty.

HADRIAN (A.D. 76–138)
Roman emperor. In addition to being a fine soldier and administrator he was a lover of the arts and did much to further these, particularly in the field of architecture. He was responsible for building the wall running across the north of England, from Wallsend to Bowness, some 73 miles.

HAGGARD, Sir Henry Rider
(1856–1925)
English novelist, born at Bradenham. He wrote many romantic adventure stories, the most popular being *King Solomon's Mines*. For a time he was secretary to the Governor of Natal.

HAHN, Otto (1879–1968)
German scientist whose work on the radio-active elements led to his discovery of nuclear fission. In this work he was associated with F. Strassmann. Hahn was awarded the Nobel Prize for Chemistry in 1944. [*See* NUCLEAR ENERGY.]

HAIG, Douglas, First Earl (1861–1928)
British soldier. Born in Edinburgh, he entered Sandhurst in 1883 and was gazetted to the Cavalry. Haig served in Egypt, South Africa and India, reaching the rank of Lieutenant-General. During the Great War he became Commander-in-Chief of the British troops in France. His main battles were at the Somme (1915), Arras and Passchendaele (1917) and in 1918 British armies under Haig drove the Germans out of France and Belgium.

HAILE SELASSIE (1891——)
Emperor of ETHIOPIA. He was educated by French monks. After making himself regent and official heir to the throne he eventually became Emperor in 1930. In 1931 he proclaimed a constitution, a new penal code and other reforms. When Ethiopia was attacked and overcome by Italy he had to leave the country (1936) and take refuge in England. Early in 1941 he returned home when his country was liberated by British soldiers.

HAITI
A republic on the island of Hispaniola which it shares with the DOMINICAN REPUBLIC. It is not much larger (10,700 square miles) than Wales but has a population of 4 million, most of which is Negro and French-speaking. The capital is Port-au-Prince. Its chief product is coffee.

HAKLUYT, Richard (c. 1552–1616)
English geographer and churchman. Born in Herefordshire, and educated at Oxford. Taking holy orders he became chaplain to the British Embassy in Paris where he collected all the material available about French and Spanish voyages to all parts of the world. Returning to England in 1588, he published the next year the *Principal Navigations, Voyages and Discoveries of the English Nation*. It is a chronicle of the adventures of the English seamen.

HALIFAX, Edward F. L. W., First Earl
(1881–1959)
British statesman. Born in Yorkshire, he was educated at Eton and Oxford. First elected to Parliament as a Conservative in 1910 he held various ministerial posts in the years 1921–1925 as president of the Board of Education and Minister of Agriculture. Viceroy of India (1926–1931), he furthered Indian development towards Dominion status. As Foreign Secretary (1938–1940) he was much criticized for the policy of appeasement towards Germany before the outbreak of war. From 1940 to 1944 he was British Ambassador to the U.S.

HALLEY, Edmund (1656–1742)
Astronomer Royal from 1720. He predicted the return in 1757 of the COMET named after him and calculated its orbit. It was last visible in 1910.

HALLOW-E'EN
October 31st, the eve of All Hallows' or All Saints' Day. In the Celtic calendar Hallow-e'en was 'old year's night', and on this night witches and ghosts are said to be abroad. There are many games, tales and superstitions connected with Hallow-e'en; for example, witches are

HADRIAN'S Wall built between Wallsend and Bowness, a distance of some 73 miles.

frightened off by anyone wearing red, or the one you will marry can be found by throwing a ball of blue wool through your window and winding it in, the lucky one will be found holding the end of the wool!

HALS, Franz (*c.* 1580–1666)
Dutch portrait painter, born in Antwerp. He painted many group portraits of soldiers and individual portraits. At the age of 84, he painted one of his greatest works *The Governors of the Almshouses*. Other famous paintings are *Archers of St. George, Archers of St. Adrian, Governors of St. Elizabeth Hospital, Married Couple, The Merry Drinker* and the *Laughing Cavalier*, all in the Wallace Collection, London. This last is one of the most frequently reproduced paintings in the world. Hals spent most of his life in poverty, owing to his extravagant habits and love of good living.

HAMMURABI (Khammurabi)
King of BABYLON about 2200 B.C. He was a powerful ruler and founded the greatness of Babylon. The Hammurabi code of laws is the earliest so far recorded. A large number of tablets bearing royal despatches from Hammurabi are in the British Museum.

HAMSTER
This small animal belongs to the RODENT family. Although not native to Britain it occurs in Europe, Asia and Africa. The European hamster is about a foot long, with a tail only 2 inches in length. It lives in burrows, containing store-rooms and nurseries, in which it sleeps during the winter. It carries food to its burrows in large cheek-pouches which it fills with the front paws, and for this reason is considered a great pest by farmers.

HANDEL, George Frederick (1685–1759)
Anglo-German composer, born at Halle. He started life as a violinist in the orchestra at the Opera House at Hamburg, spent some years in Italy and then became director of music to the Elector of Hanover. At 25 he came to London as a composer of Italian operas, and settled here without the Elector's permission. Things looked black for Handel when the Elector became King George I of England; but he restored himself to favour by writing some of his best music for the new king, including the famous *Water Music*. He became a naturalized Englishman, and when Italian opera went out of fashion took to writing oratorios, producing the greatest of all time, *The Messiah*. In his later years he went blind; he died in London and was buried with high honours in Poet's Corner, Westminster Abbey.

HANNIBAL (247–183 B.C.)
Great Carthaginian leader and son of Hamilcar. He led the armies of Carthage against Rome in the Second Punic War and from the time he crossed the Alps (218) he spent fifteen years in Italy undefeated. The historian Polybius says: 'No one can withhold admiration for Hannibal's generalship, his courage, and his power in the open field . . .' But he was recalled to Carthage and defeated by the Romans at Zama (202). Exiled from his home, he took poison and died rather than be taken by the Romans.

HANSARD
The popular name given to the Official Reports of the debates both in the House of Commons and the House of Lords. Luke Hansard was printer to the House of Commons more than 150 years ago and he did his work so well that long after his death people continued to call the reports 'Hansard'. Today anyone can buy a copy of Hansard and read the debates that take place each day that PARLIAMENT meets.

HARDIE, James Keir (1856–1915)
British labour leader. Born in Ayrshire, he had no schooling, but taught himself to read and write. He worked in a Scottish coal-pit from the age of 7 until he was 24. After a period as journalist he founded the Independent Labour Party in 1893 and entered Parliament the same year as Independent Labour member for West Ham. Later he became Chairman of the Parliamentary Labour Party. He was a prolific writer on socialism and anti-militarism.

HARDY, Thomas (1840–1928)
English novelist, born in a Dorset village. His early training was as an architect's draughtsman. In literature his preference was for poetry. Hardy always thought differently from most other people of his time; and in two novels of the nineties, *Tess of the D'Urbervilles* and *Jude the Obscure*, he expressed his differences so openly that a public outcry arose against him. He was distressed by the public anger, and after 1897 published no more novels. But for another thirty years he wrote and published poetry, and created a poetic drama of epic size, *The Dynasts,* which describes the rise and fall of Napoleon Bonaparte.

HARES
Belong to the same family (Leporidae) as rabbits but are much larger and have longer ears and hind legs. Also they do not burrow, but live in a kind of nest, called a 'form'. For safety they depend mainly on their great speed.

HARTEBEEST An antelope found only in Africa.

Hares are found in most countries with the exception of Madagascar and Australia; any in these countries have been imported.

HARGREAVES, James (? d. 1778)
Lancashire weaver who invented the spinning-jenny and revolutionized the cotton industry.

HAROUN-AL-RASCHID (c. A.D. 764–809)
Brilliant and successful Caliph of Baghdad whose fame spread to the West. He was also a scholar and a poet, but he is today known largely because of the references to him in *Thousand and One Nights.*

HARPSICHORD
Musical instrument in use in the 17th and 18th centuries. It was similar in shape to our modern grand piano (though smaller); but its strings were plucked by quills instead of being struck by hammers, which give it a thinner, more metallic sound. Sometimes it had two keyboards and occasionally a pedal-keyboard for the feet, like an organ. It gave way to the piano in the last century, but modern harpsichords are now made so that the music of such composers as Purcell and Bach may be heard as it originally sounded.

HARTE, Francis Bret (1836–1902)
American poet and writer. After becoming very popular in America he travelled to Europe and lived the last seventeen years of his life in London where he was very well known and liked. His earlier works, especially *The Luck of Roaring Camp* and *The Outcasts of Poker Flats*, are still thought to be his best.

HARTEBEESTS
Belong to the ANTELOPE family and have long narrow faces and horns with ridges across them. There are a great many species, all of which are confined to Africa.

HARVEY, William (1578–1657)
English physician, born at Folkestone. Studied at Cambridge and Padua. His discovery of the circulation of the blood was truly revolutionary, and, at the same time, laid the foundations of a new science—physiology. Harvey became physician to Charles I. He achieved great fame and even before his death a statue was erected to his honour in the Royal College of Physicians.

HASTINGS, Warren (1732–1818)
British administrator, born in Oxfordshire. He joined the East India Company as a clerk in 1750. He worked together with Robert CLIVE and gradually rose to become member of the Council of Bengal. He resigned after disputes with his colleagues, but returned to India in 1768 and in 1773 was named Governor-General. He tried to put the finances in order and improve the administration of justice during his term of office. After his return to England in 1785, he was impeached on charges of cruelty and corruption while in India. The trial lasted seven years, creating enormous public interest. Hastings was eventually acquitted and the East India Company granted him a pension.

HATHAWAY, Anne (c. 1556–1623)
Reputed to be the wife of SHAKESPEARE. The marriage is recorded as taking place in 1582. Anne Hathaway's cottage is one of the landmarks at Stratford-on-Avon today.

HAWAII [*See* U.S.A.]

HAWKINS, Sir John (1532–1595)

Elizabethan sailor. Born at Plymouth, he took to the sea as a young man and was the first Elizabethan to engage in the slave trade. After many expeditions against the Spanish and Portuguese, he was made Treasurer of the Navy (1573), when he introduced many improvements. He received his knighthood for service against the Armada in 1588. While on an expedition to the Spanish Main led by DRAKE, Hawkins caught a fever and died at sea off Porto Rico.

HAWKS

Birds of prey and closely related to the EAGLES. All have very keen eyes, powerful wings, hooked beaks and fierce talons (claws). The nests of these birds are built of sticks high in a tree or on the ledge of a cliff. Hawks do not normally catch other birds on the wing as do the eagles, but feed mostly on small mammals like mice and rats. They can glide for long periods watching out for prey and can dive at fantastic speeds.

HAWTHORNE, Nathaniel (1804–1864)

American writer, born at Salem (Mass.). He served for a time as a customs official and U.S. consul in England. His most widely-read novels are *Twice-Told Tales*, *The Scarlet Letter* and *The House of the Seven Gables*.

HAYDN, Franz Joseph (1732–1809)

Austrian composer, born at Rohrau. The son of poor country-people, he became director of music to Prince Esterhazy in Hungary; here he composed the first great string quartets and symphonies the world had ever known. He was a simple man with a strong sense of humour. When the Prince, who loved music, forgot to let his musicians go home for the winter, Haydn wrote his famous *Farewell Symphony*, in which the players left the platform one by one, leaving two violins to finish the music; the Prince, who also had a sense of humour, took the hint and let the orchestra go. Haydn later moved to Vienna, where he met MOZART, and at 60 gave concerts in London, bringing twelve symphonies specially composed for the occasion. He died in Vienna, while Napoleon's army was bombarding the city, playing the Austrian national anthem, which he had written himself. Apart from his 104 symphonies and 84 string quartets, he wrote the two famous oratorios *The Creation* and *The Seasons*.

HAZLITT, William (1778–1830)

English writer, born at Maidstone. Originally studied for the Church but turned to art and lived for a while in Paris. Later, about 1812, turned to writing after having settled in London. He wrote a great volume of work, but is particularly remembered for his essays on drama, especially Shakespearean drama. He was friendly with many of the leading writers of his time, but later critcized them, especially COLERIDGE and WORDSWORTH.

HEART [*See* HUMAN BODY]

HEAT

That form of energy of which we are normally made aware by means of our sense of touch. When heat is examined scientifically, however, instruments are used instead of the senses of the human body, and measurement is introduced. In this way the study of heat becomes a branch of physics.

Heat is normally measured in calories, one calory being the quantity of heat needed to raise one gramme of water through 1 deg. C. The

HAWK A sparrow hawk with its brood.

latter is a measure of temperature, which is the word used to describe how hot or cold anything is. Temperature is measured with a THERMOMETER, the commonest form of which is a glass tube of very narrow bore joined to a bulb containing mercury. When heat is applied to the thermometer the mercury expands and passes along the narrow tube. On this tube is marked a scale. Each unit on the scale is a degree of temperature. There are three scales in general use. In Great Britain we use the Fahrenheit scale on which the melting point of ice is called 32 and the boiling point of water is called 212, the space between being divided into 180 equal parts. In science the Centigrade scale is commonly used, on which the two fixed points already mentioned are called 0 and 100. There is also the absolute scale inferred by mathematical arguments. According to these arguments all movement causing heat in a substance cease at a certain point termed absolute zero. In practice this is the same as minus 273 degrees Centigrade.

The above arguments show that quantity of heat is not the same as temperature, for the heat given to, or taken from, a substance depends not only on the rise or fall in temperature but also on the nature of the substance and on the quantity of it. For example, much more heat is needed to boil a gallon of water than to boil a pint, yet the final temperature in each case is the same—100 deg. C. or 212 deg. F. or 373 deg. absolute.

Heat travels from one place to another in three possible ways: by conduction, by convection, and by radiation. The first is the handing on of heat from particle to particle of a substance when the particles are touching. Convection is the movement of a gas or liquid when the hot parts rise, as they do when the air of a room is heated by a fire or stove. Radiation is the transfer of heat energy by means of waves like those of light. Radiation can take place through a vacuum, whereas conduction and convection can only take place in a material. The sun's heat reaches the earth by means of radiation, but if it goes through glass into a room the air in the room is heated and begins to move and so the heat is transferred by convection.

HEAT PUMP

Device for causing heat to flow from a low-temperature region to a region of higher temperature. Every refrigerator is a heat pump, though the term is usually now applied to devices which abstract heat from the soil or rivers and employ it to warm buildings. A liquid or gaseous cooling substance is alternately compressed (by a pump) and expanded, the heat generated by the compression being transferred in a heat-exchanger to a convection system, and that lost in the expansion being made good by pumping the coolant through the pipes buried in the soil or river.

HEAVY WATER

The formula for normal water is H_2O. This means that two atoms of hydrogen are joined with one atom of oxygen to form one molecule of water. Each hydrogen atom has normally only one proton as its nucleus. If a neutron is added to this nucleus, the resulting atom is still hydrogen as far as the chemical properties are concerned, but the atomic weight is about doubled. This isotope of hydrogen is called heavy hydrogen or deuterium and is given the symbol D. If this heavy hydrogen combined

HEAT

Convection is due to the movement of particles in a gas or liquid. In a central heating system, water is heated by a furnace at A and then rises through the pipes to radiators B, C, D elsewhere in the building. It returns to A to be heated once more and in this way circulates continuously.

Radiation is the transfer of heat energy as waves. The direct heat felt from the filament of an electric fire is radiant heat, although convection also occurs in the air around the fire. The polished bowl helps to direct the heat as silvered surfaces reflect radiation while dull, black surfaces absorb it.

Conduction usually occurs in solid matter where heat can be passed from one particle of the substance to another. Metals are good conductors of heat and in a soldering iron, heat produced electrically by a filament in the handle is conducted along a length of metal to the tip where the solder is.

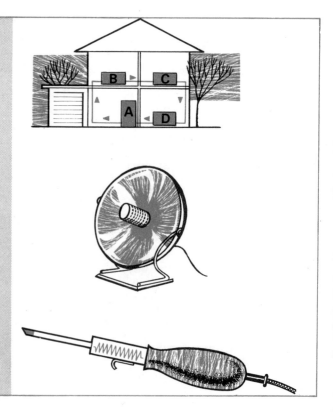

HELICOPTER

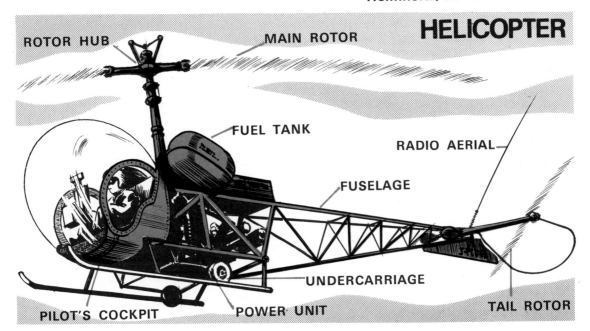

ROTOR HUB   MAIN ROTOR

FUEL TANK

RADIO AERIAL

FUSELAGE

UNDERCARRIAGE

PILOT'S COCKPIT   POWER UNIT   TAIL ROTOR

with oxygen to form water, the result is 'heavy' water, D_2O, which has a relative density of 1·1 and freezes at a temperature slightly higher than the freezing-point of ordinary water. It occurs in the proportion of one part in 5,000 in natural water, and is used in nuclear power plants.

HEDGEHOG

Species of this mammal are to be found in most parts of the world with the exception of America. It is night prowling and lives on insects, slugs, worms, eggs and even fowls. It also kills rats and snakes. The hedgehog spends the day curled up asleep, usually under dead leaves. For its winter sleep it usually finds a more secluded spot, sometimes underground. It should be noted that it is only in countries which have severe winters that the hedgehog hibernates.

HEGEL, Georg Wilhelm Friedrich
(1770–1831)
German philosopher, born at Stuttgart. His ideas are very complex and to understand them needs a great deal of study of such of his works as *Phenomenology of Mind*, *Science of Logic* and *Philosophy of Right*. However, his philosophy has had a great influence, particularly on Karl MARX, the founder of communism.

HEINE, Heinrich (1797–1856)
German lyric poet, born at Dusseldorf. Published his first volume of poems in 1821. After several journeys abroad to England and Italy

he settled permanently in Paris. In 1845 he fell victim to creeping paralysis and from 1848 until his death was bedridden. Although Heine wrote travel books, literary criticism and some poetic tragedies, his fame rests on his lyric poetry.

HELICOPTER
Type of aircraft in which lift and thrust is provided by a power-driven, horizontal rotor (usually three-bladed) located above the fuselage. It has unique flying characteristics, e.g., it can hover and ascend and descend vertically. Large designs have been built for passenger and military transport.

HELIOGRAPH
Means a 'sun-writer', and consists of a mirror and shutter and used for signalling. Signals are controlled by the shutter and are made up of long and short flashes (Morse Code) of sunlight reflected by the mirror. Radio-communication has more or less taken over the job of the heliograph.

HELMHOLTZ, Hermann L. F. von
(1821–1894)
German scientist, born at Potsdam. He did important and fundamental research into many and divers branches of science. Among his outstanding discoveries are the law of the conservation of energy (1847), the geological age of the sun (1853), a theory of organ pipes (1859), and measurement of nerve pulses (1852)—to mention only a few.

HEMINGWAY, Ernest (1898–1961)
American novelist, born at Oak Park, Illinois. He has had a very great influence on modern English writing. Hemingway attached great importance to physique and admired the manly virtues and the tough life. His style is realistic, full of clipped dialogue and physical detail. Many of his novels deal with Spain and the Spanish Civil War. His most widely read novels are *A Farewell to Arms, For Whom the Bell Tolls,* and *The Old Man and the Sea.* He was awarded the Nobel Prize for Literature in 1954.

HENRY VIII, King of England (1491–1547)
The greatest of the Tudor Kings. He ascended the throne in 1509. Together with his chief adviser, Cardinal WOLSEY, he intended to increase England's authority by keeping the balance of power between France and Spain. This meant that he needed a much larger revenue, and Wolsey procured this by heavy and unpopular taxation. Henry's determination to divorce Catharine of Aragon and marry Anne Boleyn, which the Pope would not sanction, led to the downfall of Wolsey and the break with Rome. Henry declared himself head of the Church of England in place of the Pope, but insisted, in the Statute of the Six Articles, that the doctrine of his church be otherwise unchanged. Henry next turned to the monasteries, whose valuable land he coveted, and decided that they should be abolished. This caused much misery in the countryside, and a revolt known as the 'Pilgrimage of Grace' had to be crushed. Henry's wives followed in rapid succession—Anne Boleyn was executed for infidelity; Jane Seymour died; Anne of Cleves was so ugly that Henry decided to divorce her as soon as he had married her; Catharine Howard was beheaded, charged with unfaithfulness; and only Catharine Parr survived her King. In spite of the harshness of his rule and the many judicial murders he perpetrated, Henry remained popular with most of his subjects and retained his authority in the kingdom to the end of his reign.

HERACLITUS of Ephesus (*c.* 500 B.C.)
Considered that life implies a continual change or evolution of form. Everything is in a state of flow and is always at some stage becoming something else. He was the first to distinguish clearly between the senses and reason, and taught the immortality of the soul. The senses, he believed, often mislead us, and it is by reason alone that we discover truth. Because of his pessimistic views of human beings he was known as the 'weeping philosopher'.

HERO (*c.* A.D. 100)
Also known as Heron of Alexandria. Inventor and mathematician. His book *Pneumatica* described about a hundred small machines and mechanical toys, most of which depended for their movement on the power of steam.

HERODOTUS of Halicarnassus
(484–420 B.C.)
Greek historian who was also interested in physical geography, and made a study of the fossil shells in Egypt. He made a map of the world and was the first to distinguish the continents of Africa, Asia and Europe. His largest work was a nine-volume account of the struggles between the Greeks and Persians.

HERRICK, Robert (1591–1674)
English poet. He took Holy Orders in 1627 and was appointed to a Devon village, where he served as parish priest, except during the Commonwealth when he was suspended for twelve years. The verses that he wrote were circulated in manuscript; then in 1648 a collection appeared in print under the title *Hesperides.* His poems celebrated youth, love and the countryside, and religion was conspicuously absent from them.

HERSCHEL, Sir William (1738–1822)
Anglo-German astronomer, born in Hanover. In 1757 he came to England and worked as an organist in Bath from 1766. He educated himself in astronomy, and began to build his own telescopes. In 1782 he became private astronomer to George III. He discovered the planet Uranus, many nebulae, and he found that double stars revolved round each other. He also discovered two of Saturn's satellites that had not previously been observed.

HERTZ, Heinrich Rudolf (1857–1894)
German scientist, born at Hamburg. He confirmed experimentally Maxwell's theory of ELECTRO-MAGNETIC WAVES by producing wireless (radio) waves using sparks from an induction coil. At one time radio waves were referred to as 'hertzian' waves. Hertz also did important researches on the photo-electric effect.

HESIOD (*c.* 730 B.C.)
Greek epic poet about whom little is actually known but thought to have been born at Ascra (Boeotia). Of the many works ascribed to him the best known are *Theogony, Works and Days* and *The Shield of Hercules.*

HILLIARD, Nicholas (*c.* 1547–1619)
English artist who was a goldsmith before turning to painting. His most important works

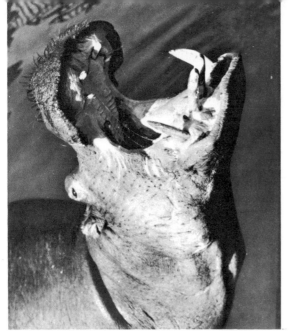

HIPPOPOTAMUS with its mouth open and showing its lower canine teeth. These can weigh up to 4-7 pounds and grow up to 24 inches long.

are portrait miniatures. He wrote one book, *The Arte of Limning.*

HIMALAYAS

A vast range of mountains that stretch for over 1,500 miles across the Indian peninsula. They consist of several ranges of peaks, separated by deep gorges through which rivers flow. Kashmir, Tibet, Nepal and Bhutan are the chief Himalayan lands. The Himalayas include the highest mountain in the world, Mount EVEREST, 29,028 feet. The great rivers Indus, Brahmaputra and Ganges rise in this range.

HINDENBURG, Paul von (1847–1934)

German soldier and second president of the German Reich. Born in Posen of a Prussian military family, he entered a cadet school in 1858. By 1911 he had reached the rank of General and retired. The Great War recalled him to duty. His victory at the battle of Tannenberg in East Prussia over the Russians (1914) made him world-famous. He was promoted Field-Marshal, and Chief of the German General Staff. In 1918 he recommended acceptance of the Armistice terms. In 1925 and again in 1932 he was elected President. In 1933 he appointed HITLER German Chancellor.

HINDUISM

The great majority of the people in INDIA are Hindus. Hinduism is both a religion and a social system. As a religion it takes many forms, sophisticated at its highest level (Brahmanism), but also tolerating more primitive beliefs. Brahma is the all-embracing spirit, with whom all people desire to be united, and this can be attained through such practices as Yoga, which frees the mind from the influence of the senses. Until he can escape from it, man follows a cycle of lives, being reincarnated at death into a higher or lower form of life according to his deeds. As a social system, Hinduism divides the faithful into 'castes' or orders—Brahmans, soldiers, farmers, servants etc.—based on the code of the Law of Manu.

HIPPARCHUS (c. 190–120 B.C.)

Greek astronomer who compiled the first star catalogue giving the position of some 1,000 stars. He calculated the length of the lunar month to within a second and the solar year to within six minutes. He invented trigonometry and used latitude and longitude to fix geographical positions. His work is recorded in PTOLEMY'S *Almagest.*

HIPPOCRATES (c. 460–c. 370 B.C.)

Greek doctor of Cos. His work established medicine as a science and has earned him the title 'Father of Medicine'. The Hippocratic Oath is still considered to represent the code of conduct or ethics of the medical profession.

HIPPOPOTAMUS

This animal is amphibious, that is, it is at home equally in the water and on land. Its muzzle is broad and rounded, with the nostrils, eyes, and ears set high to enable it to breathe, smell, see, and hear while its body is completely immersed. The skin is smooth and hairless. One important feature is the two long tusk-like teeth in the lower jaw. They feed on weeds and forest vegetation, but only at night. Hippopotami are now only to be found in Africa. Belongs to the same order (Suina) as the pig.

HIROHITO (1901——)

Former Emperor of JAPAN, now a constitutional monarch. He is descended from a dynasty that is believed to go back to the 7th century B.C. Partly educated in England, he succeeded his father in 1926, bearing the title Dai Nippon Teikoku Tenno (Imperial Son of Heaven of Great Japan). After the Japanese defeat in the Second World War he repudiated his divinity and under the new constitution he became a symbol of the state and no longer its sacred basis. He is a very skilled marine biologist.

HITLER, Adolf (1889–1945)

German dictator. Born at Braunau in Austria, the son of a customs official. After various odd jobs he went to Munich and lived as a painter

(1911). During the Great War he served in the German Army as lance-corporal. On demobilization he founded the National Socialist German Workers' Party (i.e., the Nazis) with an extreme nationalist and anti-semitic programme. An attempted uprising in Munich (1923) was suppressed and Hitler was sentenced to five years imprisonment but released after eight months. He did not become Chancellor until 1933 when he entirely suppressed German democracy, establishing concentration camps for political opponents and Jews, dissolving trade unions and abolishing free elections. Rearmament at home and expansion abroad—including the annexation of Austria (1938) and Czechoslovakia (1939)—were his chief policies. He led Germany into war in 1939 and committed suicide in April 1945 when Berlin was encircled and all hope of victory was lost. [*See* GERMANY.]

HITTITES
People who occupied Asia Minor and Syria during the period ranging from approximately 2000 B.C. to 700 B.C. The Hittites are mentioned many times in the Old Testament and recent excavations have thrown new light on Hittite civilization.

HOBBEMA, Meindert (1638–1709)
Dutch artist, particularly of landscapes. He was a close friend of RUISDAEL and much influenced by him, in fact, it is sometimes difficult to distinguish their works apart. Hobbema's work had considerable influence on English landscape painting. His *Avenue at Middelharnis* is very popular and much reproduced.

HOBBES, Thomas (1588–1679)
British philosopher, born at Malmesbury. His best-known work, *Leviathan,* which maintains the Sovereign's right to rule his subjects absolutely, so long as he has the strength to overcome their resistance, is the first great English work on political philosophy. [*See* John LOCKE.]

HOCKEY
A game played between two teams, each of 11 players, and the scoring is by goals. A hockey ground is shaped like a rectangle and is marked out with white lines, as shown in the diagram. The hockey stick has a flat face on its left-hand side only, and all the edges are rounded. Its weight must not be more than 28 ounces. The white, seamless ball must weigh between $5\frac{1}{2}$ and $5\frac{3}{4}$ ounces, and its circumference between $8\frac{13}{16}$ and $9\frac{1}{4}$ inches. The game is controlled by two umpires. Each umpire takes one half of the ground for the

whole game, and also takes the whole of one side-line. The umpires signal goals, infringements, and other causes of stoppage and resumption of play by blowing a whistle.

The game is begun by what is called a bully, which is played at the centre of the ground. One player from each side stands squarely facing the side-lines. When the whistle is blown for play to start, each player taps the ground with his stick, and then, with the flat of his stick, taps his opponent's stick over the ball; this is done three times in succession. After the third time, either of the two players may strike the ball and thus put it in play. While the bully is taking place all the other players must be in their own half of the pitch, and none of them may be within 5 yards of the ball until it has been struck into play. Centre bullies are played at the start of a game, after half-time, and to restart play after each goal is scored. Other bullies, played at the 25-yard lines and elsewhere, are subject to the same general rules. No bully may be played within 5 yards of the goal-line inside the circle.

The object of each team is to get the ball into the opposing goal by striking, dribbling, and passing. Only the flat of the stick may be used for playing the ball. In striking or stopping the ball, no part of the stick may be raised above the shoulder; otherwise the ball may be struck in the air as on the ground. The ball must not be 'undercut', i.e., driven with the face of the stick at an angle so that the ball rises with great force, but the player is allowed to use the 'scoop' stroke provided that it is not dangerous, or likely to lead to dangerous play. No player is allowed to interfere with an opponent's stick, whether by hitting, hooking, holding or striking at it, or in any other way.

The ball may be stopped on the ground or in the air with the hand. If it is caught, it must be released into play immediately. Stopping the ball intentionally with any other part of the body is not allowed. The foot or leg may not be used to support the stick in order to resist an opponent.

The correct way of moving the ball is by the use of the stick, and it must not be picked up, thrown, carried or kicked. The only exception to this is that the goalkeeper may, within his own circle, kick the ball or stop it with any part of his body, when he takes part in a penalty bully.

Charging, kicking, shoving and tripping are all forbidden, and of course no player may strike at his opponent with his stick, or use it for holding him in any way. A player is not allowed to attack from an opponent's left unless he touches the ball before the stick or person of the opponent. He is not allowed to obstruct his opponent by running in between him and the ball, nor must he interpose himself, or his stick, in any way, as an obstruction to his opponent.

A goal is scored whenever the ball passes wholly over the goal-line between the posts and under the cross-bar, provided that it was hit by, or glanced off, the stick of a player of the attacking team inside the circle.

If the ball is lodged in the goalkeeper's pads or in the clothing of any player, the umpire stops the game and orders a bully on the spot where the incident occurred.

At the moment when the ball is hit or rolled in, any player of the same side is in an off-side position if there are less than 3 opponents nearer to their own goal-line, and provided that he is nearer to their goal-line than the player striking or rolling in the ball. He cannot, however, be offside in his own half of the ground. If, while he is in this position, he gains advantage by it, or influences the play of an opponent, the umpire will award the appropriate penalty. As soon as the ball has been definitely played by an opponent the player is automatically on-side again.

Play stops whenever the ball passes over one of the side-lines, and is restarted by being rolled in by a member of the team opposed to that of the player who last touched the ball. The roller-in must stand outside the field of play, with his hand, stick, and feet all behind the side-line. He must not approach within playing distance of the ball, or take any part in the game, until the ball has been played by another player of either team. Until the ball leaves the hand of the roller-in, all the other players of both teams must have sticks and feet behind the 7-yards line.

In the case of an infringement by the roller-in, the roll-in is awarded to the opposing team. An infringement by any other player is normally not penalised, the roll-in being taken again, but if another player persistently breaks a rule, a free hit may be awarded against him.

If the ball is sent over the goal-line by a player of the attacking team, the game is restarted by a free hit to be taken by a defender 16 yards from the inner edge of that line, on a spot opposite to where the ball crossed the goal-line. The same applies if the ball is sent unintentionally over the goal-line by a player of the defending team, provided that he is at least 25 yards from the goal-line. If he is within 25 yards, a corner is awarded; if he sends the ball over the goal-line intentionally, a penalty corner is awarded.

A corner is a free hit by the attacking team, taken from any point on either line within 3 yards of the corner flag-post, on the side of the field on which the ball crossed the goal-line. When the hit is taken, all the defending team must stand with feet and sticks behind their own goal-line, while the attacking team, apart from the player taking the corner, stand with feet and sticks outside the circle. Normally in the case of an infringement of this by either side, the umpire will order the corner to be taken again. The player taking the corner is not allowed to shoot direct at goal.

There are three main penalties for infringements:

(1) A 'free hit' is awarded for an infringement outside the infringing team's circle. The ball may be hit or pushed along the ground, but not scooped. No other player of either side may stand within 5 yards of the ball when the hit is taken, and after making the hit the striker must not interfere with the play again until the ball has touched another player of either team. If the striker misses the ball completely he takes the hit again.

(2) A 'penalty corner' is awarded for in-

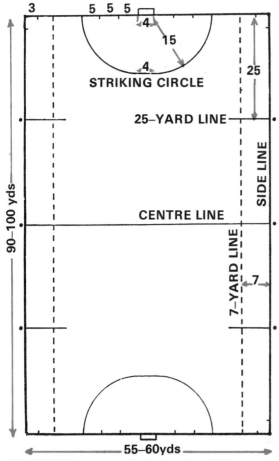

HOCKEY Diagram of the layout of a field.

fringements by defenders within their own circle or for intentionally hitting the ball over their own goal-line, as described above. It is the same as an ordinary corner, except that it may be taken from any spot on the goal-line on either side of the goal but not within 10 yards of a goal-post. No more than 6 of the defending team shall be behind their goal-line. The rest shall remain beyond the centre line until the hit has been taken.

(3) A penalty stroke is awarded for a bad breach of the rules by the defending team inside the circle, such as an intentional infringement to prevent a goal from being scored or an infringement which, though unintentional, is held to have prevented the scoring of a goal.

The penalty stroke consists of either a push, flick or scoop stroke taken from a spot 8 yards in front of the centre of the goal-line by a player of the attacking team, who, when taking the stroke, must stand close to the ball and is permitted to take one stride forward in making the stroke. He may touch the ball once only and thereafter must not approach the ball, or the goal-keeper or his substitute. While the penalty stroke is taken all the other players of both teams shall remain outside the 25-yard line. Whatever stroke is used, the ball may be raised to any height.

If, as a result of the penalty stroke:
 (i) the ball passes wholly over the goal-line between the goal-posts and under the cross-bar, a goal is scored.
 (ii) there is a breach of any rule by the goal-keeper or his substitute which prevents a goal being scored, the umpire shall award a goal, unless the offence has been induced by the striker.
 (iii) the ball come to rest inside the circle or passes outside the circle, the penalty stroke is ended. The game shall be restarted by a free hit taken by a defender from a spot in front of the centre of the goal-line and 16 yards from the inner edge of that line.

In cases of rough or dangerous play the umpire may order a player to leave the field for the rest of the game.

HOFFMANN, Ernst Theodor 'Amadeus' (1776–1822)

German writer and composer. Born at Königsberg. For some years he wandered all over Germany as composer, portrait-painter, writer and theatre manager. Was appointed Councillor of the Court of Appeal. Although prolific as a composer and painter, Hoffmann is best known as a short-story writer: OFFENBACH'S opera *Tales of Hoffmann* is based on some of these stories.

HOGARTH An engraving of 'Beer Street'. One of a series exposing the evils of drink.

HOGARTH, William (1697–1764)

English artist, born in London. At the age of 15 he was apprenticed to a silver-plate engraver. He tried to earn a living with small portraits, but achieved his first real success in 1732 with his series of moral pictures, *The Harlot's Progress*. Hogarth's talent is in the way he drew attention to the vices of his age—the terrible results of cheap drink (*Gin Lane*), the greed and arrogance of the wealthy (*Marriage à la Mode* series, *The Rake's Progress*, etc.). He also drew savage cartoons of Wilkes, Pitt and Temple.

HOGMANAY

Name given by Scottish people to New Year's Eve. Traditionally children went from house to house asking for small gifts and singing:
 Hogmanay, Trollolay,
 Gie's o' your white bread
 And nane o' your grey.

HOHENZOLLERN

Powerful German family and named after the family castle in Swabia. Closely connected with the rise and power of PRUSSIA. The last in the line was William II, King of Prussia and Emperor of Germany (1859–1941).

HOLBEIN, Hans 'the Younger' (1497–1543)

Outstanding German portrait and religious painter, born in Augsburg. As a youth, he became a friend of ERASMUS, of whom he produced many portraits. In about 1526 he came to England, where he painted a number of magnificent portraits, including those of Sir Thomas More and Sir Henry Guildford and his wife (the latter now in Windsor Castle). Holbein settled in England, and among other outstanding portraits produced those of Archbishop Warham and Christine of Denmark. Under the patronage of Henry VIII, he painted many portraits and drawings of the King and his wives. Holbein died of the plague in London.

HOLIDAYS, PUBLIC
For as long as history tells there have been holidays, though the holidays of one country and of one period differ from another. The word means Holy Days; and in Christian countries they are usually connected with Christian festivals, such as Christmas, Easter and Whitsun.

The period which today is observed in honour of the Birth of Christ has, however, been kept as a holiday period for far longer than two thousand years. For in Roman times the period December 19th to 24th was known as the Saturnalia, held in honour of the god Saturn from which we get in all probability the name Saturday. People decorated their houses with evergreens, gave one another presents and had a period of fun and merrymaking. When people became Christians they changed this holiday into a Christian festival.

The only important holiday in the Middle Ages that was not a religious one was May Day. Although May Day is still observed in Britain it is now not a public holiday as it is in many countries.

Public holidays in Britain are called Bank Holidays. This is because, since an Act of Parliament was passed in 1871, banks must close on those days.

HOLINSHED, Raphael (d. c. 1580)
English chronicler who compiled *The Chronicles of England, Scotland and Ireland*, used extensively by Shakespeare as a source of material for his historical plays. Holinshed himself wrote the section called *The History of England*, but the remainder of the work consists of translations, adaptations, and material from other hands.

HOLLAND [*See* NETHERLANDS.]

HOLST, Gustav (1874–1934)
English composer, born at Cheltenham. Much of his music was based on English folk-songs, and a certain amount inspired by ancient Indian poetry; but he is chiefly remembered for his orchestral suite *The Planets*.

HOLY COMMUNION
Service commemorating the Last Supper, and the supreme Sacrament of the Christian Church. Roman Catholics, and some Anglicans, use the term 'Mass', while to most Protestants it is known as 'The Lord's Supper'. As recorded in the Gospels and by St. Paul, it consists of repeating the action of Jesus in hallowing the bread and wine as tokens of the Sacrifice of Himself for all mankind. The bread is broken, thanks are given in prayer for the bread and the wine, after which the Communicants partake of a little of each. The Roman Church administers the Sacrament under one form only—the priest distributing the host (i.e. under the form of bread) to the laity. The Anglican Church publicly celebrates Communion every Sunday and on all Holy Days; Anglicans are expected to take Communion at Easter and at least twice again during the year. The Roman Church celebrates Mass at least once daily, encourages frequent Communion, but insists on it only once a year—'at Easter or thereabouts'. Most Free Churches celebrate Communion monthly, some weekly.

HOMER
Greek epic poet. Both the date and the place of his birth and death are not known precisely but recent research suggests a date between 1050 and 800 B.C. It has even been claimed that no such man as Homer existed and that the *Iliad* and the *Odyssey* are collections of traditional ballads and not the work of one man. In any event, they were known all over the Greek-speaking world before the 6th century B.C. The *Iliad* is an epic poem in twenty-four books and deals with fifty-one days in the last years of the siege of Troy by the Greeks. The main theme is the anger of Achilles and his withdrawal from and re-entry into the battle after the death of his friend Patroclus. The *Odyssey*, also in twenty-four books, describes the wanderings of Ulysses, a Greek seafarer, on his way back to Ithaca after the fall of Troy.

HOMO SAPIENS
Man, and the only living species of the genus *Homo*. Anatomically man resembles the higher or anthropoid apes very closely. Both are primates, but the main differences between them are that man has a larger brain, walks with an upright gait, and has hands which are capable of fashioning and using tools. Neanderthal man (*Homo neanderthalensis*) is an extinct species.

HONDURAS
A republic in Central America. It is separated from BRITISH HONDURAS by the south-east

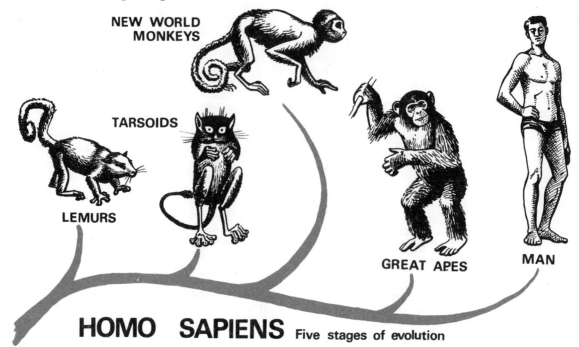

NEW WORLD MONKEYS

TARSOIDS

LEMURS

GREAT APES

MAN

HOMO SAPIENS Five stages of evolution

corner of Guatemala. It is a little smaller (43,278 square miles) than England and has a population of 2 million. The capital is Tegucigalpa. It has important silver mines.

HONG KONG
A British Crown Colony off the coast of China near the mouth of the Canton River. It is less than three times the size of the Isle of Wight but has about 3½ million inhabitants. It consists of the main island and some smaller ones together with a small part of the Chinese mainland. The capital is Victoria. Hong Kong produces large quantities of light goods—toys, shirts, plastic goods and the like.

HOOCH, Pieter De (1629–*c.* 1680)
Dutch painter. Born in Rotterdam. His paintings were mostly of bright, domestic interiors, in which field he rivals VERMEER. Most of his paintings are of rooms opening into other rooms or outdoors, and his lighting effects are very skilful. His pictures of domestic scenes are beautifully coloured, and convey a feeling of happiness. His *Interior of a Dutch House* is in the National Gallery.

HOOD, Robin
English legendary hero, supposedly leader of a band of outlaws in Sherwood Forest. Amongst his companions were 'Little' John (so called because of his huge stature), Friar Tuck (a jovial priest), and Maid Marian (his

wife). Robin Hood is first mentioned in the 14th-century poem *Piers Plowman*. He is said to have been a famous bowman who robbed the rich in order to give to the poor.

HOOD, Thomas (1799–1845)
British poet and humourist, and the son of a Scottish bookseller. He edited a number of magazines in London, and wrote some serious poetry (the *Song of the Shirt, The Bridge of Sighs*, etc.) but he is chiefly remembered today for his humorous verse like this extract from *Faithless Sally Brown*:

His death, which happened in his berth,
At forty-odd befell:
They went and told the sexton, and
The sexton toll'd the bell.

HOPKINS, Sir Frederick Gowland (1861–1947)
British scientist and discoverer of VITAMINS. He has been described as the Galileo of biochemistry. Shared the Nobel Prize for Medicine in 1929 and was President of the Royal Society in 1930.

HOPKINS, Gerard Manley (1844–1889)
English poet. He became a follower of Newman after his conversion to the Roman Church in 1866, and two years later he joined the Jesuit novitiate. None of his poems were published during his life-time, but they were collected and later published by Robert BRIDGES (1918).

Hopkins at last achieved recognition in the 1930s and is today regarded as a major poet, though rather difficult. His most famous poem is *The Wreck of the Deutschland,* and his *Notebooks* contain some beautiful descriptions of nature.

HORACE, Quintus Horatius Flaccus
(65 B.C.–8 B.C.)
Roman lyric poet, born in Venusia. Although he wrote in many forms he is perhaps best remembered for his odes. His work had a great influence on English poetry.

HORSE
Belongs to the family Equidae which also includes the ass and the zebra. It evolved from a prehistoric animal, Eohippus, which was no larger than a terrier dog. It is probable that the horse was first tamed and domesticated in Central Asia. The only real wild horse is Przhevasky's horse.

HORSE-POWER
Is the measure of the rate of doing work, and equal to 33,000 ft. lb. per min. 'Brake' horse-power is a measure of the useful work which can be performed by an engine or the like, and 'indicated' horse-power the work or energy put into it. The term and its value were adopted by James WATT after conducting experiments with dray-horses to determine their pulling power. It should be noted that although a healthy dray-horse could do this work (33,000 ft. lb. per min.) for a limited time, fatigue would reduce this figure if the horse were worked over a longer period, say a full day.

In terms of electrical power 1 h.p. equals 746 watts.

HOUDON, Jean-Antoine (1741–1828)
French sculptor, born at Versailles. Studied in Paris and Rome and was early recognized as an outstanding portrait sculptor. His models included such famous people as Voltaire, Molière, Benjamin Franklin, Rousseau and Diderot. One of his best-known works is *Girl Shivering.*

HOUSE OF REPRESENTATIVES
In the U.S.A. it is the lower House of Congress. American citizens in all the States take part in the election of members to the House. Congress passes laws concerned with defence, coinage, foreign trade, etc. Laws on marriage, education and health are made by the individual States. The lower house of the Australian Federal Parliament is also called the House of Representatives as is the New Zealand Legislature or Parliament.

HOUSMAN, Alfred Edward (1859–1936)
Classical scholar by profession, he wrote little, but a small volume which he published in 1896 under the title *A Shropshire Lad* made a deep impression on his contemporaries and on all readers since. The poems in this, and in two small books of later date, are short, pessimistic, and beautifully written. His brother, Laurence (1865–1959), was also a novelist.

HOVERCRAFT
A revolutionary kind of craft which has recently been developed for commercial and military

HOVERCRAFT was invented and made in Britain. It floats on a cushion of air as in the inset.

purposes in Britain. The hovercraft is flat-bottomed, and floats on a cushion of air, which is built up by sucking air through a funnel by means of a motor-driven fan. It can be used on either water or fairly flat ground, and jets or propellers move it forward or backward easily as it is not in frictional contact with the surface it travels over. In America hovercars are being designed.

HUDSON'S BAY COMPANY

Formed in 1668 and received its charter in 1670. Its purpose was to open up trade, particularly in furs, and chart the North-west Passage. The Company is still in existence.

HUGO, Victor Marie (1802–1885)

French poet and novelist, born at Besançon. He published his first volume of poems in 1822. Further volumes of poetry, his novel *Notre Dame de Paris,* a story of medieval Paris, and his play *Hernani* made him the leader of the Romantic school of literature. He was a very prolific writer, and poetry, novels and plays followed each other in quick succession. His best novel is *Les Misérables,* a romance of contemporary life.

HUGUENOTS

French Protestants who suffered persecution from the Catholics for two centuries. The wars began in 1562 after a congregation of Huguenots had been massacred in a barn at Vassy. A general massacre of Protestants in Paris and throughout France began on St. Bartholomew's Eve, 1572. There was a brief pause in the wars during the reign of Henry IV (1589–1610) whose Edict of Nantes (1598) gave the Protestants political and religious freedom, but the persecution was renewed by Cardinal Richelieu who took the Huguenot stronghold, La Rochelle, in 1628. Louis XIV organized 'dragonnades' to convert Protestants forcibly to Roman Catholicism, and revoked the Edict of Nantes (1685), with the result that many Huguenots fled abroad, to England or Prussia. Persecution became less severe during the 18th century, and during the Revolution the *Rights of Man* declared that everyone should have liberty of worship.

HUMAN BODY

The human body is made up of three main parts—the head, the trunk, and the limbs. The head is again divided into two regions, the skull or brain-case, and the face and jaws. The body proper, or trunk, is made up of the chest or thorax, and the abdomen, these two being separated from each other by the diaphragm or midriff. The limbs are separated into upper

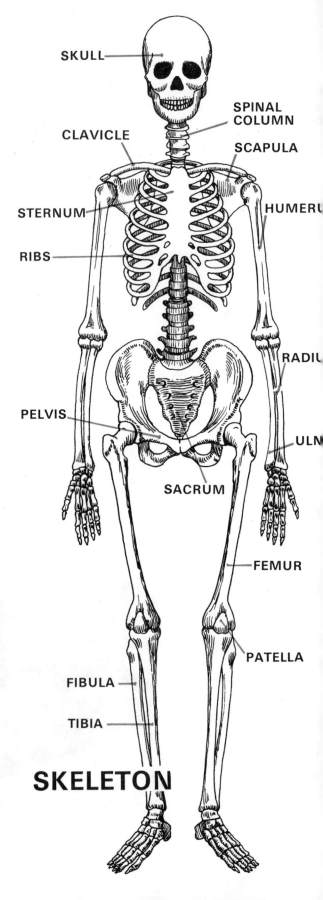

SKULL
SPINAL COLUMN
CLAVICLE
SCAPULA
STERNUM
HUMERU
RIBS
RADIU
PELVIS
ULN
SACRUM
FEMUR
PATELLA
FIBULA
TIBIA

SKELETON

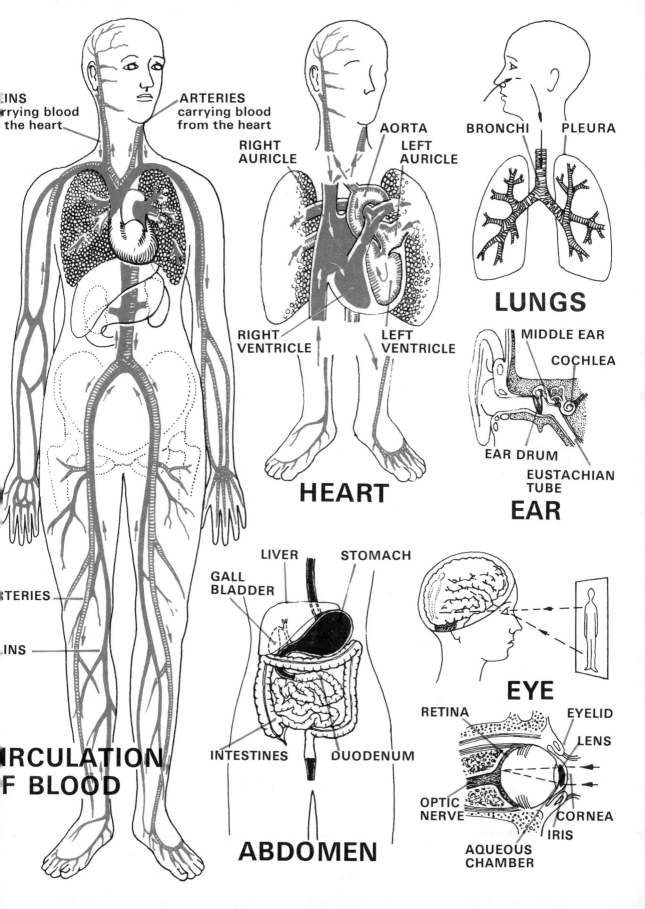

INS
rrying blood
the heart

ARTERIES
carrying blood
from the heart

RIGHT
AURICLE

AORTA
LEFT
AURICLE

BRONCHI   PLEURA

RIGHT
VENTRICLE

LEFT
VENTRICLE

LUNGS

HEART

MIDDLE EAR

COCHLEA

EAR DRUM

EUSTACHIAN
TUBE

EAR

TERIES

INS

LIVER   STOMACH

GALL
BLADDER

INTESTINES   DUODENUM

RETINA   EYELID

LENS

OPTIC
NERVE

CORNEA

IRIS

AQUEOUS
CHAMBER

EYE

**RCULATION
F BLOOD**

ABDOMEN

(arms) and lower (legs) units. The whole body is covered by skin, which may be smooth, or hairy (as over the skull). The skin has many important functions. First and foremost it is a coat of leather for purposes of protection. Secondly, it contains delicate nervous mechanisms which give rise to sensations and convey to us useful information about our surroundings. The skin also, by means of perspiration, is an important agent in regulating the temperature of the body. Just beneath the skin is a layer of what is called connective tissue, which contains fat. The framework of all these parts consists of bones forming the skeleton. The bones are held together by different kinds of connective tissue. Overlying the bones and attached to them in many places are the muscles. In the connective tissue and among the muscles are arteries and veins containing blood and numerous nerves.

If we examine the various organs and tissues under the microscope, we find that we can divide the essential constituents into groups: blood and lymph, epithelial, connective, muscular, and nervous.

Most of the body is made up of cells, but there are fibres in some organs and tissues (muscle, connective tissue, nerves). A cell is a tiny portion of living substance containing a body called the nucleus, which controls many of the functions of the cell.

It must be borne in mind that in microscopic anatomy we are dealing with very small structures, which are usually measured in thousandths of a millimetre. Thus a red blood corpuscle has a diameter of seven or eight thousandths of a millimetre.

When blood is examined under the microscope, it is seen to be a clear, transparent fluid in which float two kinds of body; (1) the red blood corpuscles and (2) the colourless blood corpuscles.

Epithelial cells cover the surface of the skin and the lining membrane of the gullet, intestines, windpipe, etc. They also build up the glands, which secrete the digestive juices and the so-called 'internal secretions'.

The connective tissues, although they contain cells, are chiefly important on account of their fibres. They form fat, gristle, tendons of muscles, ligaments round joints and bone.

If we cut through a long bone—say the humerus or femur—we see that the outer part, or 'wall', is compact; the interior is hollow and contains marrow. The ends of the bone, where they become enlarged to form the joints, are made up of a very beautiful network of plates and bars of bone. These are the cancelli and form the spongy tissue, filled, like the interior of the shaft, with marrow.

Within the rib cage lie the heart, the lungs, and the large blood-vessels coming from and going to the heart. We find here also the gullet, that part of the alimentary tube which connects the mouth with the stomach. In the abdomen is lodged the rest of the alimentary canal, the stomach and the intestine. Here also are the liver (a large gland), the spleen, the pancreas and the kidneys.

In the abdomen also are the adrenal bodies placed above the kidneys. These are small structures, but most essential for life. In both thorax and abdomen there are many important blood-vessels (arteries and veins) and nerves.

Muscles are the structures which are responsible for the different kinds of movement in our bodies. They are sometimes called the engines of the body. Muscles whose contractions are not under control of our will are called involuntary, while those, like the biceps, which are subject to direct control, are called voluntary. But some muscles, those of the eyelids, for example, are both voluntary and involuntary.

Perhaps the most important part of the body is the nervous system. This consists of the brain and spinal cord together with a large number of nerves which connect these organs with all parts of the body. The brain and spinal cord are known as the central nervous system. It is from the central nervous system that all the activities of the body are controlled and directed. The nerves act to carry messages to and from the brain and spinal cord. The function of the nervous system can best be understood by considering several examples of the way in which it works. If we wish to move an arm to pick up some object such as a glass from a table, a message is sent out from the part of the brain responsible for movement, travels down through the brain and spinal cord and leaves the central nervous system in a nerve which runs to the muscles of the arm. When the message reaches the muscles they contract and the arm moves. When the foot is put into a bath of water too hot for the body to bear it is almost immediately withdrawn. In this case messages pass to the central nervous system to tell of the painful sensation and very quickly messages are sent to the muscles of the leg to make them lift the foot out of the water. The importance of the nervous system in protecting the body from harm can thus be realized. In some instances when the nervous system has been damaged by injury or disease, messages are stopped in the nerves, brain, or spinal cord before reaching their destination. In the last example given it can be seen that if the central nervous system was not told of the painful sensation to the foot no feeling of pain would be apparent, the foot would not be withdrawn from the source of heat, and an extremely severe burn would result.

HUMBOLDT, Alexander, Baron von (1769–1859)

Famous German scientist and explorer. He made several expeditions to South and Central America. His monumental work *Kosmos* attempted to give an all-over picture of the physical universe. His brother, Wilhelm, was a great authority on ancient languages and was for a short time minister of education in Prussia. He also founded the University of Berlin.

HUME, David (1711–1776)

British philosopher, born at Edinburgh. His philosophical masterpiece is the *Treatise of Human Nature*, later simplified and called *Enquiry concerning Human Understanding*. He also wrote a six-volume *History of England*.

HUMMINGBIRDS

These magnificently-coloured birds are native to America, especially tropical areas, and range in size from 2 to 9 inches—the smallest is in fact the smallest bird in the world. There are over 300 species. Hummingbirds are remarkable fliers in that they can hover and are the only birds which can fly backwards. Their wings beat so fast (over 3,000 wing beats per minute) that they are only a blur to look at. Some have long curved bills, a few have straight ones and long tongues to reach the nectar on which they feed. Hummingbirds lay two eggs which take about two weeks to hatch and the young are ready to fly in three weeks. The smallest of this group is the 'bee' hummingbird of Cuba—about 2 inches long and the largest is the 'giant' hummingbird of the Andes which is between 8 and 9 inches long.

HUNDRED YEARS WAR

This war began in 1338, when Edward III claimed the French throne, and ended in 1453. Famous events in it were the Battle of Crécy (1346); the capture of Calais (1347), when, the story goes, six burghers offered their lives to save the citizens from massacre but were reprieved by the intercession of Edward's Queen, Philippa; the Battle of Agincourt (1415); and the resistance led by JOAN OF ARC, until she was captured and burned by the English (1431).

HUNGARY

A republic in Central Europe through which runs the River Danube. It is rather larger (about 36,000 square miles) than Scotland and has a population of over 10 million. The capital is Budapest. The language of the Hungarians is called Magyar. The country has rich wheat-growing lands. It also has coal, iron and bauxite.

Before the First World War Hungary was a much bigger country and formed part of the Austro-Hungarian Empire. As in the First World War, during the Second World War Hungary sided with Germany and afterwards accepted a Communist form of government. In 1956 a revolution occurred in Hungary against some of the harsher forms of Communist rule. The revolution was crushed with the help of Soviet armed forces. Since then there has been some improvement in conditions.

HUNT, William Holman (1827–1910)

English painter. Born in London. Was a pupil of ROSSETTI. His aim as an artist was to paint nature exactly as he saw it. Many galleries have examples of Hunt's work on exhibition and one of his most famous paintings, *The Light of the World*, hangs in Keble College, Oxford.

HUSS, John (1369–1415)

Bohemian religious reformer. He was greatly influenced by John WYCLIFFE and himself influenced LUTHER. On refusing to recant his views he was eventually burnt at the stake.

HUXLEY, Thomas Henry (1825–1895)

English biologist, born at Ealing. Although primarily a biologist, his interests and influence were very wide. He was an ardent and outspoken supporter of DARWIN and did much to popularize Darwin's work. His grandsons, Julian Huxley and Aldous Huxley have also made their mark in the world, the former as a biologist and the latter as a novelist.

HUYGENS, Christiaan (1629–1695)

Dutch scientist. He is perhaps best remembered for his invention of the pendulum clock and the marine clock for showing standard time at sea. Huygens also contributed much to optics maintaining that LIGHT was a form of wave motion as distinct from NEWTON who thought light consisted of a stream of particles.

HYDRAULICS

That branch of mechanical engineering that applies the findings of hydrodynamics to practical engineering problems, for example, hydraulic elevators, presses, servomechanisms, etc.

HYDRODYNAMICS

That branch of hydromechanics which studies the behaviour of liquids in motion. The other branch of hydromechanics is 'hydrostatics', which investigates the properties of liquids at rest or in equilibrium. The application of hydrodynamics to engineering science is known as hydraulics. It is important in all branches of ship design.

HYDROGENATION
Generally the term means treating a chemical substance with hydrogen with a resulting combination of the two. During recent years it has come to mean the production of petrol and other by-products from coal. The method of producing petrol from coal is known as the Fischer-Tropsch process. In the first stage heated coal or coke, usually the latter, is blasted alternately with air and steam, the air to bring it to a red heat, the steam to arrest the burning process and to supply hydrogen and oxygen which react with the carbon of the half-burned coke to produce the two gases, carbon monoxide and hydrogen; this mixture of gas is known as water or synthesis gas. The second stage entails passing the gas through batteries of synthetic reactors in which the carbon-monoxide molecules combine in varying proportions with hydrogen to form a mixture of vapours and gases from which the primary finished products are condensed and refined. Among these are petrol, a synthetic diesel fuel, synthetic waxes and other useful compounds.

HYDROGEN BOMB
Basis of the atomic bomb is a chain reaction (fission), but in the hydrogen bomb the process,

HYENA The scavenger of Africa and S. Asia.

although seated within the heart or nucleus of the atom, arises from the fusion or union of the nuclei (inner cores of atoms) of light atoms at enormously high temperatures. It is thought that this process of fusion, called by scientists a 'thermonuclear reaction', is similar to that which takes place in the sun to produce the great heat which it radiates. [*See* NUCLEAR ENERGY.]

HYDROMETER
A specially designed glass tube calibrated to measure the density of a liquid in which it is immersed. It is used for testing batteries.

HYDROPONICS
A technique of plant cultivation in which the roots of a plant are immersed in a nutrient solution from which they draw their food. It is sometimes referred to as 'soil-less' cultivation, and is a very successful method of growing such greenhouse plants as carnations, tomatoes and cucumbers.

HYENA
Although this animal looks very much like a dog it really belongs to the cat tribe. Hyenas are ungainly to look at because of their long neck and legs, short body, and weak sloping hindquarters. They eat small animals which they kill, or carrion left by other animals. Hyenas are known as the scavengers of Africa and Southern Asia.

HYGROMETRY
That branch of METEOROLOGY concerned with the measurement and behaviour of water vapour in the atmosphere owing to the evaporation of water from the surface of the seas, lakes, rivers, etc. The actual quantity of moisture or vapour in the atmosphere is known as 'humidity', and is measured by means of an instrument known as a hygrometer which can also be used for measuring the dew-point; the latter is the temperature at which water vapour in the air condenses to water or dew.

HYPNOTISM
A technique of putting a person into a state of sleep by repeating words in a low, monotonous voice and by movements of the hands in front of the subject or making the subject stare at a point of light. It was originally known as 'mesmerism' after a German doctor, Franz Anton Mesmer (c. 1733–1815), who first used it to treat patients. Not all people can be hypnotized and even those who can must agrée freely and be in a relaxed state. It is used to cure minor mental disorders such as stammering and sleeplessness.

I i

IBEX
Wild species of goat, agile and sturdy. It is a brownish or greyish colour and has long curving horns which are ridged. It is about 30–40 inches at the shoulder. The ibex lives in wild mountainous regions of Europe and Asia.

IBISES
These are wading birds closely related to the spoonbills. They usually live in or near marshy ground in the warmer regions of the world. There are some twenty-six known species. The most famous of this family is the 'sacred' ibis revered by the ancient Egyptians—Thoth, the Egyptian god of wisdom was portrayed with an ibis head. The most magnificent ibis is the 'scarlet' ibis of tropical South America.

IBSEN, Henrik (1828–1906)
Norwegian dramatist. Born at Skien, a timber port of southern Norway. He intended at first to study medicine, but the theatre claimed him and he became director of Bergen Theatre. In 1867 he wrote *Peer Gynt*, the first of the plays that were to make him famous. It was followed by many others including *Pillars of Society*, *An Enemy of the People*, *Rosmersholm*, *Hedda Gabler*, and *The Master Builder*. Their main theme is a satiric attack on social institutions, expressed in very skilful dramatic situations.

ICE HOCKEY
In countries where, because of the climate, there is plenty of natural ice—on lakes and ponds—ice hockey is played a great deal. Such a country is Canada. In places like Britain, however, the game is played exclusively on artificial ice, in skating rinks specially fitted out for the purpose.

An ice-hockey rink is rectangular with rounded corners. Rinks vary in size [*see* diagram], but the official rules say that the dimensions shall be 200 feet by 85 feet as nearly as possible. The rink consists of a smooth surface of ice surrounded by boards of between 3 feet 4 inches and 4 feet high. The goals are 4 feet high and 6 feet wide.

The game is played with wooden sticks. The blade which must not be more than $14\frac{3}{4}$ inches long from the heel, and 3 inches high at any point, forms an obtuse angle with the handle, which must not be more than 53 inches long

IBEX A species of wild, agile goat found in alpine regions of Europe and Asia.

from the heel. The puck is a flat, round disc of hardened vulcanized rubber. It is 1 inch thick and 3 inches in diameter.

All players wear padding for protection—shin and knee pads, elbow and shoulder pads, and usually shirts reinforced at the hips and thighs. Heavily padded gauntlets are worn to protect the hands. The goalkeeper is allowed more protection, and wears on his legs large pads, each of which may be as much as 10 inches wide.

Ice hockey is played between two teams each of 6 players; 3 forwards, 2 in defence, and 1 goalkeeper. The forwards are called right wing, centre, and left wing; the defence, simply right and left. Each team is allowed the use of substitutes. Altogether not more than 12 players may take part in a team in one game, and there must never be more than 6 (including one goalkeeper) on the ice at the same time. Otherwise changes in the players may be made at any time. The game is controlled by referees who move with the play and signal stoppages and resumptions with a whistle. There are also two goal judges, one at each end, who stand outside the rink and signal when the puck passes over the goal-line. Finally, there is the game timekeeper and a penalty time-keeper who checks the time served by penalized players.

A game consists of three periods, each of 20 minutes, with 10 minutes' rest between periods. Before the start the captains toss for ends; and the teams change ends after each period, and also half-way through the third period. Extra time may be played in competitive games.

The game begins with a 'face-off' in the centre of the rink. One player from each team stands at the centre, squarely facing his opponents' end of the rink, and with the full blade of his stick on the ice. The two players are about one stick-length apart, and the blades of the sticks are parallel to each other. All the other players must be in their own half of the rink and at least 10 feet away from the two men at the centre. To begin the game the referee blows his whistle and at the same time throws the puck between the players taking the face-off. As soon as the puck touches the ice the play begins.

Stoppages are normally caused only by in-

three zones, but it must not be passed forward from a player in one zone to a player in another zone. The only exception to this is that a player in the defending zone may pass to a player in the neutral zone, provided that the pass is completed by the receiving player on his own side of the centre line.

There is no penalty against infringements of this rule, except that the play is stopped and the puck is faced at the spot from which the off-side pass was made.

If a player in the neutral zone chases the puck passed from the same zone into the attacking zone, so that the puck crosses the blue line before he does, he is not considered offside. He must, however, have been in the

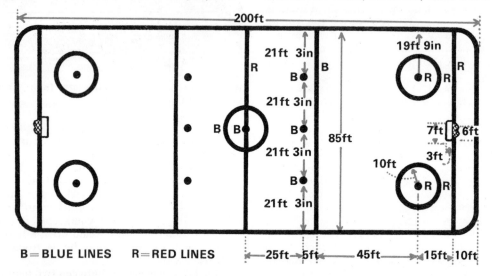

B = BLUE LINES   R = RED LINES

ICE HOCKEY Plan diagram of the layout and dimensions of an ice hockey rink.

fringements and injuries, and on the comparatively rare occasions when the puck goes over the sideboards. When this happens, the puck is faced at the point from which it was shot. In no circumstances, however, may a face-off be made within 15 feet of the goal or sideboards. The face-off is the normal way of resuming play after a stoppage, and is taken either at the place of stoppage or at one or other of the special face-off spots, according to the circumstances. When play is stopped because of infringement by a player of the attacking side in the attacking zone, the face-off is made on the nearest face-off spot in the neutral zone. When an infringement is committed by a player of the team not in possession of the puck, the referee waits till the completion of the play by the team in possession before stopping the game and punishing the offender.

The puck may be passed by any player to a player of the same side within any one of the

neutral zone at the time when the pass was made.

In no circumstances is a player of an attacking team allowed to precede the puck into the attacking zone. If he does so, the play is stopped and the puck is faced at the nearest face-off spot in the neutral zone. There is no other penalty for this form of offside. A player who, when actually propelling the puck, crosses the line ahead of it is not considered offside.

If a player shoots the puck from his own half of the ice to beyond the goal-line of the opposing team, but fails to score a goal, this is called 'icing the puck', and the game is stopped and a face-off taken at the rink-end spot of the offending team. This does not apply if the shot was made from a face-off, or if a legal pass was attempted, or if the puck touched the stick or person of any of the opposing players before passing the goal-line, or if any of the opposing players was able to play the puck, but did not do so.

The puck may be stopped and batted in the air with the hand, or hand-pushed along the ice, but not directly passed by hand to another player. It may not be held in the hand for more than three seconds, nor may it be picked up off the ice. The goalkeeper may not throw the puck forward towards his opponent's goal nor deliberately drop it into his pads.

The puck may be kicked in any zone, but a goal cannot be scored directly either from a kick or in any other way except by means of the attacking player's stick. A goal may be scored indirectly, however, when the puck is deflected by any part of a defending player (except the goalkeeper) even though it was first kicked by an attacking player.

The stick must not be raised above the shoulder, nor may it be thrown on the ice. No player (other than the goalkeeper) is allowed to fall on the puck. A player may not interfere with his opponent's play by holding, hooking with his stick, or deliberately knocking an opponent's stick out of his hand. He may not interfere with or impede the progress of any player not in possession of the puck.

Unless the puck is in the goal-crease area, no attacking player may stand in the area or on the goal-crease line. If the puck enters the net while he is in this position, the goal shall not be allowed; the game shall be stopped and a face-off taken at the nearest face-off spot in the neutral zone. No other penalty shall be imposed for this infringement.

Wasting time is not allowed; the puck must always be kept in motion. A defending player may take the puck behind his own goal once, but otherwise must always advance the puck towards the opposite goal, except when he is prevented from doing so by the opponents. A player beyond his defending zone may not pass or carry the puck back into that zone in order to delay the game. A player may not deliberately hold the puck against the boards unless he is being checked, nor may he deliberately shoot the puck out of the rink to delay the game.

There must be no holding, charging, tripping in any way, elbowing, slashing, kicking or fighting. 'Body checking' is allowed in the defence zone against an attacking player in possession of the puck, but it must be done cleanly with the chest, back, or hip, and must not be a charge, nor may it be done in such a way that the opponent is thrown violently on to the boards. 'Cross-checking', that is, checking with both hands on the stick and no part of the stick on the ice, is not allowed.

There are five different penalties for infringements:

Minor penalties involve suspension for 2 minutes, with no replacement by a substitute. Such penalties are awarded for offences like cross-checking, elbowing, hooking, and falling on the puck.

Major penalties are awarded for offences resulting in injury or likely to cause injury, and for most offences against the goalkeeper. For the first offence of this kind the penalty is suspension for 5 minutes without replacement; for the second, suspension for 15 minutes, with replacement after 5 minutes; for the third, suspension for the rest of the game with replacement after 5 minutes.

A misconduct penalty involves suspension for 10 minutes, and a game misconduct penalty suspension for the rest of the game. In each case, however, immediate replacement is allowed.

A match penalty, which is awarded only in the cases of kicking, or deliberately trying to injure a player or official, also involves suspension for the rest of the game, and replacement by a substitute is deferred for 5 or 10 minutes, according to the circumstances.

A penalty shot, which is ordered after an illegal attempt by the defenders to prevent the scoring of a probable goal, is taken by one of the attacking side from the blue line nearest the goal. It is a personal duel between the player and the opposing goalkeeper, no other players being allowed to take part until the play is completed. The player taking the shot is not obliged to shoot from the blue line, but must keep the puck in motion towards the goal until he finally shoots.

When a goalkeeper incurs a minor penalty the time is served by another player of the same side. In the case of a major penalty by the goalkeeper, no suspension is ordered, but a penalty shot is taken instead. A misconduct penalty awarded against the goalkeeper may also be served by proxy, but in the case of a game misconduct penalty or match penalty he must be replaced for the rest of the game.

ICELAND

An island republic in the North Atlantic not far from the Arctic Circle. It is considerably smaller (40,000 square miles) than England and has a population of 186,000. It used to be linked with Denmark but became independent in 1944. The capital is Reykjavik. The country depends chiefly on its fishing industry. The Icelanders claim that their Parliament, called the Athing, is older than England's and dates back to 930.

IGUANA

Large lizard which looks very like the mythical dragon. It lives in the tropical areas of South

IGUANA A large lizard not unlike the dragon of mythology. Adults grow to 6 feet.

and Central America, West Indies and on some Pacific islands. Fully grown it is about 3–6 feet long and distinguished by the ridge of scales running from neck to tail. It feeds on small animals and vegetable matter.

INCA

Empire founded about A.D. 1200 in Peru and overthrown (1533) by the Spanish Conquest led by Francisco PIZARRO. Its capital was at Cuzco. The Inca civilization was on a very high level, excelling not only in statecraft but in many skills, such as building, engineering, farming and the creative and applied arts.

INCOME TAX

A tax which people have to pay to the Government on their wages or other sources of income. If people do not have to work to earn their living, or do not get all their income through their work, they pay at a higher rate than do those whose only income is from working. Tax on earned income depends not only upon the amount of a person's wages but on such matters as whether he has to support only himself or a family as well. Income tax was first imposed in 1799 but it was withdrawn in 1816. In 1842 Sir Robert PEEL reimposed it and since then it has been an important part of the national revenue.

INDEPENDENT TELEVISION AUTHORITY

A body that, with the approval of Parliament, was set up in 1954 to provide a second television service to that already provided by the BRITISH BROADCASTING CORPORATION. The I.T.A. owns and operates the transmitting stations but the studios and equipment are owned by fourteen different companies who provide the programmes. Unlike the B.B.C., I.T.A. does not receive money from the sale of licenses. Instead the fourteen companies pay money to I.T.A. and they in turn earn money from the advertisements which are shown on the screen.

INDIA

A large republic within the BRITISH COMMONWEALTH. The country (1,173,960 square miles) is about a third the size of the United States but has more than 434 million inhabitants and so has a bigger population than any other country except China. The capital is New Delhi, other important cities being Calcutta, Bombay and Madras. The country is divided into 15 States. Goa in West India, which had been a Portuguese colony since 1510, was annexed by India in 1962. India produces much of the world's tea and also grows and manufactures cotton and jute. One of her chief minerals is coal and she is a steel-producing country. Most of the Indian people are Hindus but there are also some Moslems, Christians and Buddhists. Many languages are spoken in India, the chief being Hindi.
History :
About 4000 B.C. there were highly civilized people living in the Indus Valley and the remains of one of their well-planned cities, Mohenjo Daro, in Sind, exists to this day. About 1500 B.C. Vedic Aryans entered India from the north, and gradually they moved southwards, setting up kingdoms. It was at this time that the Indian caste system was developed. About 600 B.C. Gautama Buddha, whose teachings were to have far-reaching influence all over Asia, was born. About 270 B.C. the great Indian Emperor Asoka, one of the most enlightened rulers of ancient times, reigned. Hindu art and literature reached a high level during the 4th and 5th centuries A.D. The rulers at this time were known as the

U S S R

AFGHANISTAN

• Herat

• Kabul

• Kandahar

• Quetta

PAKISTAN

Hindu Kush

SINKIANG

K2 28250 ▲

Kunlun Mountains

• Peshawar
Rawalpindi •

• Srinagar

KASHMIR

Jammu
•

Jhelum

Lahore • • Amritsar
Ravi

PUNJAB

C H I N A

Tanglha Range

T I B E T

Nyenchen Tanglha Range

• Lhasa

Great Himalaya Range

NEPAL

Kangchenjunga
28146 ▲

• Punakha

Mt Everest 29028

Katmandu
•

Darjeeling •

Brahmaputra

ASSAM

• Shillong

Indus

Thar Desert

RAJASTHAN

• Delhi

Agra
•

Jaipur
•

• Lucknow

UTTAR
PRADESH

Ganges

Chambal

• Jhansi

Jumna

BIHAR

• Patna

BANGLA
DESH

Dacca
•

Mohenjo
Daro ⚙

Karachi ○

• Hyderabad

GUJERAT

• Ahmadabad

• Baroda

MADHYA PRADESH

WEST
BENGAL

Calcutta •

I N D I A

ORISSA

Mouths of
the Ganges

• Nagpur

ARABIAN SEA

♣ Ajanta

MAHAR ASHTRA

Bombay ○

• Poona

• Sholapur

ANDRHA
PRADESH

Western Ghats

Krishna

Hyderabad •

Eastern Ghats

BAY OF BENGAL

Panjim ○

MYSORE

ANDAMAN ISLANDS

Malabar Coast

• Bangalore   Madras ○

MADRAS

Coromandel Coast

• Mysore

KERALA

CEYLON

NICOBAR ISLANDS

Trivandrum ○

♣ •

MALDIVE ISLANDS

Colombo ○

Miles

0   100   200   300   400

Guptas. About A.D. 700 Arab traders brought the Moslem religion to north India. Then between 1001 and 1025 Moslem invasions from the north west began, and in 1526 there was founded the Mogul Empire. The Mogul emperors were the first since Asoka's time to give something like a single government to all India. The greatest of the emperors was Akbar. His successors, Jahangir and Shah Jehan, built the TAJ MAHAL and other wonderful buildings at Delhi and Agra. The power of the Moguls declined during the 18th century and this gave the British and French a chance to try to gain some control over the country. Following the Battle of Plassey in 1757, Moslem control soon came to an end and the British East India Company, under Robert CLIVE, won a victory over the French. In 1774 Warren HASTINGS became the company's first governor general. In 1857 there was a mutiny and this led the British Parliament to decide that Great Britain should take over from the East India Company. In 1887 Queen Victoria was proclaimed Empress of India. A few years later Kashmir, Burma and Baluchistan were brought within the Indian Empire. Not all India was governed directly by Britain. There were a great number of states which were allowed to have their own princes under the Viceroy.

In 1885 educated Indians formed the Indian Congress Party with the object of bringing about self-government for India. During the 20th century this demand for self government grew under the leadership of Mahatma GANDHI. At first both Hindus and Moslems worked together. Later, under Mahomed Ali Jinnah, the Moslems founded the Moslem League and eventually they demanded that those parts of northern India where the majority of the people were Moslem, should become a separate country. When, therefore, in August 1947, agreement had been reached with Britain, two separate countries India and PAKISTAN, were created.

India's first Prime Minister was Jawaharlal NEHRU who died in 1964. His successor, Mr. Shastri, did not long survive him and was succeeded in 1965 by Mr. Nehru's daughter, Mrs. Indira Gandhi.

INDIANS, AMERICAN
More often called 'Red Skins'. These tribes of peoples, and there are very many of them, occupied most of the American continent before the invasions of the Europeans. It is generally agreed by anthropologists that these tribes originated in Asia and passed over to America by way of the Bering Strait. In North America the tribes were comparatively small and fol-

lowed a simple life. In South America, however, they built up important civilisations, for example, the MAYA and INCA. The Indians in the U.S.A. and Canada who have not been absorbed into Western ways live on reservations. The only real 'wild Indians' are a few tribes which live in the Amazon jungle, and recent exploration has shown that these are not as wild as they have been made out to be.

INDONESIA
A republic in south-east Asia that is made up of several large islands and many smaller ones. The country is about four times the size of France (887,000 square miles) and its population 103 million. The largest islands are Java, Sumatra, the Celebes and most of the large island of Borneo. Since 1963 the west part of NEW GUINEA, called West Irian, has been part of Indonesia. The country was formerly ruled by the Netherlands and was then known as the Dutch East Indies. The capital is Djakarta, formerly called Batavia on the island of Java. The country is rich in minerals, including tin, coal and petroleum. It also produces rubber, tobacco and rice.

INDUSTRIAL REVOLUTION
Period, beginning in the second half of the 18th century, during which power-driven machines in factories replaced handwork. This was made possible as a result of the rapid growth of applied science, in particular the work of WATT and steam power. It brought with it a great increase in the population of this country and led to the growth of towns in which the lives of most people were squalid and miserable. Other countries which had their Industrial Revolution later than Britain carried it through with less distress. [*See* CHARTISTS.]

INFRA-RED RAY
Beam of radiation that is just beyond the visible range of the red end of the SPECTRUM. The wavelength of infra-red light is longer than 0·00007 cm. Its physical effect is to produce heat. The radiant heat felt from an electric fire or gas fire or sunlight is produced by the infra-red radiations present.

INGRES, Jean Auguste Dominique
(1780–1867)
French painter, born in Montauban. Between 1806 and 1824 he lived in Rome, where he produced many fine pencil portraits. Returning to Paris in 1824, he achieved immediate fame with his *Vow of Louis XIII*. In 1834 he returned to Rome, where he spent the rest of his life as a teacher and artist. Many of his paintings and

drawings are in the Ingres Museum in Montauban.

INQUISITION
System used by the Roman Catholic Church, particularly in the Middle Ages, for the persecution of heretics, that is, people who would not accept the orthodox teachings of the Church. JOAN OF ARC, for instance, insisted that 'voices' inspired her. She was told that this was heresy, but insisted that what she said about her 'voices' was true. She was tried, condemned and burned at the stake. The great Italian philosopher, Giordano BRUNO, was a victim of the Inquisition.

The Spanish Inquisition was well known to Englishmen who fought against Spain in the 18th century. TENNYSON in *The Revenge* pictures Sir Richard Grenville as saying he will not leave any of his sick men behind 'To these Inquisition dogs and the devildoms of Spain'. And these men

'blest him in their pain, that they were not left to Spain,
To the thumbscrew and the stake, for the glory of the Lord.'

The Spanish Inquisition was suppressed by BONAPARTE when he entered Madrid in 1808.

INSECTICIDE
Chemical compound used to destroy insects which are injurious to plants, property, and the like. In recent years great strides have been made in this branch of applied chemistry. The two main types are stomach poisons and contact poisons. One of the best known is DDT which stands for Dichloro-Diphenyl-Trichloroethane. They are applied by dusting and spraying.

INSECTS
Animals which are closely related to spiders, scorpions, crabs, lobsters and centipedes, but they differ in having the body made up of three parts, a head, thorax and abdomen, and in having three pairs of legs. Most insects have wings, either one pair as in the flies, or two pairs, as in bees and dragonflies. Beetles also have two pairs, but the front pair are hardened to form cases for the protection of the hind wings. The skeleton of an insect, unlike that of a vertebrate, is on the outside of the body and is made up of a tough skin of a substance known as chitin Most insects have large compound eyes, with many facets shaped like the cells of a honeycomb. There is no ear or nose such as we are familiar with in other animals, but there is a pair of antennae which may contain the sense of smell as well as that of touch. Some insects, like crickets and grasshoppers, 'sing' and in these we find ears, but they are either on the legs or on the sides of the body and never on the side of the head.

Insects have no lungs, but breathe through openings, known as spiracles, lying along the side of the abdomen. Air is taken in through these spiracles, and passes throughout the body through a system of tracheal tubes.

We are all familiar with the way an insect changes during its life-time. A butterfly lays its eggs on a leaf, and from each egg hatches a very small caterpillar. The caterpillar starts to feed and grow, and every so often it casts its skin, or moults, increases in size and grows another skin. In due course, when fully grown, it turns into a chrysalis. Inside the chrysalis, all the tissues break down and are rebuilt to form the fully-grown insect. This great change at the chrysalis stage is called a metamorphosis. In some insects this change is not nearly so marked. The young insect, when first hatched, resembles the adult fairly closely and although it grows by a series of moults, it does not go through a chrysalis or pupal stage. Such insects, of which the grasshopper is one, are said to have an incomplete metamorphosis.

There are about one million known species of insects. This means that they are at least four times as numerous as all other animals put together.

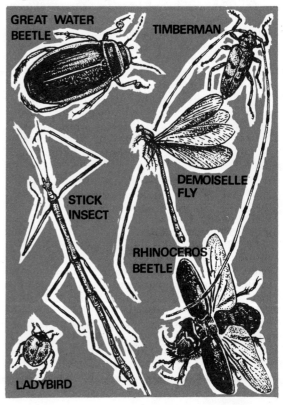

GREAT WATER BEETLE
TIMBERMAN
STICK INSECT
DEMOISELLE FLY
RHINOCEROS BEETLE
LADYBIRD

INSTINCT

Fundamental urge which seeks expression in action. There are many different kinds of instincts, such as the instinctive urge of self-preservation and the urge to feed. The aggressive urge, causing pleasurable sensations, finds a harmless outlet in such sports as cricket and football. A very fundamental urge is the sex-instinct, which is necessary for the reproduction of all animals. In human society the right balance of instincts is all important and modern psychology attaches special importance to the years of early childhood, when the character of a child is formed. Many incredible acts in animal life are instinctive, as, for instance, the migration of birds. [*See* ANIMAL BEHAVIOUR.]

INSTRUMENTS OF THE ORCHESTRA

The modern symphony orchestra is divided into four sections.

(1) The strings (instruments played with bows): usually about 28 violins (held under the chin), divided into 16 first violins and 12 second violins; 8 violas (similar to the violins, but larger and deeper-sounding); 8 cellos (held between the knees and made firm by means of a spike at the bottom which sticks into the floor); and 6 double-basses (the largest of the strings, as tall as a man, held upright resting on the floor).

(2) The woodwind (wooden tubes, played by blowing through them); usually 2 flutes (short instruments, held sideways to the mouth); 2 oboes (instruments with a piercing sound, blown endways); 2 clarinets (also blown endways, but with a mellow sound); and 2 bassoons (large tubes, blown by means of a curved mouthpiece). To these are often added a piccolo (smaller and higher-sounding flute), a cor anglais (larger and deeper-sounding oboe), a bass clarinet (larger and deeper-sounding clarinet) and a contra-bassoon (larger and deeper-sounding bassoon). Sometimes saxophones are included in the woodwind; these, which are usually found in dance bands, are made on the same principle as woodwind instruments, but are actually metal, which gives them an oily sound.

(3) The brass (brass tubes, played by blowing through them): usually 4 horns (medium-sized instruments with coiled tubes and a mellow sound); 2 trumpets or cornets (short instruments with oval tubes); 3 trombones (long instruments with sliding tubes).

(4) The percussion (instruments played by striking, plucking, or rattling them). The chief of these are drums (hollow containers with a skin stretched tight across the top, which is hit with a stick); usually 3 timpani (also called kettledrums—large drums, shaped like bowls);

a side-drum (small military drum, with a rat-tat-tat sound); and a bass drum (the big one that goes boom-boom). Other percussion instruments used are: the cymbals (round plates of metal, clashed together); the triangle (small steel triangle, struck with a small steel stick); the gong (large, round, thick plate of metal, hit with a stick); the tam-tam (a similar instrument with a more deafening sound); the tambourine (a tiny drum with metal jingles attached, held in the hand and struck with the knuckles); and the castanets (small wooden clappers, held in the hand and played by making them clack with the fingers). Also included in the percussion section are: the piano; the harp (large instrument, with long strings which are plucked); the glockenspiel (small keyboard instrument, with the keys attached to steel bars, which give a silvery sound); the celesta (a similar instrument, with an even more delicate sound); the xylophone (instrument with wooden bars arranged in the pattern of a piano keyboard and struck with hammers); tubular bells (long tubes of metal, hung on a frame, which give a sound like bells); and the vibraphone (a similar instrument, in which the tubes are kept vibrating by an electric current, giving an oscillating sound). Sometimes special effects are included in the percussion section, such as wind-machines or anvils; this probably explains why orchestral players always call this section the 'kitchen department'.

INSURANCE

Means of assuring the value of something which may be lost, stolen, damaged or destroyed by paying a regular premium. Modern insurance covers a wide field, a person's life, property from fire and burglary, ships at sea, motor-cars on the road, in fact, almost everything, even a film star's legs. Insurance of ships has been in operation since the 14th century and life insurance in England from the end of the 16th century. One of the most famous marine insurance companies is LLOYD'S. In many countries there are state insurance schemes which provide for sickness and old age, of which the National Health Insurance is an excellent example.

I.Q.

Abbreviation for 'intelligence quotient' and is a measure of intelligence compared with a standard test. It is

$$I.Q. = \frac{\text{Mental age}}{\text{Real age}} \times 100$$

i.e., if a student of 10 years reveals after test the same level of intelligence as an average student of 12 years, then the mental age of the ten-year-old student is 12 and his I.Q. 120.

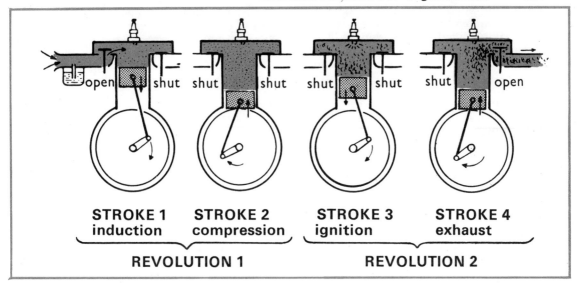

STROKE 1	STROKE 2	STROKE 3	STROKE 4
induction	compression	ignition	exhaust

REVOLUTION 1   REVOLUTION 2

INTERNAL COMBUSTION ENGINE This simplified drawing shows the cycles in a 4-stroke engine.

INTER-GOVERNMENTAL MARITIME CONSULTATIVE ORGANIZATION (IMCO)

An agency of the UNITED NATIONS, and set up in 1959. Its headquarters are in London. Its main object is to encourage the use of the highest standards of safety in navigation. It has drawn up an International Code for the Carriage of Dangerous Goods at Sea and in 1962 held an international conference on preventing the pollution of the sea by oil.

INTERNAL COMBUSTION ENGINE

The idea for this type of engine is quite as old as the STEAM ENGINE. As far back as 1678 HUYGENS proposed an engine driven by gun powder. Combustible gas had been considered as a fuel but it was not until about 1860 that a successful gas engine was built by Étienne Lenoir. The next successful gas engine, built by N. A. Otto in 1876, was a four-stroke engine (Otto's cycle). The first true petrol engine was made by Gottlieb Daimler in 1885. This had a carburettor, enclosed crankcase and splash lubrication. Rudolf Diesel's crude oil compression ignition engine was successfully made in 1897. Other engineers who made valuable contributions to internal combustion engines were Karl Benz, Wilhelm Maybach and F. W. Lanchester. [*See* STEAM ENGINES and TURBINE ENGINES.]

INTERNATIONAL CIVIL AVIATION ORGANIZATION (ICAO)

One of the UNITED NATIONS inter-governmental agencies. It was set up in 1957 and has its headquarters in Montreal. Over a hundred countries belong to it. It helps governments to plan safe, regular flights along international air routes. A network of weather ships in the North Atlantic is one of the services which I.C.A.O. helps to provide for the eighteen nations whose airlines use this route.

INTERNATIONAL COURT OF JUSTICE

This organisation sometimes called the World Court meets at the Peace Palace at The Hague, Holland. It was first set up in 1922 as part of the plans made when the LEAGUE OF NATIONS was created. When the UNITED NATIONS was set up it was re-established under new rules. There are fifteen judges from different countries but they do not act as representatives of their countries. They must give judgment impartially as must judges in national courts. They give judgment, or legal advice, on such matters as the exact meaning of clauses in treaties. The judges of the court are elected by the General Assembly of the United Nations and by the SECURITY COUNCIL.

INTERNATIONAL LABOUR ORGANIZATION

One of the specialised agencies of the UNITED NATIONS. It is older than the United Nations as it was set up as part of the LEAGUE OF NATIONS in 1919. Considerably more than a hundred countries belong to it. Its object is to improve the conditions of workers and seamen all over the world. Every year it holds a conference to which all the member countries send four delegates. Two of these represent the government of the country, one the employers and one the workers. The most important decisions taken by the Conference are laid down in rules called Conventions. These state what members must do to bring about certain improvements. This may mean making new laws to carry out what the Convention says. The I.L.O. also sends experts to countries which ask for help. These experts may help in such matters as the setting up of trade or technical schools where people can learn special skills. The headquarters of the I.L.O. are at Geneva.

INTERNATIONAL TELECOMMUNICATIONS UNION

The oldest inter-governmental agency set up by governments. It was organized in 1865 and is now an inter-governmental agency of the UNITED NATIONS with headquarters in Geneva. Its most recent task is to study space communication techniques and regulations.

INTERNATIONAL TRUST TERRITORIES

The name given to certain territories not yet able to govern themselves and which come under the direct supervision of the UNITED NATIONS. When the United Nations was first set up there were many such territories. Now nearly all of them have been given the right to rule themselves. Before the Second World War most International Trust Territories had come under the LEAGUE OF NATIONS and were called Mandated Territories. The largest remaining International Trust Territory is New Guinea and is looked after by Australia on behalf of the United Nations.

INVERTEBRATES

Include all animals without a backbone. But whereas those animals having a backbone are built more or less to the same pattern, the invertebrates make up a very mixed collection. On the one hand there are the microscopic protozoa, consisting of a single cell, very simple creatures in every sense. On the other hand, they include the insects which in many ways are more highly organized than some of the vertebrates. In between these we find the sponges, sea-anemones and corals, earthworms, starfish, oysters, slugs and snails, crabs and lobsters, and a host of others.

Apart from many insects and most spiders, the invertebrates live in water, either in the sea or in rivers and lakes, or in damp places. Except for some of the slugs and snails, they breathe by gills, and their chief danger lies in becoming dried up. The protozoa are found in large numbers in the seas and in freshwater, others live in damp earth and many live inside

plants or in the bodies of other animals, where they often cause disease. Sponges are found in the seas and freshwaters, and sea-anemones, jelly-fishes and corals are found only in the seas, although a few minute jelly-fishes and the freshwater hydra are found in rivers and lakes. All these animals have no nerves or their nervous system is of the simplest form. They have no brain, and if they have any sense-organs at all they are very simple, just a few pigment spots to serve as eyes. As we pass up the animal scale of invertebrates, through the worms, starfish and sea-urchins, the mollusca and the crustacea to the insects and spiders, we find a progressively better nervous system, more of a brain, and elaborate senses, such as eyes and antennae.

IONOSPHERE

Electrified layer surrounding the earth and extending from the stratosphere distances of between 40 and 400 miles. The electrification or ionization of this region is caused by its being bombarded by ultra-violet radiation from the sun. The existence of this region makes possible long-range radio, as it is used to reflect to earth high-frequency radio waves which would otherwise be lost in space. [*See* ATMOSPHERE.]

IRAN

Also called Persia, is a large kingdom in the MIDDLE EAST. It is about three times the size (628,000 square miles) of France and has about twenty-one million inhabitants, nearly all Moslems. The capital is Tehran and the chief port Abadan. Most of the country is desert but the country is rich in petroleum. It also produces cotton and is famous for its carpets. *History*:

Persia is one of the most ancient countries in the world. In the 6th century B.C. the Persians, a nomadic tribe, settled in the country and joined with the Medes in overthrowing the Assyrian Empire. Under Cyrus II, or the Great, the Persians captured the Medean capital, and in a very short time they had greatly extended their empire which under DARIUS I reached its greatest extent. When ALEXANDER THE GREAT rose to power in Greece the Persians were defeated at the Battle of the Hellespont in 334 B.C.

In A.D. 642 Persia came under Arab rule and was converted to Islam. During this period Persian art and science flourished. In 1037 Seljuk Turks from the Turkmen steppes ruled the country. Twenty years later Jenghiz KHAN and his Mongols arrived, and spread destruction through North Persia. For a period Persia was ruled by Hulagu, the grandson of Jenghiz

Khan, and he founded a Mongol kingdom in Persia.

In the 16th century a new line of Persian kings arose, the chief of whom was Abbas the Great. He defeated the Ottoman Turks and with English aid drove the Portuguese from Hormuz.

During the First World War Persia was occupied for a short time by both Britain and Russia. In 1921 an army officer named Reza Khan led a revolution, and in 1925 was elected Shah or king. During the Second World War both Britain and Russia accused Persia of favouring Germany, and again they occupied the country and forced Reza Khan to abdicate in favour of his son, Mohammad Reza Khan. In 1946 the troops were withdrawn. In 1951 the Persian Parliament nationalized the Persian oil industry which was controlled by a British company by agreement with the Persian Government. A new agreement was made in 1954 with British and other oil companies.

IRAQ

Once known as Mesopotamia, is in the Middle East and is 'that land between the rivers'. The rivers are the Euphrates and the Tigris. Iraq is rather more than half the size (172,000 square miles) of France and has about 6½ million inhabitants who are all Arabs. The capital is Baghdad, the city of the Arabian Nights. The ruins of Babylon are also in Iraq. The chief oil wells are around Kirkuk and Mosul and the chief port is Basra on the Persian Gulf. Near Mosul are the ruins of Nineveh. Until 1958 the country was a kingdom but in that year there was an army rising in which the King and his family and Prime Minister were murdered. Since then the country has been a republic.

IRELAND, REPUBLIC OF

An independent republic on the island of that name, rather smaller (26,600 square miles) than Scotland and with nearly 3 million inhabitants, most of whom are Roman Catholics. Many of the people are of Celtic origin. The capital is Dublin, other important towns being Cork and Limerick.

History:

Irish legends say that about 500 B.C. people from Scythia came by way of Spain and set up a kingdom in Ireland called the Kingdom of Tara. Although Roman merchants visited Ireland it was never conquered by them. Early in the 5th century Christianity was taken to Ireland by St. Patrick.

Towards the close of the 8th century Norwegians and Danes invaded Ireland. In 1014 the Scandinavians were defeated at the Battle of Clontarf. After the victory a quarrel for power occurred between chieftains. This led to the deposed king of Leinster asking Henry II of England for help and this was given. In 1172 Henry II himself landed in Ireland and established his court in Dublin. The English eventually conquered most of the island and a feudal government was set up. In the 14th and 15th centuries the Irish recovered most of their lands, but in the year 1534 Henry VIII began the reconquest of Ireland. In 1541 Parliament recognized him as King of Ireland and by 1603 English authority was supreme. A few years later Protestants were encouraged to settle in Ulster. Trouble and unrest followed and risings by the Irish were put down ruthlessly. In 1800 an Act of Parliament set up the Union of Great Britain and Ireland. During the 19th century the Irish formed a Home Rule party and this movement had many supporters in England, but it was opposed by the people of Ulster. Just before the First World War civil war seemed to be unavoidable, but when the First World War came the Irish supported the British with troops, though there was an Irish Nationalist, or Sinn Fein, rising in 1916. From 1919 to 1921 there was virtually a state of war in Ireland in which Sinn Feiners killed policemen and those in the service of the British, while British troops— Auxiliaries and 'Black-and-Tans'—killed citizens and burned houses in revenge. Peace came at last in 1921 when a treaty was signed setting up the Irish Free State in Southern Ireland. Ulster was to have her own Parliament but to remain attached to Britain.

In 1939 the Irish Free State made a new constitution for itself and in 1948 her Parliament decided to break her last ties with Britain. The following year the British Parliament passed an Act agreeing to this. Irish citizens, however, unlike other foreigners, are allowed to enter and leave the United Kingdom without passports.

IRELAND, John (1879–1962)

English composer, born at Bowden, Cheshire. He wrote two beautiful tone-poems *Mai-Dun* and *The Forgotten Rite*, a piano concerto, *A London Overture, London Pieces* for piano, and many song settings of poems by Thomas HARDY and A. E. HOUSMAN.

IRON

A silvery-white metal, chemical symbol Fe. It is very abundant in the earth's crust and mined on a very large scale. Although iron was known to have been used around 4000 B.C. in Egypt it was not until about 1000–500 B.C. that it was widely used and developed for tools

Ireland

NORTH CHANNEL

Giant's Causeway

Derryveagh Mnts

DONEGAL

Londonderry

LONDONDERRY

ANTRIM

Larne

NORTHERN

IRELAND

Kells

Donegal

Foyle

Sperrin Mnts

Lough Neagh

Belfast

Bangor

DONEGAL BAY

Omagh

TYRONE

Lurgen

DOWN

Downpatrick

Lough Erne

Enniskillen

FERMANAGH

Armagh

ARMAGH

Mourne Mnts

Sligo

LEITRIM

Monaghan

MONAGHAN

Dundalk

DUNDALK BAY

SLIGO

Lough Allen

Cavan

CAVAN

LOUTH

Lough Conn

Carrick on Shannon

Achill Head 2191

MAYO

Castlebar

ROSCOMMON

LONGFORD

Longford

MEATH

Boyne

Drogheda

Lough Mask

Roscommon

Central Plain

Lough Ree

Westmeath

WESTMEATH

Trim

DUBLIN

Dublin

Mnts of Connemara

Lough Corrib

GALWAY

Athlone

OFFALY

Tullamore

KILDARE

Liffey

Dun Laoghaire

Bray

Galway

REPUBLIC OF

Kildare

GALWAY BAY

IRELAND

Port Laoighise

Wicklow

ARAN IS

Shannon

LAOIGHISE

WICKLOW

ATLANTIC

Lough Derg

Wicklow Mnts

OCEAN

CLARE

Ennis

Nore

Kilkenny

Barrow

CARLOW

Carlow

Slaney

WEXFORD

Limerick

TIPPERARY

Kilkenny

MOUTH OF THE SHANNON

LIMERICK

Tipperary

KILKENNY

Wexford

Tralee

Galtee Mnts

Suir

Clonmel

Comeragh Mnts

Waterford

ST. GEORGE'S CHANNEL

KERRY

Knockmealdown Mnts

WATERFORD

DINGLE BAY

Killarney

Blackwater

Carrantuohill 3414

CORK

Macgillycuddy's Reeks

Lee

Cork

KENMARE RIVER

BANTRY BAY

and weapons; it is this period which is called the 'Iron Age'. The modern manufacture of steel from pig-iron is shown in the drawing illustrating the BESSEMER CONVERTER.

IRON LUNG
A mechanical device in which a person is placed when suffering from infantile paralysis to make breathing possible, that is, artificial respiration. The air pressure in the lung is changed about twelve times every minute and it is this which causes the lungs to take in air.

IRVING, Sir Henry (1838–1905)
British actor-manager and the first of his profession to be knighted. He managed the Lyceum Theatre, London, and staged magnificent productions of Shakespearean plays. His most outstanding role was as Hamlet.

IRVING, Washington (1783–1859)
American writer, born in New York. He was an author of very wide accomplishment, writing essays, biographies, tales, travel, etc., and enjoyed popularity outside the U.S.A. His best-known tale is *Rip Van Winkle*.

ISHERWOOD, Christopher (1904———)
Anglo-American novelist and playwright. His novels are written from a very personal viewpoint and much of the detail is autobiographical. His experience as a tutor in Berlin during the depression of the early 1930s gave him the material for *Mr. Norris Changes Trains* and *Goodbye to Berlin*, and one of the stories from the latter, *Sally Bowles,* was made into the film *I am a Camera*. Together with AUDEN he has written verse-plays intended as comments on the social and political scene, and his *Journey to a War* describes his travels in China.

ISLAM
Religion of the Mohammedans or Moslems who believe MOHAMMED was the great prophet. The teachings, which are said to have been revealed to Mohammed by Allah (God), are contained in the Koran. Devout Mohammedans pray five times daily and in the direction of Mecca; observe the fast of Ramadan (the ninth month of the Islamic year); make the pilgrimage to Mecca once in their lifetime if it is humanly possible to do so.

ISOTOPE
An atom consists of a nucleus and planetary electrons. The positive charge on the nucleus exactly balances the negative charge on the planetary electrons in a normal atom. The chemical properties of a substance depend on the arrangement of planetary electrons and, therefore, on the amount of positive charge on the nucleus. The particle that provides one unit of positive charge is a proton. The number of protons in the nucleus thus determines the chemical properties. The other constituent of the nucleus is the neutron (*q.v.*). This does not affect the chemical properties, but, having a mass nearly equal to that of the proton, it does affect the atomic weight. It is, therefore, possible to have atoms whose nuclei have the same number of protons (and whose planetary electrons are the same in number and conformation) and yet have different numbers of neutrons in each. These different forms are called isotopes. When isotopes of an element occur, whether natural or artificial, it is customary to distinguish them by writing the atomic (isotopic) weight after the name, e.g., uranium 235, uranium 238, carbon 14. [*See* NUCLEAR ENERGY.]

ISRAEL
A Jewish republic which occupies nearly the whole of PALESTINE. It is 10,430 square miles, about the same size as Wales, and has nearly $2\frac{1}{2}$ million inhabitants. The people speak Hebrew. The great majority are Jews, the rest being Moslems. The Israelis regard the New City of Jerusalem as their capital but larger than this are Tel-Aviv and Haifa. The chief product is citrus fruit and the chief mineral phosphates from the Dead Sea.

Before the State of Israel came into being in 1948 the whole of Palestine was ruled by Britain as an INTERNATIONAL TRUST TERRITORY of the United Nations. When fighting broke out between Arabs and Jews, many thousands of Arabs fled to Jordan and neighbouring countries where most of them and their children have been looked after by the United Nations ever since. Jews and Arabs unfortunately have remained on bad terms.

History :
The early history of the Jewish people is told in the Old Testament [*see* BIBLE]. At the birth of Christ, Judea was occupied by the Romans. There was constant unrest and in A.D. 66 there was open revolt. The putting down of this revolt led to the complete destruction of Jerusalem in A.D. 70. The Jews from then onwards had no national home. Great numbers fled to Egypt, Italy, Spain, Cyprus and elsewhere. Those who remained in Palestine made one last attempt, under Bar-Cochba, in A.D. 133, to gain their freedom but after three years' war the Romans won and forbad any Jew to enter the new city they had built on the site of Jerusalem; it was renamed Aelia Capitolina.

During the 4th and 5th centuries Jewish scholars wrote down all the Jewish laws that had been handed down by word of mouth. This collection is called the TALMUD.

In nearly all the countries where the Jews sought refuge they were treated very harshly and often suffered persecution and sometimes massacre. They were treated best by the Moors in Spain, but when the Moors were expelled, they too, had to leave that country.

Britain was one of the first countries to give the Jews rights as citizens. Because of the persecution which the Jews suffered in Russia and elsewhere, some Jews, at the end of the 19th century, began to make plans for Jews to return to Palestine. This movement was called ZIONISM. After the First World War, when Palestine became a British Mandated Territory under the League of Nations, the British Government promised to help Jews to make a national home there. The Arabs did not like this and serious trouble occurred between Jews and Arabs. In 1948 Britain decided her mandate for Palestine should end. The next day the Jews in Palestine proclaimed the setting up of the new State of Israel. The Arab States were very angry and sent troops to help the Palestine Arabs. This led to a bitter war, which only ended early in 1949. The following year the part of Palestine where most of the people were Arabs, was given to JORDAN.

ITALY

A republic in southern Europe. Included in Italy are the large islands of Sicily and Sardinia. It is 324,000 square miles, rather more than half the size of France, and has 50 million inhabitants. The capital is Rome, on the River Tiber, once the centre of the great Roman Empire. Amongst the cities famous in history are Venice and Florence whilst Naples and Genoa are today the chief ports. Milan and Turin are the chief industrial cities. Most Italians are peasant farmers and the chief crops are hard wheat, from which macaroni is made, grapes and olives. Most of the people live on the plains of Lombardy because the mountains of peninsular Italy make farming and industry difficult. Italy has few minerals but since the Second World War great quantities of natural gas have been discovered and this has greatly helped the country's industries. Other minerals found in Italy are sulphur and mercury. The country is also famous for its marble. Italy is a Member of NATO and the EUROPEAN ECONOMIC COMMUNITY.

History :

Although Rome, the capital of Italy, was the centre of an Empire that in ancient times extended over all the then known world, modern Italy did not become a single state until the 19th century.

When the story of ancient Rome began there were a number of different peoples inhabiting the Italian peninsula of whom the most important were the Etruscans. Rome began to expand in the 3rd century B.C. after a series of wars known as the Samnite wars that were followed not long afterwards by the three Punic Wars. Rome was at the height of its power shortly before the birth of Christ when Rome was ruled by Emperors, or Caesars, of whom the most famous was Julius CAESAR, who invaded Britain in 55 B.C. The story of his assassination is told in Shakespeare's play. Other famous Caesars were Tiberius, the cruel NERO, and HADRIAN who built the wall in Britain that bears his name. Constantine the Great who, in A.D. 330 made Christianity the State religion, was one of the last Roman Caesars for in 410 Rome was sacked by the Visigoths and forty years later by the Vandals.

The centuries which followed the downfall of Rome are known as the Dark Ages. During the Middle Ages there arose the City States of Italy. This was a period when art and commerce flourished in Italy. The chief City States were Venice, Florence and Genoa. These city republics gradually declined in influence following a series of European wars and the opening up of trade with the New World. By the end of the 18th century parts of the country were held by Spain and Austria, and during the Napoleonic wars most of Italy was conquered by the French. It was at this period that Italians began to dream of being united and free. About 1830 there arose an Italian patriot named Mazzini whose writings prepared Italians for action. It was the soldier GARIBALDI and the statesman Cavour who were eventually able, in a series of wars between the years 1849 and 1870, to bring about a united Italy under King Victor Emanuel I.

After the First World War, in which Italy had fought on the side of the Allies, the country, under MUSSOLINI, was the first country in Europe to become Fascist. In 1936 Italy joined with Germany and Japan in an alliance. This brought her into the Second World War against the Allies. Towards the end of the war the Italians overthrew the Fascists and Mussolini was killed. When the war was over the majority of the people decided that their country should become a democratic republic.

IVORY COAST

A republic in West Africa that is 189,030 square miles, nearly as large as France. The population is 3½ million. The capital is Abidjan. The country was formerly a French colony and became independent in 1958. The chief exports are cocoa, coffee, timber and bananas.

Jj

JACKAL
This scavanger belongs to the DOG family (Canis) and is about the size of a fox-terrier, but with a thick, coarse coat and bushy tail, and a foxy appearance. It lives on mice, birds, hares, carrion and vegetables. Jackals are still to be found in Eastern Europe, Southern Asia, India, Ceylon and Africa.

JACKSON, Thomas Jonathan (1824–1863)
American Confederate general, born in Virginia. Entered the West Point Military Academy and commissioned in the artillery. He served in the Mexican War (1845–1848). Jackson was promoted brigadier when he joined the Confederate forces at the outbreak of the Civil War. By his stubborn defence at the battle of Bull Run the same year he earned the nickname 'Stonewall' and was promoted general. He became the most trusted subordinate of General Lee and at the battle of Harper's Ferry forced over 120,000 of the Federal troops to surrender. He died after the battle of Chancellorsville in which he was accidentally shot by his own men.

JACOBITES
Those people who wanted the return of the Stuart monarchy after the expulsion of James II by William III (1688–1689), and after the accession of the Hanoverians (1714). The Jacobites twice attempted to overthrow the monarchy. In 1715 they were led by the Earl of Mar and James II's son, called the Old Pretender. In 1745 an army led by Bonnie Prince Charlie and mainly composed of Highland chiefs and their men, won the battles of Prestonpans (1745) and Falkirk (1746), but was finally defeated by the Duke of Cumberland at Culloden Moor (1746). Prince Charlie wandered in the Highlands for six months, but eventually managed to escape the English troops and flee abroad.

JADE
The name for two very hard minerals, nephrite and jadite. Used especially by Chinese craftsmen for making exquisite objects, such as amulets, pendants, vases, bowls, figures and the like. Although jade is generally linked with the colour green, it can, in fact, be any colour from black to white, yellow, brown and red. The delicate objects are made on primitive machines driven by a foot-treadle.

JAGUAR
The most powerful of the CAT family to be found in America. It is very much like the leopard in colour, pattern, voice and habit. Although not so active as this animal, either on the ground or in the trees, the jaguar is a good climber and often lies in wait for deer, capybaras and peccaries on which it feeds; it also lives on fish and fresh-water turtles.

JAMAICA
One of the largest of the West Indian Islands and a Member of the British Commonwealth. It is a little more than 4,230 square miles, about half the size of Wales, and has a population of nearly 2 million most of whom are negroes. The capital is Kingston. The next most important town is Montego Bay. The country produces sugar, rum, bananas and is the largest producer of bauxite in the world. Jamaica was discovered by Christopher COLUMBUS in 1494. It was a British Colony from the 17th century to 1962 when the country became independent.

JAMES, Henry (1843–1916)
American writer who made his home in England and became a British subject in 1915. He wrote many novels, short stories, plays and travel books. One of his best-known is the ghost-story *The Turn of the Screw*. His brother, William (1842–1910), was one of the most outstanding psychologists in America.

JAPAN
An island Empire in the Pacific Ocean made up of four large islands and many smaller ones. The country is not quite as large as France being 142,505 square miles, but has nearly 100 million inhabitants. The capital is Tokyo, the largest city in the world. Other big cities are Osaka, Nagoya, Kyoto and Yokohama, the chief port. Japan is the most important industrial country in Asia and one of the most important in the world. She is the chief ship-building country and she also produces textiles and manufactured goods like toys, bicycles and transistor radios.
History:
Although Japan has an ancient civilization it is more recent than that of China. Buddhism was taken to Japan from Korea in about the 6th century A.D. Like China, Japan for centuries did not allow foreigners to enter her

JAPAN *Above*, a view of Fuji (12,390 feet) and regarded by the Japanese as a sacred mountain. *Below*, the modern part of Tokyo, capital of Japan.

country but in 1854 Japan was forced by the United States to trade with the West and from then onwards she began to copy Western techniques. In 1905 she attacked Russia and won the war. For some years after this Japan was an ally of Britain but in 1936 she decided to make a treaty with Germany and Italy and this led her into war against the Allies. The war with Japan was brought to an end in August 1945 by the dropping of the first atom bombs on Hiroshima and Nagasaki. After the war Japan was occupied by the American army and was made to give up lands like KOREA and FORMOSA which she had occupied for many years. She also had to agree to a more democratic form of government and the Emperor abandoned his claim to divine origin.

JARGON

The kind of language which belongs to a particular group of people. Thus lawyers have a jargon, which is full of words like *aforesaid* and *heretofore*. Schoolmasters have one too, and critics, and civil servants, and even schoolboys. Sometimes the word is used, in a bad sense, of that kind of language in which a simple thing is said in a roundabout and often pompous way: a man is *the recipient* of a gift (for *receives*); they won *by the odd goal in five* (for 'by 3–2'), the books were *of a humorous nature* (for *humorous*).

JAVA [*See* INDONESIA]

JAZZ

Type of dance-music which originated at the end of the last century in America, under negro influence. Originally called 'Ragtime', it has a strong rhythmic character, though this is less clear in modern jazz than it was in the jazz of the 1930s. The players improvise on the tune of each number, either spontaneously or from an arrangement made beforehand in the case of much of the band music. Some of the well-known names in jazz are: Louis Armstrong—especially in his early numbers with the Hot Seven; Billie Holliday, the blues singer; Duke Ellington; Charlie Parker, who invented the modern style known as 'be-bop'; and the Modern Jazz Quartet.

JEANS, Sir James (1877–1946)

Born at Ormskirk and educated at Trinity College, Cambridge. Was for many years Secretary of the Royal Society. Wrote many popular books on astronomy which did much to educate the general public in such things as relativity, the expanding universe, etc. Two of his best-sellers were *The Universe Around Us* and *The Mysterious Universe*.

JEFFERIES, John Richard (1848–1883)
English essayist and naturalist, born near Swindon. He early acquired a knowledge and love of nature from his father. He became a journalist but his health failed and he spent the rest of his life in writing on natural history and agricultural topics. His essays all show great powers of observation. They were collected in such volumes as *The Gamekeeper at Home* and *Wild Life in a Southern County*. His autobiography is contained in the volume *Story of My Heart*, his most famous work.

JEFFERSON, Thomas (1743–1826)
Third President of the United States and twice elected to this office. He played a considerable part in the American revolution and drew up the 'Declaration of Independence'. He was one of America's most energetic fighters for democracy and he himself, even when President, insisted on simplicity to the point of austerity in his public and private life.

JENNER, Sir Edward (1749–1823)
English physician, born at Berkeley. Developed vaccination with cowpox VIRUS as a preventive against smallpox.

JERBOAS
Rodents about the size of rats having very long hind legs and long, tufted tails. They lie in burrows during the day and feed during the night. Jerboas walk or trot on their hind legs and can move at great speed by means of long leaps, in some cases up to several yards in length. They are to be found in North Africa, and from Central Asia to China.

JERICHO
Ancient city in Palestine which was captured by Joshua when leading the Hebrews to the Promised Land. The story of this is told in Joshua iii, 6. During recent years archaeologists have excavated the famous walls.

JERUSALEM
The holy city for Christians, Jews and Moslems. Today it is divided between JORDAN (Old City) and ISRAEL (New City). Among its sacred places are the site of the Tomb of Jesus, the Wailing Wall and the Mosque of Omar. [*See* CRUSADES.]

JESUS
'Whom say ye that I am?' Jesus asked His disciples, and Peter replied, 'Thou art the Christ, the Son of the living God.' (Matthew xvi, 15 and 16). From that day to this, men have argued, and sometimes fought, about the answer to that great question; some have refused to believe Jesus existed at all. And for the story of that life which has influenced history more than any other that the world has known, we are almost entirely dependent on the Four Gospels, which, fragmentary—and sometimes a little contradictory—as they are, still bring us into the Presence of One who 'speaks with authority' to our hearts and minds as no one else does. The name 'Jesus' is the Greek form of the Hebrew 'Josuah'; 'the Christ' is from the Greek for 'the Anointed One' (the 'Messiah' of the Prophets). Jesus was born in Bethlehem, probably four years earlier than the official dating of His birth, i.e. in 4 B.C. Apart from a few early incidents, the Gospels take up the story of His life only from about His thirtieth year onwards; their purpose being to record for the benefit of following generations the story of Jesus's public ministry and, above all, His teachings. After His baptism in the River Jordan by John the Baptist, and His Temptation in the Wilderness, Jesus chose His Twelve Disciples [*see* APOSTLES] and then went about the country preaching, healing the sick and performing a number of great miracles. Matthew, chapters v to vii, contains the great summary of Jesus's teaching known as the Sermon on the Mount. The official religious authorities in Palestine, however, became so angry at, and afraid of, Jesus's teachings and works, that they eventually had Him put to death by Crucifixion—He was nailed to a Cross made of two transverse wooden beams which was then erected in the ground, and from which He hung till He died. His Crucifixion, however, was followed by His Resurrection, and later His Ascension into Heaven. It has always been a principle of Christian doctrine that, in God's good time, Jesus will return from Heaven (the Second Advent or Second Coming) to judge Mankind and establish His Kingdom for ever. Few modern thinkers interpret this doctrine as 'literally' as the medieval and earlier theologians did. In the West, we count our CALENDAR from the official dating of Jesus's birth; A.D. standing for the Latin *Anno Domini*, 'in the year of Our Lord'—earlier dates being referred to as B.C., 'before Christ'.

JET PROPULSION [*See* TURBINE ENGINES]

JEW
A corruption of the name Judah, and originally meant an inhabitant of that kingdom. After Sargon destroyed Israel, Judah became the centre of the ancient Hebrew religion, which, in time, became known as the Jewish Religion (JUDAISM). Tyrants and persecutions have scattered the Hebrews over all the world, and

the word Jew has come to mean any Hebrew who remains faithful to his historic religion wherever he may be.

JOAN OF ARC, Saint (1412–1431)

Daughter of peasant parents at Domrémy in France. She was inspired by 'voices' which told her to rescue France from the English, and she put herself at the head of the French forces and drove the English troops of occupation out of Orleans. Later, she and her army took the dauphin through English-occupied territory so that, as Charles VII, he could be crowned at Rheims (1430). The next year she was captured, sold to the English, tried by an ecclesiastical court for heresy, and burnt at the stake. In 1920 she was canonized. Her story has been made the theme of poems and plays by many writers, among them SCHILLER, VOLTAIRE and SHAW.

JOHN, Augustus Edwin (1878–1961)

Born at Tenby and studied at the Slade School. One of Britain's most distinguished portrait painters. Although not as well known as his paintings, his etchings include a number of fine studies of W. B. Yeats, Jacob Epstein and James Joyce, to mention only a few. In 1942 he was awarded the Order of Merit. His sister, Gwen, was also a talented artist but unfortunately not so well known.

JOHNSON, Samuel (1709–1784)

Born at Lichfield, the son of a bookseller. As a child he was almost blinded by small-pox but was later able to study at Oxford. After a period as a schoolmaster he travelled to London with David Garrick, the actor. Whilst trying to earn his living as a writer he was frequently in debt and was twice imprisoned. But from 1762, when he received a Civil List pension of £300 a year, his financial difficulties were over and he became one of the best-known writers in London. Two of his most rewarding works are *The Lives of the Poets* and the *Journey to the Western Isles*, which was also recorded by his companion on the trip, James Boswell (1740–1795), in *Tour to the Hebrides*.

JOHNSON In addition to his reputation as a writer he was equally renowned as a conversationalist.

JONES, Inigo (1573–1652)
English architect, born in London. At Venice he studied the architecture of Palladio, and brought the style to England. He served James I and Charles I as an architect, and produced designs for the court masques. He was architect of the Queen's Palace at Greenwich and of the Banqueting Hall in Whitehall, and he laid out Covent Garden and Lincoln's Inn Fields.

JONGKIND, Johan Barthold (1819–1891)
Dutch artist, born at Latrop. With the French painter Eugène Boudin he was the precursor of the Impressionist Movement. He had a great influence on MANET. He lived most of his life in France and like another Dutch artist, VAN GOGH, was placed in a lunatic asylum.

JONSON, Benjamin (1572–1637)
Greatest of Shakespeare's rivals as poet and dramatist. Though brought up in poverty, Jonson received the good schooling of Westminster, acquired considerable learning, and was a hale and hearty man, given to full-blooded living. He served as a soldier in Flanders. Later in London, where he became an actor, he killed a man in a duel, but escaped hanging and lived to a ripe old age. He produced a wide range of masterly comedies, such as *Bartholomew Fair, Volpone* and *The Alchemist*, and many poems. One of his best-known lyrics is 'Drink to me only with thine eyes'. On his gravestone in Westminster Abbey an admirer of Jonson's work wrote 'O rare Ben Jonson'.

JORDAENS, Jacob (1593–1678)
Dutch artist, born in Antwerp. He was an assistant to RUBENS and much influenced by his style and subjects. Drinking scenes featured largely in his later works.

JORDAN
An Arab kingdom through which the River Jordan flows. It is about 30,000 square miles, rather larger than Scotland, and has a population of nearly 2 million, nearly half of whom are families who fled from what is now ISRAEL. The Old City of Jerusalem is in Jordan and forms the boundary with Israel. The capital is Amman. The country is an agricultural one but it produces phosphates from the Dead Sea which are exported.

JOULE, James Prescott (1818–1889)
English scientist, born at Salford. Studied the relationship between heat and mechanical work. The unit of work, the joule, is named after him and is the measure of the work done in 1 sec. by a current of 1 amp. flowing through a resistance of 1 ohm. [*See* WORK.]

JOURNALISM
A term used to describe a profession which may be exercised in many different ways. It may cover the work of a reporter for a weekly or daily newspaper, or the work of an editor or sub-editor of a newspaper or periodical, or the term may be applied to the professional freelance writer. The most recent form of journalism is the preparation of news and features for sound and television broadcasts.

There is no special academic qualification required of the would-be entrant to journalism. Most young people who want to become newspaper journalists, however, begin work on a provincial newspaper and these now all take part in a training and education scheme administered by the National Council for the Training of Journalists. Represented on the Council are newspaper proprietors and also working journalists who are members of either the National Union of Journalists or the Institute of Journalists. The training takes place partly in newspaper offices and partly in local Colleges of Further Education. It consists of a six months' probation period followed by three years of training, concluding with a proficiency test.

JOYCE, James (1882–1941)
Irish writer, born in Dublin. He was an excellent linguist and made a living by teaching languages while in France, Italy and Switzerland. He wrote long experimental books that had Dublin for their setting. The object of his books is not to tell a story but to follow the thoughts of his characters. The result, since thoughts are not orderly, is that his two great books, *Ulysses* and *Finnegan's Wake*, are like jigsaw puzzles, and in the second of these two almost every word is a jigsaw puzzle, since Joyce re-spells each word in such a way that it suggests several different words at the same time.

JUDAISM
The religion of the Jews, the growth of which is delineated in the Old Testament. The will of God is said to be revealed in the Law of Moses (Pentateuch). In the New Testament we hear of three Jewish sects—the Pharisees, the Sadducees and the Essenes—but it was the Pharisees, with their belief in the resurrection and eternal life of the good, who triumphed. In the 19th century, Jews who lived in Europe and America began to assimilate their habits to the societies around them, which sometimes

meant, for example, dropping the strict dietary laws that were part of their religion. Orthodox Jewish families are governed by a very strict code of behaviour in almost everything they do. One of the Jewish festivals is the Passover.

JUDO

Based on the centuries-old ju-jitsu unarmed fighting methods. The sport of judo was founded in the year 1882 by Dr. Jigoro Kano in Japan. It has since spread to almost every part of the world and has been an Olympic sport since 1964. It is rather important to distinguish between wrestling and judo. In wrestling, each contestant pits his strength against the other. In Judo the great thing is to let one's adversary do all the work, using his strength to bring about his defeat. This difference is an important one in practice because in wrestling it is only fair that the contestants should be more or less evenly matched in weight and strength, whereas in judo it would be quite reasonable to match a quite small man against a six-footer, for strength is not the deciding factor. A great authority on judo, Imazo Nitobe wrote this by way of explanation: 'Its feat consists in clutching or striking such part of an enemy's body as will render him numb and incapacitated for resistance.'

It is necessary to learn how to fall without getting hurt in order to beat an opponent or to break away from his hold. Having learnt to fall and to recover from a fall, the next thing is to find out how to obtain mastery over an opponent.

Judo divides itself naturally into three parts: (i) ways of throwing an adversary to the ground; (ii) locks and holds; and (iii) disabling strokes. It is a convention of all friendly judo that if an opponent feels that by continuing to resist he will suffer serious damage, he strikes on the floor or on his opponent twice with a hand or foot. The moment he does that the bout is ended and he must be allowed to free himself.

JUNG, Carl Gustav (1875–1961)

Swiss scientist, born at Basle. An early worker in PSYCHIATRY and friend of FREUD. He developed his own school of analytical psychology. He wrote a great volume of scientific works and several popular books expounding his views; one of the better known of these popular works is *Modern Man in Search of a Soul.*

JURY

A body of people who are called together to attend a trial and to give a true verdict, or opinion, on the facts to which they have listened. When they arrive at the court they have to swear to bring in a true verdict. When the time comes for them to give their verdict they retire from the court to a special room to decide what this shall be. They all have to agree on the same verdict before they declare it to the court, but there are plans to allow one or two members to disagree, and to take the majority opinion as the final verdict. Trial by jury is a very ancient right.

J.P.

This term stands for Justice of the Peace. J.P.s are magistrates who are not lawyers and who are not paid for the work they do. The office of J.P. is a very ancient one and goes back to the reign of Edward I.

JUSTINIAN (483–565)

Emperor of the Eastern Roman Empire, Byzantium. Born a barbarian, but received a first-class education at Constantinople. He had a quick brain and great energy, and he is remembered chiefly for his codification of previous Roman laws into one body of law, for the law of many modern European countries is derived from his code. He also engaged in three foreign wars. In ecclesiastical matters he believed the power of the Emperor superior to that of the Church.

JUTE

Tropical plant whose inner bark is used for making cordage, webbing, backing for carpets, oakum, tarpaulin and the like. It is made largely in Calcutta, but some is manufactured in Dundee.

JUTES

Hengist and Horsa who are said to have landed in Kent in A.D. 449 were Jutes. Like the Anglo-Saxons the Jutes were a tribe from Germany; they settled in Kent and the Isle of Wight.

JUTLAND

Peninsula of DENMARK jutting into the North Sea on the West and Skagerrak on the North. It was in the Skagerrak that the famous naval battle (1916) was fought between British (commanded by Beatty and Jellico) and German (commanded by Scheer and Hipper) navies.

JUVENAL (c. A.D. 60–c. 140)

Roman satirist. It is probable that he studied eloquence as a young man and later lived in Egypt. He is famous for his satires, sixteen of which are still in existence. They give a realistic picture of the corrupt manners of the time. It is Juvenal who coined the phrase *mens sana in corpore sano* (a healthy mind in a healthy body).

Kk

KAFKA, Franz (1883–1924)
Czech writer, born in Prague. He was a writer of unusual imagination, his works having a dreamlike quality and his characters are always searching for a haven from social forces tending to frustrate and crush them. His work has had a great influence on modern novelists in Europe and America. Two of his most famous books are *The Trial* and *The Castle*.

KALEIDOSCOPE
Optical device which if tapped or rotated gives an endless number of coloured geometrical patterns. It consists of a tube with an eyepiece at one end and at the other two mirrors set at an angle (60 deg.) to each other and a glass compartment containing bits of coloured glass.

KANDINSKY, Wassily (1866–1944)
Russian artist, born in Moscow. Originally studied law but later turned to painting, working in Germany, Russia and France. He was the first European painter to work in a purely abstract style. The largest collection of his work is in the Guggenheim Museum, New York.

KANGAROO
This MARSUPIAL is distinguished by its small and feeble front legs and large rear quarters and tail, also the pouch in which the young are kept. The small members of this family are known as 'wallabies', while the very large are called 'walleroos'. An unusual member of this family is the 'tree kangaroo', which, as the name implies, lives mostly in trees; it is about the size of a large wallaby. Found in Australia, Tasmania and New Guinea.

KANT, Immanuel (1724–1804)
German philosopher. Born at Königsberg. One of the most penetrating minds of all time, and one of the outstanding figures in the whole history of thought. Two of his most important works are *Critique of Pure Reason* and *Critique of Practical Reason*. He never moved from his birthplace and was for many years professor of philosophy at the local university.

KASHMIR
A beautiful land through which the Himalayas pass. Up till 1947 it was one of the Princely States of India. It is the same size as Great Britain but has less than 5 million inhabitants, of whom more than three-quarters are Moslems. Kashmir is famous for its fine woven woollen cloth to which the name 'cashmere' is given. Winter capital is Jammu and summer capital Srinagar.

KAUFFMAN, Angelica (1741–1807)
Swiss painter, born in Coire. Studied and worked in Rome, Venice and London. A portrait painter rather in the style of REYNOLDS with whom she was very friendly. She also painted historical pictures in a decorative manner. She was elected a member of the Royal Academy in 1768.

KEAN, Edmund (1789–1833)
English actor, born in London. One of the greatest Shakespearean actors, his most celebrated roles were that of Shylock, Lear and Richard III. His son, Charles John, was also a distinguished actor.

KEATS, John (1795–1821)
Born in London of a humble family, he went to school at Enfield, then to St. Thomas's Hospital to train as a surgeon. Teachers and friends brought the work of the English poets, first SPENSER, then later SHAKESPEARE and MILTON, to his notice, and, fired with enthusiasm for them, he worked to become a poet himself. For the eight years between 1813 and his early death in Rome in 1821, he laboured to produce a poetic masterpiece. The reviewers disliked what he published. His unhappiness at their criticisms is said to have hastened his death. SHELLEY mourned his loss in the poem *Adonais*. In the volume of Keats's works you will find at least two or three sonnets of the highest rank; five odes of great strength and richness; the *Eve of St. Agnes*, bright with decoration; and two bold attempts at a poem called *Hyperion*. Keats's letters are also much read and admired at present.

KEKULÉ, F. A. (1829–1896)
German scientist, born at Darmstadt. Originally studied architecture but turned to science, especially chemistry. His most important work was on the structure of carbon compounds and his 'ring' theory of the make-up of benzene.

KELP
Kinds of brown seaweed which grow to

enormous lengths; one species found on the southern and western seaboard of America grows to about 400 feet long. Kelps are usually found below the low-tide mark.

KELVIN, William Thomson, Lord (1824–1907)

Born in Belfast. Made Professor of Natural Philosophy, Glasgow, at the early age of 22. Kelvin was extremely active in many branches of science, electricity, heat and thermodynamics, geophysics, theory of gases, etc. He determined the absolute zero of temperature and devised the 'Kelvin' thermometric scale in which zero ($0°$ K) is equivalent to $-273°$C. Since the degrees are equal to those in the C scale, the freezing point of water is $273°$ K and the boiling point $373°$ K. He invented the modern type of mariner's compass and did much to make possible the transatlantic telephone service; for this work he was knighted. He was President of the Royal Society from 1890 to 1895. Made a peer in 1892.

KENYA

A large republic in East Africa that is a Member of the British Commonwealth. It is a little larger (224,960 square miles) than France and has a population of nearly 9 million. The capital is Nairobi and the chief port Mombasa. Although nearly all the people are negroes there are also a good many Indians and about 67,000 Europeans who have made Kenya their home. The country is famous for its coffee, and tea and cotton are also grown.

Before Kenya became independent in 1963 the country had been under British rule since 1895. In 1952 serious trouble broke out amongst the Kikuyu tribe, some of them having formed a terrorist organization called Mau Mau. The first Prime Minister and President of the country was Jomo Kenyatta.

KEPLER, Johann (1571–1630)

German astronomer, born near Stuttgart. Although an outstanding mathematician his greatest contribution to science was his work on the motion of the planets. COPERNICUS had already shown that the planets moved round the sun, but thought that they did so in true circular orbits. Kepler proved that they moved in elliptical paths with the sun at one focus and deduced three fundamental laws of planetary motion. He proposed laws regarding the refraction of light and also invented an astronomical telescope.

KHACHATURYAN, Aram (1904——)

Soviet composer, born at Tiflis and an Armenian. He has composed a great variety of music, much of which is popular in Europe and America, particularly the 'Sabre Dance' from his suite *Gayane* and the 'Waltz' from the film music *Masquerade*.

KIERKEGAARD, S. A. (1813–1855)

Danish philosopher, born in Copenhagen. Much of his writings are concerned with ethics and theories of beauty. He strongly criticized the teachings and practices of State religion believing that religion was a matter for the individual as the individual self or soul is the ultimate and only reality. His writings have had a considerable influence on many modern writers, especially SARTRE and CAMUS.

KENYA An aerial view of Mombassa, the chief port.

KINKAJOU Arboreal member of the racoon family.

KINGFISHERS
There are some eighty species of these birds, most of whom inhabit tropical forests. They range in size from the forest kingfisher about the size of a wren to the crow-sized kingfisher of New Guinea. There are only a few species in the northern hemisphere, the common kingfisher of Europe and the belted kingfisher of North America. The most unusual kingfisher is the 'kookaburra' or 'laughing jackass' of Australia.

KINGSLEY, Charles (1819–1875)
English writer, born in Holme, Devon. He was not a full-time writer, but a clergyman, being rector of Eversley, Hampshire. Kingsley wrote many novels. His best-known books are *Westward Ho!*, *Hereward the Wake* and *The Water-Babies*.

KINKAJOU
This animal belongs to the same family as the raccoons. It lives most of its life in trees, feeding by night on small animals, fruit and honey. It inhabits Central and South America.

KIPLING, Rudyard (1865–1936)
Born in Bombay and son of a British official in India. First became famous for stories describing British people of all classes, from Governors' wives to private soldiers, in the setting of India. He went on to write, with great speed and ease, short stories, longer books, poems and ballads of every kind, and pamphlets. His greatest success was *The Jungle Book*, with its curious animal and semi-animal characters, published in 1894, followed by *The Second Jungle Book* in 1895.

In *Puck of Pook's Hill* in 1906 he wrote an equally unusual fantasy for children using an English setting.

KITCHENER, Horatio Herbert, First Earl Kitchener of Khartoum (1850–1916)
Born in Ireland, he entered the Army in 1871, seeing service in many parts of the world, including Cyprus, Egypt, India and South Africa. His best-known campaign was against the Boers (1899–1902). At first Chief-of-Staff to Lord Roberts and then his successor as Commander-in-Chief he brought the campaign to a successful end by the Peace of Pretoria (1902). He was then appointed Commander-in-Chief in India and created Earl in 1914. On the outbreak of the Great War he was made Secretary for War. He died on board *H.M.S. Hampshire*, bound for Russia, when the ship struck a mine and sank.

KLEE, Paul (1879–1940)
Swiss painter, born near Berne. First studied music, his father being a music teacher, he turned to painting and studied in Munich. His work is free, full of poetic fantasy and frequently humorous, and seems to be influenced by no artist or movement.

KLIPSPRINGER
This agile little ANTELOPE is found in many mountainous regions of Africa—it has been called the African CHAMOIS. The klipspringer is about twenty inches at the shoulder and generally yellowish brown in colour. It feeds on grass, leaves and young shoots of shrubs.

KNELLER, Sir Godfrey (1646–1723)
Anglo-German artist, born in Lübeck. He studied in Amsterdam and Italy and settled in England in 1674. He was patronized by the Royal Family and many of the leading people of his time. His best-known works are the Kit-Cat Series in the National Portrait Gallery, London, and consist of 42 portraits of members of the Whig Club.

KNOX, John (1505–1572)
Scottish reformer and preacher. Born at Giffordgate, Haddington. He devoted his adult life, both in Scotland and on the Continent, to furthering the Protestant cause, especially in its Calvinist form. His triumph was achieved in 1560 when by the Treaty of Edinburgh, Papal authority was abolished in Scotland and Catholic doctrine replaced by a Calvinistic confession of faith drawn up by Knox and his colleagues. The Treaty was finally confirmed in 1567 after the flight of Mary Stuart whom Knox had frequently denounced.

KOALA

This amusing little animal is found in eastern Australia, where it lives in eucalyptus trees on whose leaves it feeds. Fully grown it is about 2¾ feet high. Like the kangaroo it is a marsupial, that is, it carries its young in a pouch.

KOCH, Robert (1843–1910)

German scientist. He discovered the germs which cause the dreaded diseases of tuberculosis, cholera and anthrax. Was awarded the Nobel Prize for Medicine in 1905.

KODALY, Zoltan (1882–1967)

Hungarian composer. Devoted much time to recording and studying the folk music of his country, some of which he has worked into his own compositions. One of his works, *Háry János*, starts off with a loud and long sneeze— which is the traditional way of starting off a very tall story.

KOKOSCHKA, Oskar (1886——)

Austrian painter, born in Pöchlarn. One of the leaders of the modern art movement in Germany. Travelled extensively but settled in Vienna until forced to leave when HITLER annexed Austria in 1934. He settled in England. His works are restless and highly colourful. Kokoschka specialized for some time in portraits but latterly turned his attention to landscapes, especially alpine landscapes.

KORAN

The sacred book of ISLAM. It contains the word of God as revealed to Mohammed by the angel Gabriel. The 114 books of the Koran are written in classical Arabic, and Moslems commit much of the work to memory.

KOREA

A republic of about 85,260 square miles on a peninsular in north-east Asia which borders on China and the Soviet Union. Since the end of the Second World War the country has been divided, the dividing line being the 38th parallel. North Korea, which is under Communist rule, is rather larger than the South but has only about 10 million inhabitants. South Korea, which is anti-Communist, has more than 26 million inhabitants. The capital of South Korea is Seoul; that of North Korea Pyongyang. The main exports are fish products, textiles, iron and some tungsten.

Korea has a very ancient civilization. It was a kingdom until Japan seized it in 1910. After the war Japan had to give up the country and whilst the Koreans were planning a Government of their own the country was divided, the Russians occupying the north and the Americans the south. When the Koreans were ready to have a general election they were not allowed to hold it in the north and so the country has been permanently divided with two separate governments. In June 1950 the North Koreans invaded the South. The United Nations agreed to help the South with troops and arms. The fighting was brought to an end in 1953 but the country remained divided as before.

KREISLER, Fritz (1875–1962)

Famous Austrian violinist who began playing at concerts when still a child. He composed much music for the violin, some of which is still very popular, for example, the short but charming *Caprice Viennois*.

KUDU

Perhaps the most magnificent ANTELOPE in Africa. The males have twisted horns of up to 60 inches long, the females are hornless. A male stands about 6 feet at the shoulder and weighs anything up to 700 pounds. The coat is greyish-brown with vertical white stripes down the body. Kudus usually live in harsh, scrubby regions. There are two species, the 'greater' kudu and the 'lesser' kudu, the latter being a remarkable jumper, covering over 30 feet in a single leap.

KU KLUX KLAN

Secret society in the U.S.A., first formed in 1866 at Pulaski, Tennessee. The cause of it was the fear of the defeated Confederates in the South that they would be dominated by the large negro population. Klan members dressed up in white robes to look like the ghosts of dead Confederate soldiers, and beat up negroes and Union soldiers at night. The Klan was revived after the First World War, grew to great strength, and not only preached the repression of the negroes, but set Gentile against Jew, Protestant against Catholic and employer against employee. It was, in fact, a thoroughly evil organization which used methods not unlike Hitler's storm-troops. Today the Klan has much less influence, though the recent Civil Rights campaigns have revived the racial feelings of the Southern conservatives.

KUWAIT

A small independent State along the shores of the Persian Gulf. It is considerably smaller (5,800 square miles) than Wales and has a population of less than half a million. The country is very rich in oil, and produces over a hundred million tons annually.

Ll

LABOUR PARTY

One of the two larger political parties represented in the British Parliament, the other being the CONSERVATIVE PARTY. Members of the party describe themselves as socialists. The first Labour members to sit in the House of Commons were John Burns and Keir HARDIE. This was in 1892. The Labour Party believes that the chief industries should be publicly owned and not left in private hands. It was they who, when they had a majority in Parliament, were responsible for the nationalization of the coal mines, railways, electricity, gas and road transport as well as planning the nationalization of steel.

On the continent there are political parties with very similar views to the British Labour Party who usually describe themselves as Social Democrats. Their chief difference from the British party is due to the fact that often their chief political opponents are the CHRISTIAN DEMOCRATS who are supported by the Roman Catholic Church and consequently the Social Democrats tend to oppose the Church.

LABRADOR

A part of the North American continent and a dependency of Newfoundland, CANADA. It is larger (112,820 square miles) than Great Britain but has a population of less than 14,000. It is rugged and desolate. Labrador is noted for its cod fisheries. Recently, in a district called Ungava, very rich iron ore deposits have been found and a 358-mile-long railway has been built to take the ore to the port.

LACROSSE

When the early French settlers arrived in Canada, they found the Red Indians playing a rather peculiar ball game called 'baggataway'. The settlers liked the game, and were soon playing it too.

The stick with which the game was played was so shaped that it rather reminded the French settlers of a Bishop's crozier; so they called it a 'crosse' and re-named the game 'lacrosse'. The stick used today is generally made of hickory wood bent to the required shape—the 'head' or net in which the ball rests, and a handle. At its widest part the stick must not be greater than 12 inches. The 4½-ounce ball is made of rubber, either black, white or yellow. A team is made up of 12 players.

The field of play can be seen from the diagram. There are no marked boundaries; these are arranged by the Captains and Umpire before a game, the object being that play can continue at the discretion of the Umpire, as far from the goals as necessary. The goals are 100 yards apart, from goal line to goal line, and are posts 6 feet apart and 6 feet high with a net attached to them and drawn to a point on the ground 6 feet behind them. The goal line is drawn from post to post. Each goal is surrounded by a circle with an 8½-foot radius taken from the centre of the goal line; this is called the goal crease. The only other marking on the pitch is the centre circle, which is 10 yards in radius, through the centre of which is a line 4 yards long parallel to the goal lines.

Lacrosse has fewer rules than almost any other ball game, which is perhaps one of the reasons why it is so popular. The object of the game is, of course, to score goals, the team scoring the most at the end of the game being the winner. What rules there are have been devised principally to keep the game going and to save injury to players. No player in Lacrosse has to bother about being off side, for there is no off side rule.

The game is started by a 'draw'—which takes the place of a bully in hockey; a game consists of two periods of 25 minutes each, with an interval not exceeding 10 minutes. For the draw, the opposing centres stand with one foot toeing the centre line, their crosses held at about hip level and the nets back to back, parallel to the centre line so that the sticks are between the ball and the goals the players are defending. The ball is placed between the sticks by the umpire, who then calls 'Ready, Draw' at which the two opponents immediately draw their crosses up and away from one another, the faster one thus propelling the ball over the head to the outside of the centre circle.

From that time on, each player tries to get the ball into their opponents' goal by carrying it in the crosse and running with it, or by passing the ball to another member of the team. Hitting another player's crosse with one's own to dislodge the ball is permitted, but no player may touch another player with the crosse, nor trip, push, charge or otherwise come into bodily contact with another player.

Finally, the player must not deliberately propel the ball with the foot or leg, or touch with the hand, unless the player is the goal-keeper acting within the crease. The goal-keeper or anyone deputizing, while within the crease may stop the ball with the hand or body as well as the stick. The player may catch the ball in the hand and put it in the crosse. One other point about the goal crease is important. No player who is attacking may score a goal if the stick or any part of the body is over the crease during or after a shot, nor after a shot may the player run into or through the crease. Any player may run through the crease to field a wide ball. The goalkeeper if outside the crease, may not take the ball back into the crease in the crosse; but is allowed to

then indicates the player to take the free position and where to take it; no other player may be within 5 yards. The player puts the ball in the stick, the umpire says "Play" and the game re-commences; the player with the ball being allowed to run, pass or shoot. A free position is never taken within 10 yards of the goal line, but should the foul have prevented an almost certain goal, the umpire may order all players including the goalkeeper from between the free position and the goal, thus allowing a clear shot.

Holding a lacrosse stick for the first time, you will soon find that, although it is not difficult to keep the ball in the stick by keeping the stick held level, this makes running, turning and dodging slow and awkward, as the ball

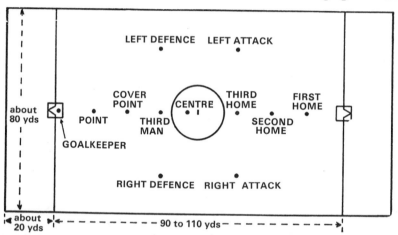

LACROSSE Plan view of a marked out pitch with the main field dimensions.

reach out from the crease and draw the ball in, provided both feet are within the crease at the time.

Should the ball go into any natural hazard, i.e. a ditch, trees or simply, in the umpire's opinion, too far from the pitch, the umpire blows the whistle and calls 'Stand' and all players must stand still wherever they are. The umpire will then either give the ball to the player nearest to it when the whistle was blown, or in the event of two opposing players being equally near, the players will take a 'Throw'. The players stand facing the game, side by side, each player nearer their own goal. The umpire stands with her or his back to the game, about 5–10 yards from the two players, and saying 'Play' throws a short high throw between the players so that they take it moving into the game.

And finally there is the problem of what happens after a foul, such as kicking the ball, rough tackling, etc. In these cases, the team against whom the foul is committed is awarded a 'Free Position'. For this the umpire blows the whistle and the players 'Stand'; she or he

tends to fly out when you change direction. For this reason players learn to 'Cradle' the ball, that is to use an easy rhythmic swinging motion of the stick from one side of the body to the other with the stick in a vertical position. This 'cradling' fits in with the running action, puts the arms and hands in a natural position for running and keeps the stick at the correct height to facilitate dodging past an opponent, turning to change direction and most important, passing to another player. The player who has a good relaxed cradling technique has the secret of being a good player.

When passing, the ball is thrown from the crosse either overarm or underarm—overarm being the best pass for length; and when receiving a pass the player reaches forward with the stick to the ball, the open face of the stick facing the ball, and the slight 'give' of the stick as the ball lands in it continues naturally into the cradling action, so that there is no slackening of speed during the pass.

Tackling an opponent's stick to get the ball needs practice—the aim being to remain balanced yourself and so able to have more than one attempt should you not succeed the first time. A series of sharp taps, either downwards on to the head of the crosse or upwards to make the ball fly into the air, is the best method. Hitting the handle of the crosse is not allowed. There are times too, when the ball must be picked up from the ground, where it may be stationary, or rolling. Here the player uses a scooping action with the feet close to the ball, lifting the stick to the cradling position as soon as the ball is in it.

LA FONTAINE, Jean de (1621–1695)

French poet, a member of the quartette of the Rue du Vieux Colombier which included RACINE, Boileau and MOLIÈRE. There are many amusing stories about his absent-mindedness, and he was very reserved in company. His writing was lively and original, and the *Fables* are still widely read today by adults and children alike.

LAMARCK, Jean Baptiste (1744–1829)

French naturalist, born at Picardy. He did important work in the field of classification, particularly of the invertebrates, (animals without backbones). He was the first to introduce a scientific theory of EVOLUTION based on his idea that a plant or an animal passes on to its offspring characteristics which it found necessary to develop in order to survive in the place in which it lived.

LAMB, Charles (1775–1834)

English poet and essayist, born in London. For more than thirty years he worked in India House, but in order to add to his normal salary he contributed essays and articles to periodicals under the name of Elia. All the essays are marked by a gentle humour and sympathy.

In 1796 his sister Mary had become insane and stabbed her mother, and for the rest of his life Lamb stayed with her and looked after her. Together they wrote *Tales from Shakespeare*.

LANDOR, Walter Savage (1775–1864)

English poet, born at Warwick. He led something of a wandering life—even raising a private regiment to fight in Spain against Napoleon. He wrote both English and Latin poetry—and prose. Among his works are *Count Julian*, *Imaginary Conversations*, *The Pentameron* and *Antony and Octavius*.

LANDSEER, Sir Edwin Henry (1802–1873)

English painter, born in London. He studied under his father who was a well-known engraver. Landseer was made a member of the Royal Society in 1831 and knighted in

LA FONTAINE 17th-century illustration to the fable by La Fontaine, *The Wolf and the Dog*.

1850. He was principally an animal-painter, especially of dogs and stags. His treatment was often sentimental, but there can be no doubt of his talent. Typical Landseer subjects are *Monarch of the Glen, The Cat Disturbed, The Old Shepherd's Chief Mourner* and *Spaniel and Rabbit*.

LANGLAND, William (c. 1332–1400)

Probably born in the region of Malvern and thought to have been a priest. His poem *The Vision of Piers the Plowman* is not only magnificent as a piece of poetic writing, but gives a detailed—and sometimes depressing—picture of English life of the period. It has been said that, 'He is the nearest approach to DANTE in our poetry.'

LANGUAGE

Man's means of communicating ideas and/or emotions, and is perhaps the most important factor distinguishing him from the rest of the animal kingdom.

Languages, like flowers and animals, have been grouped into families according to their sounds and patterns. The accompanying table shows the most important linguistic families.

Indo-European Family
Germanic (High and Low)
English, German, Dutch, Yiddish, Norwegian, Danish, Swedish.
Celtic
Welsh, Gaelic, Breton, Manx, Gaulish.
Romance or Italic
Italian, Rumanian, French, Spanish, Portuguese, Provençal, Catalan.

Hellenic or Greek
Modern and Classical Greek
Slavonic
Russian, Polish, Czech, Slovene, Slovak, Serbo-Croat, Bulgarian.
Indo-Iranian
Persian, Kurdish, Afghan
Indo-Aryan
Sanskrit, Hindustani, Urdu, Sinhalese, Kashmiri, Romany, Panjabi.
Albanian
Baltic
Old Prussian, Celtish, Lithuanian.
Armenian.
Mongolic Family
Mongolian, Buryat, Oirat.
Finno-Ugric Family
Finnish, Lappish, Morvinian, Peruvian, Magyar (Hungarian).
Malayo-Polynesian Family
Formosan, Malay, Javanese, Borneo, Balinese, Fijian, Maori, Tahitian, Hawaiian.
Semitic and Hamitic Family
Arabic, Maltese, Hebrew, Ethiopian, Berber, Riff, Somali, Galla.
Turkic Family
Turkish, Kirghiz, Uzbek, Tartar, Azerbaijanian.
Indi-Chinese Family
Chinese, Cantonese, Tibetan, Siamese, Burmese.
Dravidian Family
Tamil, Kanarese, Telugu, Brahui.
Bantu Family
Zulu, Congo, Kafir, Herero.
Such languages as Japanese, Korean, Basque, Bushman, Australian natives, etc. do not come within the above classifications. The many Amero-Indian languages of the North, Central and South American Indians are still being worked out.

LANSBURY, George (1859-1940)
British politician and leader of the Parliamentary Labour Party from 1931–1935. In addition to advocating socialism he was an ardent pacifist, asserting that differences between countries should be settled by discussion.

LAOS
An independent kingdom in the north-west of the territory formerly known as Indo-China. It is about 90,000 square miles and has a population of about 2½ million. The capital is Vientiane.
   After the Second World War Laos, together with Cambodia and Vietnam, who also used to be part of French Indo-China, fought a bitter war against France which only came to an end in 1954. Although the war with France ended then, there has been a good deal of trouble within the country itself since.

LAO-TSZE (*c.* 590 B.C.)
Chinese philosopher who was said to have founded Taoism and written its great work, the *Tao Te Ching*. Taoists believed in a return to a simple way of living and that everything about civilization was evil.

LAPLACE, Pierre Simon, Marquis de (1749–1827)
French mathematician and astronomer, born at Beaumont-en-Auge. His most celebrated work was on the movement of the heavenly bodies and presented in his book, *Mécanique Celeste*; a work said to rank with Sir Isaac Newton's *Principia Mathematica*. He maintained that the whole physical universe could be explained by the law of cause and effect so that, given enough information, both the past and the future of the universe could be determined in every detail.

LAPLAND
This arctic area is not a separate country but is a district, stretching across the north of Norway, Sweden, Finland and the Soviet Union, in which Lapps live. The district is considerably larger than Great Britain but there are only about 100,000 Lapps. They are wandering people, or nomads, who have domesticated reindeer for their food, and transport.

LASCAUX
Grotto near Montignac (south-west France) in which there are the finest cave paintings yet uncovered. They were accidentally found (1940) by a group of boys out with their dog. Although painted by our primitive ancestors some 20,000 years ago they still rank as great works of art as well as important archaeological finds.

LASER
Is an intense, narrow beam of light of uniform wavelength. As this is a recent discovery of science the technology of its applications is only now being worked out. What is certain from work already done is that they will play an important part in future systems concerned with transmission of information; already laser telephones have been developed. Another successful application is in medicine where surgeons have carried out delicate operations on the eye with a micro-fine laser beam. The word **LASER** is an acronym for **L**ightwave **A**mplification by **S**timulated **E**mission of **R**adiation.

LASCAUX An example of the painting of animals done by our ancestors at least 20,000 years ago.

LATENT HEAT

When a solid is turned to liquid by the application of HEAT, the 'latent heat of fusion', as it is termed, is the quantity of heat required to convert unit mass of substance from a solid to a liquid state without change of temperature. The latent heat of vaporisation is the quantity of heat required to convert a unit mass of a liquid to a vapour without any change of temperature.

LATHE

A machine for shaping wood and metal (and more recently plastic materials). Basically it consists of a rotating chuck in which the object to be machined is held and a flat bed which carries a fitting that takes a tool; the cutting tool can move along the object or across it. There are many types of lathe in the modern workshop, but the most widely used are the centre and capstan lathes. [See MACHINE TOOLS.]

LATIMER, Hugh (c. 1485–1555)

English Protestant and martyr. Born near Leicester, educated at Cambridge, where he took priest's orders. He was one of the clerics who declared that HENRY VIII's marriage to Anne Boleyn was lawful, and was strongly in favour of the reformed doctrine. In 1535 he was consecrated Bishop of Worcester, but his opinions were too extreme for his fellow churchmen and he was twice imprisoned, once in Chichester Palace and the second time in the Tower. On the accession of Edward VI he did not take up his episcopal duties again but devoted himself to preaching and works of charity. Under Mary Tudor he was condemned as a heretic and, together with Nicholas RIDLEY, Bishop of London, burnt at the stake at Oxford. His sermons, letters and other writings were published last century.

LATVIA

Republic of the U.S.S.R. bordering the Baltic Sea to the West. It has a population of over 2 million and its capital is Riga. Incorporated into the U.S.S.R. in 1940, but occupied by Hitler in 1941–1944.

LAUD, William (1573–1645)

English Churchman, born at Reading. He was made Archbishop of Canterbury in 1633, and, from the death of Buckingham (1628), was CHARLES I's chief adviser together with Strafford. His aim was to have an authoritarian Church of England, similar in doctrine to the Roman Catholic Church, and from which all signs of Calvinism had been purged by means of fines, exile and imprisonment. His attack on the Presbyterian Church in Scotland led to the Covenant and the Bishops' War. During the Civil War he was impeached for high treason, committed to the Tower of London and executed.

LAUDER, Sir Harry (1870–1950)

Born at Portobello. Scottish variety actor, singer and composer of Scottish songs. He was knighted in 1919.

LAVAL, Pierre (1883–1945)

French statesman. An early Socialist and twice Prime Minister in the 1930s, he later changed his political opinions. After the fall of France (1940), he worked for Marshal PETAIN's Vichy government (the French government of the 'unoccupied' zone of France, which collaborated with the Germans), and was Prime Minister from 1942–1944. He was executed in 1945 for treason against the state.

LAVOISIER, Antoine Laurent (1743–1794)

French scientist, born in Paris. He trained to be a lawyer but very early decided to devote himself to science. His greatest achievement was to prove the accepted theory of combustion wrong. In its place he gave us the theory very much as we know it today. As part of the same story he proved that the air was a mixture of oxygen and nitrogen, and that water was a compound of hydrogen and oxygen. He published his findings in a book *Traite de Chimia*, one of the greatest books on chemistry that has ever been written. Lavoisier met his end at the guillotine, in spite of protests from many scientists in France and England. He had committed no great crime, but had made enemies who brought false evidence against him.

LAW

The collection of rules which a State builds up. There are several different kinds of law. Constitutional law is concerned with how the country is to be governed. When PARLIAMENT makes a new law bringing about some change in the way Parliament does its work or saying who shall be allowed to vote and at what age, this is Constitutional law. In England the oldest type of law is Common law. This is made up of decisions given by the Courts through the centuries. Statute law is written law made by an Act of Parliament.

LAWN TENNIS

So called to distinguish it from the older game of Tennis, or Royal Tennis may be played on either a grass court or hard court. The singles game is played between two opponents; the doubles game, between two pairs of partners. The court shown in the diagram opposite is marked out for the doubles game, but can be used for singles if the players ignore the space between the 'tramlines' of 4 ft. 6 ins. on each side.

As is shown, the court is divided across the middle by a net; this is 3 feet high at the centre and held taut across the court. The lines at the end are called the base-lines, and the lines at the sides the side-lines. The lines across the court 21 feet from the net are the service lines, while the line joining their centre is called the centre service-line.

The game is played with a soft ball with a smooth outer surface and stitchless seams. It is between $2\frac{1}{2}$ and $2\frac{5}{8}$ inches in diameter and weighs between 2 and $2\frac{1}{16}$ ounces. It is made of india-rubber covered with white cloth. Rackets are made with wooden or metal frames and strung with gut or nylon, and vary in size and weight.

Before the game the players toss by spinning a racket, and the winner has the right to choose either the side of the court or whether he or his opponent shall serve first. If he chooses the first, then the loser decides who shall begin serving; if he chooses to serve or receive first, then his opponent has the choice of sides.

Before starting to serve the server must stand with both feet at rest behind the base-line and within the boundaries of the side-line and the centre of the base-line. For his first service he stands behind the right-hand court, for his second behind the left-hand court, and so on alternately throughout the game. At the start of each new game the service is taken from behind the right-hand court.

In serving, the server throws the ball into the air in any direction, and before it hits the ground, strikes it with his racket. His object is to hit the ball over the net so that it will hit the ground within the service-court diagonally opposite. If he fails to do this, the service is called a 'fault'. Particular attention should be paid to the footfault rule which states that the server shall, throughout the delivery of the service:

(a) not change his position by walking or running, and

(b) not touch, with either foot, any area other than that behind the base-line within the imaginary extension of the centre mark and side-line.

After one fault the server again serves from behind the same half of the court. If this also is a fault, the receiver wins the point.

If the ball served touches the net, but is otherwise good, it is called a 'let', and does not count in the game at all, the server serving again from the same position. The same applies if the receiver was not ready for the service and does not attempt to return it.

The object for the receiver of the service is to strike the ball with his racket over the net so that it will hit the ground within his opponent's half of the court, that is, within the area bounded by the net, the base-line, and the two side-lines. He must not hit the ball, nor must it touch him or anything he is wearing, before it hits the ground on his side of the net; but he must hit it before it bounces twice.

If the receiver succeeds in returning the ball correctly, the server now has to hit the ball back under the same conditions, that is, over the net into his opponent's half of the court, before it bounces twice. He may, however, if he wishes, strike the ball before it hits the ground in his half of the court; but if he does this he cannot afterwards claim that the ball would have pitched beyond his base-line or side-line, even though he might be standing beyond one of these lines when he strikes the ball. Striking the ball before it hits the ground is called 'volleying'.

The game continues in this way, as the players hit the ball over the net to each other, either by volleys or after one bounce, until one of them fails to make a proper return, and so loses the point.

Apart from a double fault by the server and interference with the served ball before it hits the ground by the receiver, a point is lost by either player if he:

(1) fails to hit the ball over the net;
(2) fails to hit the ball before it bounces twice;
(3) returns the ball so that it hits the ground outside his opponent's side of the court;
(4) strikes the ball in play with his racket more than once in making a stroke;

won a point in a game his score is called 'love'. After the first point, therefore, the score is '15–love' if it was won by the· server, and 'love-15' if won by the receiver.

If the same player wins the first two (or three) points in succession, the score is called '30-love' (or '40-love') if in favour of the server and 'love-30' (or 'love-40') if in favour of the receiver. When each player has scored one or two points, the score is called '15 all' or '30 all' as the case may be.

If either player scores his fourth point before his opponent has scored three points, he thereby wins the game. When, however, each player has scored three points, the score is not called '40-all', but 'deuce'. The next point scored is

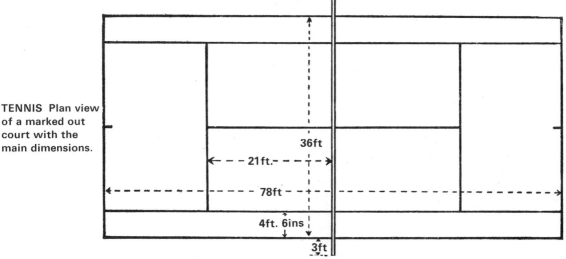

TENNIS Plan view of a marked out court with the main dimensions.

36ft

← – – 21ft.– – – →

← – – – – – – – – 78ft – – – – →

4ft. 6ins

3ft

(5) touches with his racket or his person the net, posts, or ground within his opponent's court at any time while the ball is in play;
(6) volleys the ball before it has passed the net;
(7) is touched by the ball in play on his person or clothes;
(8) throws his racket at and hits the ball.

If the ball falls on a line, it is regarded as within the court bounded by that line. If it touches the net or post, but the return is otherwise good, it is a good return. If it is returned outside the post, at any height, and falls within the court, it is a good return.

If a good return rebounds or is blown back over the net, the player receiving it may reach over the net to play the ball, provided he does not in any way touch the net or the ground in his opponent's half.

After the first point has been won, the score is called 15 for the winner; when the same player wins his second point, his score is 30, and with his third point, 40. Until a player has

'advantage' for the player who wins it; and if he wins the next point as well, he wins the game; but if the other player wins the second point after the deuce, the score is again called deuce. The game goes on this way until one of the players succeeds in scoring two consecutive points immediately after a deuce.

The player who first wins six games wins the 'set', except where his opponent has already won five games. After the score of '5-all' in games, the position in the set is similar to that of deuce in a game. To win the set, a player must obtain a clear lead of two games over his opponent, and the set continues until this is achieved.

At the end of each game the service changes. The players change ends at the end of the first, third, and every subsequent alternate game of each set, and also at the end of each set unless the total number of games in that set is an even number.

The maximum number of sets in a match is five for men and three for women. Play is governed by an umpire, whose decisions are final.

In general, the rules for the singles game apply equally to the doubles game. The partners serve alternate games, in the same order during each set. In receiving, the partners receive services alternately, so that in each game one partner receives all the balls in the left service-court and the other in the right service-court. Also, they take it in turns to receive the first service of a game, so that in fact during each set each partner is always on one side when receiving from one server and on the other side when receiving from the other server.

If the ball served touches the server's partner or his racket, it is a fault. If it touches the receiver's partner or racket before it hits the ground, the point is won by the server.

After the first return of the service, either partner may make any return; but if both partners touch the ball in succession during one return, the point is won by the opposing pair.

LAWRENCE, David Herbert (1885–1930)

English poet and novelist, the son of a Nottinghamshire miner. In spite of his poor health, he became a schoolteacher, encouraged by his mother, and then after the success of *The White Peacock* decided to live by writing. The distinctive feature of Lawrence's novels is their intense examination of intimate relationships and of the depths of human emotions. He made a tremendous impression, though not always a favourable one, on the writers and intellectuals of his day. Perhaps his most careful writing is in his poetry. Two well-known novels are *Sons and Lovers* and *The Plumed Serpent*.

LAWRENCE, Thomas Edward (1888–1935)

British soldier and author. Born in a Welsh village near Snowdon, and studied Oriental languages at Oxford. On an archaeological expedition to the Euphrates, he first discovered his profound liking and understanding of the Arab peoples. During the Great War he was persuaded to encourage and lead the Arabs in their fight against the Turks. Later, dissatisfied with what he saw as a betrayal of the Arabs at the Peace Conference, he gave up his post and joined the R.A.F. He was killed in a motor-cycle accident. He translated HOMER's *Odyssey*, and wrote *The Seven Pillars of Wisdom* and *Revolt in the Desert* about his wartime experiences. The film *Lawrence of Arabia* is about his life in the desert.

LEAD

Heavy, soft metal whose chemical symbol is Pb, atomic number 82 and atomic weight 207.21. Mechanically it is very soft, easily cut and a very poor conductor of electricity. Its principal uses are in the manufacture of paints and glass, accumulators, outer coverings of cables and roof coverings (now not so frequent because of its high cost).

People constantly using lead are liable to a disease called lead poisoning (at one time called 'painter's colic') and caused by lead getting into either the digestive or respiratory systems. Because of this disease workers in industries using lead are specially protected.

LEAD-CHAMBER PROCESS

Method of manufacturing sulphuric acid by passing a mixture of air and sulphur dioxide containing small quantities of nitrogen oxides into a lead chamber in which steam is passed. The nitrogen oxides act as catalysts and promote the rapid oxidation of sulphur dioxide to sulphur trioxide. This reacts with the water to form sulphuric acid. In normal practice there are three lead chambers and the oxidation of the sulphur dioxide takes place in the first two chambers, the third one serving mainly to dry the gases. The chambers are kept cool so that the sulphuric acid condenses on the walls and is drawn off from the floor periodically. The acid made by this process is known as 'chamber acid'; it contains between 62%–70% acid.

LEAGUE OF NATIONS

An organization of States which was the predecessor of the UNITED NATIONS. It was set up at Geneva after the First World War. People had been so horrified at the world-wide suffering caused by the war that they were determined to have some other method of settling disputes. The United States decided not to join and this weakened its effectiveness. It was able, however, to do some useful work in settling several disputes and in regard to welfare and health. But it was not strong enough to prevent Germany, under HITLER, from re-arming, or MUSSOLINI conquering Abyssinia, or Japan invading China. When Germany attacked her neighbours World War II (1939–1945) was launched and the League of Nations came to an end. After the war the United Nations was set up to replace it. One part of the League to survive, however, was the INTERNATIONAL LABOUR ORGANIZATION.

LEAR, Edward (1812–1888)

Born in London. A traveller, a painter (who taught drawing to Queen Victoria), and a writer of verse, Lear is most famous for *A Book of Nonsense*, published in 1846. It was written to entertain the grandchildren of his patron, the Earl of Derby. Many of Lear's nonsense poems are 'limericks'. In longer poems, such as *The Owl and the Pussy-Cat*, he is full of music as well as nonsense. The illustrations to his poems are as delightful as the words.

LEATHER

The tanned or dressed hide or skin of an animal. The first operation in the manufacture of leather is to remove the blood and lymph, and then the salt in which the hides or skins have been preserved. The next process is the removal of hair or wool (depilation). This is begun by 'liming' (except sheepskins) in a series of pits containing a solution of slaked lime and various sulphides. The process takes from ten to fourteen days. The liquors are kept in constant motion and when the hides are taken from the last pit their hairs are loose enough for the 'unhairing' treatment. Sheepskins are prepared for unhairing in one of two quite different ways. They may be painted on their fleshy sides with a paste of slaked lime and sulphides, or they may be 'sweated'. This means hanging them up in a warm chamber called a 'sweating stove' until the hair-roots have become loose by putrefaction. The wool is then pulled out by hand.

LEAR A page from his *Nursery Rhymes*

And wasn't that a dainty dish to set before the king?

The King was in his counting-house, Counting out his money.

The unhairing of heavy hides is also still done very largely by hand. The hides are laid on sloping boards and the hair is removed by a long two-handled knife, called an 'unhairing knife'. But sometimes this job is done in an unhairing machine. When the hairs have been removed the hides have to be 'fleshed', which may also be done either by hand or in a machine. Fleshing is the removal by knives or scrapers of all traces of adhering flesh, and when this has been done the hides or skins are known as 'pelts'. The pelts are now 'delimed'—that is, all traces of lime are removed from them by hanging them from poles in large pits containing a deliming agent.

They next go through one of four processes. The first is called 'puering', and the traditional method (still largely used) is to work the hides in an infusion of dog dung. The second alternative is similar except that fowl droppings are used, and it is called 'bating'. The third process achieves the same result by means of an infusion of fermenting bran, and the fourth alternative involves the use of synthetic substitutes for these unpleasant substances. The effect of all four methods is to render the pelts soft and supple by the decay and removal of the hair-sheaths, sweat glands and ducts, skin-muscles and elastic fibres. The pelts may now be given an antiseptic soak in borax, and are once again thoroughly washed before going to the tanning vats.

There are three groups of ordinary tan substances—one of vegetable origin, one of synthetic substances, and one of mineral salts. Vegetable tanning is the traditional method, and is still most frequently used. The active principle in vegetable tans is the group of substances known as 'tannins', of which the chief is the so-called 'tannic acid', found also in tea.

The pelts are first suspended in a very weak infusion of the tan, and then pass to stronger and stronger liquors, the final vat containing masses of the solid tan-stuff. Here they remain until tanning is complete. The process can be speeded up with smaller skins by tanning them in revolving 'paddle vats'.

The synthetic tans, or 'syntans', are derived from benzene, naphthalene, phenol, and other coal-tar products, but though they can be used alone they are often added to vegetable tans in order to speed up the tanning. The mineral tans are principally salts of chromium, but the pelts are usually pickled in dilute sulphuric acid and common salt before being 'chrometized', the process being completed by immersion in photographer's 'hypo'. The acid is then removed by a bath of washing-soda, and the pelts are thoroughly dried. Chrome leather is green, whereas ordinary vegetable-tanned leather is brown. White leather is produced by tanning with another mineral salt, alum, and is used chiefly for making such articles as gloves. Chrome leather intended for the soles of shoes is steeped in hot oils and waxes, which darken its colour considerably. All leathers go through finishing processes which usually include oiling and rolling. The last stage consists in dressing the leather with a coating of 'season' or 'finish', which produces a glazed surface when the leather is finally pressed between heavy rollers.

LEBANON

A small Arab republic bordering the eastern shores of the Mediterranean, an area sometimes called the Levant. The country is smaller (4,300 square miles) than Wales and has a population of nearly 2 million. About half the people are Christians and the other half Moslems. The capital is Beirut. The mountains of Lebanon were once famous for their cedars but not many remain.

Before the First World War Lebanon was part of the Turkish Empire. It then became a French Mandated territory under the LEAGUE OF NATIONS but became a republic during the Second World War.

LE CORBUSIER, properly Charles Jeanneret (1887–1965)

Swiss architect and artist. By his work and his books he exerted a great influence on many aspects of modern architecture, particularly on the construction of large blocks of flats. He designed Chandigarh, the new capital of the Punjab; a revolutionary block of flats in Marseilles (the *Unité d'habitation*); and was part designer of the U.N. building, New York.

LEE, Robert E. (1807–1870)

Famous American General of the Confederate Army and hero of the South. He was in command during many of the battles of the Civil War, and surrendered to General Grant at Appomattox in 1865.

LEEUWENHOEK, Antony Van (1632–1723)

Dutch scientist and father of the science of microscopy. He was the first to see and describe bacteria with his self-constructed MICROSCOPE, and gave the first description of the red cells in the BLOOD.

LEEWARD ISLANDS

A group of islands in the West Indies, some of which belong to Britain, some to France and some to the Netherlands. Included in the Leeward Islands are the Virgin Islands, some of which belong to Britain and others to the United States. The British islands include Antigua, Anguilla and Nevis. The chief French island is Guadeloupe.

In 1966 the British islands of the Leeward and Windward groups were told they could have associated status with Britain. This means that they will be allowed to manage their own affairs but Britain will look after their defence and relations with foreign countries.

LEHAR, Franz (1870–1948)

Hungarian composer. Although he composed much serious music he is best remembered for his gay operettas, *The Merry Widow* and *The Count of Luxemburg*.

LEIBNIZ, Gottfried Wilhelm (1646–1716)

Born at Leipzig and son of the Professor of Philosophy at the University of that town. His two most important books of philosophy are *Monadology* and *Principles of Nature and Grace*. He discovered the CALCULUS. For quite a long time Leibniz was accused of lifting NEWTON's work, but it is now quite certain that he discovered this branch of mathematics quite independently. He is sometimes known as the 'father of German philosophy'.

LEICESTER, Robert Dudley, Earl of (1532–1588)

Elizabethan courtier and soldier. Son of the Duke of Northumberland, and a favourite of Queen Elizabeth for thirty years, although he seems to have had little influence with her in political affairs. In 1564 he was appointed Chancellor of Oxford University, and in 1585 he commanded the English expedition to the Netherlands of which he was made governor the following year. But in 1587 he was recalled owing to inefficiency. In 1588 he was made commander at Tilbury of the land forces to oppose the Spanish ARMADA.

LEIGHTON, Frederick, Baron (1830–1896)

English artist, born at Scarborough. He studied in many European countries for the simple reason that his family were constantly on the move. He became a member of the Royal Academy in 1868 and its President in 1878. His fame started with his picture *Cimabue's Madonna carried in procession through the streets of Florence* which was bought by Queen Victoria. Leighton painted a large number of classical subjects such as *The Battle of Psyche* and *Perseus and Andromeda*.

LELY, Sir Peter (1618–1680)

Dutch-born portrait painter. After studying art in Haarlem, Holland, he came to England

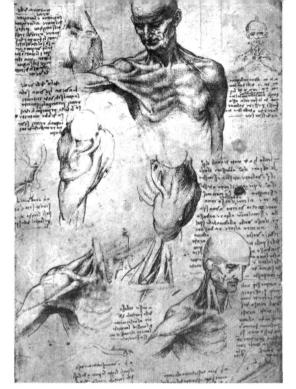

LEONARDO A page of anatomical drawings from one of his sketch books.

in 1641 as a portrait-painter. He produced portraits of all the great personalities of the reign of Charles I, Cromwell and Charles II, and the latter made him his court painter and knighted him. Many fine examples of his work are to be seen at Hampton Court and the National Portrait Gallery, London.

LEMMING

This member of the RODENT family is found in Scandinavia, usually in the mountains where it lives in burrows; in the winter it runs under the snow. At certain times lemmings migrate in swarms and if they reach the coast move into the sea and are drowned in thousands. No satisfactory explanation of this strange behaviour has yet been given.

LEMURS

These animals belong to the order of PRIMATES and generally resemble the typical monkey. They are found in the warmer parts of the Old World and are the only members of the primates found in Madagascar.

LENIN, Vladimir Ilyich (1870–1924)

Russian revolutionary. Born in Simbirsk, the son of a school-teacher, he studied law at Kazan University before being expelled for political activities. He went to St. Petersburg (now Leningrad), studied Marxism and founded a 'League for the Emancipation of the

Working Class' from which the Russian Bolshevik party finally emerged. After a period of imprisonment and exile to Siberia (1896–1898) Lenin left Russia and did not return until April 1917 when he took over command of the Bolsheviks. In October 1917 he led them to victory in the Russian Revolution. Lenin became President of the Council of Peoples' Commissars, as the new government was called. After four years of civil war (1917–1921), his 'new economic policy' was proclaimed and helped to inaugurate some reconstruction of the devastated country. But in 1922 his health began to fail and he died early in 1924. [*See* MARX.]

LENT

A period of fasting and penitence. The calendar period begins on Ash Wednesday and ends at noon on Holy Saturday, the day before Easter Sunday. Holy Week is the last week of Lent.

LEONARDO da Vinci (1452–1519)

Italian painter, sculptor, architect, musician, engineer and scientist. Born in the village of Vinci near Florence. In 1466 he was placed under the tuition of Andrea del Verrocchio, in Florence; BOTTICELLI was a fellow apprentice. The unfinished *Adoration of the Magi* reveals his early greatness. He went to Milan in about 1482, where he remained for some sixteen years. During this time he produced his famous notebooks and many architectural plans and drawings. In 1483 he painted the *Madonna of the Rocks*. One version is in the National Gallery, London, and the other in the LOUVRE. Of the two versions, it is believed that the one in the Louvre was largely produced by Leonardo himself, while the example in the National Gallery, London, was executed later, after Leonardo's design. His fresco of *The Last Supper*, one of the world's masterpieces, was begun about 1485 and finished by 1498. In 1500 Leonardo returned to Florence, where he devoted himself to mathematical and anatomical studies. In 1502, he entered the service of Cesare Borgia as a military engineer. Returning to Florence in the following year, he painted the celebrated *Mona Lisa*, now in the Louvre. In 1506 he served the French king, Louis XII, in Milan, as engineer and architect, and also investigated problems of geology, botany, hydraulics and mechanics. In 1513, he undertook architectural and engineering commissions at the Vatican. He died in France while supervising the building of a canal. Leonardo's versatility and originality mark him out as the greatest genius of the Renaissance, and perhaps of all time.

LEONCAVALLO, Ruggiero (1858–1919)

Italian composer, born at Naples. Composed a great number of operas which met with little success, except *I 'Pagliacci*, which is still a favourite opera, and his one outstanding work.

LEOPARD

This animal is sometimes called a panther and is distinguished from the lion and tiger by its spotted coat, rather long tail and smaller size. The pattern is made up of rosettes of four or five spots with sometimes one or more small black spots in the centre. However, both colour and pattern are found to vary quite a lot. The commonest variety is the black leopard of Abyssinia and the East Indies. The habits of leopards are similar to those of lions and tigers with the exception that the leopard is a tree-climber and frequently lies in branches to await its prey. It is seldom dangerous to man unless wounded or cornered. The only member of the leopard group in America is the JAGUAR.

LEPIDOPTERA

Order of INSECTS covering all the species of moths and butterflies. Their main characteristics are four wings (a few females are wingless) and complete metamorphosis, i.e., egg, larva, chrysalis to adult insect.

LEPROSY

Bacterial disease common in the tropical and sub-tropical regions of Africa, Asia, and South America. The germ may take many years to incubate and the areas infected are the skin or nerves or both. Many methods of treatment have been tried to cure this scourge, the most effective being injections of ethyl esters and sodium hydrocarpate.

LESOTHO (formerly Basutoland)

This newly-named country is in southern Africa. It is surrounded by the Republic of South Africa and so is called an enclave. It is larger (11,716 square miles) than Wales and has a population of more than half a million. The capital is Maseru.

The country was formerly a British protectorate but in 1966 it became an independent State within the British Commonwealth and took the name of 'Lesotho'.

LETTER-WRITING

Two people are concerned in the writing of a letter—the writer and the person to whom it is written. In general, letters can be divided into two main types, *private* and *business*. When we write a private letter, we 'talk', as it were, to a friend or relative; that is, we use familiar, sometimes colloquial, language. If the person we write to is not so well known to us, we use a more formal style, but nevertheless a style which suggests speech or conversation. But in a business letter we are entirely formal; we write, for example, to a person we do not know, and our chief aim should be to state our 'business' in the briefest, most straightforward, and simplest way possible. In letter-writing there are a few 'conventions' or customs to be observed. The chief of these apply to all letters; but one or two special ones to business letters only:

(i) Write your own address fully and carefully in the top right-hand corner of the paper, and under it write the date.

(ii) On the left of your paper write the name or title (e.g. 'The Secretary', 'The Manager') and address of the person to whom the letter is written. Or this may be written below the letter on the left of the paper.

(iii) Write also on the left top of the paper business references (if any), like PH/3T.

(iv) Your greeting should be 'Dear Sir' or 'Dear Madam', according to the sex of your correspondent. If you do not know the sex, write 'Dear Sir', rather than 'Dear Sir or Madam'.

(v) The beginning of your letter should be 'indented'—that is, set in from the margin; and if your letter is a long one (as it will not be normally), it should be divided into paragraphs. Take care if you are answering an advertisement (for example) that you give the exact information required.

(vi) Use a simple ending like 'Yours faithfully' or 'Yours truly', and sign your name so that it can be read.

Here is a specimen letter in answer to the following advertisement:

WANTED a Junior Clerk in office of a large engineering firm. Some knowledge of mathematics and French an advantage. Write, giving full particulars, to the Secretary, Cogs & Wheels, Ltd., Gear Lane, London, E.9.

8 *West Road,*
Eastwood,
London, N.6.
7th December, 1971

Dear Sir,

I wish to apply for the position of Junior Clerk in your office, as advertised in the Echo *of 1st December. My age is sixteen years. I shall be leaving Eastwood Secondary Modern School at the end of this term (19th December), and could therefore begin work, if I am appointed, immediately after Christmas. At the end-of-term examination I received a 'good' mark for* mathematics and a 'credit' mark for French. The Headmaster of the School, Eastwood Road, N.6., and Rev. G. Smith, Vicar, Holy Trinity Church, Southwood Lane, N.6., would be glad to give you any particulars concerning my work and character.

Yours faithfully,
Robert Brown.

The Secretary,
Messrs. Cogs & Wheels Ltd.,
Gear Lane,
London, E.9.

LEUCIPPUS (c. 430 B.C.)
Greek philosopher who believed that the primary substance of which all things are made must be eternal and changeless. His idea was that primary substance exists in the form of minute atoms, separated from one another by void (empty space). This allowed for motion and was the first statement of an 'atomic theory' of matter, though he thought that all atoms must be exactly alike.

LEVELLERS
Puritan group, led by John Lilburne (c. 1614–1657) who fought for equality in social and religious matters. Their programme of reform was contained in *The Agreement of the People* (1648). The movement was routed by CROMWELL at Burford. Lilburne was charged with treason but this was not proved. Later in his life he became a QUAKER.

LEVER [*See* PULLEYS AND LEVERS.]

LEWIS, Sinclair (1885–1951)
American novelist. His best works attack the small-mindedness and superficial intellectualism of the provinces (*Main Street*), and the complacent and conventional American, caught in the network of rotary clubs and business deals (*Babbitt*).

LIBERAL PARTY
One of the oldest parties in the United Kingdom. It developed from the old Whig Party of the 17th and 18th centuries in opposition to the Tory Party which developed into the CONSERVATIVE PARTY. The Liberal Party remained one of the two major political parties in Parliament until 1922 when it was challenged by the growth of the LABOUR PARTY. The Liberal Party, although it has for many years had fewer seats in Parliament than either the Labour or Conservative parties still plays an important role in Parliament and in British politics. The Liberal Party stands for certain progressive aims, such as the protection of individual liberties and the provision of more and better school buildings. It shares some of its aims with the Labour Party but, like the Conservative Party, it is opposed to the nationalization of industry.

LIBERIA
An independent English speaking negro republic in West Africa. It is rather smaller (43,000 square miles) than England and has a population of 1¼ million. The capital is Monrovia. The country produces rubber, cocoa, coffee and iron ore. The country was founded in 1820 as a home for American negro slaves. The President of the Republic from 1944 to 1971 was William Tubman.

LIBRARIES
Collections of books and other written matter. Ever since the days when books first came to be written there seem to have been libraries. At Nineveh the ruins of a public library and catalogues of about ten thousand documents written on tablets of clay have been found. The ancient Egyptians, Greeks and Romans all had libraries, some of them housed in fine buildings. In Rome alone there were said to have been no less than twenty-eight public libraries. The most famous and probably the largest of the ancient libraries was the one at Alexandria which was unhappily destroyed in the seventh century.

The largest library in Britain today is that at the British Museum which has in the region of six million books. Until the middle of the 19th century there were practically no free public libraries in Great Britain. Then in 1850 Parliament passed the first Act allowing towns to set up public libraries. The opening of public libraries was later on greatly helped by funds given by a millionaire named Andrew CARNEGIE. He gave enough money to build more than 2,500 public libraries in Britain and America.

Today there are many hundreds of thousands of public libraries throughout the world. During the 20th century librarians found that children wanted to use public libraries and today most public libraries have junior libraries or departments.

LIBYA
A large Arab kingdom on the Mediterranean coast of Africa. It is nearly three times larger (810,000 square miles) than France but has a population of only about 1¼ million. The country is divided into three divisions—Tripolitania, Cyrenaica and the Fezzan. There are at present two capitals—Tripoli and Benghazi but a new capital is being built at Beida in Cyrenaica. Most of the country is

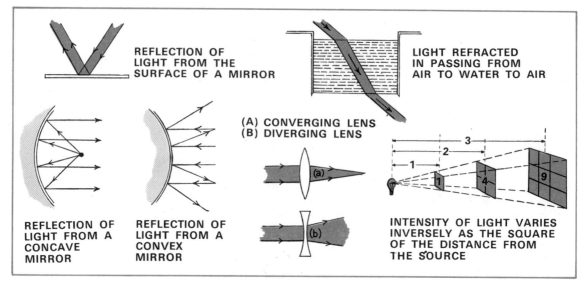

REFLECTION OF LIGHT FROM THE SURFACE OF A MIRROR

LIGHT REFRACTED IN PASSING FROM AIR TO WATER TO AIR

(A) CONVERGING LENS
(B) DIVERGING LENS

REFLECTION OF LIGHT FROM A CONCAVE MIRROR

REFLECTION OF LIGHT FROM A CONVEX MIRROR

INTENSITY OF LIGHT VARIES INVERSELY AS THE SQUARE OF THE DISTANCE FROM THE SOURCE

desert and until the discovery of oil a few years ago was one of the poorest countries in the world. Before the Second World War Libya was an Italian colony but it became an independent country in 1952.

LICHEN

Some fungi live in so close an association with certain algae (unicellular plants) that the combination is very like a single plant and such are known as lichens. These may be erect and branching or flat on the surface on which they grow. Lichens are usually grey or yellowish, and can grow and thrive in very hard conditions. The 'reindeer moss' of the Arctic is really a lichen and not a true moss.

LIECHTENSTEIN

A tiny Principality on the Upper Rhine between Austria and Switzerland. It has an area of 65 square miles and a population of a little over 18,000 inhabitants. Its capital is Vaduz.

LIE DETECTOR

An instrument which detects changes in the respiration of the body or pulse rate. These changes are thought to be caused by telling lies in answer to important questions. The instrument is used mainly in the U.S.A. This instrument should not be confused with the electro-encephalograph which records the electric currents in the brain and is in no way connected with lie detecting.

LIFEBOATS

The earliest mention of a lifeboat is in 1765 when a Frenchman built a boat which would not sink when filled with water. But it was not

until after many more sea disasters that William Wouldhave built a boat which not only floated when filled with water, but righted itself when overturned. In 1824 Sir William Hillary formed the Royal National Lifeboat Institution which today has about 250 boats positioned at Lifeboat Stations around the British Isles, where they are ready for immediate use and able to be launched with the least possible delay. Driven by powerful motor engines, they are enormously strong to withstand the buffeting of the seas. They vary between 9 and 28 tons in weight and carry from 30 to 100 persons. They are decked in and specially fitted with air tanks to give extra buoyancy so that they ride over the seas instead of plunging into them and being swamped. They carry radio telephone apparatus to keep in touch with shore stations and a searchlight to work at night. They also carry a small line-firing gun, with which they can first contact a disabled vessel and tow her away from danger or into harbour. Painted white with a topside blue and red band they are easily distinguished from any other craft.

Other types of lifeboat are those carried in merchant ships. Although these are different in pattern they have many like qualities. They are open boats (not decked in) fitted with watertight compartments to carry food, water, and first-aid kit, as it must be realised that these boats may be alone at sea for days before being found or able to make land under their own power. Some are motor driven, but many are propelled by oars and sails. They have air tanks to give buoyancy, but their weights and lifesaving capacity are much less than the shore based craft. Research is being carried out all the time to improve ships' lifeboats.

LIGHT

A form of energy. We are made aware of it through our eyes. In other words, we 'see' by means of light. The study of its behaviour is a branch of physics known as optics.

The chief natural source of light is the sun, which provides our daylight and moonlight. Artificial sources of light include the electric lamp, in which a piece of wire is made white-hot; the gas lamp, in which burning gas makes the mantle white-hot; and the oil lamp, in which the paraffin, burning with a yellow flame, provides the light. Most living animals can see. Even plants are aware of light and most of them cannot live without it, and some of them actually turn towards the light as the sun travels across the sky.

Light when not interfered with travels in straight lines. This is the first law of optics. That is why a shadow reproduces the outline of an object standing in the way of light. The law, though true for most practical purposes, is not wholly true, for light does bend sharply round the edges of objects to a slight extent. The effect is so slight that to examine it carefully one must have elaborate apparatus.

A straight line showing on a drawing the direction of travel of light is said to represent a 'ray' of light. When a ray of light meets a substance it can be turned back (reflected) or it can go through and emerge at the other side, in which case the substance is either translucent or transparent, according to whether a group of rays emerges mixed up or unchanged. Some of the light may also be used up in the substance, or, as we say, absorbed. In practice, reflection, transmission, and absorption all take place to some extent. With a mirror, which seems to reflect all the light, a little is actually absorbed. With a piece of plain glass, when all the light seems to emerge unchanged, a little is reflected and a little is absorbed.

When a ray of light passes from one transparent substance to another, as from air to glass, it is bent sharply at the surface of separation. This phenomenon is called refraction. Because of this specially shaped pieces of glass can be made, called lenses, to make the rays do what is required, such as producing an image. The eye has a lens that makes an image on the back of the eyeball. That is how we actually see the world around us. [*See* MICROSCOPE and TELESCOPE.]

LIGHTHOUSE

Lighthouses in England and Wales, the Channel Islands and Gibraltar come under the corporation of TRINITY HOUSE. Those in Scotland are provided by the Commission of Northern Lighthouses and those in Ireland

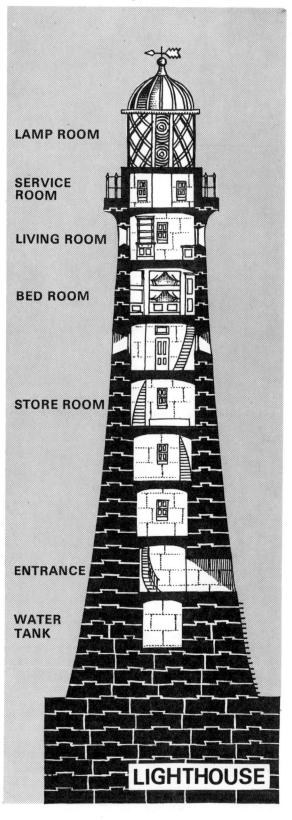

LAMP ROOM

SERVICE ROOM

LIVING ROOM

BED ROOM

STORE ROOM

ENTRANCE

WATER TANK

LIGHTHOUSE

under the Commission of Irish Lights.

There was a lighthouse in existence as early as the 3rd century B.C. at Alexandria, which consisted of a tall stone tower with an open fire burning at its summit. Similar fire-beacons were erected later at many places to guard our own shores and the last of these—at Flat Holm in the Bristol Channel—was not discontinued until 1822.

Fire-beacons were followed by candles and then oil-lamps, and it was in this period that much was done by engineers to collect as much of the light produced in the oil lamps as possible and to direct it as required. Wonderful lens systems, discovered by Augustin Fresnel and by the Stevenson family were developed by the French and English lighthouse makers. Lenses, or optics, as they are called, grew in size until a type some 9 feet in diameter, weighing many tons and revolving upon a mercury turntable, produced over a million candlepower from the oil burner at its focus. We all realize the greater brightness of an electric lamp compared with an oil lamp or candle, and when electric filaments were introduced into the old oil-burning optics, the beam increased to several million candle-power—many times the intensity produced with the oil-burners. In most places this high intensity is unwarranted because at very high powers little extra range is produced by an extra million or so candle-power.

LIGHTNING [*See* THUNDERSTORM.]

LILIENTHAL, Otto (1848–1896)
German inventor, born at Auklam. One of the founders of the science of flight. His important work was concerned with gliding. The cambered wing he invented is still the basis of modern aeroplane wing construction. He was killed during a gliding test at Rhinow.

LIMESTONE
Rock consisting almost entirely of carbonate of calcium, which may have accumulated in any of several ways. Some limestones are no more than beds of sea-shells or sea-lilies firmly compressed and cemented together. Others are formed from the skeletons of microscopic creatures which lived in the surface-waters of great oceans. When these creatures died their limy skeletons sank to the bottom and there formed an 'ooze' which eventually hardened into limestone. The material of some limestones is derived from seaweeds, while others are the remains of coral reefs. Others, again, owe their existence to chemical action, or to the agency of bacteria which are able to extract lime from the sea-water.

LISTER The father of medical antiseptics.

LINCOLN, Abraham (1809–1865)
America's 16th President and leader of the anti-slave movement, born in Kentucky. He worked on his father's farm until he was 19. After a period of study he became a leading barrister in Illinois and was elected to Congress (1847). He became recognized as the leader of the anti-slavery forces. In 1860 he was elected Republican President of America a year before the outbreak of the American Civil War when the slave-owning states in the South seceded from the Union. In his inaugural address Lincoln denied their right to do so and announced his determination to preserve the Union at all costs. In 1864, while the Civil War was still in progress, he issued a decree freeing all the slaves in the Union. He was assassinated while at a theatre by John Wilkes Booth. [*See* GETTYSBURG ADDRESS]

LINDBERGH, Charles A. (1902 ——)
American airman, born at Minnesota. He studied engineering at the University of Wisconsin and in 1922 entered the flying school at Lincoln, Nebraska. On graduation he became a pilot in the government air-mail service between St. Louis and Chicago. World fame came to him when he won a prize of £25,000 for the first non-stop air flight between

New York and Paris (1927). He was promoted to the rank of colonel in the American army, as well as receiving the prize money.

LINEN

A fabric made from FLAX, and one of man's earliest fabrics; it has been found in the form of mummy wrappings in Egyptian tombs. At the present day Ulster is one of the biggest linen producing centres and possesses about one-third of the world's flax spindles. Most of the flax for this Irish industry comes from Russia which is the principal area in the world for flax growing.

LINGUA FRANCA

Literally, the language of the Franks. In common usage it refers to the jargon which people with different languages use to communicate to each other. A good example is Pidgin-English, used by English-speaking and Chinese-speaking traders, and composed of English words, corrupted and arranged in a Chinese fashion. 'Pidgin' itself is a Chinese corruption of the English word 'business'.

LINNAEUS, Carl von Linné (1707–1778)

Swedish naturalist, born at Rashut. He is the father of the modern system of naming plants with two words. Before his day each genus had a name consisting usually of a single Latin word, but the name of the species were descriptive phrases, often many words long. As new species were discovered the descriptive names of those plants already known were altered to take account of the characters which distinguished them from the newly found plant. Thus the meadow buttercup, *Ranunculus acris*, was called by one botanist *Ranunculus pratensis erectus acris,* 'the upright, acrid ranunculus of the meadows'. Linnaeus first applied his system in his *Species Plantarum* (1753), which was an enumeration of all the plants known at that time. His system was based on grouping together those plants with the same number of stamens and carpels in the flowers, and it has long been abandoned. His two-name system, however, is still in use.

LION

This magnificent beast is distinguished from the other members of the cat family by its tawny colour, a black tuft on the tip of the tail in both sexes and a mane in the case of the male.

Lions hunt their food by day as well as by night, preying mainly on various kinds of antelopes, wild pigs, buffaloes, zebras and domestic animals near settlements. In addition to killing their own food they will feed on dead animals they find. Sometimes lions combine to kill prey.

There is an account of three full-grown lions attacking a wounded bull buffalo, which would have been more than a match for them singly.

A full grown lion (this is reached at 4 to 5 years) stands about 3 feet at the shoulder and measures about 10 feet overall, i.e., including some 3 feet of tail, and may reach a weight of 500 pounds. The lioness is always smaller, the weight being 250–300 pounds.

LI PO (c. 700–762)

Chinese poet who wrote a great volume of poetry of which some two thousand lines have been preserved. He is considered by many to be the greatest Chinese poet, his work being devoted to revealing the beauty of nature, women and wine. He led a very adventurous life and was drowned, so it is said, while trying to kiss the moon's reflection.

LIPPI, Fra Filippo (1406–1469)

Italian painter. Born at Florence and started life as a Carmelite friar. His paintings are outstanding for their colour, humanity and grace. Lippi's most famous paintings are the frescoes in the Prato cathedral. His son, Filippino, was also a famous painter and one of his pupils was the brilliant painter BOTTICELLI. BROWNING wrote of him in his poem *Fra Lippo Lippi*.

LISTER, Joseph, 1st Baron (1827–1912)

English doctor, born at Upton, Essex. Father of the science of antiseptics. He introduced carbolic acid to prevent infection (septic poisoning) during operations and discovered that instruments could be sterilized by heat.

LION The largest member of the cat family in Africa. Fully grown it can weigh 500 pounds.

LIVINGSTONE A drawing of the famous meeting between Stanley and Livingstone at Ujija.

LISZT, Franz (1811–1886)

Hungarian composer, born at Dobr'jan. He could play the piano brilliantly when still a child, and became one of the greatest pianists of all time. A generous man, he often befriended younger composers, giving them advice and help; he was also a very religious man, eventually becoming a Catholic priest. His best-known compositions are the Hungarian Rhapsodies for piano, but he wrote much striking music for orchestra, especially the *Faust* and *Dante* Symphonies; he also invented the type of orchestral composition known as the 'symphonic poem'.

LITANY

The service printed after the Athanasian creed in the Prayer book, which, since 1611, has formed part of Morning prayer. Litanies are a special form of prayer in which the clergy lead and the people make set responses. Probably originating in the 5th century, in the East, a fair number of litanies were known in East and West by the 6th century. They were originally sung in procession, in times of trouble. The English Litany is practically a translation of the ancient form still used by Roman Catholics —with prayers addressed to Mary and the Saints omitted.

LITHOGRAPHY

A process of reproduction used by artists and commercial printers, and invented by a German, Aloys Senefelder (about 1796). Basically the process consists of drawing on a stone (limestone) with a special kind of greasy crayon or ink; the drawing is in reverse to be the right way round when printed. Next the stone is washed off with a solution of turpentine and dried. The stone is sponged with water and inked with a roller. Now, the parts of the stone carrying the drawing will take the ink from the roller, but the rest, the wet part, will repel the ink. Finally the paper is pressed on the stone and takes up the inked drawing. In commercial printing a metal plate is used in place of a stone, but the process is fundamentally the same.

LITHUANIA

Republic on the Baltic Sea and now incorporated in the U.S.S.R. (1940). Capital is Vilna. Population about 3,000,000.

LIVERYMEN

Members of the City Livery Companies whose origins go back to the 14th century. Since that time they have played, and still play, an important part in the life of the City of London. The Livery Companies include the Merchant Taylors, the Goldsmiths and so on, and they have the right to wear the liveries of these ancient craft guilds. Dick Whittington (Sir Richard Whittington) was a member of one of these guilds when he was first chosen as Lord Mayor and he was chosen in much the same way as the Lord Mayor of London is chosen today. The freemen of the Livery companies meet in what is called the Court of Common Hall and at Michaelmas each year they elect the Lord Mayor for the coming year. The Liverymen also elect the City sheriffs.

LIVINGSTONE, David (1813–1873)

Scottish missionary and African explorer, born at Low Blantyre in Lanarkshire. He worked first in a cotton mill and studied at night. By dint of saving and hard work he managed to qualify as a doctor, and in 1840 sailed to Africa on behalf of the London Missionary Society. After working with the natives in Bechuanaland (now Botswana), he made many trips to the interior during which he discovered Lake Ngami and partly explored the Zambesi (1849), the Victoria Falls (1855), and Lakes Shira and Nyasa (1858–1859). From 1866–1871 when Livingstone was in search of the Nile Basin he was feared lost and a relief expedition was organized under H. M. Stanley which found him at Ujija near Lake Tanganyika. Though wasted in health Livingstone refused to return with Stanley. The reports on the slave trade that he sent to England played a large part in its suppression.

LIVY (59 B.C.–A.D. 17)
Roman historian, born at Padua. His main work was a history of Rome in 142 books of which only 35 still exist. He is renowned for his clear, masterly style of writing.

LIZARDS [*See* AMPHIBIANS.]

LLAMA
This animal belongs to the same family as the camel, but is smaller and has no hump. Llamas live only in South America on the slopes of the Andes, their feet being adapted for rocky hillsides and their thick coat protecting them from the severe cold near the snow-line of the Andes. Llamas live in herds of over a hundred individuals. In captivity they have the habit of spitting when upset.

LLOYD-GEORGE, Earl David (1863–1945)
Born in Manchester to parents of Welsh extraction. On the death of his father he was brought up in Wales by an uncle, a cobbler, who encouraged the boy in his ambition to study law. He won a wide local reputation as a solicitor and in 1890 was elected to Parliament as Radical M.P. for Caernarvon Boroughs. He made no impact at first, but later his rise was rapid. He became Liberal President of the Board of Trade (1905) and Chancellor of the Exchequer (1908). His 'people's budget' of 1909, which increased taxation on large incomes and on land in order to pay for social reforms and re-armament, was determinedly opposed by the House of Lords and, consequently, an act was passed depriving the Lords of the right to turn down permanently bills passed by the Commons. He was also largely responsible for the Unemployment Insurance Bill. During the Great War he was Premier from 1916 onwards and personified the British will to victory. He resigned the Premiership (1922) and though he remained an influential figure as leader of the Liberal Party, he never again held political office.

LLOYDS
The name of an association in London whose members deal in all kinds of insurance but chiefly in regard to shipping. It got the name Lloyd from a Mr. Edward Lloyd who in 1689 kept a coffee house in Tower Street. Three years later it moved to Lombard Street and here all those concerned with marine insurance would meet together and transact business concerning the insurance of ships and their cargoes. In 1799 a ship, named the *Lutine*, carrying gold was lost in the North Sea. Its bell and some of its cargo were recovered. The bell was taken to Lloyds and it hangs today in the centre of the underwriting rooms and above the rostrum. Whenever an important announcement is made, including the loss of a ship at sea, the 'Lutine Bell' is rung. Lloyds have created standard policies of marine insurance which are now accepted all over the world, the first of which goes back to 1779.

LOBACHEVSKI, N. I. (1793–1856)
Russian mathematician, born in Nizhnii Novgorod. He pioneered the study of non-Euclidean geometry and published examples of its uses. His work was not appreciated until after his death. He published *Pangeometry* in 1855.

LOBSTERS [*See* CRUSTACEANS]

LOCAL AUTHORITY
A body responsible for administering certain local affairs in its area. There are a number of different kinds of local authorities. The smallest is the PARISH COUNCIL which is also the oldest. Groups of Parish Councils come under RURAL DISTRICT COUNCILS. Small towns and urban areas come under URBAN DISTRICT COUNCILS; larger towns under BOROUGH COUNCILS; cities and other large towns are governed by COUNTY BOROUGH COUNCILS. These do not come under COUNTY COUNCILS but other local authorities do, with the exception of the new London Boroughs within the GREATER LONDON COUNCIL area.

LOCKE, John (1632–1704)
Born at Wrington and educated at Westminster School and Oxford. Became interested in political affairs through his friendship with the Earl of Shaftesbury. Was forced to flee to Holland (1683) and did not return to England until the accession to the throne of William of Orange. His most important works were his *Treatises on Government*, in which he maintained that a ruler only had the right to govern as long as his people agreed, in contrast to HOBBES, who thought that, since even bad government was better than no government at all, people did not have the right to change their rulers unless they were too weak to govern properly. Locke's theories were of vital importance in the French and American Revolutions.

LOCKE, Matthew (c. 1630–1677)
English composer, born at Exeter. He wrote many works for the theatre, including part of the first English opera *The Siege of Rhodes*, and music for the masque *Cupid and Death*. He wrote the music for the coronation of Charles II and many other royal occasions.

LOOM A 13th-century illustration of a simple treadle loom used throughout Europe at that time.

LODGE, Sir Oliver (1851–1940)
British scientist, born at Penkhull. For twenty years professor of physics at Liverpool, and later Principal of Birmingham University. His main interests were radio, telegraphy, physics of the electron and the ether. He was one of the few eminent scientists who ardently and sincerely believed in spiritualism.

LOGARITHM
The number 100 can be expressed as 10×10 or 10^2 (10 to the power of 2) and 1,000 as $10 \times 10 \times 10$ or 10^3. To multiply these two together all that is necessary is to add the powers i.e., $10^2 \times 10^3 = 10^{2+3} = 10^5$. The process of division is equally simple, for example, $1,000 \div 100$ becomes $10^3 \div 10^2 = 10^{3-2} = 10$, i.e., division becomes simple subtraction. Now, if all numbers are expressed in these terms then multiplication and division become a simple matter of adding and subtracting.

The definition of a common logarithm, taking the term $10^2 = 100$, is 2 is the log of 100 to the base 10. A logarithm is made up of two parts, to example, the log of $200 = 2 \cdot 3010$. 2 is termed the 'characteristic' and $\cdot 3010$ the 'mantissa'. The characteristic tells that the number lies between 100 and 1,000 and the mantissa the fractional part. The characteristic for numbers 10 to $99 \cdot 9$ is 1; for 100 to $999 \cdot 9$ it is 2, etc. For numbers less than 1, a bar is written above the characteristic. Thus from $\cdot 9$ to $\cdot 1$, it is $\bar{1}$; from $\cdot 09$ to $\cdot 01$ it is $\bar{2}$, etc.

Standard logarithm tables are the logs of all numbers calculated to a base 10 and are quite simple to use after a little instruction and practice. For example, multiply together $874 \cdot 0$ by $0 \cdot 041$. The characteristic of $874 \cdot 0$ is 2 and its log. is 9415. The characteristic of $0 \cdot 041$ is $\bar{2}$ and its log. 6128. Add the logs together:

$$\begin{array}{r} 2 \cdot 9415 \\ \bar{2} \cdot 6128 \\ \hline \bar{1} \cdot 5543 \end{array}$$

The antilog. of $\cdot 5543$ is 3583. (An antilog. is a number of which a given number is the log, and set out in tabular form following standard logarithm tables). Now, as the characteristic is $\bar{1}$, then the answer lies between 10 and 100, i.e., $35 \cdot 83$.

Note : the bar is a negative sign and follows the rule for this sign.

LONDON, Jack (1876–1916)
American writer, born in San Francisco. He led a very adventurous life being in turn sailor and goldminer. His best known stories are *The Call of the Wild, The Sea-Wolf* and *White Fang.*

LONGFELLOW, Henry Wadsworth (1807–1882)
American poet, born at Portland. He wrote quite a large amount of poetry of which the best remembered pieces are: *Excelsior, The Village Blacksmith, Paul Revere's Ride* and *Hiawatha.*

LOOMS

Machines used in the process by which materials are interlaced to form a fabric. An elementary example is the way in which a sock is darned with crossed threads to fill up a hole that has been worn in it.

In course of time man has invented ways of doing this on a large scale by mechanical means, i.e., looms, of which there are an enormous variety, from simple hand-looms made at home from a piece of cardboard to enormous power looms, such as the complicated giant Jacquard loom which can weave most intricate patterns. But whatever the size of the loom the basic principle is the same.

A number of threads, parallel and equally spaced, are wound on the yard beam of the loom. These are the warp threads, which usually run the length of the fabric. A long continuous thread, wound on a shuttle, passes backwards and forwards across the whole of the warp threads—in very simple fabrics alternately under and over each warp thread. Each time the weft thread passes across the warp threads it is 'beaten up' or pressed close to the preceding weft thread, to make a firm, even material.

To enable the shuttle to be passed across in one operation instead of 'darning' it under and over the warp threads, a heddle is used. This is a frame through which alternate warp threads are passed so that when it is raised there is a kind of tunnel or 'shed' between the threads which it holds up and those that are left free, through which the shuttle can slide along easily. For the next operation the heddle is depressed, so that the shuttle passes over the threads which it went under before. With the use of more heddles and a different arrangement of the warp threads, variety can be obtained in the actual weave of the fabric. As the material is woven, it is wound on to the cloth beam.

LORCA, Federico García (1899–1936)

Spanish poet and dramatist. One of the best known of Spain's modern poets who had considerable influence not only in his own country, but also in Europe and America. He was shot by the troops of General Franco for supposed support of the Republican Government during the Spanish Civil War. His poetry and plays have been translated into English.

LORD CHAMBERLAIN

A Peer who is head of the Royal Household and a member of the Government. On State occasions he wears a golden and jewelled key and carries a white staff. It is the Lord Chamberlain who has charge of arrangements for such ceremonies as coronations and royal weddings.

A quite different duty of the Lord Chamberlain is that of giving licences to theatres in London and Westmister. He also has to give licences for plays to be performed in public. If someone, sent by the Lord Chamberlain's office to see a play intended to be performed publicly, reports that it should not be performed without some changes being made those changes must be made or the play cannot be performed in public.

LORD CHANCELLOR

A CABINET Minister and an experienced lawyer. He presides over the House of Lords and when doing so he sits on the WOOLSACK as have Lord Chancellors for six hundred years. The Lord Chancellor is head of the judiciary which means that he has to appoint any new judges that may be needed. The Lord Chancellor is one of the chief members of the Judicial Committee of the PRIVY COUNCIL. When there is a change of government there is usually a change of Lord Chancellor.

LORD CHIEF JUSTICE

The judge who is President of the High Court of Justice. He is appointed by the PRIME MINISTER but as he is appointed for life or until he retires, it is not often that a Prime Minister has to appoint a judge to this high office. As a judge the Lord Chief Justice ranks next to the Lord Chancellor. Unlike him he cannot be a member of the Government or take part in politics.

LORD LIEUTENANT

The Queen's representative in a county. It is the PRIME MINISTER who advises the Queen when a lieutenant has to be appointed. The Lord Lieutenant, with the help of a committee, advises the LORD CHANCELLOR as to suitable people in his county to be made J.P.s. Most of the Lord Lieutenant's other duties are today ceremonial ones.

LORENTZ, Hendrick Antoon (1853–1928)

Dutch scientist. Shared the Nobel Prize for Physics in 1902. His main work was in the field of electromagnetic theory in relation to light. In addition he was much concerned with the ether; one of his theories, known as the 'Lorentz contraction' plays an important role in RELATIVITY theory.

LOUIS XIV, King of France (1638–1715)

Known as 'Le Roi Soleil'—The Sun King. Succeeded Louis XIII in 1643, and married the Infanta Maria Theresa (1660). Until 1661,

LOUIS XIV The magnificent palace at Versailles built at the instruction of Louis XIV.

when the country came under his personal rule, France was governed by Anne of Austria, his mother, and her minister, Mazarin. During this time the disaffected nobles who had not achieved high office began the civil wars of the *Fronde* ('Grumblers'). Louis made the monarchy into a harsh despotism with the help of a few brilliant and faithful men: Colbert, who put the country on a sound financial footing which enabled it to pay for Louis' numerous wars; Louvois, who reformed and strengthened the army; and Condé and Turenne, soldiers of great experience. Louis overran French Flanders and the Spanish Netherlands, captured the great German city of Strasburg, and his grandson gained the Spanish throne at the end of 'The War of the Spanish Succession'. But in achieving power abroad and despotism at home, Louis bled France of men and money, corrupted the law, and excluded the people from any participation in politics, and much of the blame for the French Revolution must be laid upon him. His most quoted remark is '*L'État c'est moi*' ('I am the State'). Under the influence of his second wife, Madame de Maintenon, he repealed the Edict of Nantes and intensified the persecution of the Protestants which caused many of them to flee the country. [*See* HUGUENOTS.] On the other hand, it was a great period for the arts in France: Mansart developed the great palace of Versailles; RACINE was writing; and Louis patronized the playwright MOLIÈRE.

LOUVRE

This building is in Paris and is one of the greatest art galleries in the world. It was the seat of the French Kings until Louis XIV built VERSAILLES and dates from the 13th century. It was added to and remodelled by Francis I, and Napoleon made some additions. Part was rebuilt during the Republic after having been burnt down during the Commune.

LOVELACE, Richard (1618-1657)

Royalist poet and lyricist, educated at Charterhouse and Oxford. In 1642 he was imprisoned for presenting a petition to the House of Commons for the restoration of the King. He was again imprisoned for Royalist activities in 1648. *To Lucasta on going to the Wars* is a superb example of his lyric writings.

LUCRETIUS (*c*. 99–55 B.C.)

One of the greatest Roman poets. His most famous work is the epic poem *De Rerum Natura* (On the Nature of Things). He believed that religion was an important source of man's troubles, and strove to achieve tranquility of mind.

LULLY, Jean Baptiste (1632–1687)

French composer, born in Florence. He was taken to Paris at a very early age. Was court musician to Louis XIV. Worked closely with MOLIÈRE on masques and ballets, and composed incidental music for some of Molière's plays. Has been called the 'father of French opera'. He composed a great volume of music, including some nineteen operas.

LUMEN
Unit of luminosity, and is measured as the quantity of light falling on one square foot of the surface of a sphere one foot radius and illuminated by an international candle at its centre. 1 lumen $= 1.496 \times 10^{-3}$ watts.

LUTE
Musical instrument in use in the 16th and 17th centuries. It was plucked like the guitar, but had a softer sound, and was often used for accompanying songs. Modern lutes are made for the performance of early music in its original form.

LUTHER, Martin (1483–1546)
German Protestant Reformer and translator of the Bible. Born in Saxony of a poor family, he was ordained a priest in 1507. The next year he became Professor of Philosophy at the new University of Wittenberg. Although disturbed at the corruption of the Papal Court at Rome which he visited in 1510, Luther was an orthodox Roman Catholic until 1517. It was then that he pinned to the church door of Wittenberg 95 theses directed against the sale of indulgences. This is generally reckoned as the beginning of the Reformation. The theses were condemned as heretical, but Luther refused to recant and even rejected a Papal summons to Rome. He was excommunicated in 1521. After defending his position at the Diet of Worms (1521) before the Holy Roman Emperor, Charles V, and a representative of the Pope, Luther realized that he could not reform the existing Catholic Church in Germany, but would have to found a new type of Church. His doctrine is formulated in the Augsburg Confession (1530).

LUXEMBURG
A Grand Duchy that borders Belgium, France and Germany. It has an area of 1,000 square miles and a population of about 400,000. Its capital is also named Luxemburg. It is rich in iron and coal and has a big steel industry. It is the headquarters of the European Coal and Steel Community. [See EUROPEAN ECONOMIC COMMUNITY and BENELUX.]

LYNX
Member of the cat family and closely related to the wild cats. One of the typical lynxes, the bob-tailed cat of North America, has been described as 'an overgrown house cat'. The best-known lynx is the common or northern

LYNX A member of the cat family. Although it looks like an overgrown house cat, it can kill animals as large as a sheep.

lynx. It is a powerful animal, at times killing animals as large as sheep, but preying mostly on small animals and birds. It is now very rare in Europe, but a few may survive in the Alps, Scandinavia and Russia. It is more plentiful in Central Asia, and in the Himalayas is found at heights of 10,000 feet and more.

LYRIC
Of all words used to denote a type of poem this is one of the most inexact, yet there is general agreement as to which poems are lyrics. If a poem has a close likeness to a song, if it is short, melodious, and descriptive, you will probably be right to call it a lyric. The poems which Palgrave collected for his *Golden Treasury* were mainly songs or lyrical poems, and a glance through this anthology will give an idea of the meaning of lyric.

LYTTON, Edward George Bulwer, 1st Baron (1803–1873)
Writer and statesman, born in London. Of his many novels the most popular were *The Last Days of Pompeii* and *Rienzi*.

Mm

MACARTHUR, General Douglas
(1880–1964)
American soldier, born in Arkansas. He graduated at the U.S. Military Academy in 1903. During the Great War he fought with the U.S. troops in France. In the Second World War he won fame for his defence of the Philippines against the Japanese (1941–1942), and for his gradual re-conquest of the south-west Pacific area (1942–1945). He drafted the new Japanese Constitution and became commander of the United Nations forces when the Korean War broke out, but was recalled on account of his political statements.

MACAULAY, Thomas Babington, Lord
(1800–1859)
British historian and politician, born in Leicestershire. He was very precocious as a boy, writing an epic at 10 and a universal history at 12. After a brilliant career at Cambridge, he was called to the bar and entered Parliament (1830). Later, as legal adviser to the supreme council of India, he helped to draw up the Indian penal code. On his return to England he again entered Parliament and became Secretary for War (1839). He was raised to the peerage in 1857 and died 1859. He is chiefly remembered for his *History of England from the Accession of James II.*

MACDONALD, Flora (1722–1790)
Scottish heroine. Born in the Hebrides. After the battle of Culloden Moor she helped Prince Charles Edward Stuart to escape in the disguise of a spinning maid. Her part in this plot was betrayed and she was placed in the Tower. Later she was released and emigrated with her husband to America. [*See* JACOBITES.]

MACDONALD, James Ramsay (1866–1937)
British politician. Born at Lossiemouth of poor parents. He was interested in socialism and joined the Independent Labour Party in 1893. Secretary of the LABOUR PARTY from its creation in 1900, he became its leader in Parliament in 1911. Through his opposition to the Great War, he was forced to resign the leadership of the party. But in 1922 he again became official leader of the opposition. He was Labour Prime Minister in 1924 and again in 1929. In the economic crisis of 1931 he formed a National Government with Conservatives and Liberals. But this lost him the support of almost all his Labour colleagues who accused him of betraying the socialist principles of the party.

MACE
A heavy club or staff about 5 feet long and is a symbol of authority. The most important mace is the one used in the House of Commons. When the House meets the Serjeant-at-Arms places the mace on the Speaker's Table. If the House goes into Committee the mace is placed on brackets under the table to show that the Members are meeting as a committee of the Commons and that the Commons itself is not in session. The House of Lords also has a mace but this is left outside the door when the House is sitting. A mace is also carried before a Mayor.

MACHIAVELLI, Niccolò (1469–1527)
Italian statesman and writer, and leading figure in the Italian Renaissance. Born at Florence. Before the restoration of the MEDICI he held many official positions in the republic. His main work is *The Prince*, and it is this book which gave him the reputation of being a hard, unscrupulous man. In addition to his political writing Machiavelli wrote poetry, plays and a *History of Florence.*

MACHINE TOOLS
This term can be applied to any tool worked from steam, oil or electric power, but is usually used to describe the power-driven tools in the engineering industry, i.e., a lathe, grinding machine, boring machinery, milling machine, shaper, drilling machine, etc.

MACH NUMBER
Speed of an aircraft or projectile measured in terms of the speed of sound as unity. Thus Mach number 2 means twice the speed of sound; Mach number 0·75 means three-quarters the speed of sound. For any given speed the Mach number varies according to the height, season and locality of the flight.

MACMILLAN, Harold (1894——)
British Conservative statesman, educated at Eton and Oxford. He worked in the family publishing company, and became an M.P. in 1924. His first cabinet post came in 1942, when he was sent as resident minister to the Allied Headquarters in North Africa, and here he showed his great ability as a mediator. When

Eden resigned over the Suez affair in 1957, Macmillan succeeded him as Prime Minister and retained power until ill-health drove him to resign in 1963. His premiership at home was marked by an expansionist policy summed up in the catch-phrase *You've never had it so good,* and he put a name to the changing conditions of Africa—*the winds of change.*

MADAGASCAR
The fifth largest island in the world lying in the Indian Ocean, 240 miles from the African coast. It is slightly larger (228,000 square miles) than France and has a population of nearly 6 million. The capital is Tananarive, or Antanaanarivo. The people are known as Malagasy and they are similar to the Malays of Malaysia. The country produces coffee and rice and its minerals include graphite and mica.

From 1895 to 1960, when it became independent, Madagascar was a French Protectorate. It is now a Member of the French Community and called Malagasy Republic.

MADEIRA
The chief of a group of islands known as the Madeiras. Only one other island, Porto Santo, is inhabited. The group forms part of Portugal from which they are separated by over five hundred miles. There are rather more than a quarter of a million inhabitants. The chief town is Funchal. The islands are famous for their excellent desert wines and their lace.

MADRIGAL
Type of musical composition for several voices, which originated in Italy and found its way to England in 1588, the year of the Spanish Armada. The singing of madrigals became very widespread during the reign of Queen Elizabeth I; anyone who could not take part in one was regarded as lacking in education. The finest madrigal writers were Thomas MORLEY, William BYRD, Orlando GIBBONS, Thomas Weelkes, and John Wilbye.

MAETERLINCK, Count Maurice
(1862–1949)
Belgian writer and dramatist, born at Ghent. He studied law at the local university, but his wealth enabled him to devote himself entirely to literature. A first volume of verse appeared in 1889 and was followed by a number of plays, including *Pelleas et Mélisande,* which was turned into an opera by Debussy, and *L'Oiseau Bleu* (The Blue Bird). The plays are marked by mystical features and are often studies in some strong emotion such as horror or despair. Maeterlinck also wrote books on the lives of bees and ants.

MAGELLAN, Ferdinand (*c.* 1480–1521)
Portuguese sailor, born at Sabrosa. He organized the first expedition to circumnavigate the earth, but was killed by natives in the Philippines before the expedition had completed its mission; only one ship completed the voyage. He discovered the Strait of Magellan, the strip of water separating the island of Tierra del Fuego from South America and gave the description 'Pacific' to the ocean of that name because of its apparent calmness.

MAGIC
Dates back to man's most primitive beginnings and is still an important part of the social life of primitive peoples living today, for example, Australian aborigines and African natives little touched by civilization. Incidentally, there is more than a touch of it in the superstitions of Western civilization.

The purpose of magic is to directly influence nature; for example, if a witch doctor performs a magical dance before a hunt, then he is not just dancing to entertain the native hunters but to make the hunters stronger, more skilful and the animals more plentiful. Magic, therefore, in primitive societies serves a very practical end.

MAGIC SQUARES
An equally divided square in which numbers are inserted and which when added across, down and diagonally make the same sum. These were introduced into Europe from the Far East and believed to have magical properties, especially in connection with astrology. A simple example is:

16	3	10	5
1	12	7	14
8	13	2	11
9	6	15	4

MAGISTRATES
These people may be described as junior judges as they serve in the lower courts of law which hear minor offences. Magistrates are of two kinds. They may be men or women who are not lawyers and are not paid for their work. These are J.P.s. The other kind of magistrates are experienced lawyers and are paid for their work. They are known as 'stipendiary magistrates'.

MAGISTRATES' COURTS
Local courts which can try small offences.

Most of such offences are tried by J.P.s. When they sit on the bench to try such cases there are usually two to seven J.P.s. Other magistrates' courts are presided over by a stipendiary magistrate who is a paid lawyer. He usually sits alone when trying cases. Most offenders are brought before a magistrates' court in the first place but if the crime is a serious one the magistrates' court does not try the case but decides whether it should go to the court of QUARTER SESSION or to the ASSIZES.

MAGNA CARTA

The Charter which King John signed at Runnymede in 1215. The need for such a charter arose because of the disappointment of the English at the loss of Normandy and the financial difficulties of the Crown, which caused John to use tactless and dishonest methods of extracting money from his barons. It was designed to guarantee certain long established rights and to put some restraints on the King's power. John repudiated the Charter after he had signed it, and some of the barons called in French help to overthrow him. He died soon afterwards, and his young son, Henry III, agreed to abide by the Charter.

MAGNETIC EQUATOR

Strength of the earth's magnetic field varies from place to place. These variations are shown on charts as an aid to navigation. Lines of equal magnetic dip are known as 'isoclinics', the line of zero dip is called the 'magnetic equator', and the two points at which the dip is 90° are called the magnetic poles. The lines of equal angle of declination, i.e., the angle between the geographical and magnetic meridians, are known as 'isogonals'.

MAGNETISM AND ELECTRICITY

Two sorts of energy. They have both been known for a very long time, for the word magnetism comes from the name Magnesia, a place on the Aegean coast and known to the ancient Greeks, and the word electricity comes from the Greek word *electron*, meaning amber. So the ancients knew that there was a sort of iron ore in Magnesia possessing unusual properties and that amber when rubbed also had peculiar properties. But both sets of properties, the magnetic and the electric, were different, and it was not until 1820 that any connection between them was shown.

One property of a magnet is that if it is made in the form of a needle and suspended freely from its middle, it always sets itself in a line running approximately north and south; and the same end always points north. So there is

evidently some difference between the two ends. They are called the poles. The end pointing north is called the 'north pole', and that pointing south is called the 'south pole'. Another property of magnets is that the north pole of one magnet will repel the north pole of another, and the south pole of one magnet will repel the south pole of another. But if the poles that are approached are of opposite polarity, attraction results. Yet another property of a magnet is that it will attract pieces of iron or iron-alloy to it. The reason for this is that all round the magnet the magnetic force is acting, and when into this magnetic 'field' a piece of iron is put, some of the energy goes into the iron and makes it magnetic for the time being. And the way in which this happens is such that the pole of the temporary magnet that is nearest the actual magnet is of opposite polarity to it. So there is attraction.

The easiest way to make a magnet is to stroke a piece of steel with a magnet. But this is not the way in which magnets are manufactured. This depends on the connection between magnetism and electricity.

The Greeks knew that if a piece of amber was rubbed it would attract tiny pieces of other substances. We know now that many other materials besides amber will show the same effect. This seems a trivial sort of effect. Yet if the rubbing is continued, and if the electric charge created can be stored up, an immense amount of electricity can be made. Today there is the Van de Graaff generator, depending on just this principle. It can build up electric charges so big that sparks like lightning flashes can be produced by it.

Most electrical phenomena, however, depend on the fact that if two charged bodies are connected by a metal lead, electricity flows from one to the other. But for this to happen the two bodies must have opposite sorts of electricity, called positive and negative. The flow is called electric current. All our electric lamps, vacuum cleaners, irons, and so on depend on the flow of electric current. The force, called the electromotive force, to make a current flow can be created by chemical action as it is in what is called a cell (a number of which together form a battery) or by a generator that depends on the connection between electricity and magnetism. This latter is used for making the electricity that is used for distribution round the country by overhead or underground cables.

The connection between electricity and magnetism was shown by the Danish scientist OERSTED, and the English scientist FARADAY. The first showed that when ELECTRIC CURRENT flowed in a wire, there was a magnetic field

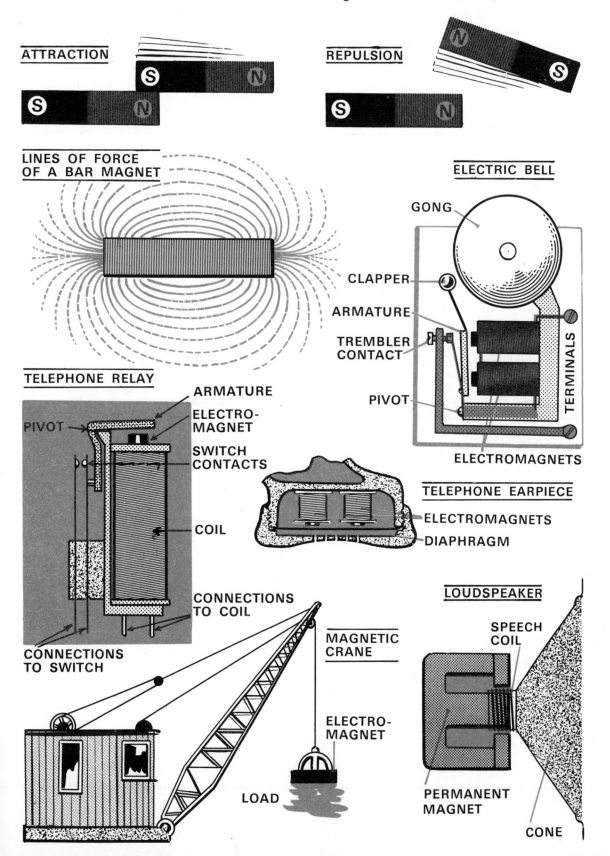

ATTRACTION

REPULSION

LINES OF FORCE
OF A BAR MAGNET

ELECTRIC BELL

GONG

CLAPPER

ARMATURE

TREMBLER
CONTACT

PIVOT

TERMINALS

ELECTROMAGNETS

TELEPHONE RELAY

ARMATURE

ELECTRO-
MAGNET

PIVOT

SWITCH
CONTACTS

COIL

TELEPHONE EARPIECE

ELECTROMAGNETS

DIAPHRAGM

CONNECTIONS
TO COIL

CONNECTIONS
TO SWITCH

MAGNETIC
CRANE

ELECTRO-
MAGNET

LOAD

LOUDSPEAKER

SPEECH
COIL

PERMANENT
MAGNET

CONE

round it. This knowledge is utilized to make an electro-magnet. The wire is wound round and round an iron core and current is passed through the wire. The result is that the whole acts as a magnet. The second scientist showed that by breaking up the magnetic field continually, an electric force could be generated. This is done in modern generators by rotating a magnet inside the magnetic field of an ELECTRO-MAGNET. The electricity so generated can be direct current (D.C.), which flows always in the same direction, or alternating current (A.C.) which flows alternately in one direction and then the other. For heating and lighting purposes both D.C. and A.C. are equally effective. It is A.C. that is mostly generated today and distributed round the country by means of a 'grid' system which allows power to be directed where it is most needed.

MAHLER, Gustav (1860–1911)

Czech-Austrian composer, born at Kalischt in Bohemia. In addition to nine symphonies he wrote a great volume of songs and chamber music. His unfinished tenth symphony was recently completed by Deryck Cooke, one of the contributors to this encyclopedia. One of his most important works is *Das Lied von der Erde* (Song of the Earth) for solo, chorus and orchestra. He was also a distinguished conductor.

MAJORCA

The largest of the Balearic Islands which form an archipelago in the Mediterranean and belong to Spain. The chief town is Palma. Other islands in the group are Minorca and Ibiza. The islands have a population of about half a million.

MALARIA

Infectious disease caused by a malarial parasite being injected into the blood stream by a mosquito (anopheles) and investigated by Sir Ronald Ross (1897). Attacks of malarial fever are treated with quinine, mepacrine and chloroquin. [*See* MOSQUITO.]

MALAWI (formerly Nyasaland)

A small State within the British Commonwealth that is rather smaller (45,746 square miles) than England. It has a population of about 3 million. The capital is Zamba but much larger is Blantyre. It was formerly a British Protectorate. From 1953 to 1963 it was part of the Federation of Rhodesia and Nyasaland. In 1964 it became independent and took the new name of Malawi. Its first Prime Minister was Dr. Hastings Banda.

MALAYSIA

A sovereign State within the British Commonwealth. It is more than half the size (130,000 square miles) of France and is made up of a Federation of thirteen States. Of these nine have their own Rulers and these elect one of their number to rule as King or Head of State of the Federation for five years. So the country changes its king every five years. Most of the States are on the Malay peninsular but in 1963 two others, Sarawak and Sabah (formerly British North Borneo) joined the Federation. For a short period Singapore belonged to the Federation but in 1965 she decided to become independent again. The Federal capital is Kuala Lumpur. Less than half the people of Malaysia are Malays. Most of the remainder are Chinese and there are also a good many Indians. The total population is nearly 9 million.

The country produces more rubber than any other country and she also produces more tin than any other country.

History :

The Portuguese were the first Europeans to visit the Malay peninsular and they were followed by the Dutch. In 1786 the East Indian Co. were given Penang Island for a trading settlement and by the early 19th century all Malaya came under British influence. During the Second World War Malaya was occupied by the Japanese. After the war there was a good deal of guerilla fighting by terrorist groups. In 1957, after peace had been restored, Malaya was given its independence. In 1963, when Sarawak and Sabah joined the Federation, it took the new name of Malaysia. Unfortunately INDONESIA objected to these two territories joining the Federation and this led to some fighting. Things began to improve in 1966.

MALDIVE ISLANDS

A chain of coral islands and atolls, about four hundred miles south-west of Ceylon. About two hundred of them are inhabited, the total population being 90,000. They form an independent State. Until 1953 they were linked with Ceylon and were a British Protectorate.

MALI

A republic in north-west Africa that is nearly three times larger (465,000 square miles) than France but much of the country is desert. Its population is about $4\frac{1}{2}$ million. It was formerly the French colony of Soudan. The capital is Bamako.

MALLARMÉ, Stéphane (1842–1898)

French poet, born at Paris. He was the founder

of a school of poetry called the 'Symbolists'. His best-known poem is *L'Après midi d'un Faune* (Afternoon in the Life of a Faun) which was the basis of the famous ballet of the same name by DEBUSSY.

MALORY, Sir Thomas (*d.* 1471)

English writer. Very little is known of him, except that he flourished in the 15th century. Through his writing of *Le Morte d'Arthur* (*c.* 1470, The Death of Arthur) he created the finest example of English prose before the Elizabethan period. It is the story of King Arthur and his Knights of the Round Table told in a connected narrative that has made the legends almost a part of English history.

MALTA

A small island in the Mediterranean that is a Member of the British Commonwealth. It is slightly smaller (95 square miles) than the Isle of Wight and has a population of about 330,000. Included with Malta are the smaller islands of Gozo and Comino. The Maltese language is descended from that of the Phoenicians who colonized the island. The people claim to have been Christians since St. Paul was shipwrecked on the island. The capital is Valletta, whose Grand Harbour is one of the finest in the world.

During the Second World War Malta was besieged and it withstood all attack. For its bravery it was awarded the George Cross.

MALTHUS, Thomas Robert (1766–1834)

English economist. Born near Guildford. Malthus was only 32 when he produced the work by which he is remembered today—*The Essay on Population*. His theories were used as an argument for not improving the conditions of the working-classes, as it was believed that better conditions would only encourage them to breed, and so create a food-shortage and, in the end, put them in a worse position than before.

MAMMALS

Warm-blooded VERTEBRATES whose bodies are covered with hair and which suckle their young for a period of time after they are born. As with everything else connected with the living world no rules can be laid down without giving many exceptions. It is easy to think of exceptions here. ELEPHANTS are mammals, but the body is covered with a tough hide and only a few bristles are found on it. WHALES are completely hairless, but the new-born whale has about half-a-dozen bristles on its lips, which are soon lost. In most mammals the young are born alive, except the Australian duckbill or PLATYPUS and the spiny anteater which lay eggs. When the young hatch, however, they feed like all other mammals on milk from the mother's teats.

In every way the bodies of mammals show an advance on the rest of the animal kingdom, particularly in the size and structure of the brain. This is most marked in human beings, whose intelligence and ability to think separate them sharply from all other living things, even though their bodies are constructed on the same plan as the higher animals.

Mammals are divided into three groups. First there are the Monotremes, which include the egg-laying platypus and spiny anteaters already mentioned. These are of particular interest because their skeletons resemble those of the reptiles, suggesting that they have evolved from reptiles. The next group is the MARSUPIALS, or pouch-animals, such as KANGAROOS, wallabies, OPOSSUMS and the rest of the Australian animals. In their skeletons, also, there are resemblances to the skeletons of REPTILES, and although they do not lay eggs the young are born at a very early stage, make their way into the mother's pouch, there to feed and grow. Both the Monotremes and the Marsupials are looked upon as primitive, which means they represent the sort of mammal that first evolved from the reptiles.

The rest of the mammals are divided into smaller groups, and classified largely by the shape of the teeth. First there are the Insectivores, including moles, shrews, and hedgehogs, with small sharp teeth for eating insects, and other small vertebrates. Then the bats (or Chiroptera), mainly insect-eating and the only mammals to fly. Flying squirrels, which are rodents, merely glide. The rest of the RODENTS include rats, mice, voles, porcupines, beavers and the ordinary squirrels. They have chisel-like incisor teeth for gnawing. The Lagomorphs, or rabbits and HARES, are similar to rodents but have four gnawing teeth instead of two in both upper and lower jaws. The rest of the mammals include the Cetacea or whales, now completely aquatic, the Carnivores such as CATS, DOGS, LIONS, TIGERS and BEARS, with teeth capable of tearing and cutting flesh, the Ungulates or hoofed animals, such as cows, horses, deer, elephants and RHINOCEROSES, with broad grinding teeth for eating grass, and the Edentates, including ARMADILLOES, PANGOLINS and SLOTHS, with no teeth at all, or a few peg-like teeth at most. Edentates feed on ants, except the sloths that eat fruit and leaves. Finally we come to the Primates, MONKEYS, APES and men, with teeth designed for eating fruit or the more delicate flesh.

MAMMOTH An extinct species of elephant. It lived about one million years ago.

MAMMOTH

Species of elephant which lived about a million years ago. Intact specimens have been found encased in ice and snow in Siberia. Several other species of mammoth lived in temperate and tropical regions.

MAN

The only living species of the genus Homo and is scientifically described as *Homo sapiens*. Anatomically man closely resembles the higher apes. Both are PRIMATES, but the main differences between them are that man has a larger brain, walks upright, has the power of speech and is capable of making and using tools. [*See* EVOLUTION.]

MAN, ISLE OF

An island in the Irish Sea and 227 square miles in area. Its population is just under 50,000. It has its own Legislature, the Tynwald, which consists of a Legislative Council and the House of Keys; the latter is one of the oldest legislative bodies in the world. The ancient language is Manx. The capital city is Douglas.

MANATEE

An aquatic mammal some 7 feet long weighing about 450 pounds. They have broad flat tails and their forelimbs have become modified into flippers. They are essentially vegetarian and peaceful. Their enemies are crocodiles and sharks. They give birth to one or two babies, born under water. Manatees are found in the coastal waters of West Africa, Caribbean and Central America.

MANET, Edouard (1832–1883)

French painter, born in Paris. After studying under Couture, his *Chanteur espagnol* was accepted by the Salon in 1861. In 1863, his *Déjeuner sur l'herbe*, shown in the Salon des Refusés, was violently attacked, and the same fate met his *Olympia*, shown in 1865. This hostility continued until his death. Manet is regarded as the greatest impressionist painter. He exerted a great influence on his contemporaries, and by the end of the 19th century, his genius was recognized.

MANN, Thomas (1875–1955)

German novelist, born at Lubeck. He was awarded the Nobel Prize for Literature in 1929. His most important novels are *Buddenbrooks* (his first book), *The Magic Mountain*, and the series of three novels on the life of Joseph. His elder brother, Heinrich (1871–1950), was also a distinguished writer. One of his works, *The Blue Angel*, was made into a most successful film—which launched Marlene Dietrich on the road to fame.

MANOMETER

Instrument or gauge for measuring gas pressures.

MANTEGNA, Andrea (1431–1506)

Italian painter and engraver, born at Vicenza in Padua. The most important painter of the early Renaissance, he produced many altarpieces and frescoes, including his masterpiece *The Triumph of Caesar*, now at Hampton Court Palace. Mantegna had a great influence on Italian art, and was also a sculptor and poet. He produced many fine drawings and copper plate engravings, and was one of the first artists to collect Greek and Roman works.

MAO TSE-TUNG (1893——)

Chinese revolutionary leader. Born in Kunan province of South China, of a family of well-to-do peasants. A brilliant pupil at school, in 1911 he was sent to the College at Changsha and in 1918 he went to Peking University where he studied Western economic and political thought. Under the influence of the Russian Revolution of 1917 he became a founder member of the Chinese Communist Party at Shanghai. He then began to organize unions amongst the peasants. In the late 20's he established the first Chinese Soviet Republic in the South-East provinces of Kiangsi and Fukien. In 1934 he was forced to ,retreat to Yennen in North-West China where he made his new capital until 1948 and the victory of his forces throughout the whole of China. He then became Chairman of the Chinese Communist Party. The two main events during his term of office have been the Great Leap Forward—the plan for Chinese economic expansion—and the Cultural Revolution.

MARAT, Jean Paul (1743–1793)

French revolutionary and scientist, born at Boudry, Neuchatel. As a young man he was considered a brilliant doctor and while living in England wrote several important papers. He was an ardent revolutionary and his writings and personal influence did much to aid the overthrow of the French monarchy. He was murdered in his bath by Charlotte Corday, a member of the Girondins, Marat's bitterest political enemies.

MARATHON

A plain some twenty miles north-east of Athens where the Persians were decisively defeated by the Athenians (490 B.C.) The news of the victory was carried by a runner. It is from this that the 'marathon race' is derived. the official distance for such a race is 26 miles 385 yards.

MARBLE

Sparkling form of limestone consisting entirely of fine crystals. Pure marble is white, and the ornamental veins in some marbles are stains caused by traces of other minerals. Sometimes the fossils in ordinary limestones show up when the rock is polished, and such ornamental stones may be called 'marble' by masons. Some of the finest marble comes from Carrara in Italy.

MARC, Franz (1880–1916)

German painter who is best known for his striking paintings of 'blue horses'. He belonged to the very modern school of painting and worked with KANDINSKY. He was killed at Verdun in the First World War.

MARCONI, Guglielmo (1874–1937)

Italian scientist and founder of the science of radio communication. Born at Bologna. Took out his first patent for wireless telegraphy in 1896. He continued his experiments in Britain and succeeded in sending a signal from Cornwall to Newfoundland in 1901. From this time on wireless developed rapidly to become the quickest and most widely used means of communication. Throughout the rest of his life Marconi continued to make important discoveries and improvements. He shared the Nobel Prize for Physics in 1909.

MARCO POLO (1254–1324)

Famous Venetian traveller and explorer. As a youth he travelled with his father and uncle to the Court of the Great Khan, the Chinese Emperor. They reached the Court in 1275, when Marco was appointed one of the Khan's envoys. He travelled in this capacity to Burma, India and Indo-China. The party finally left China for Venice, travelling via Sumatra, Ceylon and Persia. They reached their native city in 1295, having been away twenty-four years. Marco Polo dictated the record of his travels when he was taken prisoner after a sea-battle between Venice and Genoa (1298). The story was at first disbelieved, but he is now known to have brought to Europe the first knowledge of the East.

MARCUS AURELIUS ANTONINUS (A.D. 121–180)

Roman Emperor and Stoic philosopher. Much of his reign was spent in defending the boundaries of the Empire against the Parthians, the Marcomanni and the Quadi, and he has been blamed for persecuting Christians. But, among his peaceful pursuits, he endowed chairs of philosophy and rhetoric at Athens and introduced legal reforms at Rome. He was so popular that he was deified as soon as he died and his son Commodus erected the Antonine column to his memory. He is said to come nearer than any other man to ARISTOTLE's ideal of the 'philosopher-king'. His philosophical work, the *Meditations*, expresses his ideals and it is remarkable that he lived his own life according to these idealistic rules.

MARDI GRAS

French name for Shrove Tuesday and means 'fat Tuesday'. Traditionally the custom derives from the fact that as LENT starts a fast then all meats and fats should be eaten. Carnivals still celebrate Mardi Gras in Nice and Cologne in Europe and New Orleans and Rio de Janeiro in America. The date of the festival is movable.

MARIANAS ISLANDS

Group of islands in the Pacific and now a U.S. Trust Territory. The largest isle, Guam, was the scene of bitter fighting between American and Japanese forces in the Battle of the Pacific. It was recaptured in 1944 after two and a half years occupation by Japan. The principal town is Agara.

MARIE ANTOINETTE (1755–1793)

Queen of Louis XVI of France and daughter of Emperor Francis I of Austria. She was generally disliked, partly because she was an Austrian and favoured Austrian interests, but also because she opposed all new ideas, including the plan needed to solve the financial distress of the country. Her opposition to an alliance with the liberals, especially MIRABEAU, after 1789 made the eventual destruction of the monarchy by the revolutionaries inevitable. In 1793 she was tried, convicted of treason and guillotined. It is reported that in her last days she behaved with great calm, courage and dignity.

MARINER'S COMPASS

The invention of the compass is usually credited to the Chinese round about the year 1200 B.C. It was found that certain elongated stones had the property of turning round and pointing in the same direction when hung by a cord at their centre. These stones were lodestones—a type of iron ore which had become magnetized. This early type of compass was operated by placing one of these stones on a piece of wood which floated in a bowl of water. [*See* MAGNETISM.]

The Magnetic Compass of today consists of a circular bowl suspended by two hinged rings in a box or binnacle. The bowl contains a paper compass card. The card is divided into thirty-two equal parts or points and again into 360 degrees. It is attached to a magnetic needle, which, carrying the card round with them, points to the Magnetic North.

MARLBOROUGH A direct ancestor of Sir Winston Churchill, and victor of Ramillies and Blenheim.

The Gyroscope Compass. A GYROSCOPE is a wheel which can be made to revolve at high speed, and its tendency is to remain in the same direction as that in which it was set spinning. What is known as the 'master compass' is placed below the waterline, and is electrically connected with 'repeater compasses' in various parts of the ship. It is carefully adjusted and remains spinning, pointing to the True North.

The True North is the North pole of the earth. The Magnetic North is a position to the north of Canada.

MARIONETTE

A jointed doll worked by strings or wires from above.

MARLBOROUGH, John Churchill, First Duke of (1650–1722)

English soldier, born at Musbury. He entered the Guards at 17 and after service at Tangiers was promoted captain and then colonel. In 1702 he was selected by William of Orange to command the British and Dutch forces against France. Marlborough's opportunity came in 1704 when he crushed the French at Blenheim. Amongst his other great victories were Ramillies (1706), Oudenarde (1708) and Malplaquet (1709). When peace was declared and Marlborough returned to England, he was accused of misappropriating public money and dismissed from his post. He was later reinstated. He is a direct ancestor of Sir Winston CHURCHILL.

MARLOWE, Christopher (1564–1593)

English tragic dramatist and poet, born the son of a Canterbury shoemaker. He had great influence on Shakespeare's early work, and his *Edward II* compares favourably with Shakespeare's *Richard II*. His *Tamburlaine the Great* is the first great tragic drama by an English playwright, and there is superb poetry in *The Tragical History of Dr. Faustus*. He was said to have been fatally stabbed in a Deptford tavern when he was only 29 years old.

MARMOSET

Small squirrel-like monkey of South and Central America.

MARQUESAS ISLANDS

Group of islands in the South Pacific and part of the French Community. Two largest islands are Nuku Hiva and Hiva Oa; it is on the latter island that the French artist GAUGUIN is buried.

MARSHALL, General George (1880–1959)

American General and statesman, born in Pennsylvania, he became an Army officer in 1901. During the Great War he was a staff-officer and during the Second World War was Chief of Staff, United States Army. As a diplomatist, Marshall was U.S. Ambassador in China (1946) and Secretary of State the following year. He is best remembered for the project of the European Recovery Programme (1947), popularly known as Marshall Aid, whereby Marshall offered United States aid in the reconstruction of Europe after the Second World War.

MARSHALL ISLANDS

Group of coral islands and atolls in the Pacific. The main island is Kwajalein. Perhaps the best known is the Bikini atoll which was where the American atom-bomb tests were carried out. The group is a U.S. Trust Territory.

MARSUPIALS
Primitive mammals, which nourish and carry their imperfectly born young in a ventral pouch where they feed until they are more developed. The home of these animals is Australia.

MARTINI, Simone (*c.* 1283–1344)
Italian painter. A follower of DUCCIO de Buoninsegna, he was a leader of the Sienese school. He produced frescoes for the churches in Siena, Naples, Assisi and Orvieto, and decorated the papal palace in Avignon. He is noted for the colour and decorative qualities of his works.

MARTYR
Someone who upholds a faith or cause and who suffers greatly in consequence—usually losing life itself. The first Christian martyr was Stephen, whose stoning to death by the Jews is recorded in Acts, Chapters vi and vii. Before Christianity became the religion of the Roman Empire, official persecutions resulted in the martyrdoms of thousands of Christians— probably including both St. Peter and St. Paul during the first (Nero's) persecution. Alban, traditionally the first British Martyr, perished during the last (DIOCLETIAN's) persecution, about A.D. 303. Many Martyrs have later become revered as Saints. Official Christianity itself has made many martyrs; at first, a number of pagans, and, during succeeding centuries, a great number of 'heretics', who became victims of the INQUISITION.

MARVELL, Andrew (1621–1678)
English writer, born near Hull. He travelled on the Continent, mastered languages, served Lord Fairfax as tutor to his daughter, then joined the Civil Service of the Commonwealth Government, assisting Milton, the Latin secretary. Later he entered Parliament. The poems of Marvell's which are most generally known today are half a dozen anthology poems, which, beautifully written and alive, and personal in their thoughts, show the high quality of their author's work.

MARX, Karl Heinrich (1818–1883)
German philosopher and economist, founder of the international Communist movement. Born in the Rhineland. He studied history and philosophy at the Universities of Bonn and Berlin. He lived in turn at Cologne, Paris and Brussels before settling down in London where he remained until his death. His two best-

MARSUPIAL A koala, a native of Australia. It feeds only on the leaves of the eucalyptus.

known works are the *Communist Manifesto* (1847), written in collaboration with his friend and fellow-worker Friedrich ENGELS, and *Das Capital*, of which the first volume appeared in 1867 and two further volumes after his death. In them Marx proclaimed a materialist theory of history, expressing itself in the struggle between the classes, leading to the final victory of the proletariat (working class) and the abolition of private property. He founded the First International (1864), a working man's association, but never lived to see his ideas come to fruition. When LENIN and the Bolsheviks eventually set up a communist state in Russia, it was based on a considerably modified version of the original Marxist doctrine. [*See* U.S.S.R. and POLITICAL PARTIES.]

MASACCIO (1401–1428)
Italian painter, born in Florence. He was a pioneer of the Italian Renaissance. As a youth he painted a series of frescoes in the church of St. Clement in Rome. His finest and greatest work is among the frescoes in the Brancacci Chapel of the Carmine Church, Florence. Masaccio's work is regarded as the beginning of modern painting, and his frescoes were the inspiration of painters like MICHELANGELO and RAPHAEL. Masaccio treated figures and landscapes naturally, and was one of the first artists to apply the laws of perspective. Little of his work remains.

MASARYK, Thomas Garrigue (1850–1937)
Founder and first President of Czechoslovakia, born in Moravia. He studied at Vienna University and then became Professor of

Philosophy at Prague University. As a member of the Austrian Parliament to which he was first elected (1891) he advocated self-government for the Czech part of the Austria/Hungarian Empire. During the war (1914–1918) he formed a Czech National Council and a Czech Legion to work for an independent Czech Republic. When this was achieved Masaryk was elected President. Re-elected twice more, he retired from political office in 1935 on grounds of old age.

MASEFIELD, John (1878–1967)

English writer, born at Ledbury. Appointed Poet Laureate in 1930. Masefield slowly won attention as a poet after serving before the mast in an adventurous youth, then writing prose describing the sea and ships. A sense of the open air is at work in his best writing to give it rhythm and zest and a sympathy with living things. In addition to poetry he has written a number of novels and plays. He was awarded the Order of Merit (O.M) in 1935.

MASQUE

Type of stage-entertainment popular at the royal courts in the 17th century. It consisted of a play in verse, based on a legendary story, with a good deal of music and dancing, and a lot of spectacle and display. It thus differed from the opera, in which the whole play was set to music. The most famous English masque was *Comus*, by John MILTON and Henry Lawes, produced at Ludlow Castle in 1634.

MASS

If a given force acts on a series of bodies the acceleration will be different in each case, and the difference is due to that quality of the body termed mass. Mass, therefore, is measured by force and acceleration, i.e.,

$$\text{force} = \text{mass} \times \text{acceleration}$$

$$\therefore \text{ mass} = \frac{\text{force}}{\text{acceleration}}$$

Mass should not be confused with weight. The latter is the force with which the body is attracted to the earth by gravitation. Now, the acceleration of a body within the earth's gravitational field is 32·2 ft. per sec. per sec., therefore,

$$\text{mass} = \frac{\text{weight}}{32·2} \quad \text{(in grammes)}$$

It should be noted that the mass of a body is the same anywhere in the universe, but its weight is not. For example, one gramme mass on Mars weighs less than on Earth, but more on Jupiter. The reason being that the gravitational fields on these three planets vary, i.e.,

Mars's is weaker than Earth's, and Earth's weaker than Jupiter's.

For all practical purposes mass is constant, but in RELATIVITY THEORY it is considered to increase with speed.

MASTER OF THE ROLLS

The next most important Judge after the LORD CHIEF JUSTICE. His name originated in medieval times when the Master of the Rolls had to look after the 'rolls'—documents on which the statutes and the decisions of the courts were recorded.

MATISSE, Henri (1869–1954)

French painter, born at Le Cateau. His early work was influenced by CÉZANNE and SIGNAC. This led him to what is called the 'Fauve' period and characterized by bold brush strokes, distortions and explosive colour. He will probably be remembered for his studies and paintings of the nude. During the latter years of his life when his health was ailing he worked with cut-out coloured paper. One of his last and largest works was the decoration of the Chapel of Dominican Nuns at Vence.

MAUGHAM, William Somerset (1874–1965)

English novelist, born in Paris. Trained as a doctor but turned to writing as a career. His work includes novels, plays, short stories and critical studies of other writers' work. Although most of his books are extremely popular his most outstanding talent is revealed in the writing of short stories; many of these have been adapted for films, as have several of the full-length novels.

MAUPASSANT, Guy de (1850–1893)

French writer, born at Fécamp. He is considered one of the greatest masters of the short story, and his work has greatly influenced modern writers. He lost his reason two years before he died and was confined to an asylum. Many excellent translations of his stories are available in English.

MAURETANIA

A large republic in north-west Africa. It is about twice the size (322,340 square miles) of France and has a population of about a million, most of whom are Berbers and Moslems. The capital is Nouakchott. Recently rich iron ore deposits have been found in the interior and a railway has been built to take the ore to the coast for shipment. Mauretania was a French colony from 1920 till 1960 when it became independent and joined the French Community.

MAURIAC, Francois (1885–1970)

French Catholic novelist, concerned mainly with exploring the problems of the conflict between the demands of religion and human nature, and portraying the strains of unhappy relationships. He is generally regarded as a difficult novelist. *Génétrix* and *Thérèse Desqueroux* are two of his most important works.

MAURITIUS

An island in the Indian Ocean, 550 miles east of Madagascar. With its dependencies, Rodrigues and some small islands, it is nearly four times larger than the Isle of Man. The population is nearly a million. The capital is Port Louis. For some time Mauritius belonged to France but during the Napoleonic Wars it became British.

MAXIM, Sir Hiram Stevens (1840–1916)

Born at Sangerville, U.S.A. Inventor of the automatic quick-firing gun. He was brother to Hudson Maxim who experimented with, and developed, various forms of explosives.

MAXWELL, James Clerk (1831–1879)

Scottish mathematician, born at Edinburgh. Educated at Edinburgh and Cambridge. While Professor at King's College, London, became very friendly with FARADAY, then an old man, and put into mathematical form Faraday's work on electricity and magnetism. Maxwell's most important contribution was his electromagnetic theory of LIGHT. This predicted in mathematical form the existence of radio waves which were discovered experimentally a few years later by HERTZ.

MAXWELL put into mathematical form the experimental work on magnetism and electricity carried out by Faraday.

MAYA

One of the greatest Indian civilizations in South America before the Spanish Conquest. They built magnificent cities (Copan, Chichen Itza, Mayapan), composed an accurate calendar, and had a knowledge of both writing and mathematics. Perhaps their greatest achievement was building in stone which was richly and beautifully decorated.

MAYOR

The first citizen of a city or borough who presides over the BOROUGH COUNCIL. A mayor is elected by the Borough Council and serves for one year. If the mayor is a woman she will not be called mayoress, which is the title given to the wife of a mayor or other lady who undertakes the duties of mayoress. Eighteen cities, including London, are allowed to call their mayor 'Lord Mayor'.

MAZZINI, Giuseppe (1805–1872)

Italian republican patriot and revolutionary, born at Genoa. After joining The Carbonan, a secret nationalist society, he was banished from Italy. He lived for a time in France and Switzerland before he settled down in London where he devoted himself to the cause of a unified, republican ITALY. In 1848 he returned to Italy and was elected leading triumvir of the Roman Republic. When the Republic fell, Mazzini fled to London. There he spent the next ten years until he again returned to Italy. But when GARIBALDI gave the crown of a United Italy to King Victor Emmanuel, Mazzini despaired of seeing a republican Italy and he took refuge in Switzerland.

MECCA

One of the two capitals of SAUDI ARABIA and the holy city if ISLAM, being the birthplace of MOHAMMED.

MECHANICS

The study of structures and machines, from the simplest structure such as a block of wood resting on a table to the most complex machine involving the movements of interleaving teeth, the rotation of cylinders and belts and the linking of backwards and forwards motion with rotation.

Simple mechanics is usually divided into two branches: statics and dynamics (or kinetics). The first of these deals with bodies and systems that are stationary. The second deals with particles and bodies in motion.

Statics starts with the simple fact that a force can be represented on a drawing by a straight line, the length representing the size of the force and the direction indicating its direction.

MEMLING A religious triptych of the *Virgin and Child*, a typical Flemish painting of the 15th century.

The result of combining forces at a point can then be examined. This leads to the way of finding the resultant of a set of forces and conversely the way of splitting up any force into two others in any desired direction to give the same effect as the original single force. The latter operation is called the resolution of a force, one of the most useful devices for the whole of mechanics. The turning ability, or moment, of a force is then considered. After that comes the consideration of parallel forces, leading to the useful notion of a centre of gravity, a point at which the weight of any body may be considered as acting. This notion is essential to mechanics. Simple machines such as PULLEYS and LEVERS and the wheel and axle and screw can be explained with the aid of the ideas already mentioned.

Dynamics starts with the representation of a speed or velocity by means of a straight line, the length representing the size and the direction indicating the way in which the body is travelling. From this comes the idea of acceleration or rate of change of velocity. With these concepts motion influenced by gravity can be explained and NEWTON's Laws of Motion understood and applied, these laws being the foundation of dynamics.

MEDICI

Famous Italian family of fabulous wealth. This was built up by the early Medicis who were clever and astute merchants and bankers. From the time of Cosimo (1389–1464) the family exerted a great influence on the politics and life of Florence. They were generous patrons of the arts and did much to hasten the Renaissance. The last male of the line, Giovan Glastone, died in 1737. The famous Uffizi Gallery in Florence was built for Cosimo.

MELANESIA

One of the three parts into which OCEANIA

is divided. Included are the New Hebrides, Fiji, Solomon Islands and Loyalty Islands.

MELVILLE, Herman (1819–1891)

American writer, born in New York. Went to sea at an early age and obtained first-hand experience of whaling. This gave him the detailed background for his greatest novel *Moby Dick*. His other novels dealing with the Pacific islands and their peoples are not so well known. One of his novels, *Billy Budd*, has been made into an opera by Benjamin BRITTEN.

MEMLING, Hans (c. 1430–1494)

Flemish religious painter. A follower of the Van Eycks, he settled in Bruges, and became famous as a colourist. He painted many fine portraits. Most of his paintings are to be seen in the Hospital of St. John in Bruges.

MENDEL, Gregor Johann (1822–1884)

Austrian priest and natural historian. Born at Mahren and son of poor peasants. Became abbot of the monastery at Brno, where he conducted most of his work on plant breeding. His experiments were concerned chiefly with different varieties of garden peas which he showed handed from one generation to another such characteristics as tallness and shortness. His papers describing these experiments were first published in an obscure journal and went unrecognized until about 1900. [*See* GENETICS.]

MENDELEYEV, Dmitri Ivanovitch (1834–1907)

Russian scientist, born at Tobolsk, Siberia. His great contribution to science was the discovery that characteristic properties of the chemical elements recur in regular cycles in a table starting with the element of lowest atomic weight and progressing consecutively in order of weight. [*See* CHEMISTRY and PERIODIC LAW.]

MENDELSSOHN, Felix (1809–1847)

German composer, born at Hamburg. He showed genius at an early age, writing the Overture to *A Midsummer Night's Dream* when only 17. He came to England several times as pianist and conductor, played to Queen Victoria, and became a friend of the Prince Consort; his oratorio *Elijah* was first performed at Birmingham. Amongst his best-known compositions are the Overture *The Hebrides* (also called *Fingal's Cave*) and the Songs without Words for piano (including *Spring Song* and *The Bee's Wedding*.)

MENSURATION

Branch of mathematics concerned with the measurement of length, areas, and volumes. The following simple equations relate to common areas and volumes.

$$\text{Area of square} = L \times H$$
$$\text{Area of triangle} = \tfrac{1}{2}L \times H$$
$$\text{Area of circle} = \pi R^2$$
$$\text{Volume of cube} = L \times B \times H$$
$$\text{Volume of cone} = \tfrac{1}{3}\pi R^2 H$$
$$\text{Volume of sphere} = \tfrac{4}{3}\pi R^3$$

MERCATOR, Gerardus (1512–1594)

Flemish geographer and cartographer who made many maps and two globes, terrestrial and celestial. On these the surface of the earth was projected in a new way which made navigation much simpler, and this method of map representation is now known as Mercator's projection.

MEREDITH, George (1828–1909)

English novelist, born at Portsmouth. He was opposed to anything stuffy or conventional; he admired men of energy; and he delighted to invent fine women characters. He was also, all through his life, a poet. In his poem *Modern Love* some of the 'sonnets' that compose it are of memorable quality, and have found their way into the anthologies.

METEORITES

Pieces of solid matter which enter the earth's atmosphere and reach the surface; those which burn to incandescence are known as meteors or shooting stars. Many meteorites are known and some of considerable dimensions left large craters after impact. According to their contents they are classified as iron meteorites (siderites) and stone meteorites (aerolites).

METEOROLOGY

The scientific study of the weather. The weather at any moment depends on the temperature of the air, that is to say, how hot or cold it is, and the pressure, that is, how

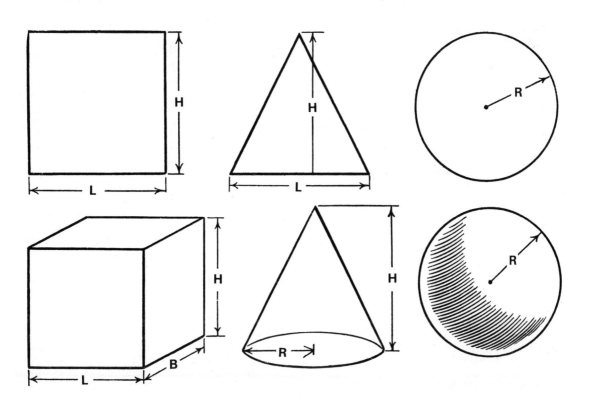

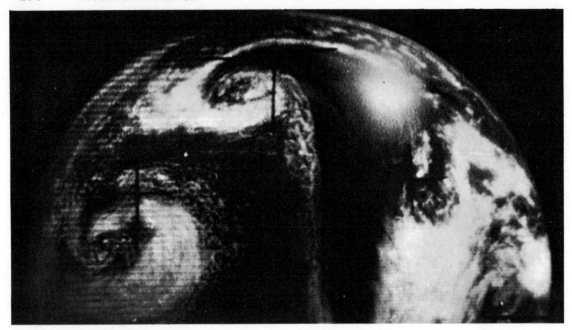

METEOROLOGY Satellite photograph of a double storm vortex forming over the Atlantic Ocean.

compressed or rarefied it is, and how these two are changing. Hot air can hold much more water vapour in it than cold air. So if hot air is allowed to take up water and then is cooled, water is deposited either in fine drops making a cloud or in bigger drops that fall as rain or in drops that freeze into ice or as fine ice-crystals that fall as snow. On the other hand, if cool air is warmed, it can take up more water and so there is no rain. Again, if the pressures in different places are unequal, air moves from the parts of high pressure to the parts of low pressure. In other words the wind blows. The rotation of the earth affects the direction of winds.

These facts are at the basis of meteorology. For industrial purposes, such as sea and air transport and agriculture, the weather is an important factor. So if it can be forecast accurately, individual people, industries, and the country as a whole benefit. WEATHER-FORECASTING is therefore the chief occupation of meteorologists, much research being done, not only on the details of actual forecasting, but also on the fundamental physics of the ATMOSPHERE. So far it has been found possible to make forecasts for a short period fairly accurately, but long-term forecasting is not yet here. The reason is that the weather at any moment is the result of complicated conditions over large parts of the world and very high up in the earth's atmosphere.

METHODIST CHURCH [*See* FREE CHURCHES]

METRIC SYSTEM

A system of weights and measures based on the gramme and metre respectively. The system was legally adopted by France in 1801 and based on the recommendations of the Academy of Sciences. The metre is a ten-millionth part of the distance between the pole and equator and equivalent to 3·2808 feet. The gramme is the weight of a cubic centi-metre of distilled water and equivalent to 15·4323 grains. Many countries now use the metric system and the remainder are seriously considering its introduction, including Britain.

MEXICO

A large republic in the southern part of North America. It is more than three times larger (758,000 square miles) than France and has a population of nearly 40 million. The people are Spanish speaking. Apart from those of European descent there are many Indians, descendants of the AZTECS, Toltecs and MAYAS. The capital is Mexico City. The country is a federal one and is divided into twenty-nine States. Mexico is rich in minerals, particularly in silver, gold, lead and petroleum. The country also produces cotton and coffee and there are many cattle ranches in the country.

MICA

Forms an important part of igneous rocks and is widely distributed throughout the world. Commercially mica mining is a large business as it is invaluable for stove windows and the

Central America

MEXICO

El Paso

Western Sierra Madre

RNIA
RORNIA

Rio Grande

Monterrey
Mexican Plateau

GULF OF MEXICO

Eastern Sierra Madre

Guadalajara

Tula
Mexico City
Popocatepetl 17887
Pueblo

Uxmal
Chichen Itza

Mitla

Palanque

YUCATAN

Belize

GRAND BAHAMA IS

NEW PROVIDENCE
ANDROS IS.
Nassau

Havana

BAHAMA ISLANDS

2

3

Guatemala City

Tegucigalpa

San Salvador

4

5

6

Managua

WEST

JAMAICA

Kingston

Port-au-Prince

Santo Domingo

11

12
1

PUERTO RICO

INDIES

LEEWARD ISLANDS

GUADELOUPE

DOMINICA

MARTINIQUE

CARIBBEAN SEA

San Jose

7

Panama Canal

Panama

8

CURACAO

Maracaibo

ST. LUCIA

ST. VINCENT

BARBADOS

GRENADA

WINDWARD ISLANDS

TOBAGO
TRINIDAD

PACIFIC OCEAN

Caracas

Magdalena

Orinoco

VENEZUELA

Bogota

COLOMBIA

GUYANA

Georgetown

Paramari

GALAPAGOS ISLANDS

Quito

Chimborazo 20577

Andes

ECUADOR

Guiana Highlands

9

Cayenne

10

1 : DOMINICAN REPUBLIC
2 : GUATEMALA
3 : BR. HONDURAS
4 : EL SALVADOR
5 : HONDURAS
6 : NICARAGUA
7 : COSTA RICA
8 : PANAMA
9 : SURINAM
10 : FR. GUIANA
11 : CUBA
12 : HAITI

MICHELANGELO'S painting of the *Madonna, Child, Saint John and the Angels*.

like, in fact, anything requiring transparent heat-resisting parts. It is also used in the manufacture of paper and paint. The largest mines are in the U.S.A., India and Russia.

MICHELANGELO, Buonarroti (1475–1564)
Italian painter, sculptor, architect and poet, and a leading figure of the Renaissance. Born at Caprese, Tuscany. At the age of 17 he came to the notice of Lorenzo de Medici, who became his patron. In 1496, Michelangelo went to Rome, where he produced his marble *Bacchus and Cupid*, followed by *Pieta* (in St. Peter's, Rome). Returning to Florence in 1501, he executed the giant *David*. His paintings on the ceiling of the Sistine Chapel make up one of the most brilliant works of art in the world, though Michelangelo undertook the task with reluctance as he preferred sculpture. Between 1513 and 1521 he produced the huge *Moses* and the two statues *Bound Slave*. From 1520 to 1534 he worked on the sepulchral chapel of the Medici in San Lorenzo, Florence. In 1529 he helped in the defence of Florence as an engineer. In 1546 he was made chief architect of St. Peter's, and it was he who planned the great dome.

MICHELSON, Albert Abraham
(1852–1931)
American scientist. His main work was concerned with measuring accurately the speed of light and experiments to discover the ether drift, the latter carried out with E. W. Morley (1838–1923) and generally known as the Michelson-Morley experiments. These disproved the existence of an all-pervading ether

and paved the way for Einstein's theory of relativity. Awarded the Nobel Prize for Physics in 1907. [*See* RELATIVITY.]

MICRONESIA
One of three divisions of OCEANIA and made up of 2,100 small islands in the West Pacific Ocean. More recently the term has been given to three of the larger groups—the Carolines, Marshall and Marianas (without Guam) which form an INTERNATIONAL TRUST TERRITORY of the United Nations which are administered by the United States. Micronesia has its own elected Congress.

MICROPHONE [*See* RADIO]

MICROSCOPE
An optical instrument that is used for viewing objects which are too small to be accurately observed by the human eye, and in some instances beyond the visual powers of the eye. The simplest form of microscope is the magnifying glass. The construction of a typical laboratory microscope is shown in the drawing. The compound microscope was first made by Z. Janssen about 1590.

MIDDLE EAST
A term used to describe those countries of Asia that are near Europe. Egypt, although actually in Africa, is generally included. The Asian countries meant by the term are Turkey, Persia, Israel, Jordan, Syria, Lebanon, Iraq and Arabia.

MILITARY AND NAVAL EVENTS
The following wars and battles were decisive in shaping and directing the course of European History.

B.C.	490	*Marathon*, Athenians defeated Persians.
	431–404	*Peloponnesian War*, between Athenians and Spartans.
	264–241	*First Punic War*, between Rome and Carthage.
	218–201	*Second Punic War*.
	149–146	*Third Punic War*.
	55	*Roman Invasion of Britain*, by Julius Caesar.
A.D.	70	*Jerusalem* razed by Titus.
	410	*Rome* sacked by Alaric.
	450	*Saxon Invasions of Britain* by Hengist and Horsa.
	630	*Mecca* captured by Mohammed.
	1066	*Hastings*, Harold defeated by William.
	1314	*Bannockburn*, Bruce defeats English.
	1346	*Crécy*, Edward III defeats French.
	1410	*Tannenberg*, Poles defeat Teutonic Knights.
	1415	*Agincourt*, Henry V defeats French.
	1455–84	*Wars of the Roses*, between Houses of York and Lancaster.
	1513	*Flodden Field*, English defeat Scots.
	1588	*Spanish Armada*.
	1642–60	*Civil War in England*, Charles I and Cromwell.
	1690	*The Boyne*, William III defeats James II.
	1704	*Blenheim*, Marlborough defeats French.
	1706	*Ramillies*, Marlborough defeats French.

JERBOAS are small rodents with highly developed rear legs. They are found in the desert regions of Europe, Asia and N. Africa.

SLOTHS are found in the tropical regions of America. There are two species, the two-toed and the three-toed, the latter is shown below. Sloths spend almost all their lives hanging upside down in trees.

BATS are mammals of the rodent family who have developed a wing-like membrane between the fore and rear limbs. In the main they fly and feed at night. In flight they guide themselves by the reflection of sound which they emit; a kind of sound radar system.

MOLE The common European mole—pictured below—lives most of its life burrowing a few inches beneath the soil in search of food, mainly earthworms and insects. They eat about twice their own weight a day.

PLATYPUS is one of the most primitive living mammals.
It is a marsupial and, like all this group, confined to
Australia. It is semi-aquatic and lives in burrows in
the banks of streams and rivers. It has a poison spur on
the heels of its rear feet. Fully grown it is about 2 feet.

ECHIDNA Another primitive mammal
and marsupial. Its beak-like
muzzle enables it to feed on
ants and termites; it has no teeth.
It is only found in Australia
and is sometimes known as the
'spiny anteater'.

KANGAROO A marsupial and native of Australia. It has powerful hind legs and a long muscular tail which it uses as a balance.

MILITARY EVENTS An 8th Army patrol in North Africa. It was here that General Rommel was defeated.

1745–46 *Jacobite Rising.*
1756–63 *Seven Years' War*, between France, Austria, Sweden, Spain, Russia and Saxony on the one side and England, Prussia and Hanover on the other.
1775–83 *American War of Independence.*
1798 *Irish Rebellion.*
1798 *Nile*, Nelson defeats French.
1805 *Trafalgar*, Nelson defeats French.
1805 *Austerlitz*, Napoleon defeats Russians and Austrians.
1808–14 *Peninsular Wars*, between French and British. (Spanish and Portuguese forces with British).
1812 *Moscow*, fired by Russians fighting Napoleon.
1815 *Waterloo*, Wellington defeats Napoleon.
1839–42 } *Afghan Wars*, caused by rivalry between
1878–81 } Britain and Russia.
1853–56 *Crimean War.*
1857 *Indian Mutiny.*
1861–65 *American Civil War.*
1865–70 *South American War*, alliance of Brazil, Argentina and Uruguay against Paraguay.

1866 *Seven-weeks' War*, between Austria and Prussia.
1870–71 *Franco-Prussian War*, between France and Prussia.
1879 *Zulu War*, between British and Zulus.
1899–1902 *South African War*, between British and Boers.
1914 *Assassination of Archduke Francis Ferdinand* and start of World War I.
1914 *Tannenberg*, Germans defeat Russians.
1914 *Ypres*, German advance stopped, also 1915 and 1917.
1914 *Marne*, 1st battle.
1916 *Verdun.*
1916 and 17 *Somme.*
1916 *Jutland*, naval battle.
1917 *Russian Revolution.*
1918 *Marne*, 2nd battle and led to defeat of German army.
1918 *Zeebrugge.*
1935 *Abyssinia* [Ethiopia] attacked by Mussolini.
1936 *Spanish Civil War.*
1939 *Poland* attacked by Hitler and start of 2nd World War.
1940 *Battle of Britain.*
1941 *Russia* attacked by Hitler.
1941 *Pearl Harbour* attacked by Japanese.
1942 *Alamein*, Gen. Montgomery defeats Rommel in N. Africa.
1942 *Guadalcanal*, Gen. MacArthur attacks Japanese.
1943 *Stalingrad*, start of German defeat in Russia.
1944 *Normandy landing.*
1945 *Hiroshima and Nagasaki* attacked with first atom bombs.
1950 *Korean War*, S. Korea and U.N. Forces against N. Korea and China.

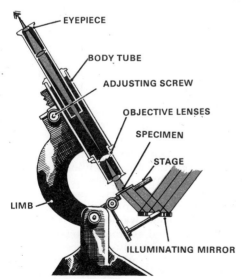

EYEPIECE
BODY TUBE
ADJUSTING SCREW
OBJECTIVE LENSES
SPECIMEN
STAGE
LIMB
ILLUMINATING MIRROR

MICROSCOPE Parts of a simple laboratory microscope and the arrangement of the lens.

MILL, John Stuart (1806–1873)

English economist and thinker, born in London. He was very precocious and could read Greek at 3 and Latin at 4. For a short time he was a Member of Parliament. Apart from writing on logic and economics, he warmly defended the rights of the working classes and woman's right to vote. He was a utilitarian, believing in happiness as the highest aim. His most important political work was *Essay on Liberty*.

MILLAIS, Sir John Everett (1829–1896)
English painter, born at Southampton. He began studying at the Royal Academy at the age of 11, and soon won all the prizes. He initiated the PRE-RAPHAELITE movement in 1848, together with W. Holman HUNT and Dante Gabriel ROSSETTI. His *Christ in the Carpenter's Shop*, painted in 1850 met with a hostile reception, but he soon gained fame and honours. His later work included portraits of Gladstone and Beaconsfield. In 1885 he was created a baronet, and in 1896 he was elected President of the Royal Academy.

MILLER, Arthur (1915——)
Important American playwright of the post-war period. *Death of a Salesman* gained him the Pulitzer Prize. In *The Crucible* the persecution of the Salem witches is used to draw attention to contemporary political persecution; and the recent *Incident at Vichy* examines the predicament of the Jews in German occupied France in the Second World War.

MILLET, Jean François (1814–1875)
French painter, born of poor parents near Greville. In 1837 he received an award which enabled him to go to Paris to study art. In 1848 he settled in the village of Barbizon, where he produced his country pictures, including such famous works as *The Gleaners*, *The Sheep-Shearers* and *The Angelus*.

MILLIKAN, Robert Andrews (1868–1954)
American scientist, born at Morrison. Has made important contributions in many fields: X-rays, cosmic rays, photoelectric effect, atomic particles, etc. He was awarded the Nobel Prize for Physics in 1923.

MILTON, John (1608–1674)
English writer, born in London. One of the greatest poets and one of the least read men in English literature. He was born and grew up with some of the contemporaries of Shakespeare still alive and active around him. From them he absorbed a living tradition, while from the books to which he devoted himself he put himself in contact with the literatures of western Europe and the ancient Hebrew, Greek, and Latin. With all these influences adding to his natural gifts for lofty language, he developed a style of English poetry which no one had used before.

He spent twelve years, following his Cambridge studies, in further study at home, then, after a visit to Italy, used his abilities in pamphlets on religion and politics. He was an ardent anti-Royalist, and served the Commonwealth as Latin Secretary. At the Restoration,

already blind, he retired to his home, where he was left in peace, if in some poverty, to his last poetic labours.

Milton had always been determined to write an English epic. He examined and discarded, several possible subjects, and at last decided to write of Man's Fall from Eden, and wrote the religious epic *Paradise Lost*. He followed it with a shorter and simpler poem, *Paradise Regained*. In his final years he wrote, perhaps with his own troubles to guide him, a play in classical form, *Samson Agonistes*, describing the distress and death of Samson among the Philistines.

MINERALS
The materials of which rocks are made, and they are often found in comparatively pure forms in cracks and cavities in the rocks. The minerals include precious stones and the ores of metals, as well as such useful substances as coal, petroleum, sulphur, gypsum and rock-salt. Minerals may occur in 'massive' beds which can be mined or dug out, or in the form of crystals lining hollows in the rocks. The crystalline minerals are grouped according to the forms of their CRYSTALS.

MINISTER
A leading member of the Government. The term Minister is also used to describe an important DIPLOMAT. [*See also* ENVOY.] Ministers who are members of the Government are appointed by the PRIME MINISTER and most of them are given a special department to look after such as the Home Office or Foreign Office. Those who do not have such a department are called 'Ministers Without Portfolio'. Some Ministers are known as Secretaries of State. These include the Home Secretary and Foreign Secretary. Others are known as Ministers of the Crown. It is from the Ministers that the Prime Minister chooses his CABINET. When a Minister is appointed he goes to Buckingham Palace to kiss the Queen's hands and to receive from her his seal of office.

MIRABEAU, Honoré Gabriel Riqueti, Comte de (1749–1791)
French orator and early leader of the Revolution. He lived the life of a libertine and was constantly in debt, which led to his imprisonment more than once. He was sentenced to death by the Parlement of Besançon because of his outspoken writings, but was later pardoned. Elected to the States-General by the Third Estate, his rousing speeches put him at the head of the National Assembly. But he remained a moderate at heart, hoping to re-arrange the government along English lines and obtain office for himself. The plan had no

chance of success, due to his declining health and the distrust he had for Queen MARIE ANTOINETTE.

MIRAGE

An optical illusion caused by the refraction and reflection of LIGHT and occurs in very hot climates, particularly desert regions. The diagram clearly shows the formation of a mirage.

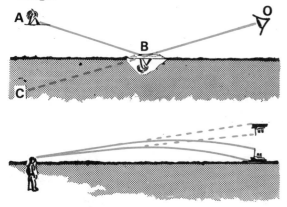

MIRAGE Light from the object A is reflected to B and the observer at O sees it along the sight line OC; the object appearing inverted. 'Looming', which is only seen over water, is also a mirage effect.

MISSIONARIES

'Go ye into all the world, and preach the gospel to every creature,' was, according to Mark— Chap. xvi: 15—the last commandment of the Risen Christ to His disciples. In a sense, all the Apostles were missionaries; but the greatest Christian Missionary of all time was ST. PAUL, who travelled more than half the Roman Empire, preaching Christianity and founding many great churches. Strangely enough, the first major heretics, the Arians, were outstanding missionaries; the Arian Bishop, Ulfilas (318–383) preached to the Goths north of the Danube, inventing an alphabet in order to translate the Scriptures into Gothic. The Irish-Scottish Celtic Church produced great missionaries, including the the 5th-century Patrick, and the 6th-century Columba and Columbanus. Probably the foremost Roman Catholic Missionaries were, and are, the Jesuits, members of the Society of Jesus. The first British (foreign) missionary society was the (Anglican) Society for the Propagation of the Gospel in Foreign Parts (the S.P.G.) founded in 1701. The Baptist Missionary Society, founded in 1792, was the first English Protestant society; one of its principal founders was William Carey, a Northampton shoemaker, who went to India,

doing magnificent work there, translating the New Testament into many native languages and dialects. Lord Wellesley appointed Carey Oriental Professor in Calcutta, in 1801. The London Missionary Society (Congregational) was founded in 1795: David LIVINGSTONE (1813–1873), the great Scottish medical missionary and explorer, was an L.M.S. Missionary. To name only a few others, The Church Missionary Society ('Evangelical' Anglican) was founded in 1799, the Wesleyan (Methodist) in 1817, and China Inland Mission (inter-denominational) in 1853.

Christian Missionaries—with, inevitably, occasional individual exceptions—have rendered an immense service throughout the world, morally, spiritually, in education, and especially within the last few decades, in medicine. A supreme modern example of a medical missionary, is Albert SCHWEITZER, Doctor of Theology, Philosophy, Music and Medicine, who gave up a successful career in Strasbourg, in 1913, to go to Lambarene, in French Equatorial Africa, where he remained until his death, attending to the sick and suffering in the district.

MISTRAL, The

A strong, cold wind that blows out to sea in the area of the north-west Mediterranean, especially around the Rhône delta, and is always accompanied by brilliant sunshine.

MITHRAISM

One of the old sun-religions, centred on Mithra, God of light and truth. It had many parallels with Christianity, including the belief in the miraculous birth and the resurrection, and the idea of heaven and hell. Sunday was Mithra's holy day too, his birth was also celebrated on December 25th, and both religions held Easter sacred. Mithraism was an important rival of early Christianity in the West, and expanded and declined with the progress and regress of the Roman armies.

MODIGLIANI, Amedeo (1884–1920)

Italian painter, born at Leghorn. Went to Paris in 1906 and soon became involved in the modern art movement, especially early Cubism. His work was mainly studies of the figure—he was an outstanding draughtsman—and portraits. He also did a number of sculptured heads with a strong feeling of African primitive art. He led a profligate life and died in poverty and obscurity.

MOGUL

Moslem empire established in INDIA from about 1526 to 1857. The founder was Babar, a direct descendant of Tamerlane, himself a descendant of JENGHIZ KHAN. One of the greatest rulers was Akbar. The Moguls were generous patrons of the arts, and perhaps their most important contribution to India's culture was in the arts of painting and architecture; the TAJ MAHAL is a living monument to the latter.

MOHAMMED (?570–632)

Founder of the religion of ISLAM, born at Mecca. After an attempt on his life he fled to Medina (622) but returned to Mecca in 630. His religious visions form the KORAN. Other forms of his name are Mahomet, Mehmet and Muhammad.

of LOUIS XIV and presented many of Molière's most famous plays, including *Tartuffe*, *Le Misanthrope*, *Le Bourgeois Gentilhomme* and *Le Malade Imaginaire*. The plays cover the whole range of comedy from delicate humour to broad farce and are often directed at pretence and hypocrisy.

MOLLUSCS

One of the most important groups in the whole animal kingdom and includes the whelk, snail, slug, limpet, oyster, clam, squid, cuttlefish, nautilus and octopus.

Molluscs are in the main slow-moving animals and rely on their shell for protection. Some molluscs have become swimmers and

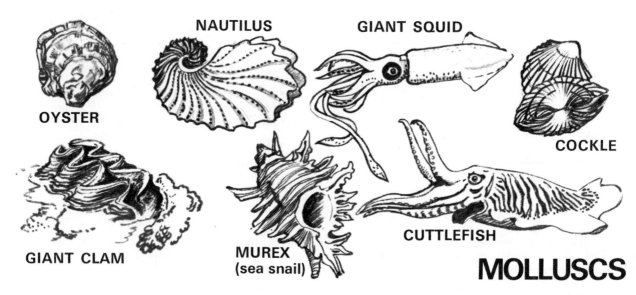

NAUTILUS

GIANT SQUID

OYSTER

COCKLE

GIANT CLAM

MUREX
(sea snail)

CUTTLEFISH

MOLLUSCS

MOHENJO-DARO

An area near the River Indus in West Pakistan where a civilization has been uncovered which flourished about 2500 B.C. From the finds already made it would appear that the inhabitants of this well-organized society were related to the SUMERIANS. The people were fine builders, potters and sculptors. What caused the decline of their civilization is as yet uncertain. The civilization is generally referred to as the Indus Civilization.

MOLIÈRE, properly Jean Baptiste Poquelin (1622–1673)

French dramatist, born in Paris. His father was upholsterer to the Court. He educated his son as a lawyer, but Molière showed more interest in the theatre. He founded his own troupe which was unsuccessful in Paris and then spent thirteen years in the provinces. On its return to Paris the troupe won the patronage

some adapted for floating, however, the majority move by crawling. They are found at great heights on mountains and equally great depths in the sea. Molluscs form an important part of the food needs of people in many parts of the world, and are the source of pearls and mother-of-pearl.

MONACO

A tiny Principality on the Mediterranean and joined with France. Its Sovereign Prince is Prince Rainier who married the film star, Grace Kelly. It is only 2 miles long and half a mile broad, and has a little over 20,000 inhabitants. It is best known for its Casino at Monte Carlo.

MONASTERIES, MONKS AND NUNS

Living alone in monasteries is known in other, and older, religions than Christianity, and is the way of life adopted by those who withdraw

from ordinary society to devote their lives t'
prayer, meditation, and the service of God.

The basic unit of a Monastery is the cell, the small, sparsely furnished room in which each monastic lives in solitude, usually leaving it only to attend communal worship, or for communal meals, or special duty. The first Christian monastics were simply composed of hermits and anchorites living in cells of rock in the Egyptian desert. St. Antony, who lived to a very great age was probably the first such 'monastic'. It was another Egyptian however, St. Pachomius, who first established a monastic community living together as one unit, according to a 'Rule' of life. Monasticism spread rapidly throughout the Greek East, where the great St. Basil of Caesarea (326–379) formulated a Monastic Rule, followed by the Orthodox monastics to this day.

In the West, monasticism never became popular until St. Benedict of Nursia (480–543) founded his famous monastery at Monte Cassino, in Italy—scene of one of the most ferocious battles in the Second World War. Benedict formulated a Rule which eventually became the principal monastic system in Western Christendom. He laid more stress on the value of dedicated work than earlier systems had done. Following Benedict's work, Monasticism became rapidly established in the West. In Scotland, North England, and North West Europe, the Celtic Monasticism of the great Irish Saint Columban (543–615)—a disciple of Columba—flourished and held its own for some time. It was eventually superseded, however, by the Benedictine Rule, especially in Britain, after the Synod of Whitby (664). Canterbury Cathedral and Westminster Abbey were both Churches of great Benedictine Monasteries: many churches in Britain have similar monastic origins. English Monasticism came to an end with the Dissolution of the Monasteries (1536–1540) in HENRY VIII's reign. In Scotland, the First Book of Discipline (1560) of the new, Reformed Church of Scotland required the abolition of abbeys, cathedral churches, monasteries, etc., in order to stamp out idolatry.

The principal building of a monastery is the church, which is usually built on the north side of the cloister—a quadrangle, sometimes of grass, surrounded by a covered passage-way called the 'ambulatory'. The other monastic buildings are usually ranged on the other three sides of the cloister, being all connected by the ambulatory, and including a 'refectory' (dining hall) 'dormitory' (sleeping quarters) and 'chapter house' (for conferences on religious and disciplinary matters): with other buildings for novices, hospitality to visitors (such as travel-lers) an infirmary, kitchens, workshops, etc.

An 'Abbey' is a monastery governed by an abbot, or an abbess.

A 'Convent' is a monastery; used more often to denote a female monastic house.

A 'Priory' is a monastery governed by a prior, or prioress.

A 'Monk' (Latin, *monachus*; from Greek meaning 'one who lives alone') is a man who adopts the monastic life, having entered a monastery and taken the Monastic Vows of 'poverty, chastity and obedience'.

A 'Nun' is a woman who adopts the monastic life. It is possible that there were women's monasteries before those for men. Most male Monastic Orders saw the establishment of their female counterparts—e.g., the Carmelite Nuns and the Franciscan and Dominican Nuns. Two female Orders in their own right were the Institute of Mary, founded in Munich in 1609 by an Englishwoman, Mary Ward, and the famous Sisters of Charity, founded in France in 1633.

A 'Friar': the early 13th century saw the first Mendicant (literally 'begging') friars. The Franciscans (1209) and the Dominicans (1215) are both Mendicant Orders. While monks normally lived and worked within one monastery all their lives, the friars moved from convent to convent, working *outside* the monastic walls; preaching, tending the sick, and so on, and living largely on the voluntary support of the people.

A 'Monastic Order': although the term 'Benedictine Order' is often used, Benedict himself never founded an 'Order'. He laid down his Rule for *all* Christian monastics who cared to follow it, and since, in time, most of them have done so, they have nearly all been Benedictine. An 'Order' is a group of monastic houses, spread, perhaps, throughout several countries, but governed by one chief monastery. All Orders have some special purpose of their own—the Knights Templar and the Hospitallers were both military religious Orders, with the purpose of freeing the Holy Land. The first Monastic Order was the Cluniac, founded at Cluny, France, in 910. Then followed the Cistercians (about 1098) and the Carthusians (1084).

MONET, Claude (1840–1926)
French painter. Born in Le Havre. In 1862 he went to Paris, where he met CÉZANNE and RENOIR. Two of his paintings were shown in the Salon in 1865. In 1870 he visited England, where he met Constable and Turner, and painted several London scenes. His *Impression : soleil levant*, which he exhibited in 1874, gave the name to the kind of paintings he and

his friends were producing—Impressionist. After living in poverty for many years, a successful exhibit in 1883 enabled him to buy a small property and retire.

MONEY

Anything which can be used to make it easy for people to exchange goods. For many centuries, however, it meant any piece of metal, usually gold, silver or copper, stamped by public authority, that could be used in trade. Until as recently as the 19th century the word money was only used to describe coins and if people wanted to include paper money as well the term 'currency' was used. Today, however, the word money is used whether it is coins, notes, or bank balances that can be used by means of cheques.

Because the most valuable metal used in coins was gold the term 'gold standard' came into use. Gold coins were freely used in Britain as payment until 1914. Even after this period Britain was still said to be on the gold standard because although no gold coins were in circulation the BANK OF ENGLAND bought and sold gold at a fixed price and this could be used to pay for goods or repayment of loans from foreign countries. Since 1945, however, the gold standard has not been in general operation and other methods are used for the payment of debts with other countries.

In 1966 the Government announced that in February 1971 Britain would change over to the decimal system, a system that is already used by most countries. The pound was divided into a hundred pence. This meant that the two shilling piece would be worth ten pence and ten shillings 50 pence. A Decimal Board was set up to make plans for making it as easy as possible to change over to the new system of currency. A similar change in currency took place in Australia recently.

The story of money is a long one. When men first lived in settled communities and began to exchange goods with one another they did it by barter. That is to say, if one man perhaps wanted some bows and arrows he might offer the man who made them a pig or some corn. As communities became bigger and more civilized this method was found to be very clumsy and inconvenient. Various tokens then began to be used such as shells and pieces of gold or silver or other metal. Even these were found to be inconvenient because metal was difficult to divide fairly and it was not always easy to tell if the metal was really gold or silver. Then about the 7th century B.C. the people of Lydia hit upon the idea of coins, stamped with a symbol of guarantee as to their value. At about the same time China also began to make coins. The study of these ancient coins tells us a good deal about the history of ancient times. The study of coins is called 'Numismatics', from numisma, the Latin word for coin. The place where coins are made is called a mint.

Most of the money used in trade and commerce is kept in banks and it is through banks that the payment of large sums of money is made. Some form of banking was practised in ancient Egypt and Greece, and it was developed by the Romans. Banking was not used in Europe after Roman times until the 15th century. The city States of Italy, like Venice and Genoa, were the first to start deposit banks. The word bank comes from the Italian word *banca*, meaning a bench, i.e., the bench at which the Italian merchants would change money and accept money for safe-keeping. They would give a receipt for the money deposited with them. Italian merchants from Lombardy set up their bench in the city of London and the street where they did business is called Lombard Street after them.

After a time people used the receipts given them by banks as payment for debts. They would sign them so that the other person could collect the money. To make this form of payment easier the bank would give a number of receipts, or notes, so that a client could pay a number of bills with them. These came to be called 'bank notes'. Bank notes used to be issued by private banks in England until 1928 when the TREASURY and the BANK OF ENGLAND together became responsible for all such notes. In Scotland commercial banks still issue notes.

Most of the money deposited in a bank is not left as coins or bank notes in its vaults or safes. It is used, or invested, to make more money. If, for instance, it is lent to the Government, the Government will pay every year money called 'interest' for the use of the money. There is, of course, no fear that the money, that is the capital, will be lost. When a Bank or private person lends money to the Government, they receive a certificate, called a 'bond', stating that so much money has been borrowed and that each year the money is on loan so much money will be paid as interest. These bonds are, therefore, valuable and they can be bought and sold like other property. The money they represent is called Government stock. It is often referred to as 'gilt edged' security because the bond used to be printed on gold bordered paper.

Apart from the Government, big firms will often borrow money in a similar way and will pay interest on the money lent to them. They, too, will issue certificates of the shares in the business that this money represents.

The buying and selling of stocks and shares is done at a 'stock exchange' which in most other countries is called a 'bourse'. The people who bring together those who want to buy or sell stock are called 'stock brokers'.

Much of the commerce of the world is done through banks. Because the payment of goods which our country buys from foreign countries is made through a bank, and because the money which foreign firms pay for British goods is also paid through a bank, it is quite easy for banks to tell whether Britain is spending more money in buying goods from foreign countries or whether she is receiving more money from foreign countries for British goods sent abroad. This way of keeping

MONKEY A rhesus monkey. It is a member of the macaque family and native of the Far East.

accounts is referred to as the 'balance of payments'. Because it is much better for a country, as for an individual, to receive more than it spends, if the balance left after the accounts are made shows that Britain has spent more foreign money than she has received, this is called an 'adverse balance'. If, on the other hand, more has been received than has been spent, it is called a 'favourable balance.'

Not all the items that appear on the account are goods to be seen and handled. Some are called invisible exports. For instance, if a foreign firm buys goods from another foreign country, but wants to hire, or charter, a British ship to carry them, the money that is paid for the use of the ship would go on the account as an invisible export.

A country that earns more money than it

spends is usually prosperous and will find that other countries are glad to have the 'currency' of that country. This means that when it is exchanged for foreign money it is found to have more value than the money of a poor country. More foreign goods can, therefore, be bought with a given amount of money than is possible when the country is thought to be hard-up, and in consequence its money of less value. A prosperous country whose money is always of the same value and so sought after by other countries, is said to have 'hard currency'. Examples of countries which have hard currencies are the United States and Switzerland.

MONGOLIA, or Mongolian People's Republic
A vast desert country to the north of China. It is about three times the size (600,000 square miles) of France but much of it consists of the great Gobi Desert. The population is only a little more than a million. The capital is Ulan Bator.

A part of Mongolia, called Inner Mongolia, is not part of the Republic but is a province of China. Many more people live there than in the Republic, the population being over 9 million.

MONKEY
The name for the group of PRIMATES in the suborder Anthropoidea, and includes baboons, capuchins, spider monkeys, howlers, marmosets, macaques, mandrills, etc.

MONMOUTH, James Scott, Duke of
(1649–1685)
English Protestant Pretender. Born in Rotterdam, and the illegitimate son of Charles II. He was created Duke of Monmouth in 1663 and appointed commander-in-chief 1674. He was in Holland when Charles died and James II succeeded to the throne. Monmouth planned to seize the throne for himself, and landed with his troops at Lyme Regis in 1685. But he was defeated at the battle of Sedgmoor, and executed at the Tower of London.

MONOPOLIES COMMISSION
A body set up by Parliament in 1948. A monopoly is an exclusive trade in a particular article. A very large manufacturing firm may succeed in gaining a monopoly by buying up smaller firms making similar articles. If this happens the Board of Trade can refer the matter to the Monopolies Commission whose findings will be reported to Parliament if the Commission believes the monopoly is not in the public interest. In 1956 another Act, the Restrictive Trade Practices Act, set up a

Restrictive Practices Court. If dealers agree with one another about, say, the price at which certain goods shall be sold the agreement must be registered so that the Court can consider any such agreements as are thought not to be in the public interest.

MONSOON

Word deriving from the Arabic (mawsin, meaning season), and refers to the winds which, in the northern hemisphere, blow for six months from the north-east and six months from the south-west. Generally it is applied to the rainy reason (June to September) in India and adjacent countries.

MONTAIGNE, Michel de (1533–1592)

Born, and lived much of his life, near Bordeaux. He was frequently at the French Court, and fulfilled a number of civic functions. He is famous for his essays, a literary form which he invented and which had considerable influence on later English writers. Montaigne's essays cover many subjects, including most aspects of life except the deeply philosophical, and are full of charm and humour.

MONTESQUIEU, Charles de Secondat (1689–1755)

French philosopher and lawyer. He became President of the Parlement of Bordeaux, but later turned to writing. His main interest was in social and political institutions, which he studied in a number of different countries including England. In *De l'esprit des lois* he showed his great admiration for the English constitution, and the *Lettres persanes* contained strong criticism of the French political and legal framework. Montesquieu had considerable influence on the men who drew up the American constitution.

MONTESSORI, Maria (1870–1952)

Italian educationalist who studied the education, first of defective, and then of normal, children. She introduced the method of teaching now known as the 'Montessori system', by which children are provided with activities and occupations to the full extent of their capacity and interest, at a very early age. Her book explaining this system, *The Montessori Method*, was published in 1912, and has been translated into many languages.

MONTEVERDI, Claudio (1567–1643)

Italian composer, born at Cremona. Organist for many years in Venice, at St. Mark's Cathedral; he died there in 1643. He wrote much church music, including the magnificent *Vespers*, but is chiefly famous as the composer

MOON A close-up photograph of the surface. Moon probes are studying this by means of scoops which are examined by cameras and the information televised back to earth.

of some of the first operas, the best known being *Orfeo*, which tells the story of Orpheus.

MONTFORT, Simon de, Earl of Leicester (1208–1265)

English statesman and soldier. As King Henry III's deputy in Gascony, de Montfort established order in the country only to be recalled by the jealous king. At home, trouble was developing because of the number of the Queen's French relatives and favourites who had come to live in the country and were supplanting the English in government. The Provisions of Oxford were drawn up by Parliament in 1258 to right these grievances, and the king agreed to abide by them but later said that the Pope had declared them void. Louis IX of France (Saint Louis) also declared in Henry's favour. De Montfort collected an army and defeated the king at the Battle of Lewes (1264), capturing the Prince Edward. The personal rule of the king was replaced by that of a commission that included de Montfort, advised by a Parliament to which representatives of the towns were for the first time invited. For this reason it is seen as the ancestor of our modern Parliament. Prince Edward eventually escaped and de Montfort was defeated and killed at Evesham (1265).

MONTGOLFIER, Joseph Michel (1740–1810)

He and his brother, Jacques Etienne, were French inventors. They experimented with, and demonstrated the use of, balloons filled with hot air. They made a number of ascents and were the pioneers of modern lighter-than-air flight.

MONTGOMERY of Alamein, Field Marshal Viscount (1887——)

British soldier, born in County Donegal, Ireland. He entered the army in 1908 and served in the First World War where he was mentioned in despatches. By 1939 he had risen to the rank of divisional commander, and took part in the evacuation of Dunkirk. Appointed lieutenant-general in 1942, he took over command of the British Eighth Army, and at El Alamein, in the Western Desert, defeated a mixed army of Germans and Italians. The victory was the first step in the conquest of the whole of North Africa. His other great war-time victory was at Normandy in 1944, when he led the 21st Army Group to the Rhine. After the war he became chairman of the commanders-in-chief of the Western Alliance and Deputy Supreme Allied Commander under the North Atlantic Treaty Organization.

MOON

Satellite of our planet. Its mean distance from the earth is 238,860 miles, it is approximately 2,160 miles in diameter and its sidereal revolution is $27\frac{1}{3}$ days. Because of the motion of the moon only one face is ever seen, but it has been photographed by lunar space vehicles. So far as is known it has no atmosphere such as our own and no form of life. [*See* SOLAR SYSTEM.]

MOORE, George (1852–1933)

Irish poet and novelist, celebrated for the brilliance of his writing. Two of his best-known works are *Esther Waters* and *The Brook Kerith*.

MOORE, Henry (1898——)

English sculptor, born at Castleford. His early work was strongly influenced by primitive art but as his work developed it took on a style which is wholly his own. Considered by many to be the greatest modern sculptor. During the Second World War he did a number of outstanding drawings of people in air-raid shelters.

MOORE, Thomas (1779–1852)

Irish poet, born in Dublin. He was educated at Trinity College, Cambridge. In 1803 he was appointed Admiralty registrar at Bermuda, the work of which was done by a deputy. His *Irish Melodies* which began to appear in 1807, with music by Sir John Stevenson, established him as the Irish national poet. They are grace-

ful and simple airs. He was very friendly with BYRON, whose biography he published in 1830.

MOORS

Dark-skinned people of North Africa who, under the inspiration of the religion of ISLAM, conquered an empire stretching from the Pamirs to the Pyrénées in the 8th century. Their occupation of Spain lasted from A.D. 711 to 1492. Although the Moors came as conquerors they left as benefactors. They made great advances in science, philosophy, mathematics, medicine and art which infused new life into European culture. To them we owe our modern system of numbers, and their ALCHEMY inspired Western minds in a direction which led to modern chemistry. To them we owe the preservation of much Greek and Roman culture and learning, for they had assimilated this knowledge while Europe was being overrun by barbarians, and brought it back to Europe when they invaded Spain and Sicily.

MOOSE [*See* ELK.]

MORE, Sir Thomas (1478–1535)

Statesman, politician and writer, born in London. He was considered very favourably by HENRY VIII, and rose to be Speaker of the House and Lord Chancellor after Cardinal WOLSEY. More was a very religious man and

MOORE'S bronze, *The King and Queen*.

would not approve of Henry's divorce from Catharine of Aragon, which led to his retirement. Later he refused to recognize Henry as supreme head of the Church, and was imprisoned in the Tower on a charge of treason and beheaded. More's best known book is *Utopia*, a political essay about an imaginary land where there is freedom of worship and universal education.

MORLEY, Thomas (1557–1603)

English composer. He was organist of St. Paul's Cathedral, but is remembered today for his gay, high-spirited songs and madrigals, of which *It Was a Lover and His Lass* and *My Bonnie Lass, She Smileth*, are typical examples.

MORMONS

American religious sect founded in 1831 by Joseph Smith, who wrote *The Book of Mormon*. Under the leadership of Brigham Young a settlement was set up in 1847 in Utah, the present Salt Lake City. For many years the settlement was opposed by the American government because of Young's idea that a man could have more than one wife. There are still over half a million mormons in the U.S.A. The correct name for the sect is 'Church of Jesus Christ of Latter-day Saints'.

MOROCCO

A kingdom in North Africa that is more than twice the size (180,000 square miles) of Great Britain and has a population of a little more than 13 million. The capital is Rabat, with Tangier as the summer capital. The largest city is the port of Casablanca. The country produces phosphates, manganese, iron ore, lead and zinc and is famous for its fine leather work. The people on the coast are chiefly Arabs and those in the Atlas Mountains chiefly Berbers.

History :

The Arabs in the 8th century founded an Empire centred on Fez and were able to conquer Spain which they ruled for centuries. After they had been driven from Spain some of the Berbers took to piracy and the coast of Morocco was named after them the Barbary coast. In 1912 most of Morocco became a French Protectorate, a small part going to Spain. In 1956 Morocco became an independent kingdom.

MORRIS-DANCE

Folk-dance probably introduced from Spain, and which has been described as '. . . a dance wherein there were usually five men, and a boy dressed in girl's habit, whom they called the Maid Marrion, or perhaps Morian, from the Italian Morione, a headpiece, because her head was wont to be gaily trimmed up. Common people call it a Morris-dance.' Up to the time of the Puritans it was popular, but they abolished it together with other so-called pagan festivals. In recent years there has been great interest in folk-dancing and there are today a number of groups who give public performances of Morris-dances—even on the busy streets of London.

MORRIS, William (1834–1896)

Born at Walthamstow. Morris loved the Middle Ages, believed that in medieval work he found beauty and good craftsmanship, and devoted his life to work intended to do away with the uglier aspects of machine civilization and replace them with finer and healthier things. He worked on fabrics and furniture to make them more beautiful; he practised the printing of more beautiful books; he took an interest in socialist politics, and wrote to convert his fellow-men to a saner way of arranging their lives together. In literature he attempted many sorts of writing; poems, pamphlets, translations, romances. His earliest volume, *The Defence of Guenevere*, published in 1858, is perhaps the most interesting.

MORRISON, Herbert Stanley (1888–1965)

English politician. Born in London. He was the son of a policeman, and was educated at an elementary school. After various jobs, including shop assistant and telephone operator, he entered local government politics. He was

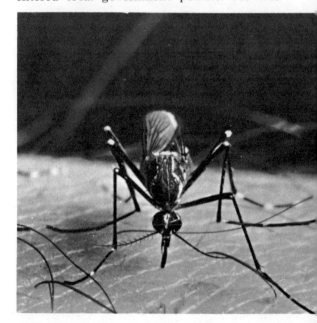

MOSQUITO feeding on a human hand.

socialist mayor of Hackney (1920–1921) and on the London County Council rose to become alderman (1931) and leader of the Council (1939–1940). He first entered Parliament in 1923. During most of the Second World War he was Minister of Home Security and was also a member of the War Cabinet (1943–1945). In the Labour Government of 1945–1950 he became leader of the House of Commons and Lord President of the Council, and was Foreign Secretary for a short while in 1951.

MORSE, Samuel Finley Breese
(1791–1872)
American inventor, born in Massachusetts. In addition to making important contributions to telegraphy he was an outstanding portrait painter. His greatest claim to fame, however, is his telegraph code, known as the Morse Code, and is:

A	· —	N	— ·	1	· — — — —
B	— · · ·	O	— — —	2	· · — — —
C	— · — ·	P	· — — ·	3	· · · — —
D	— · ·	Q	— — · —	4	· · · · —
E	·	R	· — ·	5	· · · · ·
F	· · — ·	S	· · ·	6	— · · · ·
G	— — ·	T	—	7	— — · · ·
H	· · · ·	U	· · —	8	— — — · ·
I	· ·	V	· · · —	9	— — — — ·
J	· — — —	W	· — —	0	— — — — —
K	— · —	X	— · · —		
L	· — · ·	Y	— · — —		
M	— —	Z	— — · ·		

MOSLEM [*See* ISLAM]

MOSQUITO
Member of the fly family and found throughout the world. Its eggs are laid and hatched in stagnant water. The species *Stegomyia anoples* transmits MALARIA and *Stegomyia fasciata* yellow fever. Since the foundation of the World Health Organization (W.H.O.) much has been done to stamp out these diseases by destroying the carrier mosquitoes; the most effective method is spraying the surface of the stagnant water in which they breed with oil. [*See* INSECT.]

MOTION PICTURES
This form of entertainment arose out of the development of PHOTOGRAPHY. From the middle of the 19th century many people experimented with photography to obtain moving pictures. The most important advances were made by T. A. EDISON with his invention of the 'kinetoscope' (1889) and the brothers Lumiere's 'cinematographe' (1895). In its earliest days the motion picture was not much

MOTION PICTURES Still from *Singing in the Rain*, a classic musical starring Gene Kelly.

more than a fair-ground curiosity. In 1903 E. S. Porter, an American, filmed a picture, called *The Life of an American Fireman*, and started off the film industry as we know it today; in France the work of G. Melies (1909) had a similar effect. The pioneer of Hollywood was D. W. Griffith, who produced the classic film *The Birth of a Nation* (1914). Since that time motion pictures have not only become the leading form of entertainment but a great industry, and not only in America, but in Europe, Russia, India and China.

MOTOR-CARS
As long ago as 1770 a Frenchman, Nicholas Cugnot, built a three-wheeled carriage driven by steam power. It carried two people and travelled at $2\frac{1}{2}$ m.p.h. Many other steam carriages were built later, but in Britain progress was held up by the 'Locomotives on the Highways Act' (1896) which restricted the speed of vehicles to 4 m.p.h., and required that a man with a red flag walk in front of the carriage. On the Continent where there were no such restrictions great advances were made by men like Gottlieb Daimler and Karl Benz— two names still met with. In 1896, however, the Act was abolished in Britain and the speed

BENZ 1888

ROLLS-ROYCE 1907

**FORD
Model T 1923**

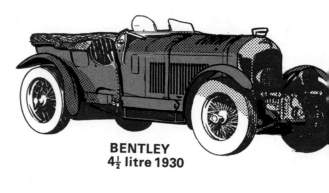

**BENTLEY
4½ litre 1930**

CITROEN 1938

MG 1947

**MORRIS
Mini-Minor 1963**

WOLESLEY 1950

FERRARI 1967

MOTOR CARS

raised to 12 m.p.h. From this time progress was rapid.

Of the many men who helped found the British motor-car industry perhaps the following are the more outstanding: H. J. Lawson (founder Motor Car Club), F. Lanchester, Herbert Austin, William Riley, J. D. Siddeley, C. S. Rolls and Henry Royce, William Hillman, W. R. Morris (Lord NUFFIELD) and W. D. Bentley. In the U.S.A. the pioneers were C. and J. F. Duryea, E. Hayes, Henry FORD, R. E. Olds and G. Selden.

MOUNTBATTEN of Burma, Admiral Louis, First Earl (1901———)

British statesman and sailor. A great grandson of Queen Victoria, he entered the Navy as a cadet in 1913. He rose to become commander of H.M.S. *Illustrious* and was then appointed chief of combined operations (1942–1943). As Supreme Allied Commander in South-east Asia (1943–1945) he achieved the reconquest of Burma from the Japanese. He became the last Viceroy of India and took a leading part in the transfer of power to the new republics of Pakistan and India. He was the first Governor-General of the new dominion. Continuing his naval career, he was appointed Commander-in-chief of the British Mediterranean Fleet, Commander-in-chief, Mediterranean, under the North Atlantic Treaty Organization and later First Sea Lord.

MOUSE [*See* RODENTS.]

MOUSSORGSKY, Modest Petrovich (1835–1881)

Russian composer and member of the musical group at St. Petersburg that included RIMSKY-KORSAKOV. His popular works are *The Song of the Flea*, the opera *Boris Godunov* and the piano suite *Pictures from an Exhibition*.

MOZART, Wolfgang Amadeus (1756–1791)

Austrian composer, born at Salzburg. A child wonder, he played the harpsichord when he was 3. At the age of 6, he and his sister (four years older than himself) were taken by their father to Paris, where they played to Queen Marie Antoinette; two years later they reached London, where Mozart composed his first symphony, at the age of 8. He spent his later life in Vienna, where he met HAYDN; he produced several operas there, including *The Marriage of Figaro* and *The Magic Flute*. He composed a vast amount of music of all kinds and of the highest quality; it has a beauty, grace, and charm which distinguish it from that of any other composer, and fully earn him his title 'the divine Mozart'.

MUIR, Edwin (1887–1959)

Scottish poet, born in the Orkneys. He moved to Glasgow when he was 14, and his unhappiness in the big city is recalled in *An Autobiography*. For much of his life he worked for the British Institute abroad. His poems are set among the harsh scenery of the Orkneys.

MULE

The offspring of an ass (male) and a horse (mare). Mules cannot be bred from mules as they are sterile. The name is also used for a machine in the cotton spinning industry.

MUNCH, Edvard (1863–1944)

Norwegian painter who strongly influenced modern German painting. His style of painting springs from GAUGUIN but is violent, neurotic and highly colourful.

MURILLO, Bartolomé Esteban (*c.* 1617–1682)

Spanish painter, born at Seville. He is most famous for paintings of religious subjects and street scenes with urchins.

MUSCAT AND OMAN

An independent Sultanate in East Arabia. It is about 82,000 square miles but has only about three-quarters of a million inhabitants. The capital is Muscat. It exports frankincense.

MUSEUMS

Places where objects of interest, often ancient and valuable, are kept and exhibited.

There are museums all over the world today, but they were unknown two or three centuries ago. In the Middle Ages kings and princes might sometimes collect curiosities, but such collections were not important enough to be called museums. One of the pioneers of museums was Robert Cotton, who lived in the reign of Elizabeth I, and who made a private collection of old books, manuscripts, coins, medals and other curiosities. This collection was not, however, given to the nation till about a hundred years later, and in the meantime the first real museum had already been opened.

A private collector named Elias Ashmole in the year 1677 gave to the University of Oxford his collection of curiosities on condition that a special building was built to house them. So the first museum, not only in England, but in any part of the world, was opened and it was called after its founder, the Ashmolean Museum. It was about twenty years later that the grandson of the Elizabethan collector, Robert Cotton, died and left the collection to the nation. So in 1700 Parliament passed an serve this collection. Later another collector, Sir Hans Sloane, who lived from 1660 to 1753 left his collection to the nation, and Parliament passed another Act in 1753 setting up the British Museum, the first *national* museum in any country. Four years later, the then King, George II, gave the Royal Library to the British Museum. It was then decided that in future a copy of every book published must be given to the British Museum Library [*see* LIBRARIES]. By this means the British Museum Library has become one of the three greatest libraries in the world.

Today there are about eight hundred museums in Great Britain and no less than two thousand in the United States; whilst in every part of the world museums have been erected to house the world's treasures.

MUSK DEER
Small deer found in Central Asia and valued for the musk perfume which is extracted from the stomach of the male.

MUSK-OX
Woolly ox-like animal with broad flattened horns which lives in the arctic regions of America and Greenland.

MUSSET, Alfred de (1810–1857)
French romantic poet and playwright. His short affair with George Sand and their visit together to Italy became famous in the literary world. His works include the dramas which he called 'armchair theatre', intending them for reading only; the autobiographical *Confessions d'un enfant du siècle*, in which he analysed the spirit of the age in France; and the lyrical verses, like *Nuits* and *Rolla*, with their self-seeking yet sympathetic characters.

MUSSOLINI, Benito (1883–1945)
Italian fascist dictator. Born at Predappio, son of a blacksmith. He passed most of his youth as a socialist propagandist. He was expelled from the socialist party when he advocated Italian intervention in the First World War. He fought at the front, and after the war founded the fascist movement (1919). In 1922 he led a march on Rome at the head of his blackshirts, forcing the King to appoint him Premier. He gradually made himself sole dictator at home, and also pursued an aggressive foreign policy. In 1935 he invaded ETHIOPIA; in 1936 he helped General Franco's revolt in SPAIN; and in 1939 he seized Albania. He did not enter the Second World War until 1940. The German collapse in 1945 was also Mussolini's collapse. He tried to escape from North Italy to Switzerland, but was arrested in April of that year in a frontier village where after "trial" he was executed by Italian partisans.

MUSTANG
When the Spanish invaded Central America many of their horses (Arab breed) escaped to form herds. These roamed the plains of Mexico and Texas, and were greatly prized by the Indians. A partly wild horse of this origin is called a mustang and one completely untamed a bronco; the latter are what cowboys try to ride and break at rodeos.

MYTHOLOGY
The study of the myths of mankind. Myths have, from the remotest times and in all places, been created by men to explain happenings that affected their lives and well-being. For example, in Babylonia harvests were sometimes killed off by the scorching heat of the sun, and at other times saved by heavy rain storms. To explain this the Babylonians imagined the rain storm to be a gigantic bird which swept down from the heavens and swallowed the sun. Similar mythical accounts have been fashioned to explain such important happenings as the creation of the heavens, the origin of man, the meaning of death.

Sometimes myths were dramatized, in fact, some ancient and colourful rituals were myths being presented in dramatic form. The same applies to many of the tribal dances of primitive peoples living today.

Many fables, legends and fairy tales contain elements which were once myths.

MYTHOLOGY Primitive people represent their mythological gods in powerful carvings. The one shown below is from the Marquesas Islands.

Nn

NABOKOV, Vladimir (1899——)

Russian-born American author. He was professor of Russian literature at Cornell University from 1948–1959. *The Real Life of Sebastian Knight* and *Pnin* established his reputation, but his best known work is the outspoken *Lolita*.

NAMES

Everybody knows that the first, or Christian, names, of a child are chosen for it by its parents, but the story of how the surname arose is less clear.

At the time of the Norman Conquest there were many Saxon names, like Edgar and Edmund, from which parents could choose names for their children. After the Norman Conquest most of these old Saxon names were no longer used and French names came to be chosen instead. Some boys' names became so popular that by the 14th century more than half the boys in the country were named either Henry, John, Richard, Robert or William. This was so confusing that nicknames used to be given to distinguish, say, one John from another; and these names developed into what we now call surnames. For instance, the colour of the hair might suggest Red (Read or Reid), White, Black, Grey or Brown. If one Henry was short and another tall, this would suggest such nicknames as Little, Long or Short. A cunning man might be given the name of Fox, a strong one Lyon (lion) or Bull and a proud one Peacock. Some animal or bird names were given as nicknames because the family kept an inn which would have a sign of perhaps a Swan or Lamb, just as many have today.

In the Middle Ages villagers used to take part in Miracle or Morality plays and often players would have to dress up as a King or Bishop or Knight and because the actors were proud of playing such parts they used them as nicknames. These nicknames were often passed on from father to son and so continued as surnames. Other people were merely referred to as, say, Robert, John's son, to distinguish him from Robert, William's son, and in time the 'son' was added to form a surname (Johnson, Williamson). But as names are often shortened as pet or diminutive names, so some names today can scarcely be recognized as derived from a Christian name. For instance, a boy named Bartholomew might be called by his family Bate, Batty, or Bartlett or even Tolly. A girl named Mary might be called Moll, and her son might be referred to as Moll's son, or Mollison. For although children were usually called after their father it was not unusual for them to be named after their mother.

Other people were referred to by their occupation—Baker, Smith, Taylor, Farmer and so on, and as such occupations were often passed on from father to son the occupation came to be a surname.

When a person moved from one part of the country and settled in another—which happened far more rarely than it does today—he might be referred to as John from London, Kent or wherever it was he came from. But sometimes such place names were local, as, for instance, if he lived on the Hill or in a Wood or on the village Green. Or if he lived in the North or West part of a town this might give rise to a surname.

Sometimes the time of year when a person was born would suggest a surname as Winter or Summers. If a person came from another country he would probably be referred to by the name of his country as Ireland, Holland or by a name connected with it, as French or Scott.

In Scotland names often begin with 'Mac' which is Celtic for son. In the same way 'O' in front of an Irish name stands for grandson.

In 1538 it became compulsory for registers to be kept by Parish Churches of those christened, married or buried. Although by this time almost everybody had got a surname as well as a Christian name, this law made certain that everybody had one that was used by the family.

Many Jewish people in Britain came to this country last century from Germany. It was not till the 19th century that German Jews adopted surnames and they did so then because new laws required them to do so. So, many of them took their Old Testament first names as surnames, such as Moses, Jacob and Levy. Some, however, chose poetic names, such as Rosenburg (rose mountain) Rubenstein (ruby) or Gluckstein (luck stone). The Rothschilds took their name from a red shield which hung over Nathan Rothschild's shop in Frankfurt.

NANSEN, Fridtjof (1861–1930)

Norwegian scientist and polar explorer. After preliminary voyages, in 1893 he reached

86° 50′ North, the most northerly point then reached by man. In 1921 he organised relief for the Russian famine victims, and was awarded the Nobel Peace Prize in 1922.

NAPOLEON [*See* BONAPARTE.]

NAPIER, John (1550–1617)
Scottish mathematician who invented LOG-ARITHMS and prepared the first logarithm tables (1614). He also invented a calculating device somewhat like an abacus, known as 'Napier's rods', and introduced the decimal point.

NARCOTIC
By definition, a narcotic is any substance producing sleep or stupor, and the term covers a wide range of drugs, though some are not directly taken for this effect. Alcohol is the commonest narcotic. The anaesthetics, such as ether, chloroform, and cyclopropane, belong to this group, as do the host of sleeping pills without which civilized man seems scarcely able to exist. Lastly comes the group of alkaloids containing morphine and Indian hemp, which because of the anti-social behaviour to which their abuse gives rise are the principal narcotics in which the police are interested. Narcotics act by slowing up activity of the cortex of the cerebrum.

NASH, Paul (1899–1946)
English artist, born in London. Many of his paintings have a dream-like quality. His best-known works are concerned with the First and Second World Wars. He was an Official War Artist in both wars. Nash was also a book illustrator and designer. His brother, John Nash (1893——), is a leading landscape painter.

NATIONAL DEBT
The money which the State borrows on the security of the taxes which it can raise. This was done as long ago as Norman times but the National Debt of today really dates back to the reign of William III. Britain in both World Wars incurred heavy debts with many countries, particularly with the United States.

NATIONAL HEALTH SERVICE
Set up in 1948 and provides for all British subjects to have free of charge hospital and specialist services as well as having medical and dental treatment outside hospital. In addition various welfare services are provided by LOCAL AUTHORITIES. By the same Act all hospitals, except a very few, were brought under the Ministry of Health. The hospitals are supervised by fifteen Regional Hospital Boards. The family doctor service is organized by local Executive Councils. The Executive Councils are also responsible for the dental and prescription services. The local authority is responsible for providing some additional services, such as running ambulances; child welfare clinics and providing health visitors. Most of the cost of the National Health Service comes from the Government and so is paid for out of taxes. Part, however comes from contributions which people pay weekly in the form of insurance stamps affixed to insurance cards.

NATIONALISM
Although nations have from the dawn of history been concerned with promoting the interests of their own people, it is only from the 18th century that this idea (nationalism) has been used as a political force. From that time on it has been one of the most powerful forces shaping the futures not only of nations but of the whole world. Perhaps the most forceful and cruel form of nationalism was HITLER's National Socialism (Nazi). In this extreme form he not only declared Germans to be supermen, but destroyed peoples he considered not fit to live, for example, the Jews, Russians, Poles, etc., during the Second World War.

NATIONAL SOCIALISM [*See* POLITICAL PARTIES.]

NATIONAL TRUST
The name of a society which owns and preserves many places of natural beauty and buildings of historic interest. There are in fact two such societies in the United Kingdom—one which acquires such sites in England and Wales and Northern Ireland and the other which acts for Scotland. Some of the places are bought by the Trust and others have been bequeathed by their owners. Between them the two Trusts own more than a hundred houses, many of which contain pictures and other works of art. These are open to the public for a small charge.

NATURAL HISTORY
The words actually mean the story of natural things. If this is accepted in a literal way then it would be necessary to say that natural history was the study of everything except the things made by man. It would have to include not only botany and zoology, but even astronomy. The only way to appreciate fully what is understood by the term is by tracing its history.

During the latter part of the 18th century and during the 19th century the great natural history museums of the world, in London,

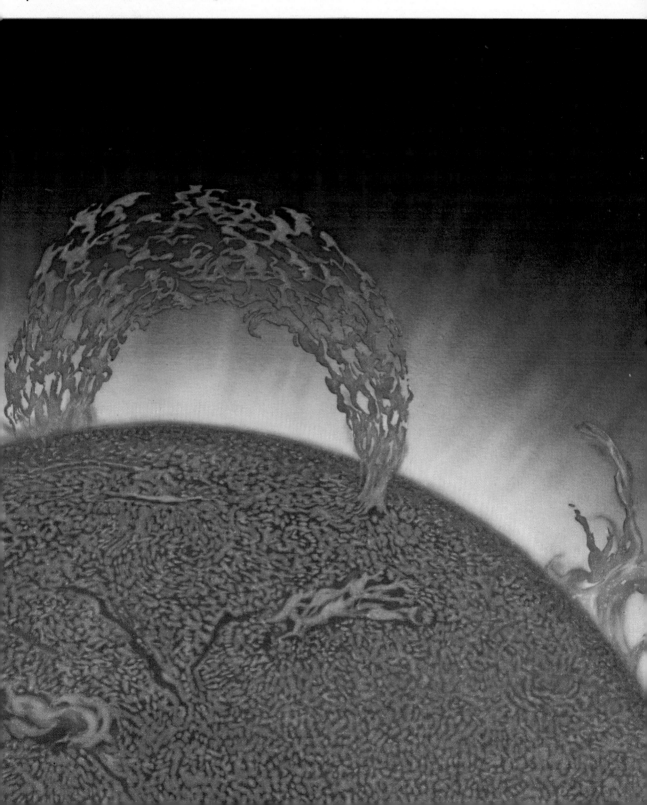

SUN The arch of flame in the illustration below is a solar prominence and rises thousands of miles above the sun's surface.

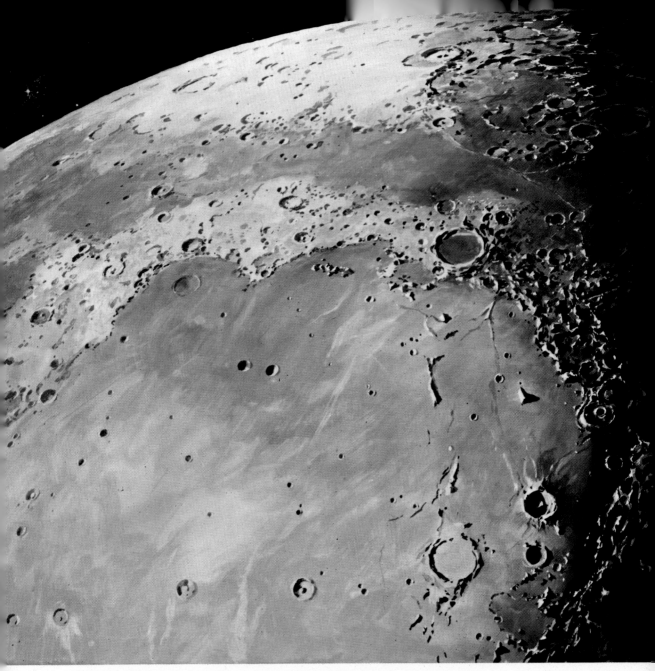

MOON A close-up of the moon's surface showing the craters
which cover great areas of this solar body. In the past
two years America and Russia have launched many probes
to study the nature of the moon's surface as it is
essential to know this before a landing by astronauts
is attempted.

NEBULAE An artist's impression of a giant spiral nebula. From observations already made it is known that there are millions of such universes beyond our own galactic system. They are the most distant objects known.

NEBULAE An artist's impression of a number of nebulae or 'island universes'. To give some idea of the remoteness of these nebulae one has only to consider the Great Nebula in Andromeda which is a million and a half light years away from our own galaxy.

NEBULAE A gaseous nebula. There is a very large one
just visible to the naked eye as a faint patch of misty
light below the three stars forming the 'belt' of Orion.

NEBULAE One theory of the origin of nebulae is that the universe
was originally a vast volume of rarified hydrogen gas, regions of
which condensed and was held together by the attraction of the
gravitational force between the atoms.

Paris, New York, and in other towns and cities, were being founded. Their purpose was to collect, describe and to classify natural objects such as plants, animals, fossils and minerals. Originally, then, natural history included these things and no more. As time went on, it was found necessary to study more and more the inner structure, or anatomy, especially of plants and animals. Also, to study how their bodies worked; this is now known as the science of physiology. Before long the sciences of anatomy and physiology were claiming more and more attention especially in the universities. At the same time, natural history became more and more to mean the study of the classification of animals and plants, as well as the study of what they looked like, how they behaved and where they lived. Moreover, the term was used more particularly for the study of animals.

At the present time there is a growing interest in natural history, both in schools and among the general public, and with its coming another change in the meaning of the term. Roughly speaking, a naturalist is a person who studies live animals in the wild state, as contrasted with the biologist who studies them in a laboratory. It is, however, becoming more and more obvious that animals cannot be studied in the wild without at the same time taking notice of the plants among which they live and on which, in many cases, they feed. This leads to the study of different soils and rocks, as well as the climate, for these in turn

NEBULA A diffuse galactic nebula or cosmic cloud in the constellation of Serpens. It is composed of fine dust and gas.

decide not only what plants we shall see in a particular piece of country, and how well they grow there, but they also exercise a considerable influence on the way animals behave. The weather is also all-important in the colour of an animal's coat. For example, in wetter regions the fur is inclined to be much darker, in colder regions it is more inclined to be white. And where there is a seasonal change in weather, the coats are apt to be brown in summer and white in winter. It seems true to say that today natural history means the study of animals, and, to a lesser extent, plants in the wild, as compared with biology which is the study of dead animals in the laboratory or animals examined for experiment or kept in captivity for closer observation. While this rough distinction can be made it should always be borne in mind that there is no hard-and-fast line to be drawn between natural history and biology.

NATURALIZATION
Describes the way a citizen of one country can become the citizen of another. If a foreigner has lived in the United Kingdom for five years he can ask to be made a British citizen. He must then give up being a citizen of his former country and promise to do his duty as a British citizen.

NEBULAE
Celestial objects resembling small luminous clouds at a distance comparable with those of the fixed STARS. Three broad classes of nebulae are distinguished. Planetary nebulae, of which the few hundreds known all belong to the galactic system, are disc-like or annular objects probably consisting of the enormously distended atmospheres of very faint stars. Galactic nebulae, which are also members of the galactic system, are clouds of tenuous gas rendered luminous by the radiations of stars within their boundaries. They are completely irregular in shape. Extra-galactic nebulae, sometimes called 'island universes,' are resolved by the camera into remote, self-contained systems of stars, comparable with the galactic system itself. They are of regular shape and usually betray a spiral structure indicating rotation. Several million are believed to exist, and they are the most distant objects known.

NEHRU, Jawaharlal (1889–1964)
Indian politician, born at Allahabad. Educated at Harrow and Cambridge. His life was dedicated to freeing INDIA, first from British rule and, when this had been achieved, the abolition of poverty and raising the standard of living of the Indian people. For the former he

was imprisoned many times. When the new Indian state was created in 1947 he was elected prime minister. During the period of the 'cold war' between the West and Russia and China he did much to ease tension. He wrote several books, the most widely read being his autobiography, *Toward Freedom*.

NELSON, Horatio, Viscount (1758–1805)

English naval commander, born at Burnham Thorpe in Norfolk. Son of a Norfolk clergyman, he went to sea at the age of 12, and by the time he was 20 was already a commander. In the siege of Calvi against the French, he lost his right eye (1794); and at the siege of Santa Cruz, Teneriffe, he lost his right arm (1797). For his victory over the French at Aboukir Bay he was created a Baron (1798). But his greatest victory was at Trafalgar (1805) where the French fleet was destroyed. Nelson himself was killed in the battle. Shortly before the action he hoisted from his flagship the famous signal: *England expects that every man will do his duty*.

NEPAL

A small independent kingdom in the Himalayas on the north-east frontier of India. It is a little larger (54,000 square miles) than England and has a population of nearly $9\frac{1}{2}$ million. MOUNT EVEREST is in Nepal. The capital is Katmandu. There are peoples of different races and religions in Nepal, one of the most important groups being the Gurkhas whose bravery is almost legendary.

NERO (Claudius Caesar) (37–68)

Succeeded the Emperor Claudius in A.D. 54. He was the son of Agrippina whom he arranged to have murdered after he became Emperor. His reign marked the first persecutions against the Christians whom he accused of firing Rome. In addition, he commanded to be murdered many leading Roman citizens, also his wife Poppaea, who at one time exercised a powerful if evil influence over him. He committed suicide after a successful revolt against his bestial rule.

NETHERLANDS, or Holland

A Kingdom in Western Europe. It is about half the size (13,500 square miles) of Scotland and has a population of over 12 million. The seat of Government is at the Hague, the chief city is Amsterdam and the chief port Rotterdam. Much of the Netherlands has been reclaimed from the sea and the Dutch are at present reclaiming an even larger area. The Netherlands is a rich agricultural country and is famous for its cheeses and flower bulbs. The

Dutch are also an important seafaring nation. A few years ago the Netherlands discovered great quantities of natural gas off the North Sea and this has been of great value to her industries.

History:

At the beginning of recorded history Holland was inhabited by people called Frisians and Batavi. The district now occupied by Holland and BELGIUM was conquered and occupied by the Romans until they in turn were driven out by the Franks. The name Holland was given to the district that still forms the provinces of North and South Holland in the 11th century. At this time the Counts of Holland had great influence. Part of Belgium at this time was

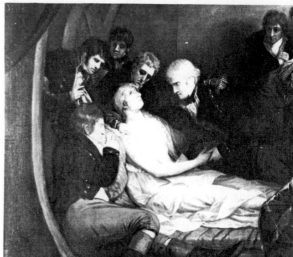

NELSON A painting depicting the death of Nelson at the Battle of Trafalgar in 1805.

united with Alsace-Lorraine, but there were many changes in the centuries that followed. The various states which made up the Netherlands passed, some by conquest and some by marriage, to the Dukes of Burgundy. Eventually they were inherited by the Emperor Charles V. His son was Philip II, husband of Mary of England, and his rule meant such oppression for the Dutch people that they rose in revolt under William of Orange. The revolt was successful in the northern provinces, but the southern provinces remained under Spain until 1714, when they eventually passed to Austria. Meantime under the House of Orange Holland was becoming a powerful country and was the rival of England in founding colonies. This rivalry led to war between the two countries under Cromwell and Charles II, but peace was made in 1678. Eleven years later William of Orange became king of Britain.

NEWCOMEN A print of Newcomen's engine used for pumping water out of mines. Built about 1717

France conquered Holland during the Napoleonic wars, but revolt soon followed, and Holland and Belgium were united as an independent kingdom, called the Netherlands. But the union did not last long, and in 1830 Belgium became a separate country. Both countries had to agree to be neutral and not make alliances with other countries. All the countries of Europe, on their part, promised to treat them as neutrals. Germany, however, broke this promise in 1914 when she invaded Belgium, and this was the immediate reason why Britain went to war with Germany then. In 1939 Germany invaded both Belgium and Holland so that neither of them could be neutral. [*See* WORLD WARS.]

NEWCOMEN, Thomas (1663–1729)
English engineer, born at Dartmouth. He was the first to develop and make use of the STEAM ENGINE. His engine was used to pump water out of the Cornish mines.

NEWFOUNDLAND
An island off the east coast of North America at the mouth of the Gulf of St. Lawrence and a province of Canada discovered by CABOT in 1497. It has a population of about 354,000. The capital is Saint John's. Included with Newfoundland is LABRADOR. The most important industries are fishing, manufacture of wood pulp for paper and the mining of iron, copper, zinc and gypsum. Gander is one of the important terminal airports on the North Atlantic air routes.

NEW GUINEA
This is the second largest (347,450 square miles) island in the world and is nearly four times bigger than Great Britain. It lies in the Pacific Ocean, north of Australia. The island is divided into three parts. The west part belonged to the Netherlands until 1963 when it became part of Indonesia. It is now called south-eastern Irian. The part which is called Papua belongs to Britain and is looked after by Australia. The third part in the north-east, belonged to Germany before the First World War but is now an International Trust Territory of the United Nations and is looked after by Australia.

British Papua (New Guinea) is nearly as large as France. The population is about 2 million. The capital is Port Moresby. The country produces gold, rubber and timber.

NEW HEBRIDES
A group of islands in the South Pacific Ocean that are called a 'condominium'. This means that more than one country rules them. In the

New Hebrides these two countries are Britain and France. There are about 66,000 inhabitants. The capital of the group is Vila on Efate Island.

NEWMAN, John Henry, Cardinal (1801–1890)
British theologian, born in London. He graduated at Oxford, and in 1828 was appointed vicar of St. Mary's Church, Oxford. There his preaching attracted wide attention. But in 1842 he resigned his position and three years later became a Catholic. He was ordained priest and appointed rector of the Roman Catholic University at Dublin. In 1879 he was created Cardinal. He wrote *The Dream of Gerontius* which ELGAR used for his oratorio of the same name. Newman also wrote hymns of which the best known is *Lead, Kindly Light*.

NEWSPAPERS
Periodical publications whose chief purpose is to give the latest information on matters of public interest.

The earliest attempts to supply a news service were the news letters, which were written by hand and were already popular in the reign of Elizabeth I. It was not till the reign of James I that the news letters began to be printed. Probably the first real newspaper was issued in 1622 and was called *Weekly News from Turkey, Hungary, Silesia, etc.* and was chiefly concerned with events of the Thirty Years War. The editors were Nicholas Bourne and Thomas Archer. In 1665 a newspaper appeared for the first time is still published regularly. This was *The London Gazette*, the official Government publication.

The first journalistic writer of importance was Daniel DEFOE, author of *Robinson Crusoe*. In 1704 he started a paper called *The Review*. In 1784 there appeared for the first time *The Times*, still the most renowned English newspaper. Its founder was John Walter. The best known journalist of the 19th century was Charles DICKENS who, in 1846, became the first editor of the *Daily News*.

Until the end of the 19th century newspapers were bought only by a few educated people and they did not cost a great deal of money to produce. Today the production of newspapers is a great national industry. There are today over 120 daily and sunday newspapers and over 1,200 weekly newspapers published in Britain. This is apart from technical papers and magazines of many kinds. The people of Britain buy more newspapers per person than any other country in the world except Sweden. Big changes in the ownership of newspapers and periodicals have taken place in Britain since the Second World War. Many of these have resulted in the closure of newspapers. Changes have also taken place in the ownership of periodicals and the International Publishing Corporation is now the largest publisher of periodicals in the world.

Because it was thought that some of these changes might be a threat to the freedom of the press, it was decided in 1953 that a Press Council should be set up. This is made up of representatives of newspaper proprietors and of working journalists, and ten years later it was decided that there should also be others not connected with newspapers. The Council not only tries to safeguard the freedom of the press but it also sees to it that newspapers and journalists maintain certain ethical standards.

NEWTON, Sir Isaac (1642–1727)
Born at Woolsthorpe, Lincolnshire. Son of a small farmer. He had a brilliant career as a student, and before he was 27 was elected Lucasian Professor of Mathematics at Cambridge. He remained for many years a university lecturer and teacher, and his early lectures on optics entirely discarded prevailing ideas about light, and substituted the results of his own research.

But already in 1666 there had occurred to him the two ideas with which his name is indelibly associated; the Laws of Gravitation, and the mathematics of fluxions, which we call the CALCULUS. It was Voltaire, the French writer, who first put into print the story of Newton, a young man in his twenties, sitting in his mother's orchard at Woolsthorpe and speculating upon the general forces which keep the planets in their courses, when he saw an over-ripe apple fall to the ground with a dull thud, pulled by the force of gravity. If the story is not true, then it ought to be, for Newton's unique contribution to man's knowledge lies in his establishment of the fact that the forces which control the fall of an apple from a tree are of the same order as those which govern the motion of a satellite round a planet, or a planet round a sun. It gave future scientists a frame upon which to work, upon which to build up more advanced theories. To express his ideas Newton developed the mathematics of fluxions, previously considered a difficult and clumsy science, so that from his day onwards mathematicians and scientists had a common language, as it were, in which they could express themselves. Newton's research laid the foundation of modern dynamics—the knowledge of how and why matter moves about in space. Newton's great work was set forth in the *Philosophiae Naturalis Principia Mathematica* (1687), generally called the *Principia*.

NEW ZEALAND
A British Dominion. It consists of a group of islands in the South Pacific Ocean, the two larger being North and South Island. These two islands are 104,000 square miles, about twice the size of England. The capital is Wellington on North Island, other important towns being Auckland, also on North Island, and Christchurch on South Island. On the Canterbury Plains on South Island are sheep which supply much mutton for Britain. New Zealand is also famous for its dairy produce. The population is about 2½ million, most of whom are of British descent but there are also a number of Maoris.

New Zealand rules a number of Pacific Islands, including the Cook Islands. She also is responsible for uninhabited land in the Antarctic Ocean.

New Zealand was discovered by TASMAN in 1642 and was explored by Captain COOK in 1769. The islands became British in 1840.

NIAGARA FALLS
One of the world's most spectacular falls located on the Niagara River between Lake Ontario and Lake Erie. The falls on the U.S. side, called American Falls, are 167 ft. high and 1,000 ft. across. On the Canadian side are Horseshoe Falls which are 160 ft. high and 2,000 ft. across. The Falls are used for the generation of hydro-electric power.

NEWTON His researches in physics and mathematics laid the foundations of modern science.

NICARAGUA
A republic and the largest country in Central America. It is 57,140 square miles, a little larger than England but has only a little over 1½ million inhabitants of whom most are of mixed Spanish and Indian origin. The capital is Managua. The country exports cotton, coffee and gold.

NICHOLSON, Sir William (1872–1949)
English painter, born at Newark. He is best known for his paintings of flowers and still-lifes. He was also a distinguished designer and with James Pryde produced a famous series of posters, they worked together under the name of 'Beggarstaff Brothers'. His son, Ben Nicholson (1894———), is a leading abstract painter.

NIETZSCHE, Friedrich Wilhelm (1844–1900)
German philosopher. Born in Prussian Saxony, and the son of a clergyman. After a brilliant university career at Bonn and Leipzig he was appointed, when only 24, professor of Greek at Basle University. This post he resigned on grounds of ill-health in 1879. He led a wandering life in Italy and Switzerland until he lost his reason. His philosophy, expressed in epigrammatic and lyrical style, is an attack on the humanitarian and democratic values of his time, and calls for a new breed of supermen to revitalise European society. His greatest work is *Thus Spake Zarathustra*.

NIGER
A large republic in Africa and takes its name from its chief river, the Niger. It is more than twice the size (484,000 square miles) of France but has a population of only about 3 million. The capital is Niamey. Except for a small area near the capital the country is mostly desert. The country was formerly part of French West Africa and became independent in 1958.

NIGERIA
On the west coast of Africa and is the largest African Member of the British Commonwealth. It is 357,000 square miles, more than three times bigger than Great Britain. There are about 55 million inhabitants who belong to three African racial groups—the Hausas, the Ibos and the Yorubas. The capital is Lagos, other important towns being Ibadan and Kano. Like NIGER the country takes its name from the River Niger. It produces cocoa, cotton and palm oil. The chief minerals are coal, tin and columbite and recently it has discovered some oil. Nigeria was formerly a British protectorate and became independent in 1960.

NIGHTINGALE, Florence (1820–1910)

Reformer of hospital nursing, known as 'the lady with the lamp'. Born in Florence. She trained as a nurse and, in spite of the opposition of her family, offered her services to the War Office when she heard of the sufferings of the wounded in the Crimean War against Russia. Accompanied by thirty-four nurses, she reached the Crimea in 1854, and gradually took over responsibility for the care of the sick and wounded. The sanitary arrangements were reformed and the death-rate from typhus, cholera and dysentery enormously reduced. She became famous thoughout Europe and her methods revolutionized British military hospitals.

NITROGEN

Symbol N, atomic number 7 and atomic weight 14·008. It is a colourless, odourless gas which makes up over three-quarters of the volume of the atmosphere, is widely distributed about the crust of the earth in combination with other elements and plays an important role in the world of plants and animals. Nitrogen is also an essential ingredient in many industrial processes, for example, dye-stuffs, ammonia, explosives, fertilizers, etc.

NOBEL, Alfred Bernhard (1833–1896)

Swedish engineer and inventor of dynamite. Born in Stockholm. Nobel was educated in Russia and the U.S.A. At first he worked with his father who was also an engineer. It was in 1867 that Nobel discovered the use of dynamite. From this and other discoveries, and his exploitation of the oil-fields at Baku in South Russia, Nobel amassed a huge fortune. On his death he left a large sum to be devoted to a fund for five annual prizes in physics, chemistry, medicine, literature and the cause of peace. They have been awareded since 1901. Their value is about £10,000 each.

NOLLEKENS, Joseph (1737–1823)

English sculptor, and one of the highest-paid artists of his age. Studied in Rome and elected to Royal Academy in 1772. Two of his best known works are busts of Dr. Johnson and Pitt. There are several tombs by him in Westminster Abbey. He and his wife were outstandingly mean.

NON-EUCLIDEAN GEOMETRY

Geometry developed out of attempts to prove Euclid's axiom: 'If a straight line falling on two straight lines makes the interior angles on the same side less than two right angles, the two straight lines, if produced indefinitely, meet on that side on which are the angles less

NIGHTINGALE Revolutionized the methods for the care and hygiene of wounded soldiers.

than two right angles.' This axiom defied proof, but led to a system of geometry which is more general, 'and in which two parallel lines can be drawn to a given line through a point, and in which the sum of the angles of a triangle is always less than two right angles'. An elementary introduction to this branch of geometry is contained in W. W. Sawyer's *Prelude to Mathematics*.

The founders of this system of geometry were Nikolai Ivanovich LOBACHEVSKY, Janos Bolyai, and Bernhard Riemann. Since the work of Albert EINSTEIN these geometrics have played an important part in modern physics and astronomy.

NON-FLOWERING PLANTS

There are many different kinds, divided into several groups. The first of these (Pteridophytes) includes the ferns, horse-tails and club mosses, all of which reproduce by means of sexual spores. They are not very large plants, but during the Carboniferous age they and their allies were large and numerous, a fact of great importance to us, for their remains were converted into coal.

The next group (Bryophytes) include mosses and liverworts, small plants, which, in addition to sexual reproduction, often have good means of vegetative reproduction. They are common inhabitants of damp banks, woods and heaths.

The next group (Algae) include green, brown, red and blue-green algae. Green algae are of many kinds, some of which consist of a single cell and some of many cells. They live on damp soil, tree trunks, and in fresh and salt water. The brown algae are the common seaweeds; some are small, but the giant kelps may reach a length of several hundred feet. The red algae are mostly marine, and some are used for food. The blue-green algae are small jelly-like plants which live in the soil.

The fungi form the next main group. They have no chlorophyll and cannot make food for themselves, so must live either as parasites (on living plants) or as saprophytes (on decaying plants or residues). They have very good means of a sexual and vegetative reproduction in addition to sexual reproduction. Typical examples include wart and blight diseases of potatoes, moulds, yeasts, mushrooms and toadstools, and rust and smut diseases of cereals.

The last group (BACTERIA) consist of minute cells, which occur in huge numbers in soil and in the digestive tracts of animals. They are useful in helping decay of plants in the soil, and in fixing nitrogen in the soil, but some cause harmful diseases, such as dysentery, diphtheria, and tuberculosis. [*See* BOTANY.]

NORDIC INVASIONS
Invasions of Central Europe by warlike tribes about 2000 B.C. Archaeologists can tell us something about them, but in Germany under the Nazis (1933–1945) these tribes were thought of as the heroic founders of their nation.

NATO
Means North Atlantic Treaty Organization. It was founded in 1949 by the countries of Western Europe and the United States and Canada as a defence against a future war. The area meant by 'North Atlantic' is described in the treaty as North of the Tropic of Cancer. The countries who joined NATO are Britain, U.S.A., France, Italy, Belgium, Netherlands, Norway, Denmark, Luxemburg, Portugal, Iceland, Turkey, Western Germany and Greece. The headquarters are in Paris but in 1966 France decided she wished to withdraw from the organization and asked for the headquarters to be removed from Paris.

NORTHERN IRELAND
Part of the United Kingdom. It is rather more than half the size of Wales and has about $1\frac{1}{2}$ million inhabitants. It is made up of six of the nine counties of Ulster. It has its own Parliament, but it also sends twelve M.P.s to the United Kingdom Parliament at Westminster. The capital is Belfast, which is famous for the manufacture of linen. [*See* EIRE.]

NORWAY
A kingdom in Northern Europe and one of the Scandinavian countries. It is more than half the size (125,000 square miles) of France but much of the country is near the Arctic and cannot produce food. There are only a little over $3\frac{1}{2}$ million inhabitants. The capital is Oslo. Norway is a very beautiful mountainous country and its forests produce timber for export. Norway has a large merchant navy and her fisheries are important.

Norway was united with Denmark from the 14th century to 1814 when it was linked with Sweden until 1905 when it became an independent kingdom.

NOVA SCOTIA [*See* CANADA.]

NUCLEAR ENERGY
This new source of power is obtained from the nucleus or central part of an atom, and has nothing to do with the electrons which revolve about it. The nucleus is extremely small; in fact, it occupies only about one million-millionth of the volume of the whole atom, but even so, it contains still smaller parts which can be separated. These are the protons and neutrons and the 'mesons' that seem to be necessary to hold the nucleus together.

In the nucleus of any atom these tiny particles are bound to each other by 'nuclear forces' of enormous strength, and the only way to separate them is to bombard them with high-speed protons, neutrons or other particles of about their own size by means of 'atom smashers' like the CYCLOTRON, but if we want to do it on a really large scale we have to make use of elements that are naturally radioactive. Such elements—and uranium is only one— keep shooting out particles on their own, without the assistance of any machinery, though the reason why they do so is not yet understood.

The most useful particles for bombarding atoms are neutrons, because they have no electric charge. Electrically-charged particles like protons have to smash their way through the barrier of electrons surrounding the atoms, but neutrons are not affected by electrons and slip through quite easily. When they strike the nucleus they may do one of two things. They may stick on to it, converting it into another isotope of the same element, or they may knock particles out of it and change it into a different element.

Now, when you have two or more things strongly bound together and force them apart, you release the force which bound them. It disappears, but it is not destroyed. Very often it takes the form of heat, but it escapes in some

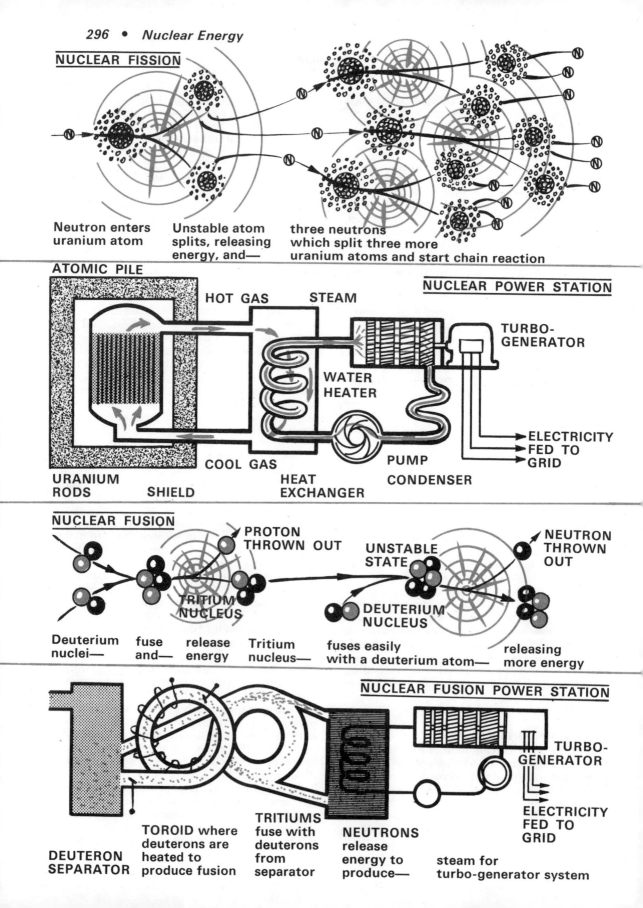

NUCLEAR FISSION

Neutron enters uranium atom

Unstable atom splits, releasing energy, and—

three neutrons which split three more uranium atoms and start chain reaction

ATOMIC PILE

HOT GAS   STEAM

NUCLEAR POWER STATION

TURBO-GENERATOR

WATER HEATER

COOL GAS

ELECTRICITY FED TO GRID

PUMP

URANIUM RODS   SHIELD   HEAT EXCHANGER   CONDENSER

NUCLEAR FUSION

PROTON THROWN OUT

UNSTABLE STATE

NEUTRON THROWN OUT

TRITIUM NUCLEUS

DEUTERIUM NUCLEUS

Deuterium nuclei—

fuse and—

release energy

Tritium nucleus—

fuses easily with a deuterium atom—

releasing more energy

NUCLEAR FUSION POWER STATION

TURBO-GENERATOR

ELECTRICITY FED TO GRID

DEUTERON SEPARATOR

TOROID where deuterons are heated to produce fusion

TRITIUMS fuse with deuterons from separator

NEUTRONS release energy to produce—

steam for turbo-generator system

form or other. Imagine two blocks of wood kept together by a strong elastic band. If you suddenly knock one of the blocks away, the elastic band will probably also fly off with considerable force. This is a picture of the binding force escaping when objects that are bound together are suddenly broken apart.

It will serve to illustrate what happens when the nucleus of an atom is broken up, though you must not, of course, apply it literally. There are no elastic bands in atoms! Instead, there are the nuclear forces and they may escape in the form of intense radiation, even more powerful than X-RAYS, or in the form of mechanical energy carried by protons, neutrons, mesons or other particles travelling away at very high speeds. This is the atomic energy that is manifest as heat in an atomic pile, and it can be used to heat the boiler of a steam-engine which will then drive an electric generator.

Each smashed atom produces an enormous quantity of energy *for its size*, but it is very, very small and to get enough to be useful many millions of millions of millions of atoms have to be smashed every second. You might think that this would mean consuming several tons of 'fuel', but atoms are so minute that the weight of a million million million of them is only about one six-millionth of an ounce! In an ounce of uranium only about 700,000 atoms break up naturally per second, and this is not nearly enough. The problem was solved when HAHN and Strassmann discovered in 1939 that a uranium atom could be split into two nearly equal portions by a fast neutron, because when that happens the smashed atom sends out *two more* fast neutrons in exchange.

This ought to start up a 'chain reaction', for each new neutron is capable of smashing another uranium atom, and at every step the number of atoms being split is doubled. The neutrons travel so fast that if you started with a few thousand you might expect to have millions of millions of millions within a fraction of a second. But there is a snag in this simple programme. It is that the neutrons suffer so many collisions that they soon lose speed and are unable to do their job. However, it was discovered that a rare isotope of uranium, known as U-235, can be split by slow neutrons, and this made the chain reaction possible.

Still another problem had to be solved before use could be made of it, because in any small piece of uranium-235 it was found that most of the neutrons escape from the surface and there are not enough left inside it to keep the chain reaction going. This difficulty was overcome in the first atomic bomb. Two pieces of U-235 were made that were not quite large enough

separately but would be more than large enough if put together. They had to be put together very quickly because of the speed at which even 'slow' neutrons travel, so one piece was shot against the other by a small charge of explosive. As soon as the two pieces met the chain reaction took place and it was all over in a fraction of a second. Though there was only a pound or two of uranium in the bomb the energy released was equal to that of 20,000 tons of T.N.T.

The next step was to find a way of releasing the energy more slowly. To do this, instead of putting lumps of U-235 close together, rods of ordinary U-238 mixed with a little U-235 were placed near to each other. The space between them was filled with graphite, and sometimes heavy water, these substances doing nothing but slow down the fast neutrons from the U-238 to the right speeds for splitting up the atoms of U-235. They are called 'moderators'.

This enabled the chain reaction to go on at a slow, steady rate, and so to release the nuclear energy as heat not much greater than is required to boil water. To make the process controllable a number of cadmium or boron rods were included among the others, for these substances are able to absorb neutrons if too many are being produced. The control rods can be moved in and out so as to keep the pile working at the required speed.

This was the first 'atomic pile' or nuclear reactor, as they are now called, and it was surrounded by a concrete shield several feet thick to absorb the dangerous gamma-rays and other radiations that are produced in enormous quantities when the pile is working. Such a pile may contain 250 tons of uranium, but every pound weight of uranium consumed gives as much heat as 1,500 tons of coal.

The 'consumption' of the uranium means the splitting of its atoms and the conversion of it into other, less useful elements. But something else goes on in the pile as well. The slow neutrons which are unable to split U-238 atoms nevertheless stick on to them and convert them into a new isotope of uranium, U-239. This is radioactive and throws off an electron, thus converting one of its neutrons into a proton and changing itself into the new element neptunium. The neptunium immediately throws off yet another electron and becomes plutonium. Now, plutonium has the same valuable properties as the rare U-235, so that the nuclear pile not only supplies heat—it also manufactures a valuable new 'fuel'.

Some modern nuclear reactors use pure U-235 or plutonium, and run at a high temperature. Others, known as 'breeder reactors', are designed especially to produce large quantities of fresh nuclear fuel, generally plutonium. Others, again, are run for the sake of the intense internal radiation they produce. Substances are put into them like cakes into an oven, so that the radiations will change them into radioactive isotopes.

Such artificially produced isotopes have many uses, both in science and industry. One, known as cobalt-60, is used in hospitals instead of the much more expensive radium for treating certain diseases. Another, caesium-137, is used by engineers for testing the soundness of metal. Still others, such as phosphorus-32, iodine-131 and iron-59, are used by chemists and biologists as 'tracers.' They can be incorporated in chemical compounds, or swallowed with food, and their readily detected radiations will then betray their subsequent positions.

The process of splitting atoms is called 'fission,' but it is also possible to obtain atomic energy by forcing atoms together. This is called 'fusion' and it takes place only at very high temperatures. If four hydrogen atoms are forced to unite to make a helium atom, a very great deal of atomic energy is released. This process is used in the hydrogen bomb, but so far nobody has discovered how to make it take place slowly so that the energy can be put to good use.

NUFFIELD, William Richard Morris, First Viscount (1877–1963)

British industrialist and philanthropist. Born in Worcester, the son of a farmer. As a young man he set up in business for himself at Cowley, near Oxford, making and repairing bicycles. He then turned to motor-cycles, and in 1912 built the first Morris Oxford cars. They were very popular and in 1925 he created a European record by producing 53,000 cars in a year. Later he established the vast Nuffield Organization to produce every type of motor vehicle. As a philanthropist he gave large sums to Oxford University to advance the study of medicine. He also founded Nuffield College and financed the Nuffield Foundation as a charitable trust.

NYASALAND [*See* MALAWI.]

NYLON

Name for a family of plastics, known as polyamides, discovered by Dr. W. H. Carothers and his colleagues in the laboratories of E. I. Du Pont de Nemours Inc., U.S.A., in 1930, and first announced to the public in 1938. The discovery was the result of scientific research to find out how and why certain molecules unite to form 'giant molecules', such as those in cotton, wood, rubber, silk, and resins. The Du Pont chemists found that they could make a kind of giant molecule which they called a 'linear polymer'. Nylon was discovered quite accidentally when a chemist found that one of the new synthetic substances being examined could, when in the molten state, be drawn into a long fibre which, even when cold, was capable of being drawn still further. The fibre formed in this way was strong, elastic and silk-like. This was nylon, the first wholly man-created fibre made from two chemical compounds, hexamethylene diamine and adipic acid. The first named chemical is made from coal (coke), air and water; from cyclohexane, a petroleum product, or from furfural, an agricultural by-product. Adipic acid is made either from coke, air, and water, or from cyclohexane. The diamine and acid are combined to form 'nylon salt', which gives molten nylon when heated. This is extruded through tiny holes in a steel plate to form filaments. These are stretched to between four and seven times their original length and twisted into a thread suitable for use by textile manufacturers. Apart from its well-known uses in the production of fine hosiery, nylon is extensively employed as brush filling or tufting materials, and nylon moulding powder is used for moulding self-lubricating bearings, unbreakable combs, washable buttons, ropes, cables, etc.

NUCLEAR ENERGY One of the first experiments in the search to unlock the energy in the atom was carried out at the Cavendish Laboratory, Cambridge, in 1932. The simple apparatus used is shown in the photograph below.

Oo

OASIS
An area in a desert region with enough water to make it fertile. This may range from a simple water hole surrounded with date palms to largish areas growing vegetables and other crops. The water may be present either by a well [*see* ARTESIAN WELL] or irrigation.

OBOE [*See* INSTRUMENTS OF THE ORCHESTRA]

O'CASEY, Sean (1884–1966)
Irish playwright, born in Dublin. Came from a very poor family, and in his early life worked as a navvy. His best-known plays are *Juno and the Paycock* and *The Plough and the Stars*.

OCEANIA
An area which extends from Australia, in the west, to the islands of POLYNESIA, in the east, and from New Zealand, in the south, to MICRONESIA and the Sandwich Islands, in the north. The area is divided into three, Polynesia, MELANESIA and Micronesia.

OCEANOGRAPHY
Study of the sea using the knowledge of all the sciences. For example: study of the ocean bed by marine geologists, chemical properties of seawater by chemists, life in the sea by marine biologists, physical properties of seawater such as temperature, pressure and density by physicists, and others such as mathematicians, geophysicists, hydrographers, botanists and meteorologists. Although oceanography is quite a young science it is becoming increasingly important, particularly now that we are looking to the sea more and more to produce foodstuffs.

OCELOT
Strongly built, savage cat of Central and South America. It has a tail that is rather short, a coat of variable pattern (leopard-like), and has a large pink nose.

OCTOPUS
Related to the squids and cuttlefish, and classified with the MOLLUSCS. It has eight arms, the tentacles found in the squid being absent. The common octopuses of European waters inhabit shallows where they hunt for crabs, which they paralyse by injecting them with a poisonous fluid. The giant octopus attains a total span of about 32 feet.

ODE
Among the ancient Greek poets the ode was stately, elaborate, and complicated, particularly as developed by the poet Pindar, many of whose great works have come down to us. The Roman poets of the age of Augustus borrowed the idea of the ode from the Greeks, but made their odes more concise, sometimes more austere, and sometimes more personal. In MILTON and his friend MARVELL we find the influence of the Latin odes of HORACE. Marvell's ode describing the execution of Charles I has simplicity and severity:

> He nothing common did, or mean,
>   Upon that memorable scene
>   But laid his comely head
>   Down as upon a bed.

At the outset of the 19th century the Romantic poets, especially KEATS, made odes which combine a traditional scheme with passionate and personal tones, and which were truly English, for example, the *Ode to a Nightingale*.

OERSTED, Hans Christian (1777–1851)
Danish scientist, born at Rudkjöbing. His most important work was to prove by experiment the connection between electricity and magnetism and founded the study of 'electromagnetism'. He was the first to isolate aluminium. Oersted also wrote books on popular science.

OFFENBACH, Jacques (1819–1880)
German-Jewish composer, born at Cologne.

OCTOPUS paralyses its victims with poison.

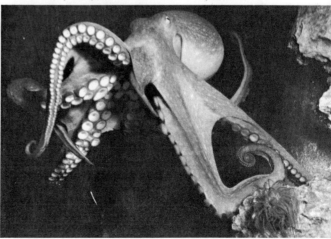

He is particularly famous for his light operas, for example, *La Belle Hélène*. Perhaps his greatest work is *The Tales of Hoffman*.

OHM, Georg Simon (1787–1854)

German scientist, born at Erlangen. His main work was concerned with electricity, and it was he who discovered the law of conduction. This is known as Ohm's Law and is: volts = current × resistance. The unit of resistance, the ohm, was named in honour of his work. The ohm is defined as the resistance offered by a column of mercury 106·3 inches long, of uniform cross-sectional area and with a mass of 14·4521 gm. at 0°C.

OKAPI

This rather rare animal is related to the giraffe, although it is much smaller and without a very long neck. It inhabits the Semliki and Ituri forests of the Upper Congo (Africa).

OLYMPIC GAMES

Competitive sports event held every four years and athletes from every country in the world compete. The games were first held (776 B.C.) at Olympia, and were in honour of the Greek god Zeus. The revival was started in 1896 at Athens.

OMAR KHAYYAM (*c.* 1050–*c.* 1123)

Persian poet, astronomer and mathematician, born at Naishapur. He helped to revise the Persian calendar, compiled astronomical tables and wrote on mathematics. He was chiefly known in Europe as author of a book on

OKAPI A rare African forest animal.

OLYMPICS 1960, a close finish to the 100 metres.

algebra until Edward Fitzgerald translated into English one of his long poems—*The Rubaiyat* (1859). It is in quatrains, and its theme is the praise of love and wine.

O'NEILL, Eugene Gladstone (1888–1954)

American dramatist, born at New York. Although born into a theatrical family he worked at various jobs (seaman, prospector, etc.) before turning to writing plays. Three of his best-known works are *The Emperor Jones*, *Anna Christie* and *Mourning Becomes Electra*; all three have been made into films. In 1936 he became the first American dramatist to be awarded the Nobel Prize for Literature.

ONOMATOPOEIA

This name, which sounds awkward in English because of its Greek origin, is used for a word, or a sequence of words, which tries to echo the sense it expresses. A number of onomatopoeic words have come into the English vocabulary—*buzz, hiss, hush, bang, clatter*. In poetry the poet often wants to imitate the sound of what he describes. Almost every poet has some skill in choosing and arranging his words to get this effect. Alexander Pope in his poem about poetry called *An Essay on Criticism* has commented on the use of it with some striking examples of how it can be done. In the 19th century Tennyson made great use of onomatopoeia.

OPERA

Stage entertainment, consisting of a play sung to music in its entirety, with no spoken dialogue at all. It originated in Italy about 1600, since when it has spread to all countries. Three of the greatest opera-composers are MOZART, WAGNER, and VERDI. English operas have been written by PURCELL (*Dido and Aneas*), Vaughan WILLIAMS (*The Pilgrim's Progress*) and Benjamin BRITTEN (*Peter Grimes*). [*See* MASQUE.]

OPERETTA

Stage entertainment of the operatic type, but lighter in character and having a certain amount of spoken dialogue. A typical example is Johann STRAUSS's *Die Fledermaus* (*The Bat*).

OPOSSUM

The most familiar member of this family is the American opossum which is found in both North and South America. It is nocturnal, i.e., it hunts food by night and sleeps during the day, usually in a hollow stump. When attacked it feigns death by rolling over on its side and lapsing into a state of 'coma'; it is from this that the saying 'playing possum' comes. Other members of this family are the crab-eating opossum, the murine opossum, and the water opossum; the latter two are found in South America.

OPPENHEIMER, J. Robert (1904–1967)

American physicist and director of the Los Almos research project which made the first atomic bomb. After the Second World War he opposed the further development and expansion of nuclear weapons and was suspected by the Committee of Un-American Activities of being a communist.

OPTICS

Branch of physics concerned with the study of light. [*See* LIGHT, MICROSCOPE and TELESCOPE.]

ORATORIO

Large-scale musical composition on a religious subject, for solo singers, chorus and orchestra; it usually tells a Bible story. The best-known of all oratorios is HANDEL's *Messiah*; other outstanding examples are Haydn's *Creation*, MENDELSSOHN's *Elijah* and, in more recent times, Sir William WALTON's *Belshazzar's Feast*.

ORCHESTRA [*See* INSTRUMENTS OF THE ORCHESTRA]

ORDERS AND DECORATIONS

For many centuries it has been the custom for the Sovereign to show favour to distinguished persons by bestowing upon them an Order of Chivalry. Some of these Orders go back to the Middle Ages. The oldest English Order is that of the Garter, which was founded by Edward III. There is a story told that the King was

dancing with the Countess of Salisbury when she dropped her garter and that as he handed it back to her the King said to his Courtiers, *Honi soit qui mal y pense* ('Shame to him who thinks evil of it'). This incident is supposed to have given the King the idea of creating the Order, but the story is only a tradition. The Garter is a ribbon of dark blue velvet with the motto in letters of gold. It is worn on the left leg below the knee. Each knight has a stall in St. George's Chapel, Windsor.

The next oldest Order is the Order of the Bath which was founded by Henry IV in 1399. Sometimes in the Middle Ages it was the custom for one who was to be made a knight to have a bath as a symbol of purification. They were then called Knights of the Bath to distinguish them from other Knights. After the reign of Charles II the ceremony fell into disuse. The Order was, however, re-formed in 1725.

The Order of the Thistle, founded in 1687, is a Scottish Order, and that of St. Patrick, founded in 1783, an Irish one.

In 1818, the Prince Regent, afterwards George IV, founded the Order of St. Michael and St. George. Letters after a Knight's name such as K.C.B. (Knight Commander of the Bath) or K.C.M.G. (Knight Commander of St. Michael and St. George) show the Order to which he belongs.

When the Sovereign bestows any of these Orders on a person and so creates him a knight she usually does it on the recommendation of the Prime Minister. There is, however, one Order which is the Sovereign's personal Order, and no Prime Minister has ever recommended any Sovereign to bestow it on someone. This is the Victorian Order, created in 1896. There are five classes in the Order, and in addition there is the Victorian Medal in three categories —silver-gilt, silver and bronze.

The last Order to be created was that of the British Empire, founded in 1917 by Georve V. This Order made it possible, for the first time, to give a title to women as well as men. There are five classes—Knights and Dames grand cross, commanders, officers, and members.

There is one Order, founded in 1902, which does not confer Knighthood. This is the Order of Merit. It is, however, one of the highest distinctions and its membership is limited to twenty-four, except for honorary foreign members.

Although all these Orders are given as awards to British civilians or Service people who have served their country or the commonwealth, an Order is sometimes given to the sovereign of another country, or some other distinguished foreigner, if it is desired to show him special honour.

Apart from the Orders of Chivalry there are many other distinctions which the Sovereign can award. Some of these are only given to those who have distinguished themselves in the armed forces. The most important of these is the Victoria Cross, created by Queen Victoria in 1856. Until 1942 Victoria Crosses were struck from the metal of the guns captured by the British at Sevastopol during the Crimean War. Now, as there is no more of this metal, the crosses are made from gunmetal from the Royal Mint. The Victoria Cross is given for conspicuous bravery, and the V.C. is worn before all other decorations.

Civilians who show conspicuous bravery may be awarded the George Medal which was instituted by George VI in 1940.

Foreign countries have their own Orders and decorations, some of which also go back to the Middle Ages.

Apart from medals and decorations awarded by the Sovereign there are some organizations, such as the Royal Humane Society, which also give medals for bravery.

ORE
Mineral mined or quarried for the extraction of a metal. Many ores, like some of those yielding iron and copper, occur in massive layers like beds of rock (strata). Others take the form of crystals lining fissures and cavities in the rocks. Such crystals are usually deposited by percolating water, but are sometimes derived from vapours and liquids of volcanic origin. Fissures thus filled with mineral ores are called 'veins' or 'lodes', and among the metals obtained from them are tin and lead. Most ores consist of a combination of the metal with either sulphur or oxygen (and sometimes carbon as well), and the process of extracting the metal is called 'smelting'.

ORELLANA, Francisco de (*died* 1546)
Spanish soldier and explorer. Discovered the Amazon river. While travelling down the river he claimed to have been attacked by a tribe of female warriors, and it is from this that the river got its name.

ORGAN
Musical instrument with one or more keyboards, the keys being attached to pipes which are made to sound by forcing air through them. In early times, organs were merely flat boxes with one keyboard; they were placed on a table and pumped by bellows, and the keys were so wide and heavy that they had to be played with the fist! Later the keys became smaller, and more keyboards with extra pipes were added; a pedal keyboard for the feet came into use in the 18th century. Large modern organs have as many as five keyboards, with thousands of pipes; the mechanism is pneumatic, and the wind supply controlled by electricity.

ORGANIC CHEMISTRY
Was at one time considered to be the branch or chemistry that dealt with organic substances, whether animal or vegetable, for it was thought that such complex substances could not be made from ordinary inorganic chemicals. But this was proved possible. Nevertheless, it is realized that all organic substances contain carbon—there are some half a million carbon compounds—and these compounds, though subject to the general laws of chemistry, have characteristics that are distinctly different from those of inorganic compounds. So organic chemistry can be taken to mean the chemistry of carbon compounds.

The characteristics of organic chemistry are several. Tnere is the enormous complexity and molecular weight of very many organic compounds, molecular weights sometimes estimated in thousands. There is the existence of complicated radicals. For example, the benzoyl radical, the first to be discovered, is represented by the formula $C_6H_5 . CO—$. This can combine with oxygen and hydrogen to form benzoic acid, with hydrogen to form oil of bitter almonds, with chlorine to form benzoyl chloride, and so on. Another feature of organic chemistry is the possibility of substitution, which is the replacement of one or more atoms by other atoms or radicals.

Peculiar to organic chemistry is the notion of shape in molecular structure in the sense that a straightforward formula is not sufficient, for it has been found that there can exist two or more compounds with the same basic formula but different properties. For example, the formula C_2H_6O has two possibilities as shown:

The two different substances, (i) is dimethyl ether and (ii) is ordinary ethyl alcohol, are said to be isomers and have to be represented by diagrammatic formulae of the sort shown. This need for pictorial formulae and the further need for three-dimensional formulae is a feature of organic chemistry.

Organic compounds are divided into two

broad types, *viz.* aliphatic, or open-chain, compounds in which the carbon atoms are linked end on end, and cyclic, or closed-ring, compounds in which carbon atoms or carbon and others are linked in a closed chain. So organic chemistry could be described as the study of aliphatic and cyclic carbon compounds.

OROZCO, José Clemente (1883–1949)

Mexican painter, born in Zapatlan. He was greatly influenced by AZTEC art and much of his work is concerned with his people's struggle for freedom from oppression. His paintings decorate many public buildings in Mexico.

ORWELL, George (1905–1950)

English writer, born in India. His writings are mainly concerned with the poor and downtrodden, and the loss of liberty of the individual. Two of his most famous books are *Animal*

porarily produced a visible pattern or wave form of some fluctuating electrical quantity such as voltage. It is employed to reveal the detailed variations in rapidly changing electric currents, potentials or pulses. It is also used to study sound waves. [*See* ELECTRONICS.]

OTTER

Belongs to the weasel family, but is easily distinguished by the features it has developed for an aquatic life. The hind feet are much larger than the fore feet, and are provided with very long, fully-webbed toes; the fore feet are also webbed. The head is flattened, with small eyes and ears, and the fur is dense and impervious to water. Otters are found almost all over the world, except Australia. The sea otter is a much more heavily-built animal. At one time it was abundant on the North Pacific coasts, but has almost been exterminated for the sake of its valuable fur.

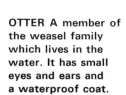
OTTER A member of the weasel family which lives in the water. It has small eyes and ears and a waterproof coat.

Farm, a satire on the course of Russian communism, and *Nineteen Eighty-Four*, a prophetic novel about a state in which science controls even man's thoughts.

OSBORNE, John James (1929———)

British playwright and actor. His play *Look Back in Anger* began a phase during which the theatre became obsessed with 'angry young men' and their attacks on the established order of life.

OSCILLOSCOPE

An instrument consisting of a CATHODE-RAY tube on the fluorescent screen of which is tem-

OTTOMAN EMPIRE

Founded by the Moslem Turkish leader Osman I (1259–1326), and reached its height in the 16th century. At its peak the Empire comprised what we know as modern Turkey, Hungary, Algiers and parts of Greece, Arabia and PERSIA. The final collapse was at the end of the First World War and under the leadership of Mustafa Kemal, called Kemal ATATURK, the modern democratic Turkey was born.

OVERTURE

A musical composition that is played before an opera or oratorio. Such a work is usually composed of tunes in the opera. The concert overture is a large-scale work played at orchestral concerts; a particularly famous one is TCHAIKOVSKY'S *Romeo and Juliet*.

OVID, properly Publius Ovidius Naso (43 B.C.–A.D. 17)

Roman poet of the Augustan age. He threw away the chance of a great legal and public career and turned to writing. As a young man he wrote a tragedy, *Medea*; some imaginary love-letters (*Heroides*); and some short poems about his mistress, Corinna (*Amores*). Later came the *Ars Amatoria*, a work that reflected the carefree standards that were fashionable at the time, and therefore challenged Augustus's plan for moral reform. This was partly responsible for his banishment nine years later, which interrupted the revising of the *Metamorphoses*, narrative poems based on legendary material, and the *Fasti*. His complaints from the town of Tomi, on the Danube, where he stayed in exile until his death, are embodied in the *Tristia* and in the *Epistolae ex Ponto*.

Ovid has been accused of lacking dignity, manliness and reverence. Nevertheless, no Roman poet displayed such kindly sincerity, such enjoyment of life and imaginative vision, and such appreciation of the beauty and forms of nature. We are indebted to him for passing on the spirit of the world of Greek romance to influence the literature of the Italian Renaissance, and to supply material for its great painters; and for his influence on Marlowe, Shakespeare, Milton and Pope.

OWEN, Robert (1771–1858)

Pioneer of social reform and the Co-operative Movement. Born at Newtown, Montgomeryshire. He founded in New Lanark a community which worked in ideal conditions and shared in the profits of the business. He wrote a large number of pamphlets on socialism, co-operative movements, child education, working conditions in factories, etc.

OWEN, Wilfred (1893–1918)

English poet, born at Oswestry. Owen, killed fighting in the last year of the First World War, left some moving poems, particularly poems dealing, like *Strange Meeting*, with the brotherhood of man as discovered even by enemies on the battlefield. The poems which Owen and certain other young soldiers like him were writing in 1918 greatly influenced later poets. Some of his poetry has been included in Benjamin BRITTEN'S *War Requiem*.

OXYGEN

Most abundant of all elements and composes about one half of the crust of the earth, by weight. Its symbol is O, atomic weight 16 and atomic number 8. Besides being a key element in water and the atmosphere, it is present in all living things. It is an essential element in the process of combustion. Ozone is a gas, the molecules of which are composed of 3 oxygen atoms (O_3). Discovered by Joseph PRIESTLEY who announced his discovery in 1774.

Pp

PACIFIC OCEAN

The largest ocean, about 70,000,000 sq. miles, and boasts the greatest known ocean depth which is located near Mindanao in the Philippines and measures 35,410 feet. Was named by Ferdinand MAGELLAN.

PADEREWSKI, Ignace Jan (1860–1941)

Polish musician, born at Kurilowka. Although he composed quite a lot of music his fame rests on his greatness as a pianist. He was a great defender of Polish liberty, and for a few years after the First World War was President.

PAGANINI, Niccolo (1784–1840)

Italian violinist, born at Genoa. He came of a poor family, but rose to be the greatest violinist of his day. He did much to further the technique of violin playing, and was also a composer, though his compositions seem to have been mainly designed to show off his own technical brilliance.

PAINE, Thomas (1737–1809)

English writer on politics and religion, born in Norfolk. Emigrated to America in 1774. There he served in the American Government and Army, supporting the war against England. He returned to England in 1787, and shortly afterwards issued the first part of *The Rights of Man*, a defence of the French Revolution, in reply to BURKE'S *Reflections*. When he issued the second part he had to flee to France to escape prosecution. Elected a member of the Convention he voted with the liberal Girondin party. This offended ROBESPIERRE and the Jacobins, and Paine was imprisoned in 1794 for eleven months. In *The Age of Reason*, published at this time, he attacked revealed religion. In 1802 he went again to America, where he died.

PAINTING AND DRAWING

These date back to the dawn of man's history and know no boundaries of race or place. Both are forms of art practised by primitive, ancient and modern men in all corners of the world.

Painting. The first paintings of ancient man so far discovered are those which decorate the grotto at LASCAUX (France) and were painted some 20,000 years ago. What should be noted is that these paintings are not just of interest to the archaeologist, but are magnificent works in their own right and still compare with any animal paintings done since. They were, however, not painted to decorate the cave, but for magical purposes.

The ancient Egyptians were great artists in paint and stone. They decorated their homes, temples and tombs with wall paintings depicting a wide variety of subjects; aspects of everyday life, religious incidents, family groups, animal life, etc.

The Classical Ages (Greek and Roman) were quite as famous for their painters as their sculptors, although the latter are much better known. The main source of our knowledge of Greek painting comes from the beautifully painted pottery. Their great contribution was to draw what they saw, and not follow a set rule as did the Egyptians.

The next stage in the history of Western art is what is called the Byzantine style, which was essentially a religious art with rigid rules of what subjects should be depicted and what form they should take. This style was to last until GIOTTO, who was the first European painter to attempt to present religious subjects with an eye to nature, and not in the style of the fixed discipline of Byzantine art. Although Giotto's works contained Byzantine elements his new vision truly opened the gates of creative activity which reached its height in the paintings of LEONARDO DA VINCI. It should be appreciated that there was intense activity in painting in most European countries during this period, in fact, one of the greatest advances in painting can be credited to Jan Van EYCK, the Flemish artist, who painted what he saw in the finest—almost photographic—detail.

From the time of the Renaissance until the Moderns there was no great revolution such as had been ushered in by Giotto or Van Eyck.

PAINTING *Above*, a Byzantine-style illustration from an early manuscript and *below*, a high Renaissance religious subject by Da Vinci.

There were, of course, great artists, but their greatness was in their vision and individual styles.

The modern revolution in painting took place in France and its greatest figure was undoubtedly Paul CEZANNE. This is strange, for he did not set out to be a revolutionary painter. His life was mainly spent at his native Aix-en-Provence where he led a quiet and orderly life. However, his greatness was soon recognized by such artists as PICASSO. After Cézanne came VAN GOGH and GAUGUIN.

The opening of the 20th century was a period of open revolt against the past and saw the birth of such schools as Expressionism, Cubism, Surrealism, Abstract art, and many other lesser styles. The greatest figure in this period is Picasso.

The development of drawing follows closely that of painting.

PAINTING *Above*, one of Paul Cézanne's powerful impressionist portraits and *below*, a cubist still-life from Pablo Picasso.

PAKISTAN

An Islamic republic within the British Commonwealth. It is divided into two parts—West Pakistan, which is by far the larger, and East Pakistan. They are separated from one another by over a thousand miles of Indian territory. The country is about four times larger (366,000 square miles) than Great Britain and has a population of about 94 million. The capital is the new city of Islamabad, near Rawalpindi. Its former capital was the important port and city of Karachi. Another famous and older city is Lahore.

In East Bengal much of the world's jute is produced. Pakistan also grows and exports cotton and tea. Pakistan has few minerals but since the Second World War she has discovered vast quantities of natural gas, chiefly near Sui, and this is greatly helping her industries.

Pakistan came into being in 1947 when British rule ended in the great sub-continent. The northern part, almost entirely Moslem, led by Mohammed Ali Jinnah, declared its wish to become a separate State. So the two countries of INDIA and Pakistan were established as separate independent States within the British Commonwealth. In March 1971 East Pakistan was declared an independent republic under the name Bangla Desh and civil war broke out. Eventually peace was restored, the new State was recognized, and Bangla Desh was admitted to the Commonwealth on 18 April 1972.

PALESTINE

The name given to the ancient Biblical lands which, since 1947, have been divided between ISRAEL and JORDAN.

PALESTRINA, Giovanni Pierluigi da
(c. 1526–1594)
Italian composer, born in Rome. The greatest composer of the Renaissance, and one of the finest church composers of all time. His most famous work is the Mass for Pope Marcellus (*Missa Papae Marcelli*) and he also composed motets, hymns and madrigals.

PALGRAVE, Francis Turner (1824–1897)
British anthologist, born at Great Yarmouth. After graduating at Oxford he became private secretary to W. E. Gladstone and then entered the Education Office. On his retirement he was appointed Professor of Poetry at Oxford (1886). He wrote many volumes of poetry and essays, but he is best remembered for his anthology of English poetry, *The Golden Treasury*, which was first published in 1861 and has frequently been revised.

PALMER, Samuel (1805–1881)
English artist, born at Newington. He was a friend of William BLAKE and his early work was much influenced by him. His best work was done whilst he was living at Shoreham, Kent, and concerned with pastoral beauty and Christian symbolism—Blake's influence. His later work, landscapes, were rather conventional and lacked the lustrous quality of the Shoreham works.

PALMERSTON, Henry John Temple, 3rd Viscount (1784–1865)
English statesman, born in Hampshire. He became Tory M.P. for Newport, Isle of Wight, in 1807, but in 1828 he switched his allegiances to the Whigs. He was Secretary for Foreign Affairs (1830–1834, 1835–1841, 1846–1851), and helped in the separation of Belgium and Holland and tried to prevent the spread of Russian influence in the East. Later came the Revolutions of 1848 and the quarrels with Spain and Greece to trouble his period of office. In 1855–1858 and 1859–1865 he was First Lord of the Treasury (i.e. Prime Minister) and proceeded with the Crimean War. He was a determined and forceful politician, which earned him the name 'firebrand Palmerston'.

PANAMA
A Central American republic through which runs the Panama Canal. Panama is about the size (31,900 square miles) of Scotland with a population of a little over 1 million. Most of the people are of mixed Spanish and Indian descent. The capital is Panama City. The country produces bananas, cocoa, coffee and rubber.

Panama used to be part of Colombia until

PANDA The giant panda found only in China.

1903 but because of a quarrel over the making of the canal it became a separate country.

PANAMA CANAL
Separates North and South America. It belongs to the Panama Canal Company and so does some land, called the Canal Zone, which borders the canal. There are about 50,000 people living in the Zone which is administered by a Governor appointed by the United States.

PANDA
There are two members of this family, the giant panda, found only in Szechwan, China, and the small cat-bear found in the Himalayas and Assam. The giant panda is very distinctive because of its white face and dark eye patches. It lives entirely on bamboo shoots and is very difficult to rear in a zoo. The cat-bear is not unlike a raccoon and has brown fur and, like the giant panda, eye patches.

PANGOLIN
The most striking thing about this animal is its protective coating of overlapping spiny scales. When attacked the pangolin rolls up like a hedgehog and emits a foul smell. The most commonly known species is the thick-tailed pangolin of India; other members of this family are to be found in China, Ceylon, Java, and Africa.

PANTHER [*See* LEOPARD]

PAPAL STATE [*See* VATICAN CITY]

PAPER
Usually refers to the substance made from fibrous materials and used in the printing of books, papers, etc. It is also used for wrapping up and protecting goods.

The ancient Egyptians used a paper made

from the papyrus plant; the name paper, in fact, comes from this. Paper as we understand it was introduced into Europe by the MOORS, who acquired their knowledge from the Chinese, who had long known the secret of making paper. From records it would appear that paper was introduced into England about the 14th century, and the first paper mill started about the beginning of the 16th century.

Today many grades of paper are made for special purposes. The highest grade of paper is made from pure rag; next is that made from a mixture of rag and wood-pulp, then that composed of esparto grass, and finally newsprint (paper on which newspapers are printed) from woodpulp; these are basic types and there are many grades in between.

The following are the standard sizes of paper:

WRITING		BOOKS	
NAME	SIZE in inches	NAME	SIZE in inches
Pott	15 × 12½	Foolscap 8vo	6¾ × 4¼
Brief	16½ × 13¼	Crown 8vo	7½ × 5
Foolscap	17 × 13½	Large Crown 8vo	8 × 5¼
Post	19 × 15¼	Demy 8vo	8⅜ × 5⅝
Demy	20 × 15½	Medium 8vo	9½ × 6
Medium	22 × 17½	Royal 8vo	10 × 6¼
Royal	24 × 19	Super Royal 8vo	10¼ × 6⅞
Cartridge	26 × 21	Imperial 8vo	11 × 7½
Elephant	28 × 23	Foolscap 4to	8½ × 6¾
Imperial	30 × 22	Crown 4to	10 × 7½
Colombier	34½ × 23½	Demy 4to	11¼ × 8¾
Atlas	34 × 26	Royal 4to	12½ × 10
Double Elephant	40 × 26¾	Imperial 4to	15 × 11
Grand Eagle	42 × 28¾	Music	14 × 10¼
Antiquarian	53 × 31		
Emperor	72 × 48		

Note

8vo means "octavo", or the sheet divided into eight.
4to means "quarto" or the sheet divided into four.

PARACELSUS, Phillippus Aureolus
(1493–1541)

Swiss alchemist and physician. Made important advances in practical medicine, recognized the value of cleanliness in medical practice. Was the first to note occupational diseases as a result of his studies of mining and smelting.

PARAGUAY

An island republic in South America through which runs a river of the same name. The country is about three times the size (157,000 square miles) of England and has less than 2 million inhabitants. Nearly all the people are farmers, rearing cattle and growing rice, cotton and tobacco. The capital is Asuncion, one of the oldest cities in South America and in 1535 was the centre from which the Spaniards colonized the continent.

PARISH COUNCIL

The smallest and also the oldest type of LOCAL AUTHORITY in England and Wales. Today Parish Councils are to be found only in villages and have little work to do, most of the duties being carried out by the RURAL DISTRICT COUNCIL. A Parish Council consists of from five to fifteen members. Although today Parish Councils have little authority, in days gone by all local government work was done by the Parish Council.

PARLIAMENT

The body which makes the laws of the land. At the head is the SOVEREIGN. Parliament consists of two Houses, or Chambers: the House of Commons and the House of Lords. All Members of the Government are Members of either the House of Commons or the House of Lords. Their seats are on the Front, or TREASURY Bench.

The name Parliament has been used since the year 1275 to describe those chosen to help the King rule. The national assembly of 1265, which Simon de Montfort summoned to Lewes, is regarded as the first real meeting of Parliament because the boroughs as well as the shires were represented. At first Lords and Commons met in the same Chamber but after a time they found it more convenient to meet separately.

The House of Lords is not elected by the people. Most of the Members are Peers and are called Lords Temporal. A few of the Members are important Judges and are called the Law Lords. They sit in the House of Lords because in addition to helping to make laws the House of Lords has also sometimes to sit as a Court of Law. The Archbishops and some of the Bishops are also Members of the House of Lords. They are called the Lords Spiritual.

The Queen's throne is in the House of Lords, and it is from here that she reads speeches to Parliament. The Chairman of the House of Lords is the LORD CHANCELLOR.

The House of Commons is elected by the people. [For the way this is done *see* GENERAL ELECTION.] The Chairman is called the SPEAKER. Since 1911 the last word as to whether a BILL shall become law or not has been with the House of Commons, and not with the House of Lords. All Bills must be discussed by both

PARTHENON The ancient Greeks built this masterpiece to crown the Acropolis.

Houses, but if the two Houses disagree at the end of about a year the House of Commons has the right to decide the matter.

Only the House of Commons can decide what is to be done with the nation's money, and for this reason the CHANCELLOR OF THE EXCHEQUER must always be a Member of the House of Commons.

The Parliamentary session usually begins in the autumn. If any Bill is not ready for the Queen's assent by the time the Parliamentary session ends, the Bill will have to be introduced into the next session of Parliament as a new Bill as the work of one session cannot be carried on from one session to another.

Parliament meets in the Palace of Westminster. In the Middle Ages this palace was the home of the King. In 1512 the palace was badly damaged by burning so the King allowed the House of Commons, which was then meeting in the Chapter House of Westminster Abbey, to move to the Chapel of St. Stephen in Westminster Palace. In 1834 the whole of the Palace, except Westminster Hall, was burned down and in 1867 a new Palace or Houses of Parliament was built on the same site. The modern building includes a great block of offices numbering eleven hundred rooms as well as a residence for the Speaker. During the Second World War the House of Commons was destroyed by a bomb and had to be rebuilt.

The bell of the Clock Tower of the Palace of Westminster is known as 'Big Ben' and named after Sir Benjamin Hall, who was First Commissioner of Works when the bell was cast.

PARMIGIANINO, Francesco (1503–1540)
Italian painter, born at Parma. He was influenced first by CORREGGIO and later by

RAPHAEL. He painted frescos in Parma Cathedral and Santa Maria della Steccata (Parma). His style was elegant and his figures are characterized by their long sweeping necks and hands. He produced etchings of many of his paintings.

PARNELL, Charles Stewart (1846–1891)
Irish nationalist politician, born at Avondale, Co. Wicklow. He entered Parliament as Member for Meath (1875) and five years later took over the leadership of the Irish Home Rule party. His aim was Home Rule for Ireland, which he hoped to obtain from the Liberal government in return for his party's support of other Liberal measures in Parliament. Parnell fell from power when he was found guilty in a divorce case (1890). GLADSTONE demanded Parnell's withdrawal and the majority of his party deserted him.

PARODY
The comic imitation of a serious work. A parody may be written by taking a well-known poem or speech, beginning with almost the same words, form and style, and then bringing in certain changes which will upset the whole intention of the original piece and convert its meaning into something different and less serious. Or it may exaggerate and imitate some peculiar mannerism which a serious author has, and using this imitation to describe a subject far from serious. In the 20th century G. K. CHESTERTON, E. V. Knox and J. C. Squire have written some amusing parodies.

PARTHENON
Doric temple to the goddess Athena built on the Acropolis of Athens. It was built between 447 B.C. and 432 B.C., and designed by Ictinus

and Callicrates under the supervision of PHEIDIAS. It was constructed of marble and is one of the great masterpieces of Greek architecture. Parts of its magnificent frieze can be seen in the British Museum. These were acquired by Lord Elgin in 1806 and are usually referred to as the Elgin Marbles.

PARTS OF SPEECH

Grammar deals with words and how they are related to one another. This relationship is seen in two ways—in their changes or 'inflections' and in their function or use in sentence structure. But we cannot properly understand this until we first understand how words are grouped or classified. We have, in fact, to learn the names and works of the *parts of speech*. But it is not much use writing all six (or seven) of them down in a list and learning them parrot fashion. The simplest way is to learn to recognize their various jobs from the very beginning:

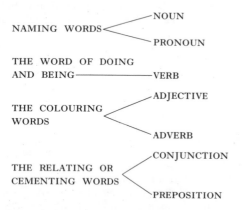

The *interjection* is left out because it is not so much a part of speech as a word attached to an exclamation mark (like *Hurrah*! and *Alas*!). 'Colouring words' and 'Relating or cementing words' are just picture phrases which explain themselves, and give us a rough idea of the work of the words concerned. With this in mind we can build up the picture in more detail:

When we learn to play cricket or tennis we have to master, first of all, one or perhaps two basic rules for hitting the ball; and having mastered these we have to put them into action in all the various circumstances that may arise. It is rather like that with grammar. Words have all kinds of uses. For example, a word which is a noun in one sentence may be an adjective or even a verb in another. Thus, in the sentence 'I was reading the paper', *paper* is a noun; in the sentence 'The book has a paper cover' it is an adjective; and in the sentence 'We are going to paper the room'

it is a verb. And sentences have all kinds of complicated shapes. But there are certain basic laws or rules of writing (and speaking) on which all the rest depend; and it is these that are of the first importance.

PASCAL, Blaise (1623–1662)
French thinker and scientist, born at Clermont. By the age of 11, without any training in the subject, he had worked out the first 23 propositions of EUCLID for himself. His main scientific work was concerned with mathematics (laid the foundations of mathematics of probability), and the physics of fluids and the atmosphere. In philosophy he belonged to what can be called the mystical thinkers. His most important philosophical work was *Pensées* which appeared in 1670.

PASSOVER
Jewish Feast commemorating their deliverance from the bondage of the Egyptians, lasting seven days, beginning on the 15th of Nizan (March–April). It is observed by the eating of unleavened bread and on certain days by readings from Exodus.

PASTEUR, Louis (1822–1895)
French scientist, born at Dôle, and of very humble parents. Founded the modern theory of bacteria and displaced the older theory that bacteria were spontaneously generated. He did outstanding work in the fight against anthrax and hydrophobia. His studies on the action of germs in wines and vinegar led to the process now called 'pasteurization', that is, heating and rapid cooling of foods to free them of bacteria. The Pasteur Institute was founded in 1888, and is one of the leading research centres in the world. [*See* BACTERIA.]

PATER, Walter (1839–1894)
English critic. His reputation was made with *Studies in the History of the Renaissance*, which showed the influence of the PRE-RAPHAELITE circle in which he moved. His later works, beginning with *Marius the Epicurean*, express his ideal of the aesthetic life, the cult of beauty.

PATMORE, Coventry Kersey Dighton (1823–1896)
English poet and associate of the PRE-RAPHAELITES. His *Angel in the House* describes a rectory courtship against a background of minute domestic details. His wife died in 1862, and two years later he became a Roman Catholic. The *Unknown Eros* and *Amelia* are very different from his early work, being devoted to political and profoundly emotional themes, and making use of the myth of Eros

and Psyche to symbolize the marriage of earthly and heavenly love. His *Collected Poetical Works* were published in 1886.

PAUSANIAS

Writer, traveller and geographer. It is known that he lived during the period of the Emperors Pius (A.D. 138–161) and Aurelius (A.D. 161–180). He is thought to have come from Lydia. He has been described as the writer of the earliest guide book. His ten volume *Itinerary of Greece* is a detailed description of peoples, customs, buildings, etc. An excellent translation in six volumes was made by Sir James Fraser.

PAVLOV, Ivan Petrovich (1849–1936)

Russian scientist, born in the district of Ryazan. His most famous work was in the study of conditioned reflexes. A simple reflex consists of a stimulus and a response without the intervention of conscious thinking; for example, show a dog food and its mouth waters. Now, if when a dog is fed a bell is rung, in a short time the dog connects food with the ringing of a bell, and by ringing a bell the dog's mouth will water; this is called a conditioned reflex and is the basis of Pavlov's important school of psychology. Pavlov received the Nobel Prize for Physiology and Medicine in 1904.

PEAT

A deposit consisting of the dead and carbonized remains of plants, partly decomposed. Peat occurs in marshes and bogs, and also on the slopes of mountains, where it is dug and burnt as fuel.

PEEL, Sir Robert (1788–1850)

English statesman, born at Bury, Lancashire. He entered Parliament as a Tory at the age of 21. As Home Secretary, he reformed the prisons, relaxed the severity of the penal code, and established the Metropolitan Police Force. Thus the policemen were popularly known as "Peelers" or "Bobbies". Peel was forced to give way on two points in which he believed very strongly. He was a fierce anti-Catholic, yet the government in which he was Home Secretary passed the Catholic Emancipation Bill (1829). He stood for the protection of English trade by tariffs, but the Irish potato famine forced his hand and he repealed the CORN LAWS (1846). He was Prime Minister in 1834 and from 1841 to 1846.

PENDULUM

Weight or 'bob' suspended from a fixed point by a string or rod, and caused to swing to and fro. The time required for a complete swing is determined by the length of the string, and is independent of the size of the weight. It is given by the formula Time $= 2\pi \sqrt{l/g}$, in which g is the acceleration due to gravity and l is the length of the string. An interesting type is the FOUCAULT pendulum which is used to show the rotation of the earth on its axis; there is one in the Science Museum, London.

PENICILLIN

Extracted from the common green mould, *penicillium notatum*, and is a species of the fungus family of plants. In 1928 Sir A. FLEMING discovered, quite by chance, that this mould destroyed harmful bacteria brought near it. During the early years of the Second World War methods were devised to produce large quantities of penicillin for the treatment of disease and wounds. It was one of the greatest discoveries in medical science, and now is the basis of the branch of medicine known as antibiotics. Many other more powerful antibiotics have since been found, for example, streptomycin and aureomycin.

PENN, William (1644–1718)

Born in London. He became a Quaker and wrote a large number of pamphlets against popery. In 1671 he went to America and founded Pennsylvania as a home for his fellow Quakers. He came back to Europe a number of times to carry on his evangelistic activities.

PENNEY, Sir William George (1909——)

British atomic scientist. Born at Gibraltar, the son of a regular soldier. He went to the Technical School at Sheerness and graduated at the Imperial College of Science, South Kensington. During the Second World War he was first asked to study the mathematical and physical aspects of explosion waves, and then invited to assist in measuring the explosive power of the first atomic bomb at Los Alamos. He was also one of the two Englishmen present at the dropping of the atomic bomb on Nagasaki. He helped to plan the atomic tests at Bikini, and in 1947 was appointed Chief Superintendent of Armament Research in the Ministry of Supply.

PENTECOST

Christian and Jewish observance. The Christian observance marks the coming of the Holy Ghost and is celebrated on the seventh Sunday after Easter (Whit Sunday). The Jewish festival Shabuoth (Feast of Weeks), occurs on the sixth of Siwan (May-June). Originally it was

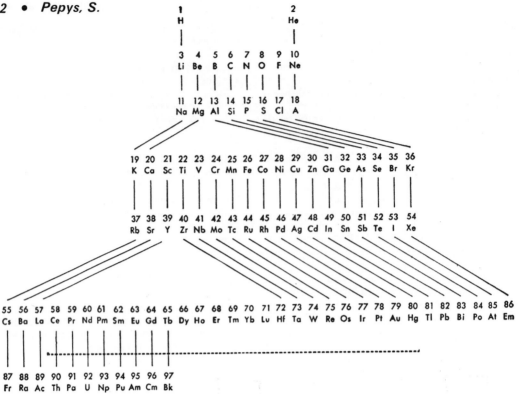

celebrated at the end of the wheat harvest, but today is chiefly concerned with the giving of the Law (Ten Commandments).

PEPYS, Samuel (1633–1703)

English diarist, born in London. Befriended by a relative, Sir Edward Montagu, he became clerk to the Exchequer and a year later entered the Navy Office, where he rose to become secretary for Naval Affairs. He was twice elected Member of Parliament (1673 and 1679). He was also twice imprisoned on false charges of being a Papist and selling secrets to France (1679 and 1690). He was President of the Royal Society (1684–1686). Fame came to him in 1825 when his diary was discovered amongst the papers that he bequeathed to Magdalene College, Cambridge. This is not only a most intimate human document showing Pepys in all his moods, but also contains much information on the court and social life of the Restoration period.

PERICLES (*c.* 490–429 B.C.)

Athenian ruler and orator, under whose administration Athens attained the peak of its greatness. He was an able general, and also a patron of art and literature, being friendly with SOPHOCLES and HERODOTUS. We have a full account of his character and life from THUCYDIDES the Athenian historian.

PERIODIC LAW

Dmitri MENDELEYEV in 1869 stated that properties of the elements recurred in regular cycles in a list starting with the element of lowest atomic weight and progressing in consecutive order of atomic weight. Henry G. J. Moseley in 1913 showed that the important thing was atomic number, not atomic weight. On this basis all the elements can be arranged in order of increasing atomic number, i.e., number of protons in the nucleus, with elements of similar chemical properties in the same vertical columns. This is known as the periodic table and the theory behind it as the periodic law. The easiest example of the working of this law is that of the elements called halogens, fluorine, chlorine, bromine, iodine, and astatine, which are found in the same vertical column and have atomic numbers 9, 17, 35, 53, and 85 respectively.

PERÓN, Juan (1896——)

Army officer who with the support of the working people rose to become President of Argentina (1946–1955). An equally important figure in the political life of Argentina was his wife, Eva, who died in 1952. He introduced many social reforms, but made many enemies. He was overthrown in the revolution of 1955 by military leaders and has been obliged to live in exile since then.

PERSIA

Also called Iran, is a kingdom in that part of Asia called the Middle East. It is about three times bigger than France, and has about 18 million inhabitants who are Moslems. Most of Persia is desert, but the country is very rich in petroleum. The oil wells were sunk and worked by a British Company in agreement with the Persian Government, but in 1951 a quarrel arose between Persia and Britain in regard to this arrangement, but it was settled in 1954. The capital is Tehran and the oil port is Abadan.

History :

Persia is one of the most ancient countries in the world. In the 6th century B.C. the Persians, a nomadic tribe, settled in the country and joined with the Medes in overthrowing the Assyrian Empire. Under Cyrus II, or the Great, the Persians captured the Medean capital, and in a very short time they had greatly extended their empire which under Darius I reached its greatest extent. When Alexander the Great rose to power in Greece the Persians were defeated at the Battle of the Hellespont in 334 B.C.

In A.D. 642 Persia came under Arab rule and was converted to Islam. During this period Persian art and science flourished. In 1037 Seljuk Turks from the Turkmen steppes ruled the country. Twenty years later Genghiz KHAN and his Mongols arrived, and spread destruction through North Persia. For a period Persia was ruled by Hulagu, the grandson of Genghiz Khan, and he founded a MONGOL kingdom in Persia.

In the 16th century a new line of Persian kings arose, the chief of whom was Abbas the Great. He defeated the Ottoman Turks and with English aid drove the Portuguese from Hormuz.

During the First World War Persia was occupied for a short time by both Britain and Russia. In 1921 an army officer named Riza Khan led a revolution, and in 1925 was elected Shah or king. During the Second World War both Britain and Russia accused Persia of favouring Germany, and again they occupied the country and forced Riza Khan to abdicate in favour of his son, Mohammed Riza Khan. In 1946 the troops were withdrawn. In 1951 the Persian Parliament nationalized the Persian oil industry which was controlled by a British company by agreement with the Persian Government. A new agreement was made in 1954 with British and other oil companies.

PERU

A republic in South America bordering the South Pacific Ocean. It is more than twice the size (531,000 square miles) of France and has a population of about 12 million, the majority of whom are descended from the INCAS or are of mixed Indian and Spanish descent. The capital is Lima. The country produces petroleum, iron ore and lead. It has recently become the chief fishing country in the world.

PÉTAIN, Marshal Henri Philippe (1856–1951)

French soldier, born in Normandy. He was a colonel at the outbreak of the Great War, eventually rising to become Commander-in-Chief of the French Army, with the rank of General. He won fame for his organization of the defence of Verdun (1916). Created Marshal (1918), he was later appointed Vice-President of the Supreme War Council and Inspector-General of the Army (1922). After 1930 he lived in virtual retirement, but in June 1940, after the French military collapse, he sought terms from the Germans and became head of the collaberationist government at Vichy which included LAVAL. In 1945 was accused of treason by the re-established French Republic. The death sentence was commuted to life imprisonment on an island in the Bay of Biscay.

PETER THE GREAT, Czar of Russia (1672–1725)

Son of Czar Alexei, born in Moscow, he became joint ruler with his brother Ivan until the latter died in 1696. In his early years he toured round Europe, and worked as a shipwright in Amsterdam, and from England he collected engineers and other trained men. At home he encouraged his country's contacts with the West, in literature and in trade. He fought major wars with Sweden and Turkey, and success against the Swedes enabled him to open up Russian trade in the Baltic. St. Petersburg was founded as the commercial centre of the area, and during his last years Peter had magnificent buildings erected in the city and made it his capital. Today it is known as Leningrad.

PETRARCH, properly Francesco di Petracco (1304–1374)

Italian poet and scholar. He became the friend of the powerful Roman family of the Colonna, and his advice and company was sought by the great rulers of the day. His ability was justly recognized by a public coronation as poet-laureate on the Capitol at Rome in 1341. He is best remembered for his love poetry and nature poetry, written in Italian, which was free from the allegory and mysticism associated with 14th-century writing. Particularly outstanding are the *Canzoniere*, in which most of the songs and poems were inspired by his pure and faithful love for Laura. His passion for collecting and preserving books, coins and manuscripts, his love of mountain scenery, and his veneration for the orators, historians and poets of ancient Rome, all reveal him to have been a man ahead of his time, and one of the founders of the Renaissance.

PETROLEUM
Mineral oil found trapped below the surface of the ground by a layer of dense rock. Boreholes sunk through this layer release the oil, which then squirts up in 'gushers'. Crude petroleum is a thick, black oil, but it is refined into petrol, paraffin, lubricating oil and grease.

PETROLOGY
Branch of geology which studies the origins of all rocks which form the crust of the earth; the description of the rocks themselves is usually termed petrography. Three main characteristics determine the nature of rocks: their composition, texture, and structure. Three main groups of rocks have been classified according to their origin, namely: igneous rocks, sedimentary rocks, and metamorphic rocks. Igneous rocks are of volcanic origin and are formed from consolidated magma. Sedimentary rocks, on the other hand, are formed from materials which were broken down by such agents as running water, frost, changes of temperature, etc. The resulting fragments were carried by water or wind to new positions where they were deposited as sediments; such things as shells or plants also form sedimentary rocks. The loose sediments are then welded together by the pressure of overlaying layers and the deposition of binding materials. Metamorphic rocks form great portions of the earth's crust, and originated with changes of environment and conditions which in turn changed and transformed the structure of the rocks.

PHEIDIAS (*c.* 500–*c.* 433 B.C.)
Greek sculptor who is thought to have been responsible for the Acropolis in Athens. No known work of his exists, his greatness resting on descriptions of his work by ancient writers.

PHILIPPINES
A large group of islands in the Pacific Ocean that together are a little more than half the size of France. There are a little more than 30 million inhabitants. Most of them are Malays but are known as Filipinos, nearly all of whom are Christians. The capital is Manila on the island of Luzon, the largest island. The country produces rice, coconuts and timber.

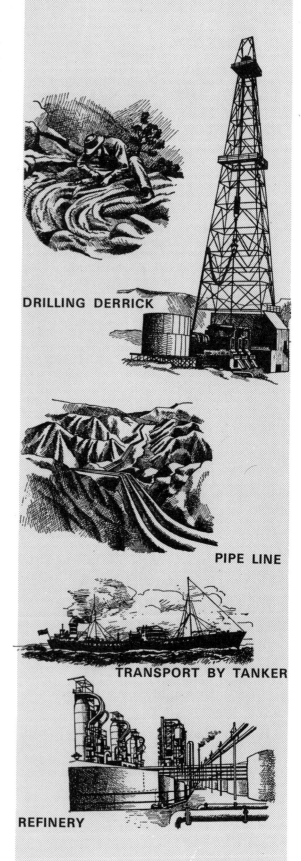

DRILLING DERRICK

PIPE LINE

TRANSPORT BY TANKER

REFINERY

The Philippines were discovered by MAGELLAN and were ruled by Spain until 1898 when they came under the rule of the United States. They became independent in 1946.

PHILOSOPHY
The pursuit of wisdom, whose aim has been described as 'to exhibit the universe as a rational system in the harmony of all its parts', that is, the universe is looked at as a whole, and not as a collection of parts, which is how the specialized sciences look at things. For example, the geologist is concerned only with the composition of the crust of the earth, the botanist with plant life, the meteorologist with the atmosphere, the electronics scientist with the movements of electrons in a vacuum, etc.

Western philosophy has its roots in Greek philosophy, and its main branches are 'ortology', the theory of the reality of ·existence; 'epistemology', the theory of human knowledge; 'psychology', the theory of mind; 'aesthetics', the theory of beauty in art; 'logic', the theory of accurate thinking; 'ethics', the theory of human conduct, particularly as regards right and wrong. Philosophy is also concerned with religion, history and politics.

It should be noted that Western philosophy is only one form of philosophy and that other parts of the world have their own philosophies, some of which, like those of China and India, are older than our own.

The following list gives the most important Western philosophers, most of whom are dealt with separately under their own heading.

Greek and Roman philosophers from c. 642 B.C. *to* A.D.180
Thales, Anaximander, Anaximenes, Xenophanes, Pythagoras, Parmenides, Zeno, Heraclitus, Anaxagoras, Leucippus, Empedocles, Protogoras, Socrates, Plato, Aristotle, Epicurus, Pyrrho, Cicero, Lucretius, Seneca, Marcus Aurelius.
Medieval philosophers from A.D. 150 *to* A.D. 1347
Tertullian, Augustine, Abelard, Aquinas, Duns Scotus, Machiavelli, Occam.
Modern philosophers from 1596 *to the present*
Descartes, Hobbes, Spinoza, Leibnitz, Locke, Berkeley, Hume, Kant, Hegel, Schopenhauer, Nietzsche, Comte, Spencer, Croce, Dewey, Bergson, Russell, Alexander, Rousseau, Bentham, J. S. Mill.

PHOTO-ELECTRIC CELL
Type of cell, usually in the form of a valve, which becomes electrically conducting when exposed to light. The element selenium possesses this property, but modern photo-electric cells utilize thin films of potassium and other metals which also emit electrons under the action of light.

PHOTOGRAPHY
As long ago as the 16th century it was known that light had a peculiar action on silver chloride (*luna cornea*), and that a small hole pierced in the darkened window of a room would admit rays of light to reproduce on a screen the view outside. The camera is, in fact, combination of these two, and unlike many other inventions cannot be said to have been discovered by one man. However, three men who played an important part in its development were W. H. Fox Talbot, Louis DAGUERRE and Joseph Niepce.

Modern photography is based on the fact that when an optical image is thrown on to a plate or film coated with a suspension of silver bromide in gelatine a latent image is formed in the emulsion and is a result of the action of the light on the silver atoms. When the plate or film is immersed in what is termed a 'developer' the latent image is fixed, that is, further action on the silver atoms by light is stopped. Fixing is simply the removal of surplus bromide. The image which remains is the 'negative'. By taking a photo-copy of this on light-sensitive paper the process is reversed and the result, called a 'positive', is similar in all respects (except colour) to the original image.

There are two main types of colour photography, the additive process in which the photograph is taken through a fine network of tiny filters, red, green and blue (the Dufay process is an example of this), and the subtractive process in which the film is made up of three layers sensitive to blue, green and red. After exposure each layer is processed to its complementary colour, dye being absorbed in proportion to the amount of silver deposited by the action of light; Ektacolour and Gevacolour are examples of this process.

PHOTOSYNTHESIS
All the dry matter of a plant, except a small percentage of mineral matter (ash), consists of organic compounds, that is, compounds of carbon along with hydrogen, nitrogen, oxygen, and sulphur. This carbon passes into the plant as carbon dioxide, either as a gas through the pores (stomata) of leaves of land plants, or as a solution in water through the skin of water plants.

The carbon dioxide, in the presence of the chlorophyll (the green colouring matter contained in the chloroplasts), and sunlight, combines indirectly with water to form organic compounds and oxygen. It is not yet fully understood how this takes place, but there is evidence that the carbon dioxide first combines with an organic compound already in the plant to form an organic acid. (Acetic acid or vinegar is a simple organic acid). The energy of the sunlight acts on water in the plant in the presence of chlorophyll and breaks it up into hydrogen and oxygen. The oxygen is set free into the air through the stomata, and the hydrogen acts on the organic acid to convert it into other compounds, especially the sugar glucose. The energy of sunlight is thus stored in glucose and other organic compounds into which glucose is afterwards converted, especially cellulose and starch, protein and fat.

PHYSICAL CHEMISTRY

The branch of science where physics and chemistry meet. PHYSICS deals with the properties of matter and is divided into branches— heat, light, sound, electricity, magnetism, etc. CHEMISTRY deals with the way in which elements combine to form compounds, and in which substances may be analyzed to find out the elements in them and their structure. But many chemical problems involve physics and hence physical chemistry.

Subjects that come under the heading of physical chemistry include the problem of solutions. Substances that dissolve in another are divided up invisibly, and little was understood about it until the physics that dealt with the electric charges on elements and radicals [see CHEMISTRY] was taken up by chemists. It was shown that many substances split up into two parts, each electrically charged, when put into a solvent such as water. For example, common salt consists of sodium and chlorine combined. When salt is put into water, each molecule of sodium chloride breaks up (or 'dissociates') into an atom of sodium, positively charged, and an atom of chlorine, negatively charged. Even in water alone some of the water molecules are dissociated into positively charged hydrogen atoms and negatively charged radicals consisting of hydrogen and oxygen combined. When an electric charge is applied to a solution containing a solute that is dissociated, one goes one way and the other the other. This is the basis of some methods of chemical manufacture and of ELECTROPLATING. None of these matters is understood with chemistry alone or physics alone. They belong to physical chemistry.

The transformation of energy belongs to physics. But chemical action involves changes in energy, usually in the form of heat, sometimes in the form of light. So the energy changes of chemical action form a part of physical chemistry. The explanation of a simple electric cell is thus to be sought in the domain of physical chemistry.

The study of colloids is a part of physical chemistry. Colloids are substances in particles not big enough to be seen or heavy enough to sink in a liquid, and yet not small enough to be molecules or atoms or radicals. The result is that a colloidal substance can be made to stay in suspension because of the bombardments of the molecules of the solvent. Such a suspension is called a sol. Under certain conditions the colloidal particles join up in rather rigid structures and the sol then becomes a gel. For instance a table jelly is quite fluid when hot but fairly solid when cold, without losing any water. In other words, it is a sol when hot and a gel when cold, the small insoluble particles being particles of gelatine.

Many organic substances lend themselves to colloidal conditions, especially substances that take part in living bodies. But the physics of surface forces and of electric charges are involved in the chemistry of colloids. So it can be seen that physical chemistry is a very important branch of science for many matters concerned with living beings.

PHYSICS

That sphere of science concerned with matter and energy and the relations between them. [*See* HEAT, LIGHT, SOUND, MECHANICS, MAGNETISM and ELECTRICITY.] The methods of general physics are applied to specialized fields and give rise to such subjects as 'geophysics' and biophysics. [*See* PHYSICAL CHEMISTRY.] The most important branch of physics today is nuclear physics which has widespread applications. [*See* NUCLEAR ENERGY.]

PIANOFORTE

A musical instrument with a keyboard; generally known as the 'piano', it was invented in the 18th century. It eventually replaced the one then in use, the HARPSICHORD, and developed into the instrument we know today. The strings are struck by hammers, enabling the pianist to play softly or loudly as the music demands, and the name of the instrument indicates this, being made up of the Italian words 'piano' (soft) and 'forte' (loud). Such a thing was impossible on the harpsichord, the strings of which were plucked by quills, and for this reason it gave way to the piano. The piano pedals were added later. The left one (the soft pedal) makes it possible to play very softly; the right one (the 'damper' pedal, often miscalled the loud pedal) lifts the dampers (pieces of felt) from the strings, allowing the notes to sound on after the fingers have been lifted from the keys.

PICASSO, Pablo (1881——)
Spanish artist, born in Malaga. After studying in Barcelona and Paris he established himself in the latter city as a painter, and became associated with BRAQUE and MATISSE. In 1910, together with Braque, he founded Cubism. Since then, Picasso has developed various styles, all of which have had a tremendous influence on modern painting. He has also produced many etchings, drawings and stage designs, and has produced a number of outstanding sculptures and pottery subjects. He is one of the most prolific artists.

PICCARD, Auguste (1884–1962)
Belgian scientist, born at Lutry, Switzerland. He is well known for his various balloon ascents into the stratosphere in the early 1930s to investigate cosmic rays, and more recently for his studies of deep-sea life, made in a bathysphere.

PIERO della Francesca (1420–1492)
Italian painter. He painted frescoes in Florence and at Loretto, and produced *The Flagellation* and other paintings for the Duke of Rimini. He was one of the first artists to paint in oil, and has been described as the greatest geometrician of his day, making many advances in the use of perspective in painting. He exerted a great influence on the art of Italy.

PIEZOELECTRIC EFFECT
Phenomena connected with the observed fact that certain crystals, such as Rochelle salt, will produce a voltage when subjected to mechanical stress and *vice versa*. One use of this is in the crystal phonograph pick-up, in which a crystal is made to vibrate with the undulations of the record grooves and so creates a varying electromotive force which can be amplified and reproduced.

PIGS
The domesticated pig as we know it was derived from the European wild boar which, up to the 16th century, roamed the wilder parts of Britain. It does not chew the cud as do cows and camels, but lives on roots, tubers and other vegetable substances, and also small animals. Perhaps the best-known of the wild pigs is the wart-hog of South Africa. It has long, ugly tusks and the skin is nearly naked, except for a mane of long hairs along its back. Species of wild pig are to be found in the Far East, most of Asia, and the West, East and Central Africa. The American wild pigs or peccaries have downward-thrusting tusks, only three toes on the hind feet, and much more complicated stomachs than the wild pigs referred to above.

PILGRIM FATHERS
A group of about one hundred Puritans who sailed in the *Mayflower* to America in 1620. They landed at what is now Plymouth, New England, and set up a colony under the leadership of William Bradford. One of its military leaders, Miles Standish, is the hero of LONGFELLOW's poem of that name.

PINTER, Harold (1930——)
British playwright, the son of a tailor in London's East End. His plays include *The Birthday Party* and *The Caretaker*, and he wrote the filmscripts for *The Servant*, *The Pumpkin Eaters*, and *Accident*.

PIPER, John (1903——)
English painter, born at Epsom. Initially a landscape painter but later turned to abstracts under the influence of modern French painters. During the Second World War painted a series of outstanding pictures of the results of bombing, especially Bath and the House of Commons. Piper is a distinguished designer and one of his most famous works in this field is the large stained-glass window in the new Coventry Cathedral.

PIRANDELLO, Luigi (1867–1936)
Italian writer, born at Girgenti. Although he wrote novels and short stories, Pirandello is best remembered by his plays, particularly *Six Characters in Search of an Author*, and his play *Henry IV* is often performed. He received the Nobel Prize for Literature in 1934.

PIRANESI, Giovanni Battista (1720–1778)
Italian architect, born in Venice. He was an outstanding etcher and his views of Rome have magnificently recorded that city in the 18th century—reproductions of the original prints are widely bought. His first love was etching the classical antiquities of Rome. His most important series of etchings is his *Vedute* published in 1745.

PISANO, Niccala (*c.* 1220–*c.* 1280)
Italian sculptor who has been described as the 'father of modern sculpture'. He worked mainly in Pisa, Perugia and Siena. His most outstanding works are reliefs, especially those on the pulpit in Pisa Cathedral. He carried out many works with his son, Giovanni, an equally great sculptor.

PITT, William, First Earl of Chatham (1708–1778)
Whig politician, and distinguished member of the House of Commons known as the 'Great

Commoner'. His policy enabled England to establish her empire in Canada and India, and his vigorous war policy against France made England the supreme maritime and colonial power.

PITT, William, the Younger (1759–1806)
English statesman and second son of the Earl of Chatham. He was an ardent reformer in his early career, attacking parliamentary corruption, abolishing many sinecure places, reforming the revenue and revising the tax system and the trade duties. Thanks to him the country was restored to financial security. He became the fierce opponent of Charles James FOX in Parliament. He led the government from 1783–1801, and for a brief spell in 1804. During the war with France his enterprises at home—the suppression of the Jacobins who sympathised with the French Revolution—were more thorough than his handling of the war. He regarded Catholic Emancipation as vital to secure a settlement in Ireland, but the measure was blocked by George III.

PLANCK, Max (1858–1947)
German scientist, born at Kiel. One of the founders, with EINSTEIN, of modern physics. His theory of 'quanta' showed that radiant energy is emitted in packets (quanta), and did much to explain the inner structure of atoms. Received the Nobel Prize for Physics in 1918. [*See* QUANTUM THEORY.]

PLANETARIUM
Could be called the theatre of the stars, and consists of a dome-like building on to whose ceiling is projected, by means of a special optical device, a replica of the northern or southern night sky. The apparatus can show not only the positions of stars and planets but also their movements. Several are installed in Europe and the U.S.A.

PLANKTON
Minute plant and animal organisms found in water, and a source of food for many species of fish, including the whale. During the past few years much scientific research has been carried out to increase the quantity of plankton as a fish food and to find out if it can be used as a food for human beings.

PLASTICS
Man-made materials produced as a result of intricate chemical reactions, mainly from the by-products of coal, lime, oil, and vegetable matter. All plastics, no matter how they are made, have one property in common—being shaped or moulded. There are many types of plastics, each type and variation having some specific property qualifying it for special applications. The first of these is known as thermoplastics. These are plastics which soften when heated and harden when cooled without undergoing any chemical change, the process being capable of being repeated indefinitely without harm to the plastic. The second group comprises the thermosetting materials. These undergo a chemical change when subjected to heat and pressure; the resins harden and can never again be softened by heat. The action of heat and pressure converts the thermosetting resin into an entirely different substance, hard and infusible. The thermoplastic group of materials includes celluloid (the first plastic discovered by Alexander Parkes in 1865), cellulose acetate or non-flam celluloid, acrylic resins, such as 'Perspex', nylon, polythene, and polystyrene. The most important of the thermosetting group is phenol formaldehyde resin which, in the form of moulding powder, is used for moulding telephone receivers, radio sets, and electric switches. Urea and melamine formaldehyde resins are used for moulding coloured bottle caps, buttons, clocks, and tableware.

Plastics are produced in several forms which include powder, sheet or liquid. The powders are fed into heavy hydraulic presses which are capable of mass-producing anything from door knobs and bottle closures to complete television cabinets. In other forms, particularly sheet, they can be drilled, turned or sawn. Such sheet plastics as 'Perspex' can also be softened by heat and then shaped over simple wood formers or blown to various contours. [*See* NYLON.]

PLATO (427–347 B.C.)
One of the greatest thinkers of all time, born at Athens. Studied under SOCRATES and travelled in Italy, Sicily and Egypt. About 388 B.C. he opened his ACADEMY in Athens. Among his students was ARISTOTLE. Plato wrote many works, all in the form of dialogues. The most important work is the *Republic* in which he put forward his ideal state. In this, men were to be permanently divided into three social classes—the guardians who would rule, the soldiers and the workers.

PLATYPUS, Duckbill
This peculiar mammal lives in long burrows in the banks of rivers and streams in Eastern Australia and Tasmania. The jaws of this furry animal are shaped like a duck's beak, and its mouth is provided with wide, horny teeth. Its eyes are small and it has no ears. An important feature is its webbed toes, at the end of which

are strong claws. The platypus spends its active hours in water, and feeds on water-snails and small crustaceans which it fetches from the bottom of the stream or river. This food is stored in a cheek pouch and eaten at leisure on the surface or on land.

PLAUTUS, Titus Marcius
(*c.* 254–184 B.C.)

Roman comic poet. At one time, when he had failed in business, he was employed by a baker, turning a hand-mill. It was then that he started to write, and twenty of his comedies survive. Shakespeare adapted the *Menaechmi* as *The Comedy of Errors*, and Molière's *L'Avare* is based on the *Aulularia*.

PLEBISCITE

A special vote to find out what people want done about some particular matter. Plebiscites are not held in the United Kingdom, but some countries, including France and Australia, have laws which make it possible to hold a plebiscite.

PLIMSOLL LINE

Another name for this is the loading line, and is a line on the side of a ship to show the depth she could be loaded to safety. The line takes its name from Samuel Plimsoll (1824–1898), a Member of Parliament who, in 1876, caused a Bill to be passed forbidding ships to overload and so become unseaworthy and a danger to the lives of seamen.

Today it is the responsibility of the Ministry of Transport to certify the Plimsoll Line on all ships as well as seeing that many other safety regulations are carried out.

PLIMSOLL LINE on a ship's side prevents dangerous overloading. The levels refer to the waters the ship will sail: TF, Tropical Fresh Water; F, Fresh Water; T, Tropical; S, Summer; W, Winter; WNA, Winter North Atlantic; LR, Lloyd's Register.

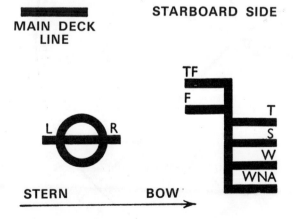

PLUTARCH (*c.* 46–120)

Greek historian and biographer. His most famous work, the *Parallel Lives*, gives biographical details of twenty-three Romans and twenty-three Greeks, arranged in pairs. They have provided the sources for the plots of many well-known dramas, including some of Shakespeare's plays.

POE, Edgar Allan (1809–1849)

American writer, born at Boston. Led a tempestuous life and died in the direst poverty. Although his best-known works are the poems, *The Raven* and *The Bells*, he wrote many stories of horror and crime. *The Murders in the Rue Morgue* is considered the earliest of modern crime stories. He also wrote *The House of Usher*.

POLAND

A republic in Eastern Europe. Since the end of the Second World War, when her frontiers were changed, the country has been rather more than half the size (121,000 square miles) of France. There are about 31 million inhabitants. The capital is Warsaw on the River Vistula and the chief port Gdansk, or Danzig.
History:
Polish recorded history begins only about the tenth century, when Christianity was introduced. In the 12th century constant fighting occurred between Poland and Prussia. In the 14th century the Polish Queen, Jadwiga, married the Grand-Duke of Lithuania and so united the two countries. By the 16th century Poland had become a powerful country. In 1683 the Poles won a brilliant victory over the Turks, and at the end of the century the Ukraine was taken from the Turks. Soon after this Russia began to interfere in Polish affairs and in 1772 Poland lost part of her territory to Russia, Austria and Prussia. By 1795 Poland had ceased to exist as a separate country, her territory being shared by these three countries.

Poland gained her independence after the First World War. She was not satisfied with the frontiers suggested by the British Foreign Secretary, Lord Curzon, and went to war with the Soviet Union in 1919 as the result of which she succeeded in taking some Russian territory. In 1939 Germany attacked Poland and it was for this reason that Britain declared war on Germany. The Russians took back the territory they lost in 1919. In return Poland was allowed some German territory. This arrangement was intended as a temporary settlement but no final agreement was reached and it is still a tender subject between Poland and Germany. Poland has had a Communist form of government since the end of the war.

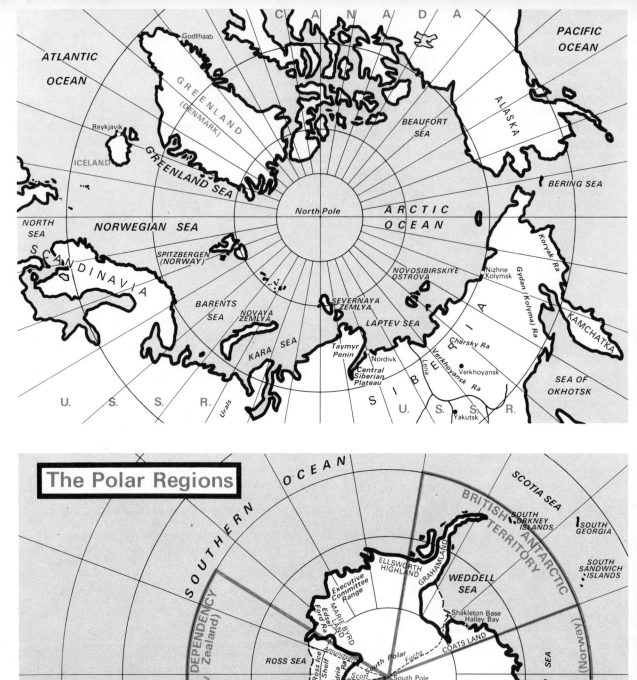

ATLANTIC
OCEAN

PACIFIC
OCEAN

CANADA

Godthaab

GREENLAND
(DENMARK)

BEAUFORT
SEA

ALASKA

Reykjavik

ICELAND

GREENLAND SEA

BERING SEA

North Pole

ARCTIC
OCEAN

NORTH
SEA

NORWEGIAN SEA

Koryak Ra

SCANDINAVIA

SPITZBERGEN
(NORWAY)

BARENTS
SEA

NOVOSIBIRSKIYE
OSTROVA

Nizhne
Kolymsk

Gydan (Kolyma) Ra

KAMCHATKA

NOVAYA
ZEMLYA

SEVERNAYA
ZEMLYA

S
I
A

LAPTEV SEA

KARA
SEA

Chersky Ra

Taymyr
Penin

Nordivk

Central
Siberian
Plateau

Lena

Verkhoyansk Ra

Verkhoyansk

SEA OF
OKHOTSK

U.   S.   S.   R.

Urals

S   U   S   S   R.

U.   S.   S.   R.

Yakutsk

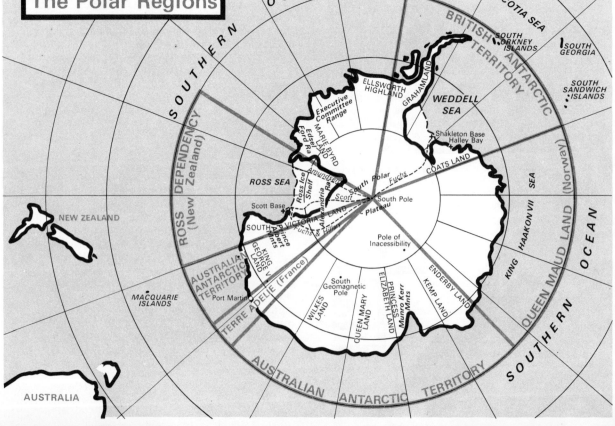

The Polar Regions

SOUTHERN   OCEAN

SCOTIA SEA

BRITISH ANTARCTIC TERRITORY

SOUTH
ORKNEY
ISLANDS

SOUTH
GEORGIA

ELLSWORTH
HIGHLAND

GRAHAMLAND

WEDDELL
SEA

SOUTH
SANDWICH
ISLANDS

Executive
Committee
Range

MARIE BYRD
LAND

Edsel
Ford Ra

Shakleton Base
Halley Bay

ROSS
DEPENDENCY
(New Zealand)

ROSS SEA

Ross Ice
Shelf

Amundsen

COATS LAND

Fuchs

KING HAAKON VII

SEA

NEW ZEALAND

Scott Base

South Polar

Scott

Plateau

South Pole

QUEEN MAUD LAND (Norway)

SOUTH VICTORIA LAND & Alexandria Ra

Fuchs & Hillary

AUSTRALIAN
ANTARCTIC
TERRITORY

SOUTH
Prince
Albert
Mnts

KING
GEORGE V
LAND

Pole of
Inacessibility

Port Martin

TERRE ADELIE (France)

South
Geomagnetic
Pole

WILKES
LAND

QUEEN MARY
LAND

PRINCESS
ELIZABETH
LAND

ENDERBY LAND

KEMP LAND

Munro Kerr Mnts

MACQUARIE
ISLANDS

SOUTHERN   OCEAN

AUSTRALIA

AUSTRALIAN   ANTARCTIC   TERRITORY

POLAR REGIONS A typical Antarctic landscape—here a glacier meets the frozen sea.

POLAR REGIONS
The North and South Poles are two opposite extremities of the axis on which the Earth revolves. The North Pole is the central point in the Arctic Circle. The North Magnetic Pole is that place where the magnetic force is vertically downward. The South Pole is at the centre of the Antarctic Circle. The South Magnetic Pole is the place where the magnetic force is vertically upward.

Antarctica is the name given to the vast ice-covered continent around the South Pole. It is thought to be about 5 million square miles, or nearly as large as North America. A large part of Antarctica is claimed by Australia and New Zealand. One of the Antarctic islands— Deception Island—is part of the British Falkland Islands, but Argentina and Chile have both disputed the claim.

In 1954 the first permanent base on the continent was set up at Mawson. It was agreed that during the Geo-physical Year, from July 1957 to December 1958, a number of countries, including the United Kingdom, should take part in expeditions to Antarctica to explore and study conditions there.

Preliminary expeditions, led by Sir Edmund Hilary and Dr. Fuchs, were sent by Britain and other countries during 1955. [See also FALKLAND ISLANDS, SIBERIA, LAPLAND, ALASKA and GREENLAND.]

POLECAT
Member of the weasel family. It has a coat of dark brown with a region of cream coloured fur on its stomach. One distinguishing point is its white ear tips. It is quite savage and kills poultry.

POLICE
Civilians who are employed to keep law and order. The police force is also called the constabulary. This is because before 1829 when the modern police force was established by Sir Robert PEEL it had been the custom for J.P.s to appoint a 'parish constable' to keep order. If he did not wish to do the work himself he could employ someone to do it for him. Sometimes such employed persons were themselves criminals or were otherwise unsuitable. Sir Robert Peel changed this state of affairs so far as the Metropolitan area of London was concerned. It is because he created the modern police force that policemen are sometimes nicknamed 'Bobbies' after him. The new police force was placed under the HOME OFFICE. When other parts of Britain also wanted to have a similar kind of police force Parliament gave counties and some other LOCAL AUTHORITIES permission to establish police forces of their own. That is how it has come about that while the police force in the metropolitan area of London is still under the Home Office, in other parts of the country the local authorities employ the police although the Home Office does have some rights of supervision. In 1966 it was decided that many of the smaller police forces should join with neighbouring ones so reducing the number of separate forces throughout the country by more than half.

POLITICAL PARTIES
Associations of citizens whose chief object is to try to get as Members of Parliament people who share their political opinions. Today nearly all those who are elected to Parliament have been chosen as candidates by one or other

of the chief political parties. It is from the party that has a majority of Members in Parliament that the Prime Minister and Government are chosen.

Parliament first became clearly divided into parties at the time of the Civil War. Afterwards the Tory Party was associated with the Stuart monarchy and the Whigs with the democratic Revolution of 1688. In the 19th century the radical position of the Whigs was inherited by the Liberals, but there is an important difference between the political parties of the 18th and the 19th century: in the 18th century, parties were composed of groups of friends and people with common interests and ambitions; but, increasingly, after the 1832 Reform Bill, parties became associations of people who subscribed to a group of particular policies.

Although political parties today choose nearly all the candidates for Parliament and although a Government will be described, for example, as Conservative or Labour, actually there is no Act of Parliament which gives political parties such rights. In other words political parties are no part of the British Constitution. No Member can be referred to in the House of Commons or the House of Lords as, say, a Liberal or a Conservative, nor is a candidate for Parliament allowed to have it stated on a voting slip during an Election which party he supports.

There are today three main political parties in Britain—Liberal, Labour and Conservative. Until 1905 there were only two parties in Parliament—Liberal and Conservative. Then the Labour Party, which had been formed at the end of the 19th century, with the help of the Trade Unions, succeeded in getting some of its supporters elected. Members of the Labour Party often call themselves Socialists. *Other Countries.* In the United States there are two main political parties. They are known as Republican and Democrat. The President of the United States is always a supporter of one or other of these two parties.

In nearly all the countries of Western Europe there are far more political parties than in Great Britain. This usually means that the Government of such countries have to be coalitions. That is to say, several parties agree for the time being to join together to form a government. In Catholic countries there is often a political party supported chiefly by Catholics, which usually has some such name as Christian Socialists or Christian Democrats.

Very often the term Left Wing or Right Wing is used to describe political opinions or groups of political parties. In the French Parliament and in some others it is usual for Members to choose their seats in the parliament building to show their political opinions instead of, as in Britain, to show whether they support or oppose the Government. Those whose opinions are conservative sit on the Right and those who have socialist views on the Left. Those who have opinions between these two sit in the Centre.

In the Soviet Union the only political party that is allowed is the Communist party. There are Communist parties in other countries which support the policy of the Soviet Union. In Great Britain the Communist party is quite small compared with the three main political parties.

The word Communism really means having things in common. For many centuries thinkers have talked of a form of society in which all the people would share everything they produced in common. There were in fact several attempts to form such communities. Karl MARX believed that a time must inevitably come when the capitalist system would break down and would be replaced by 'the dictatorship of the proletariat'—the rule of the working people. In the industrialized countries of 19th-century Europe in which Marx lived—especially in England—the contrast between the employers and the workmen was becoming more and more apparent and their interests were so totally different that it was natural for Marx to conclude that one day the group that had the larger numbers and the fewer privileges would rise up against its oppressors. Marx expounded these theories in *Das Kapital* and, together with his friend, Friedrich ENGELS, wrote a *Communist Manifesto*, which was translated into many languages and had great influence. In 1871, immediately after the Franco-German war, the people of Paris tried to set up a communist form of government which was called the Paris Commune. It did not last long, however, and it was not till towards the end of the First World War that the first successful attempt to set up a Communist form of government was made. This was in Russia in 1917 [*see* U.S.S.R.]. The leader was a Russian named Lenin, who put many of the ideas of Marx into practice, as well as introducing ideas of his own. In order to make sure that there was no change of government which would upset these plans the members of the Russian Communist Party, first under Lenin and later under Stalin, became in fact the dictators of the country. There were a good many people all over the world who sympathized with what the Russian communists were trying to do and communist parties, similar to the one in Russia, began to be formed in many countries. After the Second

World War it was these communist parties, that, with encouragement from Russia, took over the governments of the countries of eastern Europe and set up systems similar to that in the Soviet Union. China, too, set up a communist form of government.

Many people in Europe were worried by the rise of communism in Russia, particularly during the first few years when there was a period of civil war there, and great numbers of Russian people, who were opposed to communism, were killed. This fear of communism, together with serious unemployment, prepared the way for a different form of dictatorship. This was fascism which arose in Italy under MUSSOLINI in 1922. Mussolini took the word fascism from *fascio*, a bundle of rods which in the days of ancient Rome was carried by lictors ahead of the Consuls as a symbol of State power. Mussolini put down all opposition to fascism with ruthless and cruel methods. Many Italians who thought they had to choose between communism or fascism supported Mussolini. Later on HITLER in Germany decided to copy Italian fascism in an even more ruthless form. He called his form of fascism National Socialism or Nazism. Its chief difference from Italian fascism was its false teaching about the superiority of the German or Nordic race and the cruel treatment of people of other races, particularly the Jews. Fascist or Nazi parties were formed in other European countries, but after the Second World War these were made illegal. This did not mean of course that all those who had been supporters of fascism changed their opinions, though many did.

The only European country which still has a government similar to that of the fascist countries is Spain. As the Spanish Government did not enter the war against the Allies she did not have to change her government.

POLLAIUOLO, Antonio (1429?–1498)
Italian goldsmith, sculptor, painter and engraver, born in Florence of a well-known family of artists. An outstanding draughtsman, he was probably the first artist to study anatomy by dissection. His paintings are full of vitality and action. Among the most important are *Apollo and Daphne* and *The Martyrdom of St. Sebastian,* in the National Gallery, London.

POLYNESIA
The eastern division of OCEANIA. It includes New Zealand, Hawaii, Tonga and Samoa.

POPE, Alexander (1688–1744)
English poet, born in London. Son of a wealthy draper, he was privately educated. His *Essay on Criticism* and *The Rape of the Lock* established him as a writer of outstanding quality. Two of Pope's most popular works were the translations of Homer's *Iliad* and *Odyssey*; he made enough money from these two works to ensure his independence. In the *Dunciad* Pope attacked those writers and critics who had criticized his work, and, at the same time, showed his gift as a satirist. His last three major works were *Essay on Man, Moral Essays* and *Imitations of Horace*; the last has been acclaimed as his greatest work.

POPE, The
Head of the ROMAN CATHOLIC CHURCH, and considered by that church to be infallible when making pronouncements on questions of faith. The Pope regards himself as the spiritual successor of St. Peter, and the representative of Christ on earth. He resides in the VATICAN.

POPULAR MUSICAL INSTRUMENTS
Under this heading are included instruments which are rarely, if ever, employed in the modern symphony orchestra, but are much used in the home, the street, the music-hall, the pop-group, etc., for the playing of popular music.

The most numerous of these are the stringed instruments which are plucked with the fingers or with a piece of quill or metal, called a plectrum. The guitar, an instrument of Spanish origin, with six strings, now exists in three forms: the Spanish-guitar (the original instrument), the plectrum-guitar (a stronger instrument developed to replace the banjo in dance-bands), and the electric-guitar, whose sound is reinforced by an electric current. The Hawaiian-guitar was derived from the Spanish-guitar; a native of Hawaii one day slid a bolt along the strings, and liked the sound so much that he continued to play it that way. The instrument is laid on the lap, and a steel bar is used by the left hand to stop the strings; it is plucked by the thumb and the first two fingers of the right hand, to which finger-picks are attached. There is also an electric version of this instrument; it may be made in any shape, with any number of strings, and may be tuned in any way the player desires. The banjo, which was evolved in America, is a smaller instrument with a circular soundboard. It exists in four forms: the banjo proper, with five strings, plucked by the fingers; the plectrum-banjo, with four strings; the tenor-banjo; and the zither-banjo, which makes a noise somewhat similar to the zither. The mandolin is an even smaller instrument, sometimes shaped like a pear cut in half (the Neapolitan mandolin) and sometimes with a flat back; it has four pairs of strings, each pair being tuned to one note, and is played with a plectrum. (There is a whole mandolin family, including a tenor mandola, a mando-cello and a mando-bass). The ukulele is the same size as the mandolin, but shaped like a guitar; it was evolved from the normal guitar by a Portuguese living in Hawaii. The ukulele-banjo is a ukulele made in the shape of a small banjo. The zither is a Tyrolean instrument, consisting of a flat box with a large number of wires stretched across the top; it is placed on the knees or on a table, and plucked with the fingers and a finger-pick attached to the thumb.

Of instruments blown by wind, the most popular is the harmonica or mouth-organ; this consists of a small flat box, containing a series of metal reeds which, when blown with the mouth, play the notes of the major chord, and when sucked, the other notes of the major scale. The concertina is a box similar in principle to the mouth-organ, but instead of being blown by the mouth, it is placed inside a bellows which is drawn open and squeezed shut by the hands. The piano accordion is a larger instrument built on the same principle; it is strapped on to the shoulders, and has a keyboard, like the piano, for the right hand, and a set of buttons with which the left can play chords. The Jew's harp is a metal frame with a vibrating tongue attached to it; the frame is held between the teeth, the tongue is set vibrating with the forefinger, and by opening the mouth wider as in singing, it can be made to sound different notes. The barrel organ or hurdy-gurdy is a mechanical instrument on wheels, played by turning a handle. Inside, attached to the handle, is a barrel with metal spikes attached; when the barrel is turned, the spikes pluck strings or open organ pipes, which are arranged to play fixed tunes. [*See* INSTRUMENTS OF THE ORCHESTRA.]

PORPOISE
A sea mammal related to the WHALE. Porpoises travel in schools and make long, curving leaps out of the water. In recent years several American marine zoos have trained porpoises to make good and very playful pets.

PORTUGAL
A republic in Southern Europe on the western part of what is called the Iberian peninsular. It is less than half the size (34,500 square miles) of Great Britain. Included in Portugal are the islands of MADEIRA and the Azores. The population is a little over 9 million. Portuguese is one of the Latin languages. The capital is Lisbon. Portugal is famous for the wine, port, which takes its name from the port of Oporto from which it is exported. Portugal also has important sardine fisheries.

Portugal has important overseas territories.

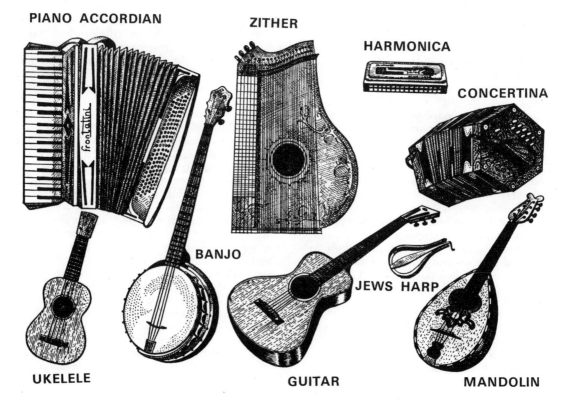

PIANO ACCORDIAN   ZITHER   HARMONICA   CONCERTINA   BANJO   JEWS HARP   UKELELE   GUITAR   MANDOLIN

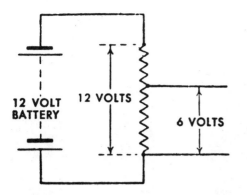

POTENTIOMETER Half the applied voltage is tapped halfway along a resistor.

In West Africa she owns Angola which is more than twice the size of France, and in East Africa Mozambique which is larger than France.

History:
Portugal was an independent kingdom from 1140 to 1910 since when it has become a republic. In the 14th and 15th centuries the Portuguese were great explorers, amongst the more famous being Prince Henry the Navigator, Bartholomew Diaz and Vasco da Gama. It was the Portuguese who in 1500 discovered and later colonized BRAZIL, retaining it until 1820. Since 1932 the Prime Minister and virtual dictator of Portugal has been Dr. Salazar.

PORTUGUESE GUINEA
A small Portuguese colony on the west coast of Africa. It adjoins the independent republic of GUINEA and should not therefore be confused with it.

POSTAL SERVICES
The writing of letters is probably as old as the art of writing itself. Letters needed to be carried by messengers or postmen to their destination. So the story of the post is in this respect very old. In ancient times the King would employ special messengers to carry his letters. The Greek writer, HERODOTUS, has described the posts of the Persians. They were well organized and rapid for an age that had to depend on horses to carry them. There are references to these posts in the Bible. The famous traveller, MARCO POLO, wrote of the posts which he found in China and which had existed for centuries. The Romans had a well organized postal service, but after the fall of the Roman Empire Europe for centuries had nothing so good as that of the Roman times. The only form of posts in the Middle Ages were those arranged by the merchant guilds and by the universities. Then in the 16th century, with the development of trade and

the discovery of the New World, the need for regular postal services became more urgent.

The first English Post Master, or Master of the Posts as he was then called, was Brian Tuke, who was appointed by Henry VIII in 1510, to organize posts along the main roads. Relays of horses were kept in readiness at points along the roads to carry the letters 'post haste'. Oliver CROMWELL was the first to appoint a Member of Parliament as Postmaster-General with an office in London known as the General Post Office. This was in 1657. The custom of putting the date of posting letters was first begun by the Post Office in 1660. Great changes were made in 1839 when Sir Roland Hill persuaded the Government to introduce the penny post and to adopt an adhesive stamp which he had invented. Up to 1839 the cost of postage depended on the distance, and usually the cost was too high for ordinary people to be able to use it.

Since 1874 the nations of the world have joined together through the Universal Postal Union to carry each other's letters by the quickest and cheapest method to any part of the world. It is through the Union that the amount of postage for letters to foreign countries is agreed upon. The Universal Postal Union is now one of the specialized agencies of the UNITED NATIONS.

POST MORTEM
This term means 'after death', and is a phrase used to describe an examination made by doctors to find out what has caused a person to die. Usually a doctor knows what has caused death, but when there is a doubt a post mortem may be held. When it is known that a person has not died from natural causes a coroner may order a post mortem to decide the exact cause of death.

POTENTIOMETER
Laboratory instrument used for the comparison of potential differences. The name is, however, commonly applied to a variable tapping resistance which is used to obtain a variable electric potential. The arrangement is illustrated in the diagram which shows the potentiometer connected across the supply voltage. The current through the resistance is constant, consequently the voltage drop is steady and at a point halfway along the voltage at the slider is half the supply voltage and so on.

POTTERY
The making of pottery is one of the oldest crafts in the world. No one knows who were the first potters. It has been suggested that primitive man originally got the idea of using

clay vessels in which to store his food and water from seeing little pools of rain water lying in hollows in clayey soil, whereas in other places the water just soaked into the ground. At first the clay vessels were probably hardened in the sun, but it may have been that in heating food in them over a fire it was found that the firing made them more durable.

Much can be learned from pieces of pottery left by peoples of bygone ages. For instance, decorated tiles, terra-cotta sculptures, earthen-ware storage jars, bricks and even drains, believed to be some 6,000 years old, have been found in the valleys of the Euphrates and Tigris, and the people there even kept their records inscribed on clay tablets. In North-West India and China pottery pipes for bathrooms were made about 2500 to 1500 B.C. The fine and beautiful Chinese glazed porcelain and stone-ware were made 3,000 years later.

From the circular shape of Egyptian pottery vases, it can be assumed that a wheel was used about 6,000 years ago. A fast potter's wheel was introduced in Greece towards the end of the Bronze Age—about 1500 B.C.

The Romans used pottery pipes for drains and water-pipes, and remains of some of them are still to be seen in this country.

The following is a description of the process of making pottery at the present time. The white clay needed for fine chinaware—which is mined in Cornwall—and another kind, called ball clay, are separately mixed with water and ground finely. The two mixtures are agitated constantly until ready for blending in the correct proportion. They are then filtered and the plastic clay left behind is then kneaded and drained in a mill, from which it emerges in an endless, snake-like roll. Suitable amounts can then be cut off for the potters.

From designs prepared in the studio, models and moulds are made. In the case of thrown articles, these are produced by the potter's skilful hands from a lump of clay rotating continually on the wheel. Some articles are made by pouring the liquid clay into moulds. Ornamentation is embossed or applied by hand. When the clay is dry and hard it is ready for the first oven firing, some of the articles being bedded in sand. Patterns de-signed for reproduction by printing are en-graved on copper with a graver or sharp-pointed tool. Prints are taken off these copper plates on specially prepared tissue paper and transferred to the chinaware, which is then passed through an electric kiln. Additional colours are sometimes applied; in other cases a free-hand design is painted on. The pottery is dipped in glaze and once more goes through an oven. After polishing, it is ready for use.

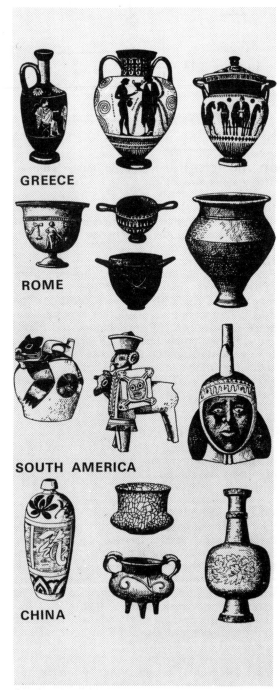

GREECE

ROME

SOUTH AMERICA

CHINA

POUND, Ezra (1885——)
American poet, born at Idaho. One of the most influential poets of his day. Pound's most important work is *Cantos*. He was sympathetic to Fascist Italy during the Second World War. When he returned to America at the end of the war he was committed to a mental home. He was released in 1958.

POUSSIN, Nicolas (1594–1665)

French painter, born at Les Andelys in Normandy. In 1624, after a hard and poverty-stricken youth, he went to Rome and there became famous. His *Golden Calf* from this period is in the National Gallery. He returned to Paris in 1640 and became painter in ordinary to Louis XIII, but, dissatisfied with the work he was charged with, he returned to Rome in 1643.

POWER

Rate of doing work. The unit of power is 1 foot-poundal per second, or (in the C.G.S. system) 1 erg-second. [*See* WORK.]

PRAYER BOOK

The Book of Common Prayer, so called because it was designed to teach *all* Church members to pray together, was a result of the demand, created by the Reformation, for Services in English instead of the then standard Latin. Its principal author was Thomas CRANMER, appointed Archbishop of Canterbury in 1533. He and his colleagues used as a foundation the old Roman Service Books, the Breviary and the Missal; and, drawing fairly heavily on Lutheran Service Books, and including some Eastern fragments too, they produced, by skilfully combining and editing their material, an English Prayer Book of great dignity. They reduced the Eight Hours (Services) of the Breviary to two—Mattins and Evensong. Cranmer attached great importance to Scripture reading, and he instituted the practice of systematically reading through the Bible each year. Cranmer produced two Prayer Books, in 1549 and 1552, both in Edward VI's reign, known as the First and Second Prayer Books of Edward VI. Cranmer made the second more Protestant in character than the First, especially in the Eucharist Service, where the word 'Mass' was replaced by 'Communion'. His work was later slightly modified in a Catholic direction in the Third (1559) and Fifth (1662) Prayer Books. The Fifth is still the official Prayer Book of the Church of England.

Its main contents are Mattins and Evensong, with Psalms for both, printed in the Great Bible translation by Miles Coverdale; the Holy Communion Service with a Collect (a special form of short prayer), Epistle and Gospel for each Sunday of the Calendar and for Saints' Days and Feasts (such as Christmas and Easter). It also contains the English Litany and Services for Baptism, Burial, Confirmation, Marriage, Consecration of Clergy, etc. Special editions of the Prayer Book are published for Anglican Congregations in Scotland, Ireland, America and elsewhere.

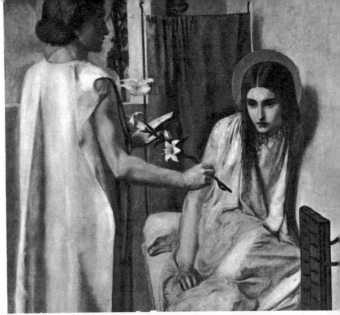

PRE-RAPHAELITES Rossetti's *The Annunciation*.

PRE-RAPHAELITES

English school of painting which flourished in the 19th century, and had as its aim the revival of the style of Italian painting before RAPHAEL, and a precision based on an exact observation of nature. Among its greatest members were Dante Gabriel ROSSETTI, Holman HUNT, Ford Maddox BROWN and William MORRIS. These men drew much of their inspiration from romantic stories and myths, from the Arthurian cycle of legends, and from religious subjects.

PRÉVOST, D'EXILES, Antoine François (1697–1763)

French novelist, born in Artois. After some years of exile in Holland and England, he published his first novel *Memoires d'un homme de qualité*. Its sequel was his best-known novel, *Manon Lescaut*. It is the story of a hopeless love ending in disaster, and has been made into both an opera and a film.

PRIESTLEY, John Boynton (1894——)

English writer, playwright and critic, born at Bradford. He is best known as a humorous novelist, two of his widely read books being *The Good Companions* and *Angel Pavement*. He has also written a number of plays, *Laburnum Grove* being particularly successful. During the Second World War he was a notable broadcaster.

PRIESTLEY, Joseph (1733–1804)

English chemist and theologian, born near Leeds. His special interest was gases. He obtained (1771) oxygen from mercuric oxide but failed to appreciate the significance of his discovery until several years later. Priestley discovered 'laughing gas' (nitrous oxide) in 1776. In religious matters he was unorthodox and eventually became a Unitarian. His sympathies with the French Revolution led to a mob storming his house. He felt himself badly used and migrated to America.

PRIMATE

The highest order of mammals and includes man, HOMO SAPIENS. They are usually divided into sub-orders in which are included: 1, man, the apes and monkeys; 2, the lemurs and 3, the tarsiers.

PRIME MINISTER

The head of the Government. He is sometimes called Premier and is always First Lord of the TREASURY. The first Prime Minister was Sir Robert WALPOLE who was an important CABINET Minister in the reign of George I. As the King could not speak English he appointed Walpole to preside over Cabinet meetings in his place and since then it has been the custom for the First, or Prime, Minister to preside over the Cabinet. It was not till 1917 that the title Prime Minister was recognized as one to describe the office of Prime Minister officially. In that year the nation, by an Act of Parliament, accepted the gift of Chequers as the country residence of British Prime Ministers. But because up till then the official title of the Prime Minister was First Lord of the Treasury, the Act accepted the gift 'for the use of the official who is popularly known as the Prime Minister'. It is the Prime Minister who personally selects the members of the Government and decides which of these shall be members of the Cabinet, in addition to those who must always be in it. The official residence of the Prime Minister is No. 10 Downing Street and it is here that the Cabinet hold their meetings.

PRINTING

Printing on soft clay by engraved rollers was practised by the SUMERIANS as early as 2500 B.C. The earliest known book printed in ink from blocks was a Buddhist sutra in A.D. 868. At about the same time the earliest printed newspaper, the Chinese *Court Gazette*, appeared. In Europe Johann GUTENBERG, of Mainz, Germany, is believed to have been the first man to print from movable cast-metal letters. This was about 1450. In Holland a similar claim is made for Laurens Janszoon Coster, of Haarlem. William CAXTON, an Englishman, learned the art of printing when he visited Cologne in 1471, and on his return set up a press of his own at Westminster in 1476.

Printing meant, of course, that instead of one document at a time being slowly written by hand, once the type was set many copies could be made for many people to read.

First of all the printer had to compose by hand, i.e., pick out the letters one by one and form words and lines in his 'stick' or case. These were then fitted together in the shape of a page and locked into formes. Later on machines were invented for casting type as it was wanted, and were worked by a keyboard, something like that of a typewriter. In the case of Monotype, holes are punched in a paper roll, afterwards transferred to another machine and the perforations control the matrix or mould through which molten metal passes to form the separate characters or letters. Linotype and Intertype machines not only mould the characters but set the words in slugs, or lines of the required width. Type sizes, once known by names, are now standardized under a points system originally introduced by a Frenchman, Pierre Simon Fournier, in 1737, and adopted by American typefounders in 1871 and, finally, by British typefounders in 1898.

In the letterpress or relief process, the faces of the characters are raised so that they become coated with ink and leave an impression when pressed on paper. The first printing machines were flat, paper was fed on to the type, pressure applied and the printed sheet removed. Now there are machines where the type is reproduced on a cylindrical metal sheet, which rotates as the paper is passed under it. Then there are the giant Miehle machines which print our newspapers from huge continuous rolls of paper—both sides simultaneously—fold and deliver them ready for despatch.

Pictures, too, are printed by letterpress—from half-tone blocks. The pictures are photographed through screen—glass frames crisscrossed by very tiny lines—and when printed on copper and treated chemically the surface consists of minute dots, which protrude in the same way as the faces of the type, and print an impression on the paper when inked. To get a coloured picture, a block has to be made for each colour used, and the blocks are printed one over the other, i.e., yellow first, then red, then blue, black, if used, and so on.

Although the relief form of printing is the most widely used, other methods are employed, some increasingly so. Gravure printing is an intaglio process, that is, the image to be printed is engraved in the surface of the printing plate and the cut out area filled with ink and the paper pressed on the plate; this is basically similar to printing engravings or etchings. Offset printing is a development of LITHO-

GRAPHY, and consists of transferring the impression of the inked plate to a rubber roller which then prints it on to the paper.

PRIVY COUNCIL

The Queen's Private Council. The Privy Council is even older than Parliament and goes back to Norman times. It was the full Council of the King's advisers that was known as the Great Council from which Parliament developed. A smaller group close to the King came to be known as the Privy Council, a term first used in the reign of Henry V.

The Queen usually presides over meetings of the Privy Council, but most of the work of the Council is done by a number of Privy Council committees and these are presided over by the Lord President of the Council. All members of the CABINET are members of the Privy Council and they remain members for life. Other distinguished people may be made Privy Councillors. All are addressed as Right Honourable.

One of the most important of the Privy Council committees is the Judicial Committee which is the final court of appeal for the colonies and for some Members of the British Commonwealth. It is also the final court of appeal for the Channel Islands and the Isle of Man.

PROKOFIEV, Sergei (1891–1953)

Russian composer, born in the Ukraine. One of the most outstanding Soviet composers, and one whose music is very popular in Europe and America, particularly his *Classical Symphony* and the musical fairy tale *Peter and the Wolf*. He wrote symphonies, concertos and ballets; of the latter his *Romeo and Juliet* is widely performed. He was also a brilliant pianist.

PROPHETS

Probably the greatest Prophets the world has ever known were the great Hebrew Prophets living in Palestine, especially between the 8th and 4th centuries B.C. After Elijah (about 870) came Amos (about 760), the first of the writing prophets, Hosea, the mighty Isaiah, Micah, Jeremiah, perhaps the greatest of them all, and Ezekiel (592). Nowadays, prophecy is usually associated with forecasting future events, but the Hebrew Prophet (the word comes from Greek meaning 'to speak before, or on behalf of') though he did often make forecasts, was primarily a religious genius, a moral teacher and a guide, a 'Man of God'. [*See* BIBLE.]

PROTECTORATES AND PROTECTED STATES

Terms used to describe territories or countries under the authority or protection of another. There is not much difference between a British Protectorate and a Crown Colony except that the inhabitants of a Protectorate are not British subjects as are those living in a British colony. A Protected State is a country whose foreign affairs are controlled by Britain but whose internal affairs are left to the ruler of the State.

PROUST, Marcel (1871–1922)

French novelist, born in Paris. Later part of his life was spent as a recluse, and it was during this time that he wrote his masterpiece *A la recherche du temps perdu* (*Remembrance of things past*) which was published in 16 volumes, and in which he portrayed his characters according to their inner emotional life, passing over their superficial appearances. His work has had considerable influence on European writers.

PROVERB

An old saying that contains a homely truth. Most proverbs began in the speech of ordinary country people. Here are half a dozen familiar ones:
A stitch in time saves nine.
Birds of a feather flock together.
It's a long lane that has no turning.
Too many cooks spoil the broth.
Fine words butter no parsnips.
A bird in the hand is worth two in the bush.

PROVOST

The chief magistrate in a Royal burgh in Scotland. His position is like that of a Mayor in England and Wales. The Provost of Edinburgh and three other Scottish cities have the right to be called Lord Provost.

PSALMS

The Book of Psalms was put together gradually, probably between the 6th and 2nd centuries B.C., and represents at least six different collections of Hebrew hymns. The word 'psalm' comes from the Greek *psalmos*, meaning 'the sound of (plucked) stringed instruments'. The Hebrew title for the whole collection means 'Book of Praises'. Our Book of Psalms contains 150 pieces; in the course of time, however, some originally single Psalms became broken up; others, originally separate, were fused together.

The majority of the Psalms date from a period during and after the Captivity. The words 'of David' represent a Hebrew literary tradition. King David was regarded as the founder of the Hebrew Psalter, and, indeed, some parts of the Book of Psalms may well have come from him; but other psalmists, writing at much later dates, continued to ascribe (perhaps dedicating) their work to David.

The Psalms are the greatest collection of religious poetry the world has seen, and they have exercised a profound influence on Hebrew and Christian thought. They are used to this day in almost every branch of the Christian Church; sometimes as they appear in our BIBLE, and sometimes in metrical (verse) versions—the first of which began to appear after the Reformation.

PSYCHIATRY

Science of the prevention, recognition and treatment of mental ill-health. The person who practises it is known as a psychiatrist. Abnormality of the mind may be due to a disease with physical symptoms, e.g., the delirium of fever; it may go hand in hand with physical disorder, a fact increasingly recognized in the new science of psychosomatic medicine. For example, the mental factor plays a great part in such diseases as gastric ulcer and asthma. Lastly, the mental abnormality may be the root cause, and is the field of psychiatry proper. The disease may have an obvious physical cause. The greatest disturbance of personality may, however, be accompanied by little obvious change in the brain. Lastly, the brain may have been abnormal from birth, this state of affairs being known as mental deficiency.

Treatment of mental disorder has been revolutionized within living memory. At one time mental patients were simply confined to a mental institution, but now the science of mental health is helping these people back to a normal way of living by such measures as electric shock treatment, and the new operation of prefrontal lobotomy, in which certain nerve fibres in the brain are cut in order to alter the patient's personality.

PSYCHOANALYSIS

A method of treating mental illness discovered by Sigmund FREUD. He claimed that there are three layers of the mind; the conscious, which contains thoughts we are aware of at any moment; the pre-conscious, which holds thoughts we can recall if need be; the unconscious (called the id), which contains thoughts we cannot recall except under the process of psychoanalysis. In treating patients the psychoanalyst has to overcome the resistance of these deep-seated thoughts to coming into the light of consciousness. The reason for wanting to reveal these 'skeletons in the cupboard' is that they are capable of haunting the patient and producing states of acute anxiety.

When they are eventually paraded before the patient and seen for what they are—and they may be very trivial things—there is a reasonable chance that the anxiety will disappear. Dreams play an important role in the treatment and in certain cases hypnotism is employed.

PSYCHOLOGY

The science of the human mind. The first psychological studies were made by ARISTOTLE in his book *On the Soul* (*De Anima*). The founder of modern psychology was Thomas HOBBES. With the development of the physical sciences psychology became an experimental science, which it still is today. Great advances have been made during the past fifty years in our knowledge of the physical construction of the BRAIN, and in the field of conscious and unconscious mind processes. Very important contributions have been made during this century by the following scientists: FREUD, JUNG, McDougall, James, PAVLOV, Watson, and, in the field of animal psychology, by Köhler.

Normal psychology deals with the intelligence, emotions, consciousness and instincts. Psychological methods are now being applied to education, industry, politics, care of children and many other branches of day-to-day life.

As distinct from the physical sciences there is no agreement amongst psychologists on the basic elements of their study. Some consider mind to be above and beyond the brain, while others tie mind and brain closely together. [*See* PSYCHIATRY and PSYCHOANALYSIS.]

PTERODACTYL

An extinct flying reptile which flourished about a hundred million years ago. It had long, toothed jaws, and a leathery skin which was stretched over the limb-bones to form wings.

PTOLEMY (*c.* A.D. 170)

Egyptian thinker of Greek origin. His great work the *Almagest* (The Great System) proved to be the most influential book on astronomy for over a thousand years. He assembled the work of earlier astronomers, and made very accurate observations of his own with the aid of an astrolabe (instrument which measures elevation of heavenly bodies). He also made advances in the fields of trigonometry, optics and geography.

PUBLIC PROSECUTOR

A lawyer under the HOME OFFICE whose duty is to see that wrongdoers are prosecuted in a court of law. A lawyer must have been a solicitor or barrister for at least ten years before he can be appointed Public Prosecutor.

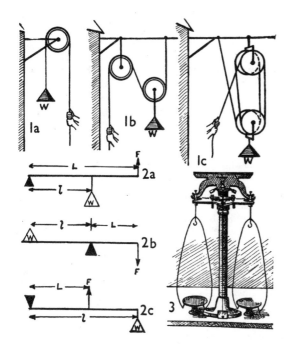

PULLEYS AND LEVERS 1a, single fixed pulley; 1b, single movable pulley; 1c, double movable pulley; 2a, b, c, principal types of lever where the formula *FL = Wl* applies. 3, laboratory balance, an application of system 2b.

PUCCINI, Giacomo (1858–1924)

Italian composer, born at Lucca. He wrote three of the most popular operas of all time, *La Bohème*, *Madame Butterfly* and *Tosca*.

PUGIN, Augustus Welby (1812–1852)

English architect, born in London, and trained in the office of his father. He helped Sir Charles Barry with the decorations and sculpture for the Houses of Parliament. He was a leading figure in the Gothic revival.

PULITZER, Joseph (1847–1911)

American newspaper proprietor and philanthropist, born in Hungary. Through his great energy and labour he became very wealthy, and subsequently endowed many prizes at Colombia University, New York.

PULLEYS AND LEVERS

A pulley is a wheel grooved round its circumference so that a rope or chain can be used to make the wheel rotate. A simple pulley is used for changing the direction of application of a force. For instance, if a single pulley is supported near the top of a house and the ends of the rope reach the ground, then a weight attached to one end can be raised to the top of the house when a man pulls downwards on the free end.

Pulleys are often arranged in systems of two or more in a 'purchase' or 'tackle'. With such a system, not only can the direction of application of a force be different from the direction of the force to be overcome, such as weight, but at the same time a mechanical advantage is obtained. This means that the resistance to be overcome is bigger than the pulling force used. (With a tackle one man alone can haul in a large sail pressed on by the wind, whereas without the tackle the resistance would be far too great for one man to overcome.) Pulley systems are often classified into the single-string system and the separate-string system, but the former is the one in general use. In practice the separate pulleys are mounted in groups in the same block, though in textbook diagrams the pulleys are shown spread out— a matter of convenience in illustration. In a system with a mechanical advantage, the distance moved by the weight to be overcome is less than the distance through which the pull must be exerted, and in the same proportion as the mechanical advantage. That is to say, with a mechanical advantage of 6, a pull of 10 pounds will lift a weight of 60 pounds, but for every foot moved by the 10 pounds, the 60 pounds moves only 2 inches.

A lever is a simple machine. This means that it has a mechanical advantage. In normal use the lever is a long rod, such as a crowbar. It is supported at one point, called the fulcrum. The force to be applied by the person using the lever has to be further from the fulcrum than the resistance to be overcome. The mechanical advantage is found by multiplying the resistance by its distance from the fulcrum, and then multiplying the applied force by its distance from the fulcrum. In equilibrium these answers are equal. Thus the resistance divided by the applied force is equal to the distance of the applied force from the fulcrum divided by the distance of the resistance from the fulcrum, and this gives the mechanical advantage. Thus a crowbar 6 feet long pivoted at a point 6 inches from one end will give a mechanical advantage at the other end of 5 feet 6 inches divided by 6 inches, which is equal to 11. So a weight just under 66 pounds placed over the shorter end could be lifted by a force of 6 pounds at the other end. An eleven-stone man using his whole weight could thus lift a weight of just under 121 stones or 15 cwt. 14 lb. This calculation, like all theoretical calculations on levers, ignores two important practical facts: (1) the strength of the lever itself, (2) the convenience or inconvenience of getting the working end of the lever into a suitable position under the weight in order to lift it.

PUN

A 'play' or joke with words. Thus Sir Robert Walpole at the outbreak of the Spanish Succession War in 1739 said, 'They may ring their bells now; before long they will be wringing their hands'. He was 'playing' on the two words *ring* and *wring* which, though of different spelling and meaning, have the same sound. In the same way Shakespeare plays on the words *soul* and *sole* when he makes Gratiano in the *Merchant of Venice* say, when Shylock is sharpening his knife on his shoe,

Not on thy sole, but on thy soul, harsh Jew
Thou mak'st thy knife keen.

Mark or Stop	Work	Examples and Notes
FULL STOP	to mark the end of a sentence.	Alice went timidly up to the door and knocked.
COMMA ,	(i) to mark off a group of words (phrase, clause) inside a sentence. (ii) to mark a slight pause between any two parts of a sentence.	After tea, when the rain had stopped, we went out into the garden. There will be, however, another chance tomorrow. There was a table set out under a tree in front of the house, and the March Hare and the Hatter were having tea at it.
SEMI-COLON ;	to mark a 'three-quarter' stop in the sentence, where two parts are neither joined nor completely separated.	It was getting dark when the blackbird at length flew off to the wood, and at once the pheasant, with head up, began walking in the same direction; then running and soon launching himself in the air he flew straight into the pines.
COLON :	used at the end of an expression that introduced something—for example, a speech or a list of items.	The Prime Minister said: The following things must be brought to camp: Answer three of the following questions: Sometimes used with a dash (:—). Many writers use the colon in much the same way as a semi-colon; but it is better limited to the work described here.
INVERTED COMMAS or QUOTATION MARKS " "	(i) placed around the *actual words spoken* in the writing down of conversation. (ii) placed around a quotation. (iii) sometimes placed around titles of books, names of ships, etc. But *see* ITALICS.	(i) "Rather!" replied the Otter, winking at the Mole. "The sight of these greedy young hedgehogs stuffing themselves with fried ham makes me feel positively famished." (ii) The valley at this time "glittered green with sunny showers", and a budding ash-tree "dipped its tender branches in the chiding stream". (iii) Dickens wrote "David Copperfield". (Notice that in conversation the other stops in the sentence come *inside* the closing quotation marks. In sentences (ii) and (iii), with quotations and titles, they belong to the main sentence and should come *outside*; though in fact most printers put them inside.)
QUESTION MARK ?	to mark the end of a *direct* question.	"Has he eaten to-day, or does he hunt empty?" said Mowgli. If we make the question indirect, the quotation marks and the question mark are not used: Mowgli asked whether he had eaten that day or was hunting empty.
EXCLAMATION MARK !	(i) used after an INTERJECTION and (ii) after an exclamation.	(i) Alas! Hurrah! (ii) How beautiful the woods are now! I suppose you want to go off in a coach and four! Sometimes, too, after commands (Attention! Sit up!) and after vocatives, that is, names called out, like this: Mowgli! Mowgli!
BRACKETS PARENTHESIS ( )	placed round a word or group of words that is only an 'aside' in the sentence.	Rikki-tikki's mother (she used to live in the General's house at Segowlee) had carefully told Rikki what to do if he ever came across white men. Brackets are often used for example, as they are in the note on the exclamation mark above.
DASHES — —	used like brackets, except that a single dash may be used before a parenthesis at the end of a sentence.	It's somebody's birthday—the Chief Weasel's, I believe—and all the weasels will be gathered together in the dining-hall. The only thing to do is to take all the furniture out of the drawing-room and put in in the bathroom—all except the piano and a few cane chairs.

PUNCTUATION

When we speak we need not bother about punctuation. Our voice does everything for us, with a little help now and then from our hand (in a movement or gesture) and eye. Punctuation means simply the 'points'—often called 'stops' or 'marks'—which we put into our sentences in order to help the *reader* who, unlike the *listener*, cannot see or hear us. Thus if we ask a question, the 'lift' of our voice at the end tells the *listener* that it is a question; but we have to show the *reader* with a mark or stop, like this: When shall we three meet again? The aim of our punctuation should be, then, to help the reader, so that we do not irritate him with too many stops or puzzle him by too few. For this reason, there can be no absolute 'rules' for punctuation. The writer himself has to decide according to the meaning he wishes to convey. But the chart on the opposite page, which shows the work of the various stops, will be a guide.

PURCELL, Henry (1659–1695)

English composer, born in London. A choir-boy of the Chapel Royal, he studied composition under Dr. John BLOW, the organist of Westminster Abbey; later he becane organist there himself. He wrote the first great English opera, *Dido and Aeneas*, several glorious Odes for St. Cecilia's Day, and much delightful music for Shakespeare's plays, especially *The Tempest* and *The Fairy Queen* (an adaptation of *A Midsummer Night's Dream*). His magnificent anthems are often heard in our cathedrals today, and his fantasias for viols and pieces for harpsichord are some of the finest ever written.

PURITANS

A group of religious people who wanted extreme purity, that is, simplicity, in church services, and observed a very strict code of behaviour with few amusements. The movement began in the reign of ELIZABETH I, and the persecution of puritans by Charles I led some to seek refuge in America; the first sailed in the *Mayflower*. Puritan support helped CROMWELL to victory, but after the restoration of Charles II they were again persecuted. Two of the great Puritan writers were John BUNYON and John MILTON.

PUSHKIN, Alexander (1799–1837)

One of Russia's greatest poets; also wrote several novels. Born in Moscow. He was a forceful character, and as a result of his liberal ideas was several times exiled. He died from wounds received while duelling. His most famous works are *Queen of Spades, Boris Godunov, Russlan and Ludmilla* and *Eugene Onegin.*

PYRAMID

In Egypt a royal tomb made out of solid masonry and built on a square base with sides sloping at an angle of about 50 deg. Perhaps the most famous of the Egyptian pyramids are those at Gizeh, the largest being the tomb of Khufu (4700 B.C.), and measuring approximately 756 feet along the base and over 480 feet high. Pyramid-like buildings were not confined to Egypt; the Assyrian ziggurat, for example, is such a structure and used as a temple. Also, the ancient peoples of South America built pyramids; in fact, two of the most magnificent of these buildings were the Temple of Tajin at Papantla, and the Temple of Tenochtitlan.

PYTHAGORAS (c. 582–c. 507 B.C.)

Greek thinker, born at Samos. Travelled in Babylonia and Egypt before settling down in Crotona, a Greek colony, and founding a religious brotherhood whose teachings had a great influence on Greek thought. Pythagoras is best known for the geometrical theorem that the square on the hypotenuse of a right-angled triangle is equal to the sum of the squares on the other two sides. He also made many contributions to the theory of numbers; he thought that everything could be reduced to numbers. He also discovered the numerical relation of musical tones.

Qq

QUAGGA

This mammal is related to the ZEBRA. Its most important distinguishing feature is the broad stripes which boldly sweep back from the middle of the flanks. Like the zebra it is confined entirely to the continent of Africa.

QUAKERS or The Society of Friends

In 1643, the 19-year-old George FOX, a native of Leicestershire and then apprenticed to a Nottingham shoe-maker, felt he had been directly commanded by Christ to 'forsake all' and dedicate himself to living a truly spiritual life, as he believed Christ had intended all His followers to do. Originally calling themselves 'Children of Light', Fox and his sympathisers were soon using the name 'Friends in the Truth', or simply 'Friends'. The Society of Friends was established as a distinct association in 1666. The name 'Quaker', originally used of a fanatical foreign sect in Southwark, was first applied to Fox, in derision, by Justice Bennett of Derby, in 1650. The name stuck, being taken up by the Friends themselves, and becoming a badge of honour.

The central principle of Quaker thought is the 'Inner Light' which dwells in every human soul, and which, if the individual develops the capacity to follow it, will guide him to salvation. Since Jesus speaks directly to every human heart, Quakers see no necessity for an organized clergy; they have no pulpits in their 'meeting houses', and no set form of service.

Since every act of a truly spiritual person should be a 'sacrament', Quakers have no official sacraments. Since no one should speak other than the truth, Quakers refuse to take an oath—which often brings them into disfavour with authority. Since war cannot be squared with spiritual life, most Quakers refuse to take arms, though their War Relief and Ambulance work is justly famous throughout the world.

QUANTUM THEORY

The theory formulated by Max PLANCK, about 1900, to account for the way in which radiation is emitted from a hot body. He showed that radiant energy could not be indefinitely subdivided but always existed in multiples of a specific unit, called a quantum (it is equal to $6 \cdot 55 \times 10^{-7}$ erg-secs and is a unit of action, that is, energy $\times$ time). The development of Planck's work is called 'quantum mechanics' and is the basis of the modern theory of the internal structure of the atom. To understand it properly needs a command of the most advanced mathematics.

QUARTER SESSIONS

These are courts which can try all but the most serious crimes. Every county has such a court and in addition 98 boroughs have similar courts. Courts of Quarter Sessions sit at least four times a year, i.e. once a quarter, and in busier places they meet much more frequently. The country courts are presided over by J.P.s but the borough ones are presided over by an important judge called a RECORDER.

QUARTZ

Also called rock crystal and is the crystalline form of silica (SiO_2) and is found throughout

the world; in fact it forms about 35 per cent of the earth's crust. It is one of the main ingredients of such igneous rocks as granite. Fused quartz can be used to make lenses.

QUATAR or Qatar

An independent State in the Persian Gulf and is known as one of the Gulf Sheikhdoms. It has had a special treaty agreement with Great Britain since 1916. The country has an area of 4,000 square miles but it has only about 55,000 inhabitants, all of whom are Arabs. The country is rich in oil.

Q.C.

This term stands for Queen's Counsel. A Q.C. is someone who has been a barrister for not less than ten years. Such barristers can apply to be appointed Queen's Counsel. As their gowns are made of silk instead of alpaca their promotion is often referred to as 'taking silk'. It is from Q.C.s that the LORD CHANCELLOR appoints judges. When the Sovereign is a King the letters used are K.C.

QUILLER-COUCH, Sir Arthur
(1863–1944)
British critic and novelist. Born at Fowey, Cornwall. With his first novel *Dead Man's Rock*, written under the pseudonym 'Q', he won great fame. This was followed by many others including *The Blue Pavilions, The Delectable Duchy, Fort Amity*. He also compiled *The Oxford Book of English Verse*. His published lectures, especially *The Art of Writing* and *On the Art of Reading* are very popular.

QUILTER, Roger (1877–1953)
British composer, born at Brighton. Composed much light music with very special appeal to children, for example, the music for the play *Where the Rainbow Ends* and the *Children's Overture*.

QUINTET [*See* CHAMBER MUSIC]

QUISLING, Vidkun (1887–1945)
Norwegian traitor and puppet minister. He formed a National Unity party in Norway in 1933, imitating the German National Socialists. After the German invasion of Norway in the Second World War he headed an administration under German control. He then made great efforts to nazify Norway but was unsuccessful. On the German defeat in 1945 he was imprisoned and executed for treachery. His name has become the general term for all who collaborate with the enemies of their country.

Rr

RABBIT

Belongs to the RODENTS, and is distinguished by the very small incisor teeth in its upper jaw placed behind a large pair in the lower. The common rabbit is found in Central and Southern Europe, and has been introduced into Australia and New Zealand. Because of the damage they cause to crops many have been killed off by infecting them with the disease myxamitosis.

RABELAIS, François (c. 1490–1553)

French satirist, born at Chinon in Touraine. He was educated for the Church, and entered first a Franciscan monastery and then the Benedictine Order. He studied medicine at Montpellier, qualifying in 1537, and practised in the hospitals of Lyons. In the meantime he had also made three voyages to Italy. He later became curé at Meudon. At intervals from 1533 onwards Rabelais published his great work—*Gargantua and Pantagruel*. It tells of the fantastic adventures of two mythical giants, and is full of the love of life. It is also a satire on the customs of the medieval Church.

RACCOON

Belongs to the same family as the KINKAJOU. The common North American raccoon is about the size of a large cat, and its fur is long, thick and grey. The face has a broad black stripe below the eyes and a white one above. It hunts for food on the ground during the night, but spends the day mostly in trees. It lives on small animals, birds, frogs, crabs, insects, fruits and berries. The crab-eating raccoon is found in South America.

RACE

Well-marked strain of an animal or plant species. In man it is usual to recognize white, yellow, brown, and black races, but this classification is based on skin-colour and does not agree with classifications based on head-form or hair-texture. The various strains of mankind which may have existed in the past have so intermingled that no pure race is believed to exist. For the purposes of studying the drifts of mankind across the globe it is convenient to speak of *Caucasian* races (Indo-Europeans, including Asiatic Indians and 'white' men), *Mongolian* races (including Red Indians and 'yellow' men), *Ethiopian* or *Negro* races ('black' men), and *Australoid* races (in-cluding the extinct Tasmanians and the aborigines). The so-called *Semitic* races contain white, black and yellow elements, and include the Bedouins, Egyptians and ancient Assyrians. Other classifications of man are in use, but it is generally agreed that the division of mankind into races is a matter of convenience, and varies according to the branch of study.

RACHMANINOV, Sergi (1873–1943)

Russian composer and pianist, born near Lake Ilman. He wrote many works, but his most popular compositions are his works for piano and orchestra. He was also an outstanding pianist.

RACINE, Jean (1639–99)

French dramatist and poet, born at La Ferté-Milon. He went to Paris where he befriended MOLIÈRE, LA FONTAINE and Boileau. Between 1667 and 1677 he wrote almost all the tragedies that made him famous—*Andromaque*, *Britannicus*, *Bérénice*, *Bajazet*, *Iphigénie*, and *Phèdre*. He was admitted into the French Academy in 1673. By 1677 he was tiring of dramatic work, and became historiographer-royal. In his last period wrote the two religious dramas *Esther* and *Athalie*.

RADAR

Originally known as 'radiolocation', was developed by a team of British scientists under the leadership of Sir Robert Watson-Watt. It is a method of detecting and positioning objects by means of reflected radio waves independent of the object itself. Short pulses of radio waves are radiated at a certain P.R.F. (pulse repetition frequency), depending upon the range required, in a narrow beam from a rotating aerial system. During the time interval between the pulses a receiver is connected to the aerial to receive the reflected signals, which are applied to a cathode-ray tube indicator. The distance to the object is determined by measuring the time interval between the transmission and reception of the reflected pulse. The reflected wave from objects one mile away is received about 10 microseconds after the transmit pulse.

With another form of radar equipment, known as P.P.I. (Position Plan Indicator), the reflected signal causes a change in intensity of the light spot on the display screen. A rotating trace on a long persistence cathode-ray tube geared to the aerial system gives a 'light' map of the area being swept out by the radio beam. An adoption of this system known as H₂S has been developed for aircraft, and this gives a recognizable map of the country over which the craft is flying. Radar equipment has been developed on similar lines to P.P.I. equipment for civilian use at harbours such as Liverpool, on ships, and at air ports (Ground Control Approach).

RADIO

Although J. C. MAXWELL mathematically described the nature of ELECTROMAGNETIC WAVES as early as 1865, and H. HERTZ showed their existence (1887) and demonstrated that they behave in a similar way to light waves, it was not until Lee de Forest (1907), an American scientist, added the grid to T. A. EDISON's lamp valve that radio became feasible. Several years went by before the true value of de Forest's work was appreciated. Broadcasting did not start until after the First World War, in 1922, when the American station KOKA

Pittsburg came 'on the air', and the B.B.C. began broadcasting from the Marconi Co. transmitter at Writtle, near Chelmsford. In the meantime radio-telegraphy had developed considerably, following the pioneer work of G. M. MARCONI, Sir A. FLEMING and Sir O. LODGE.

The basic processes in radio broadcasting are as follows. The sounds made in the broadcasting studio are transformed by the microphone into electrical signals (sound wave) which are then made to modulate a high-frequency current (carrier wave) being supplied to the aerial. These currents are induced, and are fed by the aerial as electromagnetic waves. When these reach the aerial of a domestic receiving set voltages and currents are induced, and are fed by the aerial to the receiver via tuning circuits where they are amplified and demodulated—that is, the sound wave is separated from the carrier wave. The sound wave is further amplified, and then fed to the loudspeaker which converts it to the same sounds made in the studio.

You will probably have seen or heard the

radar picture of harbour

RADAR Aircraft fitted with a radar system are given a complete picture, called a 'live map' of the area over which the plane is flying, see inset top right.

RAILWAYS A typical American steam locomotive of about 1860.

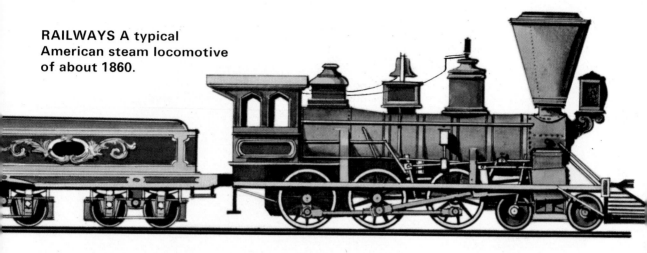

RAILWAYS A print of the opening in 1830 of the Liverpool and Manchester Railway. The 31 miles of permanent way took four years to complete. The railway was a fantastic success.

RAILWAYS A steam locomotive of the Great Northern Railway about 1870. Note the very large driving wheel.

RAILWAYS A diesel-electric
locomotive hauling a freight
train through a busy terminal.

RAILWAYS A diesel-electric
locomotive of the Canadian
National Railways hauling
an express passenger train.

RAILWAYS *Above*, the futuristic General Motors 'Aerotrain'. *Below*, the 'Kodama' electric express, one of the fastest trains in Japan. It runs between Tokyo and Osaka.

terms F.M. and A.M. used in connection with radio. A.M. means 'amplitude modulation' and describes the type of carrier wave in which the amplitude is made to vary up and down following the variation in loudness of the sounds striking the loudspeaker. F.M. means 'frequency modulation' and describes the carrier wave where the amplitude is always the same, but the frequency varies in accordance with the strength of the sound.

RADIOACTIVE ELEMENTS

The atom of any element consists of a nucleus and planetary electrons [*see* NUCLEAR ENERGY]. The nucleus is made up of protons, positively charged heavy particles, and neutrons, heavy particles without any electric charge. The protons and neutrons are bound together by very strong forces, so strong that for many years no means of releasing these nuclear forces was known.

Some elements have unstable nuclei, so that changes go on in them with the emission of particles or radiation. Such elements are said to be radioactive. This phenomenon, radioactivity, may be natural or artificial.

The best-known naturally radioactive element is radium, the first to be discovered. When a nucleus of a radioactive element emits radiation it changes into the nucleus of another element. If this is also unstable it also emits radiation and again changes, and so on through a series of changes until a non-radioactive element is reached. Thus radium finally ends up as lead, which is not radioactive. Four such radioactive series are known. The well-known radium is really a member of the uranium-radium series, the starting element really being uranium. The speed at which radiation is emitted is not the same for all radioactive elements; some are very slow, while others are very fast. The speed of breaking up is measured in terms of the half-life, that is, the time for half the nucleus to change into the next element of the series. The half-life of radium is 1,590 years, and it is the length of this half-life that makes radium seem to be permanently radioactive. Its 'daughter' element, that into which it changes when radiation is emitted, is a gas, radon, and the half-life of this is only 3·82 days. One of the elements in the uranium-radium series has a half-life of only a little more than one ten-thousandth of a second.

If we include every member of each of the three natural radioactive series then there are 49 known radioactive elements, though elements is the wrong word because some of them are forms of the same element, forms called ISOTOPES. The correct statement is therefore that there are 49 known naturally radioactive

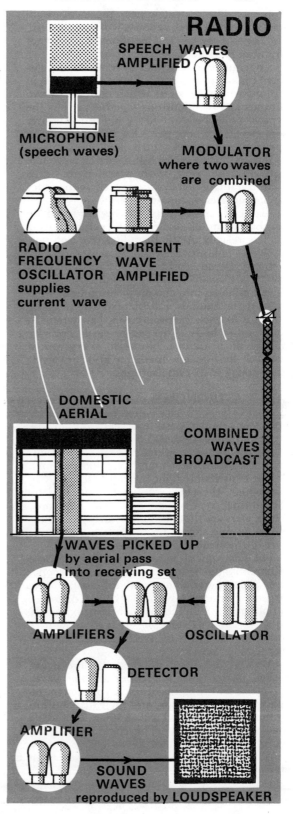

RADIO

SPEECH WAVES AMPLIFIED

MICROPHONE (speech waves)

MODULATOR where two waves are combined

RADIO-FREQUENCY OSCILLATOR supplies current wave

CURRENT WAVE AMPLIFIED

DOMESTIC AERIAL

COMBINED WAVES BROADCAST

WAVES PICKED UP by aerial pass into receiving set

AMPLIFIERS

OSCILLATOR

DETECTOR

AMPLIFIER

SOUND WAVES reproduced by LOUDSPEAKER

isotopes. The fourth series, the neptunium series, is not natural. It starts with neptunium, an element made by the bombardment of uranium with neutrons.

The radiation emitted by radioactive elements is of several sorts. One sort consists of alpha-particles, each of which consists of two protons and two neutrons together; this is the type of radiation emitted by radium. Another sort consists of beta-particles, which are high-speed electrons. A third sort is gamma-radiation, not particles but a sort of wave like light, but of very short wavelength. This gamma-radiation may be emitted with either alpha-particles or beta-particles.

Artificial radioactivity can be produced by bombardment of nuclei in a cyclotron or a nuclear reactor. Artificial radioactive isotopes, known as radioisotopes, can be made from any element. Because of this, many ordinary elements are made artificially radioactive, and then combined into chemical compounds used in food for animals and plants. The purpose of this is to trace the progress of the element in the plant or body. This can be easily done by means of a GEIGER COUNTER. Very much research in industry, medicine and biology is done today with radioisotopes.

RADIO ASTRONOMY

Branch of astrophysics which has been developed during the past few years out of the techniques of RADAR, and devoted to the study of radio waves emanating from space; particularly from dark radio stars, i.e., bodies which do not emit visible light but only radio waves, and which, therefore, cannot be observed by the normal type of astronomical telescope. These stars are thought to be nearly as numerous as visible stars, and to form a significant part of the structure of the heavens.

The instrument used to investigate these radio emissions is known as a radio telescope. It is a large aerial of parabolic shape. The largest is designed with a 250-feet diameter aerial and a bowl depth of approximately 60 feet. Also it is steerable so as to allow it to follow the bodies it is investigating; it is very like a radar aerial.

Among the most interesting 'messages' picked up by radio telescopes are the waves broadcast by the atoms of cold hydrogen in the space between the stars, and their distribution in the sky has enabled astronomers to make a map of our own galaxy. This could not be done by observing the stars because the galaxy contains so much dust or fog that most of the stars in it are invisible even through the biggest telescopes. But radio waves pass as easily through the fog in space as they do through the

fogs we have on earth.

Other radio sources, as they are called, include the hot gases blown outwards by an exploding star. Exploding stars are rare, but their gases go on broadcasting for thousands of years after the explosion and several examples are known. Sometimes the expanding gases can also be seen as a small luminous nebula, and one of the most powerful radio sources known is of this kind. It is known as the Crab nebula, from its shape, and it represents all that remains of a star that exploded in the year 1054.

The distant galaxies contain broadcasters similar to those found in our own galaxy, and these, too, can be picked up by large radio telescopes. The most powerful radio source known consists of two entire galaxies in collision. Known as Cygnus-A, it is 270 million light-years away, and it is behaving like a broadcasting station of 1,000 million million million million million million kilowatts! The great telescope at Palomar shows it only as a tiny dumb-bell-shaped patch of faint light.

Radio telescopes can penetrate into space to much greater distances than ordinary telescopes. The 200-inch reflector on Palomar Mountain can just make out objects 2,000 million light-years away, which is 12,000 million million million miles. But the big radio-interferometer at Cambridge can record waves coming from sources 10,000 million light-years distant, which is five times as far. They tell us something of what the universe was like at about the time when the sun was first formed, for they must have left their 'broadcasting stations' 10,000 million years ago!

RADIO ASTRONOMY A view of the control room of the radio-telescope at Jodrell Bank.

RADIO-CARBON DATING

Method of estimating the age of dead organic matter from the proportion of carbon-14 isotope it contains. This radioactive isotope is generated by COSMIC RAYS and absorbed by living matter, in which its proportion to ordinary carbon-12 does not vary. This proportion begins to diminish at death, the half-life [see RADIOACTIVE ELEMENTS] of carbon-14 being 5,568 years. The extent of the radioactive decay in ordinary specimens is accurately measurable for ages not exceeding 20,000 years, so that the method is suitable for dating objects of archaeological interest such as mummies, wooden articles, and papyrus.

RADIOLOGY

Science of radiology includes the study of the properties of X-RAYS and their applications. It also, by common consent, includes related subjects, such as the use of radium in medicine. Radiology is now fairly sharply divided into diagnostic radiology and radiotherapy, and radiologists tend to specialize in one or the other of these branches. The diagnostic radiologist is concerned with the use of X-rays to detect disease and to discover its nature. This he does principally by two methods; radioscopy, in which he watches through a fluorescent screen the passage of X-rays through the patient's body, and radiography, in which the rays after passage through the body are brought into contact with an exposed film, so as to make, after developing, a permanent record to be interpreted at leisure. At first radiology was concerned with bones and foreign bodies, but the use of swallowed or injected substances opaque to X-rays have made possible investigation of the stomach, bowels, bladder, kidneys, lungs, womb, and recently the heart cavities themselves.

The radiotherapist uses X-rays and the rays emitted by radium to treat disease. The bulk of his work is concerned with treatment of cancer, particularly in cases where a surgeon cannot remove the growth.

RADIO-SONDE

Sounding balloon carrying radio equipment which broadcasts signals during its ascent. The pressure, temperature and humidity of the atmosphere are calculated from the frequency of the signals and from their pitch, a separate waveband being used for determining the speed and altitude of the balloon. Radio-sondes may be sent to heights of the order of 60,000 feet.

RADIO TELEPHONY

Transmission of speech over radio links. Radio telephone links are used for communications between islands where the provision of submarine cables is either not possible or uneconomical. They are also used on the long trans-oceanic and ship-to-shore telephone services. [See TELEPHONE.]

RAEBURN, Sir Henry (1756–1823)

Scottish portrait painter. The son of a miller, he was apprenticed to a goldsmith at the age of fifteen. In 1785 he spent two years studying in Italy, and on his return to Edinburgh began producing portraits of all the Scottish celebrities of his day. Raeburn's paintings were lifelike and sincere, and he painted more than seven hundred canvases.

RAILWAYS

Most of the early railways in England were used to carry coal and stone, and belonged to private colliery and quarry companies. In 1801, however, a railway was promoted under an Act of Parliament for the carrying of 'public' traffic, and was known as the Surrey Iron Railway. Sand, stone, coal, etc. were hauled in railway wagons drawn by horses. Eventually it became derelict, although a portion was taken over by the London, Brighton and South Coast Railway.

The first 'public' railway on which locomotives were used was the Stockton and Darlington Railway. This was promoted in 1821, and on September 27, 1825 was opened for public traffic. Its first engine, *Locomotion*, is now kept on a pedestal at Darlington station. On the opening day the engine pulled six wagons of coal, one passenger carriage, twenty-one trucks fitted with seats, and six more loaded coal wagons. The speed was not high, and the long train was preceded by a man on horseback. The Stockton and Darlington became a fairly big railway before it was amalgamated with the North Eastern in 1865. It was the Liverpool and Manchester Railway, opened in 1830, which led the way to fast passenger trains. On that line thirty miles an hour was considered a wonderful speed, as it was in view of the twelve or fifteen miles an hour which represented a stage-coach horse's top speed, and the six or eight miles an hour at which coal-hauling locomotives moved.

In the United States, railways of the horse- or mule-operated type were built in 1826–1827, and by 1830 powers had been granted for the construction of many railway lines. The South Carolina Railroad had decided to use locomotives as early as 1827. The Delaware and Hudson was the first to use a locomotive, the *Stourbridge Lion*, purchased from England in 1827. The Baltimore and Ohio was the first to use American-built locomotives, starting in 1830 with Peter Cooper's experimental engine *Tom Thumb*—for which the United States claim the same honours as we do for George Stephenson's *Rocket*. The Mohawk and Hudson Railway was opened in 1831, and on this line a famous engine, the *De Witt Clinton*, was used.

Although Britain was the first country to have railways, several other countries followed closely. In France, lines somewhat similar to the English plate-ways were built as early as 1782, and in 1823 the St. Etienne Railway was authorized. This line was opened on October 1, 1828, between St. Etienne and Andrezieux, a distance of 21 kilometres. But locomotives do not appear to have been used until some time later. These early lines were worked by horses, and from illustrations of the period it would appear that both coal and passenger trains were run by gravity downhill and pulled uphill by horses.

The following are the dates when public railway traffic was inaugurated in various countries: Austria, 1827; France, 1828; Belgium, 1835; Germany, 1835; Russia, 1838; Italy, 1839; Switzerland, 1844; Spain, 1848; Sweden, 1851; Portugal, 1854; Turkey, 1860; Canada, 1836; South Africa, 1860; Australia, 1855; India, 1853; Cuba, 1834; Mexico, 1873; Japan, 1872; China, 1875; North Africa, 1852.

From these early and often crude beginnings the railway system has risen to be the most important of all forms of transport, whether of goods or passengers. This development was made possible by the engineers who were not only able to design and make engines of greater and greater power, but also rolling stock, signalling systems, permanent ways, bridges, tunnels, etc. [*See* STEAM ENGINES.]

RAINBOW

Colour effect seen when sunlight is reflected from raindrops. In passing into and out of a raindrop the LIGHT is refracted and its colours dispersed. A second bow may be seen in light which has been twice reflected within the raindrops, and in this case the order in which the colours are seen is reversed. The colours of the SPECTRUM are seldom all present, the range seen depending upon the size of the raindrops.

RALEIGH, Sir Walter (*c.* 1552–1618)

English soldier, explorer and author, born near Sidmouth. After education at Oxford he entered military service, and served in France and Ireland. Became a favourite of Queen ELIZABETH because of his charm and gallantry; from this springs the story of his throwing his mantle over a puddle of water to enable the Queen to walk dry-footed. He arranged expeditions to colonize Virginia, and himself took part in expeditions against the Spanish. In 1595 he led an exploration to South America in the hope of finding the gold mines of El Dorado. When James I came to the throne he pursued a policy of peace with Spain. This was opposed by Raleigh, who desired war with Spain, and for this and other conspiracies he was sent to the Tower. In 1617 he was released to lead an expedition to Guiana to find gold, on the condition that he in no way involved himself with the Spanish, and that should he do so he would be executed. The expedition was ill-fated, and on his return he was executed in Old Palace Yard between the Abbey and the Houses of Parliament.

RAMEAU, Jean-Philippe (1683–1764)

French composer of the time of Louis XV, born at Dijon. He was the greatest opera-composer of his time, and also wrote many delightful harpsichord pieces.

RAMSAY, Sir William (1852–1916)

Scottish scientist, born in Glasgow. Made advances in many branches of chemistry, but is most famous for his discovery of the 'inert gases', helium, argon, neon, krypton, and xenon. Also conducted important experiments with RADIOACTIVE ELEMENTS. Awarded the Nobel Prize for Chemistry in 1904.

RAPHAEL, properly Raffaello Santi (1483–1520)

Italian painter, sculptor and architect, born at Urbino. Regarded as one of the greatest artists of the Renaissance. After working in Florence from 1504 to 1508, he was summoned to Rome by Pope Julius II, where he helped in the decoration of the Vatican. His *The Crucifixion* and *The Knight's Dream* (both in the National Gallery, London) are good examples of his work at this period. His best-known work is the *Sistine Madonna*, named after the church for which it was commissioned. Appointed chief architect, Raphael designed churches, palaces, and mansions, also tapestries.

RASMUSSEN, Knud Johan Victor (1879–1933)

Danish arctic explorer, born at Jakobshavn, Greenland. Led a number of expeditions to the Arctic Circle, mainly to study the lives of the Eskimos.

RASPUTIN, Gregory (1871–1916)

Born in Siberia, and the son of a fisherman. As a young man he became a professional pilgrim, living on the alms he received. He gradually won the reputation of a saint, and in 1905 went to St. Petersburg (now Leningrad) where he acquired great influence at the Imperial Court through a mesmeric power over women. The Tsar's wife believed in his ability to cure her ailing son, and in this way Rasputin gained fantastic power at the royal court. Although banished to Siberia in 1913, he returned the next year and resumed his power, but was assassinated by members of the Court.

RAT [*See* RODENTS.]

RATES
A local tax but instead of being a tax on income they are a tax on the property a person occupies. Rates are an important contribution towards paying for services provided by LOCAL AUTHORITIES. Rates were first collected in the reign of Elizabeth I and were for the relief of the poor in a parish.

Rates are collected by all local authorities except County Councils and Parish Councils. County Councils receive from rating authorities, as they are called, a considerable amount of the money collected to spend on services for the whole county. Parish councils receive from their Rural District Council a very small grant to carry out their duties. The amount of rates to be paid on each house or other buildings is decided every five years by Valuation Officers appointed by the Board of Inland Revenue.

RAVEL, Maurice (1875–1937)
French composer, born at Ciboure in the Pyrénées. Much of his music breathes the atmosphere of fairy tales, for example the opera *L'Enfant et les Sortilèges*, the *Mother Goose Suite* and the *Pavane for a dead Infanta*. He also wrote many pieces inspired by Spain, including the famous *Bolero*.

READE, Charles (1814–1884)
British novelist and dramatist, born at Ipsden, Oxfordshire. He was educated at Oxford and began his career in writing with a play in 1851, and later wrote other plays and novels. But his reputation rests on the novel *The Cloister and the Hearth*. It is a historical novel, set in Holland, Germany, France and Italy at the turn of the 15th century, full of adventure, and depicting a wide variety of characters.

RECORDER
A musical instrument in use in the sixteenth and seventeenth centuries, and a type of flute blown endways (not sideways, like the modern flute). It had a sweet, piping sound. Various sizes existed, from treble to bass, and whole orchestras were formed, called 'consorts'.

RECORDER
A professional judge who presides over a borough QUARTER SESSIONS. He must have been a barrister for at least five years and is appointed by the LORD CHANCELLOR. There is one exception to this and that is in the case of the City of London. He is appointed by the Lord Mayor and aldermen and presides over the Lord Mayor's Court. He is also one of the Judges of the Central Criminal Court or Old Bailey.

RED CROSS
The name given to societies for the care of the sick and wounded, particularly in time of war. In Moslem countries the symbol is the Red Crescent. It was a Swiss, named Henri Dunant, who was mainly responsible for getting nations to agree to certain rules for the care of wounded soldiers. Some years before this he had helped in the founding of the first youth organization —the Young Men's Christian Association. Dunant's ideas about the care of the wounded were discussed at an international conference held at Geneva in 1864 and the first treaty, or convention, for the care of the wounded was signed then. The symbol of the Red Cross was chosen because it was a Swiss who made the plans, and the Swiss flag is a white cross on a red background. The colours were reversed so that they would not be confused with the Swiss flag. Nations who signed the Geneva Convention agree, amongst other things, to respect this sign and never to fire at a building or vehicle which is marked with the Red Cross. All countries have their own Red Cross or Red Crescent Societies. In 1929 another Red Cross Convention was signed by which nations made rules for the treatment of prisoners of war.

The Red Cross is always strictly neutral in time of war. Because Switzerland is always neutral the International Committee of the Red Cross is made up of only Swiss citizens so that they can act in time of war. Since 1909, however, there has been a League of Red Cross Societies to which all Red Cross societies belong. Its object is to encourage and help Red Cross action to relieve human suffering.

REFORMATION
The break-away from the Roman Catholic Church which took place in Europe during the 16th century. It began in Germany where Martin LUTHER, a miner's son who had become a priest, preached against the granting by the Pope of indulgences—pardons given in ex-

change for money. He attracted attention by nailing a protest to the church door in Wittenberg (1517). In England the Reformation started when HENRY VIII threw off the authority of the Pope (1534), declared himself Head of the Church and had copies of the Bible in English put into churches for all who could read. The next step was the publication of the first English Prayer Book under Edward VI. After a set-back under the Catholic Mary, the Reformation became firmly established in England during the reign of ELIZABETH I.

REGENT

Someone who acts in place of the Sovereign. This may be necessary if the Sovereign is a child or if he or she is incapable of carrying out Royal functions. This was the case in 1811 when the Prince of Wales, afterwards George IV, was appointed Regent because his father George III had become insane. This period, which lasted until 1820, is called the Regency period and Regent's Park and Regent Street are named after this Regent.

When Elizabeth II came to the throne it was decided that as the heir to the throne, Prince Charles, was then a child, a Regent should be appointed to act if he should succeed to the throne before coming of age. So in 1953 the Regency Act was passed appointing the Duke of Edinburgh as Regent in such an event. [*See* COUNSELLORS OF STATE.]

REGISTRAR GENERAL

The officer responsible for the registration of births, marriages and deaths in England and Wales. His office is at Somerset House, in the Strand, London. Every County Council has to appoint a Registrar and when a baby is born the parents have to register his birth and name with the local registrar. All marriages and deaths must also be registered with him. The local registrar sends copies of all these registrations to Somerset House.

REINDEER or caribou

Belongs to the ruminants, and is the only member of the deer family in which antlers are grown by both sexes. There are two kinds in North America, the barren-ground caribou and the woodland caribou. In Lapland the reindeer has long been domesticated, supplying the Lapps with milk, flesh, hides and a means of transport.

RELATIVITY THEORY

Created by Albert EINSTEIN, first as the 'Special' theory in 1905, then as the 'General' theory in 1915. No convincing explanation can be given of these theories without considerable mathematics. As a general and qualitative statement of them, it can be said that they resolve contradictions between certain observed facts, such as the constancy of the speed of light in a vacuum under all conditions of observation, and certain accepted theories, such as the old principle of relativity according to which the velocity of light should vary according to the speed of the observer, and they fitted anomalies of certain observed astronomical facts into a general law that had no exceptions. Two consequences of the special theory are that mass and energy are interchangeable according to a simple mathematical relationship ($e = mc^2$), and that the mass of a body increases with its speed, though the increase is negligible for such speeds as have been, until the discovery of fundamental particles smaller than an atom, observed in mechanics and astronomy.

REMBRANDT, properly **Rembrandt van Rijn** (1606–1669)

Dutch historical and portrait painter, born at Leyden. After painting members of his family in Leyden, he moved to Amsterdam in 1631, where he immediately became the most popular portrait painter. In 1632 at the age of 26 he painted his famous *Lesson in Anatomy*, a painting that showed his great talents. In 1634 he married, and about this time produced his *Portrait of an Old Woman*, *Presentation in the Temple* and *Marriage of Samson*. In 1642 the artist's fortunes changed for the worse. His wife died, and he painted the ill-fated *The Night Watch*. This group portrait was commissioned by a corporation, and the members were very disappointed to find that only a few central figures were painted clearly, the rest of the company being in shade. As a painting, *The Night Watch* is magnificent—a masterpiece of light and shade, but after its appearance Rembrandt's popularity declined rapidly. During the 1650s Rembrandt painted *John the Baptist*, *Jacob Blessing the Sons of Joseph* and the portrait of Jan Six. Among Rembrandt's last great paintings were *The Syndics* and *The Jewish Bride*. Rembrandt produced some 700 paintings and an enormous number of etchings. It is his use of light and shade, and the striking realism and delicacy of his portraits that really distinguish him.

RENOIR, Pierre Auguste (1841–1919)

French impressionist painter, born at Limoges. Renoir began work at the age of thirteen as a decorator of porcelain. In 1862 he entered an art school where he met CEZANNE, MONET and SISLEY. Up to 1870, when he began to paint portraits for a living, he lived in poverty. From

REMBRANDT
A detail of
the centre group
from Rembrandt's
painting *A Woman Taken in Adultery*.

1880 to 1882 he travelled in Italy and Algeria, and in 1882 held his first really successful exhibition, where the charming *Moulin de la Galette*, full of young dancing figures in flickering light and shade, was first seen. In 1890 he retired to Provence, where in his last years he painted with a brush tied to his paralysed hand.

REPTILES

Class of cold-blooded, air-breathing vertebrates, in which the heart is three-chambered, and the skin is protected by scales. In the evolution of the vertebrates the reptiles appear as descended from AMPHIBIANS, but are themselves ancestors of both birds and mammals. Modern species are divided into four Orders, represented by the crocodiles, tortoises, snakes, and the primitive Sphenodon (Tuatera) of New Zealand, respectively.

REPUBLICAN PARTY

The party in opposition to the DEMOCRATIC PARTY in the UNITED STATES. Formed in 1854 of anti-Federalists and people opposed to the extension of slavery. The first President of the United States drawn from the Republican Party was LINCOLN (1861–65). From the time of the Civil War until about 1930 it was the dominant political party. One of its recent Presidents was General EISENHOWER (1953–61), Supreme Commander in the Second World War.

REQUIEM

Mass for the souls of the dead. This has been set to music, the most notable being composed by PALESTRINA, MOZART, VERDI, BERLIOZ, DVORAK, FAURÉ, and BRITTEN.

RESTORATION

The re-establishment of Charles II on May 29th, 1660. After the death of CROMWELL, nearly two years earlier, there had been no firm rule in England, and Parliament finally decided to recall Charles II, who was living in Holland. May 29th was celebrated with a special service in church until about a hundred years ago. It was sometimes known as 'Oak-apple Day' because on it Charles returned thanks not only for his restoration to the throne but also for his escape in 1651 after the battle of Worcester, when he eluded the enemy for a day by hiding with one of his supporters in an oak tree. Inns called 'The Royal Oak' also commemorate this incident. Six months after the Restoration the ROYAL SOCIETY was founded and Charles became its patron. It is the oldest scientific society in Britain. A great revival began in poetry and drama.

REUTER, Paul Julius (1816–1899)

Born at Kassel, Germany. He was the founder of the news agency which still bears his name. He came to London (1851) where he set up his important business, and became a naturalized British subject.

REVERE, Paul (1735–1818)
American soldier and patriot, born in Boston, Massachusetts. Became a member of the Boston 'Anti-British Society'. He is famous for his midnight ride (April 1775) from Boston to Concord to warn the population of the approach of the British troops. The ride was made famous by Longfellow's poem *Paul Revere's Ride*.

REYNOLDS, Sir Joshua (1723–1792)
English portrait painter, born near Plymouth. After studying in London, he set up as a portrait painter in Devonport at the age of nineteen. In 1749 he went to Italy to study, and returning to London in 1752, he achieved immediate fame. On the foundation of the Royal Academy in 1768, he was elected President and knighted. Altogether Reynolds painted more than 2,000 portraits of famous people and historical paintings. His *Mrs. Siddons* is probably the finest as well as the best-known. Other fine portraits of historical interest are those of Dr. Johnson, Oliver Goldsmith, David Garrick, Edmund Burke and Charles James Fox.

RHINOCEROS
This fearsome-looking mammal is on the whole timid and prefers to avoid fighting, but if attacked blindly charges the assailant. In spite of its large size and bulk it can travel at considerable speed. Rhinoceroses are vegetable eaters, living on grasses, foliage and the like. There are five species, three found in India, Borneo, Burma and the Malay Peninsula, and two in East and South Africa.

RHODES, Cecil John (1853–1902)
South African statesman, born at Bishop's Stortford, he was eighteen when he went to South Africa. He rapidly acquired a fortune in the diamond mines of Kimberley. Rhodes dreamt of a South Africa under the British flag. He brought about the annexation of Bechuanaland (1884), and as head of the British South Africa Chartered Company and Prime Minister of the Cape Province was able to annex the territory now named after him, Rhodesia. But he was forced to retire from political life in 1896 when his associate Dr. Jameson was captured in an attempt to overthrow the Boer Government in Johannesburg. Believing in the Anglo-Saxon races, Rhodes established in his will a trust to award scholarships at Oxford to students from the Dominions, the U.S.A. and Germany.

RHODESIA
A self-governing colony in central Africa that is nearly twice the size (150,000 square miles) of Great Britain. It has a population of over four million of whom less than a quarter of a million are Europeans. The capital is Salisbury, the chief industrial town being Bulawayo. The chief river is the Zambezi which has been dammed by the building of the great Kariba Dam and lake to produce hydro-electric power. The country has many minerals and also produces tobacco.
History :
Rhodesia takes its name from Cecil RHODES who succeeded in 1890 in having the territory annexed to Britain. The territory was administered from 1890 to 1923 by the British South Africa Co. In 1923 it was allowed to be self-governing except for certain matters, particularly the protection of the African people, for which the British Parliament still retained responsibility. From 1953 to 1963 the country formed a federation with Northern Rhodesia (now ZAMBIA) and Nyasaland (now MALAWI).

RHINOCEROS
The species shown here is the one found in East Africa.

When this federation was ended and the other two countries became independent Rhodesia said she also intended to become independent even if the British Parliament did not agree. Great Britain told her that she could not lawfully do this, as Rhodesia was unwilling that the Africans should have the same right to vote as the Europeans had. In 1965, however the Prime Minister of Rhodesia announced a unilateral declaration of independence (UDI). This led Britain to stop trade with her and other Members of the Commonwealth also applied these sanctions, as such measures are called.

RICHARDSON, Samuel (1689–1761)

English novelist. His first novel, *Pamela*, is 'a series of familiar letters now first published in order to cultivate the Principles of Virtue and Religion,' and the later novels, *Clarissa* and *Sir Charles Grandison*, have the same purpose. FIELDING started his career with a parody of him (*Joseph Andrews*) but Richardson also had many admirers, including Diderot and Rousseau.

RICHELIEU, Armand Duplessis, Duc de (1585–1642)

French churchman and statesman, born in Paris. In 1622 he was named a cardinal, and in 1624 became minister of state to Louis XIII and in fact dominated the weak king for the rest of his life, holding the reins of power himself. He destroyed the HUGUENOTS as a political party, taking La Rochelle and destroying Montauban, their stronghold. Abroad he built up the power of the French crown at the expense of Spain and the Hapsburgs, but in the process destroyed the liberties and political life of the French people. The nobles hated him because of his powerful position, and tried many times to kill him. He founded the French Academy, and had literary pretensions.

RIDING

A worthwhile accomplishment for three reasons: it is wonderful exercise and helps to acquire a good upstanding presence even when the rider is not on a horse; it is a sport providing competitive interest in the many gymkhanas held in all countries; and finally the thrills of hunting are impossible without the ability to ride.

During instruction days the best and most economical dress is jodhpurs and stout shoes. An ordinary shirt or blouse with collar and tie, and a sports jacket, or a roll-neck sweater can be worn during the colder months. When buying jodhpurs, a pair with plenty of room in them is advisable.

It is essential for a rider to be on friendly terms with the horse he rides. Stroking the animal's nose, talking to him in a kindly tone and occasionally allowing him to nuzzle a piece of sugar off your hand help to establish this relationship. Avoid sudden movements as most horses are very nervous when strangers are present.

Two things should be observed about a horse's saddle and reins; that the saddle is set slightly forward, the girth going fairly close to the animal's shoulders (this brings the seat part of the saddle to the middle of the horse's back). As regards reins, the snaffle is the kind of bit which will not hurt the horse if the learner does something wrong; the curb is best left for more experienced riders, and is frequently omitted at first.

Look over the various parts of the saddle and bridle, and learn their names. Remember that girth and stirrup leathers are adjustable to prevent the saddle slipping, and to make sure that the stirrups are at the correct height.

To mount, the rider should stand by the horse's shoulders on the left side; take hold of the reins in his left hand and rest that hand on the horse's withers (just in front of the pommel); then raise the left foot and put it into the stirrup, using his right hand to turn it towards him. The foot should go well into the stirrup; almost to the heel, in fact. With his right hand on the waist of the saddle, the rider should then give a slight jump with his left foot, and when the right leg is straight, bring both heels together. After pausing like that for a fraction of a second, he should move his right hand from the waist to the pommel, then swing his right leg over the horse's back, and lower himself gently on to the saddle. Finally, he should find the right stirrup and put his foot well into it, with or without help from his right hand on the leather.

To dismount, the rider should disengage his right foot from its stirrup and swing his right foot over the horse's back until he is standing on the left stirrup with heels together. Placing his right hand firmly on the waist of the saddle and his left hand on the withers, he should take his weight on them in order to disengage his left foot from its stirrup, then let himself slide to the ground.

Mounting and dismounting should be practised continually until the whole movement becomes smooth and continuous.

When mounted, the legs should fit along each side of the saddle easily, with the stirrup leathers of such length that the knees are slightly bent. The feet should be horizontal and parallel with the horse, that is, pointing straight forward. If the legs from knees to ankles are vertical the rider will feel that he can grip the saddle and will have no fears about being able to stay on.

The back should be kept straight, the shoulders square, and the eyes should look straight to the front. The rider will learn in time to adapt himself to the motion of the horse by rising slightly in the stirrups when the horse's back rises and lowering himself when the horse's back falls. In trotting it is necessary 'to rise to the bump', quite often in a canter the weight can be taken on the stirrups.

The reins should be held one in each hand between the thumb and first finger, letting each rein lie over three fingers inside the hand and come out between the third and little fingers. The part of the rein which comes from between the third and little fingers goes to the bit and so controls the horse. Make all rein movements gently and quietly. A gentle tug on the right will turn him to the right; a similar tug on the left will turn him to the left; a slight shortening of both reins will slow him down; and a definite pull on both will bring him to a stop.

To start him walking, give the reins a shake and say a few encouraging words. Never use spurs.

RIDLEY, Nicholas (*c.* 1500–1555)

English Protestant martyr. He was Master of Pembroke College, Cambridge (1540), Bishop of Rochester (1547), and in 1550 succeeded Bonner as Bishop of London. In this office he worked hard for the reformed faith, and helped CRANMER to build up the new Church of England. At Edward VI's death he favoured the succession of Lady Jane Grey, and Queen Mary had him sent to the Tower. Condemned as a heretic at Oxford, he was burned at the stake with LATIMER outside Balliol College.

RIFLE

A type of gun in which the bore of the barrel is spirally grooved to impart a spiral movement to the bullet, and so increase its speed and accuracy of aim. Typical calibres are ·303 (service rifle), ·500 (game rifle) and ·22 (miniature rifle); calibre means the diameter of the bore in thousandths of an inch. Well-known designs are the Springfield, Winchester, Remington and B.S.A. The leading event for rifle shooting is held yearly at Bisley for the King's Prize of £250 plus a gold medal.

RILKE, Rainer Maria (1875–1926)

Austrian poet, born at Prague. During the later years of his life he was considered Germany's greatest lyric poet. For a while he was secretary to RODIN.

RIMBAUD, Arthur (1854–1891)

Belgian poet, born in the Ardennes. Showed his poetic gift at an early age, one of his most famous poems, *Le Bateau Ivre* was written when he was only seventeen. He was taken up by the famous French poet, VERLAINE, who later tried to murder him. This led the young poet to give up poetry and take to a life of adventure. He settled in Abyssinia as a trader and acquired great wealth and influence.

RIMSKY-KORSAKOV, Nicolai (1844–1908)

Russian composer, born at Novgorod. A naval officer who studied music in his spare time, he became the leading Russian composer of his time. He wrote many operas based on fairy-stories, such as *The Golden Cockerel* and *The Snow-Maiden*, and a number of brilliant orchestral suites, the most famous of which is *Scheherazade*, inspired by tales from *The Arabian Nights*.

RIVERA, Diego (1886–1957)

Mexican painter, born at Guanajuato. Worked in Paris and became very much a part of the modern art movement; was a friend of MODIGLIANI. Returned to Mexico where he became profoundly influenced by AZTEC and MAYA art. Like Orozco he painted a number of very large murals for public buildings on revolutionary themes. Rivera founded the modern school of Mexican art.

ROBERTS, Frederick Sleigh, First Earl of Kandahar (1832–1914)

Distinguished British soldier, born at Cawnpore, he entered the Army in 1851. He first saw active service in the Indian Mutiny (1857) when he was awarded the Victoria Cross. During later campaigns in Africa and India, his rise was rapid and he was appointed Field-Marshal in 1895. In 1899 he took over command of the British forces in the Boer War, turning a series of British reverses into victory. From 1901–1904 Roberts was Commander-in-chief of the British Army. When the office was abolished, Roberts was retired and became president of the National Service League, advocating a system of national military service.

ROBESPIERRE, Maximilien (1758–1794)

French revolutionary, born at Arras. On his father's death he was brought up by the local bishop. He became an advocate, but on the eve of the French Revolution went to Paris as one of the deputies for Arras. There he rapidly became a leader of the Jacobin party and a member of the Constituent Assembly and the National Convention. As head of the Committee of Public Safety, Robespierre was, more than anyone else, responsible for the executions carried out during the Reign of Terror. By April 1794 he was in effect dictator of France. But the reaction came soon afterwards. Robespierre was denounced for despotism and was himself guillotined.

ROCK

The normal material of the earth's crust. Some rocks (such as granite) are formed when the molten material inside the earth cools down. Others (such as clay and sandstone) result from the settling down of sediments in the sea. Others again (such as some limestones) consist of masses of shells or corals cemented together. Rocks sometimes get changed into new forms by the action of water, heat, or pressure. Thus, limestone may change to marble, and clay to shale or slate. [*See* GEOLOGY and PETROLOGY.]

ROCK CLIMBING AND MOUNTAINEERING

Rock climbers confine themselves to hard rock where hand and foot holds are mostly solid and secure. They climb high cliffs and outcrops of 500 feet or so, aiming to complete the climb up and down in the hours of daylight. Mountaineers, on the other hand, meet all kinds of climbing surfaces, some of them quite soft and crumbly; moreover, they frequently spend days or weeks, even longer in the case of the great mountains, on the climb, which means that they have to take substantial food supplies and bivouac equipment with them.

Two rules for rock climbing are: never go alone, and never go without the right equipment.

The two most important items of equipment are strong boots and good rope. The boots can be bought at any big sports outfitters, and while they are not of a special type they are extremely heavily built, as they have to be nailed.

The three main kinds of nails for climbing boots are called clinker, hobs and tricouni. The last are not really nails so much as plates which are fastened to the soles of the boots in various ways. The fastening is best left to an expert.

The clinker is an edge-nail; and it is driven into the sole in such a way that the bulbous end sticks out beyond the edge of the sole. Its purpose is to prevent the clinker from turning round during climbing. The purpose of the hob nail is to save wear on those parts of the sole not protected by the clinkers. Every climber has his own idea as to how a boot should be nailed.

One type of rope for climbing is known as Alpine Line. It is three-stranded and made of the best quality manilla. Other types of ropes are available but before they are bought young climbers should get expert advice. The length of rope required is 120 feet, which is considered to be enough for three climbers.

Rock climbing is very hard on clothes of any sort, and will wear out almost anything extremely quickly. Therefore buy special gear, or else go dressed in the oldest clothes available. Perhaps the most serviceable dress is a windbreaker and belted plus fours, or riding breeches. Inside the boots should be one pair of good ordinary socks and over them a pair of thick ankle socks made specially for climbing.

The remaining equipment should consist of a small pocket compass, a good knife, a really loud whistle, a small tin of first-aid dressings (especially two good-sized burn dressings) and enough food: chocolate, a few sandwiches and some hard biscuits. A small screw-capped water container of strong metal is also useful.

All these items should be stowed away in the pockets. Do not take a haversack; it will always be in the way, and its loose slings could be a positive danger if the hand got caught in them while reaching out quickly for a handhold.

Roping together is a safety scheme for climbers. In the case of a party of three the leader, the most experienced climber, selects footholds which the others, watching him as he goes upward, will find. When the leader has climbed about 30 or 40 feet he will stop, wedge his feet firmly on a rock ledge, belay (that is, make fast) his rope to a small rock nearby, and when he feels that he is nicely set he will signal to those below. The second now climbs up to the first, belays himself securely, and waits. The leader now goes on climbing for another 30 or 40 feet and belays.

Three climbers are thus roped together up the rock face at intervals of about 40 feet, the two uppermost being belayed. At this point the third who is also an experienced climber, climbs up to the second and belays. Then the second climbs up to the leader and belays; the leader climbs another 40 feet or so and belays; the tail now climbs up to the second and belays; the second climbs up to the first and belays; and so on right to the summit.

It is absolutely essential, and an unbreakable rule with three climbers that, *two must always be standing with their ropes belayed while the third is climbing.* Another equally important rule is that during climbing all slack rope must be taken in carefully, so that the balance of the climber is not upset.

In rock climbing three knots are used: the

bowline, the reef knot, and the simple noose. The important thing is that the knots must be absolutely secure; the lives of everyone on the rope depend on it. Watch particularly the reef knot, which is used for joining ropes together; the wrong version of it, the granny knot, will slip and is quite useless. The bowline is for the leader and tail, and the noose is for second. These knots should be made so that when they are drawn tight the long loops will just fit snugly around the climbers' waists.

One important tip about rope or line is that unless the ends are properly whipped they will unravel easily. A new line has the ends whipped properly and it is worth examining the whipping to see just how it is done. But in case of a break when climbing or of having to make a cut, a tight overhand knot should be tied in both of the new ends. An unstranded rope is practically useless; it has no real strength whatsoever.

Descent is known as the 'abseil', and in the opinion of many rock climbers abseiling is far more dangerous than climbing, because the climber cannot see where he is going so easily. It is in beginning the abseil that the short loop is most often used. Cut off enough rope to go round a piece of rock which can be used for a belay comfortably and make a good knot. By reef-knotting the ends of this cut-off piece together, a loop can be made to go over your belay-rock. A rope's end passed through this loop can be used as a sort of pulley. Nearly all short loops are lost—as they are left around the belay-rock; nevertheless that must not deter the climber from using the rope, doubled if necessary, for his own safety.

In the abseil climbers descend either in the same order or in the reverse order to the climb. For the reverse order, assuming that all three climbers are together at the top of their climb, the tail goes first. He climbs down about 30 or 40 feet and belays. Then comes the second to join him. Then the tail goes on down and belays again. Now the leader comes down to second; second goes down to tail; tail goes down another 30 to 40 feet; and so on until the bottom is reached.

Good belays are doubly important on the abseil. Plenty of feet slip on the way down, and quite often a man has to lean right out, his feet sort of walking downwards. For that reason, on the descent, the next man waiting to go takes the slack of the rope over his shoulders and watches his companion go down, paying out the rope gradually. Then if the abseiler suddenly throws the whole of his weight on the rope there is no difficulty.

The great thing about successful climbing is to be as sure as possible of both handholds and footholds, and if a climber should find himself sliding down a rope he should on no account let go, even if his hands are severely skinned in the process.

ROCKEFELLER, John Davison (1839–1937)
American industrialist, born at Richford, New York. He entered the oil refining industry when it was in a very precarious condition, and in a matter of a few years became extremely wealthy. He is, in fact, said to have been the richest man in the world. In later years he was a benefactor on a large scale, and endowed many institutions in the United States.

ROCKET
A missile propelled by the reaction to the expulsion of gases from its rear, and not, as sometimes thought, the result of the gases pushing on the surrounding air. Rocket flight is, in fact, an excellent example of Newton's third law of motion: 'to every action there is an equal and opposite reaction'.

Rocket motors have several advantages over other forms of propulsion, the chief of which is their ability to operate in rarefied air. Prime movers which draw their oxygen from the atmosphere sooner or later lose power with height, but the output of rockets remains constant, and in consequence their propulsive efficiency increases with height because air resistance grows less.

According to records that have come down to us rocket propulsion has been known for at least 750 years. The Chinese used gunpowder rockets with devastating effect upon the enemy at the siege of Kai-fung-fu in 1232. For many years afterwards rockets were used only for signalling, but in 1780 Raja Hyder Ali armed his legions with metal-cased rockets, which were larger and had a greater range than the compressed rockets of the Chinese. The British developed the rocket still further, and gained considerable advantage with it in various wars in the eighteenth and nineteenth centuries. But the gun ultimately outranged the rocket and proved to be more accurate. Its chief role was that of carrying a line from the shore to wrecked ships for the setting up of breeches buoy rescue apparatus. Between the 1st and 2nd World Wars much experimental work was done, particularly in Germany; in fact, the Germans laid the foundations for what was one of their most important weapons, the flying bomb and the V-2.

In nearly all the practical applications of rocket propulsion, until about 1939, only solid fuels were used—gunpowder or cordite. These fuels contain their own oxygen, and once ignited continue to burn until the charge is

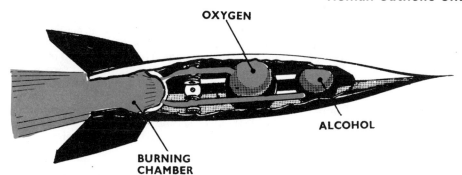

OXYGEN

ALCOHOL

BURNING CHAMBER

ROCKET
Drawing of a basic design of rocket propelled by a mixture of oxygen and alcohol.

used up. Modern rockets for military and space research use liquid fuels such as alcohol and liquid oxygen. Both America and Russia are carrying out extensive research on rocket motors and for reasons of security not very much is known of the details.

Undoubtedly the next step in rocket propulsion will be the application of nuclear power. A 'photon' motor has already been suggested, and quite recently money has been allocated to active research in this field in the United States. Exactly what direction this will take is hard to assess, but what is certain is that before man can really start exploring the outer reaches of space he will need some such propulsive power.

RODENTS
Found practically throughout the world. There are two sub-orders; the double-toothed rodents which include the hares and rabbits, and the single-toothed rodents which include the squirrels, beavers, dormice, rats, mice, voles, jerboas, flying squirrels, porcupines, cavies, agutis and capybaras [*see* separate entries].

RODIN, Auguste (1840–1917)
French sculptor, born in Paris. Between 1863 and 1877 he worked as an architectural sculptor, and in the Salon of that year he exhibited a male figure, *The Age of Bronze*. This figure caused an artistic storm, and as a result Rodin secured the patronage of Turquet, Under-Secretary of Fine Arts. The French government provided him with a studio in Paris, where he worked for the rest of his life. His most famous creations were: *Adam, Eve, The Thinker*, and *The Burghers of Calais*, intended for the unfinished bronze door for the Musées des Arts. Rodin produced many fine portrait busts and symbolic groups, including *The Kiss*. Rodin is regarded as the most important sculptor of the 19th century.

RODNEY, George Brydges, First Baron (1719–1792)
English sailor, born in London. Rodney

entered the Navy when he was 14, and at 24 was already a captain. After serving with distinction in various parts of the world, his greatest success was the defeat of the Spanish fleet off Cape St. Vincent (1780). He also defeated the combined French and Spanish fleets off Martinique (1782). On his return to England he was created Baron.

ROMAN CATHOLIC CHURCH
According to an ancient tradition, St. Peter founded the Christian Church at Rome. Matthew xvi: verse 18, tells us that Jesus called Peter the 'Rock' on which He would build His church, and from earliest times, Bishops of Rome (Popes) have claimed for their office a direct succession from the great chief Apostle. The word 'POPE' is just a version of 'Papa', and was first applied, sarcastically, to Callistus, Bishop of Rome (219–233) by Tertullian.

Leo I (440–461) was the founder of the Papacy as a power in its own right. The collapse of the Western Empire was followed by great missionary activity from Rome, especially in Europe. Clovis, King of the Franks, was baptized by the Bishop of Rheims

RODENT A pair of voles. This particular species is found only on the island of Skomer.

in 496. The Papacy was considerably strengthened by Gregory I (590–604)—who sent Augustine to England. But the Papacy reached the summit of its spiritual and political power between the 11th and 14th centuries.

The Pope's residence, the Vatican City, in Rome, was recognized by the Lateran Treaty of 1928 as an Independent State. The Roman Catholic Church claims that the teaching of the Church in matters of faith and morals is infallible, that is, free from all possibility of error. The Vatican Council of 1870 proclaimed that when the Pope, speaking in his Apostolic capacity, makes a pronouncement in such matters, his teaching is infallible.

There are about 350,000,000 Roman Catholics in the world today, the Church being especially strong on the Continent, in Eire, and in the South Americas.

ROMANOV

Royal family of Russia. Michael, whose family originated in Prussia, was elected Czar by the Russian boyars in 1613. The successive Czars of Russia were all descended from him, down to Nicholas II who was murdered in 1917.

ROMMEL, General Erwin (1891–1944)

German soldier. He fought as a junior officer in the Great War, and became an early member of the Nazi party, belonging to Hitler's bodyguard. After commanding an armoured division in Poland (1939) and France (1940) he was appointed commander of the Afrika Korps in North Africa (1941). His greatest success came in 1942 when he captured the fortress of Tobruk, and reached a point only 80 miles west of Alexandria. But he was then defeated by MONTGOMERY, and had to retreat right across Africa. In 1944 he commanded an army group defending the Low Countries and Northern France, but died from injuries received by bombing in October the same year. He was known as the 'desert fox'.

ROMNEY, George (1734–1802)

English portrait painter, born in Lancashire. After setting up as a travelling portrait painter in Kendal, he moved to London, where he quickly became one of the most fashionable portrait painters. From 1773 to 1775 he studied in Italy, and on his return to London, he became the rival of Sir Joshua Reynolds. Towards the end of his life he gave up portrait painting for ideal subjects, including *Milton and His Daughters* and *Scene from 'The Tempest'*. Romney's portraits—particularly of society women—are famous for their grace and charm.

RONSARD, Pierre de (1524–1585)

French Renaissance poet, born at La Poissonnière, Vendôme. After a period of study he became a court page. He lived in Scotland and England (1538–1541), and on his return to France moved in court circles, but devoted much of his time to poetry. He did much to revive French verse, and is best remembered for his *Odes*, *Hymns* and *Amours de Marie*, which are graceful and direct lyrical expressions of feeling.

RÖNTGEN, Wilhelm Conrad von (1845–1923)

German scientist, born at Lennep in Prussia. He discovered X-RAYS for which he was awarded a Nobel Prize in 1901.

ROOSEVELT, Franklin Delano (1884–1945)

Great American statesman, born at Hyde Park, New York. Roosevelt was elected to the Senate in 1910. Under President Woodrow Wilson he was Under-Secretary of the Navy. Although partially crippled by paralysis in 1921 he continued his public activities, and in 1929 was elected Governor of New York. In 1933 he was elected President for the Democrats at the height of the world economic depression. He was re-elected President in 1936, 1940, and 1944. He died April 1945, having been the only President to serve more than two terms. Roosevelt's main peace-time policy was the New Deal, a programme of public works to deal with unemployment. In war-time he introduced the Lend-Lease Act to aid Britain. Roosevelt was an outstanding internationalist and liberal.

ROSETTA STONE

Found (1798) by a French artillery officer near the Rosetta mouth of the Nile, and passed into British hands in 1801. It is now in the British Museum. It consists of a piece of black basalt measuring 45 inches by $28\frac{1}{2}$ inches; it is only part of the original monument. On it are inscribed 14 lines of hieroglyphics (ancient Egyptian writing), 32 lines of demotic (a simplified form of hieroglyphic writing) and 54 lines of Greek. It was this Greek writing which gave scholars the key to understanding and deciphering Egyptian hieroglyphics.

ROSSETTI, Dante Gabriel (1828–1882)

English poet and painter born in London. Is often regarded as the leading spirit of the Victorian group of painters and writers who called themselves the PRE-RAPHAELITE Brotherhood—by which name they meant that they wished to achieve in their own work the startling simplicity of the early Italian painters who preceded Raphael. He was both painter and poet, and indeed a writer of two prose-tales as well. His sister, Christina, was a writer of lyrics and of religious poetry.

ROSSINI, Gioacchino (1792–1868)
Italian composer, born at Pesaro. He was the most popular opera-composer of his day. *The Barber of Seville*, written at the age of twenty-four, brought him fame. He is chiefly remembered for this opera and the overtures to his other operas, especially that to *William Tell*. After writing the latter work at the age of thirty-seven, he gave up music, and for the rest of his life (thirty-nine more years) took things easy, indulging his favourite hobby of cooking.

ROSTAND, Edmond (1868–1918)
French poet and playwright. His comedy *Cyrano de Bergerac*, set in the 17th century, was translated into English, German and Russian, and has remained a favourite to this day.

ROUSSEAU, Henri (1844–1910)
French primitive painter, born at Laval, Mayenne. First went into the army, serving in the Franco-Prussian War, he later became a clerk in the customs service. He began painting about 1880 and exhibited at the Société des Artistes Indépendants. His work was greatly appreciated by most of the modern artists of that period, especially PICASSO. Rousseau painted a wide range of subjects, portraits, still lifes, family groups, landscapes, etc. His most outstanding paintings are his exotic works featuring jungles, nudes and wild animals. Because of his job in the customs service he is often known by the name 'Le Douanier'.

ROUSSEAU, Jean Jacques (1712–1778)
Swiss thinker and writer, born at Geneva. He was much concerned with the freedom and rights of the common man, in fact, he was a champion of the cause of democracy and greatly influenced the leaders of the French Revolution. His most important work was *The Social Contract*, and his *Confessions* is considered one of the greatest pieces of autobiographical writing.

ROWING
A general term which covers the propulsion of a boat by means of oars, no matter what the style of rowing used. In rowing you lean forward, raise your hands to dip the blades of the oars in the water, pull as you lean back, lower the hands to pull the blades out, and go forward once more to repeat the process all over again. Rowing in the best sense is that displayed at, say, the Oxford and Cambridge Boat Race. Here it is one man to one oar and sliding seats are used to give greater reach. In 'sculling' the rower handles two light oars (called sculls); in this type of rowing there are 'singles' and 'doubles'. In rowing and sculling the blades are 'feathered', that is, the blade is upright while pulling against the water, turned flat the moment it is lifted out of the water and held like this until ready to be dipped into the water again at the beginning of the stroke. For the beginner at sculling the best speed of stroke is a matter of experience. Speeds are measured by numbers of strokes per minute: 20 is a steady pace; 24 will give you a fair turn of speed; and 30 to 36 is definitely a racing pace. In terms of time per complete stroke, 24 per minute means a complete stroke in 2·5 seconds; 30 p/m, 2 seconds; 36 p/m, 1·66 seconds.

ROWLANDSON, Thomas (1756–1827)
English artist, born in London. Studied in Paris and London and originally intended to be a conventional painter. He led a gay, rumbustious life—and was forever in debt. To pay off his debts he produced hundreds of drawings of contemporary life and manners. These are exuberant, humorous and display masterful draughtmanship. One of his best-known series is the set of illustrations to *Dr. Syntax*. A great volume of his work was reproduced as prints.

ROYAL CHARTER
A written document given by the Sovereign which grants certain rights and privileges. The most famous Royal Charter was MAGNA CARTA. When a town wishes to become a BOROUGH it petitions the Queen to grant it a Royal Charter of incorporation. If the petition is granted the Chairman of the Town Council becomes the Charter MAYOR, as the first Mayor of the town. Sometimes societies are given Charters in which case they can, if they wish, put the word 'Royal' in front of the society's name, such as the Royal Society for the Prevention of Cruelty to Animals. Other public bodies may also be given Royal Charters. Present day examples are the British Broadcasting Corporation and the BANK OF ENGLAND. A Chartered Accountant is a member of a society that has a Royal Charter. In olden times trading companies were given Royal Charters as in the case of the East India Company and the Hudson Bay Company.

When the Queen grants a Royal Charter she does so by Letters Patent through a sub-committee of the PRIVY COUNCIL. They are given under the Great Seal which is the emblem of sovereignty. The Great Seal—first introduced by Edward the Confessor—is held by the LORD CHANCELLOR and may not be taken out of the country. A Lord Chancellor obtains his office from the Queen when she delivers into his hands the Great Seal.

ROYAL FAMILY [*See* SOVEREIGN.]

ROYAL SOCIETY

Most important scientific society in Great Britain, and to be elected a Fellow (F.R.S.) is an honour of great distinction. It was started by a group of learned men for the purpose of discussing science, and received its ROYAL CHARTER in 1662 when it was known as the Royal Society of London for Improving Natural Knowledge. A similar society was formed in Edinburgh in 1783, and Fellows have the initials F.R.S.E.

RUBBER

Gummy substance exuded by a wide variety of trees and plants, especially the trees *Hevea brasiliensis,* and several other species of *Hevea* which grow in the East Indies, particularly the Malay peninsula, and other parts of the world. Rubber is also obtained from the large tree *Castilla elastica,* found in Mexico. So-called dandelion rubber is derived from the roots of various species of dandelion plant *Taraxacum,* chiefly Kok sagyz, etc., grown in Turkestan, U.S.S.R.

Rubber trees are tapped and the latex, a milk-like juice, containing about 30–40% rubber, is coagulated by exposing it to heat and wood smoke, or by mechanical means, so as to separate the rubber from the water, mineral salts, sugars, resins, and protein matters. The rubber obtained in this way is known as 'crude'. Latex is also extensively used in industry for making foam rubber products, footwear, dolls, etc. Untreated crude rubber is naturally soft and lacks the requisite strength for making into manufactured articles. To improve its strength and usefulness it is vulcanized or heated with sulphur, the proportion of sulphur used determining the hardness and elasticity of the rubber. Fillers such as carbon black or channel black are also vital constituents of rubber, particularly tyre rubber. About 75% of the rubber produced goes into the manufacture of tyres, the remainder being utilized for cable sheathing, wire covering, footwear, flooring, proofing of clothing, togs, upholstery material, hose, etc. Latest developments include bullet-proof tyres, non-tear rubber for fuel tanks, flame-proof hose, suits for frogmen.

RUBENS, Peter Paul (1577–1640)

Flemish painter, born in Siegen, Westphalia. In 1598 he joined the painters' guild in Antwerp, and two years later went to Italy, where he served the Duke of Mantua. He returned to Antwerp, where he immediately became the most famous painter in the city. Here he produced the *Adoration of the Magi* and the *Raising of the Cross* and *Descent from the Cross.* Between 1620 and 1625 he executed many commissions for the French court. In 1626, he entered the diplomatic service, and later went to Spain on a mission to Philip III. After painting the Spanish royal family in Madrid, he went to London, where he painted the ceiling at Whitehall and *The Blessing of Peace* (now in the National Gallery, London). Rubens produced paintings of every kind—landscapes, portraits, animals, religious and allegorical works. His output was colossal, and although he employed an army of assistants, the final touches he put on his works made them the products of genius. More than 2,000 paintings have been attributed to him.

RUGBY

Ball-game played with teams of two strengths: Rugby Union, 15 players; Rugby League, 13 players. The rules which follow apply only to Rugby Union.

The field is 110 yards long between goal-lines and 75 yards wide. The in-goals are a maximum of 25 yards deep, measured from the goal-line. The posts must not be less than 11 feet high, and the crossbar 10 feet above ground-level. The distance from post to post, along the ground, must be 18 feet 6 inches.

A rugby football is between 11 and $11\frac{1}{4}$ inches long, its length-circumference must be 30 to 31 inches, its width-circumference 24 to $25\frac{1}{2}$ inches, and its weight $13\frac{1}{2}$ to 15 ounces when dry. Finally, it is of leather and hand sewn, with not less than 8 stitches to the inch.

Once the game has started any player may either kick or pick up the ball and run with it. The ball must *never* be handled in a scrummage or immediately after it has been dropped following a tackle. The ball may be passed from one player to another of the same team, but *never* forward. And if a player is tackled while holding or running with the ball, he must at once put the ball on the ground between himself and his opponents' goal-line.

If the ball goes into touch, that is, either it or the player carrying it goes voluntarily over one of the touch-lines, it is at once out of play until it is brought into play again by a player of the opposing team; but if a player when carrying the ball is forced into touch by an opponent, then the ball belongs to the team of the man

SHIPS A Roman merchantman of about A.D. 300. Traders from Rome ventured as far as the Baltic Sea and sailed regularly round the Mediterranean. They built much bigger vessels than that shown below, especially ships for carrying grain from Egypt to Rome.

SHIPS *Above*, the *Henry Grâce à Dieu* or the *Great Harry*.
First built by Henry VIII in 1514 and rebuilt in 1536–39.
She was flat-sterned and had a large forecastle which
projected over the bows. The *Great Harry* was about
1,000 tons and very heavily armed. *Below*, the *Great Britain*
designed by I. K. Brunel. She was built of iron, driven by
a six-bladed propeller and made an average of 12 knots.

HOVERCRAFT A passenger-carrying hovercraft. This revolutionary craft is supported on a cushion of air beneath the floor of the vessel. It is propelled by means of propellers in the style shown in the model above or jets.

SHIPS A 'lakotoi' of New Guinea. This primitive but seaworthy craft is built up of several dug-out canoes lashed together and covered with a bamboo platform.

SHIPS A missile destroyer firing a guided weapon. This class of ship is being rapidly developed by the world's leading naval powers.

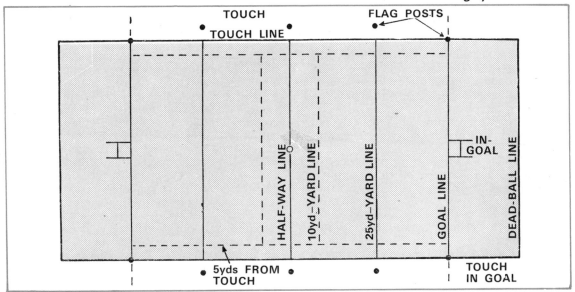

TOUCH

TOUCH LINE

FLAG POSTS

IN-GOAL

HALF-WAY LINE

10yd–YARD LINE

25yd–YARD LINE

GOAL LINE

DEAD-BALL LINE

5yds FROM
TOUCH

TOUCH
IN GOAL

RUGBY A rugby pitch should be 110 yards between goal lines and 75 yards wide.

who went into touch. The ball is brought back into play by a player standing with both feet beyond the touch-line and throwing the ball in at right-angles so that it touches either another player or the ground within 5 yards of the touch-line. When the ball goes into touch-in-goal it is brought back into play again by a '25'.

A player is offside whenever he is nearer to his opponent's goal-line than a player of his own team who has just touched or kicked or who is carrying the ball. A player can be offside in his opponents' in-goal, but not in his own, except where one of his side takes a free kick from behind his goal-line, when all of his own side must be behind the ball at the time it is kicked.

A player is also offside if he, (a) enters a scrummage from his opponents' end of the field, or (b) is in front of a line at right-angles to the place from where a throw-in is being made before the ball has touched the ground or another player. For either of these offences, a penalty-kick will be awarded to the opposing team.

The great thing to remember when a player finds himself in an offside position during actual play is that he must not do anything while in that position to take part in the play. This means not only that he must leave the ball severely alone, but also that he must not do anything which obstructs an opponent or helps one of his own side; in fact he must keep at least 10 yards away from any opponent who is waiting to receive the ball. If he does take part in the play in any way, a penalty kick will

be awarded to his opponents, or a scrummage where the ball was last played by the offending team, at the option of the other team.

A player who is in an offside position becomes onside again if:
(1) One of his own team runs ahead of him, that is, runs nearer to his opponents' goal-line with the ball.
(2) One of his own team kicks the ball when behind him, and then runs ahead of him to follow the ball up.
(3) Any opponent kicks, intentionally touches, or runs 5 yards with the ball.

A fair catch is a catch direct from an opponent without the ball touching the ground between opponent and catcher, and it does not matter whether the opponent has kicked, thrown or knocked-on the ball. When a player has made a fair catch, he at once claims it by making a mark with his heel in the ground at the spot where the catch was made, calling out 'Mark' at the same time. The player is then entitled to a free-kick from the place he has marked.

Any free-kick may be (at the kicker's choice) a place-kick, a drop-kick or a punt. It must always be in the direction of the opponents' goal-line, and all players of the kicker's side must be behind the ball at the moment the kick is taken (except one player to place the ball when a place-kick is taken). The differences between the various kicks are these: in the place-kick, the ball is placed on the ground by a player in such a way that the kicker will be able to kick it to the best advantage; in a drop-kick, the kicker drops the ball to the ground and kicks it after it has bounced once; and in a punt, the kicker drops the ball and kicks it before it has touched the ground.

In theory, a scrummage is formed when one or more players from each side close up in readiness to allow the ball to be thrown on to the ground between them. In actual practice, however, most scrums are formed by eight forwards from each team, the ball being put between them by a player known as the scrum-half.

The players in a scrum must not touch the ball with their hands, except when the scrum is formed in goal, when any player may attempt to save a touch-down or try. The ball must always come out of the scrum as the result of footwork by the second player of the front row of the scrum.

The penalty generally awarded against a team committing an offence against the rules is a penalty kick. The kick is awarded for:

(1) Handling the ball, intentionally falling down, holding the ball with legs, or illegally lifting a foot from the ground while in scrummage.

(2) Picking up the ball after it has been put on to the ground by a tackled player, or failing to put the ball on the ground immediately on being tackled.

(3) Being on the ground, failing to get up at once; or doing anything to prevent an opponent from getting up or from putting the ball down on the ground.

(4) Tackling an opponent who is not in possession of the ball.

(5) Putting the ball unfairly into a scrummage or returning it to a scrummage after it has come out lawfully.

(6) Wilfully hacking or tripping up an opponent.

As in all games, it is the referee who decides when there has been an infringement of the rules, and his decision is absolutely final. In particular the referee will decide whether there has been foul or dangerous play, and is empowered to caution a player for a first serious offence, although he could order the player off the field immediately. However, the referee must order him off if the offence is repeated or if a player continually commits breaches of the rules. Further, a referee will stop play if a player is injured; it is restarted by a scrummage.

The object of the game is, of course, to score points for one's side, and these points are scored either by goals or by tries. A goal is scored when the ball passes between the posts above the cross-bar—it does not matter at what height. A goal may be scored in two different ways: (i) from a place-kick after a try has been scored (see the next paragraph for this); (ii) from a drop-kick or a free-kick—score, 2 points.

A try is achieved when a player takes the ball across his opponents' goal-line and puts it down on the ground in their in-goal, or when, the ball already being in the opponents' in-goal, a player puts his hand upon it as it lies upon the ground. The score is 3 points. After a try the ball is placed before the opponents' goal-line directly opposite to where the try was achieved and a place-kick is taken. If, as a result of this kick, the ball passes between the posts above the cross-bar, then a goal is scored and a further 2 points taken by the successful team.

All that you have just read is a summary of the rules and objects of Rugger. The time has now come to consider some of the ways in which individual players, and players as a team can best score points and so win the game. In considering these matters, a few additional definitions known to all good Rugger players will be helpful. Here they are:

Touch-down is when a player grounds the ball within his own in-goal. The ball is brought into play again by a '25' (see next paragraph). But if a player deliberately passes, kicks, knocks or carries the ball back across his own goal-line, the other side may demand that the ball be taken to the place from where the ball was last played on the field and there scrummaged.

A 25 is a drop-kick by the defending side from behind their own 25-yard line. The kick must carry beyond the 25-yard line, and all defending players must be behind the kicker; if any are not, the defending side will be penalised under the offside rule.

A knock-on is made by propelling the ball forward in the direction of the opponents' dead-ball-line by knocking it with the arm or hand. The penalty is a scrummage.

The kick-off is a place- or drop-kick from the centre spot. It is made to begin the game, after half-time, after a goal, and after failure to turn a try into a goal.

Selling the Dummy is when a player, about to be attacked by an opponent, pretends to make a pass, but retains the ball and runs on. It is very good play when successful.

Handing off is the process of pushing away an attacker who attempts to tackle. It is made with the flat of the hand, generally against the opponents' head.

Above, it was said that there are two Rugger games—Union and League. Union is the game which is confined to amateur players only. The League variety—extremely popular in the North of England, France, Australia and New Zealand—is played by amateurs too and schoolboys but also permits professionalism.

Professionalism in the League game is confined to thirty senior club teams. There are regular interchanges of visits between the Rugby League organisations in England, France, Australia and New Zealand. In Sydney, Australia, Test Matches are played on the famous Cricket Ground and attract capacity crowds.

Briefly, League Rugby differs from Union in the following respects: in League there are only 13 players in a team as against 15 in a Union team; in League, ground cannot be gained by kicking the ball into touch on the full. If a kick does go directly into touch then a scrum is formed where the ball was kicked. The effect of this particular rule is to reduce touch play in League as compared with Union and it also produces more handling. When a man is tackled in League Rugby, he is allowed to get to his feet, drop the ball to the ground, after which it can be played with the foot. Invariably the tackled player heels the ball and a passing movement can then be easily started. There are also minor differences in the Laws relating to the scrum and the re-starting of play after dead-ball. In both games, a try counts as 3 points but in League, any type of goal, whether from penalty-kick, drop-kick or converting a try, counts only 2 points.

RUHR

District in north-west Germany. One of the most important industrial centres in Europe, contains the world's richest anthracite coalfields. Its name comes from the river Ruhr, a tributary of the Rhine. The most important towns are Dortmund, Essen and Duisberg. Because of its importance to Hitler it was devastated by the Allied air forces during the Second World War.

RUISDAEL, Jacob van (1628–1682)

Dutch painter, born in Haarlem. One of the pioneers of European landscape painting. His works, although typically Dutch, have a sad melancholy about them. Towards the end of his life he took a doctor's degree and it is thought that he practised in this profession for some time.

RUMANIA

A republic in east Europe that is a little larger (91,600 square miles) than Great Britain and has a population of over nineteen million. The capital is Bucharest at the mouth of the River Danube. The plains of Transylvania are rich wheat growing lands. The country is rich in minerals, particularly petroleum.
History:
The name of the country comes from Roman

and in Roman times much of it formed Roman provinces. In modern times most of what is now Rumania was ruled by Turkey until 1866. It became an independent kingdom in 1878. After the First World War the size of the country was greatly increased, Transylvania being taken from Hungary and given to Rumania. After the Second World War the country ceased to be a kingdom and became a Communist republic. Bessarabia and North Bukovinia, which had been part of Rumania since the end of the First World War, were ceded to the Soviet Union.

RUMFORD, Benjamin Thompson, Count (1753–1814)

Anglo-American scientist, born in Massachusetts. Came to England in 1776, and later entered the service of the Elector of Bavaria. Although he studied many branches of science his most lasting work was concerned with the theory that heat is a form of energy. He was also a very capable administrator.

RURAL DISTRICT COUNCIL (RDC)

The LOCAL AUTHORITY that does for people living in the country the kind of work that is done for towns by BOROUGH COUNCILS and URBAN DISTRICT COUNCILS. RDCs are made up of parishes, each one having from twenty to thirty parishes. [*See* PARISH COUNCIL.]

RUSKIN, John (1819–1900)

British writer and art critic, born in London. As a young man he travelled widely in Britain, France, Switzerland and Italy. His first publication was an essay on the paintings of TURNER. This was followed by other volumes on art and architecture, including *Modern Painters*, *The Stones of Venice* and *The Seven Lamps of Architecture*. He always put the emphasis on the moral and religious element in art. He was also interested in social and economic reform, and supported the Working Men's College (founded 1854). In a number of works, such as *Sesame and Lilies* and *The Crown of Wild Olives*, he denounced the crushing influence of industrial civilization upon art and morality.

RUSSELL, Bertrand Arthur William, Third Earl (1872–1970)

British philosopher and mathematician. Born in Trelleck, he was educated privately and at Cambridge. He served for a year as attaché to the British Embassy in Paris, but then took up an academic career and has lectured and travelled widely. Amongst his many publications are *Principles of Mathematics*, *Principia Mathematica* (in collaboration with A. N. Whitehead) and *An Enquiry into Meaning and*

Truth. He was awarded the Order of Merit in 1949 and the Nobel Prize for Literature in 1950. All his work is marked by wit and clarity. As a philosopher he stresses the value of logic and anti-mysticism. He has also written on social questions such as peace, education and marriage.

RUSSIA [*See* U.S.S.R.]

RUTHERFORD, Ernest, First Baron (1871–1937)

British scientist, born near Nelson, New Zealand. Worked under Sir J. J. THOMSON at the Cavendish Laboratory. He was in turn professor at the universities of McGill (Canada) and Manchester, and took over the position of his teacher, Thomson, at the Cavendish Laboratory. His most outstanding work was in the field of RADIOACTIVE ELEMENTS, particularly radium; for this he received the Nobel Prize for Chemistry in 1908. He was one of the greatest experimental scientists, following in the tradition of Faraday. Many of the present-day nuclear scientists were his students.

RWANDA

A small republic in Central Africa that was formerly an INTERNATIONAL TRUST TERRITORY administered by Belgium. The country is 10,000 square miles, only a little larger than Wales, and has a population of a little more than 3,000,000. About 50,000 of these are pygmies.

Ss

SAAR, or Saarland

A territory in Central Europe near Alsace Lorraine. It takes its name from the river of the same name. There are less than a million inhabitants. The Saar is the centre of coal mining and great steel works. The people are Germans, but after the Second World War they decided by a vote that they would have their own government. Later they united with Germany. The capital is Saarbrucken.

SABATINI, Rafael (1875–1950)

Anglo-Italian writer of exciting adventure stories. Particularly well-known are *Captain Blood* and *The Sea Hawk*.

SACCHARIN

White crystalline powder, almost three hundred times as sweet as cane sugar, and used as a substitute for SUGAR in foodstuffs. Saccharin is made from toluene and permanganate of potash. Its chemical formula is $C_6H_4SO_3CONH$.

SAGA

Epic in verse or prose about Icelandic heroes and legendary people. One of the most famous is the *Volsung Saga*, recounting the life and adventures of Sigurd and Gudrun. Richard Wagner included parts of this saga in his opera cycle, *The Ring*.

SAHARA

The world's largest desert. It covers a large area in North and Central Africa that is about the same size as the United States. It includes the Libyan and Nubian deserts. Parts of Algeria, Chad, Libya, Mali, Mauretania, Niger, the Sudan, Tunisia and the United Arab Republic form the desert.

SAINT

Someone of outstanding holiness and virtue. St. Paul called all Christian believers Saints, but the word soon referred almost exclusively to especially devout individuals. After 1170, the Popes alone have declared, in a solemn ceremony known as 'canonization', which historical figures shall be specially revered by Roman Catholics as Saints. Since the early 17th century, Jesuit scholars, known as 'Bollandists', have worked at recording the lives of the Christian Saints; so far over 20,000 lives have been included. A Patron Saint is a Saint who, usually for some legendary reason, is regarded as having special concern for a country, class or occupation—e.g. St. George (England), St. Denis (France), St. Anne (housewives—and miners), etc.

ST. HELENA

A solitary island in the South Atlantic Ocean and a British Crown Colony. It is about 1,200 miles west of Africa. It is 47 square miles, a little more than twice the size of the Isle of Wight, but has less than 5,000 inhabitants. It is famous for having been the place to which the Emperor NAPOLEON was exiled after the Battle of Waterloo. St. Helena has two dependencies—Ascension Island and TRISTAN DA CUNHA.

SAINT-SAËNS, Camille (1835–1921)

French composer, born in Paris. Composed a wide variety of music of which the following are frequently played: *Danse Macabre* (symphonic poem), *Samson and Dalila* (opera) and the highly entertaining *Carnival of Animals*.

SAKI, pseudonym of Hector Hugh Munro (1870–1916)

British novelist and short-story writer. He worked as a correspondent in Russia and in Paris. *Reginald*, *The Chronicles of Clovis*, and *Beasts and Superbeasts* are collections of stories, while the novels *The Unbearable Barrington* and *When William Came* are satires on the Edwardian upper classes.

SALADIN (1137–1193)

Sultan of Egypt and Syria. Son of a Kurdish general. Spent most of his youth in Damascus where he was born. For five years he fought the Christians in Egypt, eventually making himself ruler of the country (1174). The same year Saladin also made himself Sultan of Syria. In 1187 he won a great victory over the Christians at Tiberias, and captured Jerusalem. This led to the Third Crusade, and in 1191 Saladin was defeated, losing Jaffa and Caesarea. However, he remained in possession of Jerusalem, when the Third Crusade ended (1192).

SALLUST, or Gaius Sallustius Crispus (86–35 B.C.)

Roman historian and follower of Caesar in the Civil War. His oppressive rule as governor of Numidia earned him great riches. His works include a history of Catiline's conspiracy; a history of the Roman war against Jugurtha; and *Histories* of the years 78–67 B.C., of which little survives.

SALT

A compound of sodium and chlorine. In its natural state is found in salt flats or lakes and rock salt which has to be mined.

Salt is an essential item of the human diet, and an important raw material in many industries. In CHEMISTRY the term 'salt' is used to describe the compound where all or part of the hydrogen of an acid is replaced by a metal, for example, sulphuric acid and copper give the salt copper sulphate.

SALVADOR (or El Salvador)

A Central American republic that is (7,700 square miles) about the size of Wales. It has a population of over 3 million and so is one of the most densely populated countries in the New World. The capital is San Salvador. Its chief product is coffee.

SALVAGE

The saving of ships and goods from wreck, fire, or enemies. It is also the term used for the reward made to those by whose means the ship and goods have been saved. Specially designed ships are built for the sole purpose of salvage, these being fitted with diving apparatus to enable divers to go down and help to recover ships and valuable cargoes from the sea bed. A most notable feat of salvage of ships was the raising of the German High Seas Fleet of 72 vessels, including battleships, cruisers, and destroyers, which had been scuttled by their crews at Scapa Flow in 1919. Amongst the most notable instances of the recovery of valuable cargoes from sunken ships are the *S.S. Laurentic*, from which nearly £5,000,000-worth of gold was salvaged, and the *S.S. Egypt*, from which nearly £1,000,000 in gold was brought to the surface. But salvage does not operate only in the case of wrecks. In the case of a ship being unable to proceed under her own power, owing to damage or machinery breakdown, she may be brought to safety by being towed into port by another ship, or ocean-going tugs specially equipped for this service.

SALVATION ARMY

The name of a religious organization which was founded by William BOOTH in 1865. It is called 'army' because it is organized in a military manner; it has generals, officers and soldiers. Its members wear a uniform and march to a military type of band. The Salvation Army does a great deal of work helping people who are destitute and does rescue work amongst those who have been guilty of crime. It also does welfare work amongst the British armed forces serving abroad. There are branches throughout the world.

SAMOA (American)

A group of islands in the Pacific Ocean that belong to the United States. The population is a little over 100,000. The capital is Pago Pago.

SAMOA (Western)

A Member of the British Commonwealth and the first fully independent Polynesian State. The chief islands are Savai and Upolo and the capital is Apia. The islands were formerly an INTERNATIONAL TRUST TERRITORY administered by New Zealand. They became independent in 1962.

SAND, George (1804–1876)

French writer, born in Paris. One of France's outstanding women novelists. She led a very tempestuous life, and dressed in a manner which was considered outrageous at the time. She exerted a great influence over the composer CHOPIN. Her real name was Aurore Dupin and she came of an aristocratic family.

SANDBURG, Carl (1878–1969)
American poet, born at Galesburg. Led a varied life as labourer, soldier and journalist. His early poems were concerned with Chicago, and written with a force and gusto new to American poetry. He has also written the standard life of Abraham LINCOLN.

SAN MARINO
A tiny hilly republic on the Adriatic Sea that legend says was founded by a Dalmatian stonecutter in the 4th century. There are only 17,000 inhabitants and its land area is only 27 square miles.

SANTAYANA, George (1863–1952)
American philosopher, born in Madrid. One of his most important philosophical works is *Realms of Beauty*. He also wrote a number of poems and one novel, *The Last Puritan*.

SAPPHO
Greek poetess who lived about the 6th century B.C. Although only fragments of her poetry have survived, they are sufficient to show her outstanding gift as a lyric poet.

SARGASSO SEA
Region in the North Atlantic (lat. 20° to 35° N.) which is the comparatively calm centre of several ocean currents. It is rich in sea-weeds, and at one time it was thought ships sailing into it would become entangled in these and never get out.

SARTRE, Jean-Paul (1905—)
French philosopher, playwright and novelist, one of the leading exponents of existentialism. He was a member of the French Resistance Movement during the war. He is prominent in left-wing intellectual circles in France and since his student days at the Sorbonne he has been closely associated with the existentialist writer Simone de Beauvoir. *Intimacy* is a selection of short stories, and some of the material is based on war experiences, which also provided background detail for the play *In Camera*. Perhaps his greatest literary work is the trilogy that includes *The Age of Reason*, *Iron in the Soul* and *Reprieve*.

SASSOON, Siegfried (1886–1967)
English writer. During the First World War he achieved fame as a poet who showed up the horrors and wasteful destruction of war. One of his most widely read books is *Memoirs of a Foxhunting Man*.

SATIRE
Poking fun at or mocking such things as correct manners, social institutions, rigid ideas, formal people, etc. It can take the form of poetry, art, novel or drama. Its purpose is not evil or destructive, but usually to render ridiculous in as funny a way as possible; sometimes however it can be unkind.

SAUD, Abdul Azziz, Ibn (c. 1880–1953)
King of Saudi Arabia. Born in Central Arabia, his early years were spent in conflict with neighbouring territories and the Turks. By 1926 he succeeded in having himself proclaimed King of the Hejaz. In 1927 the territory of Nejd and its dependencies were added. In 1932 the two were united under the name of Saudi Arabia. He succeeded in establishing a stable country, and exploiting the rich oil reserves. Succeeded by his son.

SAUDI ARABIA
A vast desert kingdom that occupies most of the Arabian peninsular. It is 927,000 square miles, four times larger than France, but has a population of only about 6 million. It has two capitals—MECCA and Riyadh. It is very rich in oil.

SAVONAROLA, Girolamo (1452–1498)
Italian reformer, born at Ferrara. Started life as a monk (Dominican Order), and because of his outstanding oratory rose to great power, particularly in Florence. He was later tortured, and finally hanged for attacking Pope Alexander VI. He called for reforms in the conduct of churchmen who lived in a way far removed from that expected of men of religion.

SAXONS
Group of Germanic (or Teutonic) people who invaded Gaul, Germany and parts of Roman territory, and who later (6th century A.D.) occupied parts of South-East England forming, with the Angles, the Anglo-Saxon areas of Sussex, Wessex and Essex.

SAXOPHONE [*See* INSTRUMENTS OF THE ORCHESTRA]

SCANDINAVIA
A peninsula in north-west Europe on which are NORWAY and SWEDEN. The peninsula of DENMARK is very close to these two countries, and when Scandinavia is spoken of, the three countries are generally taken together. Sometimes FINLAND is also included.

History :

When the recorded history of the countries we know today as Sweden, Norway and Denmark began the inhabitants were seafaring folk who made themselves known to all the countries of Northern Europe as Vikings, a word meaning 'people of the fiords'. At the end of the 8th century they tried to conquer England, but eventually made peace with King Alfred. Later, other Vikings from Denmark, under Canute, did succeed for a brief time. Canute's son, Sven Estridsen, became the first of a line of Danish kings which ruled for four centuries. In 1293 Sweden conquered Finland and about a hundred years later, by the Union of Kalmar, Denmark, Norway and Sweden were united under the Danish Queen, Margaret. Iceland, too, came under Danish rule and continued to be linked with Denmark until 1944. The union of Kalmar came to an end in 1523 when Gustavus I became King of Sweden. Norway, however, in spite of a revolt, did not succeed in becoming free and remained under Danish rule until 1814.

The greatest of the Swedish kings was Gustavus Adolphus who ruled from 1611 to 1632, and who became the recognized champion of Protestantism in Europe. As the result of conquest, Sweden greatly increased her dominions under this king.

At the beginning of the 19th century Sweden had to yield Finland to Russia, but because Denmark had opposed Britain during the Napoleonic wars she was forced to give Norway to Sweden. It was only in 1905 that Norway became a separate kingdom.

During the First World War all three Scandinavian countries were neutral. When the Russian Revolution occurred in 1917 Finland was given her independence and became a republic. During the Second World War Sweden was again able to remain neutral. In 1940 Germany invaded Norway, and so Norway became one of the allies. German troops also invaded Denmark, but in this case there was no fighting.

SCARLATTI, Domenico (1685–1757)

Italian composer, born at Naples. Famous for his short harpsichord sonatas, of which he wrote over five hundred. His father, Alessandro Scarlatti (1660–1725), was one of the first opera-composers, and several of his songs are still sung.

SCHILLER, Johann Christoph Friedrich Von (1759–1805)

German dramatist and poet, born in Württemberg. Educated at the local military school, studying first law and then medicine. In secret he also wrote a play *Die Raube* (*The Brigands*) which was produced at Mannheim with immediate success. But Schiller had to flee from Württemberg and take refuge at Mannheim. He settled in Jena (1780) and later in Weimar (1800). There he wrote his major dramas, mainly on historical subjects, such as Mary Stuart, Joan of Arc, and William Tell, the greatest of all. They are all in blank verse and embody a high conception of human nature and morality.

SCHÖNBERG, Arnold (1874–1951)

Austrian composer, born in Vienna. Driven out of Austria by the Nazis, he settled in the U.S.A. At about thirty, he gave up writing music of the usual kind, and invented an entirely new way of composing, the 'twelve-note system'; most people find it difficult to understand the music that results from it. He once found a record of one of his pieces in a penny-in-the-slot gramophone in a café; the proprietor told him that the children loved it, because it sounded like Chinese music! He has had a great influence on many younger composers, but their music, together with his own, has yet to be widely appreciated.

SCHOOLS

Places for education or instruction. The word 'school' comes from a Greek word meaning leisure because the Greeks liked to spend their leisure time learning new things from their philosophers.

The earliest schools of which we know were those of ancient Egypt. Egyptian children's exercise books have been found with their teachers' corrections in them. The Chinese, too, had schools about this time. In ancient Greece boys were sent by their parents to teachers in the care of slaves. One teacher called a *grammati* (from which comes our word grammar) taught reading, writing and arithmetic. Another teacher would teach music, and a third gymnastics. The Romans copied many of the Greek ideas about schools and education, and usually employed Greeks as teachers for their children. When the Roman Empire came to an end it was the monasteries which took over the tasks of education. The oldest schools and universities in Europe were founded by monks. Two of the oldest British schools which still exist were founded not so very long after the fall of Rome. They are King's School, Canterbury, founded in A.D. 600, and King's School, Rochester, founded four years later. St. Peter's, York, was founded a few years later, in A.D. 627.

Many of these old schools, still called today Public Schools, such as Eton and Winchester, were originally founded by monks for the education of poor boys, but the education the boys received was often so much better than that given elsewhere that rich parents would offer the monks money for their monasteries if they would educate their sons. In this way the schools came to charge fees and so were able to continue after England became Protestant.

Most of the schools for the children of working people in Britain were provided by religious organizations until it became the law for all children to attend school. The law making school attendance compulsory was passed in 1870.

The schools of today are subject to the Education Act of 1944 which provided for many reforms, some of them to be introduced gradually. By this Act parents have to see that their children have efficient full-time education between the ages of 5 and 15. In 1970 the school-leaving age will be raised to 16. All forms of education in England and Wales are the responsibility of the Secretary of State for Education and Science. There are nearly 9 million children and young people all receiving full-time education at schools, universities, training and technical colleges.

The actual provision of schools is the responsibility of LOCAL AUTHORITIES, chiefly COUNTY COUNCILS and COUNTY BOROUGH COUNCILS. In the Greater London area the London Boroughs are responsible for schools, except for the twelve Inner London Boroughs which together form a single education authority. The local education authorities build schools and colleges, pay the teachers and provide materials, etc. Part of the cost is paid for by the local education authority and part by the Department of Education.

There are two types of schools for which the authorities are responsible. For one type the authority is entirely responsible. For the other the responsibility is shared by another organization, usually religious. [*See* UNIVERSITIES.]

SCHOPENHAUER, Arthur (1788–1860)
German philosopher, born at Danzig. Travelled widely in Europe, but spent the latter part of his life in seclusion. His great work is *The World as Will and Idea*. He was a close friend of the German writer GOETHE.

SCHUBERT, Franz (1797–1828)
Austrian composer, born in Vienna. He earned his living as a schoolmaster for a time, but the urge to compose was so strong that he threw up this job and devoted himself to music. His compositions were not accepted by music publishers, and he struggled against poverty; but his friends helped to support him. His inspiration worked at top speed, most of his 600 songs (some of the world's greatest) being the work of a few minutes; the famous *Hark, hark, the lark* was scribbled on the back of a menu-card in a restaurant! He also wrote nine symphonies, including the well-known *Unfinished*, much fine chamber music, and a number of piano sonatas.

SCHUMANN, Robert (1810-1856)
German composer, born at Zwickau. He wanted to be a concert pianist and, having a weak finger, devised a machine to strengthen it; unfortunately, the machine went wrong and broke his finger. He then turned to composing and produced much beautiful piano music, including the famous *Carnival*. He also wrote four symphonies, one of the best-known piano concertos and many lovely songs. The end of his life makes a sad story; he lost his reason and died in an asylum. Schumann and his wife did much to help BRAHMS.

SCHWEITZER, Albert (1875–1964)
Alsatian doctor, writer, religious thinker and musician, born at Kaiserberg. One of the truly great men of modern times who gave himself wholly to the service of his fellow men. Although he could quite easily have become a wealthy doctor he preferred to become a doctor-missionary in French Equatorial Africa, and devote his skill to the welfare of the backward and neglected coloured people. He was also an outstanding musician, being one of the greatest authorities on J. S. BACH. Schweitzer was awarded the Nobel Prize for Peace in 1954 and the Order of Merit in 1955.

SCILLY ISLES, or Isles of Scilly
A group of islands, five of them inhabited, which lie some twenty-five miles off the south-west coast of Britain. The main island is St. Mary's and the chief town Hugh Town. Because of the warm climate early vegetables and flowers are grown and exported to the mainland.

SCOTLAND
A kingdom, in the north of Great Britain, which forms part of the United Kingdom. The greatest length is 274 miles and the greatest breadth is 154 miles. When speaking of the length of Great Britain the site of John O' Groat's house, Caithness, is taken as the most northerly point in Great Britain. There are, however, important groups of islands—the Orkneys, Shetlands and the Hebrides—that are also part of Scotland. There are over 5

million Scots in Scotland. Like the Welsh and Irish, they are Celts. Their ancient language, Gaelic, is now spoken by only a few people, chiefly in the West Highlands and the islands. The capital of Scotland is Edinburgh, but the largest city is Glasgow. Scotland's chief river is the Clyde, one of the important rivers of the world and one of the great centres of ship-building. Because of the beauty of the country tourism plays an important part in the country's economy.

History :

Archaeological finds show that man has occupied Scotland since the Old Stone Age. During the New Stone Age people of Mediterranean origin settled, and built such monuments as the Circles of Callanish and the Ring of Brogar. At about the same time people from the Rhineland also settled; they are thought to have introduced 'bronze culture'. Agricola entered Scotland in A.D. 80, but only as a defensive measure. After the departure of the Romans four kingdoms were set up: 1, the Scots from Ireland, 2, the Britons (Strathclyde), 3, the Angles (Northumbria) and 4, the Picts (North). Out of these four elements a united monarchy emerged. The main factors which caused this were the conversion to Christianity, the raids of the Norsemen and the rise of the Scoto-Pictish kings. The first to bear the title of the King of Scotland was Malcolm II. With the capture of William the Lion Scotland came under the power of England. Two leaders who revolted against this were William WALLACE and Robert BRUCE. During this period Scotland maintained close ties with France. James IV married Margaret, daughter of Henry VII. Mary, Queen of Scots, daughter of James V, claimed the throne from Elizabeth I. On the death of Elizabeth, James I, son of Mary, succeeded to the throne, thus uniting the two crowns. The REFORMATION was introduced to Scotland by John KNOX. The Act of Union giving Scotland representation in Parliament was made in 1707. The Jacobite Rising of 1715 was an attempt to destroy this Union.

SCOTLAND YARD

The headquarters of the Metropolitan Police Force. The original headquarters occupied a site where formerly there had been a Palace where the Kings of Scotland used to stay. When new premises were built on a different site the name New Scotland Yard was adopted. It is at Scotland Yard that the Criminal Investigation Department is housed whose detectives and other services can be used by other police forces in the detection of serious crime. Criminal records are also kept at Scotland Yard. [*See* POLICE.]

SCOTT, Captain Robert Falcon (1868–1912)

British explorer, born at Davenport. Entered the Navy in 1882, and by 1900 had reached the rank of commander. He organized and led an Antarctic expedition (1900–1904) in his ship *Discovery*. In 1910 he led another expedition in the *Terra Nova*. It was on January 25th, 1912 that Scott's party of four men reached the South Pole, shortly after the Norwegian explorer Roald AMUNDSEN. But on the return journey to base camp Scott and his party perished, when only eleven miles from safety.

SCOTT, Sir Walter (1771–1832)

Scottish novelist, born in Edinburgh. Scott spent his youth familiarizing himself with the wilder parts of the Border country, with the Border people, and with their ballads. Eventually he put together a collection of ballads called *Minstrelsy of the Scottish Border*; and was led to write some imitations of the ballads, and then, further, to attempt historical narrative poems. He had great popular success with *The Lay of the Last Minstrel* and with subsequent similar poems. He did not start writing the historical novels, for which we know him best, until late in life, and he did not set his name to them. The first was *Waverley* in 1814, and its successors were published as 'by the author of *Waverley*'.

SCULPTURE

Probably the oldest of the arts, starting when primitive man had gained proficiency in shaping tools out of stone and bone. The earliest art objects yet found are statuettes of woman, thought to be images of a mother goddess, and animals.

In the Western hemisphere the Egyptians, Assyrians and Babylonians early mastered the art of sculpture, and applied it extensively to glorify religious beliefs. Some of the finest Egyptian sculpture is devoted to perpetuating the greatness and godliness of dead pharaohs—for example, the beautiful head of Tutankhamen rising from a lotus, or the colossal head of Rameses.

The greatest sculptors of ancient times were the Greeks. They considered sculpture to be the highest of the arts, and greatly encouraged its practice. One of the outstanding Greek sculptors was PHEIDIAS who, during the reign of PERICLES, decorated the new Acropolis. Perhaps the greatest was Praxiteles.

Roman sculpture is best represented by the portraits of great emperors and citizens. These are almost photographic in their likenesses, and in the Greek tradition.

Early Christian art was Greek in style, but

with the moving of the centre of Roman life by Constantine to Byzantium (Constantinople) it became influenced by the work of oriental craftsmen, and, further, the Church laid down hard and fast rules on how artists should treat their subjects.

With the rise to power of Christianity in Europe, sculpture served wholly the purposes of religion: Now, as the Church was the centre of religious life, sculpture became the hand-maiden of architecture. The climax of this development is in the Gothic period, a period of enormous output of the sculptor's art.

When the merchant-princes of northern Italy became the patrons of the arts in the 14th century, the sculptor (as did the painter) turned his eyes to the work of classical times. This new movement, the Renaissance, set the style of sculpture in the Western world for the next five hundred years. Among the greatest sculptors of this period were MICHELANGELO, BERNINI, DONATELLO and CELLINI.

The 20th century heralded a great revolution in sculpture as in painting. The ideas and styles which had held since the Renaissance were swept aside. Where the Renaissance artist had turned his eyes to the classical, the 20th-century sculptor turned his to the arts of prehistoric and primitive people, in addition to experimenting with abstract and geometrical forms. Of the modern sculptors whose work has achieved wide recognition the best known are RODIN, EPSTEIN and Henry MOORE.

Sculpture has also played an important part in other cultures, particularly India, China and South America (Aztec, Maya and Inca). Sculpture also plays an important part in the life of primitive peoples, particularly in their magical ceremonies. A large amount of modern sculpture owes a great deal to West African carving.

SEALS
Belong to the family of fin-footed flesh-eating animals. They have large flippers, and can turn the hind flippers forward and use their soles for walking in a waddling fashion. Seals have small ears, and swim by means of powerful strokes of their fore flippers. They feed mainly on fish, and grow (males) to some 8 feet in length. There are a number of species of which the most prized, for its fur, is the Northern or North Pacific fur seal.

SEASONS
The four divisions of the year, arising from the inclination of the earth's axis. As the earth moves round the sun on its inclined axis the amount of heat falling on a given surface will vary through the year.

SEAWEEDS
Belong to the family of plants known as 'algae'. One group, the 'brown algae' are olive-brown, and owe their colour to the presence of a brown pigment in addition to chlorophyll. They range from the small delicate seaweeds to the giant kelps. A familiar type is the 'bladder wrack' which grows between tide-marks. Iodine is obtained from this group. Another group, the 'red algae' are found below the low-tide mark, and they reach deeper levels in the sea than the other groups. A well-known species is the 'gulf weed'. Red algae are used as food in the East and the United States, and to a limited extent in Britain. Commercially they are used in the manufacture of agar, a jelly-like substance, used in making the familiar jelly sweet.

SEISMOGRAPH
An instrument for detecting earthquakes, and also used in prospecting for petroleum.

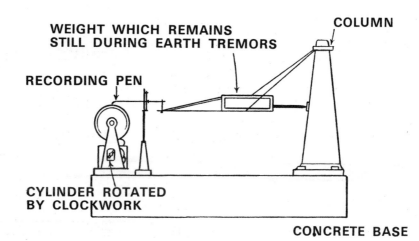

SEISMOGRAPH
When an earthquake occurs the resulting vibrations affect the apparatus but not the delicately balanced weight which remains still. This movement is recorded on a graph attached to the revolving cylinder.

WEIGHT WHICH REMAINS STILL DURING EARTH TREMORS

COLUMN

RECORDING PEN

CYLINDER ROTATED BY CLOCKWORK

CONCRETE BASE

SENECA, Lucius Annaeus (c. 4 B.C.–A.D. 65)
Roman philosopher, dramatist and statesman, born in Cordova, Spain. He was brought to Rome at an early age, and later adopted a public career. He gained a reputation as lawyer, and in A.D. 49 was appointed tutor to the Emperor Nero. He used his position to amass enormous wealth but, falling into disfavour, was forced to commit suicide. His tragedies, of which only ten remain, had great influence on early Elizabethan drama.

SENEGAL
A republic in West Africa that is rather larger (77,810 square miles) than England and Wales. Its population is a little over 3 million. Its capital is Dakar.

Before it became an independent State in 1958 it had been under French rule since the 17th century and was France's oldest colony. In the 14th century Senegal had been an independent kingdom.

SEPTET [*See* CHAMBER MUSIC]

SERBIA [*See* YUGOSLAVIA]

SERJEANT-AT-ARMS
An officer of the House of Commons who has to keep order. If the Speaker says a Member must leave the House because he has not kept the rules, the Serjeant-at-Arms must see that he obeys the Speaker.

SEVEN WONDERS OF THE WORLD
Were the pyramids of ancient Egypt, the Hanging Gardens of Babylon, the Temple of Diana at Ephesus, the tomb of Mausolus at Halicarnassus, the Colossus of Rhodes, the statue of the Greek god Zeus at Olympia, and the Pharos at Alexandria (lighthouse built by Ptolemy II).

SEXTANT
Instrument used for measuring the angular distance between two objects or points. It works on the principle of the double reflection from two mirrors. The sextant is used for the navigation of ships, and for surveying land.

SEXTET [*See* CHAMBER MUSIC]

SEYCHELLES
A group of small islands in the Indian Ocean which are a British Crown Colony. There is a population of about 37,000.

SHACKLETON, Sir Ernest Henry (1874–1922)
Antarctic explorer, born at Kilkee in Ireland.

He served first in the mercantile marine and joined Scott's Antarctic expedition of 1900, though he was forced to return through illness. He commanded two later Antarctic expeditions, in 1907–1909, and 1914–1917. The former was the first to reach the South magnetic pole, and attained a point only 100 miles from the South Pole itself. On his third expedition to the Antarctic Shackleton died of heart-failure following influenza while on board his ship *The Quest*.

SHAFTESBURY, Anthony Ashley Cooper, Seventh Earl of (1801–1885)
English philanthropist. Devoted his life to improving the conditions of the poor and humble. In 1828 he secured various reforms in the treatment of lunatics. In 1833 he turned his attention to mill-workers, and after many years framed a bill introducing the ten-hour day, and giving protection to children working in factories (1847). He also succeeded in banning employment underground for women and children. For forty years he was president of the Ragged Schools for Poor Children.

SHAKESPEARE, William (1564–1616)
English dramatist, born at Stratford-upon-Avon. Not much is known about his early life, or about any part of his life that closely relates to the plays which have won him the name of the greatest poet of all time. He came from Stratford to London in the period when the first professional theatres were drawing excited audiences, and the English drama was coming into flower. (The lifetime of this first and most vigorous of all periods of English drama lasted

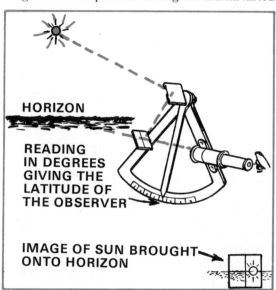

SEXTANT An instrument for angular measurement.

SHAKESPEARE An early portrait engraving.

and becoming an almost legendary figure. He knew how to surprise and stimulate the public. He also knew how to write good parts for actors, who always enjoy performing such plays as *Saint Joan, Candida,* and *Captain Brassbound's Conversion.*

SHEEP

Belong to the hollow-horned cud-chewers (ruminants), and are closely linked with the goats. They range very widely in Middle East, Central Asia and the Rocky Mountains. There are many different species and local races, the latter generally confined to particular mountain ranges. The origin of the domesticated sheep is obscure, but it has been suggested that it was descended from the mouflon with other strains. The fleece has been developed by selective breeding.

SHELLEY, Percy Bysshe (1792–1822)

English poet, born at Warnham, Sussex. For many people Shelley will always represent the poetic temperament, with its difficulties and its triumphs. From his earliest days he longed to reform the world, and spent his youth writing, printing and distributing pamphlets intended to bring reforms about; his *The Masque of Anarchy* is typical of his crusading zeal. His efforts for liberty involved him in clashes with the law, and he met personal troubles over his marriage. Moving to Switzerland and Italy, he lived mainly in these countries from 1814 to 1822, engaged in the writing of poetry. He was drowned, while sailing, in the Mediterranean. Perhaps his greatest works are *Prometheus Unbound* and *The Cenci.*

SHERIDAN, Richard Brinsley (1751–1816)

British dramatist, born in Dublin. In addition to being an outstanding dramatist and director of the Drury Lane Theatre, he was a brilliant speaker and prominent Member of Parliament. His plays are full of gaiety and wit, and include *The School for Scandal, The Rivals* and *The Critic.*

SHERIFF

This term comes from two words 'shire reeve', meaning a county governor. Today sheriffs are appointed to hold office for a year. It is an appointment of honour, a sheriff being the first citizen in a county. His duties today are chiefly connected with civic ceremonies although he does have to carry out certain duties during a General Election. Ever since the reign of Edward II sheriffs have been chosen in the same way. The Judges, the Lord Chancellor and the Chancellor of the Exchequer meet in the Queen's Bench Division of the High Court

not more than sixty years—from 1580 to 1640). There are twenty-six plays in the usual collections of Shakespeare's works. They won the admiration of his own contemporaries, and they have gone round the world, providing in themselves material for hundreds of books. *Twelfth Night* may be mentioned as a supreme example of the comedies; *Henry IV* and *Henry V* among the histories; *Julius Caesar* among the plays with a Roman theme; while there are four tragedies each so fine that it would be hard to say which is greatest—*Hamlet, King Lear, Macbeth, Othello.* They are, after three hundred and fifty years, as much alive on the stage as in the printed book. Every season in the larger cities of the world some of the plays are performed, and prove, by the scope they give to the actors, and producers, how strong a sense of the stage Shakespeare had, and by the pleasure they give the audiences with his deep understanding of human beings.

SHAW, George Bernard (1856–1950)

Born in Dublin. Settled in London as a young man of twenty. He worked as a politician in the then youthful Socialist movement, and drew attention to himself by his clear thinking and powerful speaking. He wrote novels, and became a music-critic and dramatic-critic. It was not evident at first that he was going to make his name as a dramatist, for his first play, *Widowers' Houses*, was not produced till he was 36, and his immediately subsequent plays found it difficult to get public performance. But between 1904 and 1907 there were striking performances of his works which established him as the most intelligent, amusing, and forceful of the then living dramatists. For over thirty years after that he went on writing numerous plays, adding pungent prefaces to them, making provoking public statements, on November 12th. There they suggest the names of three people for each county. These names have to be submitted to the Queen on February 3rd. On this day she pricks with a bodkin the name of the person she chooses for each county, usually the first on the list.

SHERMAN, William Tecumseh
(1820–1891)
American general (Union side) during the Civil War. He was responsible for the destruction by fire of Atlanta (1864) after its capture; he also burned other areas after capture. He put forward the idea that it was necessary in war not only to defeat the opposing army, but to break the resistance of the ordinary people as well.

SHINTO
Religion of Japan. The name comes from the Chinese 'Shin To' meaning 'the way of the gods'. There are two forms of shinto: 1, is the form of religion followed by the ordinary people, consisting of a mixture of primitive beliefs, Buddhism and Confucianism, and 2, state shinto, which is more political than religious, in fact, this form of shinto did much to bring about the way of thinking which led Japan into the Second World War with its ideas of world conquest. [*See* JAPAN.]

SHIPS
When man made his first attempts to travel over water he probably did so seated with his legs astride a log, propelling himself with his hands. Later, when he had mastered the art of making and using tools, he hollowed out a tree trunk and sat inside, using lengths of wood as oars. To prevent capsizing an outrigger was later added, i.e., a length of wood fixed parallel to the length of the boat. Craft of this type are still made by primitive peoples.

Pictures on pottery show that almost six thousand years ago sailing boats with flat hulls and long flat bows were used by the Egyptians on the Nile. The Phoenicians constructed really seaworthy vessels, and voyaged as far south as the Cape of Good Hope, through the Mediterranean to the Scilly Isles. Greeks and Romans used galleys, often with several decks and propelled by slaves chained to the oars. At the time of the Roman invasion (55 B.C.) Britons were using basket boats, known as coracles. Dug-out boats have been unearthed in Northern Europe, and some with planks fastened along the side (the forerunner of the keel), and the long ships of the Vikings.

At the time of the Crusades ships were rather in the nature of floating castles. The introduction of gunpowder in 1372 started the develop-

ment of two different types of ship; the man-of-war and the merchant ship. The need for greater weight and speed brought about an increase in the number of masts and sails. Henry VII gave an impetus to English shipbuilding with the *Sovereign*, which carried 30 large guns and 111 serpentines (small guns). So did Henry VIII with his *Great Harry*, which had 4 masts, a forecastle lower than that of medieval ships, because cannon did away with ramming and boarding as a method of fighting. 34 large guns were arranged on two decks in alternating rows. The 3- and 4-masted ships of the line in Nelson's time were less ornate, and eventually gave place to the smaller and faster frigates and corvettes.

Competition in trade in the 17th and 18th centuries saw the rise of fully rigged ships, i.e., barques, brigs, barquentines, brigantines, schooners and sloops, and later clippers.

Early in the 18th century experiments were made with steam engines for the propulsion of ships, and they were first fitted to old wooden sailing vessels. Later iron ships were built, but at the beginning of the next century the tall-masted clippers could often make faster time. The first successful steam crossing from America to Ireland was made in 1827 by the American ship *Susannah*. The *Great Western*, designed by I. K. BRUNEL (1806–1859), and rigged as a schooner, was the first British steamship to cross the Atlantic. Sir Samuel Cunard (1787–1865), founder of the famous shipping line, had four small wooden-paddle steamships built, and one of these, the *Britannia*, left Liverpool on 4th July 1840 and reached Boston in fourteen days. In 1853 an iron steamer of 3,000 tons, the *Himalaya*, was ordered by the P and O Line, and her success renewed the faith of the steam-ship pioneers. The *Great Eastern*, at that time the greatest ship ever built, was a complete failure, but it gave a lead which has since been followed and developed, and justified in such magnificent ships as *Queen Mary*, *Queen Elizabeth*, *United States*, etc. In the main large modern ships are propelled by steam TURBINES or diesel engines; small craft generally use petrol-driven outboard motors. The most recent development is nuclear power which is now used in SUBMARINES. Two non-military uses of nuclear power are the Russian ice-breaker *Lenin* and the American merchant ship *Savannah*.

SHORTHAND
The name given to any system of writing by brief signs which makes it possible to record speech as quickly as it is spoken. It is sometimes called stenography, which means narrow writing.

The earliest form of shorthand known is that invented by Tiro, a friend of Cicero's, in the year 63 B.C. By this system the speeches of CICERO, SENECA and other senators were taken down verbatim, just as today are the speeches made in Parliament. This system was used for many centuries. Many of the trials of the early Christians were reported by shorthand writers who were employed by the Church for that purpose.

The first system of English shorthand was invented by Dr. Bight during the reign of Elizabeth I, and was dedicated to her. Some years later John Willis invented in 1602 the first system based on the alphabet. Another similar system was invented in 1630 by Thomas Shelton, and it was this which was used by Samuel Pepys for the writing of his famous Diary.

During the 18th century a number of people invented various methods of writing shorthand by sound, that is phonetic shorthand. It was in 1837, the year Queen Victoria came to the throne, that the most famous and still most widely used system of phonetic shorthand was invented by Isaac Pitman. Other systems, notably that of John Gregg in 1888, have been invented since then and are in limited use at the present day.

SHOSTAKOVICH, Dmitri (1906—)

Russian composer, born in Leningrad. One of the greatest living Soviet musicians whose music is popular the world over. He has composed a large number of symphonies; the 7th was composed in Leningrad when the city was under German attack and the composer helping in its defence. He has written much music for films, notably *Hamlet*.

SHREWS

These small mammals belong to the order 'Insectivore'. A few species are adapted for life in water, but the majority live on land, are mostly nocturnal and live on insects, worms, snails and the like. They have long sensitive snounts, small eyes and soft fur. The largest is about the size of a small rat, and the smallest is the tiniest of all living mammals. They are found in many countries, but not in Madagascar or Australia.

SIAM or THAILAND

A kingdom in south-east Asia, about 198,240 square miles and nearly as big as France, and has more than 31 million inhabitants. The capital is Bangkok. Most of the people are farmers; their chief crop is rice. Siamese cats were originally brought from Siam where they were Royal pets.

SIBELIUS, Jan (1865–1958)

Finnish composer, born at Tavastehus. At 32, he was given a yearly allowance by the Finnish Government, so that he need not worry about earning a living, but could devote all his time to composing. Many of his compositions are inspired by Finnish legends, especially his gripping tone-poems *Tapiola*, *En Saga* and *The Swan of Tuonela*. He has also written seven outstanding symphonies.

SICKERT, Walter Richard (1860–1942)

English artist. A pupil of Whistler in his youth, he came under the influence of Degas in Paris. He was an outstanding painter of interiors, and specialized in scenes of everyday life. About 1911 he helped found the Camden Town Club. In 1934 he was made a R.A., but resigned in the following year. He was President of the Royal Society of British Artists 1928–1929. One of his best-known works is *Ennui*.

SIDNEY, Sir Philip (1554–1586)

Poet and soldier, and a favourite courtier of Queen Elizabeth. Born at Penshurst. He was a man of great ability, a brave soldier and a fine poet. He is now best-known for his writings,

SHREW The smallest of all living mammals, it belongs to the family of insectivores.

SHIPS

EGYPTIAN NILE
SAILING SHIP 2000BC

VIKING "DRAKKAR"

14th CENTURY
COASTING SHIP

HULLOT
38-GUN FRIGATE 1790

MAURETANIA TYPE c1907

1858 THE GREAT EASTE

ROTTERDAM 1960
TYPICAL NEW 'LINES'

EARLIEST TYPE OF BOAT
MADE OF BOUND REEDS

CHINESE SAILING JUNK

ENGLISH GALLEON 1545

SAIL PLAN OF FULL-RIGGED
SHIP (CLIPPER TYPE) 1890

THE *ELSIE*: FIRST STEAMBOAT
TO CROSS THE CHANNEL 1816

SMALL CHANNEL PACKET
AND MAIL BOAT

US NUCLEAR SHIP *SAVANNAH*
MAIDEN VOYAGE 1964

of which the sonnets *Astrophel and Stella* are the most famous. His essay *Apologie for Poetry* was a significant step in the development of formal poetical writing.

SIENKIEWICZ, Henryk (1846–1916)

Polish novelist. Travelled extensively in America, Africa and Europe. In 1905 he was awarded the Nobel Prize for his novel *Quo Vadis*, which concerned Rome under the rule of Nero. During the First World War he organized relief for Polish victims, and died in Switzerland while still carrying out this most humanitarian work.

SIERRA LEONE

An independent State in West Africa within the British Commonwealth. It is about 27,930 square miles, nearly as big as Scotland and has a little over 2 million inhabitants. The capital is Freetown, one of the chief ports in the African continent. The town got its name because it was a refuge for freed slaves before slavery was abolished. The country produces diamonds, including some of the largest found anywhere, and also iron ore.

SIKHS

Group of people in the Punjab (India) who follow the religion of Baba Nanak (born 1469). Under the leadership of Ranjit Singh they became a powerful military force which opposed the British in the Sikh Wars (1845–1849). The sikhs wear a turban and never cut their hair. The sikh regiments in the Indian army (British period) were among the most gallant in the forces.

SIMOOM

Hot, dry, wind occurring in the Sahara and Arabian deserts. It often forms a vortex and raises immense clouds of sand, but seldom lasts more than twenty minutes.

SINGAPORE

An island Member of the British Commonwealth and lies off the tip of the Malay peninsular. It is less than three times the size of the Isle of Wight. It is one of the chief ports within the British Commonwealth. It has a population of about $1\frac{1}{2}$ million, nearly all of whom are Chinese. For about two years Singapore joined the Federation of MALAYSIA but then decided to become a separate State again.

SINGER, Isaac Merritt (1811–1875)

American engineer who developed and patented a single-thread and a chain-stitch sewing machine, and founded the world-famous Singer Sewing Machine Company.

SIPHON

Tube so bent that one end can be immersed in a vessel containing a liquid while its other end is outside the vessel and at a lower level. Once the tube itself is filled, the vessel is automatically emptied by atmospheric pressure acting on the surface of the liquid.

SIROCCO

Hot, dry wind which blows north from the Sahara across Libya and the Mediterranean, reaching Italy as a warm, moist wind.

SITWELLS

Family of writers and poets. Dame Edith Sitwell (1877–1964) was one of Britain's foremost poetesses. She wrote a large volume of poetry, several critical studies on modern poetry, and much miscellaneous writings. Her set of poems entitled *Façade* was set to music by William WALTON and later turned into a very successful ballet. Sir Osbert Sitwell (1892–1969) was a poet and novelist. His series of autobiographical books are highly thought of as is his novel, *Before the Bombardment*. Sacheverell Sitwell (1897—) is an outstanding poet and art critic, and has written important studies of LISZT and MOZART.

SKATING

Like riding a bicycle, skating is primarily a matter of balance and confidence. Ordinary walking is done with a heel-and-toe action, and most beginners try to skate forward in the same way. At best, they will not move at all.

Skates have two sharp edges, and all movement depends on the use of these. By bending the feet over slightly the beginner will feel the edges 'bite' the ice, and this will give him a feeling of security.

In skating the knees should be slightly bent, so that the weight of the body is supported on the muscles at the top of the thighs. Stiffness must be avoided. The beginner will find it easier to keep his balance if he leans slightly forward. When skating on the left foot, the right arm and shoulder should swing forward, while on the right foot the position is reversed. The important thing, however, is to see that all skating 'effort' comes from below the hips.

To get into a starting position the skater should stand with heels together and toes pointing outward. If he or she keeps on the inside edges of the skates there will be no difficulty in keeping balance. Now move the right skate so that the right heel is against the middle of the left skate, the feet being at right-angles. Bring the right skate on to the flat of the runner, press on the inside edge of the left skate, lifting the foot off the ice as the right skate glides forward. When the right skate stops moving, the left skate is placed at right-angles against it, and the same movement is done with the other foot.

Figures require backward as well as forward skating, and this should be learned at the beginning. The simplest way is by the two-footed method. The skates are placed close together with the toes turned in, and the skater presses on each inside edge alternately. Each skate will make a small curve, and the skater will be able to move backward without lifting either foot off the ground. Soon, however, it will come natural to lift the free foot, and the curves will get longer.

The use of the inside edges is learned more easily than the use of the outside ones because they give the skater a greater feeling of security. To get on the outside edge of a skate means leaning over away from the second foot; thus it calls for greater confidence. It can, however, be learned gradually, and will develop naturally from the proper movement of the arms and shoulders. When the beginner glides forward on the outside edge instead of the flat of the skate, it will be found that a curve is described and not a straight line, and if the skater leans towards the curve a complete circle can be executed.

SKELTON, John (*c.* 1460–1529)

English poet, born at Diss, Norfolk. We know all too little of this poet who was a strong and forceful writer. Much of his work is known only by name. But the poems of his which we do have show how energetic his ideas were, and how skilful his writing. A form of verse of which he was fond was that in which several short vigorous lines rhyme together, followed by several short lines on a new rhyme, and so on. Verses with this form are called 'skeltonics' after him.

SKI-ING

In some countries ski-ing is not only a sport but a normal means of transport. It consists simply of travelling over snow on narrow boards or planks, usually of ash or hickory wood, which are fastened to the feet with leather straps or metal clips. There are various types of ski, but the most general type is thick at the centre, tapering towards both ends, and bulges upward in a curve at the middle. When the weight of the body is placed on the ski this bulge is straightened out so that the weight of the skier is evenly distributed over the whole surface. The tip or front rises up in a curve, and is very springy. The length of skis varies according to the skier's height and weight.

The skier uses ski-sticks to push himself forward. These are usually made of a light wood, such as bamboo; they are pointed and have a small disc near the bottom end and a looped leather strap at the top. They should be long enough to reach as high as the armpits.

One of the first essentials in ski-ing is suppleness of the knees and hips, and the aim in walking should be a rhythmic, continuous gliding movement without any jerkiness. There are two common methods of climbing a slope. Direct climbing, which is used for gentle slopes, and the herring-bone or side-stepping method for steeper slopes. The run down, the most exciting part of ski-ing, may be done in four positions. The upright; the telemark, or striding position; the semi-crouch and crouch. Before any complicated manoeuvres can be attempted the skier must master the important snowplough position which acts as a brake.

SKUNK

A flesh-eating mammal found only in America. It is not unlike the badger, being mainly nocturnal and feeding upon smaller mammals, frogs, insects, etc. When attacked skunks discharge from glands beneath the tail a very offensive smell. Their fur is highly valued.

SLATE

Hard rock which splits easily into thin leaves suitable for use as roofing-tiles. Slate was formed from clay by enormous pressure, which rearranged all its particles in layers. These are not the original layers in which the clay settled down, but new ones which often run at right-angles to the beds of rock.

SLESSOR, Mary (1848–1915)

One of Britain's most outstanding women missionaries. Born at Aberdeen of very humble parents, and started life working in a mill. She was self-educated. Went to West Africa where she did great work in caring and educating the native population.

SLOTH

An animal wholly adapted to life in trees, and is practically helpless on the ground. It moves hanging down from branches, suspended by its claws; it also sleeps in this position. The food of the sloth consists of the leaves of the trees it inhabits. There are two kinds, the two-toed and the three-toed. Both are found in South America, particularly Brazil.

SMITH, Adam (1723–1790)

Scottish economist, born at Kirkcaldy. His *The Wealth of Nations* (1776) was the first scientific work on the principles of economy. Smith's main theme was the need for the division of labour, whereby every country would produce what it was best fitted to produce. The book was very influential in the 19th century and was the basis of Britain's manufacturing prosperity.

SMITH, Sir Matthew (1879–1959)

English painter, born in Halifax. Studied in London and Paris, and was greatly influenced by artists like MATISSE. Smith's work was almost all done in oils and was of landscapes, still-lifes and the nude. His colours were rich and daring.

SMOLLETT, Tobias (1721–1771)

British novelist, born at Dalquhurne, Scotland. For the first part of his life he was a naval surgeon, but later turned to writing. His most famous books are *The Adventures of Roderick Random*, *The Adventures of Peregrine Pickle* and *The Expedition of Humphry Clinker*.

SMUTS, Field-Marshal, Jan Christiaan (1870–1950)

South African statesman, born in Cape Colony. Son of a prosperous Boer farmer, he was educated in South Africa and Cambridge. Admitted to the Bar in 1895 he had risen to the post of State Attorney of the South African Republic by 1898. In the Boer War (1899–1902) he was a commando leader against the British, but when the Boers lost he was the first to work for reconciliation. In the Great War he commanded British forces in East Africa, and served as a member of the Imperial War Cabinet (1917–1918). In 1919 he was elected South African Prime Minister but was defeated at the polls in 1924. After a period in opposition he again became Prime Minister in 1939, and was instrumental in bringing South Africa into the Second World War. A strong supporter both of the League of Nations and the United Nations Organization.

SMYTH, Dame Ethel Mary (1858–1944)

Britain's foremost woman composer, born at Foots Cray, Kent. She was a great fighter for women's rights and spent a short spell in prison for her militancy. Her best-known works are the two operas, *The Wreckers* and *The Boatswain's Mate*.

SNAKES

Belong to the order 'Ophidea', and some two thousand species are known. They are reptiles and closely related to the lizards. Their main features are the absence of limbs, very long body, absence of ear openings and movable eyelids, and long cleft tongue. Snakes move by means of muscles which are fixed to the many ribs and pull the skin backwards and forwards in a kind of wave-motion. The scales on the under-surface grip earth, branch or whatever else it may be travelling over. Another method of moving is by twisting the body sideways in loops and wriggling along, pressing the body against projections in its path. The outer skin is cast periodically, usually in a single piece. The structure of the jaws is such that the reptile can eat its food whole. Less than one-third of living snakes are known to be poisonous. Those which are do not 'sting' with the tongue (this is an organ of smell) but with the fangs.

SNOOKER

A game played on the same table as BILLIARDS but with 22 balls. The first part of the game consists of potting the reds. When a red has been potted (1 point) it stays in the pocket, and the player is free to pot any colour he chooses. Should he pot this it must be replaced on its spot position, and the player try to pot a further red, and so on. The second part of the game starts when the 15 reds have been potted, and consists simply of potting the 6 colours in the following order: yellow (2), green (3), brown (4), blue (5), pink (6), and black (7). The numbers in brackets are the point scores for each colour. In play the term 'snooker' means placing the ball such that it cannot be directly hit. Should the player miss he gives away 4 points, and if he hits another colour he gives away points to the value of the colour.

SNOW

Crystallized water vapour of the air which has formed about a dust particle at a temperature below freezing point. There exists a large variety of the two basic types of snow crystals; the columnar and the tabular forms.

SOANE, Sir John (1753–1837)

English architect and collector, born near Reading. Among other things he was architect to the Bank of England, which he rebuilt and enlarged as it is now. He left his house in Lincoln's Inn Fields with an endowment, and his library, pictures and works of art, to the nation, and it is now open to the public.

SOAP

Made from beef, mutton tallow and olive oil, but palm oil, coconut oil, cotton-seed oil and many others are also used, for a soap can be made by boiling any fat with any alkali. The manufacture of soap is carried out in large iron pans heated by steam-pipes. About half a ton of clarified fats and oils are mixed with a

INDIAN PYTHON   **BOA CONSTRICTOR**

SNAKES

ADDER

GRASS SNAKE   **KING COBRA**

RUSSELLS VIPER

hundredweight and a half of caustic soda in solution (lye) and boiled. The result is a clear brown liquid containing half a ton of soap and a hundredweight of glycerine. The soap is now separated by adding salt, which causes it to float to the surface as a white curd. The liquid below (the spent lyes) is drawn off, and used for the extraction of its glycerine. The soap is now heated once more till it forms a pasty mass which can be pumped off into frames, where it cools and sets. It can now be resoftened, scented, and cast into moulds or ornamental cakes.

SOCCER

Association football (called soccer for short) was invented in England, and has spread right round the world. It is doubtful whether there is any place where soccer of some sort is not played. English teams tour the Americas, much of Europe, and of course, the Commonwealth; the game is played in the icy wastes of the Arctic and (barefooted) in the tropics.

Apart from the fact that each team has a goal-keeper, there is nothing in the Laws which insists upon the positions of the players on the field. But long experience has shown that the best arrangement is to have 5 forwards, 3 half-backs and 2 full-backs, placed as shown in the diagram of the pitch. Incidentally, in the diagrams for this chapter, abbreviations for players are as follows:

Forwards: OL = outside-left; IL = inside-left; CF = centre-forward; IR = inside-right; OR = outside-right. Half-backs: LH = left-half; CH = centre-half; RH = right-half. Backs: LB = left-back;

RB = right-back; G = Goal-keeper.

The referee is a most important official, for he is the one who controls the game. He starts it, times it, and brings it to an end. He also decides whether or not a goal has been scored, whether there have been any breaches of the laws of the game, and when and where penalties shall be awarded. The referee's decision is absolutely final.

The referee is assisted by two linesmen whose duty is to run up and down the pitch just outside the touch-lines, signal when the ball goes out of play, and to see that the throw-in is taken correctly.

First, the two captains (one to each team) toss up, and the winner of the toss has the choice either of ends or kick-off. Then the referee places the ball on the centre-spot, looks round to see that everyone is ready, and then blows his whistle as a signal for the game to begin. At the same moment he notes the time, for the game will last for 90 minutes in all, plus 10 minutes for an interval at half-time, plus any time lost because of stoppages. After the half-time interval the teams change ends.

The ball has to be not less than 27 inches or more than 28 inches in circumference. When it is dry and clean, it must weigh between 14 and 16 ounces. Incidentally, it must not have anything on it, such as wire lacing, which could cause anyone serious injury. No player shall wear anything which could be dangerous to other players. Studs or bars on boots must not project more than half an inch, must not be pointed in any way, and must be so nailed that the heads of the nails are buried. Studs or bars can be of leather or soft rubber.

When the ball is in play it is the purpose of

every player to put it, or help to put it, into his opponents' goal. The players can propel the ball with any part of their bodies except their hands and arms (from the shoulders); they may kick it, head it, thump it with their chests, and so on.

There are certain things they must not do, or they will be penalized.

(1) Kick, strike, jump at, trip, or attempt to trip an opponent. If you bend down suddenly so that an opponent falls over you that is just as much tripping as if you stick out your foot.

(2) Handle the ball or use any part of the arm in an attempt to stop it, or carry it.

(3) Hold or push an opponent with hand or arm extended from the body. This does not prohibit a fair shoulder-charge so long as the charge is made with your arm close to your side. But you must not charge in a violent or dangerous manner; nor must you charge an opponent in the back.

The goalkeeper is a specially privileged person, but only *so long as he is within his own penalty area.* Within that area he may handle the ball as much as he likes, but he must not carry it for more than four steps without bouncing it on the ground. Incidentally, it is an offence to charge a goalkeeper unless he is actually carrying the ball or unless he is outside his penalty area.

A player is in an offside position if, when not actually playing the ball, he is nearer to his opponents' goal-line than two of the opposing players. In other words, you should have at least the opposing goalkeeper, and, say, one of the backs between you and the goal-line before receiving the ball from a player of your own side.

You are not in an offside position, whether there are two opposing players between you and their goal-line or not, if:

(1) You play the ball after it was last touched or played by an opponent.

(2) You are in your own half of the field of play.

(3) You are onside when the pass is made.

(4) You receive the ball direct from a goal-kick, a corner-kick, a throw-in, or a drop by the referee. We will come to those special kicks and so on in a minute.

(5) You can be in an offside position just as much as you like, without penalty to your side, so long as you make no attempt to play the ball or obstruct an opponent.

A goal is scored when the ball *lawfully* goes over the opponents' goal-line between the goal-posts, no matter which player puts it there; which means that if one of your opponents is so obliging as to put the ball into his own goal, so much the worse for the opposing team.

For the goal to be a good one, the whole of the ball must go right over the line; it is not enough that it shall go just half-way over. This applies to all other lines: the ball is out of play when the whole of it goes over a goal-line or a touch-line, no matter how high it is travelling.

Getting a ball back into play after it has gone over a goal-line or a touch-line is done in four ways:

(1) If a goal has been scored, then there is a kick-off from the centre-spot by the centre-forward of the team which had the goal scored against it.

(2) If the ball went over a touch-line, it is thrown in by a player of the team which did *not* send it out of play.

(3) If the ball was sent over a goal-line by the attackers, a player from the defending team makes a goal-kick; that is, he kicks it from his goal-area to some place beyond his penalty area.

(4) If the ball was sent over a goal-line by a defender, a player of the attacking team makes a corner-kick; that is, he kicks the ball from within the quarter-circle at the nearest corner flag-post, towards the defenders' goal, or anywhere into the field of play. A goal can be scored direct from a corner kick.

The ball is sent into play again either from part of the touch-line where the ball went out of play, or from the other half of the goal-area or the corner-circle on that side of the goal where the ball went over the line.

There is just one other way of getting the ball back into play, and that is by the referee dropping it after a stoppage of the game because of injury to a player or from some other cause. The referee simply lets the ball fall at the spot where the play was stopped, and the moment it touches the ground it is in play again.

There are three kinds of ordinary penalty which can be awarded against an offending team. These are: an indirect free-kick, a direct free-kick and a penalty-kick. A goal cannot be scored directly from an indirect free-kick, the ball must first be touched by a player other than the kicker. A goal can be scored directly from a direct free-kick. A penalty-kick is always taken from the penalty-mark of the offending team. Incidentally, when any of these kicks is being taken, all other players of the opposing team, except the defending goalkeeper, must stand outside the penalty area and must not approach within ten yards of the ball until it has been kicked, except that, in the case of direct and indirect free-kicks, defenders may line up between their goal-posts

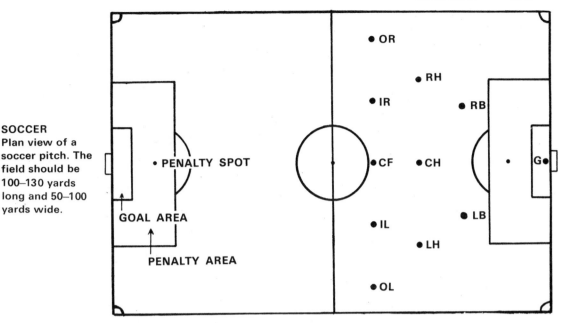

SOCCER
Plan view of a soccer pitch. The field should be 100–130 yards long and 50–100 yards wide.

GOAL AREA

PENALTY AREA

PENALTY SPOT

if the kick is being taken from within ten yards of their goal.

And now for the penalties which are awarded for each type of offence, a subject on which there is nearly as much argument as on the offside law:

For kicking, striking, jumping at, or tripping an opponent; for handling the ball; for charging violently or otherwise playing in a dangerous manner—a direct free-kick.

For any of the above offences by a defending team within their own penalty area—a penalty-kick.

When playing as goalkeeper, for carrying the ball more than four steps without bouncing it on the ground—an indirect free-kick.

For charging a goalkeeper when he is not actually carrying the ball—an indirect free-kick.

There are other offences which are not easily defined, but which come under the heading of ungentlemanly conduct, for example, repeatedly fouling an opponent, arguing with the referee, and so on. In these cases a referee may either caution a player or send him off the field altogether. Play is resumed afterwards by an indirect free-kick by the opposing side.

There are just one or two points about the pitch which, because of scale, could not be shown on the diagram. Here is a brief list of them:

(1) The lines must not be more than 5 inches in width, and must be marked clearly on the surface, but they must *not* be cut into the ground. Whitewash lines are the best.

(2) There are small flags at the corners; these must be on posts at least 5 feet high, and the posts must *not* be pointed at the top. Two more posts can be placed just outside the touch-lines to mark the halfway-line if required, but these are not compulsory.

(3) Each goal must be 8 feet high (from the centre of the cross-bar to the ground), and the width and depths of posts, and cross-bar must not exceed 5 inches. Goalnets are not compulsory, but they are very convenient in an important match, for they leave no doubt whether a ball has or has not entered the goal when it has gone near to a post or a cross-bar.

SOCIETY ISLANDS
Group of French islands in the Pacific, including the LEEWARD ISLANDS and WINDWARD ISLANDS. Named after the Royal Society, members of which accompanied Capt. COOK on his 1769 voyage of research.

SOCRATES (469–399 B.C.)
Greek philosopher, and considered one of the greatest thinkers of all time. Born at Athens. Socrates committed nothing to writing and our knowledge of him comes from the writings of his pupil PLATO. His greatness lies in his love of truth and virtue, in fact, his main contention was that 'virtue is knowledge'. His way of getting at truth was by means of dialogue in a question and answer form. Socrates would first describe exactly what the subject was and then question his audience until every aspect of the subject was aired. His teachings were consider-

ed dangerous to the Athenian rulers, and they arrested and charged Socrates with corrupting the youth of Athens and denying the existence of the gods. Although he took the charge lightly, he was condemned to death and elected to die by drinking hemlock.

SODDY, Frederick (1877–1956)

English scientist, born at Eastbourne. A pioneer in the study of radioactive substances, and proposed a theory that elements have isotopes. Was awarded the Nobel Prize for Chemistry in 1921.

SOIL

Organic and mineral materials which form the surface of the earth and in which perceptible horizontal layers can be distinguished. A number of biological and physical actions develop the soils in different ways. Weathering process of minerals, chemical and biological decomposition strongly affect soil development and environmental factors play an outstanding role. Soil scientists first pointed out that the character of each soil depended on the environment and the material from which it originated. Soil studies now form a special subject, pedology, in which the physical nature, the chemical and biological properties, productivity, etc., are investigated.

SOLAR SYSTEM

Includes the sun and all the surrounding bodies that revolve about it. They consist of the planets, comets and meteor swarms.

SOLENOID

Coil of wire which produces a magnetic field when an electric current passes through it. The solenoid coil is extensively used in many types of electrical instruments, and such things as motor-car starters, magnetic brakes, switches, etc. [*See* ELECTRO-MAGNET.]

SOLOMON (died *c.* 932 B.C.)

Son of David and Bathsheba, and third King of the Hebrews *c.* 972–*c.* 932 B.C. His period of rule was marked by peace and great expansion of trade. Several books of the BIBLE are considered to have been written by him, *Proverbs*, *Ecclesiastes* and *Song of Solomon*. Traditionally his name is connected with wisdom. He built the Temple at Jerusalem.

SOLOMON ISLANDS

An archipelago in the Pacific Ocean. Nearly all the islands are a British Protectorate. The chief island is Guadacanal. Two of the northern islands are an International Trust Territory and are looked after by Australia. The population of the islands is about 160,000.

SOLSTICE

Either of the two points in the earth's orbit at which the noonday sun is overhead at the maximum distance (north or south) from the equator. At the present time the solstices very nearly coincide with the positions of perihelion (22nd December) and aphelion (21st June), the times when the earth is nearest to and furthest from the sun.

CHARACTERISTICS OF THE SOLAR SYSTEM

Name of Planet				Distance from Sun in millions of miles	Orbital Period ('year')	Rotation Period	Diameter in Miles	Mass (earth = 1)
Mercury	.	.	.	36	88·0 days	88 days	3,100	0·037
Venus	.	.	.	67	225 days	20–30 days	7,700	0·810
Earth .	.	.	.	93	865·26 days	23h. 56 m.	7,900	1·000
Mars .	.	.	.	142	1·88 years	24h. 37 m.	4,200	0·109
Jupiter	.	.	.	484	11·86 years	9h. 55 m.	89,000 84,000	317·00
Saturn	.	.	.	887	29·46 years	10h. 14 m.	75,000 68,000	95·0
Uranus	.	.	.	1783	84·02 years	10h. 45 m.	32,000	14·7
Neptune	.	.	.	2793	164·79 years	15h. 40 m.	31,000	17·2
Pluto .	.	.	.	3670	248·43 years	—	7,700?	0·7

NOTE.—Jupiter and Saturn are flattened at the poles so two diameters are given, the equatorial and the polar. The flattening of Earth is 26 miles. Between the orbits of Mars and Jupiter lie the orbits of some 2,000 minor planets.

SOMALIA, or Somali Republic

An independent State in East Africa that is a little larger (246,000 square miles) than France and has a population of a little over 2½ million. The capital is Mogadishu. It produces and exports fruit and vegetables. It was created an independent State in 1960 when British Somaliland and the International Trust Territory of Somaliland, administered by Italy, joined together to form the new State. Its neighbour is French Somaliland.

SONAR

This is similar to RADAR but uses sound waves instead of radio waves. Detects presence of objects near a boat in a fog and is also used to find depth of the ocean bottom. (The bat is guided by a system similar to sonar using extremely high pitched sounds that are beyond the range of human hearing.) The sound is sent out at regular intervals and the time required for the sound to be returned by reflection is measured. Knowing the speed of sound, it is easy to determine the distance.

SONATA

Type of musical composition for one or two instruments, created in the 18th century; it is usually divided into several sections, called movements. The first is normally built on the following pattern: an 'exposition', in which two contrasting groups of themes are played, followed by a 'development', in which the various themes are varied and modified, and a 'recapitulation', in which the themes are played again more or less in their original form. Sometimes some of the other movements follow this pattern. The usual number of movements is four, the first being quick, the second slow, the third a minuet or 'scherzo', and the last quick again. The order may be changed, and the third movement is often omitted. This description applies in general to the classical sonatas of Mozart, Haydn and Beethoven; modern sonatas follow this pattern roughly. Compositions of the sonata type written for more than two instruments are given the general title of chamber music, and those written for orchestra are called symphonies. [*See* CHAMBER MUSIC and SYMPHONY.]

SONG

Musical composition for a solo singer, with or without accompaniment. It is probably the oldest form of music, as the voice was the only instrument given by nature to man. Early songs, composed by the ordinary people, were usually unaccompanied; these are called folk-songs, and have been arranged and provided with accompaniments in modern times. In the time of Queen Elizabeth, songs were accompanied by the lute, and in Purcell's time by the harpsichord; the modern type of song with piano accompaniment was established by Schubert.

SONNET

One of the most celebrated forms in the poetry of many European languages. A true sonnet is fourteen lines long, these being divided into a first group of eight, known as the octet, and a second group of six, known as the sestet. Often there is a paragraph-break or change in mood between the octet and the sestet.

Sonnets were first introduced into England by Sir Thomas Wyatt in the reign of King Henry VIII, and were modelled on a rhyme-scheme he had found in Italy, so that afterwards when our poets followed the same scheme their works were called Italian sonnets. Here is a sequence of rhymes in an Italian sonnet by MILTON: *rings, praise, amaze, kings, brings, raise, displaies, wings, hand, breed, freed, brand, bleed, land.* Later, since the English language has not so many words rhyming on one sound as the Italian has, poets began to introduce a change of rhyme into the fifth and sixth lines, and so arose the so-called English sonnet. A sonnet by John Clare framed on this pattern rhymes: *bush, round, thrush, sound, guest, day, nest, clay, dew, flowers, blue, hours, fly, sky.* Do not be surprised at any mixtures you may come across of these two dominant forms. Variations always creep in. You may even hear the sixteen-line verses of Meredith's *Modern Love* described as sonnets.

SOPHOCLES (*c.* 496–*c.* 406 B.C.)

Greek dramatist, born at Colonus. He introduced a number of new ideas into Greek drama, and twenty times won first place in the Athenian dramatic contests. His first conquest was over the famous dramatist AESCHYLUS. Seven of his works survive of which the most famous are *Antigone, Oedipus Rex* and *Electra.*

SOUND

A form of energy. It is the form that we are aware of through our ears. Everything we hear is sound. The ear is a complicated instrument, but the essential part, without which no normal hearing is possible, is a tiny stretched skin called the drum. Movement of this drum makes us hear. This fact shows that all sound that we hear must consist of air movements. In fact, sound will not travel through a vacuum.

The sort of air-movements that make sound is easily shown. All that need be done is to rotate a toothed wheel rapidly and hold a piece of card lightly against the teeth so that the card is flipped by each tooth. If the speed is enough, the result is a recognizable musical note. This shows that a succession of pulses of air makes a recognizable note. If the speed of the wheel is changed, so is the pitch of the note, and the faster the speed the higher is the pitch. The number of pulses every second is called the frequency. So the first fact in the science of acoustics, or the study of sound, is that the pitch of a note depends on the frequency. A frequency of about twenty cycles per second gives just about the lowest note that can be heard as a note. A frequency of about twenty thousand cycles per second gives just about the highest note that can be heard. This range of audibility varies with the person and with age. The note A in the treble clef, the tuning note used by orchestras and choirs, has a frequency of 440 cycles per second by international agreement.

Anything travelling in a succession of pulses is usually described as a wave. As soon as this change is made, the mathematics of waves can be applied. This is the usual way in which the theory of sound is investigated.

Sound travels at about 1,100 feet per second in air, the actual value depending on the temperature and pressure. It travels at different speeds in different substances, being much faster in solids. Though the speed may be greater in a substance, this does not mean that the substance is necessarily a better conductor of sound, for the loss of energy in travel may be great. Substances that are poor conductors are used in buildings for absorbing sound between rooms and floors in order to make rooms and flats somewhat soundproof. Such a poor conductor, for example, is glass wool. Any substance that is a poor conductor of heat is also a poor conductor of sound.

SOUSA, John Philip (1854–1932)
American composer, born at Washington. He is particularly famous for his military marches, so much so that he was known as 'The March King'. Among his best-known works are *Stars and Stripes Forever*, *The Washington Post* and *El Capitan*.

SOUTH AFRICA, Republic of
A large independent State at the tip of the African continent. It is more than twice the size (472,360 square miles) of France but its population is only 16 million. Only a little over 3 million of these are white people, nearly 11 million are Africans and the rest are either of mixed race or are Asians. Most of the white people are Afrikaans speaking, a language derived from Dutch, but a large number are English speaking. There are two capitals—

Pretoria in the North is the administrative capital, i.e. where the Government departments are centred; and Cape Town where Parliament meets. More than half the world's gold comes from South African mines, chiefly those near Johannesburg. The country also produces diamonds, coal and iron.

History:
The first European settlers in South Africa were the Dutch who settled in the Cape in the 17th century. During the Napoleonic Wars the British took the Cape and many of the Dutch, or Boer, settlers trekked inland to find what later became the Boer republics of the Transvaal and the Orange Free State. At the end of the 19th century war broke out between the Boers and the English. After the war the whole of South Africa came under British rule. In 1907 the country became a self-governing British colony and in 1961 elected to become an independent republic.

SOUTH ARABIA, Federation of
A British Protectorate. It lies at the southern end of the Arabian peninsular. It is about 60,000 square miles, slightly larger than England and Wales, but with only about three-quarters of a million inhabitants. The federation is made up of the former colony of Aden and thirteen sultanates and amirates. The port of Aden at the entrance to the Red Sea is the most prosperous of the States forming the federation. There has been a good deal of unrest in the Federation since it came into existence in 1958, partly because the neighbouring country of the YEMEN does not approve of the new form of government then set up.

SOUTHEY, Robert (1774–1843)
English poet and writer. At Oxford he met COLERIDGE and later settled at Keswick, with some money from a friend and later a grant from the government. In 1813 he became poet-laureate.

His longer poems are rarely read nowadays, but some of the shorter pieces remain popular —*The Battle of Blenheim* and *The Inchcape Rock*, for example. He also wrote light and comic verse. The *History of Brazil* and the *History of the Peninsular War* are among his most useful prose works.

SOVEREIGN, or MONARCH
The name used to describe the Head of State when the country is a kingdom. The reigning sovereign may be either a King or Queen.

Queen Elizabeth II succeeded to the throne in 1952. She is not only Queen of Great Britain and Northern Ireland but Queen of the DOMINIONS as well. Thus, in Canada or

SOVEREIGNS OF ENGLAND

Sovereign	Born Date	Born Place	Died Date	Died Place	Reign From	Reign To	Married
Saxon and Danish Monarchy							
Egbert	c. 775		839		827	839	Raedburgh
Ethelwulf	—		858		839	858	Osburg
							Judith
Ethelbald ⎱			860		858	860	Judith (Father's widow)
Ethelbert ⎰	—		866		858	866	
Ethelred I	—		871	Merton	866	871	
Alfred	c. 849	Wantage	901	Farringdon	871	901	Eahlswith
Edward the Elder	c. 870		925	Farndon	901	925	Ecgwyn
							Elfleda
							Edgiva
Athelstan	c. 895		940		925	940	
Edmund I	c. 922		946	Pucklechurch (Glos.)	940	946	Aelfgifu
							Ethelflaed
Edred	—		955	Frome	946	955	
Edwy	—		959		955	959	
Edgar	944		975		959	975	Ethelfleada
							Elfrida
Edward the Martyr	c. 963		978	Corfe Castle	975	978	
Ethelred the Unready	c. 968	London	1016	London	978	1016	Elfleda
							Emma of Normandy
Edmund II	980	Islip (Oxford)	1016	Oxford	1016	1016	Algitha
Canute	994		1035	Shaftesbury	1017	1035	Alfwen
							Emma of Normandy
Harold I	—		1040	Oxford	1035	1040	
Hardicanute	1019		1042	London	1040	1042	
Edward the Confessor	1004		1066		1042	1066	Edgitha
Harold II	c. 1022		1066	Hastings	1066	1066	Ealdhyrh
House of Normandy							
William I	1027	Falaise	1087	St. Gervais	1066	1087	Matilda of Flanders
William II	1057	Normandy	1100	New Forest	1087	1100	
Henry I	1068	Selby (Yorks)	1135	Normandy	1100	1135	Matilda of Scotland
							Adelaide of Louvain
Stephen	1104	Blois (France)	1154	Dover	1135	1154	Matilda of Boulogne
House of Plantagenet							
Henry II	1133	Mans (France)	1189	Chinon (France)	1154	1189	Eleanor of Aquitaine
Richard I	1157	Oxford	1199	Châlus (France)	1189	1199	Berengaria of Navarre
John	1166	Oxford	1216	Newark	1199	1216	Isabella of Gloucester
							Isabella of Angoulême
Henry III	1207	Winchester	1272	Bury St. Edmunds	1216	1272	Eleanor of Provence
Edward I	1239	Westminster	1307	Burgh-on-the-Sands	1272	1307	Eleanor of Castile
							Margaret of France
Edward II	1284	Caernarvon	1327	Berkeley Castle	1307	1327	Isabella of France
Edward III	1312	Windsor	1377	East Sheen	1327	1377	Philippa of Hainault
Richard II	1367	Bordeaux	1400	Pontefract	1377	1399	Anne of Luxemburg
							Isabel of France
Henry IV	1366	Bolingbroke	1413	Westminster	1399	1413	Mary of Bohun
							Joan of Navarre
Henry V	1388	Monmouth	1422	Bois de Vincennes	1413	1422	Katherine of France
Henry VI	1421	Windsor	1471	Tower of London	1422	1461	Margaret of Anjou
House of York							
Edward IV	1442	Rouen	1483		1461	1483	Elizabeth Woodville
Edward V	1470	Westminster	1483	Tower of London	1483	1483	
Richard III	1452	Fotheringay Castle	1485	Bosworth	1483	1485	Anne Neville

Sovereigns of England (cont.)

Sovereign	Born		Died		Reign		Married
	Date	Place	Date	Place	From	To	
House of Tudor							
Henry VII	1457	Pembroke Castle	1509	Sheen (Surrey)	1485	1509	Elizabeth of York
Henry VIII	1491	Greenwich	1547	Westminster	1509	1547	Katherine of Aragon
							Anne Boleyn
							Jane Seymour
							Anne of Cleves
							Katherine Howard
							Katherine Parr
Edward VI	1537	Greenwich	1553	Greenwich	1547	1553	
Mary I	1516	Greenwich	1558	Greenwich	1553	1558	Philip II of Spain
Elizabeth	1533	Greenwich	1603	Richmond	1558	1603	

SOVEREIGNS OF BRITAIN

Sovereign	Born		Died		Reign		Married
	Date	Place	Date	Place	From	To	
House of Stuart							
James I	1566	Edinburgh	1625	Theobalds (Herts)	1603	1625	Anne of Denmark
Charles I	1600	Dunfermline	1649	Whitehall	1625	1649	Henrietta of France
Period of the Commonwealth 1649-1659							
Charles II	1630	St. James, London	1685	St. James, London	1659	1685	Catherine of Portugal
James II	1633	St. James, London	1701	St. Germain's	1685	1688	Anne Hyde
							Mary d'Este
Period of the Interregnum 1688-1689							
William III	1650	Hague	1702	Kensington	1689	1702	Mary, daughter James II
Mary II	1622	St. James, London	1694	Kensington	1689	1694	
Anne	1665	St. James, London	1714	Kensington	1702	1714	George, Prince of Denmark
House of Hanover							
George I	1660	Hanover	1727	Osnabruck	1714	1727	Sophia Dorothea of Zell
George II	1683	Hanover	1760	Kensington	1727	1760	Caroline of Brandenburg-Anspach
George III	1738	London	1820	Windsor	1760	1820	Charlotte of Mecklenburg-Strelitz
George IV	1762	London	1830	Windsor	1820	1830	Caroline of Brunswick
William IV	1765	Windsor	1837	Windsor	1830	1837	Louisa of Saxe-Meiningen
Victoria	1819	Kensington	1901	Isle of Wight	1837	1901	Prince Albert of Saxe-Coburg and Gotha
House of Saxe-Coburg							
Edward VII	1841	London	1910	London	1901	1910	Princess Alexandra of Denmark
House of Windsor							
George V	1865	Marlborough House	1936	Sandringham	1910	1936	Princess Mary of Teck
Edward VIII	1894	Richmond			1936 (abdicated)		Mrs. Wallis Simpson
George VI	1895	Sandringham	1952	Sandringham	1936	1952	Lady Elizabeth Bowes-Lyon
Elizabeth II	1926	17 Bruton St. London			1952		Prince Philip of Greece, Duke of Edinburgh

Australia she will be referred to as Queen of Canada or Queen of Australia. She is not Queen of other countries who are Members of the Commonwealth. They recognize her only as Head of the Commonwealth.

In the United Kingdom and in the Dominions all government is carried out in the name of Her Majesty, although the Sovereign no longer has to decide matters for herself, but acts on the advice of her ministers. No new law can be made by PARLIAMENT without the Sovereign's signature to it. The Sovereign is supreme head of the Church of England, also the head of the Army, Navy and Air Force.

The Sovereign summons Parliament and prorogues it, that is, puts an end to each of its sessions. When there is a GENERAL ELECTION the Sovereign dissolves Parliament. When the result of the election is known the Sovereign must send for the head of the party which has a majority of seats in the House of Commons and ask him to form a government.

SPACE-SHIP

Man has for a long time dreamt of exploring outer space, and with the rapid development of ROCKET flight there is every possibility of this dream becoming a reality in the not too distant future.

The two most important factors in space flight are 1, developing sufficient speed to escape from the earth's gravitational field, and 2, developing means of making a two-way journey.

To escape the earth's gravitational pull a space-ship must travel at about 26,000 miles per hour. To attain this, space scientists have developed the 3-stage rocket, that is, a ship incorporating three sets of rocket motors which fire successively; the first two stages are jettisoned and the third carries the astronaut module. It is not intended to use such ships for travelling beyond, say, the Moon or Mars, and for the building of space-stations which will act as refuelling points.

Another important factor which is now being rigorously studied by doctors is whether men can stand up to the terrific strain that will be experienced during the period that the ship is escaping from earth's gravity. From the experience of both Russian and American cosmonauts there is still much work to be done in this field.

Once in outer space the journey is uneventful except for the absence of gravity, that is, men and objects tend to float about in space unless anchored by some means. Drinking is especially difficult, and to do this satisfactorily means sucking all liquids through tubes from a closed flask. From the flights already made to the Moon it is reasonable to suppose that within the next few years man will set foot on one or more of the planets. As for more adventurous probes beyond the Solar System, much has still to be done with propulsion systems and space-ship design.

SPAIN

A republic in Southern Europe on what is called the Iberian Peninsular. It is more than twice the size (196,700 square miles) of Great Britain and has over 31 million inhabitants. Spanish is a Latin language. The capital is

SPACE-SHIP Artist's impression of a space station. Stations such as this will be absolutely essential before man can seriously begin to explore even our solar system.

Madrid, other important cities being Seville and Barcelona. Spain is famous for her oranges and she produces the wine called sherry. Her minerals include iron, coal, lead and zinc.

Spain possesses the Balearic Islands which include MAJORCA and Minorca, and the CANARY ISLANDS. She also has some colonies in Africa.

History :

The earliest inhabitants of Spain and Portugal were Iberians, whose descendants still inhabit the Basque Provinces. The peninsula is still called Iberia after them.

About 500 B.C. Celtic tribes entered the peninsula and mingled with the Iberians. They were followed by the Carthagenians who founded Cartagena, and in 201 B.C. came the Romans. Spain remained a Roman province till the 5th century when the Vandals and Suevi overran the peninsula. These invaders were overcome by the Visigoths who ruled the whole peninsula till the beginning of the 8th century when the MOORS, or Saracens, arrived from North Africa. For a time almost the whole peninsula was ruled by the Moors, and they ruled parts of Spain for eight hundred years. Castile and Aragon were eventually able to become separate kingdoms. The capital of the Moorish kingdom is Granada where the Moors built the beautiful palace of the Alhambra.

In 1479 Isabella of Castile married Ferdinand of Aragon and so the two Spanish kingdoms were united. Together Ferdinand and Isabella were able to drive the Moors from Spain. It was they who sent Christopher Columbus on his voyage of discovery. This was followed by the conquest of South and Central America by the Spanish and Portuguese. Spain also for a time ruled the Netherlands. In this way she became the most powerful country in the world. Her power began to decline when her ARMADA, sent to conquer England, was defeated in 1588.

In the 19th century Napoleon forced the Spanish King, Charles IV, to resign, and he put his own brother, Joseph Bonaparte, on the Spanish throne. This led to the Peninsular Wars from 1808–1814. With the defeat of Napoleon the throne was restored to the Spanish King. Soon after this Spain lost her American colonies, and in 1898 there was a war between Spain and the United States in which Spain was defeated and lost more territory.

In 1911 there was a revolution in Portugal and the country became a republic. This encouraged republicanism in Spain. Soon after the First World War the King of Spain, Alfonso XIII, suspended parliament and appointed a soldier as dictator. This led to

discontent and when, after seven years, the dictatorship came to an end the people voted for a republic, and so in 1931 the King abdicated. Early in 1936 the army, under General FRANCO, revolted. A terrible civil war followed during which General Franco received help from Hitler and Mussolini. It ended in victory for General Franco in 1939.

SPANISH GUINEA

A Spanish possession in the Gulf of Guinea, West Africa. It consists of the island of Fernando Po and some other islands and of Rio Muni on the mainland. Spanish Guinea is rather larger (10,000 square miles) than Wales and has a population of a little over a quarter of a million. The capital is Santa Isabel on Fernando Po.

SPARTACUS (died 71 B.C.)

Leader of the slaves in the Servile Wars (73–71 B.C.). He was trained as a gladiator. This revolt of Roman slaves was strong, and for a short while occupied a large part of Southern Italy before it was suppressed by Pompey and Crassus who murdered thousands of the slaves taken prisoner.

SPEAKER, THE

The name given to the Chairman of the House of Commons. There has been a Speaker for nearly as long as there has been PARLIAMENT. In the early days of Parliament the King only called together the Commons when he wanted them to collect money for him. The Commons would choose one of their number to 'speak' to the King on behalf of the rest. Often the Commons would agree through their Speaker to bargain with the King. They would agree to give the King money he wanted if he would give them certain rights in return. In this way Parliament gradually came to have the right to make laws. The King and the Commons often quarrelled, and it was the Speaker who would be blamed by the King. So no one wanted to be Speaker and the one chosen had usually to be dragged to the chair. To this day when a new Speaker is elected he has to pretend to be afraid to accept and is dragged by two Members to the Speaker's Chair.

Although the Speaker is elected in the same way as other M.P.s and will have been chosen as their candidate by one of the POLITICAL PARTIES, once he has been chosen speaker he takes no part in party politics. He expresses no opinions in regard to the matters discussed by the House of Commons. His sole duty is to maintain order and to be fair to all Members.

The Speaker has a splendid residence within the Palace of Westminster.

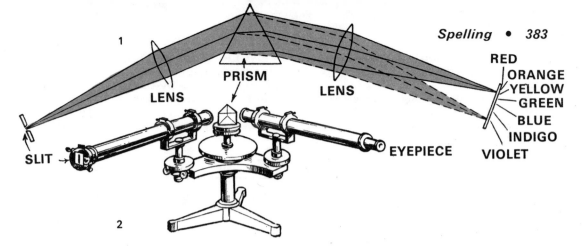

LENS   PRISM   LENS

1

RED
ORANGE
YELLOW
GREEN
BLUE
INDIGO
VIOLET

SLIT →

EYEPIECE

2

SPECTRUM 1, is a diagram showing how a beam of white light is split up into its constituent colours by a prism. 2, a simple laboratory spectroscope.

SPECIFIC GRAVITY
Ratio of the density of a substance to that of water.

SPECIFIC HEAT
Ratio of the quantity of heat required to raise 1 gm. of a substance 1°C. to the quantity required to raise 1 gm. of water 1°C.

SPECTRUM
When light is passed through a glass prism it is bent twice from its original direction, at the first glass surface and the second. If the incoming light is ordinary white light, as from the sun or an incandescent electric lamp, there is a further effect. The experimenter looking at the light through the prism sees a band of colours. This was the effect that Sir Isaac NEWTON set out to investigate in about 1665.

He found that the colours appeared only in the plane in which the rays were doubly bent round by the non-parallel faces of the prism. His conclusion was that the incoming light consisted of a mixture of rays, each of which was bent round to a different extent, and each of these separate rays caused a colour sensation in the eye. This historic conclusion is the basis of the physics of COLOUR. Today we say that each ray of light has a different wavelength, and so the colour of light depends on the wavelength of the wave by means of which it travels.

The spread-out band of colours is called a spectrum. The sort that Newton observed was a *white-light* spectrum, but it is possible to get the spectrum of any sort of light by means of a prism. For accurate observation it is better to have the prism in an instrument called a spectroscope. The observed spectrum is then really a series of images of the slit through which the light is first passed, each image corresponding to one wavelength. In the white-light spectrum there is an infinite number of

such images touching each other in succession, so that a continuous band of light is seen grading from red at one end to violet at the other. Newton thought he could see seven different colours—red, orange, yellow, green, blue, indigo, violet. These are called the seven colours of the spectrum or of the rainbow. Actually careful experimenting shows that more than a hundred separate hues can be discerned, but for ordinary discussion we still make use of Newton's seven colours.

If the incoming light has only one wavelength, or is, as it is said, monochromatic, then the spectrum consists of only one bright line on a dark background. If the incoming light has several separate wavelengths, then the spectrum consists of a number of bright lines on a dark background, one line per wavelength. If the incoming light is white but is passed through a coloured filter before it reaches the slit of the spectroscope, the spectrum consists of a part of continuous spectrum with a part missing corresponding to the light absorbed by the filter.

These different sorts of spectrum have been used for very fine analysis of materials because it is found that only a few parts in a million of a substance need be present in the source of light in order to produce its characteristic spectrum. This fine analysis is called 'spectrum analysis'.

SPELLING
English spelling is difficult for two main reasons:
(i) because we are apt to spell words according to their history or derivation rather than according to their sound. Thus a guttural or 'throat' sound represented by *gh* once existed in the word *bough*, but we have lost it altogether today. We get our word *debt* from the

Latin *debitum*, and we keep the *b* in spelling though we no longer pronounce it.

(ii) because in our ALPHABET one letter can stand for more than one sound, and one sound can be represented by more than one letter. Thus *c* can be 'soft' like *s* or 'hard' like *k*, *i* can have the various sounds represented in *bin*, *line* and *machine*, and the sound that we have in *seed* can be represented also by *ea*, *ei*, *e*, *ie*, *i*, *eo*.

Since this is so, rules for spelling are hard to make. One or two are helpful like '*i* before *e* except after *c*', provided you remember that this applies only to words in which *ie* and *ei* are pronounced like *ee*, and that there are exceptions (*weird* and *seize* are the chief). But spelling rules, with their numerous exceptions, may make things more difficult rather than easier. It is better to recognize the two main difficulties given above, and then help yourself to spell by

(i) learning to 'see' the shape and pattern of words. Sometimes, even then, you will 'see' wrongly; but this training of the eye by what is called in schools the 'look and see' method can save you from foolish mistakes.

(ii) learning to build words. The 'root', which may be an actual word, or part of a word taken from another language (usually Latin), may have added to it at the beginning a PREFIX and at the end a SUFFIX, like this:

PREFIX	ROOT	SUFFIX
dis-	agree	-ment

It is a good thing to build such words, beginning with the root, rather than to try to 'see' them whole. Above all, we have to remember that something may happen at the joins, especially—

(1) a *y* may change into an *i* and
(2) a consonant may double.

(iii) using the dictionary wisely, and especially by looking up the derivation of the word (from Latin, for example, or French). This will often give you a direct clue to the spelling, and sometimes an indirect clue, through the original meaning. Thus if you discover the Latin word *scio* ('know'), you will realize that there is *sc* in *science* and *conscious*.

Here are a dozen difficult words to 'see':

ANONYMOUS	EMBARRASSMENT	NECESSARY
CATECHISM	FORFEIT	PARAFFIN
CEMETERY	GAUGE	PARALLEL
PRECEDE	REMEMBRANCE	SYLLABLE

SPENCER, Herbert (1820–1903)
British philosopher, born at Derby. Was very much influenced by the theory of evolution, which he applied to other branches of knowledge. His principal works are *The Principles of Psychology*, *The Principles of Sociology* and *The Principles of Ethics*.

SPENCER, Stanley (1891–1959)
English painter, born at Cookham. Trained in London and served in Macedonia during the First World War. His experiences during this period are featured in a series of paintings he was commissioned to do for Burghelere Chapel. Most of his large paintings are devoted to religious subjects presented in contemporary setting, an outstanding example of this is his *Resurrection*.

SPENGLER, Oswald (1880–1936)
German philosopher, born at Blankenburg. His most important work, *The Decline of the West*, was very influential after the First World War. His idea was that every civilization, like a living body, passed through a cycle of birth, growth, maturity, decline and death. His ideas were greatly admired by the Nazis.

SPENSER, Edmund (1552–1599)
English poet, born in London. He was educated at Cambridge. In 1578 joined the household of the Earl of Leicester, and shortly afterwards published his first important poem, *The Shepheard's Calendar*. Apart from occasional short visits to England he spent the rest of his life in Ireland after 1580. His chief poem, *The Faerie Queen*, began to appear in 1579. It introduces the Virtues, Holiness, Justice and Courtesy as characters, and relates the adventures of Una and the Red Cross Knight. It bridges the gap between the medieval and the modern.

SPIDER
An invertebrate and belongs to the order 'Araneae'. The head and thorax (cephalothorax) is separated from the abdomen by a waist. Spiders are a large group, and are distributed throughout the world. In the main they live on the land, but there are a few who live in water, e.g., the water spider passes nearly the whole of its life under water, breathing air from a bubble attached to the long hairs of its abdomen. The food of spiders consists mainly of insects, but some species prey on such animals as lizards and mice. Another important feature of the spider is the organ (spinneret) for spinning silk for the capture of prey, making cocoons, and lining the inside of its nest.

SPONGE

An INVERTEBRATE belonging to the group 'Porifera', and is so named because of the pores that occur over the surface of the body. Sponges are abundant in all seas and at nearly all depths. Generally they are fixed to the bottom, or to rocks or weeds. The common bath sponge is a skeleton from which the flesh has been removed.

SQUASH

This game is played by striking a ball against a wall as in FIVES, although the ball is struck with a racket instead of with the hand.

The dimensions shown on the diagram are those of a squash court. On the front wall three horizontal lines are marked. The lowest one is 19 inches from the ground and is known as the 'play line' or 'board', the second is 6 feet high and is known as the 'cut line', and the top line is 15 feet high and is the 'court line'. On the back wall one horizontal line is marked at a height of 7 feet, and the ends of this line are joined to the 'court line' on the front wall by sloping lines on the side walls. These lines mark the upper limits of the court. If the ball is struck so that it hits on or above these lines the striker loses a point as will be seen later.

The racket weighs between 8 and 12 ounces; the length is limited to 27 inches and the strung face must not be greater than $8\frac{1}{2}$ inches by $7\frac{1}{4}$ inches. The ball which is used has also to be of a certain weight and size, and should be marked by the S.R.A. (Squash Rackets Association) as having the correct size, weight and bounce.

The serve. A match generally consists of five games, each game being 9 points up, that is to say, the player who first wins 9 points wins the game, except that, if the score becomes 8 all for the first time, hand-out (the player who receives the service) may, if he chooses before the next service is delivered, set the game to 2, in which case the player who first scores 2 more points wins the game.

Scoring. Points can only be scored by the server, known in Squash as the 'hand-in'. When a player fails to serve or make a good return according to the rules, the opponent wins the stroke. When 'hand-in' wins the stroke he scores a point; when 'hand-out' wins the stroke he becomes 'hand-in'.

Service. The right to serve first is decided by the spin of the racket. Thereafter the server continues to serve until he loses a stroke, whereupon his opponent becomes the server, and so on throughout the match.

Before being struck by the server the ball must be thrown into the air and must not touch the floor or the walls. The ball must be

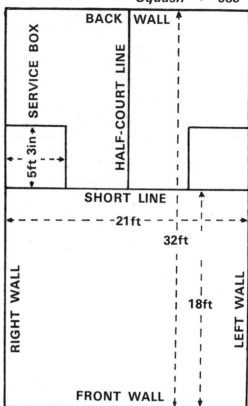

SQUASH Plan view of a court. The front wall is 15 feet high and the rear 7 feet.

struck directly on to the front wall between the cut line and the court line so that on its rebound it shall fall to the floor in the half court furthest from the server. At the beginning of each game, and of each hand, the server may serve from either box, then change to the other box, and so on as long as he remains hand-in. If a service is made from the wrong box there is no penalty, but hand-out may, if he has not attempted to take the service, ask for it to be served from the other box.

It is most important to appreciate the difference between hand-in serving a fault and losing the service to hand-out. A service is a fault if:

(a) Server does not have a least one foot in his serving box; called a foot fault.

(b) The ball strikes the front wall on or below the cut line.

(c) The ball first touches the floor on or in front of the service line.

(d) The ball served rebounds and first touches the floor in the wrong half court, that is, the half court on the same side as the server.

The server loses the service to hand-out if:

(a) The ball is served on or below the play-line or board, or out of court; that is, if

STARS
A photograph showing the density of stars in our galaxy. Also shown is a spiral nebula, or 'island universe'

the ball strikes any of the walls on or above the court line, or against any part of the court before striking the front wall.

(b) He fails to strike the ball or strikes it more than once.

(c) He serves two consecutive faults.

After a good service the players return the ball alternately until one of them fails to make a good return. A return is good if the ball, before it has bounced twice upon the floor, is returned by the striker:

(a) On to the front wall above the play line or board.

(b) Is not hit more than once.

(c) Does not hit on or above the court line.

You may notice that on its return the ball may rebound off any other wall provided it hits under the court line and finally hits the front wall above the play-line.

There are just one or two other points in the rules which a player must know.

In the first place each player shall, after playing the ball, get out of his opponent's way so as to give him a fair view of the ball and plenty of room in which to play it. Another point is that if the ball hits a player or his racket while on its way to the front wall, then:

(a) If the ball would have made a good return to the front wall, without glancing off a side-wall first, the striker wins the stroke.

(b) If the ball would have made a good return, but would have glanced off a side-wall first, the rally is cancelled and the stroke is played for again.

(c) If the ball would not have made a good return, the striker loses the stroke.

SQUIRREL

A 'single-toothed' RODENT of which there are a large number of families. Typical climbing squirrels have long bushy tails, are expert climbers and quite at home on the ground. They live mainly on fruit, nuts, buds, seeds, birds' eggs and sometimes insects. Ground squirrels live in burrows and differ from the ordinary squirrel in having cheek pouches; a typical example is the CHIPMUNK.

STALACTITE

A mineral deposit of carbonate of calcium on the roof of a limestone cave. It hangs from the roof like an icicle, and consists of fine sparkling crystals. The water which deposits stalactites drips on to the floor beneath, where a second deposit, called a stalagmite, grows upwards in the form of a pillar.

STALIN, Joseph Vissarionovitch
(1879–1953)

Russian communist leader, born at Gori, Georgia. The son of a cobbler, he studied at a theological seminary before joining the revolutionary movement. He became the leading Bolshevik in the Caucasus area, and by 1913 had been arrested eight times and had escaped six times. His greatest interest was in the problems of the various non-Russian peoples. In the civil war (1918–1922) he played a prominent part in the defence of Tsaritsya (renamed Stalingrad). After Lenin's death (1924) he used his position as General Secretary of the Communist Party to make himself supreme and to ensure that his aim of socialism in one country be achieved. To this end he inaugurated the First Five Year Plan (1927) and the collectivization of agriculture (1930-1932). When the Second World War came he directed the Russian defence. Not long after his death he was denounced as a tyrant, but recently this attitude has been moderated.

STANLEY, Sir Henry Morton (1841–1904)

British explorer, born at Denbigh. Stanley started his career as a soldier in the American Civil War, and afterwards became an explorer and author of travel books. He went in search of LIVINGSTONE, whom he believed to be alive, and with him explored the northern end of Lake Tanganyika. He also discovered the course of the river Congo. He is unaccountably well known for a remark on meeting Livingstone in the jungle: 'Dr. Livingstone, I presume', but there is no authority for this.

STARS

Vast condensations of matter poised in space, of which large numbers are incandescent and visible. The SUN is a fairly typical star, the next nearest to the earth being four light-years distant. Few stars exceed three times the sun's mass, and very few either exceed ten times or fall below one-tenth the sun's mass. In diameter the stars vary from more than one hundred times that of the sun (the red giants) to less than one-hundredth (the white dwarfs). In luminosity they vary from 300,000 times to 1/300,000th the luminosity of the sun. In recent years radio astronomers have shown the existence of non-incandescent stars from observations with the radio telescope. [*See* RADIO ASTRONOMY.]

STATUE OF LIBERTY

A national monument on the Isle of Bedloe in the entrance to New York harbour. It is made of copper and stands 150 feet high. It was erected to mark the American and French revolutions and was designed by F. A. Bartholdi.

STEAM ENGINE

Two Englishmen, Thomas Savery and Thomas NEWCOMEN, must be given the credit for devising the first practical steam engine. In the 17th century flooding of coalmines was causing very serious problems, and thousands of horses had to be used to operate pumps to keep the mines dry. In Newcomen's engine, steam, generated in a boiler, was admitted by a tap to a cylinder containing a piston. The steam pressure raised the piston, which was coupled by a rod to a large rocking beam, pivoted at the centre. To the other end of the beam was attached a rod which operated the piston of a pump. Thus when the steam was turned on the engine piston rose and the pump fell, ready for the pumping stroke. Water was then poured on to the engine cylinder to condense the steam, causing a partial vacuum within the cylinder; the engine piston was forced down by atmospheric pressure and the pump piston was raised to pump water from the mine. Before the process could be repeated it was necessary to open a second tap, connected to a pipe in the base of the engine cylinder, to draw off the condensed water from the cylinder. It was soon found, however, that the steam could be condensed more quickly by spraying water into the cylinder, and that the action could be speeded up by fitting valves to admit the steam and remove the water. For many years this type of engine did good service and rendered work possible in deep mines.

It was James WATT who was responsible in 1769 for the development of the forerunner of the modern steam engine, when he hit on the idea of a separate condenser for the steam,

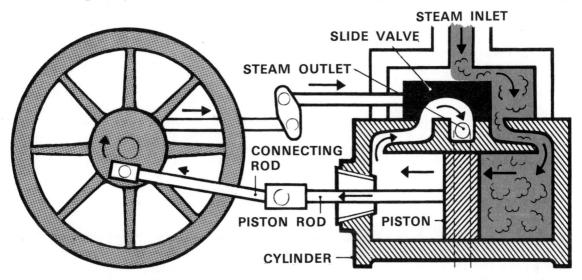

STEAM INLET

SLIDE VALVE

STEAM OUTLET

CONNECTING ROD

PISTON ROD

PISTON

CYLINDER

STEAM ENGINE Simplified diagram showing how steam operates a piston in a cylinder and the mechanisms by which this motion is transmitted to a driving wheel.

instead of condensing it inside the cylinder. This led to the basic design which is still used today; a cylinder fitted with a piston and provided with two holes or 'ports', one to admit the steam as the piston moved downwards and the other to allow the steam to be forced out into the condenser as the piston rose. A sliding valve, operated by the engine, uncovered each port at the right moment. It will be evident that in this engine a new principle was introduced: power was obtained from expansion of the steam in the cylinder instead of making use of atmospheric pressure. In order to raise the piston at the end of the power stroke, it was necessary to couple the rocking beam to a crank attached to a heavy flywheel, the momentum of which provided the energy to drive the piston upwards and expel the exhaust steam. The next idea which occurred to Watt was to use expanding steam to drive the piston in both directions. This design, which is widely used today, is termed a double-acting engine. In time the heavy rocking beam gave place to a short connecting-rod, coupled directly to the crank, resulting in a much more compact engine and allowing higher speeds to be obtained. Designers soon realized that the exhaust steam still contained a certain amount of useful energy, particularly if steam was admitted to the cylinder at a high pressure of, say, two hundred pounds per square inch. The logical course, therefore, was to lead this steam into a second, larger cylinder, containing a piston coupled to the same crankshaft, forming an engine known as a double-expansion type. In triple-expansion engines the exhaust steam from the second cylinder is led to yet another and still larger cylinder.

STEEL

Iron is obtained from ore in a blast furnace, and turned into steel by reducing the amount of carbon from about 3–4% to 0·15–0·25%; with certain grades of steel small percentages of alloying elements, such as nickel and chromium, are added. The most widely used method of steel production is the open hearth process. This can be visualized as a shallow swimming bath surrounded by walls, and an arched roof made of heat-resisting bricks. At one side are charging doors through which the raw materials, mainly pig-iron, scrap and limestone, are loaded. At each end are openings which direct gas and air directly on to the bath of steel, and lead the spent gases away through the regenerators to the chimney. Regenerators are built under the furnace, and are used to preheat the air and gas before they enter the furnace, thus using up the heat that would otherwise be wasted. At intervals the flow is reversed. The

complete process takes from ten to fourteen hours. Special steels are made in electrically heated furnaces, but the quantity is very small, in fact, only about 4% of the total output of steel. The BESSEMER process accounts for only a very small proportion of the output.

STEINBECK, John Ernest (1902–1968)

American novelist. His greatest work is *The Grapes of Wrath*, a harrowing story of the landless poor in California, continually threatened with disaster. The book so powerfully communicated their distress that it persuaded the authorities to take action, and Steinbeck was awarded the Pulitzer Prize as a result. His other books include *Tortilla Flat*, *Of Mice and Men* and *Cannery Row*. In 1962 he was awarded the Nobel Prize for Literature.

STENDHAL (1783–1842)

French novelist. His real name was Henri Beyle. Born at Grenoble and served in Napoleon's army. Although he was one of the greatest novelists of his or any other time, his work was not recognized or appreciated until after his death. His most outstanding work is *The Charterhouse of Parma*.

STEPHENSON, George (1781–1848)

Born near Newcastle, and son of a miner. Is generally regarded as the 'father of the railway'. In 1814 he built his first steam locomotive, the 'Blucher'. It was not till 1823 that Stephenson was asked to build the first RAILWAY from Stockton to Darlington. Other railways were proposed, notably the line running from Liverpool to Manchester, and it was for this that Stephenson built the famous 'Rocket'. He became a very celebrated man, building railways in Britain and abroad. He was buried in Westminster Abbey.

STERNE, Laurence (1713–1768)

British novelist, born at Clonmel, Ireland. Educated at Cambridge. He began his literary career with *The Life and Opinions of Tristram Shandy*, of which the first two volumes appeared in 1760. It was an immediate success, and Sterne became as famous in Paris as in London. The final volumes appeared in 1765. Shortly before his death he published *A Sentimental Journey Through France and Italy*, based on his own travel experiences.

STETHOSCOPE

The familiar instrument used by a doctor for sounding the heart and lungs, and is, in fact, a simple sound amplifier. It was invented by a French physician, Dr. R. Laennec (1781–1826).

STEVENSON, Robert Louis (1850–1894)
Scottish novelist and essayist, born at Edinburgh. A traveller in search of health, Stevenson wrote essays, stories, and poems. He is best known for the adventure books which are read by children everywhere today: *Treasure Island*, in particular, and *The Black Arrow*. His strange story *Dr. Jekyll and Mr. Hyde* has also made a mark on the popular imagination.

STOAT
Belongs to the same family as the weasel, but is larger although of much the same colour. From the farmer's point of view it is a pest, since it kills game-birds and poultry. In winter its fur turns to white, and is known as 'ermine' —the valuable fur used to trim civic robes, etc.

STONE AGE
Covers the earliest periods of man's life on earth. It is divided into two periods, the Old Stone Age (Paleolithic) beginning perhaps some 500,000 years ago and the New Stone Age (Neolithic) approximately 10,000 years ago. During the Old Stone Age man lived by gathering food where he could find it and used crude stone implements. In the New Stone Age man had advanced sufficiently to cultivate plants and breed domestic animals, it was, in fact, a period of food-producing.

STONE OF SCONE
Also called the Coronation Stone, it is now in Westminster Abbey. Originally this Stone was at Scone, the seat of the Scottish Kings, and was removed by Edward I. The last Scottish king to be crowned at Scone was Charles II (1651).

STRADIVARI
Family of famous violin makers who lived and worked in Cremona, Italy. The craft was started by Antonio Stradivari (1644–1737), and continued by his two sons. Stradivari violins are highly prized by concert violinists of today.

STRATOSPHERE
Region of the atmosphere above the zone of winds. Its lower layers are at a height of about 7 miles, rising to 11 in equatorial regions. [*See* ATMOSPHERE.]

STRAUSS, Johann (1825–1899)
The great Austrian waltz-king, born in Vienna. As well as many famous waltzes, such as *The Blue Danube* and *Tales from the Vienna Woods*, he wrote the sparkling and ever-popular operetta *Die Fledermaus* (The Bat).

STRAUSS, Richard (1864–1949)
German composer, and no relation to Johann Strauss. Born at Munich. One of the great writers of 'programme music' (music that tells a story), he was such a master of the orchestra that he could make it imitate actual sounds; for example, in his symphonic poem *Don Quixote*, the horns imitate the bleating of sheep, and in his *Domestic Symphony*, the gurgling sound of water running out of a bath is heard. His most popular compositions are the symphonic poems *Till Eulenspiegel's Merry Pranks* and *Don Juan*, and the opera *Der Rosenkavalier* (The Knight of the Silver Rose).

STRAVINSKY, Igor (1882–1971)
Russian composer, born at Oranienbaum. He startled the world just before the 1914-1918

STEPHENSON'S *North Star* built in 1837. His first locomotive was *Blucher* built in 1814.

war with his fantastic ballets *The Firebird*, *Petrouchka* and *The Rite of Spring*. The music for the latter was so advanced that the ballet was hissed and shouted off the stage; it has since become very popular, and was used by Walt Disney in his film *Fantasia*. Stravinsky settled in the U.S.A. and is now an American citizen. Later successes include the *Symphony of Psalms* and the opera *The Rake's Progress*.

STRINDBERG, August (1849–1912)

Swedish writer, born at Stockholm. Although he produced short stories and novels, his most important work was in the field of drama. Strindberg wrote some seventy plays, many of which were centred around his own life and marriages. One of his best-known plays is *Miss Julie*, which has also been produced as a film.

STROBOSCOPE

Instrument which enables a moving part of a machine to be observed while in rapid motion. An intermittent light permits the part to be seen momentarily in the several successive positions of its motion. The views seen are not actually consecutive, but each is separated from the next by one or more entire cycles of the motion, the effect being a slow-motion picture of the action. Instead of an intermittent light, an intermittent view of the object may be seen through a slot in a rotating disc, the speed of which can be varied.

SUBMARINE

A naval vessel which can operate under water and, although experiments were made as long ago as the 17th century, it was developed by R. Fulton (1765–1815) and S. Lake (1866–1945). Submarines were first used in the First World War and very extensively by Germany (termed U-boats). In the Second World War they were employed by the Allies, Germany and Japan. One-man and midget submarines were also developed during the Second World War. The most recent type of submarine is the nuclear-powered submarine, usually armed with ballistic missiles.

SUDAN

A vast republic in Africa, the SAHARA desert forming a large part of it. It is more than four times the size (977,000 square miles) of France and has a population of a little over 12 million. The capital is Khartoum on the River Nile. The people living north of the Sahara are mostly Arabs and Muslims. Those south of the Sahara are chiefly negroes and are either Christians or pagans. The Sudan produces cotton.

SUEZ CANAL

Separates Africa from Asia, and is the gateway to the Indian Ocean. It was opened in 1869, is 101 miles long, and belongs to a private company. Britain was given the right to guard the canal with her soldiers because of its importance during the First and Second World Wars. Egypt is now responsible for running and guarding this valuable strip of water.

SUFFRAGETTES

Before the First World War, many women became very discontented because they did not have the vote, and believed that it was time they stopped being second-rate citizens. The Women's Social and Political Union was formed to persuade Parliament to enfranchise women, and its members worked peacefully at first, but later, when they found that they were making no impression, they became more and more militant. Suffragettes chained themselves to the railings of Buckingham Palace to attract attention to their cause; one of them threw herself under the King's horse at the Derby; others destroyed pillar-boxes, lobbied their M.P.s, and, when imprisoned, went on hunger strike. Their demands were at last satisfied in 1928.

SUGAR

The name for a group of substances (carbohydrates) which possess a sweet taste. The most important of the sugars is cane sugar (sucrose) which occurs in sugar cane and to a lesser extent in sugar beet. Apart from its use for sweetening foods it is also an important raw material in the manufacture of alcohol and many other chemical products.

SUBMARINE HMS *Dreadnought*, Britain's first nuclear-powered submarine. 1, reactor compartment; 2, reactor control room; 3, auxiliary machinery; 4, diesel generator; 5, escape hatch; 6, main steam condenser; 7, main turbine; 8, electric propulsion motor (alternative drive); 9, rudders; 10, after hydroplane; 11, surface navigating bridge; 12, periscope; 13, radar and radio aerials; 14, snort; 15, control room; 16, electric batteries; 17, crew's quarters; 18, officers' quarters; 19, electrical equipment; 20, forward hydroplane; 21, torpedo space; 22, torpedo tubes; 23, stowed anchor; 24, galley; 25, store rooms and refrigeration space

SULLIVAN, Sir Arthur Seymour
(1842–1900)

English composer, born in London, and son of a military bandsman. He composed church music, grand operas, songs, oratorios, etc., but his fame rests on the comic operas generally known as the GILBERT AND SULLIVAN operas. These include *H.M.S. Pinafore*, *The Pirates of Penzance*, *The Mikado*, and *The Gondoliers*.

SUMATRA [*See* INDONESIA]

SUN

Star of the 5th absolute magnitude about which revolve nine major planets and several smaller bodies. It is about 330,000 times as massive as the earth, and a million and a quarter times its volume. Its surface temperature is about 6,000°C., and it radiates energy at about 50 h.p. per sq. in. of its surface per second. Its temperature is maintained by thermo-nuclear reactions, i.e., the building up of helium atoms from hydrogen atoms, but many other atomic reactions are believed to occur. [*See* SOLAR SYSTEM.]

SUNSPOTS

The sun as normally seen with the naked eye is a yellowish disc. If examined with a telescope, however, black spots are sometimes seen not far from the sun's equator. These are sunspots. They are not seen all the time, and there is not the same number of them every time they are seen. The sunspot activity reaches a maximum and then decreases to a minimum in just over six years and then increases to a maximum in another period of between four and five years. Thus the time from maximum to maximum is about eleven years.

Sunspot activity is associated with certain phenomena experienced on our earth. Sunspots themselves emit wireless waves of a few metres wavelength. A remarkable instance of this occurred in 1942 when military radar apparatus suffered from serious interference, the cause of which was traced to the emission of wireless waves from the sun during intense sunspot activity. Sunspot activity also coincides with magnetic storms in the earth's atmosphere and with severe fading of wireless waves.

SUN YAT-SEN (1866–1925)

Chinese statesman, born near Canton. He was trained as a doctor, but in 1893 he abandoned medicine for politics. After leading an unsuccessful revolt in 1895 in Canton he was an exile from CHINA until 1911. All this time, as the leader of the Young China Party, he was preparing the revolution of 1911 which overthrew the Manchu dynasty. He then became president of the newly established Chinese Republic, but resigned the next year. In 1917 and again in 1921 he was elected President at Canton of the southern Chinese states in revolt against the central government at Peking. He organized the Kuomintang party to achieve a centralized government in China, but this was successful only after his death. [*See* CHINA.]

SUPPÉ, Franz von (1819–1895)

Austrian composer, born in Dalmatia. He wrote a great number of operas which are no longer performed. However, two of his overtures *Poet and Peasant* and *Light Cavalry* are still popular and frequently played—particularly by brass bands.

SURINAM

That part of Guiana that belongs to the Netherlands. It adjoins Guyana. Surinam is rather larger than England but has a population of less than half a million. It produces bauxite for the making of aluminium. Surinam is governed as part of the Netherlands West Indies which includes Curaçao.

SUTHERLAND, Graham (1903—)

English painter, born in London. His early work was influenced by BLAKE and PALMER. After a stay in South Wales his style changed. He brought a new vision to bear on nature, thorns, hedges and insects. His greatest work is the tapestry in the new Coventry Cathedral.

SWAZILAND

A British protectorate in southern Africa. It is 6,700 square miles, smaller than Wales, and has a population of a little over a quarter of a million. In 1966 it was given the right to manage its home affairs and before 1970 it will probably become quite independent.

SWEDEN

A kingdom in north-west Europe on the eastern half of the Scandinavian peninsula. It is more than twice the size (173,000 square miles) of Great Britain but has only a little over $7\frac{1}{2}$ million inhabitants. The capital is Stockholm and the next largest city the port of Gothenburg. The country has many minerals, particularly iron ore. Her forests, which cover half the country, make her an important timber and paper producing country.

SWEDENBORG, Emanuel (1688–1772)

Swedish religious thinker, born at Stockholm. Up until 1747 his life was concerned with science and he wrote many outstanding scientific works. He then turned to religion, and because of mystical experiences thought that he was chosen to express the voice of God. After his death a sect was formed in London (1788) to expound his religious teachings; it was called 'Church of the New Jerusalem'.

SWIFT, Jonathan (1667–1745)

Irish writer, born in Dublin. Brought up by an uncle, and educated at Trinity College, Dublin. He came to England and won the interest of the Tory politicians. With their defeat he was left with little but the post of Dean of St. Patrick's in Dublin, to which he retired. He was pamphleteer, poet, politician, letter-writer; but he is famous above all as the author of *Gulliver's Travels*. The first two books of the *Travels* have become regular reading for children, but the book was written, as becomes clearer towards its end, not as entertainment but as an angry attack on the follies and (as Swift sees it) the monstrosities of the behaviour of men and women in Gulliver's country—that is, in England.

SWIMMING

The means by which man and animals propel themselves through the water. The movements are natural and, with confidence, can be quickly and easily learned. The principal strokes are breast, front-crawl, back-crawl and butterfly.

Diving is entering the water head-first or feet-first and this can be done in a variety of ways. The following descriptions are given: 'plunge', 'plain header' or 'swallow' dive, 'pike' dive or 'jack-knife', 'somersaults', 'twists' and various combinations.

Survival in water is important to everyone. Such skills as treading water, swimming a distance of quarter to half a mile, surface diving, swimming underwater, entering the water from a height, and inflating articles of clothing to aid flotation, are recognized. Every swimmer should know something about life-saving so as to be able to go to the rescue of another swimmer who may be in difficulties.

There are several ways of towing a person to safety, e.g. using two hands or one hand, with arms bent or straight, holding the patient's head, arms or trunk, and the rescuer swimming on the back or on the side.

SWINBURNE, Algernon Charles (1837–1909)

English poet, born in London. Free from financial difficulties, Swinburne was able to devote his life to poetry. He left a great quantity of work behind him. One of his best-known is *Atalanta in Calydon*. His critical studies of Shakespeare are still valuable.

SWITZERLAND

A republic in Central Europe, 16,000 square miles, about half the size of Scotland, with a population of nearly 6 million inhabitants. It is the most mountainous country in Europe, the chief range being the Alps. The highest peak in the Alps, Mt. Blanc, is not, however, in Switzerland, but lies between France and Italy. Switzerland is famous for its clocks and watches, and also for its natural beauty which attracts many tourists from all over the world. The capital is Berne, but Zurich, Basle and Geneva are even better known. There are 22 cantons and the country is ruled by a Federal Assembly made up of two Chambers. The three main languages are German, French and Italian, the majority of the people speaking German.

SYMPHONIC POEM
Musical composition for orchestra which tells a story. Built on a different plan from the symphony, it was invented by Liszt and developed by many other composers; another title for it is 'tone-poem'. Popular examples of the form are Richard Strauss's *Don Juan* and Tchaikovsky's *Romeo and Juliet*.

SYMPHONY
Musical composition for orchestra, built on the same pattern as the SONATA. Some of the most famous composers of symphonies are HAYDN, MOZART, BEETHOVEN, SCHUBERT, BRAHMS, TCHAIKOVSKY, SIBELIUS and VAUGHAN WILLIAMS.

SYNAGOGUE
Jewish place of worship, and originally a place where Jews gathered either for social or other purposes. [*See* JEWS.]

SYNGE, John Millington (1871–1909)
Irish dramatist, born at Rathfarnham near Dublin. He travelled extensively on the Continent, although he spent most time in Paris. Synge returned to Ireland in 1902 and devoted himself to writing plays, poems, translations and prose. His plays are written in the language of everyday speech. The most important plays are *The Shadow of the Glen, Riders to the Sea, The Tinker's Wedding, The Well of the Saints*. In 1907 *The Playboy of the Western World* had a controversial reception and is perhaps his masterpiece, though *Deirdre of the Sorrows* is a close rival.

SYNONYM
Two (or more) words of the same meaning, like *small-little, begin-commence, gift-donation* are called *synonyms*. But in fact no two words are exactly the same in meaning and use. Thus we should never say 'I am *commencing* to feel hungry', or 'The shop window is full of Christmas *donations*'. It is an important and difficult rule of all writing and speaking that only *one* word is the 'right' word in a particular context—that is, in its particular surroundings, as it were. If, for example, we think of a number of synonyms like *happy—merry—glad—jolly—bright—felicitous*, we shall see, with a moment's thought, that though these words mean roughly the same thing, each has a definite use of its own.

We must remember also that one word may itself have more than one meaning and use, like *tall* in the phrases 'tall man', 'tall story', 'tall order'. This is easy to see when we consider the *antonym*, or 'opposite', of a word. The antonyms of the word *tall* in these three phrases

clarify its original meaning:
> *tall* man—*short* man
> *tall* story—*credible* or *believable* story
> (not *short* story)
> *tall* order—*modest* or *reasonable* order.

SYRIA
A republic in that part of Asia called the Levant. It is 71,000 square miles, bigger than England and Wales and has a population of nearly 5 million, most of them Arabs and nearly all Moslems. The capital is Damascus, the oldest city in the world, next in importance being Aleppo. The country produces and exports cotton.

SUTHERLAND The tapestry in the new Coventry Cathedral designed by Graham Sutherland.

Tt

TABLE TENNIS

A ball game which used to be called 'ping-pong'. That was in the days when the game consisted of patting a ball over a net on the dining-room table. Now it is a fast and strenuous game, with a highly developed technique.

The regulation table is 9 feet long, 5 feet wide and 2 feet 6 inches high. It must be of dark colour with a white line about $\frac{3}{4}$ inch wide around each edge. It is divided across the middle by a net 6 feet long with its top 6 inches above the playing surface. The ball is of white celluloid, between $4\frac{1}{2}$ and $4\frac{3}{4}$ inches in circumference; it has to weigh between 37 and 39 grains. The bat (referred to as 'racket' in the Rules) can be of any size, shape or weight so long as its blade is made of wood and its covering, if any, is rubber of specified types and thickness. It must be dark in colour and must not have a shiny surface.

The scoring is by points, and the game is won by the first player to reach 21, unless both players score 20, in which case the game is won by the first to secure a lead of 2 points.

The players toss for choice of ends and service, as in LAWN TENNIS. Service changes after every five points, but if the score reaches 20-all, service then changes at every point. Service and playing-end alternate with each game, but in a match of a single game or the deciding game of a match the players change ends at the score of 10. The service is made as in lawn tennis, the server putting the ball into the air with his hand and striking it with his racket. Both ball and racket must be behind the server's end-line at the time, and the server is not allowed to impart finger-spin to the ball. But—and here is a difference from lawn tennis —for a service to be good the ball must first bounce once in the server's court, then pass over the net and bounce in his opponent's court. The server has only one service, and a fault counts as a loss of a point. If the served ball touches the net but is otherwise good, 'let' is called and the service does not count. A 'let' may also be called if the receiver is not ready for the service, or if play is interrupted for any reason.

After service, play consists of alternate strokes by the players, who hit the ball across the net to each other until the rally ends. Volleying is not allowed, and the ball must be struck before it bounces twice. No player may strike the ball twice in succession. If the ball touches but goes over the net during a rally the stroke is good. If a player touches the net, or moves the playing surface with his racket or clothing or any part of his person, he loses the point. If the ball hits a player over the table surface before it bounces, he loses a point. In the absence of any of the infringements already mentioned, the rally continues until one of the players hits the ball off the table or into the net, when he loses the point.

In the doubles game the table is marked with a line running the length of the table midway between the two side-lines, and in the service the ball must bounce diagonally from the server's right half-court to the receiver's right half-court. After a good service and a good return, the players must strike the ball in strict rotation, making returns alternately.

The normal grip is similar to that used in lawn tennis, the thumb and forefinger forming a V. The thumb rests on the forehand face of the racket, to guide it in backhand strokes, and the forefinger rests on the backhand face to guide the racket in the forehand strokes. An alternative grip is the so-called 'pen-holder', in which the racket is simply held as if it were a pen. This style was used in the early days of table tennis but gradually fell out of favour until the arrival of the world-beating Japanese and Chinese players a few years ago. It is still not widely adopted by Western players although the success of the Asiatic nations is causing some 'orthodox' stylists to think again about its possibilities. Service may be backhand or forehand. Because the ball must bounce first in the server's court, it is not possible to serve with great speed. It is a good thing when serving to send the ball just over the net so that it will bounce deep in the opponent's court, frequently varying the actual direction of the service.

TACITUS, Cornelius (c. A.D. 55–c. 120)

Roman historian, born probably at Rome. He occupied a number of important public posts, and was a consul and senator. He wrote the *Germania*, the first account of the people who inhabited Central Europe at the beginning of the Christian era. In *Agricola*, a biography of his father-in-law, he gives an account of Roman Britain. But his chief work, although only about half if it survives, is the Histories and Annals—Rome's history from A.D. 14.

TAGORE, Sir Rabindranath (1861–1941)

Indian poet and author, born in Calcutta. He was partly educated in England, where he also studied law. He began writing poetry as a young man, and in 1913 was the first Indian to be awarded the Nobel Prize. He actively supported the Indian national movement, especially social reforms and one of his poems— *Lord of the Heart of the People*—was chosen as the national anthem of the Republic of India. He believed that India's task was to set an example of brotherly co-operation of races and creeds. His numerous volumes of poetry, plays and essays express a belief in the power of love to achieve man's freedom.

TAHITI

The chief island in French Polynesia and is one of the SOCIETY ISLANDS in the Pacific Ocean. The population is 77,000 and its capital is Papeete.

TAJ MAHAL

A palatial tomb in Agra, India, and one of the gems of architecture in INDIA. It was built by Shah Jahan for his wife, Mumtaz Mahal, between 1630 and 1650. One of the most beautiful buildings in the world, it is a perfect example of MOGUL style.

TALLIS, Thomas (c. 1505–1585)

English composer. He has been described as 'the father of English church music'. Organist at Waltham Abbey, near London, he went to the Chapel Royal of Henry VIII when the monasteries were dissolved. His setting of the Responses for the Church Service is still in use today, and so are many of his great anthems.

TALMUD

The book of the Oral Law of the Jews and compiled of the Mishnab and Gemara. 'Its method of instruction is by means of story, saga, legend, fable, parable, homily, maxim, proverb, wise saying. Its aim is to edify, inspire and elevate, and to supply those finer qualities of heart and mind that shall move man to the right action and right conduct . . .' (Rabbi I. Epstein, *Judaism*).

TAMERLANE (1336–1405)

Also known as Timur. Mongol conqueror. Born near Samarkand, a direct descendant of the Mongol leader GENGHIZ KHAN. In 1369 crowned King of Samarkand. He then began a series of invasions conquering Persia, Georgia and Armenia. Later he extended the Mongol Empire to Moscow (1394), the mouth of the Ganges (1398) and to Egypt (1401). He died whilst preparing to invade China.

TANK

A heavily armoured vehicle used in modern warfare for breaking the defence of an enemy and establishing strongholds. It usually runs on caterpillar or crawler tracks, and mounts one or more powerful guns. The first tank was made by the British during the First World War, and went into action on 15th September 1916 on the Somme. This proved their value in modern war, and they have been developed by every major country since that time. They played a leading role in the Second World War, particularly in the Western Desert under the leadership of then General MONTGOMERY.

TANZANIA (Tanganyika and Zanzibar)

A republic in East Africa within the British Commonwealth. It is 362,688 square miles in area but has a population of only 10 million. The country's largest lake is Tanganyika which gave its name to the territory. The capital is Dar-es-Salaam. Mount Kilimanjaro, Africa's highest mountain, is in Tanganyika near the town of Moshi. Tanganyika's most valuable export is diamonds. The country also produces cotton and coffee. The island of Zanzibar produces most of the cloves used in the world.
History:
Lake Tanganyika was discovered in 1858 by two explorers, Burton and Speke. From 1891 to 1918 Tanganyika was a German protectorate. It then became a Mandated territory under the League of Nations and was administered by Great Britain who continued to look after it when it became an INTERNATIONAL TRUST TERRITORY under the United Nations. The territory became independent in 1961 and in 1964 it joined with the former British protectorate of Zanzibar to form the State of Tanzania.

TAPIR

The main feature of this mammal is its long upper lip and snout which looks very like a trunk, and is used for hooking foliage into the mouth. Tapirs are timid creatures, browsing on forest foliage, and dashing into the undergrowth when alarmed. They are expert swimmers. Tapirs are found in America and East India.

TASMAN, Abel (c. 1603–1659)

Dutch explorer. Led an expedition to circumnavigate AUSTRALIA. He discovered Tasmania, which he named Van Dieman's Land, but in 1853 the island was renamed after its discoverer. Tasmania is now one of the six States of the Commonwealth of Australia. It is separated from the mainland by the Bass Straits.

TASMANIAN DEVIL

A chubby bear-like MARSUPIAL found only in Tasmania but once roamed much of Australia. Normally it feeds on small animal life but when its natural food is in short supply will kill domestic animals. It has a coarse brown coat with patches of white. An adult is about 3 feet long with a tail about 12 inches.

TASSO, Torquato (1544–1595)

Italian poet, born at Sorrento. After studying literature and philosophy at Padua, he entered the service of the Duke of Ferrara. Three years later he finished his epic poem *Gerusalemme Liberata* (Jerusalem Delivered). It tells the story of the First Crusade and the capture of Jerusalem by Godfrey of Bouillon.

TCHAIKOVSKY, Peter Ilich (1840–1893)

Russian composer, born at Votkinsk. He began life as a civil servant, and did not begin to compose seriously till he was 23. He made little money by his music, but when he was about 37, a wealthy lady named Nadejda von Meck, a music-lover who had heard of his poverty, wrote to him, offering to support him for the rest of his life. There was one condition; that Tchaikovsky should never try to meet her. He accepted, and although they exchanged many letters and became the firmest of friends, they never saw one another. His compositions include six symphonies (the last of which is known as the 'Pathetic'), many orchestral pieces, such as *Romeo and Juliet*, much music for ballets, especially *Swan Lake* and *The Sleeping Princess*, the well-known *Nutcracker Suite*, and the most famous of all piano concertos.

TEA

Harvested from the evergreen plant, *Camellia sinensis* or *Thea sinensis*, which grows in a climate which is warm and dry in winter and hot and wet in summer. Only the fresh green leaves, known as 'flush', are used in tea making. Plucking consists of taking two leaves and a bud, and is carried out at intervals of twelve to fourteen days. After the leaves are picked they are heaped and covered with matting when they ferment and turn black. Also they become limp which allows them to be rolled up. They are next dried in pans over a fire and packed for market.

TELEGRAPHY

Term first used by Claude Chappe to describe his system of mechanical semaphore signalling towers, but it is now applied to all systems of sending written information and pictures by means of electrical signals from one place to another over wires or wireless links. One modern telegraph system uses teleprinters which are similar in appearance to a typewriter. The pressing of a letter key on the keyboard sends out a special five-unit code signal which is received at the distant-end, re-translated, and printed by another teleprinter.

TELEPHONE

Electro-mechanical device which converts sound waves into electrical signals. These are conveyed over conductors or wireless links to distant points, to be reconverted to sound waves which are a replica of the original.

The science of telephony deals with the provision of interconnecting cable networks, junction cables between towns and automatic systems of connecting telephone subscribers together.

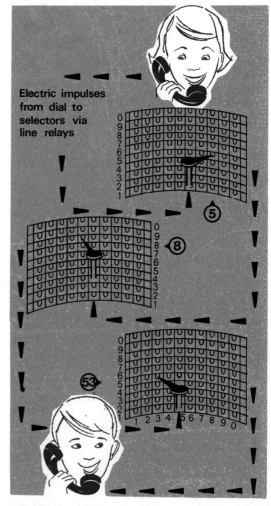

TELEPHONE The heart of an automatic system lies in the selectors. The simple diagram above shows the number 5853 being selected.

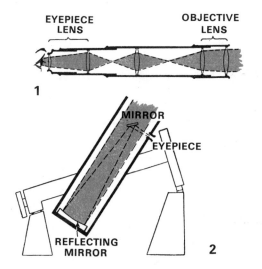

EYEPIECE LENS   OBJECTIVE LENS

1

MIRROR

EYEPIECE

REFLECTING MIRROR   2

TELESCOPE Two basic types: 1, a refracting telescope and 2, a reflecting telescope.

TELESCOPE

Instrument for enlarging the appearance of distant objects. In general, an image produced by a convex lens (the object-glass) is examined by a simple MICROSCOPE (the eye-piece). The insertion of a field-lens in front of the eye-lens serves to gather the rays towards the centre of the eye-lens and widens the field of view. Such a telescope gives an inverted image and is of little use except to astronomers. For terrestrial use a further convex lens, usually in the form of two plano-convex components, called the 'erectors', reinverts the image before it is dealt with by the eye-piece. In the reflecting telescope the objective consists of a concave mirror. In the opera-glass, or Galilean telescope, the eye-piece consists of a single biconcave lens. No real image is formed, but the eye sees an erect virtual image. [*See* LIGHT.]

TELEVISION

As television plays so important a part in our lives we should know as much about it as possible and it is for this reason that this article is longer and more detailed.

Television means 'seeing at a distance', and it is made possible because some substances are able to change light into electricity, and other substances are able to change the electricity back into light again. While it is in the form of electricity it can be broadcast as radio waves and picked up by receivers. The instrument that changes the light into electricity is called an emitron camera, and the instrument that changes it back into light is the 'tube' in your television set. A television or 'emitron' camera has a lens in front, just like an ordinary camera. This produces a small 'image' of the scene being televised, and it is really this image that is converted into electricity and broadcast. Let us see how it works.

If you hold a magnifying-glass an inch or two away from the wall of a room opposite a window, you will see a little picture of the window on the wall. In an ordinary camera such a picture is cast on to a film, which holds it permanently, but in a television camera it is cast on to a special screen, called a 'mosaic'. It is this which changes it into electrical signals so we must describe it carefully.

The first thing to realize is that you cannot hope to transmit a whole picture at once, for there are different degrees of light and shade in every part of it. So small portions of it have to be broadcast separately, one after the other. They have also to be reproduced in all their right places in the receiver, and the whole process must be done so quickly that you see them all at almost the same time. The mosaic first breaks the picture up into suitable parts, and these are tiny dots much like the dots in a picture in a newspaper, which you can easily see with your magnifying-glass.

The mosaic consists of a sheet of mica or other electrical insulating material, but the side of it on to which the picture is to be cast is sprayed thinly with an alloy of caesium and silver, so that it is covered with a few million tiny globules of metal. Caesium-silver is very sensitive to light and when light shines on it, it becomes charged with electricity. When the picture is cast on it by the camera lens, the metal globules all acquire different electric charges according to the brightness of the part of the picture which falls on them.

Now, the back of the sheet of mica is covered by a metal plate called the 'signal plate', and when the globules on the other side are electrically charged they attract the signal plate through the mica so that it also becomes charged. If a few of the globules are then discharged—that is, made to lose their electricity —the signal plate shows a similar change. By discharging a few of the globules at a time, until we have covered the whole of the picture, we can make the signal plate give a whole train of electrical signals which will represent the different degrees of light and shade in every part of the picture. These are the signals that are broadcast and picked up by television receivers.

But the signals must be sent out in some regular order, so that a receiver can reproduce them in exactly the same way, and it must all be done fast enough for us to see them altogether instead of one after the other. Fortunately, electricity moves so swiftly that the speed presents no special problems. The entire television picture is actually transmitted 25 times

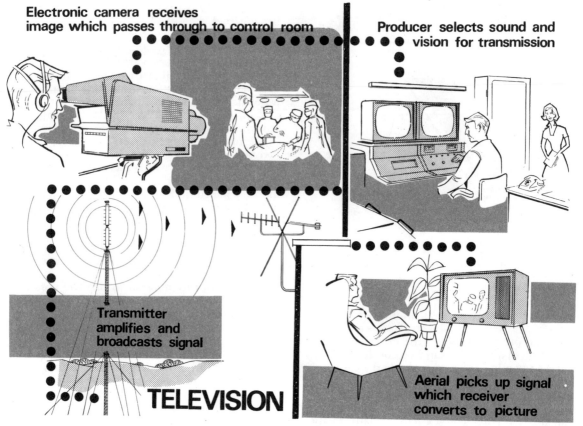

Electronic camera receives image which passes through to control room

Producer selects sound and vision for transmission

Transmitter amplifies and broadcasts signal

TELEVISION

Aerial picks up signal which receiver converts to picture

every second, so that you cannot possibly tell what is happening but see the picture complete.

The problem is to arrange for the globules on the mosaic to be discharged in strict order so that the signals never get mixed. This is done by 'scanning' the mosaic with a narrow beam of cathode-rays, which sweeps across it so as to draw a series of parallel lines, one under the other. The globules are thus discharged in rows or 'lines', 405 lines being used in British television.

A CATHODE-RAY is a stream of electrons passing through a vacuum tube from a negative pole or 'cathode' to a positive pole or 'anode'. The electrons travel very quickly, and if a hole is made in the centre of the anode some of them shoot straight through. This device is called an 'electron-gun' and it produces a long, narrow beam of electrons. Such a beam travels in a straight line, but it can be bent by passing it between the poles of a magnet.

To make such a beam scan the mosaic screen in parallel lines two electro-magnets are used. One causes it to move from left to right across the screen, and the other drags it downwards so that each line comes just underneath the previous line. In actual practice, the cathode-ray first draws every *other* line, making

$202\frac{1}{2}$ lines as it moves down the screen. It then starts again and fills in the missing $202\frac{1}{2}$ lines. This enables the lines to be put closer together without getting mixed.

The electrons in the beam discharge the globules on the mosaic as soon as they touch them, and so the globules send their signals to the signal plate at the exact rate at which the cathode-ray passes over them. The signals are then broadcast exactly as in ordinary radio.

In the receiving set there is a similar cathode-ray, drawing exactly the same number of lines, in exactly the same order, as the one in the emitron camera. Only this time the ray strikes against a fluorescent screen, which lights up whenever electrons hit it. This screen is made by simply coating the inside of the glass of the cathode-ray tube with zinc sulphide or some other 'phosphor'.

Now, the picture signals are received and fed to the cathode-ray as a train of electrical impulses of various strengths. The ray thus contains more or less electrons according to the signals, and as it passes over the screen it produces different degrees of brightness according to the light and shade in the various parts of the picture being broadcast.

Every time the cathode-ray completes its

line across the screen it is cut off—or 'blanked out'—while it returns to the other side to start the next line. Otherwise you would see it streak back and the picture would be spoiled. Similarly, when it gets to the bottom of the picture it is blanked out while it streaks back to the top to start a fresh picture. These blanked-out periods are so brief that you cannot detect them, but they provide an opportunity for the transmitting station to send out a special signal called 'sync pulse'. This prevents the cathode-ray in the receiver from starting its lines until the cathode-ray in the transmitter is ready. In this way, the two rays are 'synchronized', or made to keep in perfect time.

Pictures transmitted and received in the manner described appear in black and white. The apparatus required for colour television is more complicated but you can grasp the general principle without difficulty. It should be noted that the system described below is only one of several and that much work on colour television is still being done.

The colour television camera has to contain three separate tubes instead of only one. Emitron tubes are too clumsy, so a neater form called an 'orthicon' is used. Mirrors are employed to make the lens of the camera provide three images instead of one, and each image is cast on the screen of a separate orthicon. But the light of these images is first passed through three differently-coloured 'filters'. These are simply like pieces of coloured glass, one stopping all except the red rays, one stopping all but the green, and the third stopping all but the blue.

The three differently coloured pictures are broadcast separately, but in the receiver they are all projected on to the same screen so that the red, green and blue from the view being televised are put together again. This is a very tricky business, because the receiving screen has to be coated with three different phosphors, one of which will shine with a red light when the electrons strike it, one with a green light and the third with a blue light. The difficulty is to make them shine only when the signals belonging to their right colours arrive, but the method of doing this is too complicated to explain simply.

But when all the colours are thus shown together in the same picture, the view appears in its natural colours, for not only do the red, green and blue parts come out clearly, but where the red overlaps the green you get yellow, and all the other shades are produced in a similar way. This may puzzle you if you have a box of paints, for you know that it is impossible to make yellow with paints, and red and green make a dirty black. But in tele-vision it is not paints that are being mixed but coloured light, and the mixing rules for light are quite different.

TELL, William (14th century)

Swiss hero who is regarded in that country in much the same way as is Robin Hood in Britain. The best known incident of his life is that in which he shoots the apple from his son's head with a bow and arrow to gain his pardon from execution by order of a powerful bailiff, Gessler.

TEMPLARS

A military order founded in 1119 during the Crusades. They took solemn vows to defend pilgrims going to the Holy Land from attack by the Saracens. During the 13th century the Order became so rich and powerful that it was abolished in 1307 by Pope Clement V.

TEMPLE

A building erected to the honour of a god, or as a place of public worship. Perhaps, the most famous temple in history was SOLOMON'S Temple at Jerusalem. This was razed to the ground by Nebuchadnezzar's soldiers in 587–586 B.C. The Second (Zerubbabel's) Temple was completed on the same site in 516 B.C., and stood until it was replaced by the Third and most magnificent Temple of all—that of Herod the great, in the courts of which Jesus walked and taught. Herod's temple shared in the general destruction of Jerusalem by Titus in A.D. 70. The Tabernacle in the Bible was a movable place of worship used during the wanderings of the Hebrews.

TENIERS Family

A family of Flemish artists. The elder, David Teniers (1582–1649), painted in the style of RUBENS and on religious subjects. His son, also David (1610–1690), is best-known for his paintings of peasant life, interiors of picture galleries and religious subjects. There has always been a big demand for his pictures. A son of the last Teniers, also David (1638–1685), was also a painter and worked in the style of his father.

TENNYSON, Alfred, First Baron (1809–1892)

English poet. Brought up in a Lincolnshire rectory, and one of a circle of serious young undergraduates when at Cambridge. Tennyson devoted himself throughout a long life to the profession of poetry, and became Queen Victoria's most honoured poet and respected by the nation; Poet Laureate (1850–1892). He was marvellously skilful in the writing of onomatopoeic poetry, and there was always a dignity in what he wrote, and sometimes a music never heard before. The poem on which he worked longest and most intently was *In Memoriam*, brooding on the early death of his gifted university friend, Arthur Henry Hallam. Other famous poems are *The Charge of the Light Brigade, Maud* and *Idylls of a King*.

TENRECS
A group of small insect-eating mammals confined to the island of Madagascar. The common tenrec measures 12–16 inches fully grown and has a yellowish-brown coat. It lives in holes in mountainous regions and feeds on insects. It rears a large family—sometimes as many as twenty young. The 'rice' tenrec lives very much like a mole and the 'marsh' tenrec has webbed feet to enable it to live in the water.

THACKERAY, William Makepeace
(1811–1863)
Born in Bengal. Was sent to England at six to a lonely schooling, his father having died and his mother remarried. After studying at Cambridge, he spent some time abroad. For the London papers he wrote stories, sketches, and verses under various and curious pen names. Then, under his own name, he produced a number of novels, of which at least two are masterpieces—*Vanity Fair* and *Henry Esmond*.

THAILAND, or Siam
A kingdom in South-east Asia that is 198,245 square miles, nearly as large as France, and has a population of 30 million. The capital is Bangkok. Most of the people are farmers and rice and rubber are the chief exports. The country's chief minerals are tin and lignite. Siamese cats were originally brought from Siam where they are royal pets. The country, unlike its neighbours, never came under European rule.

THALES (*c.* 636–*c.* 546 B.C.)
Greek philosopher, born at Miletos. With the philosopher Anaximander was the founder of the Greek school of philosophy known as the Milesian. This school is considered to be the root of European thought and natural science.

THEATRE
The Greeks were the first to erect a special building for the performance of plays. It was in the form of an open-air arena built of stone, and consisted of three sections; the auditorium where the audience sat, the orchestra where the players acted, and the scene which was usually an architectural background.
During the Middle Ages there were no

theatres, the mystery and miracle plays being performed on carts. In the 16th century plays were produced in the courtyards of inns. The first theatre to be authorized to perform plays in London was erected at Shoreditch by the great Shakespearean actor, Richard Burbage. He later pulled this down and built the *Globe Theatre* at Southwark.
The first modern theatre was built at Parma in 1618. Here, for the first time, the stage was separated from the U-shaped auditorium by a curtain. This plan was adopted throughout Europe, and has persisted until the present time. During the present century many experiments have been made in theatre design, particularly with a view to bringing the audience into closer contact with the players. One type of theatre arising from this is the 'theatre in the round', a circular auditorium with a simple low stage near the centre. No scenery is used and only the simplest stage effects, e.g. a chair or a table.

THEODOLITE
Small telescope used in surveying, mounted on a level stand so that its angles of direction and elevation can be read on graduated scales.

THEOPHRASTUS of Lesbos (368–284 B.C.)
He succeeded ARISTOTLE as head of the Lyceum at Athens. He wrote a *History of Plants* in which he attempted to do for the plant world what Aristotle did for the animal kingdom.

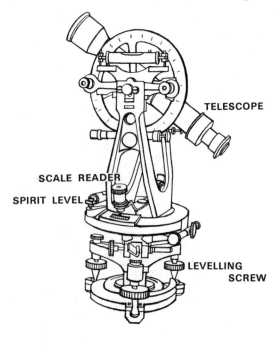

TELESCOPE

SCALE READER

SPIRIT LEVEL

LEVELLING SCREW

THEODOLITE An optical surveying instrument.

He also wrote works on minerals and their classification, weather-lore and an important book on fire.

THERMOCOUPLE

Consists of a pair of dissimilar metal wires joined end to end, and with their outer ends also joined. If one junction becomes hotter than another an electric current flows round the loop. A battery of thermocouples form a thermopile, and is used for measuring temperatures, when it is not possible or convenient to use a THERMOMETER.

THERMOMETER

An instrument for measuring the degree of temperature of a body by the expansion of a liquid. Alcohol or pertane is used in low-temperature thermometers, mercury in ordinary-temperature and gallium in very-high-temperature thermometers. The three main types of thermometer are, the CENTIGRADE, which measures from 0° to 100°, the FAHRENHEIT, which measures from 32° to 212°, and the RÉAUMUR, which measures 0° to 80°.

THERMOSTAT

An automatic device for controlling temperature. It is used in such things as electric irons, furnaces, water heaters and the like. It is based on the fact that the expansions of dissimilar metals are unequal.

THOMAS, Dylan (1914–1953)

Welsh poet, born in Swansea. His first published work, *Eighteen Poems* (1934), was immediately acclaimed. His collected poems for the period 1934–1952 were published in 1952. His most widely-known work is *Under Milk Wood*, a radio play. Thomas's unfinished novel *Adventures in the Skin Trade* was published in 1955. He was a fine reader of poetry.

THOMSON, Sir J. J. (1856–1940)

English scientist, born at Cheetham. At the early age of 28 was made Cavendish Professor at Cambridge. He was awarded a Nobel Prize for Physics in 1906, and was President of the Royal Society from 1915 to 1920. Most of his life was devoted to studying the nature of the ELECTRON whose mass and electrical charge he was the first to measure.

THOREAU, Henry David (1817–1862)

American naturalist and writer, born at Concord. A great friend of EMERSON. His greatest work is *Walden*, and recounts his experiences of living alone in a cabin at Walden Pond. His writings have had a great influence on fellow writers since his death.

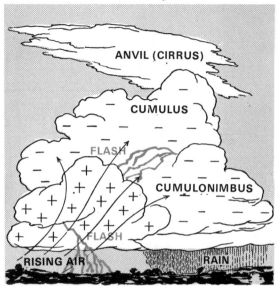

THUNDERSTORM The positive and negative electric charges which cause a lightning flash.

THUCYDIDES (*c.* 460–399 B.C.)

The first historian, and an Athenian. Little is known about his life, but his writings are valuable accounts of the time in which he lived. His longest work is a history of the Peloponnesian War, which, apart from its historical significance, has great literary and dramatic merit.

THUNDERSTORM

Electric storm caused by the breaking up of rain-drops in a strong up-current of air which prevents their descent to the ground. The process of buffeting gives them a positive charge and the surrounding air a negative charge. In such a system, a cloud which retains its rain gradually acquires a high positive charge, while parts from which the rain has fallen have a high negative charge, a discharge between them taking place when the potential difference is of the order of a hundred million volts. A discharge may also take place between the positive cloud and the earth. Lightning is the flash of the discharge, and thunder the atmospheric vibrations set up by the sudden expansion of the heated air, and their echoes.

THYLACINE

A flesh-eating MARSUPIAL which was once found in Australia but now confined to Tasmania. It is a savage hunter and will attack sheep and poultry. It is about the size of a collie dog with distinctive chocolate-brown stripes across the rear of its back. Because of its savage disposition it is also called a 'marsupial' wolf or 'marsupial' tiger.

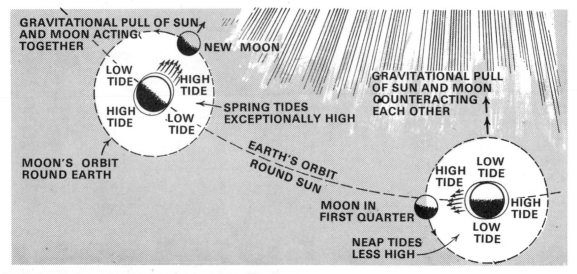

TIDE This diagram shows how the gravitational pulls of the sun and moon cause tides

TIBET

A large mountainous country in Asia of 463,000 square miles, that is more than twice the size of France but with a population of less than 1½ million. About every fifth man in the country is a Buddhist monk. The capital is Lhasa. Most of the people are farmers. The country exports borax and musk.

History:

From the 9th to the 18th centuries Tibet closed her doors to foreign countries. In the 18th century China claimed some rights over Tibet but did not interfere with it. In 1904 Great Britain compelled Tibet to agree to trade with other countries. In 1950, after China became a Communist country, that country sent an armed force to occupy Tibet. Tibet was allowed to manage most of her own affairs until 1959 when some of the Tibetans rose in revolt. The Tibetan ruler, the Dalai Lama, and many of his followers fled to India.

TIDE

Phenomenon of the sea, and to a slight extent of the atmosphere, due to the gravitational influences of the sun and moon. The surface of the earth facing the moon is subject to a greater gravitational force than its centre, and water, being mobile, is therefore drawn visibly towards the moon, the surface of the ocean rising a few feet. Water on the further side from the moon is attracted to a lesser degree than the rigid earth, and is freely subject to the centrifugal force of the earth's monthly revolution about the common centre of gravity of the moon and earth. It is, therefore, thrown outwards and its surface also rises, these two opposite accumulations of water being termed high tides. The earth rotates beneath them once every 24 hours, and since the water rotates with it they travel over the surface as slight waves, visible in all coastal districts as two tides per day (approximately). They are called 'spring tides' when augmented by the sun's influence (at new and full moon), and 'neap tides' when the solar effect tends to counteract the lunar tides (at first and last quarters).

TIEPOLO, Giovanni Battista (1696–1770)

Venetian painter. His early frescoes won him international fame. In 1750 he was called to Wurzburg, where he decorated the archbishop's palaces with frescoes and altarpieces. In 1763 he went to Madrid, where he spent the rest of his life. There he decorated the Royal Palace, and produced many oil paintings.

TIERRA DEL FUEGO

Group of islands off the tip of South America, belonging to ARGENTINA and to Chile. Two principal towns are Ushuaia and Magallanes.

TIGER

A member of the CAT family (Felidae). It is distinguished by bright yellowish orange colouring, vertical black stripes and white belly. Tigers are found only in Asia where they occur as far north as Mongolia and as far south as Java. They habitually frequent forest and thick jungle with which their colour harmonizes; not open bush as does the lion. Their food is mainly deer, wild pigs, cattle and goats, but when hungry they will eat carrion and small animals. Generally tigers are afraid of men, and in the case of man-eaters it is thought that they turn to this as a result of injury which prevents their living on their normal prey.

TIME
Mode by which we perceive the succession of events and the phenomenon of change. There is probably no absolute time, but the standard time of physics is measured by the periodic rotation of the earth in relation to the sun at noon, the unit of one second being defined as 86,400th of the mean solar day.

TINTORETTO (1518–1594)
Italian painter, born in Venice. His real name was Jacopo Robusti. The name Il Tintoretto was given to him because of his father's trade; it means 'little dyer'. Tintoretto was influenced chiefly by TITIAN and MICHELANGELO, and in 1548 painted his famous *Miracle of St. Mark*. In 1564, in San Rocco in Venice, he commenced work on a series of more than 60 paintings dealing with scenes from the Passion, including the vast and grandly-conceived Crucifixion (1565). Tintoretto's works in San Rocco, along with Michelangelo's ceiling in the Sistine Chapel and Raphael's Vatican Stanze are the greatest artistic achievements of the Renaissance.

TIPSTAFF
An officer of the High Court who is appointed by the LORD CHANCELLOR. If a person misbehaves himself in court the judge can order him to be arrested and this must be done by the Tipstaff.

TITHES
A church or ecclesiastical tax. In olden times the tithes a farmer had to give each year to the church consisted of a tenth of his farm produce.

TITIAN (1477–1576)
Italian painter, born at Pieve di Cadore in the Dolomites. Real name Tiziano Vecellio. Studied at Venice under GIORGIONE, became head of the Venetian school, and one of the most celebrated painters in Venice. He painted many of the great people of his day. With MICHELANGELO and RAPHAEL, he led the Italian Renaissance.

TITICACA, LAKE
The highest lake in the world being some 12,500 feet above sea-level. It is situated on the borders of Peru and Bolivia, and is over 3,000 square miles in area.

TITO, Marshal Josip (1892——)
Yugoslav revolutionary and national leader. Born in Croatia, son of a locksmith. He fought for the Austrians in the First World War. Afterwards he went to Russia and on his return to Yugoslavia (1923) joined the Communist Party. He was imprisoned for illegal political activities 1928–1934. In July 1941 he emerged as Yugoslav national leader in the war against the German invaders. He became commander-in-chief of the Yugoslav army in 1946 and head of the country's communist form of government.

TOADS [*See* AMPHIBIANS]

TOBACCO
Obtained from the plant *Nicotiana tabacum*. This is sown as seed and the young plants afterwards are planted out in the tobacco fields. When in full leaf the point of the centre shoot is cut off to prevent flowering. As soon as the leaves begin to turn yellow they are collected, dried and fermented. This plant is one of the principal crops of sub-tropical lands; for example, America grows some 2,200,000,000 pounds yearly. In recent years tobacco in the form of cigarettes has been named as one of the main causes of lung cancer.

TOBOGGANING
The toboggan, so named by the Red Indians of Canada, is perhaps the simplest of all vehicles for travelling over snow and ice. There are two types, the toboggan and the bob-sleigh. In the toboggan there is one pair of runners which go the whole length from front to stern, but in the bob-sleigh the runners are arranged in two pairs, back and front. The back ones are fixed securely to the board on which the passenger lies, and may extend from the stern to about half-way to the front. The front ones, generally quite short, are mounted on a separate piece of board which is joined to the board by a swivel; these runners are used for steering, and they are worked by a rope which is used as a drag-rope for hauling and a steering rope when running. To steer to the left the rope is pulled so that the left steering runner goes back and the right one comes forward; and *vice versa*.

TOGO
An independent republic on the Gulf of Guinea in West Africa. It is smaller (21,000 square miles) than Scotland and has a population of 1½ million. The capital is Lomé. The country produces coffee, cocoa and cotton.

Togo was part of a German colony before the First World War and then became a Mandated Territory under the League of Nations and later a United Nations International Trust Territory administered by France.

TOLSTOY, Count Leo Nikolaievich
(1828–1910)

Greatest Russian novelist, born on the family estate at Tula. In 1851 he joined the Russian Army in the Caucasus, and later fought in the Crimean War against England. After two journeys to Western Europe he settled down on the family estate. Apart from devoting himself to the welfare of his peasants, about whom he wrote many stories, he wrote his two masterpieces—*War and Peace* (1865–1869) and *Anna Karenina* (1875–1876). The first of these is an epic study of the Napoleonic invasion of Russia. In 1881 Tolstoy passed through a period of inner crises, from which he emerged as moralist and religious teacher inspired by his own form of Christianity. In 1895 he renounced his property and wealth in order to live the life of an ordinary peasant.

TONGA [*See* FRIENDLY ISLANDS]

TORNADO

Small thermal cyclone of great intensity which occurs most frequently in the central plains of the Mississippi, but is known also in Australia. A tornado may measure only a few hundred feet in diameter, and usually travels at about 30 m.p.h., but its speed of rotation is so high that within it winds of 200 m.p.h. have been recorded. The partial vacuum in the centre of the tornado can uproot trees or cause buildings to collapse.

TORPEDO

A naval weapon used mainly in submarines and destroyers to attack enemy ships. It travels under water, having its own small engine, and explodes with great force when it hits its target. It travels, at any depth required, at a speed of about 50 knots. It is fired from a torpedo tube, submerged in submarines and above water in destroyers. The direction in which the tube is trained at the moment of firing gives the torpedo the course on which it will run, and a steering device inside the torpedo keeps it steady on its course.

TORQUEMADA, Thomas de (1420–1498)

Founder of the Spanish Inquisition, born at Valladolid. He became a Dominican monk, and afterwards confessor to Queen Isabella of Spain and her husband, Ferdinand. In 1478 he secured the establishment of the Inquisition in Spain, and in 1483 was made inquisitor-general, a post which he held for eighteen years. During this period several thousand people were put to death. Torquemada was also one of the main instigators of the expulsion of the Jews from Spain. [*See* INQUISITION.]

TORRICELLI, Evangelista (1608–1647)

Italian physicist who discovered the pressure of the atmosphere and suggested how a BAROMETER might be constructed and carried out by his friend Vincenzo Viviani. Torricelli also made advances in microscope and telescope design.

TORTOISE [*See* TURTLE]

TOSCANINI, Arturo (1867–1957)

Italian musician and one of the greatest conductors of all time. Born at Parma. In his early days he was a cellist, but soon proved his ability as a conductor. He conducted at La Scala, Milan, and most of the leading opera houses in Europe and America. He openly opposed the dictatorship of Mussolini.

TOULOUSE-LAUTREC, Henri de
(1864–1901)

French painter, born at Albi. Was dwarfed because of an accident to his legs when he was about 15. He showed an early talent for art, and went to Paris in 1882 to continue studies. His most important works are of singers, dancers and other entertainers of the Paris scene of that time. They are outstanding for their human insight and unsentimental observations. He will always be associated with the vigorous can-can dancers at the Moulin Rouge. Lautrec was also a pioneer in modern poster design.

TOUSSAINT L'OUVERTURE, François Dominique (c. 1744–1803)

Negro patriot of Haiti. He was leader of a negro revolt which kept the Spanish and English at bay, and eventually occupied Santo Domingo. Later he successfully defended the island from the attacks of Napoleon's army, but was betrayed and transported to France where he died.

TOWER OF LONDON

The central keep or White Tower was built by William the Conqueror in 1078. The inner wall with its thirteen towers was added in the 13th century. Richard I added the moat, Henry III made extensive additions, Edward I surrounded the whole with a second wall with towers commanding the river, and Henry VIII added the rounded bastions on the north side. In its time the Tower has served as a fortress, a palace and a prison. It has ceased to have any direct association with royalty, except for the fact that the CROWN JEWELS are kept in the Wakefield Tower. The Tower is guarded by Beefeaters (Yeomen of the Guard) who still dress in traditional Tudor uniform.

TOWN CLERK

The clerk, or secretary of a BOROUGH or COUNTY BOROUGH COUNCIL. His office is the Town Hall and all those employed there will come under him. He is a lawyer and will advise the Mayor and Councillors on legal matters, and so must attend meetings of the Council. He is a paid official and is not elected as are the members of the Council. County Councils have similar officers and they are called Clerks to the Council.

TRADE UNIONS

The name given to organizations of work people, the purpose of which is to secure good pay and conditions of work for their members.

In the Middle Ages craftsmen used to form 'guilds' to protect their interests, but they were different from the modern trade unions. It was the changes brought about by the Industrial Revolution in the 18th century that made work people feel the need to organize. At first this was very difficult because laws, called the Combination Laws, made it a crime to belong to a trade union. In 1834 six labourers of Tolpuddle, Dorsetshire were deported to Australia because of the part they had taken in a trade union. These men are spoken of today as the Tolpuddle Martyrs. Things improved soon afterwards and workers were allowed to organize in trade unions. One of the first of the big trade unions to be formed was the Amalgamated Society of Engineers which was founded in 1851. In 1868 the many different trade unions which had by then formed, decided to meet together for certain purposes, and this led to the formation of the Trades Union Congress. Today the T.U.C. plays an important part in the life of the nation. When the Government wants Parliament to make some new factory or other law affecting workers, it always first finds out what the T.U.C. thinks about it. When the INTERNATIONAL LABOUR ORGANIZATION holds a conference it is always the T.U.C. that is asked to choose the workers' delegate. Today there are trade unions in all the industrial countries of the world. [*See* POLITICAL PARTIES.]

TRADE WINDS

Permanent atmospheric convection currents at the surface of the earth, generated by equatorial heat. Hot air over the equator rises, and cooler air is drawn in from about latitudes 30° N. and S. Owing to the rotation of the earth these 'trade winds' blow in from the north-east and south-east respectively.

TRANSISTOR

A small, sturdy electronic device which is replacing the old glass vacuum tube. It is based on the amplifying properties of semiconductors (silicon, selenium, germanium, etc.). Constructionally it consists of a simple cylinder and two extremely fine wires whose points rest on a small dot of semi-conductive material soldered to a metal base. The transistor has been shown to produce amplifications as high as 100 to 1 (20 decibels).

TREASURE TROVE

Most people, including many young people, have at some time or other discovered some article that has been lost by some unknown person. Very often when such articles are handed over to the police the owner is found and so is able to recover the article. Such lost articles, however, are not treasure trove. Treasure trove are coins or gold or silver objects that have clearly been hidden by their owner although it is no longer possible to discover who that was. All treasure trove belongs to the Crown and not to the person who finds it. If the treasure trove is valuable the local coroner will hold an inquest, or enquiry, about it. The Government will often then give back the articles to the finder or if they are wanted for a Museum the finder will be given some money as a reward. People who find treasure trove and do not report it can be punished.

TREASURY, THE

The chief department of the Government. The heads of the Treasury are seven Lords Commissioners who form the Treasury Board. Today, however, the Board never meets so it is only nominally in control. The First Lord is now always the PRIME MINISTER and the Second Lord the CHANCELLOR OF THE EXCHEQUER. The work of the Treasury is now carried out by the Chancellor who is helped by the Chief Secretary who is also a Cabinet Minister. There is also a Financial Secretary and a Parliamentary Secretary to the Treasury. The Parliamentary Secretary is also the chief Government WHIP in the House of Commons. The first row of seats in the House of Commons, on the Speaker's right, is called the Treasury Bench because the chief members of the Cabinet sit there.

TREATY

A signed agreement between two or more States. Although the word treaty is the one most often used for such a signed agreement there are other words used as well. The most common of these is Convention which is often used for an agreement which any nation which wishes may sign. There are, for instance, Red Cross Conventions about the treatment of wounded soldiers and prisoners of war. There are also Conventions about conditions of work agreed to at conferences of the INTERNATIONAL LABOUR ORGANIZATION. Then there is the word Charter, such as the Charter of the UNITED NATIONS and the word Protocol which, however, is more often used to describe something that is added to a treaty. Other words for a treaty that have been used include Covenant and Pact.

After countries have signed a treaty or Convention they have to ratify it. This means that a country accepts what its representative undertook when he signed it. Each country makes its own rules as to what shall be done before a treaty is ratified. In Britain important treaties are brought before Parliament so that Parliament can say if it agrees with the treaty before it is ratified. It is usual for Parliament to agree.

TREE

A perennial woody plant which sheds its leaves in the autumn, and for this reason is described as 'deciduous'. However, in tropical climates many deciduous trees do not shed their leaves as they do in temperate climates. The 'evergreens' do shed their leaves, but not all at once, and it is for this reason that they appear to bear their leaves all the year round. Perhaps the most important physical feature of a tree is the single supporting trunk which distinguishes it from a shrub. Many trees can be identified by their shape as viewed from a distance. For example there is no mistaking the tall, spear-shaped poplar, or the bulbous chestnut. Not all trees can be definitely identified by their shape. Often it is necessary to know such things as leaf shape, flower and fruit.

TREVITHICK, Richard (1771–1833)

English inventor, born in Cornwall. One of the first to realize the practical uses of the steam engine. He invented the high-pressure steam-engine, and applied it to mining, carriages and even a threshing machine. [*See* STEAM ENGINE.]

TRIGONOMETRY

The branch of mathematics concerned with the relations of the sides and angles of triangles. A triangle has three sides and three angles. Generally speaking, if three are known (sides or angles) it is possible to find the other three. Trigonometrical tables are essential and are worked out for the sine, cosine and tangent of all angles between 0–90 deg. Trigonometry is essential in such subjects as navigation and surveying.

TRINIDAD AND TOBAGO

An independent State and a Member of the British Commonwealth. The two islands together are less than a quarter of the size of Wales. The population is less than a million, most of whom are of negro descent but there are also many Indians. The capital of Trinidad is Port of Spain. It exports asphalt, petroleum, citrus fruit, cocoa and sugar. Trinidad was discovered by Christopher Columbus on Trinity Sunday—hence its name. Trinidad became British in 1802 and Tobago twelve years later. The country became independent in 1962.

TRINITY HOUSE

The authority which provides and maintains LIGHTHOUSES around the coasts of England and Wales and the Channel Islands and also Gibraltar. Trinity House received its first Royal Charter from Henry VIII. It is administered by important persons called Elder Brethren who are elected from the Royal Navy and the Merchant Navy. Trinity House is also responsible for most pilots in England and Wales.

TRISTAN DA CUNHA

British island in the South Atlantic and a dependency of St. Helena. It has a population of less than 250, and its main importance lies in the radio and weather stations which are situated on the island. Several years ago all the people were evacuated because of volcanic activity, but most returned later.

TROLLOPE, Anthony (1815–1882)

English novelist, born in London. Spent many years as an official in the Post Office, but managed to write some fifty novels besides other works. His most famous novels were *The Warden* and *Barchester Towers*. His father and brother were also well-known writers in their day.

TROTSKY, Leon Davidovitch (1879–1940)

Russian revolutionary leader. Born in the Ukraine, and the son of a farmer, he studied at Kiev University and soon joined the revolu-

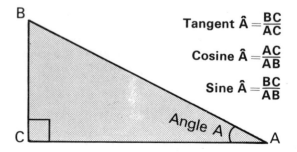

Tangent $\hat{A} = \dfrac{BC}{AC}$

Cosine $\hat{A} = \dfrac{AC}{AB}$

Sine $\hat{A} = \dfrac{BC}{AB}$

Angle A

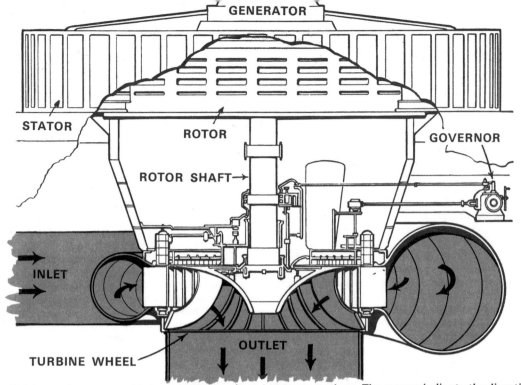

TURBINE A reaction-type turbine used in hydro-electric power-stations. The arrows indicate the direction of the flow of water that drives the rotor shaft.

tionaries. He was prominent in the first Russian Revolution of 1905, but was later exiled to Siberia. Together with LENIN he was the principal organizer of the 1917 Revolution.

After Lenin's death he quarrelled with STALIN on whether the Revolution should be national or international. He was finally exiled from Russia in 1927 and after periods of residence in Turkey, France, Norway and Mexico was assassinated by unknown hands in Mexico City.

TRUCIAL STATES
Seven independent Sheikhdoms along the shores of the Persian Gulf. They have had special treaty arrangements with Great Britain since 1820. The total area is a little larger than Scotland but the population only a little over 100,000. The largest of the States is Abu Dhabi and the largest town and chief port is Dubai. In all the States oil companies are searching for oil and some has been found.

TRUMAN, Harry S. (1884———)
American politician and President. Born in Missouri, and went to school in Independence, Missouri. Served in the American Army in France in the First World War. After losing all his money in a business venture in Kansas City, he turned to politics and by 1934 was elected to the U.S. Senate for the Democrats. Ten years later he was elected Vice-President,

becoming President on President ROOSEVELT'S death (1945). In 1948 he was re-elected President against all the predictions of the forecasters. In 1952 he announced his retirement from politics.

TUATARA
A survivor of that group of prehistoric reptiles to which the DINOSAURS belonged. It is confined to a few islands of New Zealand. A fully-grown adult is about 24 inches long. It lays some 10–14 eggs which it buries in the ground; the hatching period is nearly a year. Tuataras live in bare rocky regions and feed on small animal life.

TUNISIA
An Arabic-speaking republic on the coast of North Africa. It is nearly as large as England and has a population of over 4 million. The capital is Tunis. The country grows and exports dates. Its chief mineral is phosphates.
History:
Tunisia was conquered by the Turks in 1574 but allowed its own monarch called a Bey. In 1881 it became a French protectorate and in 1956 it became independent. The following year it became a republic.

TURBINE
A device in which steam, water or hot gases are used to generate power or drive a machine.

A steam turbine consists of two major parts, the rotor, or moving part, and the stator, or stationary portion. The rotor takes the form of a drum to which are attached a number of rows of curved blades, each acting, in effect, as one blade of a small windmill when the steam strikes it at high pressure. Depending on the manner in which the steam is directed on to the blades of the rotor, turbines are divided into two types, impulse and reaction. In the simple impulse turbine a number of wheels, each carrying one row of blades, are attached to a common shaft. In front of each wheel is a stationary circular metal plate provided with openings which form nozzles to direct jets of steam on to the blades of the wheel behind it. After the steam has passed through the blades of the first wheel, it is directed by a second set of nozzles on to the next wheel, and so on through successive stages, until the useful energy in the steam has been used up.

In the reaction type of turbine, on the other hand, the nozzles are replaced by rings of stationary blades between the rows of rotating blades, power being obtained chiefly from the reaction set up by the steam as it passes between the fixed and moving blades. Since the steam loses some of its force after passing through each ring of blades, succeeding blades are made larger and larger to obtain the maximum turning effort from the lower pressure of steam in each stage. In many cases two or more turbines are combined.

The gas turbine operates on a similar principle to the steam turbine, with the exception that the rotor blades are forced round by a mixture of heated air and gas. Since very large quantities of air are required to burn the fuel and to provide huge volumes of gas, the gas turbine requires an air compressor, which is driven from the rotor shaft. This may be similar in design to the rotor, with successive rings of rotating blades and stationary guide vanes of gradually decreasing size, the largest vanes being at the end at which air is drawn into the compressor, and the smallest at the end at which it is discharged into the combustion chamber, so that the air is progressively compressed as it passes through each stage. The jet engine is one of the most outstanding examples of this type of turbine.

The water turbine is the modern descendant of the primitive water-wheel. The type which most closely resembles the water-wheel is the Pelton design. The wheel, or runner, as it is termed, has a number of cast-steel buckets attached to its rim. One or more nozzles project high-speed jets of water against the buckets, thus rotating the wheel.

This is termed an impulse turbine. In a widely used type of Pelton turbine there are two runners on a common shaft, with two nozzles to each runner. The speed of the turbine is controlled by varying the force of the jets by means of needle valves in the openings of the nozzles. Should the load on the turbine drop suddenly, overspeeding is prevented by deflectors which divert the jets away from the buckets, followed by a gradual closing of the needle valves. These actions are automatically controlled by a governor.

Another type of turbine is the Francis

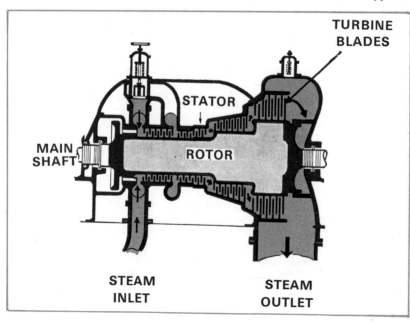

TURBINE Section through a steam turbine showing the direction of the steam flow that drives the rotor shaft.

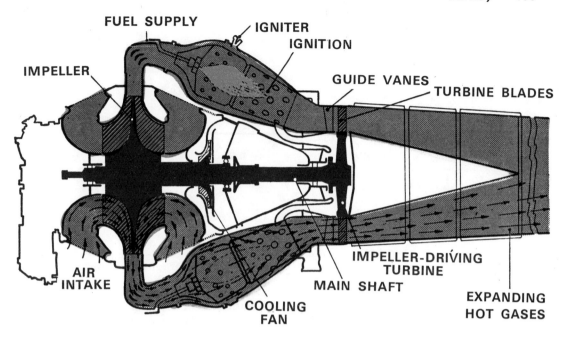

TURBINE Basic design of gas turbine of the type used to propel jet aircraft.

design which is installed in the majority of the new hydro-electric generating stations. The Francis turbine is a reaction type in which the water reacts against vanes in the runner, which may be arranged vertically on large turbines, or horizontally on small and medium-sized machines. The water enters a spiral casing surrounding the runner and is directed by movable inlet guide vanes against the runner vanes. The turbine speed is controlled by varying the angles of the guide vanes, and thus altering the angle at which the water meets the vanes of the runner and the amount of 'push' imparted to them.

A third type of turbine is the Kaplan, in which the water flows through the blades of a propeller—similar in general design to a ship's screw—attached to the end of the runner shaft. The reaction of the water against the propeller blades drives the electric generator coupled vertically to the upper end of the runner shaft.

TURGENEV, Ivan Sergeievitch
(1818–1883)

Russian novelist, born at Orel. His first important work was *A Sportsman's Sketches* (1852) dealing with country life and the plight of the Russian serfs. Incurring the displeasure of the Tsar he left Russia voluntarily in 1885, and apart from brief return visits, spent the rest of his life in Baden (Germany) and Paris. Of his novels the best known is *Fathers and Children* which he wrote in 1862.

TURKEY

A republic, part of which is in Europe but far the larger part is in Asia. The country covers an area of about 296,000 square miles, more than three times bigger than Great Britain, and has over 30 million inhabitants. The capital is Ankara but larger and more famous is Istanbul, or Constantinople, on the Bosphorus. Another important town and port is Izmir, or Smyrna. Turkey grows tobacco, sultanas and figs and makes Turkish delight and carpets. It has a number of minerals of which coal is the most important.

History :

The land now inhabited by the Turks is one of the oldest peopled regions of the world. Its ancient cities included Ephesus, Antioch and Tarsus. The Ottoman or Osmali Turks, however, did not arrive in what is now Turkey from Central Asia until the 14th century. Until then Constantinople had been the seat of the Byzantine Empire, the successor state to the Roman Empire. In the 14th century the Turks conquered a large part of the Balkan peninsula. By the 16th century under Suleiman the Magnificent, Belgrade and Rhodes were conquered, and the Hungarians defeated at the Battle of Mohacs. Soon afterwards Cairo, Algiers, Tripoli, Egypt, Syria, Mesopotamia were all brought within the OTTOMAN EMPIRE. It was in the 19th century that the Ottoman Empire began to decline rapidly, first Greece and then other Balkan countries gaining their

TURNER An example of one of his paintings in which he anticipates the French Impressionists.

independence. In the First World War Turkey sided with Germany, and this led to her losing the whole of what remained of her empire. It was soon after the war that the Turks found a great leader, KEMAL ATATURK, who made his country a modern republic and became its first president. Towards the close of the Second World War Turkey declared war on Germany and so became one of the allies. In 1960 a military uprising led to the execution of the Prime Minister and other Cabinet Ministers and the setting up of a new government.

TURNER, Joseph Mallord William
(1775–1851)
English landscape painter. Born in London, and the son of a barber. Studied at the Royal Academy of Arts, elected an Associate of the Royal Academy at 24, and made an Academician at 28. In 1808 he was appointed Professor of Perspective at the Academy. From 1802, when he painted the famous *Calais Pier*, he travelled extensively in Europe, making drawings and sketches from which he produced oil and water-colour paintings in his studio. Turner lived quietly all his life, despite his huge success. He was much criticized towards the end of his life owing to the increasingly abstract quality of his work. In his will he left over 19,000 water-colours, drawings and oils to the nation, and most of them are now in the National and Tate Galleries, London.

TURPIN, Richard (1706–1739)
Notorious highwayman. He was first a horse thief and later leader of a gang of criminals. Some popular writers have tried to picture Turpin as a romantic adventurer. This is not in keeping with historical fact which reveals him as a robber—and often very brutal—who was hanged.

TURTLES
Reptiles, closely related to the terrapins and tortoises, in fact, there is very little difference between them. They may be aquatic, semi-aquatic or terrestrial. In the aquatic species the limbs are paddle-shaped, in the terrestrial club-shaped, and in the semi-aquatic intermediate between the two. The body is short and stout, and is protected above (carapace) and below (plastron) by a bony framework, usually covered with horny shields into which head, neck, limbs and tail may be withdrawn. All these reptiles hatch their young from eggs. The marine turtles lay their eggs in the sand on the shore some distance from the sea, and the land tortoises bury theirs in the ground, but the aquatic tortoises lay theirs under water or in the mud on the banks. Most land species are vegetable eaters, while the aquatic ones are either mixed eaters or entirely flesh-eating.

TUSSAUD, Marie (1760–1850)
Founder of the famous waxwork exhibition in Baker Street, London, which she started in 1802. Marie Tussaud was of Swiss origin, and started her collection of wax heads while a prisoner during the French Revolution.

TWAIN, Mark (1835–1910)
American writer, born at Hannibal, Missouri. In his early days was a pilot on the Missouri and later a journalist. He travelled in Europe and the Middle East, and wrote one of his most popular stories from these experiences, *Innocents Abroad*. Twain's most famous novels are woven round his boyhood experiences, they are *The Adventures of Tom Sawyer* and *The Adventures of Huckleberry Finn*. Another popular—and often filmed—novel was *A Connecticut Yankee in King Arthur's Court*. He also wrote travel books. His real name was Samuel Langhorne Clemens.

TYLER, Wat (*d.* 1381)

Leader of the Peasants' Revolt of 1381 against Richard II. The revolt was provoked by the poll-tax and the oppressive conditions of serfdom. Over 100,000 peasants from Kent and Essex followed Tyler to London. They met the King at Smithfield where promises were made to the peasants but never fulfilled. Tyler himself was killed by the Lord Mayor of London. [*See* FEUDALISM.]

TYPEWRITER

A machine for writing mechanically consisting of a keyboard the keys of which, when depressed, actuate levers at whose ends are type characters. The paper moves round a platen or roller, and between it and the type face is an inked ribbon which transfers the image to the paper.

The idea of a mechanical writer dates back to the 18th century when Henry Mill patented such a device (1714), however, the machine was never made. Two of the earliest machines were the Progin (Xavier Progin was a Frenchman) which was patented in 1833 and the Thurber (Charles Thurber was an American) machine on which a patent was taken out in 1843. From that time great and many advances were made, in fact, are still going on, for office machinery is a very important part of modern commercial life. The latest designs are electrically operated.

TYPHOON

Eastern name for the tropical cyclone of the western Pacific which occurs in the autumn. The typhoon is the eastern equivalent of the West Indian hurricane.

Uu

UGANDA

A republic in Central Africa within the British Commonwealth. It is 94,000 square miles, rather bigger than Great Britain, and has a population of $6\frac{1}{2}$ million. The capital is Kampala. The chief exports are coffee, cotton and timber. Part of Lake Victoria is in Uganda and the Nile flows northwards from there to the Sudan and Egypt. The Owen's Falls dam, which was opened in 1954, not only supplies the industrial town of Jinja, near the dam, with hydro-electric power but it also supplies Kenya as well.

UKRAINE

Except for the Russian Federal Republic is the richest and most populated of the fifteen republics which make up the SOVIET UNION. It and Belorussia are treated differently from the other republics as they are allowed to become Members of the United Nations and other inter-government organizations as if they were independent States. The Ukraine is larger (232,000 square miles) than France and has about 42 million inhabitants. The capital is Kiev, other big cities being Kharkov and Odessa. The chief river is the Dnieper on which is a large electric-power dam.

ULTRASONIC SOUND

Sound waves with a very high frequency and short wavelength. They can be produced by any flat surface that vibrates backwards and

forwards in the direction in which the wave is sent. One method of generating ultrasonic sound is by applying an electric force across the faces of a thin slab of crystal (quartz or Rochelle salt). The effect of this is to change the thickness of the crystal. Now, if an alternating current is applied the thickness gets thicker and thinner in succession. If the slab is in contact with, say, water, then an ultrasonic wave is transmitted. This method is called the piezo-electric effect.

A narrow beam of ultrasonic sound has several uses, e.g. it can be sent downwards from a ship and then be reflected from the seabed or from any obstacle. The time it takes for this journey depends on how deep the reflecting obstacle is. Thus a diagram of the seabed can be made on which the depths of water are clearly shown. This is echo-sounding. It can be used also for the detection of wrecks and submarines.

ULTRA-VIOLET LIGHT

Narrow band of light just beyond the visible range at the violet end of the SPECTRUM and with a wavelength of less than 0·00004 cm. It affects a photographic plate, and causes vitamin D to be produced in the human skin. It will not pass through ordinary glass.

UNDSET, Sigrid (1882–1949)

Norwegian woman writer. She wrote two outstanding works, *Kristin Lavransdatter*, which dealt with life in medieval Norway, and *The Master of Hesviken*, a set of novels marked by deep religious feeling. She received the Nobel Prize for Literature in 1928.

UNESCO

Stands for United Nations Educational, Scientific, and Cultural Organization. It brings together educationists, scientists and artists of many kinds. One of its main objects is to help countries to fight illiteracy. Illiteracy and poverty go together and one way of ending poverty is to bring education and training to all people. Amongst other things UNESCO aids countries who need such help to provide teachers' training colleges and to send experts who can show how adults who have never been to school can best be taught to read and write and obtain other necessary knowledge, in the simplest and most practical way.

UNESCO publishes many books and pamphlets on cultural subjects and a periodical *Courier* which should have a place in every school library. The headquarters of UNESCO are in Paris.

UNION OF SOVIET SOCIALIST REPUBLICS, or Soviet Union

A union of fifteen republics of which the Russian Federal Republic is by far the largest. Soviet is a Russian word meaning Council. The country is the largest in the world being 8,599,806 square miles, and more than twice the size of the United States and the population nearly 227 million. The country stretches across Europe from the Polish border to the Pacific Ocean and so is partly in Europe and partly in Asia. About half the Soviet Union— that stretching from the Ural Mountains to the Bering Straits—is called Siberia but it is not itself one of the republics. After the Russian Federal Republic the most important republics are the UKRAINE and BELORUSSIA, both of which are Members of the United Nations. The other republics are: Uzbekistan, Kazakstan, Latvia, Kirghizia, Georgia, Azerbaidjan, Lithuania, Moldavia, Tadjikstan, Turkmenistan, Estonia and Armenia.

The capital of the Soviet Union is Moscow, the next most important city is Leningrad, which used to be called St. Petersburg. The most important river is the Volga. The highest mountain in Europe is Mt. Elbruz in the Caucasus. On the Black Sea is the Crimea, some of the historic places there being Sevastopol, Balaclava and Yalta. The Caspian Sea is a saltwater lake and is the largest lake in the world. In recent years the Soviet Union has dammed many of her rivers to produce hydro-electric power and this has created some of the largest artificial lakes in the world. The Soviet Union has many minerals and much oil and she is one of the chief wheat producing countries.

History:

For many centuries after the birth of Christ Russia was a land of mystery. It is now known that by the 5th century, tribes of Slav people began to settle on the great Russian plains. After some time they began to build cities, the biggest of which were Kiev and Novgorod. In the 9th century the North Slavs were conquered by Norsemen who founded a kingdom which they called the kingdom of the Russ, from which the people of Russia got their name. After a time differences between Slav and Norsemen disappeared and they became one people. It was only in the 10th century that the Russians accepted the Christian faith and became part of the Orthodox Church.

In the 13th century Russia was divided as the result of two invasions. The Lithuanians in the north succeeded in conquering a large part of Russia, whilst from the east the Mongols or Tartars set up a kingdom, called the Golden Order, in the south. Eventually the princes of Moscow were able, at the end of the 15th century, to free themselves of the Tartars, and the Prince of Moscow took the title of Tsar or Caesar. The greatest of the Russian tsars was Peter the Great who came to the throne in 1698 and made Russia a great European country. He established the Russian navy, and built St. Petersburg. But he was very ruthless and, like all the tsars, a despot.

During the reign of Nicholas I there occurred a war between Russia and Britain which is generally referred to as the Crimean war, (1854–1856). It was in this war that Florence NIGHTINGALE started the nursing service. At this time the vast majority of the Russian people were serfs but in the year 1861, under Alexander II, serfdom was abolished. The last of the Russian tsars was Nicholas II. It was during his reign that in 1903 a secret political party, called Bolshevik (from the Russian word meaning 'majority'), was formed with the object of introducing a communist form of society. In 1917, guided by LENIN, they were able to seize power and they have remained in control ever since.

In June 1941 Germany without warning attacked Russia and thus brought Russia into the war on the side of the Allies. They suffered stupendous losses in both people and materials. Soon after the war was over, however, serious differences occurred between Russia and the other allies, particularly on the question of the future of GERMANY.

In 1953 STALIN died and not long afterwards

laws which had made criticism of any kind almost impossible, were administered much less harshly. Meantime differences between the Soviet Union and CHINA began to develop and by 1965 these had become open and serious.

UNITED ARAB REPUBLIC, or Egypt
A republic in North Africa of 386,110 square miles, more than twice the size of France. The population is over 27 million, nearly all of whom are Arabic speaking. All are Moslems except for one million who belong to what is called the Coptic Church. The capital of Egypt is Cairo, other important cities being the port of Alexandria and Port Said at the entrance to the SUEZ CANAL. Egypt has hardly any rainfall and depends entirely on the River Nile, which has no tributaries, for its water. This means that the Egyptian people nearly all live near the river. It is because of the unusual situation as regards water that Egypt has placed so much importance on the building of the new Aswan dam across the Nile. The dam will increase the amount of Egypt's farm land by more than a quarter and will give her hydro-electric power. Egypt produces cotton and her minerals include coal, manganese and some oil. Egypt also earns money from many tourists who visit the country to see the monuments of ancient Egypt, of which the pyramids, the Valley of the Kings and the Sphinx are the best known.

History :
Egypt can trace back a continuous civilization to the year 4241 B.C. It was in this year that Egypt adopted the CALENDAR. There were about thirty dynasties, or lines of kings, between then and Alexander the Great who conquered Egypt. Egyptian culture reached a high peak during the IVth dynasty, 2900 B.C., which is the age of the great pyramids. After Alexander's conquest the family of a Greek ruler named Ptolemy reigned in Egypt for two centuries. Then about 58 B.C. Rome began to gain control. CLEOPATRA, daughter of Ptolemy XI, tried without success to win back power for Egypt. She was in fact, the last independent sovereign of Egypt until the 20th century. Egypt remained under Rome for several centuries. Then the country was conquered by the Arabs.

In 1798 Napoleon occupied Egypt but was defeated by Nelson outside Abukir in 1801. There then arose a remarkable Egyptian soldier named Mohamed Ali who was made pasha of Egypt by the Ottoman Sultan. He conquered the Sudan and introduced many reforms in Egypt. It was one of his descendants who was made king of Egypt as Fuad I, in 1922. One of Mohamed Ali's successors, Ismail Pasha,

sold his shares in the SUEZ CANAL to Britain. After the First World War Egypt, as the result of a treaty with Britain, was given her independence. The treaty still left the control of the Suez Canal to Britain and it arranged that Britain and Egypt should rule the SUDAN together.

Britain defended Egypt during the Second World War but when it was over Egypt demanded that all British troops should be withdrawn from the Canal Zone and in 1954 this was done. But in 1956, when Egypt took over the Canal, a more serious quarrel arose between the two countries. Meantime, Egypt, which had been a monarchy since it became independent, became a republic. From 1954 to 1971 the President had been Colonel Nasser.

UNITED KINGDOM
The kingdom which unites ENGLAND, WALES, SCOTLAND, Northern IRELAND and many islands around the coasts of Great Britain. When Britain speaks to other countries in the name of the United Kingdom she does so not only on behalf of these countries but also for her CROWN COLONIES and PROTECTORATES. Her Dominions speak for themselves.

UNITED NATIONS
The international organization which was set up after the Second World War to replace the LEAGUE OF NATIONS. It was set up by a treaty or charter, signed in San Francisco in 1945. By 1966 there were 117 States belonging to it, or nearly all the independent countries in the world. Every year, for about three months, representatives of all these Member States send delegates to the General Assembly of the United Nations. This Assembly decides what shall be the chief work of the organization during the next twelve months. The United Nations has a special body called the Security Council whose work is to try to settle disputes between nations and is made up of fifteen countries. Five of these—the United Kingdom, the United States, the Soviet Union, France and China—are permanent members but the others have to be elected by the General Assembly and serve for two years. The United Nations also has a World Court or INTERNATIONAL COURT OF JUSTICE. This meets at The Hague, Holland.

The United Nations does a great deal of work for the general benefit of mankind because much of this can only be done when nations agree to work together to carry it out. Some of this work is described under the following headings: UNICEF, UNESCO, UPU, WORLD BANK, WHO, FAO, ILO, IMCO, ICAO, ITU, IAEA.

UNICEF (United Nations Children's Fund)
Set up by the UNITED NATIONS in 1946 to provide food and other necessities for children who had suffered in the Second World War. Later it was decided it should help all suffering children in all parts of the world. Many millions of children have received milk or other essential foods with money provided by UNICEF. No fewer than 162 million children and young people have been provided with vaccine against tuberculosis and millions more have been treated for malaria and other diseases. In these tasks UNICEF works closely with the WORLD HEALTH ORGANIZATION. UNICEF get its money partly from Governments and partly from voluntary contributions, including money collected by school children all over the world.

UNITED STATES OF AMERICA
A republic and union of 50 states, as well as the Dist. of Columbia. All are on the mainland except Hawaii which is the smallest and most recent to join. All the other States are as large, or larger, than England and Wales. The largest is Alaska which is nearly three times bigger than France. The United States stretches across the continent from the Atlantic to the Pacific and from the Canadian border to Mexico. Its total area is about 3,548,970 square miles. The Great Lakes—Superior, Huron, Erie and Ontario—form part of the border with Canada. There are over 183 million inhabitants. Although the language they speak is English because the first settlers came from Britain, the ancestors of most of them come from many other European countries as well. There are also about nineteen million negroes whose ancestors were brought from Africa as slaves a century or two ago. There are also about half a million Red Indians.

The capital of the United States is Washington, District of Columbia, but the largest is New York, the second largest city in the world. The next largest American city is Chicago, on the shores of Lake Michigan. Other important cities include Los Angeles, on the Pacific coast, Philadelphia and Detroit. Cattle from the plains of the Middle West, where cowboys work, are brought to the great meat packing factories of Chicago. Beyond the Rocky Mountains is Hollywood, California, famous for its film studios.

The United States has two great rivers, the Mississippi and the Missouri, which join one another and the two together are longer than the Amazon. Many rivers have been harnessed for the production of electric power, particularly the Colorado (Hoover Dam) and the Tennessee (Tennessee Valley Authority).

The United States has many minerals. She produces more coal, iron, petroleum, lead and zinc than any other country. She also produces most cotton and tobacco.

The United States form of government has served as a pattern for a number of other countries, particularly in Latin America. It is a federal form of government which means that each State makes its own local laws. The laws for the whole country are made by CONGRESS which, like the British Parliament, has two Houses—Senate and House of Representatives. The President of the United States is not chosen by Congress but by the people of the United States in a special election, held every four years. As Head of State he does the kind of work the Queen does in Britain and also the work which a Prime Minister does.

History :
Many thousands of years ago people from Asia made their way across the Bering Straits to the continent which today we know as AMERICA. Their existence, and the land they had found, remained a secret until a few centuries ago. In the 11th century Vikings from Greenland chanced upon the northern coast of America, although it was not till recent times that it was known that the land they had reached was in fact a new continent. It was not, therefore, until 1492 that Christopher COLUMBUS, sailing in search of a new route to India, discovered America. He thought, however, that he had reached India which is the reason why to this day the original inhabitants are still called Indians. It was another navigator, named Amerigo VESPUCCI, who gave his name to the continent.

About sixty years after South America had been discovered, the English sailor, Sir Francis DRAKE, and after him, Sir Walter RALEIGH, made possible the colonization of North America. The first colony was in Virginia, and in 1620 a hundred men, women and children set out in the little sailing ship called the *Mayflower*, and founded a colony which they called New Plymouth. These settlers, who were Puritans, are referred to as the PILGRIM FATHERS.

By the year 1763 there were thirteen separate colonies along the eastern shore of North America. The people were developing a sense of nationhood and they resented paying taxes to Britain. The colonists found a great leader in George WASHINGTON, who succeeded in bringing together the thirteen Colonies to fight for their independence. On July 4th these United States, as they decided to call themselves, issued a Declaration of Independence, but it was not till 1781 that the war came to an end. Some years later, in 1787, these States

drew up a Constitution by which they became a single nation and George Washington became the first President.

In 1823, Russia, Austria and Prussia decided to help Spain get back some of her colonies in South America but the American President, James Monroe, issued a Statement warning European countries that if they interfered in American affairs the United States would regard it as an unfriendly act. On their part America would not interfere in European affairs. This Statement became known as the Monroe Doctrine.

At this time Americans were pressing into the interior of the continent, and more settlements were growing up into States and joining the Union. In 1860 war broke out between the southern States and the central government in the north. The President at this time was Abraham LINCOLN. One result of the Civil War, when it ended by victory for the north, was that the negro slaves were freed.

As America became richer and more powerful, and vast numbers of immigrants from all over Europe settled in the new land, she came to acquire more territory. As the result of war with Spain in 1898 the United States acquired the Philippines, which she held till after the Second World War when, freed of Japanese occupation, they became an independent State.

The United States joined the allies in the war against Germany in 1917 but although the President, at that time Woodrow WILSON, had much to do with the founding of the League of Nations, the United States decided not to become a member as her people were still guided by the Monroe Doctrine. It was the attack by Japan on Pearl Harbour in the American colony of Hawaii, in December 1941, that brought the United States into the Second World War on the side of the Allies. This time, when it was decided to set up the UNITED NATIONS to replace the LEAGUE OF NATIONS, the United States decided to join and to take a leading part in world affairs. Since the end of the Second World War the United States has been concerned in two wars—that in KOREA and that in VIETNAM.

UNIVERSAL POSTAL UNION
One of the oldest international organizations set up by the governments of the world. It was founded in 1874 and its headquarters are at Berne in Switzerland. Until the setting up of U.P.U. all countries used to compete with one another to get the the business of carrying letters from one country to another. This meant that the quickest way was usually the dearest. As the result of plans made at inter-

national conferences it was agreed that all countries would let letters go through their countries in the quickest and cheapest way possible. This meant that there could be a single price for a stamp on a letter going abroad whether the country was near or far. Although countries may increase the postage rates inside their own countries the charge for letters going abroad is changed only by agreement with the other countries belonging to U.P.U. Today almost all countries belong to U.P.U. In 1948 it was agreed that U.P.U. should come under the UNITED NATIONS.

UNIVERSITY
A college, or group of colleges, that has the right to give degrees to students.

The three oldest universities in Europe were founded in the 12th century. They were Paris, Bologna in Italy, and Oxford. Cambridge was founded in the 13th century.

Until 1832 when Durham University was founded the only English Universities were Oxford and Cambridge. Scotland, however, at this time had four, all founded in the 15th and 16th centuries. Today there are thirty-three universities in Britain, by far the largest being London with about 27,000 students. Most of the new universities, founded since the Second World War, consist of a single college and are non-residential. About 85 per cent of students at British Universities are able to obtain a maintenance grant from the State or County education authority.

Amongst the most famous Universities outside Britain are three in the United States—Harvard, Yale and Princeton, the oldest of these being Harvard which was founded in 1636. North Africa, however, can claim a University older even than those of Europe. For in the 10th century the MOORS built at Fez a Moslem University, called the Karouine, for the teaching of Moslem theology. The University is still carried on in much the same way as it was then.

UPPER VOLTA, or Voltaic Republic
An independent State in West Africa. It is about 100,000 square miles, larger than Great Britain, and has a population of over 4 million. It takes its name from the River Volta. The capital is Ouagadougou. Most of the people are farmers. The country's chief mineral is gold. Upper Volta was formerly a French colony and became independent in 1960.

URALS
Mountain range in the U.S.S.R. and extremely rich in minerals. Its highest peak, Navoda, is about 6,200 feet high. Some of the largest

industrial towns are situated in the Urals, one such is the town of Magnitogorsk. The range also forms the boundary between European and Asiatic Russia.

URANIUM

Chemical element of atomic number 92, and the last of the naturally occurring RADIO-ACTIVE ELEMENTS. Symbol U. Since the discovery of nuclear fission it has become one of the most important raw materials in the world and every country is making intense efforts to find deposits of this valuable mineral. [*See* NUCLEAR ENERGY.]

URBAN DISTRICT COUNCIL (U.D.C.)

The LOCAL AUTHORITY responsible for local government in small towns. It does much the same kind of work as a BOROUGH COUNCIL and its councillors are elected in the same way. It has, however, no mayor or aldermen and has at its head a Chairman. Like a Borough Council it comes under its County Council.

URUGUAY

A republic in South America. It is the smallest country in the continent, 72,170 square miles, not much larger than England and Wales. A river of the same name forms the boundary with Argentina. Its population is a little over $2\frac{1}{2}$ million, most of whom are of European descent. The capital is Montevideo. Most of the people are farmers and wool is the chief export.

UTOPIA

An ideal society where such evils as poverty do not exist. The subject of a work by Sir THOMAS MORE.

UTRILLO, Maurice (1883–1955)

French painter, born in Paris. His mother, Suzanne Valadon, was a talented artist and it was she who taught her son to paint. He led a wild life, drinking and drug-taking, and was many times confined in hospital. His paintings were mainly street scenes of his native Paris.

Vv

VACCINATION

Injections of anti-serums, as a means of protection against disease-producing BACTERIA. Only since the discoveries of PASTEUR and LISTER in the last century was the significance of bacterial infection fully realized. Some bacteria kill by invading the body and destroying the tissues, others by producing poisons, which are called toxins. Anti-toxins are produced by injecting the toxins into animals. These are used to neutralize the poison of the bacteria and to produce immunity against certain diseases. Diphtheria immunity is now produced by inoculation, without affecting the health of children.

VACUUM BRAKE

Type of brake used to bring railway trains to a halt or slow them down. The system consists of a cylinder located under the coach or van in which is a piston, the piston-rod of which is connected to a system of push rods and levers to the blocks suspended on both sides of each wheel. The cylinder is linked by means of pipes to a pump in the locomotive. When the air is pumped out of the system the brakes are off and when it re-enters they are applied to stop the train.

VACUUM FLASK

A double-walled container, the surfaces of which are silvered, and the enclosed space between the walls evacuated of air. The factors keeping a body hot are: 1, the silvered walls which allow little or no heat to radiate away, and 2, the vacuum which prevents loss of heat by conduction. By the same process it can be used to keep substances cold. It is sometimes referred to as a Dewar flask, after Sir James Dewar (1842–1923) who was the first to liquefy hydrogen.

VANBRUGH, Sir John (1664–1726)

English dramatist and architect, born in London. He studied architecture in France, where he was arrested as a spy and imprisoned in the Bastille. His first comedy *The Relapse* was produced in 1696. Other comedies followed, including *The Provoked Wife* and *The Confederacy*. They are marked by witty dialogue, a loose plot and great comic invention. In his later years he turned to architecture and designed Blenheim Palace and Castle Howard.

VANDALS

War-like Germanic or Teutonic peoples who between the 5th and 6th centuries invaded

Gaul, Spain and North Africa. They sacked Rome in A.D. 455. Their leader was Genseric. They were barbarians, and wantonly destroyed priceless treasures of literature and art. Ever since then the senseless destruction of beautiful things has been described as 'vandalism'.

VATICAN CITY, or Papal State

It is also called the Holy See and is the home of the Pope. The part of Rome in which the Vatican is, which includes St. Peter's, does not belong to Italy but is a tiny State under the Pope. Although there are only about a thousand inhabitants the Pope can send ambassadors, called nuncios, to foreign countries. The General Council of Roman Catholic leaders from all over the world called to the Vatican by the late Pope John in 1962 was only the second in history to be held in the Vatican.

VAUGHAN WILLIAMS, Ralph (1872–1958)

English composer, born at Down Ampney, Gloucestershire. His music draws its inspiration from four sources: love of nature (*Pastoral Symphony*), English folk-songs (many of which he has arranged, including *Greensleeves*), the music of the Elizabethan composers (*Fantasia on a theme of Thomas Tallis*) and the Bible (the masque for dancing, *Job*). He has written eight symphonies, several operas, including *The Pilgrim's Progress* and *Sir John in Love* (the latter based on Shakespeare's *Merry Wives of Windsor*), and many lovely songs, such as *Linden Lea* and *Silent Noon*. He also wrote the music for the film *Scott of the Antarctic*.

VEGA CARPIO, Lope Felix de (1562–1635)

Spanish dramatist and poet. He served in the Armada against England, continuing to write even during his time at sea. Later he became an officer of the INQUISITION, and devoted almost the whole of his large income to charities and the Church. The *Dragontea* celebrates the death of DRAKE and *Corona Tragica* is an epic about Mary Stuart. But his poetry and ballad writing was little more than competent and though his plays are exciting and full of complicated turns in the plot, the characters do not stand out. About 440 plays remain, though this is only a part of his original output. Lope has had considerable influence on European literature, above all in France.

VELÁZQUEZ, Diego Rodriguez de Silva y (1599–1660)

Spain's most celebrated painter, born at Seville. After an apprenticeship in Seville, he went to Madrid in 1622, where he became court painter within two years, and was given a studio in the Royal Palace. He produced many fine portraits of the King (Philip IV) and other royal personages. On a visit to Italy in 1630, Velázquez painted his well-known figure compositions *The Forge of Vulcan* and *Joseph's Coat*. Between 1631 and 1649, he painted the famous *Surrender of Breda*. Between 1650 and 1660 Velázquez painted the portraits of Queen Mariana and the Infanta Margarita, and the portrait of King Philip as an old man and *Venus With a Mirror*, now in the National Gallery, London. Velázquez was a master of colour values, and his portraits have never been equalled. Most of them are in Madrid.

VENEZUELA

A republic in the north of South America. It is about four times bigger (352,050 square miles) than Great Britain but has only a little over 8 million inhabitants. Most of the people are Spanish-speaking but in the forest regions there are some Indian tribes. The capital is Caracas and the chief river the Orinoco. Along the shores of Lake Maracaibo are some of the richest oil wells in the world and oil is Venezuela's chief export.

VERDI, Giuseppe (1813–1901)

Italian composer and one of the most outstanding opera composers of the 19th century. His operas are very dramatic and highly musical. Amongst his best-known works are *Rigoletto* (1851), *Il Trovatore* (1853), *Aida* (1871) and *La Forza del Destino* (1862). He was devoted to Shakespeare and composed three operas based on his plays; *Macbeth* (1847), *Otello* (1887) and *Falstaff* (1893). He wrote a magnificent *Requiem Mass*.

VERLAINE, Paul (1844–1896)

French poet. Formed a school of poetry, called the 'Symbolists', which had a great influence on modern poetry. He led a very wild life, even attempting to murder his friend, the poet RIMBAUD.

VERMEER, Jan (1632–1675)

Dutch painter, born at Delft. Neglected in his lifetime, Vermeer is today regarded as one of the greatest of the Dutch masters, and an unsurpassed colourist. Most of his subjects were paintings of interiors and courtyards, and were painted with the utmost care.

VERNE, Jules (1828–1905)

French writer, born at Nantes. He wrote extravagant adventure stories, which have been translated into many languages and are uni-

South America

PACIFIC OCEAN

ATLANTIC OCEAN

Branco

RIO BRANCO

AMAPA

Negro

Japura

Amazon

Amazon

Belem

PARA

Fortaleza

Manaus

Maranon

Jurua

ACRE

AMAZONAS

Madeira

Tapajos

Xingu

Araguaia

Tocantins

S. Francisco

Huascaran 22,211 ▲

MONTANA

Madre de Dios

BRAZIL

BAHIA

Lima

Cuzco

MATO GROSSO

Plateau of
Mato Grosso

Campo

Salvador

A P E R U S

Lake
Titicaca

Illampu 21,490 ▲

La Paz

Santa Cruz

BOLIVIA

Brasilia

Brazil Plateau
MINAS GERAIS

Belo Horizonte

Pilcomayo

PARAGUAY

Paraguay

Parana

SAO PAULO

CHILE

Llullaillaco 22,150 ▲

CHACO

Asuncion

Sao Paulo

Rio de Janeiro

A N D E S

Tucuman

Uruguay

RIO GRANDE
DO SUL

Porto Alegre

Aconagua 23,080 ▲

Cordoba

Santa Fe

Valparaiso

Mendoza

Rosario

URUGUAY

Santiago

Buenos Aires

Montevideo

ARGENTINA

Bahia Blanca

Negro

ATLANTIC OCEAN

CHONOS
ARCHIPELAGO

PATAGONIA

Port Stanley

FALKLAND
ISLANDS

TIERRA
DEL FUEGO

CAPE HORN

versally popular; he is rightly called one of the first science-fiction writers. Among the best known are *Round the World in Eighty Days* and *Twenty Thousand Leagues Under the Sea*. He also wrote a few plays, of which *Michael Strogoff* was the only one to be widely popular.

VERONESE, Paolo (1528–1588)
Italian painter, born at Verona. After settling in Venice in 1553, his genius soon became apparent. About 1560 he produced the *Supper at Emmaus*, the first of the many religious feast scenes he was to paint. Among these feast subjects was the famous *Marriage at Cana*. In 1573 the Inquisition objected to certain of the details in one of his feast paintings, and Veronese was called before them and told to alter the picture. His real name was Paolo Cagliari.

VERROCCHIO, Andrea del (1435–1488)
Italian sculptor, painter, silversmith and engineer, born in Florence. His most famous painting is *The Baptism of Christ at Florence*, and his best pieces of sculpture the bronze group *Incredulity of St. Thomas* and the bronze equestrian statue of Bartolomeo in Venice. He was a teacher of LEONARDO DA VINCI.

VERSAILLES, Treaty of (1919)
A treaty between the Allies and Germany after the First World War. The conditions of the Treaty were discussed and decided at the Paris Peace Conference (1918–1919). The principal

VERMEER A typical example of this artist's concern for the details of an interior.

countries concerned were Britain, France, United States and Italy. The Treaty imposed REPARATIONS on Germany, re-distributed many of its territories: for example, the Saar under French control and the former German colonies under LEAGUE OF NATIONS mandate, and limited German armaments.

When HITLER came to power he repudiated most of the conditions of the Treaty.

VERSE
Used with the following different meanings: (a) strictly it means a line of poetry with a rhythmical succession of sounds. But you will not often hear the words used so absolutely strictly, unless you are in a Latin lesson. (b) more often, verse means a number of such rhythmical lines together, and then it means much the same thing as stanza. (c) very loosely, verse is used to mean poetry. 'He writes verse' means 'he writes poetry'; or 'his verse' can mean 'his poems'. (d) when used in connection with the BIBLE a verse means one of the sections into which a chapter of the Bible is divided.

VERTEBRATES
All animals having a backbone which is made up of separate bones called vertebrae. They comprise one of the two main groups into which the animal kingdom is divided, the other being the INVERTEBRATES. We are more familiar with vertebrates because their members are larger and more obvious, and include the four-footed beasts, birds and fish, that serve us as pets or sources of food. The main way in which the vertebrates differ from the invertebrates is in having an internal skeleton made up of a framework of bone, or in the case of some fishes such as sharks, of cartilage. There is usually an outer skeleton also, of scales, feathers or hair.

The vertebrates are often referred to as the higher animals, not only because they have larger and more complicated bodies, but because they rank higher in the animal scale in the development of their nervous system. They are also unlike the invertebrates in having a true brain. This is an enlarged part at the forward end of the spinal cord, the main nerve cord of the body. From both brain and spinal cord other branch nerves run out to serve the other parts of the body.

In their methods of movement we find another marked difference between the vertebrates and invertebrates. The latter are usually found in water, except for many insects and most spiders, and, if they move at all, progress by a swimming action which involves movements of the whole body, or else have numerous swimming legs, as in lobsters and shrimps.

VICTORIA and children. A painting by Landseer, friend and painter to the Queen.

Insects have six legs and spiders eight. Land vertebrates have two pairs of main legs, and fishes have two pairs of main fins, the pectoral and the pelvic fins, and it is believed that the transformation of these fins into walking legs in some fish-ancestor led to the EVOLUTION of the four-legged land vertebrates. As usual, of course, there are exceptions, as in snakes and slow-worms which have lost all four limbs, whales which have lost the hind-limbs, and birds and bats in which the fore-limbs are converted into wings.

VESALIUS, Andreas (1514–1564)
Belgian physician, and founder of the science of anatomy. Studied at Louvain and Paris, and at the early age of 22 became a professor at Padua. His most important work was *On the Fabric of the Human Body*. He later became court physician to Emperor Charles V.

VESPUCCI, Amerigo (1454–1512)
Italian discoverer. Made several voyages to the New World and discovered the Amazon (1499). America was named after him.

VESUVIUS
Volcano overlooking the Bay of Naples, and one of the few still active in Europe. The ancient Roman towns of Pompeii and Herculaneum were destroyed by the eruption of Vesuvius. It is nearly 3,900 feet high.

VICTORIA, Queen (1819–1901)
Daughter of Edward, fourth son of George III. She was crowned in 1837 and had the longest reign in English history. She married Prince Albert of Saxe-Coburg to whom she was completely devoted and by whom she had nine children. His early death was a great blow to her and she mourned him three years. Victoria's reign saw the rise of Britain's wealth and imperial power.

VIETNAM
Formerly part of French Indo-China and covers the three countries of Tonkin, Annam and Cochin-China. It and Cambodia and Laos became independent only after war with France, a war that lasted seven years. It ended in 1954 and resulted in great changes in what had been Indo-China. Because the northern part of Vietnam had come under Communist control, it was decided at a conference held in Geneva in 1954 that Vietnam should be divided into two zones—North and South—until elections had been held to settle the country's future. These elections have not taken place so the country has remained divided with two separate governments. South Vietnam is 66,280 square miles, larger than England and Wales, and has a population of about 16 million. The capital is Saigon. North Vietnam is 63,000 square miles, a little larger than the South, and has a population of 17 million. The capital is Hanoi.

VIKINGS
Sea-raiders from Scandinavia (*c.* A.D. 800–1000) who not only attacked Britain and northern Europe, but penetrated the Mediterranean as far as Constantinople and made a settlement in what is now Russia. Westwards they settled in Greenland and one of them, Leif Ericsson, probably reached America. One of their ships which lay buried for hundreds of years can now be seen in a museum in Norway. It has room for fifteen oarsmen on each side and is steered by an oar at the stern.

VILLA, Francisco (*c.* 1877–1923)
Mexican revolutionary leader whose military conquests did much to bring about the victory of Francisco Indalecio Madero, the democratic president of MEXICO. After the death of Madero he became something of an outlaw, being particularly bitter to American citizens resident in Mexico. He was assassinated.

VILLA-LOBOS, Heitor (1887–1959)
Brazilian composer, born at Rio de Janeiro. Brazil's greatest composer, who has created a great volume of music of all types. Most of his music is strongly flavoured with Brazilian folk tunes.

VILLON, François (*c.* 1431–*c.* 1463)
French poet, born of poor parents in Paris. Attended the University of Paris. He then became leader of a party of robbers and thieves, and was sentenced to death for killing a priest in a street brawl (1455). But he was reprieved, only to spend the rest of his days in alternating between prison sentences and a reckless life.

As a poet his masterpiece is *Le Grand Testament* (1461) written at the age of 30.

VIOLA [*See* INSTRUMENTS OF THE ORCHESTRA]

VIOLA DA GAMBA [*See* VIOLS]

VIOLIN [*See* INSTRUMENTS OF THE ORCHESTRA]

VIOLS
Musical instruments of the 16th and 17th centuries, similar to the modern violin family which replaced them but having a softer sound. There were several sizes, from the small treble-viol to the larger viola da gamba and bass-viol. The smaller ones were held on the knees while they were played, the larger ones on the floor, like the modern cello and double bass. A set of them was called a 'chest of viols', and an orchestra a 'consort of viols'.

VIRGIL (Full name Publius Vergilius Maro) (70–19 B.C.)
Roman poet, born near Mantua, he was educated at Cremona, Milan and Naples, studying rhetoric and philosophy. Through influential friends he was relieved of financial cares and was able to devote himself to poetry. His works comprise the *Eclogues*, a series of short and graceful pastoral poems on the Greek model, the *Georgics*, a poetical work on agriculture, and the *Aeneid*, the greatest of all. It is an epic poem in twelve books describing the wanderings of Aeneas (the legendary founder of Rome) after the fall of Troy. It glorifies the Roman Empire of Virgil's day and became the Roman national epic.

VIRGINAL
A musical instrument in use in the 16th century. It was similar to the harpsichord, which replaced it in the reign of Charles II, but was smaller and had only one keyboard.

VIRGIN ISLANDS
A group of islands in the West Indies. The larger part belongs to the United States and has about 27,000 inhabitants, the others are part of the British West Indies and have a little over 7,000 inhabitants.

VIRUS
Most elemental form of life. Viruses have only been discovered in recent years and are still being extensively studied. They seem to occupy an intermediate position between living and non-living matter. All viruses are smaller than the smallest BACTERIA and pass through the finest filters. With the introduction of the ELECTRON-MICROSCOPE it has been possible to

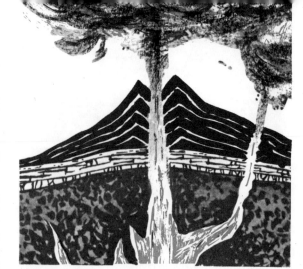

VOLCANO Section through a volcano showing how a conical crater is built up.

examine certain types. Among the diseases known to be caused by these agents are influenza, infantile paralysis, common colds, measles, foot and mouth disease, and yellow fever.

VITAMINS
Food substances of widely varying composition, small quantities of which are essential for health. More than a dozen vitamins are known, and some are man-made on a commercial scale. The main vitamins are: A, found in fish, milk, butter and vegetables, essential to growth of children. B, found in yeast, eggs and some meats, essential for digestion, appetite and growth. C, found in oranges, tomatoes and raw cabbage, prevents scurvy. D, found in fish and animal livers, prevents rickets. K, found in lettuce and wheat germs, essential to clotting of the blood.

VIVALDI, Antonio (*c*. 1680–1743)
Italian musician, born in Venice. Composed a great volume of instrumental music. Was highly thought of by J. S. BACH.

VOLCANO
Conical mountain consisting of ashes, scoria and lava ejected from the interior of the earth through a vent in the crust. The vent opens in a crater at the summit, but the precise form of the mountain varies with the nature of the ejected matter, lavas rich in iron and magnesium being more fluid than those consisting largely of silica. The lava is highly charged with steam and gases, which are often released with explosive violence. Lava containing bubbles of gas cools to form pumice. A volcano which is not active may be dormant (if further eruptions are expected) or extinct (if activity is not likely to recur).

VOLTA, Alessandro, Conte (1745–1827)

Italian scientist who did a great deal of research into the nature of electricity, and invented the ELECTROPHORUS and the voltaic cell. The electrical unit volt was named in his honour.

VOLTAIRE (1694–1778)

French writer, born in Paris. Educated by the Jesuits. He assumed the name Arouet de Voltaire and then studied law for a while but soon turned to literature. His witty satires on persons in authority earned him several terms of imprisonment. At different times he lived in England (1726–1729), at a country house in Champagne (1734–1749) and at Berlin with Frederick the Great, King of Prussia (1750–1753). He finally settled down at Ferney, in France but close to Geneva. There he became the wealthiest and most popular man of letters of the 18th century. His literary output was enormous, and includes several works of history, epic poems, fifty plays, novels, volumes of philosophy and political pamphlets. But he is best-known today for his vast correspondence with all the most distinguished men of his time, and his novel *Candide*.

VOLTMETER

Instrument used for the measurement of electric voltage. The instrument usually consists of a moving coil ammeter connected in series with a high resistance. The resistance of the meter being fixed the current passing through it will be directly proportional to the voltage at the points where it is connected and so the instrument can be calibrated in volts.

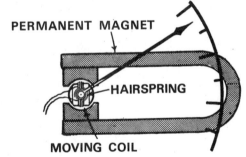

PERMANENT MAGNET

HAIRSPRING

MOVING COIL

VOLTMETER Main parts of a simple voltmeter.

VOLUNTARY SOCIETIES

Groups of people who have joined together for some special object. British people have brought about many reforms by such societies, and have done much to bring help to those in need. There are today thousands of such societies many of them with branches in different parts of the country.

One of the oldest of these societies that still carries on its good work is the Royal Humane Society which was founded in 1774. You may see their boatmen by lakes and waterways in or near London. Every year the society gives medals to hundreds of people, including boys and girls, who have saved the lives of others. Another of these early societies still doing valuable work is the Royal National Lifeboat Institution. [*See* LIFEBOATS.] A society in which young people who keep pets are specially interested is the Royal Society for the Prevention of Cruelty to Animals. The society employs great numbers of inspectors who make enquiries if people report that some person is treating an animal cruelly or neglecting it. They also have clinics where sick animals can be treated. Then there is the National Society for the Prevention of Cruelty to Children which also employs inspectors. Their work is to see that children are not neglected or ill treated.

There are a number of societies which care for orphan children, of which the best known is Dr. Barnardo's Homes. There are special societies for the care and welfare of the handicapped, such as the Royal National Institute for the Blind and the Royal National Institute for the Deaf.

Many of the national organizations concerned with welfare work are linked together through the National Council of Social Service. It was this Council which set up Citizen's Advice Bureaux of which there are now about 430 in Britain. Citizens who want answers to their problems, or who want to know what voluntary organization might be willing to help them can get advice through their Citizen's Advice Bureau.

There are a number of voluntary organizations specially for women, of which the largest are the Women's Institutes, of which there are 8,700 in the villages of Britain.

There are many societies which have been started by Christian people. They are amongst the oldest voluntary societies still doing the work for which they were founded. The first of these is the Society for Promoting Christian Knowledge, founded in 1698. Then came the great missionary societies which between them have sent thousands of missionaries to non-Christian lands. The first was the Society for the Propagation of the Gospel in Foreign Parts (S.P.G.) which was founded in 1701. It was followed by the Baptist Missionary Society in 1792, and the London Missionary Society in 1795, which later sent David LIVINGSTONE to Africa, and then by a number of other societies, including the British and Foreign Bible Society which has translated the Bible into more than 800 languages and distributed many millions of copies.

Ww

WAGNER, Richard (1813–1883)
German opera-composer, born at Leipzig. His step-father being an actor and playwright, he took an early interest in the theatre, and at 29 became conductor at the Dresden Opera House. Here he achieved fame with the operas *Rienzi*, *The Flying Dutchman*, *Tannhauser* and *Lohengrin*. He took part in the revolution of 1848, however, and had to leave Germany for Switzerland, a price being placed on his head. He then began to write in an entirely new style, starting with the great work entitled *The Ring of the Nibelung*; this consists of four operas in one, and tells the legends of Siegfried and the old Norse Gods. The 19-year-old King of Bavaria, Ludwig II, supported him in this venture, and a special theatre was built at Bayreuth for the production of *The Ring* and Wagner's later operas, *The Mastersingers*, *Tristan and Isolde* and *Parsifal*.

WALES
A Principality in the west of Great Britain that is part of the United Kingdom. It is, at its greatest width, 92 miles and at its greatest length 136 miles. There are about $2\frac{1}{2}$ million inhabitants. The Welsh people and their language are called Celtic and belong to the same group as the Scots and Irish. Wales is a hill country and has one of the highest peaks in Great Britain—Mount Snowdon. In the south there are important coal mines and iron foundries. The capital is Cardiff.
History:
At the time of the Roman Invasion the Celtic tribes who lived in Wales took part in wars against the invaders. However, not much is known about the history of Wales until the arrival of the Anglo-Saxons in Britain when there were fierce border wars. King Offa is said to have built Offa's Dyke to mark the boundary between Mercia and Wales. When the Normans invaded England they found it impossible to conquer Wales, and as a result William the Conqueror gave earldoms to some of his followers on condition that they protected his kingdom from the Welsh. There was constant fighting between England and Wales, but in 1282 Edward I succeeded in defeating the Welsh prince, Llewelyn ap Griffith, and conquering the whole of Wales. Edward I gave his baby son to the Welsh as their prince, and since that time the eldest son of the sovereign has always been created Prince of Wales.

In 1400 Owen Glendower led a revolt against Henry IV, but it achieved nothing. In 1536 an Act of Union joined England and Wales, and since that time the histories of the two countries have been closely connected. Wales elects 36 M.P.s to the House of Commons and the British Government appoints a Minister for Welsh Affairs. Since the end of the Second World War Monmouthshire has been added to the Principality.

WALLACE, Edgar (1875–1932)
British novelist. As a boy was a newspaper seller, and later became a journalist in Britain and South Africa; his experiences in Africa provided the background for such stories as *Sanders of the River*. He wrote many detective and racing stories (*The Four Just Men* and *The Council of Justice*). He was also successful as a playwright.

WALL STREET
The name of the street in New York where the United States Stock Exchange has its building. The first settlement built in Manhattan in the 17th century was on this site. A wall was built around it to protect it from the Indians. Hence the name of the street.

WALPOLE, Horace, Fourth Earl of Orford (1717–1797)
Youngest son of Robert Walpole, he entered Parliament in 1741, but we remember him mainly for his letters, in which he describes the political and social life of the period. Strawberry Hill, his house near Twickenham, he had redesigned in a gothic style (1753–1776), and this heralded the end of the classical style of architecture and was a powerful influence on the Victorian architects.

WALPOLE, Robert, First Earl of Orford (1676–1745)
English statesman, born at Houghton. Had a dramatic career in politics; at one time was placed in the Tower for corruption. He was Prime Minister for over twenty years. Walpole managed to clear up the financial confusion caused by the collapse of the South Sea scheme —known as the South Sea Bubble—and to protect the reputations of the important people, including King George I, who had been involved in it. This earned him the title of 'Skreen-Master General'. He reformed the

WALRUS A young specimen. This species is found only in the Arctic Ocean.

system of import duties, and tried to increase the revenue from the excise, but was restrained by Parliament. Nevertheless, his measures did much to improve British trade and to put the country on a sound economic footing.

WALRUS

Although it resembles the seal in general form and use of the hind feet, it differs in that it has no external ear (only a hole) nearly naked skin and, more particularly, large downwardly projecting tusks in male and female. The walrus is confined to the waste and ice floes of the Arctic Ocean and seldom ventures out into open sea. It is a bottom-feeder, i.e., lives mainly on clams and other shell fish, which it tears off rocks or digs from the mud with its tusks.

WALTON, Izaak (1593–1683)

English writer and angler, born at Stafford. He was apprenticed to a London ironmonger, and after a successful business career retired to Staffordshire (c. 1644). He spent his leisure in writing biographies of his friends, but he is best remembered for *The Compleat Angler* (1653), the first English nature book. It is devoted to the art of angling and in it three characters, Piscator (the Angler), Venator (the Huntsman), and Auceps (the Falconer) talk about the country. The style is simple and the humour gentle.

WALTON, Sir William (1902—)

English composer, born at Oldham. He made his name with *Façade*, a suite of witty music written to accompany the recital of some of EDITH SITWELL'S poems through a megaphone, and later used for a ballet. He has written a symphony, concertos for violin and viola, the march *Crown Imperial* (for the coronation of King George VI), music for the films *Henry V*, *Richard III* and *Hamlet*, an oratorio *Belshazzar's Feast*, and an opera *Troilus and Cressida*.

WAPITI

Member of the deer family and a typical stag. It is bigger than the red deer, and found in North America and Central Asia.

WASHINGTON, George (1732–1799)

American statesman of English descent, born at Bridges Creek, Virginia. He became commander-in-chief of the American army, and after being instrumental in the founding of the Republic, became the first President of the UNITED STATES in 1789. He was re-elected for a second term of office, but the third time refused to stand for election. He is unfairly represented by legend as being unable to tell a lie.

WATER

Chemical compound made up of hydrogen and oxygen (H_2O). Water is essential to life and is widely distributed. It occurs in different states, liquid, solid as ice or in vapour form. Sea water contains many chemical substances; such as, magnesium and sodium chloride (27%). So-called 'hard' water contains soluble salts of magnesium and calcium (bicarbonates), chlorides, and sulphates.

WATER POLO

Aquatic game not unlike soccer in many ways, except that it is played in a swimming bath and the ball is propelled with the hand. The game is much shorter—4 periods of 5 minutes each actual play with 2 minutes interval between periods, the teams changing ends each period.

The field of play or pool has to be between 20 to 30 yards in length and 8 to 20 yards in width. These dimensions allow a field of play to be marked out across the deep end of a reasonable-sized swimming bath, which is presumably why they have been chosen. The markings are quite simple, as you can see from the diagram. Sometimes a centre-mark is used. This is a ring of cork on which the ball can be placed, and it is anchored to the bottom exactly half-way across the half-distance line.

Teams consist of 7 players each, and they are generally distinguished in the water by means of coloured caps—dark-blue for one team, white for the other. Each team has 4 reserves who may be substituted. Goalkeepers always wear red caps. An important point is that caps have to be fastened by means of chinstraps; losing a cap during play means

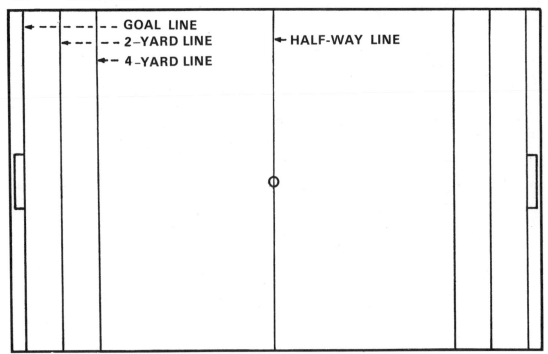

GOAL LINE
2-YARD LINE
4-YARD LINE
HALF-WAY LINE

WATER POLO can be played in a pool 20 to 30 yards long and 8 to 20 yards wide.

losing one's team-identity.

The ball itself is similar to a soccer ball—leather-covered, waterproof, and 27 to 28 inches in circumference. It must not be greased in any way, and it has no lacing, a spiral valve being used for inflating it.

And lastly, there is a referee in charge of the game, and his decision on everything connected with the game is absolutely final. In addition there are 2 goal judges, one for each end, and a time-keeper.

It has already been said that the ball is propelled with the hand—one hand only (except in the case of the goalkeeper, who may use both hands). The ball may be pushed along the surface of the water (dribbled) or thrown (passed or shot for goal), but only with the flat of the hand, never with the fist. Also during play a player *must* swim; he is not permitted when in shallow water to walk along the bottom or use his feet against the bottom to shoot himself high out of the water.

There are just one or two other simple rules to remember. For example, a player is not allowed to splash water into an opponent's face, tackle any opponent who is not in possession of the ball, tackle in such a way as to get hold of an opponent or pull him under the water or kick him, or hold the ball under the water when tackled.

For the 'kick-off', players swim to their own ends of the bath, where they remain about one yard apart on their goal-lines and clear of their goals. If there is a centre-ring, the ball is placed in it beforehand; if not the referee throws the ball into the centre of the field of play. Then he blows his whistle, and the players swim as hard as they can after it, the intention of each team being to propel it into the opponents' goal.

While play is going on, should there be any reason for stoppage, such as the ball going out of bounds or a foul being committed, the referee blows his whistle.

Under previous rules, every player had to stop swimming and stay exactly where he was, but now players can continue swimming in order to get into good position for the restart.

When the ball goes into touch or across the goal-lines, the rules about returning it to play are the same as in SOCCER. There are free-throws from goal, from a corner, or from the place where the ball went over a side-line. In a free-throw, a player of the team designated simply picks up the ball with one hand and throws it to another player (one of his own team, naturally) or towards the goal in the case of a penalty-throw.

The goalkeeper is the only one who is allowed to stand (if he can reach the bottom); he may do so to defend his goal. But in all other respects he is treated as an ordinary player, except that he must not throw the ball beyond the half-distance line.

After a goal is scored players take up positions anywhere within their respective halves of the field of play, and the side that had the goal scored against them start the play, as in soccer.

WATT

Practical unit of electric power. It is a measure of the amount of energy expended per second by an electric current of one ampere flowing under a pressure of one volt. One watt equals one volt multiplied by one amp. One horse-power is equivalent to 746 watts.

WATT, James (1736–1819)

Scottish inventor, born at Greenock. Worked for a time as an instrument maker at Glasgow University. He improved and extended New-comen's steam engine which was very wasteful of power. He was not interested in its applica-tion as a means for driving locomotives. [*See* STEAM ENGINE.]

WATTEAU, Antoine (1684–1721)

French painter and engraver, born at Valen-ciennes. In 1702 he went to Paris, where he lived in poverty until he came to the attention of the painter Claude Gillot. Although he died at the age of 37, he exercised a profound in-fluence on his contemporaries and successors. His small paintings of people in pastoral settings make him one of the greatest of all colourists.

WATTS, George Frederic (1817–1904)

English painter and sculptor, born in London. He studied art at the Royal Academy and in Italy. Among his early works was the large fresco *Justice* in Lincoln's Inn, London. He is best known for his allegorical paintings and portraits, most of which are in the Tate Gallery, London. Many of his portraits are in the National Portrait Gallery, London. His sculptural memorial, *Physical Energy*, to Cecil Rhodes, is at World's View in Southern Rhodesia.

WAUGH, Evelyn Arthur St. John (1903–1965)

British author, educated at Oxford. He was converted to Roman Catholicism. Such novels as *Vile Bodies* and *Decline and Fall* are satirical studies of the social life of the inter-war period. Later his novels became more serious, the two best known being *Brideshead Revisited* and *The Loved One*.

WAVELL, Archibald Percival, First Earl (1883–1950)

British soldier, born at Colchester. Served in the South African War and First World War, but won fame in the Second World War for his defeat of the Italians in Cyrenaica. He was later Viceroy of India (1943–1947). A man of wide cultural interests, he compiled an anthol-ogy of poetry, *Other Men's Flowers*.

WEASEL

One of the smallest flesh-eating animals to be found in Europe, but not in Ireland. It is brown in colour with a stripe of white down the middle of the belly. Found in hedgerows and about farms. It is a danger to poultry, but it feeds mainly on field mice and other small creatures.

WEATHER FORECASTING

Weather study is concerned above all things with the ATMOSPHERE. At sea-level the air exerts a pressure of $14\frac{3}{4}$ lb. per square foot, such pressure of course diminishing with in-creasing height. It is measured either by an aneroid BAROMETER, or by a standard mercurial barometer. The lines on a weather map, 'isobars', connect places where for the time being the pressures are equal, after conversion to sea-level value, so as to give uniformity. On such a line the pressure is represented in inches and decimal fractions thereof: also, in most cases, in 'millibars' (mb.), of which $33·9 = 1$ inch, these decimal units being more conveni-ent for scientific purposes.

Inspection of a typical weather map will show that isobars are often arranged in con-centric curves, and here we can distinguish between two types: (a) a 'cyclone', with a low pressure area in the middle, a 'trough' as it were, and (b) an 'anticyclone', with a central region of high pressure.

The typical weather associated with cyclones and anticyclones was worked out in the latter part of last century. The former move quickly along certain paths, usually reaching this country from the west or south-west, and this is associated with the familiar wireless an-nouncement 'further outlook unsettled', while anticyclones are more deliberate and commonly mean a spell of fair weather.

The direction and force of the WIND are definitely related to the arrangement of the isobars. There is a spiral movement in both cyclone and anticyclone, anticlockwise in the former and clockwise in the latter in the north-ern hemisphere, while the converse is true for the southern. The primary cause of such movement is the rotation of the earth on its axis. If, in the northern hemisphere, you stand with your back to the wind, the pressure, as recorded by the barometer, is lower on your left. The force of the wind is greater when the isobars are close together, as in a cyclone, and

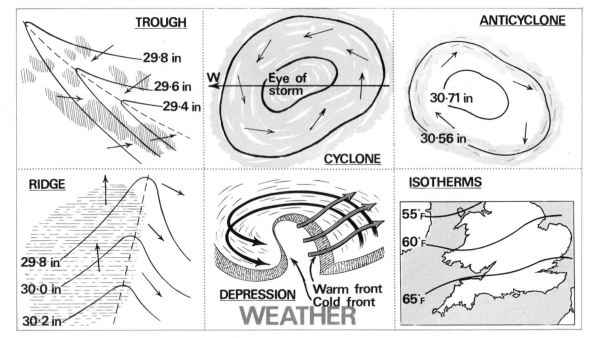

on the map the arrows indicating the direction are proportionate in strength to the number of 'feathers' on their shafts. One feather means 2 miles an hour (a light air), while 4 indicate 15 miles an hour (moderate breeze), and so on, as laid down in the 'Beaufort Scale'.

Weather observers are much concerned with moisture of the air, in various states. It condenses into fog, mist, dew and hoar-frost on the ground: rain, hail, and snow, in the sky. Details are given in a report. Rain is measured in a gauge, and the amount is put down, for a period of 24 hours, in inches or millimetres (1 in. = 25·39 mm.), being the depth of the layer it would form on a non-absorbent surface. [See CLOUDS.]

The hours of sunshine are reckoned automatically by a sunshine recorder. A method has also been devised of calculating the amount received of the invisible ultra-violet rays, to which so much importance is now attached. Thermometers of various kinds are used for temperature determinations. It may be added that some of the meteorological instruments, besides the one used for calculating the amount of sunshine, are self-recording. [See RADIO-SONDE.]

WEBB, Sidney James (1859–1947) and
Beatrice (née Potter) (1858–1943)
English social reformers, historians and economists. Sidney joined the Fabian Society, for which he wrote a number of tracts, and became a reforming member of the L.C.C. Later he became a Labour M.P., and eventually Colon-

ial Secretary (1930–1931). He accepted a peerage in 1929, but his wife refused to adopt any title. Beatrice's interest in social problems began when she was a rent-collector. Together with her husband, she wrote the *History of Trade Unionism, Industrial Democracy, English Local Government* and many other books, and devoted her life to the Labour movement. Together the Webbs began *The New Statesman,* and helped found the London School of Economics.

WEBER, Carl Maria Friedrich Ernst von (1786–1826)
German composer, born near Lübeck. Although he composed a wide variety of music his fame rests on his operas, particularly *Der Freischütz, Euryanthe* and *Oberon.* One of his most popular orchestral works was *Invitation to the Waltz.*

WEBSTER, John (c. 1580–1625)
English dramatist about whom very little is known. His fame rests on his two plays *The White Devil* and *The Duchess of Malfi,* both of which are full of horror and strong passions.

WEDGWOOD, Josiah (1730–1795)
English potter, and founder of the Wedgwood potteries. Born at Burslem. Of his designs the blue and white are the most famous although red, black, green and other colours were used with white in traditional Wedgwood designs. Josiah Wedgwood was also a pioneer in the development of social and civic services.

WEIGHTS AND MEASURES
(BRITISH AND METRIC)

AVOIRDUPOIS
7000 grams	1 pound
16 drams	1 ounce (oz.)
16 ounces	1 pound (lb.)
14 pounds	1 stone (st.)
28 pounds	1 quarter (qr.)
4 quarters	1 hundredweight (cwt.)
20 hundredweights	1 ton (tn.)

BRITISH LINEAR MEASURE
12 inches (in.)	1 foot (ft.)
3 feet	1 yard (yd.)
2 yards	1 fathom (f.)
$5\frac{1}{2}$ yards	1 pole (rod or perch)
4 poles	1 chain
10 chains	1 furlong (fur.)
8 furlongs	1 mile (m.)
	(1,760 yds.)

SQUARE MEASURE
144 square inches	1 square foot
9 square feet	1 square yard
$30\frac{1}{4}$ square yards	1 square pole
40 square poles	1 rood
4 roods	1 acre
640 acres	1 sq. mile

CUBIC MEASURE
1,728 cubic inches	1 cubic foot
26 cubic feet	1 cubic yard
$24\frac{3}{4}$—25 cubic feet	1 solid perch
	(mason's measure)

CONVERSION TABLE—BRITISH TO METRIC
1 inch	25·399 millimetres
1 foot	30·479 centimetres
1 yard	0·914 metre
1 chain	20·1164 metres
1 furlong	201·164 metres
1 mile	1·609 kilometres
1 square foot	9·29 sq. decimetres
1 acre	0·405 hectare
1 square mile	2·599 sq. kilometres

IMPERIAL DRY MEASURE
2 glasses	1 noggin (5 oz.)
4 noggins	1 pint (1 lb. 4 oz.)
2 pints	1 quart (2 lb. 8 oz.)
4 quarts	1 gallon (10 lb.)
2 gallons	1 peck (20 lb.)
4 pecks	1 bushel (80 lb.)
8 bushels	1 quarter (640 lb.)

METRIC MEASURE
1 metre	
1 decametre	10 metres
1 hectometre	100 metres
1 kilometre	1,000 metres
1 myriametre	10,000 metres
1 decimetre	$\frac{1}{10}$th of a metre
1 centimetre	$\frac{1}{100}$th of a metre
1 millimetre	$\frac{1}{1000}$th of a metre

METRIC SQUARE MEASURE
1 are	100 square metres
1 decare	10 ares
1 hectare	100 ares
1 deciare	$\frac{1}{10}$th of an are
1 centiare	$\frac{1}{100}$th of an are

METRIC CUBIC MEASURE
1 litre	
1 decalitre	10 litres
1 hectolitre	100 litres
1 decilitre	$\frac{1}{10}$th of a litre
1 centilitre	$\frac{1}{100}$th of a litre
1 millilitre	$\frac{1}{1000}$th of a litre

CONVERSION TABLE—BRITISH TO METRIC
1 grain	0·0648 gramme
1 ounce	28·33 grammes
1 pound (avoird.)	454 grammes
1 pound (troy)	373 grammes
1 hundredweight	50·8 kilos
1 ton	1,016 kilos
1 pint	0·568 litre
1 gallon	4·546 litres
1 peck	9·087 litres
1 quarter	2·908 hectolitres

METRIC WEIGHT
1 gramme	
1 decagramme	10 grammes
1 hectogramme	100 grammes
1 kilogramme	1,000 grammes
1 myriagramme	10,000 grammes
1 decigramme	$\frac{1}{10}$th of a gramme
1 centigramme	$\frac{1}{100}$th of a gramme
1 milligramme	$\frac{1}{1000}$th of a gramme

TROY WEIGHT
24 grains	1 pennyweight (dwt.)
20 pennyweights	1 ounce
12 ounces	1 pound

APOTHECARIES' WEIGHT
20 grains	1 scruple (scr.)
3 scruples	1 dram (dr.)
8 drams	1 ounce (oz.)
12 ounces	1 pound (lb.)

CONVERSION TABLES— METRIC TO BRITISH
1 millimetre	0·0394 inch
1 centimetre	0·3937 inch
1 decimetre	3·937 inches
1 metre	39·3701 inches
1 kilometre	0·6214 mile
1 centiare	1·196 square yards
1 are	3·954 square poles
1 hectare	2·471 acres
1 decigramme	1·543 grains
1 gramme	15·432 grains
1 hectogramme	3·527 ounces
1 kilogramme	2·2046 pounds
1 litre	1·76 pints

Note: 1 metre is the length of a platinum-iridium bar kept at a temperature of the melting point of ice, and housed in the International Bureau of Weights and Measures, Paris. 1 gramme is a thousandth part of the International Prototype Kilogramme, and was formerly the weight of a cubic centimetre of water at 4 deg. C. 1 litre is the volume of one kilogramme of water at 4 deg. C.

WELLINGTON, Arthur Wellesley, First Duke of (1769–1852)

British soldier and politician, born in Ireland. He entered the Army as a young man in 1787. He first saw active service in India where he showed such military skill that when he returned to England in 1805 he received a knighthood. Wellington's most famous campaign was against the French in the Peninsular War. In the years 1809 until 1814 he secured a number of distinguished victories which finally drove the French from Spain and Portugal, at the same time sapping Napoleon's strength elsewhere. It was at the Battle of Waterloo (1815) that Wellington, aided by the Prussian Marshal Blücher, finally defeated Napoleon. As Tory Prime Minister (1828–1830) Wellington was responsible for the Bill of Catholic Emancipation.

WELLS, Herbert George (1866–1946)

English writer, born at Bromley. In the main he was self-educated, but took a science degree at London University. Bad health made him unable to teach, so he turned to writing. His scientific fantasies like *The War of the Worlds* and *Time Machine* won great success. Later he preferred to write about politics and the importance of changing our society into a saner one. At the end of the First World War he thought people would see their mistakes more clearly if they understood world history, and wrote alone a full-length account of the story of mankind called the *Outline of History*. In his later years he grew angry for, as he thought, man was doing nothing to avoid the old mistakes, and there is a bitter, sarcastic tone in his late novels.

WESLEY, John (1703–1791)

English preacher, and founder of the Methodist Church. Born at Epworth. While at Oxford he and his brother Charles formed a group who were sarcastically called 'Methodists', because of the methodical way in which they pursued their religious studies. He travelled widely as an evangelist giving, it is said, some 40,000 sermons. His brother Charles was also an ardent evangelist, but is more well known for the large volume of hymns, two of the best known being, *Jesus Lover of my Soul* and *Hark the Herald Angels Sing*.

WEST INDIES

Groups of islands in the Atlantic which stretch between the coast of Florida, U.S.A. and Venezuela. They separate the Gulf of Mexico and the Caribbean Sea from the Atlantic. There are three main groups—the Greater Antilles, in which are CUBA, Hispaniola [*see* HAITI and DOMINICAN REPUBLIC], JAMAICA and PUERTO RICO; the BAHAMAS; and thirdly, the Lesser Antilles which include TRINIDAD and BARBADOS and also the Leeward and Windward Islands. Apart from Trinidad and Jamaica, which are independent Members of the British Commonwealth, there are a number of other islands that together are referred to as the British West Indies. In 1966 it was agreed that these smaller British West Indian islands should be given new rights to manage their own home affairs. The West Indies were discovered by Christopher COLUMBUS in 1492. He gave them their name thinking he had found the western route to India.

WEST IRIAN

The name which the Indonesians give to their part of the island of NEW GUINEA which is in the west part of the island. It is more than half the size of France and has a population of three-quarters of a million. West Irian formerly belonged to the Netherlands but came under Indonesian rule in 1962.

WESTMINSTER ABBEY

Traditionally the first church was built between A.D. 605–610 by Sebert, King of the East Saxons. Being built on the west side of the City of London it was called 'West Minster'. However, Edward the Confessor is generally regarded as the founder of the church. Like all great historic buildings, the Abbey has undergone many changes during its long history. In the main the present building is the work of Henry III who pulled down the eastern part of the Confessor's church. The western portions were added at various periods between 1340 and 1483. The north and west cloisters, and the Jerusalem Chamber were built in the reign of Edward III. The chapel at the eastern end is famous for its magnificent fan vaulting which was added by Henry VII. The west towers were added in 1738–1739. Many minor alterations have been made as a result of keeping the fabric in repair.

WEST POINT

Site of the United States Military Academy, and situated on the west bank of the Hudson, New York. It was founded in 1802 for the training of officers of the American army.

WEYDEN, Roger van der (1399–1464)

Flemish painter, born at Tournai. He settled in Brussels, where he became official city painter. After a period in Italy he returned to Brussels, where he produced such outstanding works as his *Last Judgment*, *Nativity* and *Adoration of the Magi*.

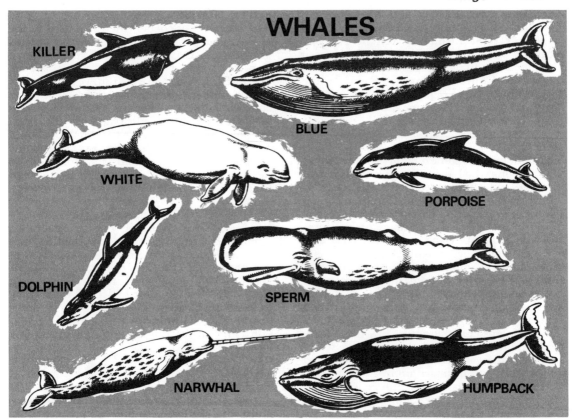

WHALES

KILLER

BLUE

WHITE

PORPOISE

DOLPHIN

SPERM

NARWHAL

HUMPBACK

WHALE

A marine mammal and not a fish. The shape is fish-like and all trace of hind limbs has disappeared; the fore-foot is converted into a flipper. There are no external ears, only a hole, the eyes are minute and the nostrils are situated on top of the head. Whales swim by means of up and down strokes of the powerful tail, the flippers and fin acting as balancers. Whales are classified on the basis of their way of eating: Baleen whales (small marine life and plankton) and toothed whales (seals, birds, large fishes, etc.).

WHEATSTONE, Sir Charles (1802–1875)

English scientist, born near Gloucester. He carried out important work on the telegraph system and other branches of electrical engineering, but is especially remembered for the Wheatstone bridge which he invented for the measurement of electrical resistance, (see diagram).

WHIGS

The two opposing parties in Parliament under Charles II were named 'Whigs' and 'Tories'. The Whig party contained those who had supported Cromwell in the Civil War. Its

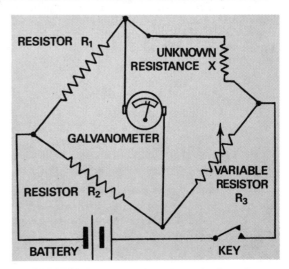

WHEATSTONE bridge is based on the fact that no current flows between points of the same voltage and that when the same current flows through two resistances the voltage drop is proportional to their resistances. The bridge is balanced by the variable resistance and the unknown

$$X = \frac{R_1}{R_2} \times R_3$$

sympathies were Puritan and its nickname, short for 'Whiggamore', had first been applied, insultingly, to Scottish Presbyterians. Its exact meaning is uncertain. 'Tory' was an Irish word for a bandit which came to be applied to the royalist Church of England Party. In the 19th century the Whigs became the Liberal Party and the Tories became the Conservative Party. [See POLITICAL PARTIES.]

WHIP

The name given to some members of the House of Commons who have to see that members of their particular parties who are M.P.s are in their places in the House of Commons when a vote has to be taken. The Chief Whip for the Government party is also Parliamentary Secretary to the TREASURY and is paid a salary. The five assistant Government Whips, who are called Lords Commissioners, are also paid. Whips for the Opposition parties are not paid.

The notices sent by Whips telling Members when they may have to vote are also called Whips. If it is very important that Members should be present, the notice has three lines scored under it and is called a three-line whip. Less important notices have two lines scored under them and ordinary notices one line.

If an M.P. disregards the wishes and opinions of his fellow M.P.s in the same party they may consider that he should no longer be a member of their party. To make it clear he is no longer a member he will be told that the party's whip will be withdrawn from him. He would then have to decide whether to be an independent M.P. or to 'cross the floor of the House' and join the M.P.s who belong to the party in opposition to his own.

WHISTLER, James Abbott McNeill (1834–1903)

American artist, born at Lowell, Massachusetts. In 1855 he went to Paris, and later settled in London. There he achieved fame as a wit and eccentric, before his artistic talents were recognised. An outstanding colourist, Whistler was himself influenced by Japanese prints and the works of VELÁZQUEZ. He painted some famous portraits, including one of his mother and one of Thomas Carlyle, and more than 400 brilliant etchings. He also produced lithographs, water colours and pastels, and wrote brilliant essays, including *The Gentle Art of Making Enemies*.

WHITEFIELD, George (1714–1770)

English preacher, born at Gloucester. Originally a follower of WESLEY, and like him was a powerful orator. Whitefield travelled extensively in Britain and America. Later led the group known as Calvinistic Methodists.

WHITE HOUSE

The official residence of the Presidents of the U.S.A., and located in Pennsylvania Avenue, Washington, D.C.

WHITMAN, Walt (1819–1892)

American poet, born at Long Island. He studied, and was influenced by, the classic poets, but his own originality of spirit gave his work great freshness and vitality. His first book of poetry, *Leaves of Grass* (published in 1855), attracted considerable attention and is still thought to be his greatest work. For almost the last twenty years of his life Whitman was an invalid.

WHITTINGTON, Richard (1358–1423)

Lord Mayor of London, born at Pauntley, Gloucestershire. He came to London and made a fortune as a mercer. He was Mayor of London 1397–1398, 1406–1407, 1419–1420. He also lent large sums to Henry IV and Henry V. When he died he left all his fortune to London charities. The legend about him is not mentioned until 1605 and lacks all foundation. The tale of the cat is found in the folk lore of many countries.

WHITTLE, Sir Frank (1907—)

English inventor, born at Leamington. He entered the Royal Air Force as a boy apprentice and won a cadetship to Cranwell College. As a cadet he was interested in jet propulsion and in 1930 he lodged his patent. In 1936 he was placed on the special duties list and the following year his first jet engine ran. By 1941 it was ready to power the Gloster E 2839. The invention of jet-propulsion revolutionized aircraft design, and made possible longer flights and faster speeds. [See TURBINE ENGINE.]

WHITWORTH, Sir Joseph, First Baronet (1803–1887)

English mechanical engineer and inventor, born at Stockport. His inventions include a knitting machine (1835) and a street-sweeping machine. He also made experiments to improve the accuracy of rifles (1857), and he improved molten steel for guns by fluid compression (1869). He established the Whitworth scholarships for the training of mechanical engineers.

WILBERFORCE, William (1759–1833)

English statesman, born at Hull. His life was dedicated to the abolition of slavery, and with the aid of such important political friends as Pitt, Fox and Burke was able to see his fight realized. The bill abolishing the slave trade was passed in 1807, and an act freeing slaves in the British Empire was passed in 1833, the year of his death.

WILDE, Oscar Fingall O'Flahertie Wills (1854–1900)

British writer, born at Dublin. His career was abruptly cut short by a libel case, as a result of which he suffered two years' imprisonment at Reading, and then retired to France where he died in poverty and obscurity. For the stage he wrote four dazzling comedies, including *The Importance of being Earnest* and *Lady Windermere's Fan*. In prose he wrote essays and a novel, and the best known of his poems is *The Ballad of Reading Gaol*.

WILLIAM II, Kaiser (1859–1941)

Third German Emperor and ninth King of Prussia. Born the eldest son of the Kaiser Frederick III, on whose death he ascended the throne (1888). His first important action was to dismiss his Chancellor BISMARCK. His nationalist public speeches did a great deal to alarm Europe about German aims and he became identified with the spirit of German militarism. Thus, although he had little to do with the conduct of the First World War he was forced by the Allies to abdicate on the German defeat in 1918. He spent the rest of his life in exile at Doorn, Holland.

WILLIAMS, Tennessee, properly Thomas Lanier (1914—)

American playwright. The backgrounds of his plays often show the underprivileged, corrupt and seamy side of American life, and his interest in the abnormal comes over in his characterizations. His plays include *A Streetcar Named Desire*, *Cat on a Hot Tin Roof*, and *Suddenly, Last Summer*. Most of his works have been filmed.

WILSON CLOUD CHAMBER

Apparatus for the detection and measurement of the tracks of small particles, especially fundamental particles invisible in microscope or electron microscope. The principle of it is that a perfectly dust-free atmosphere is brought to a super-saturated state and then any ionizing particle produces ions along its path and these form the nuclei of small water drops, which are visible. It was invented by Dr. C. T. R. Wilson. It is an indispensable tool of nuclear physics. A more recently developed device known as the *bubble chamber* is even more effective for the detection of fast moving sub-atomic particles.

WILSON, James Harold (1916——)

British Labour statesman, educated at Huddersfield, in Cheshire and at Oxford, where he became a lecturer in economics. He entered Parliament in 1945, and later became President

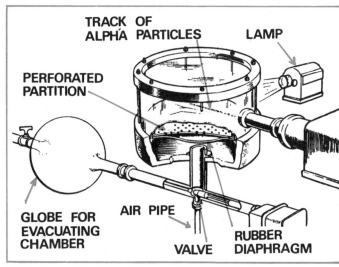

WILSON CLOUD CHAMBER Schematic drawing of a chamber for photographing atomic particles.

of the Board of Trade, the youngest man ever to hold the post, resigning with Aneurin BEVAN in 1951. He became the chief Opposition spokesman on Economics in the late 1950s, and succeeded Hugh Gaitskell on his death in 1963 as leader of the party. He became Prime Minister in 1964, and his party was again returned in 1966. His main concerns have been with economic stability and industrial productivity at home, and with the breakaway Government of RHODESIA.

WILSON, Richard (1714–1782)

English landscape painter. After studying in London he became known as a portrait painter, but later turned to landscapes. The exhibition of his *Niobe* in 1760 brought him praise, and he was elected a member of the Royal Academy. Wilson's work was not appreciated until after his death, and he became embittered by poverty.

WILSON, Thomas Woodrow (1856–1924)

American politician, born in Virginia. After a period as lawyer he entered on an academic career and became President of Princeton University (1902–1911). Already known in politics as Democratic governor of New Jersey, he was elected President of the United States 1912. When the First World War broke out Wilson at first tried to keep America neutral, but in 1917 was compelled to join the Allies because of the German anti-submarine war. In 1918 he proclaimed his famous Fourteen Points as the basis for peace. The following year he represented the U.S.A. at the Versailles Peace Conference, but of all his proposals he only succeeded in securing the foundation of the League of Nations, although the United States refused to join. Defeated in his attempt at re-election as President, Wilson died a broken man.

WIND
Air current occurring naturally and flowing parallel with the surface of the ground. Winds are caused by local differences of atmospheric pressure, and are classified according to their velocity. Permanent differences in atmospheric pressure occur at different latitudes, and these give rise to the permanent winds, which include the Trade Winds, the Roaring Forties and the Westerly Variables. In addition, there are seasonal winds, which depend upon seasonal changes, and include monsoons and land and sea breeze. Local winds, which are due to the special geographical characteristics of a region, include the Fohn and Sirocco.

WINDSOR, Duke of, Edward Albert Christian George Andrew Patrick David (1894———)
The eldest son of King George V and Queen Mary. He succeeded to the throne in January 1936 and abdicated in December of the same year, before being crowned, in order to be able to marry Mrs. Wallis Simpson, an American divorcee, such a marriage not being permissible for a king. The marriage took place in June 1937. Since his abdication the Duke of Windsor has lived mainly in France and America, and was Governor of the Bahamas from 1940–1945. He was succeeded on the throne by his brother, the late King George VI.

WITAN
Meant 'wise men' and was the Council of the Anglo-Saxon kings. It was not elected, but consisted of nobles or churchmen whom the king summoned to give him advice. The Witan also confirmed the appointment of the successor designated by the previous king.

WODEHOUSE, Pelham Grenville (1881———)
English humorous novelist. Bertie Wooster and his pompous valet, Jeeves, are his famed creations. His books include *The Inimitable Jeeves* and *The Code of the Woosters*.

WOLF
Belongs to the same family (Canidae) as dogs and foxes. At one time it was widely distributed over the northern hemisphere. Wolves frequently hunt in packs, and when pressed by hunger will attack man.

WOLFE, James (1727–1759)
English soldier, born at Westerham. Served in several campaigns, but won immortal fame by defeating the French on the Plains of Abraham and thus securing CANADA (New France) for England. He was killed during the battle, as was the opposing French general, Montcalm.

WOLF-FERRARI, Ermanno (1876–1948)
German-Italian composer, born in Venice. Of his many operas the most successful were *The Secret of Suzanne* and *Jewels of the Madonna*.

WOLSEY, Thomas (1475–1530)
English churchman and statesman. Son of an

WOLF The species of wolf shown here is found in Europe, Asia and North Africa.

Ipswich butcher. He was educated at Oxford and then entered the Church. Under Henry VII and Henry VIII his rise to power was rapid. In 1515 he was appointed Lord Chancellor and virtually acted as Henry VIII's Prime Minister and Ambassador. His aim was to make England the arbiter of Europe by balancing power between France and the Holy Roman Empire. But he fell from grace in 1529 when he was unable to compel the Pope to annul Henry's marriage with Katherine of Aragon so that he might marry Anne Boleyn. The next year he was charged with treason but died on the way to meet his accusers.

WOLVERINE
Also known as 'glutton', is related to the martens, although it has the general appearance of a small bear. It inhabits the forested districts of the Northern Hemisphere and is mainly terrestrial. It is one of the most cunning of animals, and is disliked by trappers whose traps a wolverine will rob for food.

WOMBAT
In appearance this animal resembles a large guinea-pig. Its teeth and mouth are formed for gnawing in much the same way as rats and other rodents. It is nocturnal, lying up in deep burrows which it digs by day, and feeding on grasses, roots and bark at nights. It is found in eastern Australia.

WOOD, Sir Henry Joseph (1869–1944)
English conductor, born in London. At the early age of 25 was the first conductor of the Queen's Hall Promenade Concerts, a position he occupied for fifty years. He did much to improve and broaden musical taste and encourage young composers. He composed a few works under the name 'Klenovsky'.

WOOL
Material obtained from domestic sheep and widely used in the manufacture of cloth. It has for long been a leading industry in Britain—a token of this is the 'WOOLSACK' on which the Lord Chancellor sits in the House of Lords. As a material it is strong, elastic and retains warmth as it is a bad conductor of heat.

After the fleece has been sheared from the sheep it is cleaned to remove dirt and greasy impurities after which it is gilled or carded, that is, the cleaned wool is run between rollers which are studded with pins which drag the fibres apart. The carding machine automatically oils the wool, so that the fibres will come free without breaking. The next stage is done in a combing machine which separates the fibres in long (used for worsted goods) and short (used for woollen goods) lengths. From the combing machine the wool emerges as a thick rope which is twisted sufficiently to hold it together. It is then spun in a spinning frame or mule and automatically wound on bobbins. The yarn, as it is now called, is finally treated with moisture and dyed before being woven.

WOOLF, Virginia (1882–1941)
English novelist. In novels like *Mrs. Dalloway* she broke away from the conventional narrative novel, and experimented in the realm of impressionistic writing, reflecting and penetrating the thoughts of her characters rather than describing their actions. She played a considerable part in the development of the modern novel.

WOOLSACK
The seat of the LORD CHANCELLOR in the House of Lords. He presides over its discussions from this seat. The Woolsack faces the throne where the Queen sits when she opens Parliament. Six hundred years ago when the Lord Chancellor was first given a sack of wool for his seat in the House of Lords, England was an agricultural country and most of the wealth of the nation came from wool. So it was a symbol of the nation's wealth.

WOOLWORTH, Frank Winfield (1852–1919)
American trader who started the 'five-and-ten-cent stores' which grew to the world-famous chain of stores of that name. In this he was so successful that at his death he was estimated to be one of the richest men in the world.

WORDSWORTH, William (1770–1850)
English poet, born at Cockermouth. After studying at Cambridge, he spent a period in France, where he witnessed the outbreak of the Revolution. Later he returned to England, and, with the help of a legacy from a friend, was able to settle down to writing poetry. He has told his own story in the autobiographical poem *The Prelude*, and there stressed the importance of growing up among mountains. His sense of the permanent things in nature helped him to write poetry with a simplicity and solemnity which set all poets on a new path of exploration. COLERIDGE helped him in this development, while he in return gave help to Coleridge. He lived long and consistently went on writing.

WORK
Effect of expending energy, especially in causing motion in a body. The unit of work is the

foot-pound, which is the work done in lifting 1 lb. a distance of 1 foot against gravity. The absolute unit (i.e., independent of variations in gravity) is the foot-poundal, which equals the work done by a force of 1 poundal in moving 1 lb. a distance of 1 foot. The corresponding units in the C.G.S. system are the gramme-centimetre and centimetre-dyne or erg, respectively.

WORLD BANK

Also known as the International Bank for Reconstruction and Development it is an agency of the UNITED NATIONS. It helps the poorer countries to develop their natural resources by lending them money. For instance, it has helped countries to produce electricity by building great dams on rivers where hydro-electric power can be generated. It has also helped countries with loans to build new roads and railways and other big and very expensive projects. Usually such development means that the country is able to earn a good deal of extra money after a few years and so can repay the loan. The headquarters of the World Bank are in Washington, D.C.

WORLD GEOGRAPHY [*See* next page]

WORLD HEALTH ORGANIZATION (WHO)

An agency of the UNITED NATIONS. It helps nations to fight disease on a world-wide scale. In the case of diseases which particularly affect children and young people it works closely with UNICEF. For instance in a single year, with such help, 32 million were tested for tuberculosis in 28 countries and 11 million of these were vaccinated. Another big campaign has been undertaken by the two organisations against malaria and as a result a number of countries no longer have the disease and in others the problem is much less serious. WHO has established April 7th as World Health Day. The headquarters are in Geneva.

WORLD WARS

First World War. On the 28th June 1914 Archduke Francis Ferdinand, heir to the Austro-Hungarian Imperial throne, was assassinated by a Serbian at Sarajevo. This incident set off a train of events which culminated in the start of the First World War. Britain entered the war against Germany on the 4th August 1914, and for the reason that Germany invaded Belgium, a neutral country that Britain was pledged to help in the event of attack. For three years fierce battles were fought in Flanders; those of the Marne and Ypres being the biggest. In Eastern Europe the Germans attacked

Russia. The terrible losses suffered by the Russians was one of the chief factors leading to the Bolshevik Revolution, and the Soviets concluding a peace with Germany. The United States joined Britain and her Allies in April 1917. In the Middle East Germany was aided by Turkey, but, under the leadership of T. E. LAWRENCE, the Arabs revolted against Turkish rule; this action led to the break-up of the Turkish Empire. Important naval actions were fought at Heligoland (1914), Jutland (1916) and Zeebrugge (1918). The armistice was signed on the 11th November 1918, and the Peace Treaty at Versailles in January 1920.

Second World War arose as the result of the war-like plans of Adolf HITLER to conquer first the principal countries of Europe, and later the world. Hitler showed his intentions by annexing Austria in 1938 and Czechoslovakia in April 1939. On September 1st 1939 the German Army marched into Poland, and on September 3rd Britain and France declared war on Germany. In April 1940 Germany occupied Denmark and Norway, and in May overran France, Holland and Belgium. It was during this period that the British Army was evacuated from the beaches of Dunkirk. Preliminary to invading Britain Hitler let loose the German Air Force which was decisively beaten by the R.A.F. in the Battle of Britain, fought over the Southern Counties. Meantime the Germans were attacking the Balkan countries, and Italy (who allied herself with Germany in 1940) was engaged in North Africa and Greece. In June 1941 Hitler launched a full-scale attack against Russia, so bringing that country to the side of the Allies. The United States did not enter the war until attacked by the Japanese at Pearl Harbour. Britain was given help, however, in terms of arms and supplies. The first major Allied victory was at El Alamein where in October 1942 General MONTGOMERY defeated General ROMMEL. The Allies pressed forward through North Africa and into Italy. On the Eastern Front Russia won a great battle at Stalingrad, and from there rolled the German Army back to Berlin. In June 1944 the Allies under General EISENHOWER landed in Normandy and defeated the Germans. On the 7th May Germany surrendered unconditionally. After atomic bombs had been dropped on Hiroshima and Nagasaki Japan surrendered on August 14th 1945.

WREN, Sir Christopher (1632–1723)

English architect, born at East Knoyle. Like many men of his period, Wren's interests were wide and productive. He was an inventor, a Member of Parliament, a mathematician of note, an agriculturalist, etc. In London he was given the opportunity to design 52 churches including St. Paul's Cathedral, following the great fire of 1666.

WRIGHT, Frank Lloyd (1869–1959)
American architect, born at Richland Centre, Wisconsin. America's most outstanding architect, and one whose influence has extended beyond his own shores. One of his most important buildings is the Imperial Hotel, Tokyo. It survived the severe earthquake of 1923.

WRIGHT, Orville (1871–1948) **and Wilbur** (1867–1912)
American pioneers of flying. Started life as bicycle mechanics, but became interested in flying and built their own aeroplane, *Kitty Hawk*, which made its first controlled flight on 17th December 1903.

WYCHERLEY, William (*c.* 1640–1716)
English dramatist of the Restoration. His two most famous plays are *The Country Wife* and the *Plain Dealer*.

WYCLIFFE, John (*c.* 1324–1384)
English churchman, born at Hipswell, Yorkshire. After leaving Oxford he was ordained and became one of the most influential churchmen of his time. He felt very strongly against the Roman Catholic Church, and made many enemies among its leaders. He was one of the forerunners of the Reformation, and had it not been for the protection of John of Gaunt, would have received more drastic treatment than he did. He was a scholar, and one of his greatest works and labours was the translation of the BIBLE into English, the first such translation to be undertaken.

WORLD GEOGRAPHY

Table 1   Oceans and Seas

Sea or Ocean	Area in square miles	Greatest Depth in feet (approx.)	Sea or Ocean	Area in square miles	Greatest Depth in feet (approx.)
Antarctic Ocean		28,150	Gulf of Alaska	2,000	
Arctic Ocean	5,440,000	17,850	Gulf of Bothnia	61,833	380
Atlantic Ocean	31,530,000	27,500	Gulf of California	62,500	6,000
Indian Ocean	28,350,000	26,400	Gulf of Finland	20,000	350
Pacific Ocean	64,000,000	36,200	Gulf of Mexico	700,000	12,700
Adriatic Sea	52,000	4,035	Gulf of St. Lawrence	100,000	450
Aegean Sea	69,000	6,000	Gulf of Siam	135,000	
Andaman Sea	300,000	10,000	Gulf of Tonkin	450,000	
Arabian Sea	150,000	17,000	Hudson Bay	475,000	845
Baffin Bay	183,800	9,000	Irish Sea	17,000	840
Baltic Sea	160,000	1,520	Java Sea	120,000	
Banda Sea	285,000	21,000	Kara Sea	108,000	650
Barents Sea	520,000	600	Laptev Sea	210,000	
Bass Strait	30,000	230	Ligurian Sea	800,000	9,300
Bay of Bengal	459,000	3,000	Mediterranean	900,000	14,695
Bay of Biscay	53,000	1,200	Mozambique Channel	500,000	10,000
Beaufort Sea	180,000	10,000	North Sea	221,000	2,165
Bering Sea	878,000	13,420	Persian Gulf	90,000	300
Black Sea	159,000	7,360	Red Sea	170,000	3,840
Caribbean Sea	750,000	22,790	Sea of Okhotsk	580,000	11,140
Celebes Sea	69,280		South China Sea	895,000	15,300
Coral Sea	1,021,000		Tasman Sea	900,000	
English Channel	35,000	300	Timor Sea	13,070	1,200
East China Sea	480,000	8,920	Weddell Sea	770,000	
Flores Sea	28,000		White Sea	47,345	300
Great Australian Bight	158,400		Yellow Sea	160,000	
Greenland Sea	217,000				

Table 2   Islands

Name	Area in square miles (approx.)	Name	Area in square miles (approx.)
Andaman Islands	2,508	Japan	183,000
Anglesey	276	Java	50,400
Antilles	100,000	Luzon	41,000
Auckland Islands	234	Madagascar	228,000
Azores	890	Malta	122
Baffin Island	236,000	New Britain Island	14,600
Bahamas	4,401	New Caledonia	8,550
Barbados	166	Newfoundland	42,750
Bathurst Island	785	New Guinea	347,400
Bermuda	21	New Zealand	104,737
Borneo	286,968	Novaya Zemlya	35,000
Canary Islands	2,910	Orkney Islands	360
Cape Breton Island	3,120	Pelée	4,430
Cape Verde Islands	1,559	Philippine Islands	115,000
Capri	4	Prince Edward Island	2,185
Celebes	69,280	Prince of Wales Island	13,740
Ceylon	25,000	Sardinia	9,300
Channel Islands	750	Shetland Islands	551
Christmas Islands	223	Sicily	9,930
Crete	3,237	Skye	670
Cuba	44,210	Solomon Islands	16,000
Cyprus	3,500	Southampton Island	16,940
Devon Island	21,610	South Georgia	1,450
Ellesmere Island	77,390	Sumatra	161,612
Falkland Islands	4,620	Tahiti	402
Fiji	7,100	Tasmania	26,215
Formosa	13,890	Tierra del Fuego	18,000
Galapagos Islands	2,997	Timor	13,070
Greenland	840,000	Trinidad	1,863
Hainan	13,000	Tristan da Cuna	40
Hawaiian Islands	6,420	Vancouver Island	13,049
Hispaniola	30,000	Victoria Island	80,340
Iceland	39,710	West Indies	72,000
Isle of Man	221	W. Spitsbergen Island	23,658
Isle of Wight	148	Zanzibar	1,020
Jamaica	4,410		

Table 3   Mountains and Peaks

Mountain range	Highest peaks	Height in feet to nearest ten	Country of Peak
Ahaggar Plateau	Tahat	9,840	Algeria
Alps	Mount Blanc	15,780	France/Italy
	Monte Rosa	15,220	Italy/Switzerland
	Dom	14,940	Switzerland/Italy
	Matterhorn	14,710	Switzerland
	Finsteraahorn	14,030	Switzerland
	Breithorn	13,690	Switzerland
	Jungfrau	13,670	Switzerland
	Weisshorn	14,600	Switzerland

Altai Mountains	Bieluka Peak	12,800	Siberia
Andes	Aconcagua	22,830	Argentina
	Huascaran	22,210	Peru
	Sorata	21,500	Bolivia
	Sajama	21,480	Bolivia
	Illimani	21,220	Bolivia
	Chimborazo	20,500	Ecuador
	Llullaillaco	20,240	Argentina/Chile
	Cotopaxi	19,610	Ecuador
	Antisana	18,850	Ecuador
	Tolima	18,320	Columbia
Appalachians	Mount Mitchell	6,680	U.S.A.
	Mount Rodgers	5,720	U.S.A.
	Mount Marcy	5,340	U.S.A.
	Mount Katahdin	5,270	U.S.A.
	Brasstown Bald	4,780	U.S.A.
	Big Black Mountain	4,150	U.S.A.
	Sassafras	3,550	U.S.A.
Apennines	Mount Corno	10,740	Italy
	Mount Edna	9,580	Italy
Atlas Mountains	Tizi-n-Tamjurt	14,500	Morocco
Australian Alps	Mount Buller	5,910	Australia
Balkan Mountains	Shipka-Pass	7,780	Bulgaria
Barisan Mountains	Koerinji	12,940	Sumatra
Berwyn Mountains	Aran-Mawddwy	2,720	Wales
Black Mountains	Pe-Y-Gaver-Fawr	2,600	Wales
Black Mountains	Carmarthen Van	2,630	Wales
Black Mountains	Brecon Beacons	2,910	Wales
Cantabrians	Pena Vie Ja	8,740	Spain
Carpathians	Tatra	8,740	Czechoslovakia
Cascade Range	Mount Rainer	14,420	U.S.A.
	Mount Hood	11,250	U.S.A.
Caucasus Range	Mount Ararat	16,950	Turkey
Cheviots	Cheviot Hill	2,680	Scotland
Colorado Plateau	Humphrey's Peak	12,800	U.S.A.
Cordillera de Los	Tupungato	21,490	Chile
	Maipo	17,460	Chile
Dinaric Alps	Dinari	6,010	Jugoslavia
Dovreffeld	Snohetta	7,360	Norway
Elburz Range	Demavend	18,550	Iran
Front Range	Mount Evans	14,260	U.S.A.
Grampians	Ben Nevis	4,400	Scotland
	Ben Macdhui	4,290	Scotland
Great Basin	Boundary Peak	13,150	U.S.A.
Great Dividing Range	Koskiusko	7,730	Australia
Himalayas	Nanga Parbat	26,630	Tibet
	Mount Everest	29,000	Tibet
	K.2	28,250	Tibet
	Kinchinjanga	28,150	Tibet
Iran Mountains	Kinabalu	13,450	Borneo
Kunlun Mountains	Godwin Austin	28,250	Tibet
Mountains of Mourne	Slieve Donard	2,800	Ireland
North West Highlands	Mam Soul	3,860	Scotland
Owen Stanley Range	Mount Victoria	13,120	New Guinea
	Mount Simpson	9,970	New Guinea
Pennine Chain	Cross Fell	2,930	England
Pindus Mountains	Mount Olympus	9,790	Greece
Plateau of Ethiopia	Kilimanjaro	19,320	Ethiopia
Pyrénées	Pic de Aneto	11,170	Spain
	Mount Perdu	10,990	Spain
Rocky Mountains	Mount Elbert	14,430	U.S.A.
	Mount Massive	14,420	U.S.A.
Salmon River Mountains	Borah Peak	12,660	U.S.A.

Sa Nevada	Mount Whitney	14,500	U.S.A.
Snowdon	Snowdon	3,560	Wales
	Carnedd Llywelyn	3,490	Wales
Southern Alps	Mount Cook	12,350	New Zealand
	Mount Tasman	11,480	New Zealand
Southern Uplands	Mount Merrick	2,770	Scotland
Taurus Mountains	Ala Dagh	11,000	Turkey
Wicklow Mountains	Lugnaquillia	3,040	Ireland

Table 4   Rivers

River	Length in miles (approx.)	Country	River	Length in miles (approx.)	Country
Altamaha	150	U.S.A.	Loire	630	France
Amazon	4,050	South America	Mackenzie	2,300	North America
Amur	2,500	Mongolia	Madeira	2,000	South America
Amu Darya	1,350	U.S.S.R.	Magdalena	1,060	South America
Araguaia	1,000	South America	Mekong	2,800	China
Assiniboine	1,500	Canada	Missouri-Mississippi	3,760	U.S.A.
Barrow	115	Ireland	Murray	1,610	Australia
Blackwater	100	Ireland	Niger	2,600	French Guinea
Brahmaputra	1,680	Tibet	Nelson	460	Canada
Choctawhatchee	180	U.S.A.	Nile	4,160	Africa
Colorado	2,000	U.S.A.	Nith	70	Scotland
Columbia	1,400	North America	Nore	70	Ireland
Congo	3,000	Africa	Obi	2,700	U.S.S.R.
Connecticut	450	U.S.A.	Oder	560	Moravia
Coppermine	475	Canada	Onega	140	U.S.S.R.
Danube	1,725	Europe	Orange	1,300	Africa
Darling	1,160	Australia	Orinoco	1,500	Venezuela
Dnieper	1,330	Russia	Ottawa	686	Canada
Don	1,150	Russia	Ouse	155	England
Douro	500	Spain	Pahang	298	Siam
Drave	450	Yugoslavia	Peace	1,100	Canada
Drina	300	Yugoslavia	Red	1,600	U.S.A.
Ebro	466	Spain	Rhine	770	France
Elbe	724	Germany	Rhone	505	France
Ems	207	Germany	Rio Grande del Norte	1,800	U.S.A.
Essequibo	620	British Guiana	Sabine	500	U.S.A.
Euphrates	1,700	West Asia	Salween	1,800	Tibet
Ganges	1,556	India	Sao Francisco	1,800	Brazil
Garonne	377	France	Saone	300	France
Godavari	900	India	South and North Saskatchewan	700 and 810	Canada
Guadiana	510	Spain/Portugal	Sava	550	Yugoslavia
Hoangho	2,600	Asia	Savannah	450	U.S.A.
Housatonic	150	U.S.A.	Seine	480	France
Hudson	144	U.S.A.	Senegal	1,000	West Africa
Humber	40	England	Severn	220	England
Indus	1,700	India	Shannon	225	Ireland
Irrawaddy	1,300	Burma	Spey	107	Scotland
Jordan	65	Palestine	St. Lawrence	1,800	Canada
Kistna	800	India	Suir	160	(Eire) Ireland
Kuban	450	Russia	Syr	1,500	U.S.S.R.
Lena	2,800	Siberia	Thames	210	England
Limpopo	1,000	Africa			

Tigris	1,100	Iraq		Volga	2,400	U.S.S.R.
Tiza	750	U.S.S.R.		Wear	65	England
Trent	170	England		Wye	130	Wales-England
Tweed	98	Scotland		Yangtse Kiang	3,500	China
Uruguay	850	South America		Yenisei	3,300	Siberia
Ural	1,500	Russia		Yukon	2,000	Canada
Vistula	650	Poland		Zambezi	1,632	Africa

Table 5 Volcanoes

Name	Height in feet	Country		Name	Height in feet	Country
Aconcagua	22,830	Chile/Argentina		Llullaillaco	20,250	Chile
Antisana	18,850	Ecuador		Mauna Loa*	13,680	Hawaii
Asama*	8,200	Japan		Mikeno	14,780	Congo
Chillan*	10,500	Chile		Mount Wrangell*	14,000	U.S.A.
Chimborazo	20,500	Ecuador		Ng Uaru Hoe	7,520	New Zealand
Cotopaxi*	19,610	Ecuador		Nyamuragira*	10,150	Congo
Demavend	18,600	Persia		Nyiragongo*	11,560	Congo
Elbruz	18,530	U.S.S.R.		Orizaba	17,400	Mexico
Erebus*	13,000	Antarctic		Popocatapetl	17,540	Mexico
Etna	10,800	Sicily		Ruapehu*	9,175	New Zealand
Fujiyama	12,400	Japan		Soufriere	4,430	St. Vincent Island, West Indies
Guntur	7,300	Java				
Haleakala	10,300	Hawaii		Stromboli*	3,000	Lipari Islands, Italy
Hecla*	5,100	Iceland		Tarawera	3,650	New Zealand
Iliamna*	11,000	Aleutian Islands		Tongariro	6,460	New Zealand
Karisimbi	14,780	Congo		Two-Shima	2,480	Japan
Kilauea*	4,090	Hawaii		Vesuvius*	3,700	Italy
Kilimanjaro	19,340	Tanganyika		Volcanello*	2,500	Lipari Islands
Krakatoa	2,600	Sunda Strait		*denotes an active volcano		

Table 6 Lakes

Name	Area in square miles (approx.)	Country		Name	Area in square miles (approx.)	Country
Amadjuak	4,000	Baffin Land		Constance	207	Switzerland/ Germany
Aral	26,165	U.S.S.R.				
Athabasca	3,059	Canada		Dead Sea	460	Palestine
Baikal	11,700	Siberia		Erie	9,940	Canada
Balaton	225	Hungary		Eyre	3,700	Australia
Balkhash	7,050	U.S.S.R.		Gairdner	3,000	Australia
Bangwenlo	2,000	Africa		Geneva	108	Switzerland
Caspian Sea	170,000	Asia		Great Bear	11,660	Canada
Chad	6,000	Africa		Great Slave	11,170	Canada

Huron	23,010	North America
Issyk-Kul	2,250	Turkestan
Koko-Nor	2,300	Tibet
Ladoga	7,100	U.S.S.R.
Loch Lomond	27	Scotland
Lough Neagh	150	Ireland
Manitoba	1,817	Canada
Maracaiba	8,300	South America
Michigan	22,400	North America
Nettling	5,000	Baffin Land
Nicaragua	3,000	Central America
Nyasa	14,200	Africa
Onega	3,765	U.S.S.R.
Ontario	7,540	North America

Reindeer	2,440	Canada
Rudolf	3,500	Africa
Superior	31,820	North America
Tanganyika	12,700	Africa
Titicaca	3,200	South America
Torrens	2,400	Australia
Van	2,500	Asia Minor
Vanern	2,150	Sweden
Victoria	25,000–26,000	Africa
Victoria Nyanza	26,200	Africa
Winnipeg	9,398	Canada
Winnipegosis	2,086	Canada

Table 7   Waterfalls

Name	Height in feet	Country
Angel Falls	3,210	Venezuela
Bridalveil	620	Yosemite, U.S.A.
Gavarnie	1,385	Pyrénées, Spain/France
Gersoppa	830	India
Guayra	90–130	Brazil
Iguassu	220	Brazil
Kaietur	740	British Guiana
Kalambo	704	Malawi
Khon Cataracts	50–70	Indo-China
King Edward VIII	840	British Guiana
Malet Sunyane	630	Basutoland
Nevada	594	Yosemite, U.S.A.
Niagara	158–175	Canada-U.S.A.
Ribbon Fall	1,612	Yosemite, U.S.A.
Skjeggedalsfoss	525	Norway
Staubbach	980	Switzerland
Sterling	505	New Zealand
Sutherland	815	New Zealand
Upper Yosemite	1,430	Yosemite, U.S.A.
Vettis Foss	856	Norway
Victoria Falls	236–345	Rhodesia
Wollomombie	1,100	New South Wales

Xx

XENOPHANES (*c.* 520 B.C.)

Greek poet-philosopher. He made observations of raised beaches and concluded that the land was once submerged. He also studied fossils. He thought that the universe could be understood only by considering it as a single whole, and not as a collection of separate things.

XENOPHON (*c.* 430–*c.* 355 B.C.)

Greek historian and soldier. He was a student of SOCRATES and much of our knowledge on this great philosopher comes from Xenophon's two books *Symposium* and *Memorabilia*. His greatest work, however, is *Anabasis*, which is a thrilling account of the retreat after the battle of Cimaxa (401 B.C.) at the head of an army of Greeks who enlisted in the army of Cyrus the Younger of Persia in his war against his brother Artaxerxes. Although an Athenian he was banished from Athens for fighting with the Spartans.

X-RAYS

In 1895 Professor W. C. RÖNTGEN of the University of Wurzburg produced evidence of an invisible sort of radiation that could penetrate solid substances. It could produce light on certain fluorescent materials, and affect a photographic plate. It penetrated substances to different extents, being absorbed by the denser substances. Thus if the radiation passed through a hand and a photographic plate was held on the opposite side to that of the radiation, the result was a photograph showing the actual bones of the hand. This penetrating radiation he called X-rays; so called because they were similar to other rays in travelling through space, and labelled 'X' to distinguish them from other known rays, such as cathode rays and light rays.

The obvious use for such radiation was in medicine, and the X-ray examination of the inside of the human body is today a routine procedure. But X-rays have also been used in the examination of crystal structures and metallic flaws. X-rays consist of radiations similar to that of visible light, but of very much shorter wavelength. It is the shortness of the waves that enables X-rays to penetrate into substances opaque to visible light. The rays are formed when high-speed electrons (negative particles) strike a target. In the usual X-ray tube this target is a metal disc.

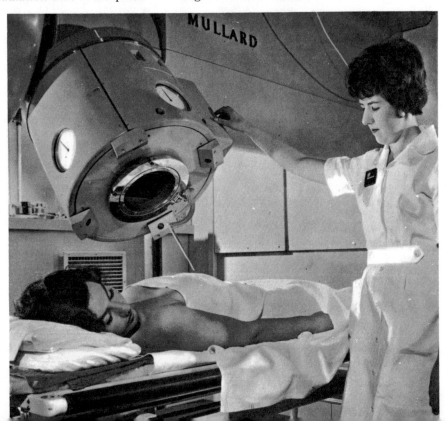

X-RAYS
A modern linear accelerator for producing X-rays for the treatment of deep-seated cancer.

Yy

YAK

Long-bodied, short-legged ruminant, with a thick fringe-like mane on the throat and belly, a tuft on the tail and long hooked horns. Its home is the high plateau and mountains of China and Tibet where it ascends mountains to a height of 15,000 to 20,000 feet during the summer.

YEAST

Consists of single-cell fungi which are able to break down carbohydrates. A few species are used for converting sugar into alcohol in the manufacture of beer, cider, wine, etc. It is also used in the making of bread; it is the release of carbon dioxide from the dough which causes bread to rise.

YEATS, William Butler (1865–1939)

Irish poet and dramatist, born in Dublin. Yeats belonged by birth to a remote country district of Ireland, and his poetry was full of the language, the beliefs, and the features of the country people, though at the same time he was also interested in the magical rituals of the East. He grew up in Ireland at a time when it was struggling with England for freedom, and when its literature and drama—both in old Irish and English—were suddenly flourishing. In his writings he both took a passionate part in Ireland's struggle, but kept his distance from it so as to comment as a thoughtful individualist on what he saw. While having some skill as a painter, he was wrapped up in poetry. Throughout his long life he wrote at least a stanza daily. Except for his poetical plays, his poems are almost all short. The greater part of Yeats' writings are contained in *Collected Works*.

YEMEN

A country in south-west Arabia, near the Federation of SOUTH ARABIA. It is 74,000 square miles, nearly as large as Great Britain, and has a population of 4 million. The capital is Taiz but San'a is larger and Mocha is better known. The country's chief export is coffee.

In 1958 the Yemen joined Egypt in the United Arab Republic but a dispute arose between the two countries and an Egyptian army entered the Yemen to aid a revolt. There has been a good deal of trouble since then within the Yemen between the Yemen and the Federation of South Arabia.

YIDDISH

A Germanic language, composed of German and Hebrew with words and phrases collected from other languages. It is largely spoken by Jews in Europe. It is written in Hebrew characters.

YOUTH

A term which in its plural form is used to describe boys and girls who are between childhood and adulthood, though those above twenty-one are often included.

There are many VOLUNTARY SOCIETIES in Great Britain whose members are entirely, or chiefly, young people. Altogether there are about twenty-seven national voluntary youth organizations which between them have a total membership of about 3 million. Amongst the largest of these are the BOY SCOUTS and Girl Guides. Two smaller groups whose members also wear uniforms and which are, like the Scouts and Guides, also to be found in other

YAK A woolly ruminant of high altitudes living in China and Tibet.

The Middle East

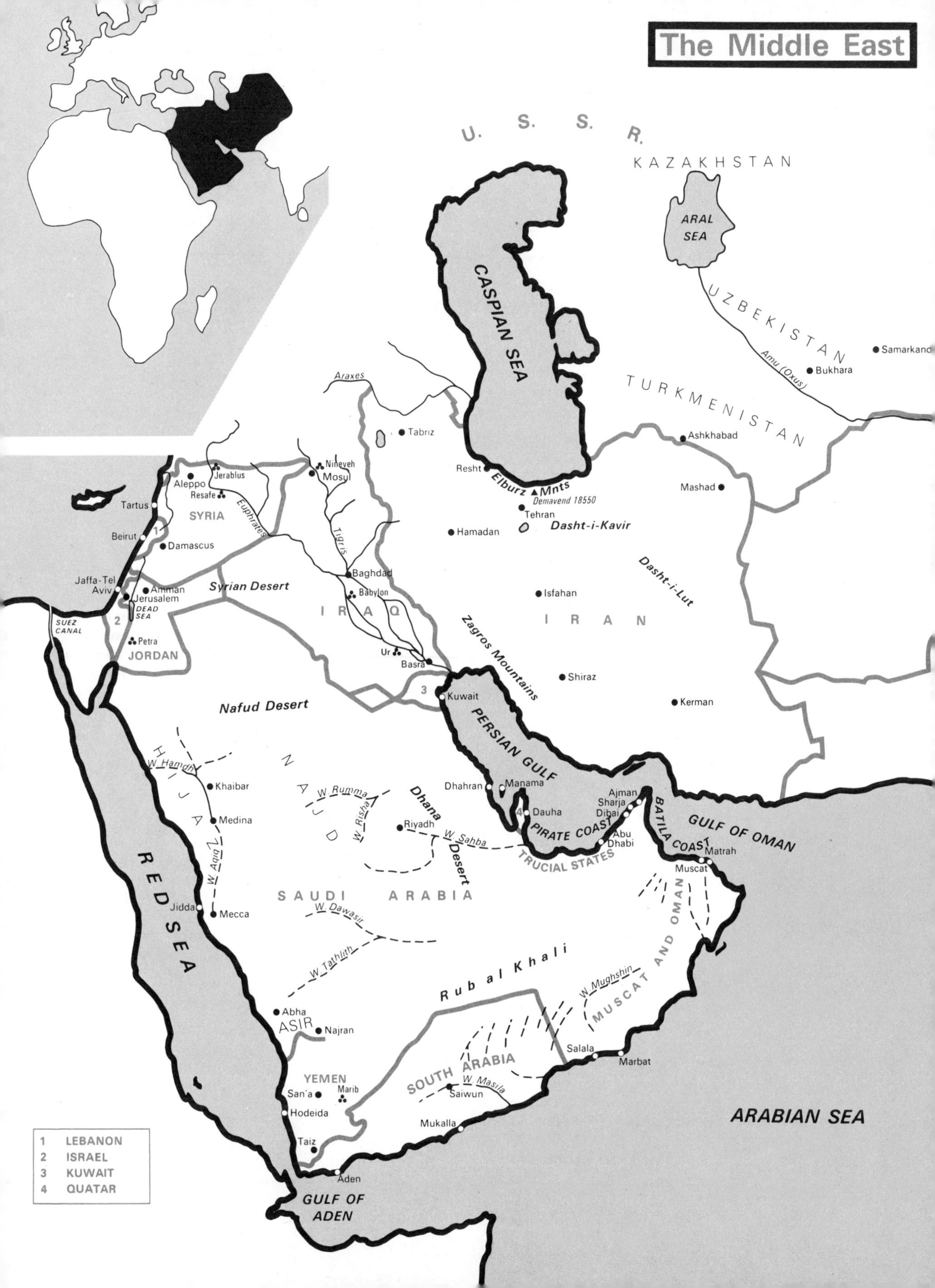

U. S. S. R.

KAZAKHSTAN

ARAL SEA

UZBEKISTAN

• Samarkand

Amu (Oxus)

• Bukhara

TURKMENISTAN

CASPIAN SEA

Araxes

• Tabriz

• Ashkhabad

Nineveh
Mosul

Resht Elburz ▲ Mnts
Demavend 18550

• Mashad

Jerablus
Aleppo
Resafe

Tartus

SYRIA

Tehran

Dasht-i-Kavir

Beirut
1

Damascus

• Hamadan

Dasht-i-Lut

Euphrates

Tigris

Jaffa-Tel
Aviv

Amman
Jerusalem
DEAD
SEA

Syrian Desert

Baghdad
Babylon

• Isfahan

I R A N

SUEZ
CANAL

2

Petra

JORDAN

I R A Q

Zagros Mountains

• Shiraz

Ur
Basra

Nafud Desert

3 Kuwait

• Kerman

H I J A Z

W. Hamdh

• Khaibar

N A J D

W. Rumma

PERSIAN GULF

Dhahran • Manama

Ajman
Sharja
Dibai

BATINA COAST

GULF OF OMAN

Medina

W. Rishq

Dhana

4 Dauha

PIRATE COAST

Abu
Dhabi

Matrah

W. Aqiq

Riyadh

W. Sahba

Desert

TRUCIAL STATES

Muscat

R E D   S E A

SAUDI

ARABIA

W. Dawasir

MUSCAT AND OMAN

Jidda
Mecca

W. Tathlith

Rub al Khali

W. Mughshin

• Abha

ASIR

• Najran

SOUTH ARABIA

Salala

Marbat

YEMEN

San'a •

Marib

W. Masila

Saiwun

ARABIAN SEA

Hodeida

Mukalla

Taiz

Aden

GULF OF
ADEN

1	LEBANON
2	ISRAEL
3	KUWAIT
4	QUATAR

YUGOSLAVIA A view of Dubrovnik, an ancient walled city on the southern Adriatic coast.

countries, are the Boys' Brigade and the Girls' Brigade. They are in fact considerably older than the larger and better-known bodies and are attached to Protestant Churches. The National Association of Boys' Clubs, with over 2,000 affiliated clubs and 152,000 members, and the National Association of Youth Clubs, with 2,500 affiliated clubs and 200,000 members provide recreation, mainly for those between 14 and 20.

One of the newer big youth organizations is the Youth Hostels Association which was formed in 1930. This provides cheap youth hostels so as to encourage young people to go for cycling and hiking trips. There are similar youth hostel organizations in other countries and this makes it possible for young people to visit foreign countries cheaply. Another organization which aims at helping children and young people to enjoy their playtime in safety is the National Playing Fields Association of which the Duke of Edinburgh is President. Since it began in 1925 it has helped to provide about 8,000 playing grounds. These range from large sports centres to small children's playgrounds and cricket pitches.

The oldest societies for young people were started for young men and young women. They are the Young Men's Christian Association and the Young Women's Christian Association whose signs are triangles, the Men's red and the Women's blue. This is meant to show that they provide for the physical, mental and religious needs of young people. This is largely done by providing hostels and clubs. The Y.M.C.A. was formed in 1844 and both societies have now spread all over the world.

There are many school societies, some of which encourage hobbies of various kinds. Others, like school debating societies, encourage public speaking. One of the largest school societies is the Council for Education in World Citizenship. Its object is to encourage friendship amongst boys and girls all over the world, to study world problems, and in particular the work carried out by the UNITED NATIONS ORGANIZATION.

YUGOSLAVIA

A federal republic in south-east Europe that is a little larger (95,500 square miles) than Great Britain and has a population of over 19 million. It is made up of six States: Serbia, Croatia, Slovenia, Montenegro, Macedonia and Bosnia-Herzegovina. The capital is Belgrade. Yugoslavia is a very mountainous country and it is one of those through which the River Danube flows. About half the people are farmers but the country has many minerals, including coal, iron and lead, and in recent years much more use has been made of them.
History:
Yugoslavia was created in 1918 after the First World War. There had been two small countries—Serbia and Montenegro—and they joined together and with some other territory that had formed part of the Austro-Hungarian Empire, they formed the new State of Yugoslavia. It was a kingdom until after the Second World War when it adopted a Communist form of government under its war-time leader, Marshal TITO.

YUKON

A cold, bleak territory in north-west Canada. In spite of its uninviting climate it has attracted many writers, of whom the best known is Robert Service (*Songs of a Sourdough*). This desolate territory first became famous because of the Klondike gold rush of the 1890s. Gold, silver and lead mining is carried on there, also large-scale fishing and fur-trapping.

Zz

ZAMBIA

Republic in Central Africa with an area of 298,580 square miles and population of nearly four millions. The capital is Lusaka. It is rich in copper which is its main export.

ZANZIBAR

A small island off the coast of East Africa which was a British Protectorate until 1963. Now a part of the United Republic of TANZANIA. It is ruled by a Sultan. There are about 150,000 inhabitants. Nearly all the cloves we use come from Zanzibar.

ZARATHUSTRA or ZOROASTER
(c. 660–c. 583 B.C.)

Persian prophet, and founder of the religion known as Zoroastrianism. The religious book for this faith is the 'Zendavesta' which was partly written by Zarathustra. It consists of hymns, prayers, sayings, religious instructions, etc. Zoroastrianism is still practised by the Parsis of India.

ZEBRA

Belongs to the same family (Equidae) as the horse and ass. It is found only in Africa. The largest, and some think the handsomest, is Grevy's zebra; two other species are Hartmann's Mountain zebra and Chapman's quagga.

ZEBU

It is a ruminant which differs from European cattle in having a fatty hump on the shoulder and a large dewlap. Although originally an Indian animal it has been exported to many tropical countries. There are many breeds.

ZENO OF CITIUM (c. 340–c. 265 B.C.)

Greek philosopher, and founder of the school of philosophy known as the 'Stoics'. He committed suicide when very old as he considered his useful life had run its full course.

ZENO OF ELEA (490–430 B.C.)

Greek philosopher, and follower of Parmendides. It was Zeno who presented the famous paradox of 'Achilles and the tortoise', that is, if a tortoise were given a start in a race against Achilles that Achilles would never be able to beat the slow-moving tortoise. Zeno argued that at every point Achilles would need to travel one-half of the distance between the tortoise and himself, and so on *ad infinitum*.

ZEBU
This animal is a ruminant and came originally from India. It can be distinguished from other cattle by its large dewlap and fatty hump near its shoulders.

ZEPPELIN

A type of rigid airship first built by the German inventor Graf von Zeppelin in 1900, and used as a weapon of war in the First World War by the Germans.

ZODIAC

Zone in the celestial sphere in which the sun, moon and planets trace their paths. It is divided into twelve sections according to the apparent positions of the sun during the twelve months of the year. These sections are known by the 'signs of the zodiac', named from the appropriate constellations.

ZOLA, Emile Eduard Charles Antoine
(1840–1902)

French novelist, born in Paris. He began his literary career as a journalist in Paris, but he soon took to novel-writing and with his series of twenty novels on the family of Rougon-Macquart, became the leader of the realistic school of writers. His aim was to trace with social and psychological methods the influences on a certain family of heredity and environment. *L'Assommoir* (1877) which shows the effect of drink upon the life of an artisan family, is the best known. Zola is also famous for his championing of DREYFUS against the false accusation of treason.

ZOOLOGY

The science that deals with the study of animals. It can be said to have begun with the writings of the Greek philosopher ARISTOTLE, who is usually called the 'Father of Zoology'. For many centuries after he had lived, however, very little that was new was added to our knowledge until the 18th century, when the classification and naming of animals and plants was put into order by the work of the Swedish botanist LINNAEUS. Before we can study any collection of different objects we must so arrange them that we can find each one easily. So the science of taxonomy or classification became of first importance in zoology. Then we must know what part of the world they came from, how numerous they are and how far they range. This is dealt with under the study of zoogeography, or the distribution of animals. In a very short time other subdivisions of the science of zoology began to make their appearance. Morphology deals with the study of their form, anatomy with their internal structure, physiology with the way their internal organs work, as in digestion, breathing and so on. Then came the study of the tissues of which the organs are composed, a study known as histology, and the study of the structure of the cells, or cytology. During the last century the study of heredity, known as genetics, has taken a prominent place. Each of these is worthy of being called a science, but because they are so dependent upon each other, and interlock one with the other, it is usual to include them all under the one term, zoology.

ZODIAC The traditional way of showing the twelve signs. Reading anti-clockwise they are: Aquarius, Pisces, Aries, Taurus, Gemini, Cancer, Leo, Virgo, Libra, Scorpio, Saggittarius, and Capricorn.

ARCTIC
OCEAN

18

128

81

PACIFIC
OCEAN

NORTH
ATLANTIC

55

87

32

10

127

56

75

39

118

103

114

82

84

3

124

115

109

80

79

42

(28)

(52)

(33)

(47)

(48)

(63)

(107)

(53)

(91)

(96)

(27)

(34)

24

131

(123)

(49)

12

(50)

(44)

11

97

5

SOUTH
ATLANTIC

51

110

62

1

9

72

122

31

43

41

40

(22)

(100)

(129)

THE WORLD

1 Afghanistan
2 Albania
3 Algeria
4 Angola
5 Argentina
6 Australia
7 Austria
8 Lesotho
9 Botswana
10 Belgium
11 Bolivia
12 Brazil

13 Bulgaria
14 Burma
15 Burundi
16 Cambodia
17 Cameroon
18 Canada
19 Central Africa
20 Ceylon
21 Chad
22 Chile
23 China
24 Colombia

25 Congo
26 Congolese Rep.
27 Costa Rica
28 Cuba
29 Cyprus
30 Czechoslovakia
31 Dahomey
32 Denmark
33 Dominican Rep.

34 Ecuador
35 Egypt
36 Ethiopia
37 Finland
38 Formosa
39 France
40 French Polynesia
41 Gaboon
42 Gambia

43 Ghana
44 Surinam
45 Germany
46 Greece
47 Guadeloupe
48 Guatemala
49 Guyana
50 French Guiana
51 Guinea
52 Haiti
53 Honduras
54 Hungary
55 Iceland
56 Irish Republic
57 Italy
58 India